D1571524

INJUNCTIONS IN PATENT LAW

Patents are important tools for innovation policy. They incentivize the creation and dissemination of new technical solutions and help to disclose their working to the public in exchange for limited exclusivity. Injunctions are important tools of their enforcement. Much has been written about different aspects of the patent system, but the issue of injunctions is largely neglected in the comparative legal literature. This book explains how the drafting, tailoring and enforcement of injunctions in patent law works in several leading jurisdictions: Europe, the United States, Canada, and Israel. The chapters provide in-depth explanation of how and why national judges provide for or reject flexibility and tailoring of injunctive relief. With its transatlantic and intra-European comparisons, as well as a policy and theoretical synthesis, this is the most comprehensive overview available for practicing attorneys and scholars in patent law. This book is also available as Open Access on Cambridge Core.

JORGE L. CONTRERAS is Presidential Scholar and Professor at the University of Utah S.J. Quinney College of Law.

MARTIN HUSOVEC is Assistant Professor at the London School of Economics and Political Science, LSE Law School.

Injunctions in Patent Law

TRANS-ATLANTIC DIALOGUES ON FLEXIBILITY AND TAILORING

Edited by

JORGE L. CONTRERAS
University of Utah S. J. Quinney College of Law

MARTIN HUSOVEC
London School of Economics and Political Science

CAMBRIDGE
UNIVERSITY PRESS

CAMBRIDGE
UNIVERSITY PRESS

University Printing House, Cambridge CB2 8BS, United Kingdom

One Liberty Plaza, 20th Floor, New York, NY 10006, USA

477 Williamstown Road, Port Melbourne, VIC 3207, Australia

314–321, 3rd Floor, Plot 3, Splendor Forum, Jasola District Centre, New Delhi – 110025, India

103 Penang Road, #05–06/07, Visioncrest Commercial, Singapore 238467

Cambridge University Press is part of the University of Cambridge.

It furthers the University's mission by disseminating knowledge in the pursuit of
education, learning, and research at the highest international levels of excellence.

www.cambridge.org
Information on this title: www.cambridge.org/9781108835619
DOI: 10.1017/9781108891103

First published 2022

A catalogue record for this publication is available from the British Library.

Library of Congress Cataloging-in-Publication Data
NAMES: Contreras, Jorge L., editor. | Husovec, Martin, editor.
TITLE: Injunctions in patent law : Trans-Atlantic dialogues on flexibility and tailoring / edited by Jorge
L. Contreras, University of Utah S.J. Quinney College of Law; Martin Husovec, Department of Law, The
London School of Economics and Political Science (LSE).
DESCRIPTION: Cambridge, United Kingdom ; New York, NY : Cambridge University Press, 2022. |
Includes bibliographical references and index.
IDENTIFIERS: LCCN 2021040633 (print) | LCCN 2021040634 (ebook) | ISBN 9781108835619 (hardback) |
ISBN 9781108812955 (paperback) | ISBN 9781108891103 (epub)
SUBJECTS: LCSH: Patent suits. | Injunctions.
CLASSIFICATION: LCC K1536 .I55 2022 (print) | LCC K1536 (ebook) | DDC 346.04/86–DC23
LC record available at https://lccn.loc.gov/2021040633
LC ebook record available at https://lccn.loc.gov/2021040634

ISBN 978-1-108-83561-9 Hardback

Contents

Notes on Contributors   *page* vii
Preface   xvii

1   Introduction: Patent Remedies in the Global Landscape   1
     Jorge L. Contreras and Martin Husovec

2   Injunctive Relief in Patent Law under TRIPS   5
     Graeme B. Dinwoodie and Rochelle C. Dreyfuss

3   European Union   26
     Matthias Leistner and Viola Pless

4   Injunctions in European Law: Judicial Reflections   65
     Sir Richard Arnold

5   Canada   70
     Norman Siebrasse

6   Finland   97
     Marcus Norrgård

7   France   124
     Thibault Gisclard and Emmanuel Py

8   Germany   142
     Peter Georg Picht and Anna-Lena Karczewski

9   Israel   171
     Orit Fischman-Afori

10   Italy   194
      Alessandro Cogo and Marco Ricolfi

11   Netherlands   218
      Willem A. Hoyng and Léon E. Dijkman

12   Poland   237
      Rafał Sikorski and Tomasz Targosz

13   United Kingdom   261
      Lionel Bently and Sir Richard Arnold

14   United States   291
      John M. Golden

15   Issuing and Tailoring Patent Injunctions: A Cross-Jurisdictional
      Comparison and Synthesis   313
      Jorge L. Contreras and Martin Husovec

Notes on Contributors

Sir Richard Arnold, MA (Oxford), Hon. DL (Westminster), is Lord Justice of Appeal in England and Wales, an external member of the Enlarged Board of Appeal of the European Patent Office and a visiting professor at the University of Westminster. He was called to the Bar of England and Wales in 1985 and became a QC in 2000. Previously, he was chairman of the Code of Practice for the Promotion of Animal Medicines Committee from 2002 to 2008, an appointed person hearing trademark appeals from 2003 to 2008 and a deputy high court judge from 2004 to 2008. He also served as a judge of the High Court, Chancery Division from October 2008 to September 2019 and judge in charge of the Patents Court from April 2013 to September 2019. He is the author of *Performers' Rights* (6th ed., Sweet & Maxwell, 2021), is the editor of the *Halsbury's Laws of England* title *Trade Marks and Trade Names* (5th ed., Butterworths, 2014), was the editor of *Entertainment and Media Law* from 1993 to 2004 inclusive and has published numerous journal articles and book chapters.

Lionel Bently, BA (Cambridge), is the Herchel Smith Professor of Intellectual Property Law and Deputy Director of the Centre for Intellectual Property and Information Law, Faculty of Law, University of Cambridge, and a professorial fellow of Emmanuel College, Cambridge. He is a barrister and door tenant at 11 South Square, Gray's Inn, London. Previously, he has held visiting posts at Murdoch University, Queensland University of Technology, University of New South Wales, National University of Singapore, Columbia University, University of Amsterdam and University of Technology, Sydney. He is co-director of the AHRC-funded Primary Sources on Copyright in five (now eight) jurisdictions (www.copyrighthistory.org), and was one of the principal investigations on the HERA-funded project "Of Authorship and Originality" (with the universities of Bergen and Amsterdam) and the AHRC-funded project on Copyright and News in the Digital Environment (with Ian Hargreaves). Professor Bently is the coauthor of (with Brad Sherman) *The Making of Modern Intellectual Property: The British Experience* (Cambridge University Press, 1999); *Intellectual Property Law* (1–4 eds., with Brad Sherman; 5th ed., with Brad Sherman, Dev Gangjee and Phil Johnson, Oxford University Press, 2018); *Gurry on Breach of Confidence: The Protection of Confidential Information* (with Tanya Aplin, Simon Malynicz and Phill Johnson, Oxford University Press, 2012) and *Global Mandatory Fair Use: The Right of Quotation in International Copyright Law* (with Tanya Aplin, Cambridge University Press, 2020).

Alessandro Cogo, PhD (University of Pavia and Ludwig Maximilian University), JD (University of Turin), is an associate professor of business law and intellectual property at the Turin Law School and partner of the law firm CVPM Legal. Professor Cogo is the scientific director of the Intellectual Property Master organized by WIPO and Turin University with the support of ITC-ILO. His writings include *I contratti di diritto d'autore nell'era digitale* (Giappichelli, 2010); *L'armonizzazione del diritto patrimoniale d'autore* (AIDA, 2016); *Appunti sulla contraffazione indiretta* (Giuffrè, 2019); *Online Content-Sharing Platforms as Users of Copyrighted Contents* (AIDA, 2019).

Jorge L. Contreras, JD (Harvard), BSEE (Rice University), BA (Rice University), is a presidential scholar and professor of law at the University of Utah with an adjunct appointment in the Department of Human Genetics. His research focuses, among other things, on intellectual property, technical standards and science policy. He is the author of more than 100 scholarly articles and book chapters that have appeared in scientific, legal and policy journals including *Science, Nature, Georgetown Law Journal, NYU Law Review, Washington Law Review, Harvard Journal of Law and Technology, Antitrust Law Journal* and *Telecommunications Policy.* He is the editor of six books, including the *Cambridge Handbook of Technical Standardization Law* (2 vols., Cambridge University Press, 2017, 2019). He has been quoted in the *New York Times, Wall Street Journal, Economist, Washington Post* and *Korea Times,* and has been a guest on NPR, PRI and BBC radio shows and various televised broadcasts. His work has been cited by the US Federal Trade Commission, European Commission and courts in the United States and Europe. Before entering academia, Professor Contreras was a partner at the international law firm Wilmer Cutler Pickering Hale and Dorr LLP, where he practiced international transactional and IP law in Boston, London and Washington, DC. He currently serves as co-chair of the Interdisciplinary Division of the American Bar Association's Section of Science & Technology Law and a member of the American Antitrust Institute's Board of Advisors. He has previously served as a member of the National Academy of Sciences (NAS) Committee on IP Management in Standard-Setting Processes, the National Institutes of Health (NIH) Council of Councils, the Councils of the National Human Genome Research Institute (NHGRI) and the National Center for Advancing Translational Sciences (NCATS).

Léon E. Dijkman, PhD candidate (European University Institute), LLM (University of California, Berkeley, School of Law), LLM (Utrecht University), LLB, BA (Utrecht University), is an associate at the Amsterdam office of HOYNG ROKH MONEGIER. His doctoral research focuses on flexibility and tailoring injunctive relief in EU patent cases and in 2020, one of his early articles on the subject was awarded the Dutch AIPPI chapter's prize for best article by an author under 35. He teaches intellectual property law at the Erasmus School of Law in Rotterdam and is a member of the editorial board of *IER* (Kluwer), one of the Netherlands' oldest specialized journals. He also holds a research position at the European University Institute's Robert Schuman Centre for Advanced Studies and previously held a visiting position at the Max Planck Institute for Innovation and Competition.

Graeme B. Dinwoodie, LLB (University of Glasgow), LLM (Harvard), JSD (Columbia), is the Global Professor of Intellectual Property Law at Chicago-Kent College of Law. He returned full-time to Chicago in 2018 after nine years as the Professor of Intellectual Property and Information Technology Law at the University of Oxford, where he was also director of the Oxford Intellectual Property Research Centre and a professorial fellow of St. Peter's College. He remains a visiting professor of law at the University of Oxford. Immediately prior to taking up the IP Chair at Oxford, Professor Dinwoodie was for several years a professor of law at Chicago-Kent College of Law and, from 2005 to 2009, also held a chair in intellectual property law at Queen Mary College, University of London. Professor Dinwoodie has held a number of visiting or honorary positions, including as the Yong Shook Lin Visiting Professor of Intellectual Property Law at the National University of Singapore, a global professor of law at New York University School of Law, an honorary professor of law at the University of Strasbourg, the George P. Smith II Distinguished Visiting Chair at Indiana University Maurer School of Law, and a visiting professor of law at the University of Pennsylvania School of Law. He was elected a member of the American Law Institute in 2003, and served as president of ATRIP from 2011 to 2013. In 2008, INTA awarded Professor Dinwoodie the Pattishall Medal for Teaching Excellence in Trademark Law. In addition to his book *A Neofederalist Vision of TRIPS: The Resilience of the International Intellectual Property Regime* (Oxford University Press 2012), co-authored with Rochelle C. Dreyfuss, he is the author of five casebooks. His scholarship has appeared in several leading law journals and is widely cited by scholars in Europe, the United States and elsewhere.

Rochelle C. Dreyfuss, JD (Columbia Law School), MS (University of California, Berkeley), BA (Wellesley College), is the Pauline Newman Professor of Law at New York University School of Law and co-director of its Engelberg Center on Innovation Law and Policy. She recently held the Arthur Goodhart Visiting Professorship in Legal Science at Cambridge University and she has also visited

Swinburne University, Oxford University, the National University of Singapore, the University of Washington School of Law, the University of Chicago School of Law, and the Max Planck Institute. She served as a law clerk for Chief Judge Wilfred Feinberg (2d Circuit) and Supreme Court Chief Justice Warren E. Burger. She was a co-reporter of the ALI Project on Intellectual Property: Principles Governing Jurisdiction, Choice of Law, and Judgments in Transnational Disputes and served on National Academies of Sciences Committees on Intellectual Property in Genomic and Protein Research; on Intellectual Property in the Knowledge Based Economy; and on Science, Technology and Law. She was also a member of the National Institute of Health Advisory Committee on Genetics, Health and Society. Her writings include *A Neofederalist Vision of TRIPS: Building a Resilient International Intellectual Property System* (with Graeme B. Dinwoodie, Oxford University Press, 2012) and *Balancing Wealth and Health: The Battle over Intellectual Property and Access to Medicines in Latin America* (with César Rodríguez-Garavito, Oxford University Press, 2014). With Justine Pila, she edited *The Oxford Handbook of Intellectual Property Law* (Oxford University Press, 2018). Her recent work focuses on private international law, particularly in trade secrecy cases, and on state-to-state and investor–state dispute settlement.

Orit Fischman-Afori, LLD (Hebrew University of Jerusalem), LLM (Hebrew University of Jerusalem), LLB (Hebrew University of Jerusalem), is a law professor at the Striks School of Law, College of Management, teaching a variety of courses and seminars in the fields of intellectual property, law and technology and the mandatory course in corporate law and is often invited to lecture in Israel and worldwide. Professor Fischman-Afori also currently serves as a director of the Heth Center for the Research of Regulation and Competition Law, and as a member of the Israeli Competition Law Tribunal (District Court, Jerusalem). Previously, Professor Fischman-Afori served as Dean of the Striks School of Law beginning in 2016 through 2019, was a guest researcher at University of California, Berkley in 2007, and a guest researcher at Cambridge University in 2013. Her doctorate dissertation focused on derivative works in copyright law and was published as a book in 2005. Professor Fischman-Afori's main fields of research are intellectual property, law and technology, information law and human rights. Professor Fischman- Afori publishes extensively in Israel, Europe and in the US. Her world-wide published studies present multidimensional examination of intellectual property law. Professor Fischman-Afori's publications include the development of the interface between intellectual property and human rights, emphasizing the importance of remedies in the development of substantive law, and promoting open standards along with practical tools for developing intellectual property law.

Thibault Gisclard, PhD (Sorbonne & Max Planck Institute), MS (University of Nancy), is Associate Professor of intellectual property law and comparative law at the University of Lille, where he supervises the university diploma in Industrial Property

Law. Professor Gisclard is notably the coauthor of a book on legal methodology, now at its 5th edition (LexisNexis, 2020). He also teaches biotechnological and pharmaceutical patent law at the University of Poitiers, and is a member of the European Intellectual Property Teachers Network. After an MSc in Biomedical Sciences and a Magister Juris in European Business Law, he devoted his PhD thesis to the subject of comparative analysis of the right of publicity. Professor Gisclard now focuses his research and publications mostly on biotechnological and pharmaceutical patent law, and on the interactions between the law of obligations and IP law, notably as regards damages for infringement of IP rights. He is a member of the European Law Institute.

John M. Golden, JD (Harvard Law School), PhD (Harvard), AB (Harvard), is the Edward S. Knight Chair in Law, Entrepreneurialism and Innovation at the University of Texas at Austin. Professor Golden has taught administrative law, contracts, patent law, and writing seminars relating to innovation and intellectual property. Since 2011, he has served as faculty director of the Andrew Ben White Center in Law, Science and Social Policy. His research has focused primarily on issues relating to innovation policy, institutional design, patents, and remedies. Before joining the faculty of the University of Texas School of Law, he clerked for the Honorable Michael Boudin of the United States Court of Appeals for the First Circuit and then for Associate Justice Stephen Breyer of the United States Supreme Court. He also worked as an associate in the intellectual property department of Wilmer Cutler Pickering Hale and Dorr LLP.

Willem A. Hoyng, PhD (Tilburg University), JD (University of Leiden), is a partner at HOYNG ROKH MONEGIER. Professor Hoyng's practice primarily consists of litigating in the field of intellectual property law. He acts before all the national courts (the courts of first instance, the courts of appeal and the Supreme Court), and regularly litigates before the Court of Justice of the European Union (CJEU) and the European Patent Office (EPO). Professor Hoyng is a member of a select group of lawyers admitted to appear before the Dutch Supreme Court. Professor Hoyng is also involved in advising on European patent strategies and coordinating and conducting European patent proceedings. He is the advisor of many innovative Dutch and foreign multinationals, including pharmaceutical and biotechnological companies. He is a member of the drafting committee of the Rules of Proceedings of the future Unified Patent Court (UPC) and member of the advisory committee of the UPC Preparatory Committee. He also advises the Dutch Ministry of Economic Affairs on UPC matters. Professor Hoyng has been teaching intellectual property law at the University of Tilburg since 1988.

Martin Husovec, PhD (Ludwig Maximilian University & Max Planck Institute), Masters and Bachelor (Pavol Jozef Safarik University), is an Assistant Professor at the London School of Economics and Political Science, LSE Law School. His scholarship deals with questions of innovation policy and digital liberties, in particular regulation of intellectual property and freedom of expression. Professor Husovec is also a fellow at CREATe, Stanford Center for Internet & Society (CIS), and Tilburg Law and Economics Center (TILEC). Previously, he was an assistant professor at Tilburg University in the Netherlands, appointed jointly by Tilburg Institute for Law, Technology, and Society (TILT) and Tilburg Law and Economics Center (TILEC), and held visiting appointments at Stanford Law School (2014), the Japanese Institute for Intellectual Property (2015), the Central European University (2018), the European University Institute (2018) and the University of Cambridge (2019). He is the author of a monograph, *Injunctions against Intermediaries in the European Union*, published by Cambridge University Press in 2017.

Anna-Lena Karczewski is a junior associate at Reetz Sohm Rechtsanwälte (Zurich) and a former research assistant to Professor Peter Picht at the University of Zurich. Ms. Karczewski had her first practice experience with a focus on international intellectual property law at the law firm Heuking Kühn Lüer Wojtek in Hamburg as well as at the law firm Meyerlustenberger Lachenal in Zurich.

Matthias Leistner, PhD (Ludwig Maximillian University), LLM (Trinity Hall Cambridge), is a professor of private law and intellectual property law with information and IT law at Ludwig Maximilian University (LMU). Apart from his chair at LMU Munich, he is a member of the faculty of the Munich Intellectual Property Law Center (MIPLC), and a guest professor for European Intellectual Property Law at the University of Xiamen, and at the Tongji University. Previously, Professor Leistner was head of the Commonwealth Unit at the Max-Planck-Institute for Intellectual Property and Competition Law. From 2007 to 2016 he was the Professor of Civil Law, Intellectual Property Law and Competition Law and director of the Institute for Commercial and Economic Law at the University of Bonn. In the spring term 2020, he was short-termi visiting professor at Columbia Law School. His specialties are intellectual property law (in particular copyright and patents), unfair competition law and internet law. He has published ten books and numerous articles in these fields and has been consulted on IP matters by various government departments and nongovernmental organizations as well as international institutions.

Marcus Norrgård, LLD (University of Helsinki), juris kandidat (University of Helsinki), is professor of law at the University of Helsinki, Vaasa Unit of Legal Studies. Professor Norrgård has served as director of the IPR University Center in Helsinki 2018–2020, as chairman of the Finnish Copyright Council (Tekijänoikeusneuvosto) 2008–2020 and as the editor-in-chief for *Tidskrift, utgiven av Juridiska föreningen i Finland*. Before joining the University of Helsinki, Norrgård was Professor of Intellectual Property Law at the Hanken School of Economics. Professor Norrgård specializes in intellectual property law with a special interest in enforcement issues. He is the sole author of three books and over seventy journal articles and other publications. He has co-edited three books.

Peter Georg Picht, LLM (Yale), PhD (Munich University/Max Planck Institute), is the Chair for Economic Law, Chairman Center for Intellectual Property and Competition Law (CIPCO) at the University of Zurich. Professor Picht is an affiliated research fellow at the Max Planck Institute for Innovation and Competition in Munich. Professor Picht is also a counsel in Schellenberg Wittmer's Competition Group and IP Group. Having worked with the EU Commission's Directorate General for Competition, he joined the Max-Planck-Institute for Intellectual Property and Competition Law in 2008, did his PhD (Promotion) in antitrust law with Professor Drexl and is currently a senior research fellow at the MPI. His academic teaching and writing, as well as his counseling activity, focus on intellectual property law, competition law, international private and procedural law.

Viola Pless is a research fellow with Prof. Dr. Dr. Mackenrodt at the Professorship of Law of Digital Goods, Commerce and Competition at TUM School of Management, Technical University Munich. She has previously held a position as research fellow at Professor Leistner's Chair for Private Law and Intellectual Property Law with Information Law and IT Law (GRUR Chair) at Ludwig Maximilian University Munich. She studied law in Munich and completed her legal clerkship at the Higher Regional Court of Munich. During her studies she was a scholar of the German National Merit Foundation and worked as a student research assistant at the Max Planck Institute for Innovation and Competition in the department of Professor Dr. Josef Drexl. Her further professional experience includes working in the competition law department of international law firms in Brussels and Munich.

Emmanuel Py, PhD (University of Strasburg – CEIPI), is an associate professor of private law at the University of Burgundy, and a member of the European Intellectual Property Teacher's Network and of the Centre Innovation & Droit. Professor Py notably teaches IP law, property law and civil procedure law at the university of Burgundy, and at the CEIPI (Strasburg) and Sciences Po Law School Paris. He is the director of the "Smart Cities and Data Governance" chair and of the eponymous master's degree. His research mostly focuses on patent law, IP litigation and trade secrets. He is the author and coauthor of many articles and books, including "Sanction des conditions de brevetabilité: à propos de la décision d'annulation," in *Les grands arrêts de la propriété intellectuelle*, M. Vivant (ed.), Dalloz 2020; "La contrefaçon transfrontalière d'une invention de procédé: approche de droit comparé," in *Les inventions mises en œuvre par ordinateur*, LexisNexis, 2019; *Droit de la propriété industrielle* (LexisNexis 2016, with J. Raynard and P. Tréfigny); and *La protection des secrets d'affaires: enjeux et perspectives* (LexisNexis 2015, with J.-M. Garinot).

Marco Ricolfi, LLM (Yale), JD (Turin University), is a professor of business law and intellectual property at the Turin Law School, partner of the law firm Weigmann Studio legale, and co-director of the Nexa Center on Internet and Society of the Turin Polytechnic. He is currently the president of the Comitato Consultivo permanente per il diritto d'autore set up at the Ministry for Culture. He was chairman of the Copyright subgroup of the EU High Level Expert Group for the Digital Libraries Initiative (2006–2007) and member of the *Fachbeirat* of the Max Planck Institute for Innovation & Compation. From 2000 to 2015, he was director of the Intellectual Property Master organized by WIPO and the Turin University. Publications include: *Trattato dei marchi: Diritto europeo e nazionale*, Giappichelli, 2015; "I segni distintivi di impresa: Marchio ditta insegna," in P. Auteri et al., *Diritto industrial: Proprietà intellettuale e concorrenza*, Giappichelli, 2020; "Le operazioni di garanzia su macho," *Giurisprudenza Commerciale*, 2020; "Security Rights over Intellectual Property," *Annuario di diritto comparato e di studi legislativi*, 2018; "The Internet of Things and the Ages of Antitrust," *Concorrenza e mercato (Giuffrè)*, 2017; "La protezione doganale della proprietà intellettuale," *Annuario Italiano Diritto d'Autore*, 2016; "Trademarks and Human Rights," in P. Torremans (ed.), *Intellectual Property Law and Human Rights*, Wolters Kluwer, 2015.

Norman Siebrasse, LLM (Chicago), LLB (Queen's), BS (Queen's), is a professor of law at the University of New Brunswick, having previously clerked for the Honourable Madam Justice McLachlin at the Supreme Court of Canada. His research and writing focuses on patent law, in particular pharmaceutical patent law, patent remedies and the intersection of IP law and commercial law. He is a co-editor of *Patent Remedies and Complex Products: Towards a Global Consensus* (Cambridge University Press, 2019). His blog, "Sufficient Description," comments on recent Canadian patent cases and is widely read by the Canadian patent bar. Professor Siebrasse's work is regularly cited by the courts in patent cases.

Rafał Sikorski, PhD (Adam Mickiewicz University), LLM (Central European University), is a professor of law at the Adam Mickiewicz University in Poznań (Poland). His major research areas include patent remedies, the nexus between IP and competition law, standard essential patents, as well as various forms of private ordering in IP and particularly patent law. He has published on patent pools, access to standard essential patents, patent remedies, conflicts-of-law rules for IP contracts and IP infringement as well as copyright law. Results of his research appeared in books published by, for example, Edward Elgar, Cambridge University Press, Wolters Kluwer and C. H. Beck. At the Law Faculty of Adam Mickiewicz University, he teaches various courses on IP, civil law, private international law and European Union law. Rafal Sikorski is also an attorney-at-law at one of the leading Polish law firms where he advises clients in matters related to licensing and protection of IP.

Tomasz Targosz, PhD (Jagiellonian University), LLM (Catholic University of America) is an assistant professor in the Chair of Intellectual Property Law at the Jagiellonian University in Krakow. Professor Targosz is also a partner at Traple Konarski Podrecki & Partners specializing in intellectual property law, in particular in copyright and patent law, and in unfair competition and antitrust. He has represented clients in precedential disputes concerning the protection of pharmaceutical patents and copyright protection on the internet, as well as in proceedings before the President of the Office of Competition and Consumer Protection, and in litigation related to appeals against the body's decisions, in cases involving the abuse of a dominant position, competition-restricting agreements, and practices infringing collective consumer interests. Previously, he was a member of the Graduate College of the universities of Krakow, Heidelberg and Mainz, and a visiting fellow at the Max Planck Institute for Intellectual Property, Competition and Tax Law in Munich. He is the author and co-author of scientific publications on civil and commercial law, copyright law and new technologies law, including internet law, advertising and promotion law, media and personality rights including: *Handbuch des Persönlichkeitsrechts*, the monographs *Abuse of Legal Personality*, and *Copyright Transfer Agreements*, a *Commentary on the Act on Copyright and Related Rights*, and many articles in legal journals. He has been a speaker at conferences and training courses in Poland and elsewhere. He has had individual recommendations in Chambers Europe 2020, The Legal 500, Europe, Middle East & Africa 2020, and IP Stars 2020/21.

Preface

We are delighted to present this book. It is the result of a three-year project that was made possible thanks to the generosity and enthusiasm of our authors and other participants in our dialogues.

The project began in 2017. We had each been involved in prior projects that investigated remedies in intellectual property cases on a comparative international basis. Husovec's monograph *Injunctions against Intermediaries in the European Union* (Cambridge University Press, 2017) focused on injunctive relief in intellectual property cases against intermediaries, and Contreras covered injunctions in patent cases in contributions to the edited volumes *Patent Law Injunctions* (Rafał Sikorski, ed., Wolters Kluwer, 2019) and *Patent Remedies and Complex Products* (C. Bradford Biddle et al., eds., Cambridge University Press, 2019). In comparing notes, however, we realized that scholarship on the comparative aspects of flexibility and tailoring of injunctions under patent law continues to pose many unanswered questions.[1] Since the issue was growing in importance, we decided to organize a workshop with a number of leading patent law experts from various jurisdictions to consider the scope of the issues.

This first dialogue was held in June 2018 at Tilburg University, Netherlands, and was entitled *Mapping Flexibilities for Injunctive Relief in Patent Law: What Can the Member States of the European Union and the United States Learn from Each Other?* The discussion included most of the jurisdictions represented in this book, with the exceptions of Finland, Israel and Canada. Each jurisdiction was represented by two experts. One expert was asked to draft a detailed report summarizing

---

[1] While the subject of flexibility in injunctive relief has been addressed briefly in prior work, it has not previously been the subject of an in-depth study. *See, e.g.,* Cotter 2013, 247–48; Siebrasse et al. 2019, 155–56; Sikorski 2019, 242–47.

the law of injunctions in their jurisdiction, and the second to comment on and validate the findings of that report. In this way, we tried to build solid ground for personal dialogues with the primary goal of deepening common understanding and facilitating the exchange of ideas. This process allowed our Tilburg dialogues to be highly focused, which we hope is also apparent from the contributions in this book.

The participants in the workshop then offered to commit their valuable time to a book project whose goal was to expand the discussion and offer its fruits to a broader readership. To initiate this second phase of the project, we organized a second meeting, this time in beautiful Vienna in conjunction with the annual meeting of the European Law Institute.

To keep the work manageable, we limited our comparative exercise to the transatlantic space only, omitting important jurisdictions in Asia and elsewhere. The book draws its insights from a representative sample of European countries steeped in different legal traditions, the United States, Canada and Israel.[2]

As with any project, we wish some things had worked out differently. The lives of our contributors were deeply impacted by COVID-19, which made the finalization of the project particularly challenging and prevented us from holding a final symposium to discuss and announce our results, which we hope to conduct once the world has returned to a more normal state.

Therefore, we are particularly grateful to eminent patent judges, including Sir Richard Arnold, Dr. Klaus Grabinski and Dr. Peter Block, who shared their views, whether in writing or as participants in one or both of our workshops. We are also grateful to the other participants in our workshops, in particular Colleen Chien, Lisa van Dongen, Florian Schuett, Matěj Myška, Andreas Wiebe, Franz Hofmann, Alain Strowel and Luke McDonagh. We are also grateful for the able assistance of student research assistants Sydney Hecimovich and Matthew Whitehead at the University of Utah, who helped with the preparation of this book.

Last but not least, we wish to acknowledge the financial support of Qualcomm, which funded the organization of the initial Tilburg workshop through the Tilburg Centre for Law and Economics (TILEC), and Intel, which provided funding for the workshop in Vienna, along with open access publication of the book, via the Tilburg Institute for Law, Technology, and Society (TILT). We have contributed all royalties from sales of this book toward making it available on an open access basis to all interested readers. We hope that it will continue to advance the important dialogue on international patent remedies.

---

[2] This is not a comprehensive comparison of European law or litigation. For a comprehensive review, *see, e.g.*, EPO 2016.

REFERENCES

Cotter, Thomas F. 2013. *Comparative Patent Remedies: A Legal and Economic Analysis.* Oxford University Press.

European Patent Office (EPO). 2016. Patent Litigation in Europe: An Overview of National Law and Practice in the EPC Contracting States.

Siebrasse, Norman V., Rafał Sikorski, Jorge L. Contreras, Thomas F. Cotter, John Golden, Sang Jo Jong, Brian J. Love, & David O. Taylor. 2019. "Injunctive Relief" in C. Bradford Biddle, Jorge L. Contreras, Brian J. Love and Norman V. Siebrasse, eds., *Patent Remedies and Complex Products.* Cambridge University Press.

Sikorski, Rafał. 2019. "Between Automatism and Flexibility: Injunctions in Twenty-First Century Patent Law," in Rafał Sikorski ed., *Patent Law Injunctions.* Wolters Kluwer.

1

Introduction

Patent Remedies in the Global Landscape

Jorge L. Contreras and Martin Husovec

Despite their outward differences, all modern legal systems share a number of fundamental features. One of these features is the availability of remedies for injuries that are proven to an adequate legal standard. As explained by Douglas Laycock, one of the preeminent scholars of common law remedies: "The choice of remedy and the measure and administration of the remedy chosen pose a distinctive set of questions – logically separate from the liability determination and usually considered subsequent to that determination – focused on what the court will do to correct or prevent the violation of legal rights that gives rise to liability."[1]

The law recognizes a wide array of remedies, both civil and criminal, ranging from monetary damages and fines to orders constraining future conduct to imprisonment.[2] A legal system, embodied by the legislative, executive and judicial branches of government, selects remedies for particular types of harms based on a range of considerations including compensating the injured party, punishing the injuring party, constraining future conduct by the injuring party, and deterring future injurious conduct by others. It is seldom the case that all available remedies are imposed for a single injurious act, but remedies issued in combination are not at all uncommon.

Like most other areas of the law, patent law offers remedies to injured parties – those whose validly issued patents are infringed by others. Broadly speaking, remedies in patent law fall into two categories – damages, calculated by a variety of measures, and injunctions, which legally restrain the infringer's future conduct. It is not obvious, as a purely logical matter, which of these remedies is preferable in a given situation, or as a general matter. Each has its purposes and can shape

---

[1]   Laycock 2008, 164.
[2]   Criminal penalties for commercial activities should not be underestimated. In the United States, at least, criminal penalties are routinely imposed for antitrust law violations, copyright infringement and trade secret misappropriation.

individual behavior as well as broader societal incentives and deterrents. This being said, injunctive relief is highly valued by patent holders, sometimes far surpassing the perceived value of monetary relief.[3]

Over the years, different jurisdictions have emphasized one form of remedy over another based on the internal structure of their laws, the position that patents occupy within that structure, and the role that judges, lawyers and political bodies play in making legal determinations. In some jurisdictions, patent law has a manifestly instrumental purpose. For example, patents are authorized under the US Constitution for the express purpose of promoting the progress of science and the useful arts (US Const., Art. I, Sec. 8, Cl. 8). In other jurisdictions, patents are regarded as property rights inherent to individual acts of invention. As a result of differences like these, there is a diversity of approaches to injunctive relief in patent cases.[4] One aim of this book is to highlight the differences among jurisdictions in this regard, whether rooted in legal doctrine, broader institutional structures or social and professional norms.

In no jurisdiction that we studied is the issuance of injunctions in patent cases a purely automatic process. Even the most rigid legal system provides some degree of discretion or flexibility in this regard under certain circumstances. Flexibility at the remedial stage of an action can help to alleviate inefficiencies otherwise caused by uniformity within the patent system. That is, because patents extend a uniform term of protection, and uniform rights to enforce against infringers, to all patented inventions irrespective of their degree of innovation or usefulness, "society pays too much for numerous innovations that would have been created with less robust protection, while in other cases patent rights are less extensive than would be necessary to induce the creation of certain costly but socially desirable inventions."[5]

This is the problem of uniformity cost – when the law affords the same legal rights to all inventions, some are invariably protected too much and some are protected too little, resulting in a cost to society with respect to these inventions. But because it is impossible to tailor patent grants to the societal value of individual inventions, tailoring mechanisms that can be deployed in the area of remedies can help to address inefficiencies resulting from uniformity cost.[6] However, as remedies cannot redefine the scope of patent rights by going beyond the baseline of protection set by the legislature, tailoring and flexibility of remedies are more likely to resolve

---

[3] We do not address in this book the use of so-called anti-suit injunctions – interjurisdictional procedural remedies that have been used with increasing frequency in certain patent disputes. See Contreras 2019. While these injunctions are used in some patent suits, they are not, themselves, remedies flowing from patent law, but from interjurisdictional competition. As such they fall outside the scope of this book.

[4] *See, e.g.*, Cotter 2013; Siebrasse et al. 2019; Sikorski 2019.

[5] Carroll 2007, 423.

[6] Id. at 425. See also Burk & Lemley 2009, 137–41 (referring to judicial flexibility in the issuance and tailoring of injunctions as a "policy lever" that can help to alleviate the inherent costs associated with the uniformity of legal protection in different industries).

situations when inventions are protected too much (i.e., a remedy may be tailored to award the rights holder less than the full scope of its legal entitlement, but cannot be tailored to give the rights holder more).[7]

Thus, another goal of this book is to explore the degree to which judges in different jurisdictions employ tools of flexibility and tailoring in the imposition of patent law injunctions. As with the decision to issue injunctions, this set of tools is highly subject to the doctrinal, structural and normative background of individual jurisdictions. Hence, we observe a variety of approaches, both to the issuance of injunctions and to the tailoring of injunctive remedies after the decision to issue them has been made. This variety also demonstrates varying degrees of institutional openness towards judicial reconciliation of fundamental trade-offs implicit in the patent system.

It is not a goal of this book, however, to suggest that strict uniformity among jurisdictions is possible or even desirable. Like other scholars who have considered the issue, we do not suggest that an international treaty or harmonization of legal regimes is a desirable or even feasible goal.[8] This book demonstrates that injunction practices are embedded in the institutional makeup of each jurisdiction, such that simple legal transplants would be inadequate to address perceived deficiencies in the practices of any given jurisdiction.

Rather, we seek to elucidate existing flexibility mechanisms within the legal frameworks that have developed around the world, to identify their similarities and differences, their probable driving forces, and to analyze trends that may emerge as patent litigation becomes an increasingly global and interconnected enterprise.[9] We hope that this comparative and analytical study will assist judges and litigators to learn from the diverse approaches to patent injunctions taken by different jurisdictions.

REFERENCES

Burk, Dan L. & Mark A. Lemley. 2009. *The Patent Crisis and How the Courts Can Solve It.* University of Chicago Press.

Carroll, Michael W. 2007. "Patent Injunctions and the Problem of Uniformity Cost," *Michigan Telecommunications and Technology Law Review* 13: 421–43. University of Chicago Press.

Contreras, Jorge L. 2019. "The New Extraterritoriality: FRAND Royalties, Anti-Suit Injunctions and the Global Race to the Bottom in Disputes Over Standards-Essential Patents," *Boston University Journal of Science and Technology* 25:251–90.

Cotter, Thomas F. 2013. *Comparative Patent Remedies: A Legal and Economic Analysis.* Oxford University Press.

---

[7] See Dobbs 1993, 113.

[8] See Cotter 2015, 2 ("a treaty that goes into greater detail about when injunctions must or should be granted ... would not be a good idea").

[9] *See, e.g.,* Contreras 2019 (describing global litigation in the area of standard-essential patents).

2015. Patent Remedies: Recommendations for International Best Practices. Minnesota Legal Studies Research Paper No. 16-40.

Dobbs, Dan B. 1993. *Dobbs Law of Remedies Vol. 1* (2nd ed.). West Publishing.

Laycock, Douglas. 2008. "How Remedies Became a Field: A History," *Review of Litigation* 27:161–267.

Siebrasse, Norman V., Rafał Sikorski, Jorge L. Contreras, Thomas F. Cotter, John Golden, Sang Jo Jong, Brian J. Love & David O. Taylor. 2019. "Injunctive Relief," in C. Bradford Biddle, Jorge L. Contreras, Brian J. Love and Norman V. Siebrasse eds., *Patent Remedies and Complex Products*. Cambridge University Press.

Sikorski, Rafał ed., 2019. *Patent Law Injunctions*. Wolters Kluwer.

2

Injunctive Relief in Patent Law under TRIPS

Graeme B. Dinwoodie and Rochelle C. Dreyfuss

Traditionally, intellectual property's right to exclude has implied that injunctive relief should always be available at the conclusion of a successful infringement action.[1] However, in recent years that view has evolved. As discussed in Chapter 14, in the United States, the 2006 Supreme Court decision in *eBay Inc. v. MercExchange* imposed a four-part test requiring the plaintiff in a patent case seeking a permanent injunction to demonstrate "(1) that it has suffered an irreparable injury; (2) that remedies available at law, such as monetary damages, are inadequate to compensate for that injury; (3) that, considering the balance of hardships between the plaintiff and defendant, a remedy in equity is warranted; and (4) that the public interest would not be disserved by a permanent injunction."[2] While this standard appears to impose quite a restrictive test, several members of the court emphasized that even under this discretionary standard, injunctive relief should remain available in the vast majority of cases.[3]

Furthermore, Justice Kennedy wrote a concurring opinion delineating specific areas where such relief might be appropriately withheld. First, he suggested that the availability of injunctive relief may furnish firms that use patents primarily to obtain licensing fees (so-called patent assertion entities or PAEs) too much bargaining power in licensing negotiations and that since they are only interested in fees, monetary relief is usually sufficient to compensate them.[4] Second, he stated that when a patent is "but a small component" of a larger product, the opportunity for holdups creates undue leverage. As a result, injunctive relief in such cases could undermine the public interest.[5] Third, he argued, giving the example of business

[1] Cf. Simpson 1936, 183.
[2] *eBay* (2006, p. 391).
[3] Id. at 395 (Roberts, J., concurring, joined by Justices Scalia and Ginsburg); at 396 (Kennedy, J. concurring, joined by Justices Stevens, Souter, and Breyer).
[4] Id. at 396.
[5] Id. at 396–97.

method patents, that injunctions may be withheld when the asserted patents are vague and of "suspect validity."[6]

As the other chapters in this volume attest, many countries have now adopted a similar discretionary approach to the award of injunctive relief. The question we address in this chapter is whether that position is consistent with the Agreement on Trade-Related Aspects of Intellectual Property Rights (TRIPS or the TRIPS Agreement).[7] To be sure, the TRIPS Agreement is largely conceptual in character and the section addressing enforcement (Part III of TRIPS) is of a very general nature. However, the Agreement does require member states to give courts the authority to order parties to desist from infringement,[8] it requires remedies to deter future infringements,[9] it imposes national treatment and most-favored-nation (MFN) obligations,[10] and it bars discrimination by field of technology.[11] In addition, it cautions member states that protection exceeding its standards is allowable, but only if such a measure "does not contravene the provisions of [the] Agreement."[12] Thus, TRIPS also sets a ceiling on right-holder protection. Since empirical evidence on the effect of *eBay* in US patent litigation shows that its impact falls disproportionately on certain right holders (not surprisingly, PAEs in particular) and on specific industries,[13] all of these TRIPS obligations are implicated.

In this chapter, we first outline what we regard as the conceptual features of TRIPS. We then consider the individual provisions touching on enforcement and how they might be interpreted. Finally, we discuss specific applications of the discretionary approach and ask whether World Trade Organization (WTO) decision makers would find any of the outcomes incompatible with TRIPS obligations. Our analysis draws heavily on our book, *A Neofederalist Vision of TRIPS*.[14]

A. TRIPS AND ENFORCEMENT

Several features of the TRIPS Agreement (and indeed of international intellectual property law generally) would appear to limit its relevance to the question whether an *eBay*-like approach to injunctive relief is TRIPS-compliant. First, like most norm-setting international instruments in the field, the TRIPS Agreement largely imposes

---

[6] Id.
[7] Agreement on Trade-Related Aspects of Intellectual Property Rights (TRIPS), Apr. 15, 1994, Marrakesh Agreement Establishing the World Trade Organization, Annex 1C, Legal Instruments – Results of the Uruguay Round, Vol. 31, 33 ILM 81 (1994) [hereinafter TRIPS Agreement].
[8] Id. art. 41(1).
[9] Id. art. 41(1).
[10] Id. arts. 3 & 4.
[11] Id. art. 27(1).
[12] Id. art. 1(1).
[13] *See, e.g.*, Seaman 2016; Gupta & Kesan 2016; Lim & Craven 2009, 798.
[14] Dinwoodie & Dreyfuss 2012.

only minimum standards. Thus, Article 1(1) of TRIPS provides that "Members may, but shall not be obliged to, implement in their law more extensive protection than is required by this Agreement, provided that such protection does not contravene the provisions of this Agreement." Under a minimum standards regime, the possibility of noncompliance would arise directly only when a jurisdiction fails to make injunctive relief available,[15] fails to offer remediation that deters further infringement,[16] or interferes with the structural features of TRIPS, such as its various bars on discrimination. And to the extent TRIPS sets a ceiling, excessive enforcement could also raise compliance issues.

Second, TRIPS was one of the first multilateral forays into questions of patent (or indeed any intellectual property) enforcement other than at a very general level.[17] As such, it is perhaps inevitable, if not desirable, that the text of the provisions on remedies has little detail, and that the plain language of the Agreement affords WTO members substantial flexibility. In other words, this part of the Agreement allows member states more latitude than one finds in areas where there has been a century or more of serial international convergence among nation states.[18] Indeed, this cautious attitude has been emphasized by both a WTO dispute settlement panel and the WTO Appellate Body in the WTO TRIPS reports to date that have interpreted provisions in the enforcement section of the Agreement.[19] (Reflective of this fact, post-TRIPS, developed countries have tried to ratchet up the level of

---

[15] Art. 44(1).

[16] Art. 41(1).

[17] See Gervais 2012, 564; World Trade Organization 2012, 136; Roffe & Seuba 2015, 18–19. Some provisions on enforcement were contained in the trademark sections of the Paris Convention, see Paris Convention for the Protection of Industrial Property, Jul. 14, 1967, 21 UST 1583, 828 UNTS 305 [hereinafter Paris Convention], arts. 9–10, but these were focused primarily on border measures. Likewise, the adequacy of intellectual property enforcement options in the United States had been successfully challenged under the predecessor to the World Trade Organization, the General Agreement on Tariffs and Trade, but this had been on national treatment grounds. See Panel Report, United States – Section 337 of the Tariff Act of 1930, L/ 6439 (Nov. 7, 1989) [hereinafter *US – Section 337*].

[18] See Taubman 2011, 110; Reichman 1997, 344 ("The enforcement provisions of the TRIPS Agreement have been drafted in terms of broad legal standards rather than as narrow rules. Their very ambiguity, allows … dispute-settlement panels to take local circumstances and diverse legal philosophies into account when seeking to mediate actual or potential conflicts between states").

[19] See Appellate Body Report, United States – Section 211 Omnibus Appropriations Act of 1998, WT/DS176/AB/R (Aug. 6, 2001) [hereinafter *United States – Section 211*] at para. 8.97 ("Prior to the TRIPS Agreement, provisions related to enforcement were limited to general obligations to provide legal remedies and seizure of infringing goods"); Panel Report, *China – Measures Affecting the Protection and Enforcement of Intellectual Property Rights*, WT/DS362/R (Jan. 26, 2009) [hereinafter *China – Enforcement*] at para. 7.241 ("[Prior to TRIPS,] the pre-existing international intellectual property agreements contained comparatively few minimum standards on enforcement procedures beyond national treatment and certain optional provisions"). In contrast, Article 61, on criminal procedures, uses the formulation "Members shall provide for criminal procedures and penalties to be applied," a phrase the panel in the Saudi Arabia – IPR dispute interpreted as requiring states to do more than merely adopt a written law

international enforcement obligations through plurilateral and bilateral initiatives, such as the Anti-Counterfeiting Trade Agreement or ACTA.[20]) Amplifying that point, this characterization of the enforcement provisions might also to a lesser extent be applied to the substantive patent provisions, which are arguably newer and less prescriptive than parallel sections of the Agreement on copyright or trademark.[21]

For example, although Article 41(1) mandates that specific enforcement procedures delineated in the subsequent provisions of the Agreement are available to courts, the general principles applicable to enforcement matters that are outlined in Article 41 appear more in the nature of standards than rules. This latitude is also reflected in the textual structure of the specific remedial provisions. Thus, many of the remedial articles (including Article 44 on injunctions, but also those addressing damages and other remedies) contain the formulation "the judicial authorities shall have the authority."[22] As the WTO panel in *China – Enforcement* put it on reading the same language in Article 59, "the obligation is to 'have' authority, [it is] not an obligation to 'exercise' authority."[23] Likewise, the Appellate Body in *United States – Section 211* adopted a relatively narrow reading of Article 42, which generally requires that civil judicial procedures must be "made available" to enable right holders to protect against infringement.[24] Accordingly, while Article 44 requires that judicial authorities have "the authority to order a party to desist from an infringement" and Article 50 uses similar language regarding provisional remedies, neither mandates that injunctive relief (preliminary or mandatory) be awarded in all cases. Nor do they fully dictate the detail or form of that relief.

Third, Article 1(1) of the TRIPS Agreement explicitly endorses the longstanding principle of international intellectual property law that different WTO member states should be able to implement their international obligations in ways best suited to their jurisprudential tradition.[25] That position is reinforced in the enforcement section by Article 41(5), which states that this part "does not create any obligation to

---

authorizing criminal penalties. See Panel Report, Saudi Arabia – Measures Concerning the Protection of Intellectual Property Rights, WT/DS567/R (Jun. 16, 2020), at paras. 7.207–09.

[20] See Anti-Counterfeiting Trade Agreement, Mar. 31, 2011 Text, available at https://ustr.gov/acta [hereinafter ACTA]; see also Roffe & Seuba 2015, 18 (discussing Free Trade Agreements).

[21] Post-TRIPS efforts at reaching agreement on more detailed substantive patent law have stalled. See Reichman & Dreyfuss 2007.

[22] See TRIPS, arts. 44–46.

[23] *China – Enforcement*, at para. 7.236. Article 59 requires that "competent authorities shall have the authority to order the destruction or disposal of infringing goods." See TRIPS, art. 59.

[24] See *United States – Section 211*, at para. 215 ("Making [civil judicial enforcement] available means making it 'obtainable', putting it 'within one's reach' and 'at one's disposal' in a way that has sufficient force or efficacy"); id. at para. 216 (noting that TRIPS reserved "a degree of discretion to Members on this, taking into account 'differences in national legal systems'," and commenting that "no Member's national system of civil judicial procedures will be identical to that of another Member").

[25] See TRIPS Agreement, art. 1(1) ("Members shall be free to determine the appropriate method of implementing the provisions of this Agreement within their own legal system and practice").

put in place a judicial system for the enforcement of intellectual property rights that is distinct from that for the enforcement of law in general, nor does it affect the capacity of Members to enforce their law in general."

Taken together, these features ensure that the TRIPS Agreement serves only to define in very general terms the substantial policy space in which WTO member states can themselves devise a variety of different approaches to the grant or structure of injunctive relief. Moreover, when the WTO's Dispute Settlement Body (DSB) interprets TRIPS, it sometimes looks beyond the text or the history of particular provisions and considers the national practices then in force.[26] Accordingly, in disputes concerning TRIPS compliance with enforcement, the national practices revealed by the chapters in this volume, which address the situation in different countries, may contribute to the adjudicators' understanding of the meaning of TRIPS. Given the many differences in these practices, one might expect the DSB would allow different member states substantial room to implement their obligations in varying ways between the minimum and maximum.[27]

That said, a relatively deferential approach to the detail of member states' choices on patent injunctions reveals a paradox. One of the principal motivations behind TRIPS was a sense among developed countries that many countries had enacted substantively compliant intellectual property regimes that were rendered nugatory by ineffective remedies.[28] Indeed, the principal WTO decisions to date addressing enforcement issues have highlighted this point.[29] But one must distinguish between the motivation for TRIPS and the content of what was finally agreed, especially when moving beyond the treatment of pirated or counterfeit goods (which nominally was the most urgent enforcement challenge justifying the developed world putting enforcement on the TRIPS agenda). However, as the next section discusses,

---

[26] See Panel Report, Canada – Patent Protection of Pharmaceutical Products, WT/DS114/R (Mar. 17, 2000) [hereinafter *Canada – Pharmaceutical Patents*], at para. 7.69. In *Canada – Pharmaceutical Patents*, given a lack of consensus on the question at issue, the panel took a deferential approach to the question of Canadian compliance. See id. at para. 7.82.

[27] See Dinwoodie & Dreyfuss 2012, 37 ("the provisions on remedies ... require legal systems to provide the 'authority' to order discovery, injunctions, damages, and other relief, but these provisions do not mandate particular forms of relief in individual cases, thus leaving it to local decision-makers to tailor remedies to local conditions"); see also Sarnoff 2010; Malbon et al. 2014, para. 41.13.

[28] See *Taubman* 2011, 109–10; *Malbon et al.* 2014, 615.

[29] *See, e.g., United States – Section 211*, at para. 8.97 ("The inclusion of this Part on enforcement in the TRIPS Agreement was one of the major accomplishments of the Uruguay Round negotiations as it expanded the scope of enforcement ... of intellectual property rights"); *China – Enforcement*, at para. 7.241 ("One of the major reasons for the conclusion of the TRIPS Agreement was the desire to set out a minimum set of procedures and remedies that judicial, border and other competent authorities must have available to them. This represented a major advance in intellectual property protection"); see also TRIPS, recital 2(c) ("Recognizing ... the need for new rules and disciplines concerning ... the provision of effective and appropriate means for the enforcement of trade-related intellectual property rights, taking into account differences in national legal systems").

the standards are not toothless. Combined with substantive provisions that have received more scrutiny (such as the cornerstone guarantees of national treatment and MFN), there are specific obligations to which member states must adhere.

B. PROVISIONS IN TRIPS SPECIFICALLY RELEVANT
TO PATENT INJUNCTIONS

The TRIPS Agreement includes several provisions relevant to the question of how much discretion courts (and member states) enjoy when remediating infringement. Article 41 sets out the general obligations on enforcement. Subsection (1) requires that remedial measures must be "effective," "expeditious" and "constitute a deterrent to further infringements."[30] And they must "be applied in such a manner as to avoid the creation of barriers to legitimate trade and to provide for safeguards against their abuse."[31] The procedural protections of Article 41(2)–(4) are similarly framed: procedures must be "fair and equitable," and "not . . . unnecessarily complicated or costly, or entail unreasonable time-limits or unwarranted delays."[32]

Article 44 deals specifically with injunctions. Subsection (1) requires that "the judicial authorities shall have the authority to order a party to desist from an infringement, inter alia to prevent the entry into the channels of commerce in their jurisdiction of imported goods that involve the infringement of an intellectual property right, immediately after customs clearance of such goods."[33] In some respects, this statement simply affirms that the measures required of member states under Article 41(1) should include the authority to offer injunctive relief. As noted, as per the *China – Enforcement* panel report, all that is required is that the authority to award such relief exists; it does not have to be exercised in any individual case. The power to deny injunctive relief is also evident in Article 44(2), which deals with the

---

[30] See TRIPS, art. 41(1).

[31] See id.

[32] See TRIPS, art. 41(2) ("Procedures concerning the enforcement of intellectual property rights shall be fair and equitable. They shall not be unnecessarily complicated or costly, or entail unreasonable time-limits or unwarranted delays"); id. art. 41(3) ("Decisions on the merits of a case shall preferably be in writing and reasoned. They shall be made available at least to the parties to the proceeding without undue delay. Decisions on the merits of a case shall be based only on evidence in respect of which parties were offered the opportunity to be heard"); id. art. 41(4) ("4. Parties to a proceeding shall have an opportunity for review by a judicial authority of final administrative decisions and, subject to jurisdictional provisions in a Member's law concerning the importance of a case, of at least the legal aspects of initial judicial decisions on the merits of a case"). See also TRIPS art. 42 ("Members shall make available to right holders civil judicial procedures concerning the enforcement of any intellectual property right covered by this Agreement. Defendants shall have the right to written notice which is timely and contains sufficient detail, including the basis of the claims").

[33] Article 44(1) also limits this obligation as regards innocent infringement, providing that "Members are not obliged to accord such authority in respect of protected subject matter acquired or ordered by a person prior to knowing or having reasonable grounds to know that dealing in such subject matter would entail the infringement of an intellectual property right."

specific issue of government use. It creates a general right for governments (and authorized third parties) to use an invention upon the payment of "adequate remuneration in the circumstances of each case, taking into account the economic value of the authorization."[34] Although Article 50, on provisional relief, is somewhat more detailed, courts necessarily have more discretion over the decision to order such relief while the case is *pendente lite* – before the defendant is found to be an infringer – than after its liability is adjudicated.

Taken together, these provisions suggest that, other than possibly the question of the adequacy of monetary relief to deter infringement, the WTO might give scant scrutiny to challenges concerning the denial of injunctive relief. Indeed, Nuno Pires De Carvalho, a commonly cited commentator on the patent provisions of TRIPS, does not include in his introductory narrative a separate section on remedies or enforcement. He simply identifies enforcement as the source of a "cluster of flexibilities," representing "a very strong commitment by Members towards accommodation of different legal regimes."[35] Even ACTA, which attempted to delineate signatory states' obligations on enforcement in far greater detail, nonetheless acknowledges that its enforcement requirements must take into account "differences in [states'] respective legal systems and practices."[36]

Nonetheless, there is language in the Agreement that constrains member states at both ends. Thus, one might treat the juxtaposition of the requirements that measures must be "effective," "expeditious" and "constitute a deterrent to further infringements" with the caution found in Article 41(1) that remedies "be applied in such a manner as to avoid the creation of barriers to legitimate trade and to provide for safeguards against their abuse" as articulation of some standard of proportionality.[37] This would at least allow such considerations to be taken into account, and might even prohibit disproportionate injunctive relief.[38] De Carvalho takes this argument one step further. He notes that in contrast to the substantive "standards of protection – which are generally enunciated as *minimum standards* – many provisions in Part III of the TRIPS Agreement [on Enforcement] are phrased in a way that leaves WTO Members no alternative to the measures thereby established and thus do not provide for *minimum standards* but provide instead for *mandatory standards*. The reason for this, as enunciated in the first paragraph of the Preamble as well as in Article 44.1, is to avoid enforcement measures becoming abusive and constituting themselves as barriers to legitimate trade."[39]

---

[34] The provision specifically cites art. 31(h) for the standard of compensation government must pay.
[35] See De Carvalho 2010, 64.
[36] ACTA, supra note 20, recital 4.
[37] Cf. Taubman 2011, 110.
[38] See *infra* text accompanying notes 42–44.
[39] See De Carvalho 2010, 64 (emphasis in original).

While the distinction drawn by De Carvalho between "minimum" and "mandatory" is perhaps too stark, given the latitude that is incorporated via the broad language of the enforcement standards,[40] there are provisions that support the view that there is something of a ceiling on enforcement – or at least that states can create one. Article 7, which articulates the objectives of the Agreement, stresses that TRIPS is intended to "contribute to the promotion of technological innovation and to the transfer and dissemination of technology, to the mutual advantage of producers and users of technological knowledge and in a manner conducive to social and economic welfare, and to a balance of rights and obligations." To accomplish that balance, Article 8(1) permits members "in formulating or amending their laws and regulations, [to] adopt measures necessary to protect public health and nutrition . . . provided consistent with the Agreement." Article 8(2) notes that "appropriate measures, provided that they are consistent with the provisions of this Agreement, may be needed to prevent the abuse of intellectual property rights by right holders or the resort to practices which unreasonably restrain trade or adversely affect the international transfer of technology," and Article 40(2) authorizes WTO members to address anticompetitive licensing practices or conditions and adopt appropriate measures to prevent or control such practices.

It can even be argued that excessive enforcement might itself create a possible TRIPS violation.[41] Notably, in 2010, India filed a WTO complaint against the European Union and the Netherlands regarding repeated seizures (based on alleged patent infringement) of generic drugs originating in India but transiting through ports in the Netherlands to third-country destinations. India alleged violation not only of the General Agreement on Tariffs and Trade (GATT) but also various provisions of TRIPS including Articles 41 and 42.[42] The dispute has not been resolved. However, the complaint suggests that the provisions in Part III can be seen as imposing some maximum as well as minimum levels of protection for right

---

[40] See Reichman 1997, 348–49 ("the relevant enforcement provisions – unlike the substantive standards set out in the TRIPS Agreement – are truly minimum standards, as attested by the loose and open-ended language in which they are cast"). Professor Reichman is here using "minimum" to refer to the low level of harmonization that is required relative to the substantive standards.

[41] Cf. *United States – Section 211*, at paras. 206–07 (noting that sections 1–2 of Part III "[introduce] an international minimum standard which Members are bound to implement in their domestic legislation").

[42] Cf. Request for Consultations, European Union and a Member State – Seizure of Generic Drugs in Transit, WT/DS408/1 (May 11, 2010); EU, India Drop Generics Dispute to Focus on FTA Talks, *FDAnews*, Jan. 24, 2011, available at http://fdanews.com/newsletter/article?issueId=14404&articleId=133690; Request for Consultations, European Union and a Member State – Seizure of Generic Drugs in Transit, WT/DS409/1 (May 12, 2010) (complaint by Brazil); see generally Grosse Ruse-Khan 2011.

holders.[43] Article 1(1) does not preclude this argument because protection beyond that mandated must still be "consistent with the Agreement."

The analysis of the discretion member states enjoy over injunctive relief is additionally complicated by the possibility that the DSB might also consider other provisions of the TRIPS Agreement. These include the guarantees of national treatment and MFN in Articles 3 and 4, Article 27(1)'s bar on discrimination by field of technology, and the conditions attached to grants of compulsory licenses found in Article 31.

Because of the conceptual similarity between ordering monetary damages in lieu of injunctive relief and granting a compulsory license, Article 31 arguably imposes the most stringent and detailed limits on the exercise of discretion.[44] While that provision authorizes states to order compulsory licenses, it includes a long set of conditions.[45] Thus, member states must consider applications for licenses on their individual merits after efforts to obtain permission from the right holder; the decision must be appealable; the license must be limited to the authorized purpose; it must be nonexclusive and nonassignable; it must be terminable when the circumstance leading to the authorization ends; and it can extend only to supply of the domestic market of the authorizing state.[46] The provision also requires the payment of "adequate remuneration in the circumstances of each case, taking into account the economic value of the authorization."[47] (This condition is referenced in Article 44(2) on government use.)

To some extent, a decision to deny injunctive relief complies with these conditions. The adjudication constitutes a consideration of the case on its individual merits and both the merits and the remedial award can be appealed. The denial of the injunction is limited in that it is framed by the claims in the complaint and, in some cases, it is also accompanied by specific conditions. Monetary damages are similar to court-ordered royalties and thus arguably serve as compensation (whether the compensation is adequate is taken up in Section C.1). However, except for cases where the infringer initially tried to license the patent, it is difficult to consider the institution of an infringement action a substitute for an effort to obtain authorization. And while this condition uses the term "may" rather than "shall," the subsection also appears to limit a waiver of this requirement to national emergencies or other urgent circumstances. Moreover, because decisions in infringement cases bind only the litigants, the use by the defendant is not, at least as a technical matter,

---

[43] See Taubman 2011, 110 ("TRIPS imposes positive obligations not unduly to hamper trade that does not infringe IP rights, even while recognizing that firms should expect credible and effective means of appropriately enforcing their IP rights"); Malbon et al. 2014, para. 41.25 (quoting Grosse Ruse-Kahn).

[44] See Dinwoodie & Dreyfuss, 2012, 76–78; Gervais 2012, para. 2.539 at 578.

[45] See Dinwoodie & Dreyfuss 2012, 77.

[46] See TRIPS, art. 31. The limit to use by the authorizing state was lifted by art. 31bis, but only as it pertains to protecting public health.

[47] TRIPS, art. 31(h).

"non-exclusive." Furthermore, the order likely runs to those in privity with the defendant, including assignees; as a final decision, it may not be terminable; and the award may not include specific geographic limitations.

To be sure, under Article 31(h), some of these conditions are not applicable to practices determined to be anticompetitive. Furthermore, the reference to antic-ompetitive behavior is supplemented by Article 8(2) on the right to prevent abuse and unreasonable restraints and by Article 40(2) on anticompetitive licensing prac-tices. In addition, Article 31(l) permits compulsory licenses to deal with blocking patents. These present problems very similar to that posed by the owner of a patent on a small component of a large product trying to hold up development of the product, where Justice Kennedy suggested injunctions are inappropriate. However, it is an open question whether the DSB would read these provisions to include practices, such as PAE suits, which can have abusive aspects but do not rise to violations of a state's competition (antitrust) law. Nor is it clear whether it would consider hold-up problems sufficiently akin to the blocking situation to trigger the application of subsection (l).

Of course, the DSB might adopt a more formalistic approach, and confine assessment of a denial of injunctive relief to the mandates of Articles 41 and 44. It might also reason that since the enforcement part specifically references Article 31 (h), but not any of the other conditions set out in Article 31, the rest is not relevant. However, one cannot be entirely confident that this is how WTO adjudicators would approach the task. Experience to date suggests that panels tend to examine compliance under every conceivable provision. One notorious example is *Canada – Pharmaceutical Patents*. There, the panel first assessed the TRIPS compatibility of Canada's two challenged exceptions under Article 30, which creates a three-step assessment of the permissibility of domestic exceptions in patent law.[48] By its terms, such exceptions must be "limited" and one way in which Canada's exceptions were limited was that, as a practical matter, they applied only to pharmaceuticals (see Chapter 5 on Canada). However, the panel also subjected the exceptions to the rigors of Article 27(1), which prohibits discrimination against a particular field of technology, but which was arguably intended only to guarantee protection for a variety of subject matter previously unprotected by patent in a number of coun-tries.[49] Elsewhere, we have heavily criticized the approach of the *Canada – Pharmaceutical Patents* panel,[50] and this discussion, showing how Article 31 could undermine the latitude built into the enforcement part, supports the notion that WTO adjudicators should be cautious when applying provisions cumulatively. Not

[48] See TRIPS, art. 30 ("Members may provide limited exceptions to the exclusive rights conferred by a patent, provided that such exceptions do not unreasonably conflict with a normal exploit-ation of the patent and do not unreasonably prejudice the legitimate interests of the patent owner, taking account of the legitimate interests of third parties").
[49] *Canada – Pharmaceutical Patents*, at para. 7.91; see also id. at para. 4.6 n. 27.
[50] See Dinwoodie & Dreyfuss 2012, 66–67 & 71.

all provisions are like the Basic Principles in Part I, which are meant to apply to the Agreement as a whole. Nonetheless, the prospect that a panel or the Appellate Body might apply Article 31 cannot be dismissed, in which case some denials of injunctive relief are suspect.[51]

The applicability of other guarantees that arguably constrain judicial discretion is highly dependent on the impact of denials of injunctive relief. We now consider them, along with the question of the adequacy of relief.

C. APPLICATION OF A DISCRETIONARY APPROACH TO INJUNCTIVE RELIEF

Putting the application of Article 31 to one side, it can readily be argued that the approach the US Supreme Court articulated in *eBay* would satisfy TRIPS standards. Indeed, several scholars have explored the issue and concluded that *eBay* is likely consistent with TRIPS.[52] Although, as illustrated in the other chapters of this volume, the approach to the issue of injunctive relief varies quite widely among member states, sometimes for reasons related to the character or organizations of particular legal systems, we reach similar conclusions as to the variations described in this volume. The structural features of TRIPS noted earlier, as well as experience with WTO adjudicators hesitating to go far beyond the text and resolving contested policy choices, suggests that future decisions are likely to allow continued room for such choices unless they violate a clear textual dictate.

Yet, as noted, there are a few clear textual requirements. Injunctions must be available in at least some instances; that is evident from Article 44. And Article 41(1) sets out general requirements according to which decisions to grant, deny or condition relief must be assessed: the relief must be effective and expeditious, and remedies must be sufficient to deter future infringement. These are the TRIPS standards that are most likely to be engaged by any approach to injunctive relief, but discretionary decisions can have differential impacts that might raise issues under other provisions in the Agreement. Thus, our conclusion comes with several caveats.

1. *The Adequacy of Monetary Damages*

Article 41(1) requires that the relief granted – under *eBay* this would be something short of an injunction – must be effective and sufficient to deter future

---

[51] Not everyone agrees. See Knowledge Ecology International, General Statement to the 15th Standing Committee on the Law of Patents (SCP) (Oct. 12, 2010), available at www.keionline .org/21393 ("Finally, KEI notes that the experts failed to distinguish between compulsory licenses that are granted under the procedures of Part II of the TRIPS, concerning patent rights, and those granted under Part III of the TRIPS, concerning the remedies for infringement of those rights"); Sarnoff 2010, 58 & 59.

[52] *See, e.g.,* De Carvalho 2010, 64; Sarnoff 2010, 48; Malbon et al 2014, paras. 44.04–44.05.

infringement. So, will offering the patentee damages in lieu of an injunction meet this standard? To be sure, the four-factor test set out in *eBay* requires the court to consider whether the right holder could be adequately compensated with money damages and presumably other countries do the same. Yet adequate compensation may not always be enough to deter infringement. A rational actor may believe that there is a strong probability that its infringement will not be discovered and that if it is, the award of damages will be no less burdensome than royalties. Indeed, awards in the future may be considerably lower than royalties. After all, courts tend to make their calculations by reference to comparable licensing arrangements,[53] but comparable rates may fall over time as potential licensees come to understand the circumstances in which they will not be enjoined and, in those circumstances, refuse to pay what the patent holder demands. As a result, these judicially established royalty rates may come to set a ceiling on the price patent holders can negotiate from licensees.[54]

Whether that violates TRIPS may depend on the rationale cited to withhold relief. One concerns PAEs. Christopher Seaman's work shows that the impact of *eBay* on them is considerable.[55] Since one of the justifications for denying an injunction in these cases is that the PAE industry was developed "primarily to obtain licensing fees"[56] and that the fees demanded with threats of injunctive relief were "exorbitant,"[57] awarding them damages at a low rate may not raise difficult questions. Normatively, their return on investment should be lower than their exorbitant demands. But since Justice Kennedy was likely thinking about patent trolls – right holders who send demand letters to naïve defendants in the hope they will quickly capitulate and pay up[58] – denying injunctive relief could be thought of as a safeguard against abuse, which, as we saw, is specifically mentioned in Article 41 (1), as well as in Articles 8(2) and 40(2).

However, it is not clear that all entities that earn their revenue through assertions are the bad actors the Supreme Court had in mind. For one thing, there are organizations that specialize in inventing. For example, universities and government laboratories are largely engaged in fundamental research; they do not commercialize their work themselves. In some cases, they may assign their patents and turn over enforcement to assignees. Since they are strongly encouraged to license on a nonexclusive basis, enforcement will largely be up to them.[59] To courts, they may

---

[53] *See, e.g.,* Cotter 2018, 164.
[54] Venkatesan 2009; Lim & Craven 2009, 817.
[55] See Seaman 2016, 1988 (noting that PAEs prevailing on liability were awarded injunctions in 16% of the cases as compared to other patentees, who were successful in 80% of their cases).
[56] *eBay* (2006, p. 396) (Kennedy, J., concurring).
[57] Id.
[58] *See, e.g.,* Lemley & Melamed 2013, 2163 (describing "bottom-feeder trolls"); Johnson 2014, 2033 (describing the problem in Vermont and its response in Act of Jul. 1, 2013, No. 44, § 6, 2013 Vt. Legis. Serv. 44 (West) (codified at Vt. Stat. Ann. tit. 9, §§ 4195–99 (2013))).
[59] See AUTM 2007, Points 1 & 2. *See, e.g., Textile Productions* (Fed. Cir. 1998).

then appear to be PAEs. Yet it is hard to argue that the fees demanded for using fundamental discoveries are exorbitant or that they are abusing the system.[60]

In addition, Seaman's study shows that to a significant extent, *eBay* is applied to deny relief to patent holders who are working their invention, but are not in direct competition with the infringer (for example, a party who holds rights on a patent to manufacture lenses and makes lenses for cameras but not for eyeglasses is not in direct competition with infringing eyeglass manufacturers).[61] These patentees are also not abusing the system. It may be true that, like PAEs, they rely only on monetary returns and that in the markets that they are not exploiting there are no subsidiary nonmonetizable benefits, such as developing a loyal customer base or selling ancillary products. Still, a system that depresses royalties can deny inventors fair compensation in markets to which their inventions contributed. Furthermore, such a system will fail to deter infringement.

But these considerations may be better directed to national lawmakers than to WTO adjudicators. The effect of withholding injunctive relief depends on how damages are calculated and it may be difficult to challenge such calculations under TRIPS. Article 45 provides little guidance on how to determine appropriate relief and we doubt that WTO adjudicators would consider relief on a case-by-case basis: a systemic analysis that looks at cases and licensing practices over a period of time, appears more consistent with the purpose of TRIPS and the WTO. Furthermore, as long as licensing negotiations occur, it is unlikely that the DSB would find deterrence inadequate.

A second rationale concerns holdups. Justice Kennedy was concerned that when a product was made up of many components, the holder of a patent on any one of them could demand high royalties and the leverage of an injunction would allow it to extract a disproportionate share of the value (or, of course, the product might simply not come to market). The adequacy of compensation is a problem here as well, in part because experience shows that determining the appropriate royalty rate for a small component in a large product is notoriously difficult. In the United States, it has been the subject of multiple cases and considerable uncertainty.[62] Which way this difficulty cuts is, however, another question. It suggests that the compensation awarded could easily be inadequate and fail to deter infringement. But since there is no generally accepted way to calculate royalties in these situations, the WTO is unlikely to step in and declare any particular method incompatible with TRIPS.

---

[60] In many cases, research institutions transfer their patents to aggregators who specialize in licensing and enforcement, at prices that are a function of the rewards the aggregator can extract. Treating these aggregators as PAEs will depress what they are willing to pay and reduce the return on fundamental research. *See, e.g.,* Chien 2014.

[61] Seaman 2016 (21% of prevailing noncompetitive patentees vs 84% of patentees who were in competition with the infringer).

[62] See Clemons 2014; Kappos & Michel 2017, 1433.

Justice Kennedy also suggested a third justification for withholding injunctive relief: patents are sometimes vague and of suspect validity.[63] In the United States, courts appear to be applying this criterion. Thus, holders of software patents – which raise significant validity questions – suffered the lowest grant rate of injunctive relief in Seaman's study.[64] But denying injunctive relief to take account of "suspect validity" is a cheap way to solve the problem of low-quality patents. Article 28 requires member states to grant the same set of rights to all patentees. Thus, it would seem that a court must either invalidate such a patent or treat it, for purposes of awarding final relief, the same as every other patent. While it thus strikes us that denying an injunction on this ground is a clear violation of TRIPS, we do not believe that problem will arise often. Under Article 52 of the European Patent Convention, programs for computers claimed as such are not patentable. Significantly, within a few years after *eBay*, US Supreme Court decisions in a group of cases relating to patent-eligible subject matter also made it extremely difficult to patent not only the business methods specifically mentioned by Justice Kennedy, but also computer software inventions.[65]

Although not among Justice Kennedy's justifications for denying permanent injunctive relief, the public's interest in health, safety and employment may provide other rationales for allowing infringers to continue their operations. Justice Kennedy's failure to mention health and safety may have stemmed from the fact that these considerations were well recognized as rationales for denying injunctions even before *eBay*.[66] However, in the United States, these cases are rare and depend on a demonstration of necessity. Seaman, for example, found that post-*eBay*, injunctions were awarded in 100 percent of the biotechnology cases and 92 percent of the pharmaceutical cases, likely on the theory that the public interest favors maximizing incentives to invent in these sectors, and thus supports granting injunctions.[67] But in some countries, courts may deny injunctions on such grounds. Whether a denial based on public interests is compatible with TRIPS may depend on the specifics of the situation. It is noteworthy that the *Canada–Pharmaceutical Products* panel never considered the public interest once it found that Canada's stockpiling exception was not "limited" and therefore violated the first part of Article 30 three-step exception test.[68] Moreover, Article 31 specifically contemplates the public interest in subsection (b), where it singles out only "national emergencies or other circumstances of extreme urgency" for special consideration. While the WTO's Doha Declaration emphasized the interest in health and stressed the right

---

[63] *eBay* (2006, p. 397).

[64] Seaman 2016, 1985 (grant rate of 53%, compared to 100% in biotechnology).

[65] *Alice Corp.* (2014); *Bilski* (2010).

[66] Examples include *Vitamin Technologists* (9th Cir. 1945); *City of Milwaukee* v. *Activated Sludge* (7th Cir. 1934).

[67] Seaman 2016, 1985 & 2004.

[68] *Canada–Pharmaceutical Products*, para. 7.38.

of every country to determine for itself what constitutes an emergency,[69] it remains likely that very close scrutiny will be given to a practice of denying injunctions on public interest grounds. First, the determination of an emergency may not be entirely self-judging.[70] Second, the size of the monetary relief awarded in lieu of an injunction may loom large in the determination. For example, awards of the sort contemplated as remuneration by the World Health Organization may not be considered sufficient.[71]

2. *National Treatment and MFN*

As noted above, patentees not in competition with infringers are not awarded injunctions at the same rate as those that exploit the patent in the infringer's field. To the extent that patent holders are more likely to license (rather than practice) in remote jurisdictions, they may find themselves treated differently from local right holders. Such cases arguably raise challenges under the national treatment or MFN obligations in TRIPS.[72] For example, it may be more convenient for US and Canadian holders of US patents to exploit their patents in the United States than it is for a Japanese holder of a US patent, who will have to expend resources to develop support materials in English and acquaint itself with North American preferences. If the Japanese right holder is considered a PAE, it could be treated differently from the American (a national treatment violation) and the Canadian (an MFN problem).

Admittedly, there is no *de jure* discrimination in this scenario: all patent holders that sue noncompetitors are subject to the same discretionary rule, based on the notion that monetary damages are sufficient to compensate. However, in the *EC-GI* case,[73] a panel held that *de facto* discrimination may also constitute a violation of TRIPS. The regulation at issue made it easier for those producing foodstuffs in the EU to obtain EU geographical indications (GIs) than those producing foodstuffs elsewhere.[74] Although the discrimination was not based on the nationality of the producer, the panel reasoned that "the vast majority of natural and legal persons who produce, process and/or prepare products according to a GI specification within the

<hr/>

[69] WTO Ministerial Conference, Declaration on the TRIPs Agreement and Public Health, WT/MIN(01)/DEC/2, paras. 4 and 5(c) (Nov. 20, 2001) [hereinafter Doha Declaration].

[70] See *Saudi Arabia – IPRs*, para. 7.230 (requiring interpretation of the security exception of TRIPS Article 73 to meet a standard of plausibility).

[71] World Health Organization 2005, 6 ("When countries are facing difficult resource constraints, and cannot provide access to medicines for all, royalty payments should normally not exceed a modest fraction of the generic price").

[72] See TRIPS, arts. 3–4.

[73] Panel Report, European Communities – Protection of Trademarks and Geographical Indications for Agricultural Products and Foodstuffs, WT/DS174/R (Mar. 15, 2005) [hereinafter EC–GI].

[74] EC Council Regulation (EEC) No. 2081/92 of Jul. 14, 1992 on the protection of geographical indications and designations of origin for agricultural products and foodstuffs, as amended.

territory of a WTO Member party to this dispute will be nationals of that Member," and that accordingly, "the Regulation ... will operate in practice to discriminate between the group of nationals of other Members who wish to obtain GI protection, and the group of the European Communities' own nationals who wish to obtain GI protection, to the detriment of the nationals of other Members."[75] Arguably, the same would be true of a rule that awards injunctive relief based on whether the plaintiff exploited the patent or licensed it. If it could be demonstrated that the vast majority of those exploiting the patent in the relevant field were locals, the denial of relief on the basis of whether the patent holder was in competition with the infringer could be considered *de facto* discrimination.

But such a finding is far from certain. The *EC–GI* panel found that discrimination was "a feature of the design and structure of the system."[76] It was also impressed by the link between "persons, the territory of a particular member, and the availability of protection."[77] Here, the reasoning is that if monetary damages are sufficient to compensate for the injury (as discussed in Section C.2), injunctive relief is not required to make any patent holder whole. Since injunctions can promote abusive practices, courts should have the discretion to deny a form of relief that could injure the public and which the plaintiff does not need. Protectionism is not a feature of such a system. Moreover, GIs are meant to signify a connection between product and territory; patents lack that symbolic connection.[78]

3. Discrimination by Field of Technology

Justice Kennedy argued that patents should also be denied when the "patented invention is but a small component of the product" produced.[79] As suggested earlier, his concern was holdup: that the patent holder could use the threat of an injunction for "undue leverage."[80] Because not all products are made up of components, the impact of this provision is highly field-dependent. Thus, Seaman found that post-*eBay*, the rate at which injunctions were granted was lower for medical devices, electronics and software, where products often have multiple patented components, than is the rate in fields like biotechnology and pharmaceuticals, where the

---

[75] *EC–GI*, at para. 7.194.
[76] Id.
[77] Id. at para. 7.189.
[78] A country might also allow a firm that is employing locals to work the patent to continue its operations when a foreign patent holder relies on importation rather than domestic production. This would similarly raise national treatment problems. It would also raise concerns about compatibility with the local working provision in art. 5 of the Paris Convention, which are beyond the scope of this chapter. See Dinwoodie & Dreyfuss 2012, 43–45.
[79] *eBay* (2006, p. 397).
[80] Id.

patent-to-product ratio is much lower.[81] The holders of patents on medical devices are particularly hard hit because the demand for an injunction can also fail under the fourth factor in *eBay*: given the number of people dependent on medical devices such as hip and heart valve replacements, an injunction could have severe public interest consequences. Of course, biotech and pharmaceutical inventions raise similar public interest concerns. However, as Seaman notes, in both fields, the risks and costs associated with bringing products to market are high, courts see strong patent rights as so necessary to encourage innovation that interest dominates over the interest of the public.[82]

Does this difference in treatment violate Article 27(1), which prohibits "discrimination as to … the field of technology"? As we saw, the *Canada–Pharmaceutical Products* panel was highly sensitive to the issue of field discrimination and applied the provision in a manner similar to the way the cornerstone obligations of national treatment and MFN are handled – as an overarching consideration. At the same time, however, the panel also recognized that fields can raise unique problems. As long as the principle at issue is "also applied to other areas where the same problem occurs," the differential treatment does not violate TRIPS.[83] Indeed, the panel saw this approach to developing the law as "a common desideratum in many legal systems."[84] Here, holdup concerns and holdup-like concerns would presumably be treated the same way in any field – indeed, Seaman's study found three fields affected by this approach. Furthermore, the same rule is sometimes applied to holdout and holdout-like situations, where the user refuses to accept a license. Consider, for example, FRAND licenses, which are common in fields, such as communication technologies, where interoperability is a concern. In these fields, standard-setting organizations choose the inventions that will constitute the standard, and often require the holders of rights over these inventions to license their so-called standard essential patents on fair, reasonable and non-discriminatory (FRAND) terms. Disputes often arise as to what constitutes FRAND terms and some jurisdictions argue that a patentee bound by a FRAND promise cannot be awarded injunctive relief when the implementer rejects the license on the ground that the patentee is asking too much – that its offer of a license is not FRAND.[85]

Other arguments also support the failure to award injunctive relief in such cases. Refusing a FRAND license is essentially an attempt to extract disproportionate royalties; as such, it is a form of abuse in that it either diverts rewards from other

---

[81] Seaman 2016, 1985 (comparing the injunction rate for biotech patents (100%) and pharmaceuticals (92%) with the rates for electronics (67%,), medical devices (65%) and software (53%)).
[82] Id. at 2005.
[83] *Canada–Pharmaceuticals*, para. 7.104.
[84] Id.
[85] *See, e.g., Apple, Inc.* (ND Ill. 2012)(Posner, J.,), aff'd in part, rev'd in part and remanded, 757 F.3d 1286 (Fed. Cir. 2014); *Microsoft Corp.* (9th Cir. 2012); *Huawei Techs. Co. Ltd.* (CJEU 2015); *Unwired Planet Int. Ltd.* (EWHC 1304 (Pat.) 2017). See also Brankin et al. 2015; Epstein & Noroozi 2017, 1381.

worthy inventions or stymies the development of products consumers might enjoy. Similarly, holdouts abuse the patent holder's promise and divert revenue from the inventor to the implementer. The denial of injunctive relief in these situations can also be analogized to an effort to deal with blocking patents, which is permissible under Article 31(l). Finally, denials here may be justified under the Objectives and Principles of the Agreement. Because these behaviors can prevent manufacturers from bringing product improvements to market, they implicate Article 7 and its objective of promoting technological innovation and seeking the "mutual advantage of producers and users." Furthermore, Article 8 allows states to protect public health, which is a concern for medical devices.

Admittedly, the weight to be afforded to Articles 7 and 8 was cast into some doubt by the report of the WTO panel in *Canada–Pharmaceutical Patents*. However, the Doha Ministerial Declaration buttresses their invocation. Admittedly, the precise status of the Ministerial Declaration is uncertain.[86] However, the Appellate Body in the *Australia–Plain Packaging* dispute supported the panel decision's emphasis on Articles 7 and 8, if not its reliance on the Ministerial Declaration itself.[87] Thus, as Daniel Gervais has suggested, post-Doha panels may give these provisions a "somewhat higher normative profile," and be more receptive to flexibilities when cast in terms of public health.[88] In addition, the Doha Declaration, like Article 8, is directed at heath and "promoting both access to existing medicines and research and development into new medicines."[89] Thus, while it may support the denial of injunctions in medical device cases, the nature of the interaction between TRIPS and fundamental (human) rights outside the sphere of healthcare is more contested.[90]

D. CONCLUSION

Over time a country may be able to show systematic denials of rights, or inadequate compensation in lieu of injunctions, based upon patterns of decisions granting or denying injunctive relief. But the mere fact that courts have the discretion to deny injunctive relief that might result in the failure to meet the standards will not of itself constitute a TRIPS violation. The Appellate Body has made clear that panels should not assume that member states will exercise discretion inconsistently with their

---

[86] In Appellate Body Reports, *Australia – Certain Measures Concerning Trademarks, Geographical Indications and Other Plain Packaging Requirements Applicable to Tobacco Products and Packaging*, WT/DS435/AB/R and WT/DS441/AB/R (Jun. 9, 2020), the Appellate Body refused to opine on the panel's view that the Declaration is a subsequent agreement between the parties and binding under the Vienna Convention on the Law of Treaties, para. 6.626.

[87] Id.

[88] Gervais 2008, para. 2.87; Gervais 2012, paras. 1.66–1.67 at 62–63; Gervais 2007, 19.

[89] Ministerial Declaration, para. 17, WT/MIN(01)/DEC/1, Nov. 20, 2001.

[90] See generally Helfer & Austin 2011.

TRIPS obligations.[91] Thus, compliance will only become an issue when a pattern or practice emerges that reveals that a rule has evolved out of the nominal discretion.[92] And the *China–Enforcement* panel put a heavy burden of proof on the United States in this regard.[93]

REFERENCES

Cases

Alice Corp. Pty. v. CLS Bank Int'l, 573 US 208 (2014).
Apple, Inc. v. Motorola, Inc., 869 F. Supp. 2d 901 (ND Ill. 2012).
Bilski v. Kappos, 561 US 593 (2010).
City of Milwaukee v. Activated Sludge, Inc., 69 F.2d 577 (7th Cir. 1964).
eBay Inc. v. MercExchange, LLC, 547 US 388 (2006).
Huawei Techs. Co. Ltd. v. ZTE Corp. (C-170/13) (CJEU 2015).
Microsoft Corp. v. Motorola, Inc., 696 F.3d 872 (9th Cir. 2012).
Textile Productions, Inc. v. Mead Corp., 134 F.3d 1481 (Fed. Cir. 1998).
Unwired Planet Int. Ltd. v. Huawei Techs. Co. Ltd., [2017] EWHC 1304 (Pat).
Vitamin Technologists, Inc. v. Wisconsin Alumni Research Found., 146 F.2d 941 (9th Cir. 1945).

Regulatory and Legislative Materials

Agreement on Trade-Related Aspects of Intellectual Property Rights (TRIPS), Apr. 15, 1994, Marrakesh Agreement Establishing the World Trade Organization, Annex 1C, Legal Instruments – Results of the Uruguay Round, Vol. 31, 33 ILM 81 (1994). [TRIPS Agreement]
Anti-Counterfeiting Trade Agreement, Mar. 31, 2011, http://trade.ec.europa.eu/doclib/docs/2011/may/tradoc_147937.pdf [ACTA]
Appellate Body Report, Australia – Certain Measures Concerning Trademarks, Geographical Indications and Other Plain Packaging Requirements Applicable to Tobacco Products and Packaging, WT/DS435/AB/R and WT/DS441/AB/R (Jul. 9, 2002).
Appellate Body Report, United States – Section 211 Omnibus Appropriations Act of 1998, WT/DS176/AB/R (Aug. 6, 2001). [*United States – Section 211*]
EC Council Regulation (EEC) No. 2081/92 of Jul. 14, 1992.
Ministerial Declaration, WT/MIN(01)/DEC/1, Nov. 20, 2001.
Panel Report, Canada – Patent Protection of Pharmaceutical Products, WT/DS114/R (Mar. 17, 2000). [*Canada – Pharmaceutical Patents*]
Panel Report, China – Measures Affecting the Protection and Enforcement of Intellectual Property Rights, WT/DS362/R (Jan. 26, 2009). [*China – Enforcement*]

[91] See *United States – Section 211*, at para. 259 (citing Chile–Taxes on Alcoholic Beverages, para. 74, WT/DS87/AB/R, WT/DS110/AB/R (WTO Appellate Body, 2000)).
[92] See Dinwoodie & Dreyfuss, 2012, 74; see also Reichman 1997, 346–48 (arguing for a ripeness doctrine).
[93] See *China – Enforcement*, paras. 7.289–7.291 & 7.297.

Panel Report, European Communities – Protection of Trademarks and Geographical Indications for Agricultural Products and Foodstuffs, WT/DS174/R (Mar. 15, 2005). [*EC – GI*]

Panel Report, Saudi Arabia – Measures Concerning the Protection of Intellectual Property Rights, WT/DS567/R (Jun. 16, 2020). [*Saudi Arabia – IPR*]

Panel Report, United States – Section 337 of the Tariff Act of 1930, L/6439 (Nov. 7, 1989). [*United States – Section 337*]

Paris Convention for the Protection of Industrial Property, Jul. 14, 1967, 21 UST 1583, 828 UNTS 305.

Request for Consultations, European Union and a Member State – Seizure of Generic Drugs in Transit, WT/DS408/1 (May 11, 2010).

Request for Consultations, European Union and a Member State – Seizure of Generic Drugs in Transit, WT/DS409/1 (May 12, 2010).

Understanding on Rules and Procedures Governing the Settlement of Disputes, Marrakesh Agreement Establishing the World Trade Organization, Annex 2, Apr. 15, 1994, 33 ILM 1226. [DSU]

WTO Ministerial Conference, Declaration on the TRIPs Agreement and Public health, WT/MIN(01)/DEC/2 (Nov. 20, 2001). [Doha Declaration]

Books, Articles and Online Materials

AUTM. 2007. Nine Points to Consider in Licensing University Patents. https://autm.net/about-tech-transfer/principles-and-guidelines/nine-points-to-consider-when-licensing-university.

Brankin, Sean-Paul, Salomé Cisnal de Ugarte & Lisa Kimmel. 2015. "Huawei: Injunctions and Standard Essential Patents – Is Exclusion a Foregone Conclusion?," *Antitrust* 30 (1):80–87.

Chien, Colleen V. 2014. "Holding Up and Holding Out," *Michigan Telecommunications and Technology Law Review* 21(1):1–42.

Clemons, Alexander L. 2014. "Beyond the Smallest Salable Unit: How Surveys Provide a Path from Recent Case Law to an Appropriate Royalty Base," *Landslide* 6(5):36–39.

Cotter, Thomas F. 2018. "Patent Damages Heuristics," *Texas Intellectual Property Law Journal* 25(2):159–214.

De Carvalho, Nuno Pires. 2010. *The TRIPS Regime of Patent Rights*. Wolters Kluwer.

Dinwoodie, Graeme B. & Rochelle C. Dreyfuss. 2012. *A Neofederalist Vision of TRIPS: The Resilience of the International Intellectual Property Regime*. Oxford University Press.

Epstein, Richard A. & Kayvan B. Noroozi. 2017. "Why Incentives for 'Patent Holdout' Threaten to Dismantle FRAND, and Why It Matters," *Berkeley Technology Law Journal* 32(4):1381–432.

FDA News. 2011. "EU, India Drop Generics Dispute to Focus on FTA Talks," *FDAnews*, Jan. 21, 2011. http://fdanews.com/newsletter/article?issueId=14404&articleId=133690.

Gervais, Daniel. 2007. "TRIPS and Development," in *Intellectual Property, Trade and Development: Strategies to Optimize Economic Development in a TRIPS-Plus Era*. Oxford University Press.

2008. *The TRIPS Agreement: Drafting History and Analysis*. Oxford University Press (3d ed).

2012. *The TRIPS Agreement: Drafting History and Analysis*. Oxford University Press (4th ed.).

Gupta, Kirti & Jay P. Kesan. 2016. "Studying the Impact of eBay on Injunctive Relief in Patent Cases," University of Illinois College of Law Legal Studies Research Paper No. 17-03. https://papers.ssrn.com/sol3/papers.cfm?abstract_id=2816701.

Helfer, Laurence R. & Graeme W. Austin. 2011. *Human Rights and Intellectual Property: Mapping the Global Interface*. Cambridge University Press.

Johnson, David Lee. 2014. "Facing Down the Trolls: States Stumble on the Bridge to Patent-Assertion Regulation," *Washington and Lee Law Review* 71(3):2023–76.

Kappos, David & Paul R. Michel. 2017. "The Smallest Salable Patent-Practicing Unit: Observations on Its Origins, Development, and Future," *Berkeley Technology Law Journal* 32(4):1433–56.

Knowledge Economy International. 2010. "KEI General Statement to the 15th Standing Committee on the Law of Patents (SCP)," www.keionline.org/21393.

Lemley, Mark A. & A. Douglas Melamed. 2013. "Missing the Forest for the Trolls," *Columbia Law Review* 113(8):2117–90.

Lim, Lily & Sarah E. Craven. 2009. "Injunctions Enjoined; Remedies Restructured," *Santa Clara Computer and High Technology Law Journal* 25(4):787–820.

Malbon, Justin, Charles Allen Lawson & Mark J. Davison. 2014. *The WTO Agreement on Trade Related Aspects of Intellectual Property Rights: A Commentary*. Edward Elgar.

Reichman, Jerome H. 1997. "Enforcing the Enforcement Procedures of the TRIPS Agreement," *Virginia Journal of International Law* 37(2):335–56.

Reichman, Jerome H. & Rochelle Cooper Dreyfuss. 2007. "Harmonization without Consensus: Critical Reflections on Drafting a Substantive Patent Law Treaty," *Duke Law Journal* 57(1):85–130.

Roffe, Pedro & Xavier Seuba. 2015. "ACTA and the International Debate on Intellectual Property Enforcement," in Pedro Roffe and Xavier Seuba eds., *The ACTA and the Plurilateral Enforcement Agenda*. Cambridge University Press.

Ruse-Kahn, Henning Grosse. 2011. "A Trade Agreement Creating Barriers to International Trade? ACTA Border Measures and Goods in Transit," *American University International Law Review* 26(3):645–726.

Sarnoff, Joshua D. 2010. "Lessons from the United States in Regard to the Recent, More Flexible Application of Injunctive Relief," in Carlos Correa ed., *II Research Handbook on Enforcement of IP under WTO Rules* 60. Edward Elgar.

Seaman, Christopher B. 2016. "Permanent Injunctions in Patent Litigation after Ebay: An Empirical Study," *Iowa Law Review* 101(5): 1949–2020.

Simpson, Sidney Post. 1936. "Fifty Years of American Equity," *Harvard Law Review* 50:171–251.

Taubman, Antony. 2011. *A Practical Guide to Working with TRIPS*. Oxford University Press.

Venkatesan, Jaideep. 2009. "Compulsory Licensing of Nonpracticing Patentees after Ebay v. Mercexchange," *Virginia Journal of Law and Technology* 14(1):26–47.

World Trade Organization. 2012. *A Handbook on the WTO TRIPS Agreement*. Oxford University Press.

World Health Organization. 2005. *Renumeration Guidelines for Non-Voluntary Use of a Patent on Medical Technologies / James Love*. World Trade Organization. https://apps.who.int/iris/handle/10665/69199.

3

European Union

Matthias Leistner and Viola Pless

A. EU LAW FRAMEWORK

1. *Overview*

The regulation of patent enforcement in Europe is characterized by the typical multi-layered EU law system of primary EU law, secondary EU law, i.e. unification and harmonization of member states' laws by way of regulations and directives, and member states' laws which in particular implement the EU directives into national law.[1] Primary EU law, insofar as it is similar to written constitutional law, establishes the competence and baseline for all EU legal actions. Secondary legislation is based on the competences of the EU established in primary law and unifies certain areas of law (by way of directly applicable unitary regulations) or harmonizes member states' laws by way of directives that are not directly applicable but addressed to the member states and that typically leave the member states certain leeway for manoeuvre when they implement such directives in their national law systems. Both EU primary and secondary legislation take primacy over national law; this so-called principle of primacy of EU law has been developed by the Court of Justice of the European Union (CJEU) in its case law[2] and is meanwhile also laid down in a declaration concerning primacy,[3] which is part of the Treaty of Lisbon.[4]

Primary law consists, first, of the Charter of Fundamental Rights of the European Union (CFR) which is an integral part of primary law according to Art. 6(1) of the Treaty on European Union (TEU). Secondly, the competences and structure of the

---

[1] *See* for a general overview of the EU legal system Chalmers et al. 2019, 113 et seq.; Furlong & Doe 2006, 137.

[2] *Costa* v. *ENEL* (CJEU 1964, 1268 et seq.); *Amministrazione delle Finanze* v. *Simmenthal* (CJEU 1978, paras. 17 et seq.); *Marleasing* (CJEU 1990, paras. 8 et seq.).

[3] *See* declaration 17 *Annexes Consolidated EU Treaties.*

[4] Art. 51 TEU.

EU as well as the establishment of the unitary market through the fundamental freedoms are laid down in the EU Treaties, i.e. the Treaty on the Functioning of the European Union (TFEU) and the TEU. Thirdly, certain so-called general principles of EU law have been developed by the CJEU mainly on the basis of the comparative law method, the principle of proportionality[5] as well as the principle of good faith.[6]

While directly applicable regulations do not play an important role for patent enforcement in the EU,[7] the ground rules for enforcement of intellectual property (IP) rights in Europe are laid down in the Enforcement Directive. The Directive harmonizes enforcement of intellectual property rights in member states' laws following a principle of so-called minimum harmonization.[8] Consequently, generally the Enforcement Directive establishes only minimum standards for enforcement and leaves certain leeway for implementation by the member states in their respective national laws. Nonetheless, certain principles and elements of the Directive also establish ceiling standards or conclusive mechanisms and will have to be interpreted in an autonomous unitary way throughout the European Union.[9] In general, the Directive has to be interpreted in conformity with primary EU law, i.e. interpretation in conformity with the CFR's fundamental rights as well as with the fundamental freedoms; establishing the unitary market according to the TFEU is an important method for the construction of the Enforcement Directive's provisions.

Further, the E-Commerce Directive provides for additional sector-specific rules in regulating certain aspects of online services. As this practically relates mainly to internet providers, it has hitherto not played a central role in patent enforcement cases. However, in EU law patent remedies can be neither understood nor interpreted as isolated rules because on principle the Enforcement Directive applies equally to copyright, trademark and patent law injunctions. It will be shown below[10] that the overall context of constitutional and primary law rights and principles as well as the relationship to other areas of IP law provide for a multifactorial normative methodology and framework guiding the application of injunctive relief in the CJEU's case law where principles from neighbouring areas of law can also instruct the area of patent injunctions in the framework of the method of contextual interpretation. For this reason, the CJEU's case law on the E-Commerce

---

[5] *See* for cases on copyright law decided by the CJEU *Promusicae* v. *Telefónica* (CJEU 2008, para. 70); *LSG* v. *Tele2* (CJEU 2009, para. 28).

[6] The principle of proportionality is meanwhile expressly laid down in Art. 5(4) TEU.

[7] Except of course concerning international jurisdiction (which is uniformly regulated in the *Brussels Ia Regulation* (2012)) and choice of law (which is uniformly regulated in the *Rome II Regulation* (2007)).

[8] *Cf.* on minimum and maximum harmonization through directives in *Summary of Article 288 TFEU*.

[9] *See* Section A.4.

[10] *See* Section A.5.

Directive is relevant for patent enforcement as well because it has established certain methodological approaches and fundamental principles (in particular on the necessary balancing of fundamental rights) which are not only relevant in internet copyright and trademark infringement cases, but are of a more general nature for IP enforcement in the EU.

In addition, of course, the TRIPS Agreement[11] has to be taken into account. It lays down international law standards for the protection of intellectual property rights. As for the Enforcement Directive, it was the clear intention of the European legislator to fulfil the obligations of the TRIPS Agreement imposed on the EU as a contracting party when enacting the Directive.[12] Nonetheless, in certain respects the guarantees in the Enforcement Directive also go beyond the requirements of the third part of the TRIPS Agreement (Arts. 41–50 TRIPS).[13]

2. *EU Legal Framework for Patent Injunctions, in Particular Art. 11 of the Enforcement Directive*

The Enforcement Directive is the centrepiece of EU law in the area of patent enforcement and intellectual property rights enforcement in general (with the exception of trade secrets[14]). The adoption of the Enforcement Directive in 2004 should implement the third chapter of the TRIPS Agreement in European law and provide for a minimum standard of "measures, procedure and remedies" for the infringement of intellectual property rights.[15] The explicit objective of the Enforcement Directive is to approximate the previously divergent[16] national legal systems in order to ensure high, equivalent and homogenous protection in the internal market.[17] In that regard, the adoption of the Enforcement Directive was clearly influenced by a general tendency in the 1990s to expand intellectual property protection and by the massive increase of product piracy and counterfeiting which benefited from technological progress and the globalization of trade.[18]

---

[11] *TRIPS* (1994); *see* Chapter 2 for further discussion on TRIPS.

[12] *Bericap Záródástechnikai Bt.* v. *Plastinnova* (CJEU 2012, paras. 72 et seq.).

[13] *Cf.* in more detail Heinze 2012, 932 with examples. See Chapter 2 (TRIPS) for discussion on the WTO.

[14] The enforcement of trade secrets is governed by Art. 6 et seq. *Trade Secrets Directive* (2016) which establishes a modern approach to enforcement measures including numerous open standards, defences and further flexible elements to curtail overly broad injunctions.

[15] *See* Art. 2(1) of the Enforcement Directive; Heinze 2012, 930; for a detailed history of the origins of the Enforcement Directive see Petillion et al. 2019, 4 et seq. with further references.

[16] Despite the various enforcement provisions in the TRIPS Agreement, there were considerable discrepancies in national legislation which caused uncertainty and a difference in enforcement levels between the EU member states, see Petillion et al. 2019, vii et seq.

[17] *See* Recitals 7–10 of the Enforcement Directive. *See* on the implementation of the Enforcement Directive in the member states, Petillion et al. 2019, 12 et seq. with further references.

[18] *See* Heinze 2012, 931 with further references.

According to the general standard of Art. 3 of the Enforcement Directive, the measures must be effective, proportionate and dissuasive[19] to ensure the enforcement of intellectual property rights. The Enforcement Directive does not contain any further substantive or procedural provisions about the specific design of injunctive relief. On the contrary, it expressly leaves the exact conditions and procedures to the member states.[20]

The Enforcement Directive's Art. 11 provides for an obligation on the EU member states to ensure that judicial authorities may issue an injunction against the infringer of an intellectual property right aimed at prohibiting the continuation of the infringement. The member states are also obliged to provide for the possibility of interlocutory (i.e. preliminary) injunctions against the alleged infringer in order to prevent any imminent infringement according to Art. 9(1) of the Enforcement Directive. Art. 11 of the Enforcement Directive provides for injunctions against so-called intermediaries (i.e. any secondary infringers and further accountable but not liable persons contributing to the infringement). Concerning this liability of intermediaries, Recital 23 of the Enforcement Directive expressly leaves the design of the conditions and procedures relating to such injunctions against intermediaries to the member states.

EU law does not specifically provide for automated compliance fines in the initial grant of an injunction. Sentence 2 in Art. 11 of the Enforcement Directive stipulates though that where provided by national law, non-compliance with an injunction shall, where appropriate, be subject to a recurring penalty payment.

3. *Basic Principles of Construction of Art. 11 of the Enforcement Directive*

In line with the general method of minimum harmonization, the wording of Art. 11 of the Enforcement Directive only requires member states to foresee injunctions aimed at prohibiting the continuation of the infringement on principle. Further details of injunctive relief are not specified in the provision.

Consequently, the text of the Enforcement Directive does not contain an express or implied obligation that injunctive relief is mandatory in all cases of infringement.[21] The wording of Art. 11 of the Enforcement Directive ("may") is not conclusive in that regard. Against this background, on the one hand, the principles of purposive construction and *effet utile* in EU law[22] require that the Directive is

---

[19] This element reflects the requirement of deterrent measures in Art. 41 TRIPS in a more general form.

[20] *See* Recital 23 Enforcement Directive.

[21] Von Mühlendahl 2007, 377.

[22] The principle of "effet utile" is a rule of interpretation according to which all member states are obliged to interpret EU law in such a way as to ensure its practical effectiveness; see for example *Zuckerfabrik Suederdithmarschen* (CJEU 1991, paras. 15 et seq.). The "principle of effet utile" follows directly from the primacy of EU law over the national law of the member states; *see* on primacy of EU law Section A.1.

interpreted in a way which allows states to reach the harmonization goal and to ensure the practical effectiveness of the Directive. On the other hand, as for possible discretion of the court, it has to be taken into account that the principle of proportionality (which is a so-called general principle of EU law)[23] would be undermined if Art. 11 of the Enforcement Directive were interpreted to force the courts in all member states to grant final injunctions even in cases of evident disproportionality.[24]

Further, as a harmonizing measure the Directive also has to be construed in light of the comparative law method taking into account that the EU consists of member states that follow the common law tradition as well as civil law member states. In the common law system, injunctive relief is an equitable remedy. At least in principle, therefore, it is only subordinately available. To be sure, in practice injunctive relief is awarded on a regular basis in terms of patent infringement in common law jurisdictions.[25] Nonetheless, against this background, a strict approach obliging courts to grant injunctions in every case of infringement without any flexibilities would hardly be compatible with the flexible nature of equity.[26] By contrast, in civil law systems injunctive relief is the basic remedy for IP infringement and will automatically be granted in normal cases.[27]

Against the background of these differences in national law, the wording as well as the contextual interpretation of the Directive (which is more specific in other sectors) allow for the assumption that the Directive only requires that national courts have the authority to grant injunctive relief, while the specific conditions for granting it are not fully harmonized. With that in mind, a necessarily EU-wide, autonomous approach, taking into account the principle of *effet utile*[28] as well as a basic comparative law understanding, seems to lead to the conclusion that in atypical cases, the courts may refuse to grant injunctive relief due to considerations of proportionality, whereas in typical infringement cases it should be available due to Art. 11 of the Enforcement Directive.[29]

4. *Considerations of Proportionality*

The legal concept of proportionality is recognized as a general principle of EU law.[30] More specifically, according to Art. 3(2) of the Enforcement Directive, in the realm of enforcement of intellectual property rights, all measures provided by the

---

[23] *See* Section A.4.
[24] Ohly 2009, 265.
[25] Heath & Cotter 2015, 31 et seq. *Cf.* also Chapters 5 (Canada), 13 (United Kingdom) and 14 (United States).
[26] Ohly 2009, 264 et seq.
[27] For a comparative overview see Heath & Cotter 2015, 31 et seq.
[28] *See* on "effet utile" above in footnote 22.
[29] Ohly 2009, 266 et seq.
[30] *See* Art. 5(4) TEU.

member states shall be effective, proportionate and dissuasive. Hence, as a general mandatory obligation for the implementation of the Enforcement Directive, the principle of proportionality should not only be considered by the member states when implementing the Directive but also in regard to the specification of injunctive relief granted by the member states' courts.[31] It has been argued that the character of the Directive as an instrument of minimum harmonization excludes this construction of the principle of proportionality as a maximum (ceiling) of possible enforcement measures in national law which fall into the scope of harmonization of the Directive.[32] However, in a number of cases the CJEU – which typically emphasizes the goal of effective harmonization – has expressly used the principle of proportionality under the Enforcement Directive as a ceiling and limitation on possible enforcement measures granted to the rightsholder under national law of the member states.[33] Also, the prevailing opinion in literature[34] and member states' case law[35] follows this approach, albeit with considerable differences concerning the details.

Recital 17 of the Enforcement Directive specifies that the measures should take into account the specific characteristics of the case, including the specific features of each intellectual property right and, where appropriate, the intentional or unintentional character of the infringement. Against the backdrop of the broad impact an injunction may have on business, consumers and the public interest, the European Commission emphasizes that the proportionality assessment by judicial authorities needs to be done carefully on a case-by-case basis when considering the grant of measures, procedures and remedies provided for in the Enforcement Directive.[36] This shows the Commission's general acceptance of and even requirement for an individual case-by-case approach, taking into account proportionality considerations.[37]

Respective national provisions which implement the Enforcement Directive into the different member states' laws have to be construed in conformity with the Directive. Therefore, more recent case law of different member states' courts on injunctions and proportionality is also of indirect relevance to the question of whether Art. 3 of the Enforcement Directive must be considered mandatorily in the construction of provisions of national law which fall into the scope of application

---

[31] *See* O'Sullivan 2019, 543 et seq.; but see Stierle 2019, 877; Stierle 2018, 304 et seq.; Marfé et al. 2015, 181.

[32] But see Stierle 2019, 877; Stierle 2018, 304 et seq.; Marfé et al. 2015, 181.

[33] *L'Oréal* v. *eBay* (CJEU 2009, paras. 139 et seq.); *Tommy Hilfiger* v. *Delta Center* (CJEU 2015, paras. 34 et seq.) (both cases concerning injunctions against intermediaries in trademark law); *Stowarzyszenie* (CJEU 2017, para. 31).

[34] *See* Husovec 2013, para. 8; Ohly 2008, 796 et seq.; O'Sullivan 2019, 543 et seq.

[35] *See* for a couple of illustrative examples in the following text and more comprehensively in the respective chapters on national law.

[36] *Guidance on Enforcement Directive* (EC 2017, 9 et seq.); *EU Approach to SEPs* (EC 2017, 10).

[37] Osterrieth 2018, 990 et seq.

of the Enforcement Directive. In the English *Edwards Lifescience* v. *Boston Scientific Scimed* case,[38] Justice Richard Arnold pointed out that in accordance with Art. 3 of the Enforcement Directive the principle of proportionality *must* be considered. According to the judgment, proportionality is the *key consideration* in Art. 3 and sets the analytical framework for the consideration of all the other factors.[39] Consistently, on the facts of the case (which concerned the infringement of a patent on certain transcatheter heart valves) the High Court ordered a twelve-month stay of the granted injunction to allow for the necessary re-training of medical personnel to use non-infringing transcatheter heart valves.[40] In contrast, in parallel proceedings before the Regional Court of Düsseldorf on the same patent in the *Herzklappen* case,[41] the court denied such a delayed injunction and instead granted an immediate injunction despite reasonable public interests to the contrary. While this does not on principle exclude proportionality considerations in regard to the encroachment of an injunction on the defendant's rights and interests in certain exceptional cases in German law, it certainly shows the comparative reluctance of German practice to consider public interests in the framework of proportionality considerations concerning injunctions.[42]

In sum, under the Enforcement Directive according to the proportionality principle as well as the general prohibition of abuse of rights (as a general principle of European Union law which also expressly applies to the enforcement of intellectual property rights[43]), the denial or curtailing of injunctive relief is possible due to proportionality considerations and will even be required by the law in exceptional cases. According to the prohibition of abuse of rights, the enforcement of intellectual property claims has an abusive character if the economic loss on the infringer's side is entirely disproportionate to the economic potential to be realized by the patent holder.[44] This can in particular be applied to injunctive relief which practically leads to entire closure of manufacturing and thus to disproportionately substantial losses. The main factors to be balanced are the relative insignificance of the patented invention in relation to the whole product, the infringer's level of negligence as well as the question of whether the plaintiff exploits the patent without

---

[38] *Edwards Lifescience* v. *Boston Scientific Scimed* (EWHC 2018, 1256).

[39] Id., paras 15 et seq.; *see* for further analysis Chapter 13 (United Kingdom).

[40] *Edwards Lifescience* v. *Boston Scientific Scimed* (EWHC 2018, 1256, paras. 64 et seq.).

[41] *Herzklappen* (LG Düsseldorf 2017).

[42] Recently proportionality considerations have been expressly established in sec. 139 para. 1 of the German Patent Act. *See* further Chapter 8 (Germany). *Cf.* also Section A.6.

[43] *Bayer* v. *Richter* (CJEU 2019, paras. 67 et seq.). The principle is expressly laid down as a limitation to enforcement measures in Art. 3 (2) of the Enforcement Directive and has been relied on by the CJEU as a maximum ceiling for admissible enforcement measures when these are so clearly disproportionate to the rights and interests of the claimant that their effect could constitute an abuse of rights; *see Stowarzyszenie* (CJEU 2017, para. 31).

[44] *Cf. Stowarzyszenie* (CJEU 2017, para. 31); Ohly 2008, 796; Blok 2016, 59 et seq.; for approaches in the United States to fight abusive court proceedings, in particular with means of fee-shifting, *see*, *e.g.*, Morton & Shapiro 2016, 7 et seq.; Voet 2018, 15 et seq.

facilitating their own research or production activities.[45] In contrast to the idea of abuse of rights, the denial of injunctive relief due to proportionality considerations allows for a differentiation between injunctive relief and financial compensation and thus for a more flexible curtailing of injunctive relief as well as compensation in lieu of an injunction.[46] However, it has to be noted that any objections relating to proportionality considerations are limiting the effect of injunctive relief, thus partly depriving the intellectual property right of its essential function and curtailing *ex ante* incentives for inventive activity. Therefore, such objections need to be rigorously considered in each case individually, and generally be treated with caution.[47]

5. *Considerations of Fundamental Rights*

According to Recital 32, the Enforcement Directive respects the fundamental rights and observes the principles recognized in particular by the CFR. In consequence, according to the European Commission, the rules set out in the Directive must be interpreted and applied in a way that safeguards not only the intellectual property right pursuant to Art. 17(2) of the CFR but also fully considers and respects other conflicting fundamental rights of the infringer and/or third parties at issue.[48]

In practice, this means that in any enforcement case which is governed by the Enforcement Directive and/or other instruments of EU law (e.g., also the GDPR[49]) the relevant instrument of EU law will have to be interpreted in conformity with the CFR. Typically, when interpreting open standards laid down in EU regulations and directives a balancing of the fundamental rights and interests of the parties against each other will have to be carried out. In this regard, the basic methodological principles have hitherto mainly been developed by the CJEU in copyright and trademark cases. However, under the contextual method as it is applied by the CJEU it can safely be assumed that the same methodological approach would also apply to patent infringement cases under the Enforcement Directive.

The basic principles for balancing the fundamental rights and interests of the parties against each other in IP infringement cases have been established by the CJEU in the field of copyright law, inter alia in the *UPC Telekabel*[50] case on injunctions against intermediaries as well as in the older *Promusicae* v. *Telefónica* case,[51] the latter relating to the denial of a claim to information according to Art. 8 of the Enforcement Directive due to considerations in regard to the protection of

---

[45] Ohly 2008, 798.
[46] Id., 796. *See also* Section A.11.
[47] Id., 797.
[48] *Guidance on Enforcement Directive* (EC 2017, 10).
[49] *General Data Protection Regulation* (2016).
[50] *UPC Telekabel Wien* (CJEU 2014).
[51] *Promusicae* v. *Telefónica* (CJEU 2008).

personal data.[52] For the aforementioned reasons, the basic methodology developed in these cases clearly has an impact on the general question of how to consider and balance the fundamental rights of the parties when applying and specifying injunctions according to Art. 11 of the Enforcement Directive.

In the aforementioned judgments, the CJEU held that when enacting the measures implementing a European Union directive in national law, the authorities and courts of the member states must not only interpret their national law in a manner consistent with the directive but must also ensure that they do not rely on an interpretation of it which would be in conflict with fundamental rights of the concerned parties or with other general principles of EU law, such as the principle of proportionality.[53] Therefore, the CJEU requires that national courts take into account the requirements following from the protection of the applicable fundamental rights in accordance with Art. 51 of the CFR.[54] The involved fundamental rights will have to be fairly balanced against each other taking into account the principle of proportionality. In practice this means that neither of the parties must be deprived entirely of their fundamental rights and that any encroachment on the relevant fundamental rights of one party has to be justified as necessary and reasonable with regard to the protection of the relevant fundamental rights of the other party.

With regard to injunctions against intermediaries in the *UPC Telekabel* case, the CJEU sought to find a balance primarily between the protection of copyrights and related rights on the one hand, and the freedom to conduct business (of internet providers) as well as the freedom of information (of internet users) on the other.[55] When assessing the consistency of the injunction in question with EU law, the CJEU claimed that measures under the InfoSoc Directive's provisions on injunctions must be "strictly targeted"[56] and that the design of the injunction must not affect the very substance of the freedom at issue (i.e. the freedom of the internet provider on principle to conduct its legitimate business).[57]

---

[52] In particular Art. 7 CFR (respect for private and family life) and Art. 8 CFR (protection of personal data).

[53] *UPC Telekabel Wien* (CJEU 2014, para. 46); *Promusicae* v. *Telefónica* (CJEU 2008, para. 68).

[54] Id., para. 45.

[55] Id., para. 47.

[56] Id., para. 56.

[57] Id., para. 51. From the court's viewpoint an open-ended injunction, leaving the implementation of measures to block the accessibility of the site to the provider, was in line with that requirement since it left certain leeway for implementation to the provider. Admittedly, of course, in this case the concerned internet provider was not the primary infringer, but instead only liable as a secondary infringer (if at all); nonetheless, it can be assumed that the CJEU would apply the same basic approach if the legitimate commercial activities and interests of an infringer of an intellectual property right were concerned, although of course in such a case the outcome of the balancing procedure might be different and tend to be more favourable to the rightsholder.

The line of case law, started in the *Promusicae* v. *Telefónica* and *UPC Telekabel* judgments, was further strengthened and developed in subsequent decisions[58] and meanwhile gives consistent principled guidance on how to strike a fair balance between the different conflicting fundamental rights of the parties in IP enforcement cases. Essentially, in patent cases the right to protection of intellectual property (Art. 17 (2) of the CFR) will have to be balanced against the right to freedom to conduct a business (Art. 16 of the CFR) under the guiding principle of proportionality. This reasonable balancing of fundamental rights, which must not lead to an outcome where one of the parties is entirely deprived of their rights or freedoms, had to be carried out, first, by the member states when implementing the Enforcement Directive in their respective statutes. Secondly, the proportionate balancing of the rights to protection of intellectual property and freedom to conduct a business will also have to be taken into account by the member states' courts when applying these implementation provisions to the facts of a given case. The latest relevant judgments in *Pelham* v. *Hütter*,[59] *Funke Medien* v. *Germany*[60] and *Spiegel Online* v. *Beck*,[61] all from July 2019, are in line with these principles and bring further essential guidance on the influence and methodological treatment of different fundamental rights systems in this respect (i.e. the CFR on the EU level and the different constitutions of the member states which overlap in many cases).[62] Essentially these judgments further clarify the methodological delineation between the EU's fundamental rights framework (CFR and ECHR[63]) and the member states' constitutions. In sum, if EU secondary law leaves discretion to the member states in implementing a directive, the CJEU under certain conditions (compliance with the level of protection afforded by the CFR) does accept the prevalence of the member states' constitutions. By contrast, if a certain field of law is fully harmonized by EU law (such as in the case of EU Regulations or provisions of EU Directives which leave no discretion to member states in the implementation process), the EU fundamental rights will apply exclusively and take primacy over the respective member states' constitutions.

Although the cited cases were issued in the specific context of copyright litigation, as has been said, the requirements set up by the CJEU regarding a fair balance between fundamental rights in the light of the Enforcement Directive apply *mutatis mutandis*[64] to all cases within the Enforcement Directive's scope, i.e. any

---

[58] E.g., *Bonnier Audio* v. *Perfect Communication Sweden* (CJEU 2012); *Coty Germany* v. *Stadtsparkasse Magdeburg* (CJEU 2015).

[59] *Pelham* v. *Hütter* (CJEU 2019).

[60] *Funke Medien* v. *Germany* (CJEU 2019).

[61] *Spiegel Online* v. *Beck* (CJEU 2019).

[62] Leistner 2019a, 1014 et seq.; Leistner 2019b, 720.

[63] European Court of Human Rights.

[64] *See* footnote 57 on possible differentiation if a direct infringer is concerned, as opposed to merely secondary infringers or other intermediaries.

enforcement of intellectual property rights in the EU.[65] Hence, (1) under EU law, given the requirement of a fair balance between the involved fundamental rights, taking into account the general principles of EU law, in particular the principle of proportionality, an injunction, which does not lead to a complete cessation of the infringement, can be consistent with the requirements of EU fundamental rights.[66] What is more, respective qualifications and limitations might even be required by EU law in certain cases. If these general requirements under the CFR regime are met, however, (2) the specifics of the fair and proportional balance can be developed on the basis of the respective member state's constitutional order since the Directive undoubtedly leaves discretion to the member states in this field and therefore their fundamental rights and constitutional principles can be applied by the national courts.

6. *Considerations of Public Interest*

The wording of Art. 11 of the Enforcement Directive as well as the recitals do not provide for specific guidance on how to consider public interest. However, in the related area of enforcement of unitary EU trademarks, the CJEU's assertions in the *Nokia* v. *Wärdell* case[67] show that the CJEU is generally rather reluctant to deny injunctive relief due to mere general considerations of public interest.

The decision dealt with "special reasons" for denying injunctive relief based on Art. 130(1) of the Trade Mark Regulation.[68] In particular, it was asked whether the national EU trademark court could refuse to issue a permanent injunction as the alleged infringer had never committed such an act before and could only be accused of carelessness.[69] The CJEU highlighted the need for prohibitions against infringement for the purpose of EU-wide intellectual property rights when asserting that the term "special reasons" must be given a uniform interpretation and has clearly to be understood as an exception to the obligation for prohibition orders.[70] As a result, the CJEU denied an interpretation according to which the prohibition against further or threatened infringement would be conditional on an obvious or not merely negligible risk of recurrence of infringing acts as this would lead to the risk of varying scope of protection depending on the respective court's assessment of that risk of recurrence.[71] This shows that as far as EU-wide unitary protection titles

---

[65] *EU Approach to SEPs* (EC 2017, 10 et seq.).
[66] *Cf. UPC Telekabel Wien* (CJEU 2014, para. 63).
[67] *Nokia* v. *Wärdell* (CJEU 2006).
[68] *See* Art. 130(1) Trade Mark Regulation: "Where an EU trade mark court finds that the defendant has infringed or threatened to infringe an EU trade mark, it shall, *unless there are special reasons* for not doing so, issue an order prohibiting the defendant from proceeding with the acts which infringed or would infringe the EU trade mark."
[69] *Nokia* v. *Wärdell* (CJEU 2006, para. 17).
[70] Id., paras. 26, 28, 30.
[71] Id., para. 34.

are concerned, the CJEU favours a general rule that obliges the courts to grant injunctive relief, unless there are circumstances specific to the case, which would allow a clear conclusion that further infringement will not occur.[72] In fact, this slightly less flexible approach – as often occurs in EU IP law – seems less guided by genuine IP-specific considerations than by the general objective of uniform application of EU law in the internal market.

However, in line with general EU law principles, it must still be possible to restrain a court order due to considerations of public interest. An explicit guidepost on how to consider public interest can be found in Art. 52(1) of the CFR which states that limitations on the exercise of rights and freedoms may be made only if they are necessary and genuinely meet the objectives of general interest recognized by the EU. This is based on well-established general case law of the CJEU, according to which restrictions may be imposed on the exercise of those rights, "in particular in the context of a common organisation of a market, provided that those restrictions in fact correspond to objectives of general interest pursued by the Community and do not constitute, with regard to the aim pursued, disproportionate and unreasonable interference undermining the very substance of those rights."[73] The reference to general interests recognized by the EU covers both the objectives mentioned in Art. 3 of the TEU and other interests protected by specific provisions of the EU Treaties such as Art. 4(1) TEU and Arts. 35(3), 36 and 346 TFEU.[74] Thus, the goals must be enshrined in EU law, but the reference to Art. 4 TEU, including national identities and their fundamental political and constitutional structures, shows that a broad understanding of public interests that are not explicitly named in the EU Treaties is possible.[75]

Given the increasing importance of fundamental rights for the specification of open-ended terms in the IP directives, particularly in copyright law, it will have to be seen whether the aforementioned general principles will lead to a more flexible consideration of public interest as a basis for denying or modifying injunctive relief in IP cases in the future. This is even more so, since the latest judgments in *Pelham*, *Funke Medien* and *Spiegel Online* show a certain, tentative tendency to leave the member states some more discretion than before (at least in certain not fully harmonized areas of IP law).[76]

7. *Competition Law Considerations*

The CJEU has dealt several times with the question of whether and how the competition law-based objection of the abuse of a dominant market position

---

[72] Von Mühlendahl 2007, 380; *Nokia v. Wärdell* (CJEU 2006, para. 35).
[73] *Karlsson* (CJEU 2000, para. 45).
[74] *Explanations Relating to the CFR* (2007, 16).
[75] Streinz & Michl 2018, Art. 52 CFR para. 17.
[76] Leistner 2019a, 1012.

(according to Art. 102 TFEU) by the rightsholder because of a refusal to license the underlying intellectual property right can be raised by the defendant in injunction proceedings. The leading CJEU's cases are *RTE* v. *Commission/Magill*[77] and *IMS Health*.[78] In these cases, the CJEU established that a duty of a dominant undertaking to grant compulsory licences can be based on Art. 102 of the TFEU under certain exceptional circumstances. This requires specifically that a licence in the (primary) licensing market (which can be a purely hypothetical market if the rightsholder does not license the intellectual property right at all) is indispensable for the offer of a new product or service in a (secondary) product or service market and if the rightsholder unjustifiably refuses to license the intellectual property right in order to exclude competition in that secondary market. These rather strict requirements hitherto prevented the instrument of compulsory licensing and of objections relating to claims to a compulsory licence from having a large practical impact on patent infringement injunctions in EU law.

In the specific sector of standard essential patents (SEPs) which are essential to the implementation of a certain technical standard and where the SEP holder has committed vis-à-vis the standard-setting organization (SSO) to grant licences to any interested party under fair, reasonable and non-discriminatory (FRAND) terms, the CJEU has recently applied more stringent competition law standards in its *Huawei* v. *ZTE* judgment.[79] Typically, in the area of telecommunications or consumer electronics standards, the SEP holder will have declared their preparedness to license the patent under FRAND terms as the standardization organizations in these sectors require such FRAND declarations as a necessary precondition of the possible inclusion of the patent in the standard. Consequently, for such SEPs (in particular in the telecommunications and consumer electronics sector but also in other areas which are characterized by the necessity of technical standardization) the competition law objection according to *Huawei* v. *ZTE* is now the most important tool for curtailing injunctive relief in the EU.

The *Huawei* v. *ZTE* case concerned an action for alleged infringement brought by Huawei, seeking injunctive relief on the basis of a SEP which was subject to a FRAND commitment by Huawei. Despite long negotiations, the parties had not been able to agree on licence terms. In the resulting litigation, the defendant ZTE claimed that the plaintiff Huawei abused its dominant position according to Art. 102 of the TFEU by refusing to grant a licence for the SEP on FRAND terms. Essentially, the CJEU placed substantial negotiation obligations (including the obligation to propose respective FRAND offers) upon both parties. As regards injunctions based on alleged infringements of SEPs, in practice these come down to requirements on the patent holder seeking an injunction to first notify the alleged

[77] *RTE* v. *Commission/Magill* (CJEU 1995).
[78] *IMS Health* (CJEU 2004).
[79] *Huawei* v. *ZTE* (CJEU 2015).

infringer of the alleged infringement and then – if the alleged infringer at least signals its general willingness to take a licence – to make a licence offer on FRAND terms before proceeding with any action for an injunction against the alleged infringer. The specifics of this procedural regime of enforcement in the sector of SEPs have been discussed extensively in the literature, and meanwhile been specified by different national courts, namely in the United Kingdom and Germany, with some differences remaining.[80] To describe the details of this balanced procedural step-by-step approach for the enforcement of SEPs in the EU would go beyond the description of general EU competition law tools presented in this section. Suffice it to say that SEP holders seeking an injunction in an EU member state against standard implementers (who use their SEP) now have to follow the *Huawei v. ZTE* regime (and namely first make a FRAND licence offer to the implementer and await the reaction) before proceeding with an action for an injunction.

8. *Injunctions against Intermediaries*

The Enforcement Directive's Art. 11 obliges member states to provide the possibility of injunctions against "intermediaries whose services are used by a third party to infringe an intellectual property right". The provision does not only concern internet intermediaries but covers any service which is used by a third party to infringe an intellectual property right. Consequently, the CJEU has also applied Art. 11 to "intermediaries" in the sense of providers of physical infrastructure, such as a business subletting market stalls to traders which infringed trademark rights in these premises,[81] which explains the potential relevance of the provision and the respective case law of the CJEU for secondary liability cases in patent law.

Firstly, Art. 11 of the Enforcement Directive sets a minimum standard for what are typically secondary liability cases in EU member states' laws.[82] However, the provision gives no further detailed guidance for what has been shaped as "primary" and "secondary" liability in many member states' laws and to which extent injunctions have to be qualified or limited (in the realm of secondary liability).[83] In fact, the Directive does not even expressly define the term "intermediary". Thus, it leaves the scope of the area of minimum harmonization as unclear as the crucial question of whether remedies other than injunctive relief, especially a claim for damages, should be applicable against secondary infringers.[84] Moreover, secondly, it has been

---

[80] *See* for an overview of post-Huawei judgments in Germany and the United Kingdom (including further explanation of the remaining differences) Leistner 2018; Picht 2017a; Picht 2017b; Lawrance & Brooks 2018; Cross & Strath 2017; *see* for an overview over latest judgments outside the EU, Block & Rätz 2019, 798 et seq.

[81] *Tommy Hilfiger* v. *Delta Center* (CJEU 2016, para. 29).

[82] Id.; Cabrera Rodríguez 2018.

[83] Id.; Cabrera Rodríguez 2018.

[84] Leistner 2014, 76, 88; see also the comparison between the member states regarding liability for indirect infringement of second medical use patents, England 2016, 426.

convincingly argued in literature that Art. 11 of the Enforcement Directive goes further than that and effectively establishes a category of accountable but not liable intermediaries which have to assist in preventing third-party infringement although they are not liable under any doctrine of secondary liability.[85]

Despite gross differences in detail regarding structure and legal consequences of secondary liability between the member states, certain common elements can be identified. Specifically, as objective factors, the degree of the (objective) risk caused by the secondary infringer as well as the degree of control the secondary infringer has in relation to the acts of direct infringement, play a significant role in assessing contributory liability.[86] Moreover, the (objective) design of a business model of an intermediary, most of all where the business model is specifically designed to profit from direct acts of infringement, might give grounds for liability. Subjectively, actual and specific knowledge (or mere constructive knowledge in certain cases) of particular infringements can be an important factor with a lot of differences in detail.[87]

In the ruling in the influential *L'Oréal* v. *eBay*[88] case, the CJEU held that Art. 11 of the Enforcement Directive – in the case at hand concerning injunctions against an internet host provider as an intermediary pursuant to Art. 11, sentence 3, of the Enforcement Directive – must be interpreted as requiring the member states to ensure that the national courts with jurisdiction in relation to the protection of intellectual property rights are able to order the intermediary to take measures which contribute not only to bringing the specific infringements of those rights to an end but also to preventing further infringements.[89] In this field (the case concerned trademark infringement[90]), the CJEU clearly differentiates between injunctions granted against infringers aimed at prohibiting the continuation of the infringement pursuant to Art. 11, sentence 1, of the Enforcement Directive and the injunction against intermediaries pursuant to Art. 1, sentence 3, of the Enforcement Directive. The situation of an intermediary, which is to be understood broadly as "a service capable of being used by one or more other persons in order to infringe one or more

---

[85] *See* comprehensively Husovec 2017, 65 et seq. In addition, there is a large number of academic articles on this, although they mostly relate to copyright and trademark infringements on the internet and the liability or accountability of internet service providers and thus have little direct relevance for patent law.

[86] Leistner 2014, 88.

[87] *See* in detail id. This chapter will not cover the specific situation in copyright law, where the CJEU has extended the communication to the public right under the *InfoSoc Directive* so that the resulting infringement concept effectively covers what would be mere secondary liability in many member states' laws. This is because this case law, obviously, is specifically related to the concrete scope of the economic rights under the *InfoSoc Directive*, and even more particularly to the CJEU's concept of the communication to the public right. Therefore, any impact on the patent law sector, where neither harmonization nor comparable infringement standards do exist in EU law, would be far-fetched to say the least.

[88] *L'Oréal* v. *eBay* (CJEU 2011).

[89] Id., para. 144.

[90] *See* on the very specific situation in copyright law above in footnote 87.

intellectual property rights",[91] by means of which the infringement is committed, would be more complex and lends itself to other kinds of injunctions.[92] Therefore, in respect of effective protection of intellectual property rights, the court holds that Art. 11, sentence 3, of the Enforcement Directive must allow national courts to order an online service to take measures that provide for the prevention of further infringements detached from the specific act of infringement which gave rise to the injunction.[93] The court emphasizes the general guidelines for the imposed injunctions to be effective, proportionate, dissuasive and not to create barriers for legitimate trade.[94] This is to be applied equally to physical marketplaces as intermediaries.[95] The CJEU judgments allow the conclusion that injunctions according to Arts. 9(1)(a) and 11 of the Enforcement Directive against intermediaries are neither limited to a specific group of intermediaries nor to certain sectors.[96]

Within this legal framework, undoubtedly, both generally formulated "obey-the-law" commands as well as more specific court orders are possible on the level of the different member states. This is in line with the basic ideas of the CJEU rulings[97] concerning the liability of intermediaries in the field of copyright law infringements, based on Arts. 3 and 8(3) of the InfoSoc Directive, where the CJEU has explicitly accepted open-ended "obey-the-law" injunctions against intermediaries according to national law.[98] Taking into account the general principle not to grant injunctions that go beyond what is appropriate and necessary in the light of the facts and circumstances of the case at hand, the conceivable scope of injunctions might vary. In certain cases, an injunction not causing a complete cessation of the infringement will be reasonable and obligations can also include certain preventive measures, such as password protection or identification of direct infringers if and to the extent that this is possible under European data protection law.[99] Also stay-down duties – i.e. duties to prevent future comparable infringements – can be ordered, where such preventive measures can be implemented on the basis of automated search tools and technologies without having to carry out an independent assessment.[100]

While such more specific intermediary liability problems will be rare in patent law (though not inconceivable in cases where patent-infringing products are sold via internet platforms), the general principles of the cited case law are also applicable, *mutatis mutandis*, to other cases where injunctive relief against physical intermediaries (e.g., shippers, infrastructure suppliers, trade fair organizers) is concerned.

---

[91] *Tommy Hilfiger* v. *Delta Center* (CJEU 2016, para. 23).
[92] *L'Oréal* v. *eBay* (CJEU 2011, paras. 128 et seq.).
[93] Id., para. 131.
[94] Id., para. 144.
[95] *Tommy Hilfiger* v. *Delta Center* (CJEU 2016, para. 36).
[96] *Guidance on Enforcement Directive* (EC 2017, 17).
[97] *UPC Telekabel Wien* (CJEU 2014).
[98] Leistner 2017, 757.
[99] *See, e.g., McFadden* v. *Sony Music Entertainment* (CJEU 2016, paras. 99 et seq.).
[100] *Glawischnig-Piesczek* v. *Facebook* (CJEU 2019, para. 53).

Accordingly, in the *Tommy Hilfiger* case, cited above,[101] the CJEU applied the same general principles in regard to the tenant of a market hall who – as an intermediary in the sense of Art. 11 of the Enforcement Directive – sublet sales points to market traders some of whom committed trademark infringements in these pitches.

9. *Scope of Injunctions Regarding Non-Infringing Activities*

Specific CJEU decisions on the Enforcement Directive itself have not yet addressed a situation where a (collateral) prohibition of non-infringing activities came along with injunctive relief. However, certain general principles can be derived from the *UPC Telekabel*[102] judgment on injunctions against intermediaries under the InfoSoc Directive's copyright provisions on injunctions which are essentially similar to the provisions in the Enforcement Directive. The case dealt with the proportionality of website blocking orders addressed to internet service providers (ISPs) in cases of copyright infringements. In particular, the CJEU had to decide whether injunctions issued against ISPs requiring them to effectively block access (thus without ordering *specific* measures) to certain websites, that provide content exclusively or predominantly without the rightsholders' consent, were compatible with the InfoSoc Directive and the CFR's fundamental rights.[103] Inter alia, the CJEU stated that the freedom to conduct a business is not infringed when the (open-ended) injunction leaves the enjoined party to determine the specific measures to be taken in order to achieve the result sought.[104] The measures taken by the subject of the injunction must be sufficiently effective to ensure genuine protection of the IP owner's fundamental right to intellectual property so that the measures would at least have to have the effect of making a further infringement more difficult.[105]

The question, referred to by the Austrian court in the *UPC Telekabel* case, clearly would have also included situations where the material on the blocked website was predominantly provided without the rightsholders' consent (and not completely illegal). In this respect, the CJEU held that "the measures adopted by the internet service provider must be strictly targeted, in the sense that they must serve to bring an end to a third party's infringement of copyright or of a related right but without thereby affecting internet users who are using the provider's services in order to lawfully access information. Failing that, the provider's interference in the freedom of information of those users would be unjustified in the light of the objective pursued".[106] However, since compliance with this qualification in a strict sense

---

[101] *See* above footnote 95.
[102] *UPC Telekabel Wien* (CJEU 2014).
[103] Id., para. 17.
[104] Id., para. 52.
[105] Id., paras. 62 et seq.
[106] Id., para. 56.

would obviously have been impossible, as the absolutely overwhelming part of such infringing websites also has a certain share of legal content, in the referred case this begs the question how much incidental effect on third parties' interest would still have to be accepted as *de minimis*. Hence, the crucial question at this point is which concrete measures in which concrete cases would on balance not unnecessarily and disproportionately deprive internet users of their possibility to lawfully access the information available, and thus could still be permissible under the CJEU's ruling. The court has left these questions open, and essentially gave only a procedural answer concerning the affected users' right to due process: At a minimum, affected users must have legal standing in proceedings for injunctions in order to defend their lawful rights. In another case on blocking injunctions within this general framework, the English High Court accepted 6 per cent of illegal content on a website for which a blocking order was granted as *de minimis*.[107]

10. *Flexibility Regarding NPEs*

The widely discussed and particularly relevant case of patent assertion entities (PAEs)[108] undoubtedly shows that non-practising entities (NPEs) can use injunctive relief as a threat. As they are less exposed to counterclaims on the side of the defendant, patent enforcement by NPEs is prone to a higher risk of abuse which can erect obstacles for innovation leading to market failure.[109] Consequently, there has been discussion of denying injunctive relief to NPEs in certain cases. The Enforcement Directive does not explicitly mention the possibility of denying injunctive relief to a certain type of plaintiff as such. Justifiably, therefore, courts in Europe seem to hesitate to apply patent or competition law tools in order to deny injunctive relief based solely on the fact that a party is an NPE since such a categorical differentiation is not really laid out in the legislative framework. Instead the law seems to require a flexible case-by-case analysis taking into account all the relevant factors in a given case[110] so as to conduct the key analysis of proportionality.

While a specific statutory justification for treating NPEs differently does therefore not exist in European law in general, the European litigation system seems to offer sufficient safeguards to protect against the potentially harmful effects of NPEs' enforcement practices in the EU.[111] Apart from competition law remedies, in

---

[107] *Twentieth Century Fox v. BT* (EWHC 2011, paras. 48 et seq., 186).

[108] *See* the comprehensive examination of the business model in the United States and Europe in US Fed. Trade Commission 2016; European Commission Joint Research Centre 2016; Love et al. 2015.

[109] Ohly 2008, 791; Ullrich 2012a, 33 et seq.; Osterrieth 2009, 542 et seq.; Lemley & Melamed 2013, 2153 et seq.

[110] Stierle 2019, 875; Contreras & Picht 2017, 3 et seq., Morton & Shapiro 2016, 21 et seq.

[111] European Commission Joint Research Centre 2016, 12 et seq.; *EU Approach to SEPs* (EC 2017, 11).

particular the abuse of dominant position according to Art. 102 of the TFEU,[112] as well as the general principle of abuse of rights in civil law (and as a common principle of European Union law also expressly laid down in Art. 3(2) Enforcement Directive), the denial of injunctive relief might also be possible due to proportionality considerations in certain cases.[113]

Nevertheless, these instruments only give the necessary leeway for member states' laws to deny injunctive relief to NPEs in certain cases, specified in a case-by-case approach. The European Commission also stated explicitly in its communication regarding the EU approach to standard essential patents that the application of the proportionality principle by courts provides another safeguard in NPE cases.[114] By contrast, a general exemption with regard to an entire category of rightsholders is rightly not foreseen in the Enforcement Directive. Arguably, such a general exemption would not even be compliant with the Directive if it was foreseen in the national law of a member state for the reasons mentioned.

11. *Grant of Compensation in Lieu of Injunctions*

Hitherto, national courts of the EU member states approach the issue of alternative measures, such as compensation in lieu of injunctions, very differently.[115]

Art. 12 of the Enforcement Directive gives the option to the member states to foresee that in certain cases and at the request of the infringer, the court may order pecuniary compensation to be paid to the injured party instead of an injunction if that person acted unintentionally and without negligence, if the injunction would cause the infringer disproportionate harm and if pecuniary compensation to the injured party appears reasonably satisfactory.[116] In the original Commission proposal for the Directive, this provision was intended to be mandatory for the member states.[117] The Commission presented this element of the proposal as providing a "safeguard against unfair litigation".[118] Subsequently, this concept of pecuniary compensation in lieu of an injunction was criticized inter alia because in most civil law systems, an obligation to pay damages is made dependent upon a certain degree

---

[112] *See* above Section A.7 on competition law.
[113] *See* above Section A.4.
[114] *EU Approach to SEPs* (EC 2017, 12).
[115] Blok 2016, 56; Marfé et al. 2015, 181 et seq.; Bennett et al. 2015. *See* further Chapters 6 (Finland), 7 (France), 8 (Germany), 10 (Italy), 11 (Netherlands) and 12 (Poland).
[116] Art. 12 *Enforcement Directive*: "Alternative measures: Member States may provide that, in appropriate cases and at the request of the person liable to be subject to the measures provided for in this section, the competent judicial authorities may order pecuniary compensation to be paid to the injured party instead of applying the measures provided for in this section if that person acted unintentionally and without negligence, if execution of the measures in question would cause him/her disproportionate harm and if pecuniary compensation to the injured party appears reasonably satisfactory."
[117] *See* Art. 16 *Enforcement of Intellectual Property Rights Proposal* (2003, 40).
[118] *Frequently Asked Questions Proposed Directive* (2003, 9).

of fault or negligence.[119] In consequence, in the final version of the Enforcement Directive, the possibility to foresee compensation in lieu of injunctions became purely optional for the member states.[120]

Art. 12 of the Enforcement Directive contains a specific rule, providing for compensation in lieu of an injunction.[121] Concerning the requirements laid down in this provision (i.e., the infringer acting unintentionally and without negligence, the injunction causing disproportionate harm to the infringer, reasonable possibility to satisfy the rightsholder by way of pecuniary compensation), it is the subject of discussion whether the enumeration of these requirements has to be understood to establish a set of alternative or cumulative conditions.[122] While the wording of the English version is open for interpretation, the German version[123] points clearly towards a cumulative understanding, even if this limits the application to very exceptional cases.[124] This interpretation would be in line with the general under-standing of injunctive relief as a core tool to enforce intellectual property rights and in striving for a strong judicial protection of the latter.[125]

The heading "Alternative measures" and wording "instead" show clearly that the compensation described in Art. 12 of the Enforcement Directive is an alternative to the prohibitory injunctions of Art. 11 and the corrective measures of Art. 10 of the Enforcement Directive.[126] Consequently, the compensation payment for continu-ing infringement can only be granted if the court has already determined an infringement according to Art. 10 or 11 of the Enforcement Directive. However, the establishment of an infringement by the court does not necessarily state whether the infringer acted unintentionally or non-negligently. The possibility to grant an injunction does not depend on the wilful or negligent fault of the (alleged) infringer; the mere objective fact that a patent infringement has occurred will generally suffice in the EU for granting an injunction.[127] When taking the wording of Art. 12

---

[119] Blok 2016, 57.

[120] Recital 25, sentence 1 *Enforcement Directive* also expressly underlines the character of the provision as a pure voluntary option for the member states: "Where an infringement is committed unintentionally and without negligence and where the corrective measures or injunctions provided for by this Directive would be disproportionate, Member States should have the option of providing for the possibility, in appropriate cases, of pecuniary compensation being awarded to the injured party as an alternative measure."

[121] *See* above footnote 116.

[122] Blok 2016, 59.

[123] The German version of Art. 12 of the Enforcement Directive reads as follows: "[S]ofern die betreffende Person weder vorsätzlich noch fahrlässig gehandelt hat, ihr aus der Durchführung der betreffenden Maßnahmen ein unverhältnismäßig großer Schaden entstehen würde und die Zahlung einer Abfindung an die geschädigte Partei als angemessene Entschädigung erscheint."

[124] Blok 2016, 59; cf. also for an analysis of the rare application of the parallel provision in section 100(1) German Copyright Act: Sonnenberg 2014, 170 et seq.

[125] Blok 2016, 59.

[126] Id., 58.

[127] Explicitly for intermediary liability *Guidance on Enforcement Directive* (EC 2017, 16).

seriously, therefore, it is necessary to ask under which conditions the infringer will fulfil the requirement of acting unintentionally and without negligence. However, under many member states' laws, it is hardly conceivable that someone would infringe a patent without any intention or negligence since courts in the EU member states, in particular in civil law countries such as Germany, interpret the requisite level of care very strictly. Especially in situations dealing with SEPs and taking into account the *Huawei* v. *ZTE* obligations, the infringer will be put on notice with the first warning letter[128] sent by the patentee. At least from this moment, continued use by the alleged infringer will generally establish intention or negligence. In addition, if courts claim an infringement as the basis for an injunction, any further use of the patent will establish liability for wilful or negligent fault. Hence, it seems that the requirements can only be understood as a reference to the *initial* act of infringement because otherwise an unintentional and non-negligent act would hardly be conceivable in European practice. Another possible avenue to guarantee the applicability of alternative measures would be a more restrictive interpretation of fault (i.e., intention or negligence) in the sense of Art. 12 of the Enforcement Directive. Since these are autonomous terms of EU law, different practice in the context of infringement proceedings in member states' laws would on principle not hinder a more flexible application of Art. 12 of the Enforcement Directive; whether such a split interpretation of one and the same term in different contexts would really be convincing from a viewpoint of contextual interpretation, however, remains in doubt.

Since the provision is a mere option for the member states, applicability in national law requires an implementing provision in national law in order to give Art. 12 of the Enforcement Directive effect in a member state. In that regard it has to be noted that numerous member states have not implemented Art. 12 of the Enforcement Directive at all.[129] Accordingly, the conditions and design of alternative measures are still very ambiguous and diverse in the different EU member states. In the EU-wide proportionality discussion, the focus is therefore rather on the general proportionality standard of Art. 3 of the Enforcement Directive and on the question of how the *general* principle of proportionality can be applied in order to create more flexibility in the realm of injunctions.

To further elucidate Art. 12 proper, it might be helpful to have a look at comparable provisions in national law, which actually were the model for the provision. In this regard Section 101(1) (now Section 100) of the German Copyright Act stands out.[130] This provision aims to protect the interests of the defending party having acted without intent or negligence. Such defendants can pay compensation in lieu of an injunction when the execution of measures in

---

[128] *Huawei* v. *ZTE* (CJEU 2015, paras 60 et seq.); see Section A.9.
[129] *Analysis of Application of Enforcement Directive* (EC 2010, 5 et seq.).
[130] Explanatory memorandum Art. 16 *Enforcement of Intellectual Property Rights Proposal*, 23.

question would cause disproportionate harm to them and if pecuniary compensation to the injured party appears reasonably satisfactory. The German legislature intended to create an exemption for cases that are particularly complex from a factual or legal point of view and therefore lead to infringement without being based on the defendant's fault.[131] The criterion of disproportionate harm leads to a proportionality test, weighing regular measures against the harm on the defendant's side.[132] The principle of proportionality certainly demands that such exceptional cases be treated differently, but it has to be emphasized that disproportionality and subsequently financial compensation instead of injunctive relief have remained a very rare exception even under this express provision in German copyright law.[133] Also, the Enforcement Directive does not contain any specification for the calculation and the amount of pecuniary compensation and there is no case law on this at the EU level yet. Again, further specification could arguably be based on the model of Section 100, sentence 2 of the German Copyright Act. According to this provision, compensation shall total the amount that would constitute equitable remuneration in the case of a contractual granting of the right.[134]

B. AGREEMENT ON A UNIFIED PATENT COURT (UPCA)

1. *Overview and Current Status*

The lengthy efforts to establish the Unified Patent Court as a court with competence for legal claims for traditional European patents and in particular the newly created European patents with unitary effect are back on track after delays, with operations expected to begin mid-2022. In contrast to the European patent characterized by granting a bundle of various national patents in a unified procedure, the European patent with unitary effect (Unitary patent) would be one of a kind, unitarily covering the territories of the EU member states that became members of the UPCA (i.e. all EU member states except for Poland and Spain). An international agreement was necessary (instead of an EU regulation proper) because the Unified Patent Court (UPC) shall also have limited jurisdiction over European patents and future European patents with unitary effect will be granted by the European Patent Office (EPO). Thus, the European Patent Organisation (EPO) and the contracting states of the European Patent Convention[135] (EPC) had to be part of the underlying international law framework. Consequently, a complex set of partly overlapping, interfering and similarly worded provisions deriving from different sources of law (the UPCA as an international agreement, EU law, such as the Enforcement

---

[131] *Draft of German Copyright Act* (1962, 150); Wimmers 2020, para. 26.

[132] Klein 2012, 371; Amschewitz 2008, 197.

[133] Ohly 2009, 266 et seq.

[134] *Cf.* Amschewitz 2008, 197.

[135] *See* the preamble of the *UPCA*.

Directive, but also primary EU law as well as national law of the contracting states) give rise to problems of interpretation and scope of application of these different legal regimes.[136]

Essentially, as for European patents and European patents with unitary effect, the UPCA and the accompanying EU regulations[137] shall establish a single Unified Patent Court with exclusive jurisdiction over actions for infringement (including provisional and protective measures and injunctions), for declaration of non-infringement, for revocation and respective counter-claims – all this with certain optional exceptions ("opt out") for "classic" European patents during a transitional period of seven years which can be prolonged up to a further seven years.[138] The UPC will be structured as follows: (1) A decentralized Court of First Instance with local and regional divisions located in the contracting member states and a central division with its seat in Paris and a section in Munich and (2) a common Court of Appeal and a Registry which will have their seat in Luxembourg.[139]

The relationship between the UPCA as an international agreement and EU law is complex. According to the UPCA, the UPC applies EU law in its entirety and shall respect its primacy (Art. 20 UPCA). Accordingly, questions concerning the interpretation of overriding EU law will have to be referred by the UPC to the CJEU (Art. 21 UPCA, Art. 267 TFEU). In practice, however, the enforcement of patents will be governed primarily by the provisions of the UPCA (see Art. 82(3) UPCA) and, where the UPCA leaves gaps, by national law (which in turn is partly harmonized on the basis of the Enforcement Directive). Practically, this means that notwithstanding the legal primacy of EU law, primarily concerning patent enforcement, the UPC will have to apply and interpret the UPCA, while in cases of gaps in the agreement, national law of the *loci protectionis* (the member state for which protection is sought) will apply and will have to be construed in conformity with the Enforcement Directive.[140] If open questions of interpretation of the Enforcement Directive are relevant in that context, the UPCA will have to refer such questions to the CJEU for a preliminary ruling.

Meanwhile, the United Kingdom's official declaration stating that it will not apply the UPCA after Brexit[141] put an end to the discussion in legal literature

[136] Ullrich 2012b; Cabrera Rodríguez 2018.
[137] *Unitary Patent Protection Regulation* (2012) and *Unitary Patent Protection – Applicable Translation Arrangements Regulation* (2012).
[138] *See* further Art. 83 UPCA; *see also* Art. 32 UPCA and further Section B.2.
[139] Art. 9 et seq. 5 UPCA. See for a concise practical overview www.epo.org/law-practice/unitary/upc/upc-faq.html.
[140] Leistner 2016, 220 et seq.
[141] On 27 February 2020 the United Kingdom published a government report titled "The Future Relationship with the EU – The UK's Approach to Negotiations" in which the UPCA is not mentioned and the CJEU is expressly excluded from any jurisdiction in the United Kingdom. The fact that the United Kingdom does not seek involvement in the UPC system has been expressly confirmed by a UK government spokesperson on 28 February 2020. See *Letter to Lord Morris*. On 20 July 2020 the United Kingdom has deposited a withdrawal notification of

whether this would have been legally possible in the first place.[142] This leads to follow-up problems as the seat of one of the central sections of the Court of First Instance should have been in London. Further delays occurred as a result of the constitutional complaint against the German act of approval[143] and the declaration of its nullity by the German Federal Constitutional Court in its Decision of 13 February 2020[144] as the German ratification is mandatory for the entry into force of the UPCA alongside that of France and Italy according to Art. 89(1) of the UPCA. [145] Even though the German UPC Act of Approval II entered into force 13 August 2021[146] after a new legislative procedure and the rejection of two applications for preliminary injunctions,[147] the ratification of one further participating UPC member state is still required until the necessary number of 13 member states is reached. At the time of writing, the Preparatory Committee[148] has estimated that the UPC will start operations mid-2022.[149]

2. *Legal Framework*

The UPCA lists the main substantive claims for which the UPC has competence in Art. 32(1) of the UPCA. At the top of the list stands the action for injunction pursuant to Art. 32(1)(a) of the UPCA. The same structure and the dominant position of injunctive relief is reflected as well in Art. 63 of the UPCA where it leads the articles on the contents of the final decisions of the UPC. Art. 63 of the UPCA requires that the court, first, finds that an infringement has occurred. In a second step, it considers related defences. In a third step, it orders certain remedies, namely grants an injunction, preferably including a warning to the effect that a penalty may be handed down by the court in case of non-compliance with the terms of the injunction. In a fourth step, if the infringer does not comply with the terms of the

ratification with the UPCA Council Secretariat (see www.unified-patent-court.org/news/uk-withdrawal-upca) and a *Parliamentary Written Statement* in the House of Commons has been made.

[142] *See* for the discussion in legal literature, e.g., Tilmann 2016b; Dinwoodie & Dreyfuss 2017, 6 et seq.; Ohly & Streinz 2017; Leistner & Simon 2017; Jaeger 2017; Gandía Sellens 2018; Broß & Lamping 2018; Lamping & Ullrich 2018; Dijkmann & Paddenburgh 2018.

[143] *Draft of German UPC Act of Approval I* (2017).

[144] *EPGÜ-ZustG I* (BVerfG 2020).

[145] The latest ratification details can be found at: www.consilium.europa.eu/en/documents-publi cations/treaties-agreements/agreement/?id=2013001&DocLanguage=en.

[146] *German UPC Act of Approval II.*

[147] *EPGÜ-ZustG II* (BVerfG 2021).

[148] The Preparatory Committee consists of expert representatives of all the signatory states to the UPCA and is tasked with the practical establishment of the new court including the preparation of the UPC's rules of procedure (UPCRoP). It is not expressly foreseen in the UPCA but has been established by the UPCA's signatory states in order to oversee the UPC's workstream: www.unified-patent-court.org/content/preparatory-committee.

[149] *See* www.unified-patent-court.org/news/what-decision-german-federal-constitutional-court-means-unified-patent-courts-timeplan.

injunction, the court shall set a recurrent penalty payment (see on penalties Art. 63 (2) UPCA).[150]

As to the protection of the addressee of an injunction, Art. 82(2) of the UPCA provides for the general rule that, where appropriate, enforcement of any court decision may be subject to security or an equivalent assurance to ensure compensation for any damage suffered by the addressee of an (unjustified) injunction.

3. *Discretion of the Court?*

The final (permanent) injunction pursuant to Art. 63(1) of the UPCA, according to which the court "may" grant an injunction against the infringer aimed at prohibiting the continuation of the infringement, emulates the wording of Art. 11 of the Enforcement Directive. Consequently, the question arises whether the word "may" instead of "shall",[151] which is usually used for mandatory obligations, gives the court discretion. On the one hand, the wording indicates the non-mandatory character of the provision.[152] When interpreting the provision from a contextual point of view it has to be noted, however, that for both the provisional injunctions which are regulated in Art. 62 (1) of the UPCA and the permanent injunctions (Art. 63(1) UPCA), the wording in regard to the Court's position is "may", while only in Art. 62(1) of the UPCA on provisional injunctions is the court expressly instructed to execute a balance of interests of the parties and in particular to take into account the potential harm for either of the parties resulting from the granting or refusal of a (provisional) injunction.[153] In the wider context of EU law one might also consider a contextual argument resting on the identical wording of the UPCA and the Enforcement Directive for which latter it is uncontentious that generally injunctions shall be granted in cases of infringement.[154] However, this is not necessarily a compelling argument as the Enforcement Directive, other than the UPCA, does not have direct effect but is addressed to the EU member states which have to implement it.[155]

In the materials relating to the genesis of the UPCA there is no clear evidence that the court is intended to have discretion to deny the exercise of an injunction pursuant to Art. 63(1) of the UPCA.[156] However, in the explanation of why the alternative measure of granting damages in lieu of injunctions was removed, the

[150] Tilmann 2016a, 414.
[151] *See* the wording in Art. 65(1) UPCA for the decision on the validity of a patent and Art. 68(1) UPCA for the award of claims.
[152] Schröer 2013, 1107.
[153] Reetz et al. 2015, 216; Marfé et al. 2015, 187; Bennett et al. 2015, 26.
[154] *See* Sections A.2, B.2.
[155] *See* Sections A.11.
[156] Reetz et al. 2015, 217; Marfé et al. 2015, 188.

Legal Group of the Preparatory Committee seemed to assume discretion of the court when stating:

> Where the Court finds an infringement of a patent it will under Article 63 of the Agreement give order of injunctive relief. Only under very exceptional circumstances it will use its discretion and not give such an order. This follows from Article 25 of the Agreement which recognizes the right to prevent the use of the invention without the consent of the patent proprietor as the core right of the patentee. When exercising this discretion, the Court can also consider the use of alternative measures.[157]

In sum, the question of mandatory injunctive relief is not finally determined by procedural law but the answer has to be found in substantive law on patent protection and enforcement contained in Arts. 25–28 of the UPCA and in the Enforcement Directive.[158] In that regard, Arts. 25–28 of the UPCA do not name a claim for injunctive relief explicitly but merely determine the scope of patent protection in infringement cases which does not necessarily fully determine the remedies.[159] Hence, from the authors' viewpoint the question of discretion with regard to court orders granting injunctive relief is governed by common principles of substantive law of the contracting member states, i.e. the EU member states (see Art. 2(a) UPCA). As the substantive law of the member states in this area is, in turn, governed by the overriding Enforcement Directive, the respective principles of the Enforcement Directive on injunctive relief have to be taken into account. This leads to the tentative conclusion that in principle injunctive relief has to be granted by the court, except that under exceptional circumstances, where the granting of an injunction is clearly disproportionate, it can execute its discretion to deny an injunction.[160]

The more specific limitations of Art. 3(2) of the Enforcement Directive (abuse and other measures creating barriers to legitimate trade; EU competition law pursuant to Arts. 101, 102 TFEU) are applicable in any case. If these limitations apply, an injunction can also be denied.[161] The applicability of the principles of the Enforcement Directive (as European Union law) is made explicit in Art. 1 of the UPCA when stating that the court shall be "subject to the same obligations under Union law as any national court of the Contracting Member States". This is in line with Art. 24 of the UPCA according to which EU law, in particular directly applicable provisions of EU law pursuant to Art. 24(2)(a) of the UPCA, is a source of law the court shall base its decisions on.

[157] *Table with Explanatory Notes to the Changes of the Rules of Procedure* (2014), 11. Particularly with regard to the definition of the court's discretion, the aforementioned explanatory notes may serve as an instrument for a historical interpretation of the law.
[158] Tilmann 2016a, 416; Yan 2017, 157.
[159] Meier-Beck 2014, 147; Hüttermann 2017, para. 659; Marfé et al. 2015, 187.
[160] But see Tilmann 2016a, 416: no discretion.
[161] *See also* id., 416.

4. *Considerations of Proportionality*

A general principle according to which the court may grant permanent injunctive relief only within the frame of proportionality cannot be found in the UPCA text.[162] The claim for a fair balance between the legitimate interests of all parties and the provision for the required level of discretion of judges made in Art. 41(3) of the UPCA only refers to the procedure and the judicial remedies but not to the court order itself. Pursuant to Art. 56 of the UPCA the court may make its orders subject to conditions in accordance with the Unified Patent Court Rules of Procedure (UPCRoP). However, such conditions are not established for Art. 63 of the UPCA.

If the Court of Appeal considers the question of injunctive relief, it is urged by the UPCA to take its decision about the so-called suspensive effect of the appeal (i.e. the staying of an injunction pending appeal) in a fair and equitable manner according to Arts. 74(1) and 42(2) of the UPCA. This could have the effect of procedural discretion as to considerations of fairness but which has to be differentiated from proportionality in terms of substantive law on remedies.[163]

Ultimately, with regard to the primacy of EU law expressly laid down in Arts. 20 and 24(1) of the UPCA, the requirements of Art. 3(2) of the Enforcement Directive as to shaping effective, proportionate and dissuasive measures must be respected in all cases.

5. *Competition Law Considerations*

Arts. 20 and 24(1)(a) of the UPCA declare respect for and the primacy of EU law in its entirety. Therefore, competition law, in particular the antitrust principles of compulsory licence and abuse of rights pursuant to Arts. 101 and 102 of the TFEU, have to be taken into account as a limitation on injunctive relief, provided that their conditions are met in the particular case (Arts. 25 and 26 UPCA).[164] Furthermore, it is also conceivable that the denying or modification of injunctive relief could draw upon the general principle of the abuse of rights.[165]

6. *Injunctions against Intermediaries*

According to Art. 63(1) of the UPCA permanent injunctions may also be addressed to intermediaries whose services are used by a third party to infringe a patent. Furthermore, Art. 62 of the UPCA, in line with Art. 32(1)(c) of the UPCA, stipulates

---

[162] Reetz et al. 2015, 218.
[163] Id., 219.
[164] Id., 217.
[165] The doctrine of abuse of rights is one of the accepted common principles of EU law, derived from common legal principles in the member states, *see generally* de la Feria & Vogenauer 2011, 33 et seq. For the UPCA, *see* Reetz et al. 2015, 218; Yan 2017, 158.

the competence of the court to grant provisional injunctions by way of order against an alleged infringer or against an intermediary, intended to prevent any imminent infringement. National approaches to indirect infringement actions are very different within the EU member states (as the Enforcement Directive only partly harmonizes this area[166]) and the law is constantly evolving in this field.[167] It will be for the UPC to draw its own conclusion from the rather open-ended EU framework as well as national doctrines and to make a contribution to further harmonization in its future case law within the framework set by the Enforcement Directive.

7. *Flexibility Regarding NPEs*

If Art. 63(1) of the UPCA is understood to comprise discretion of the court, one could at least theoretically consider denying injunctive relief to a certain group of plaintiffs. However, if there is discretionary scope for the court, this would also be limited to exceptional cases. Therefore, it seems highly questionable whether an exception for an entire group of plaintiffs could indeed be grounded on possible discretion under Art. 63(1) of the UPCA.[168] Eventually, absent a more specific rule, injunctive relief can only be denied in specific individual cases with a view to a comprehensive analysis of all circumstances of the case at hand.[169]

Several structural features of the UPC system – for example, loser-pays fee-shifting rules, a lack of judicial review and possible shift to jurisdictions that are most patentee-friendly for unitary-wide claims – should give occasion to closely observe whether NPE activity will rise under the future UPCA regime and whether current unitary patent remedies will be sufficiently balanced to deal with this.[170]

8. *Grant of Compensation in Lieu of Injunctions*

The sixteenth draft of the 31 January 2014 UPCRoP, Rule 118.2[171] contained the possibility for the court to award damages or compensation instead of an injunction under certain conditions similar to the criteria of Art. 12 of the Enforcement Directive. In the seventeenth draft, the content of Rule 118.2 was removed without

---

[166] *See* Section A.1.
[167] *See* Section A.
[168] But cf. Schröer 2013, 1107.
[169] *See also* Sections A.4, B.3.
[170] Tietz 2019; Love et al. 2017, 18 et seq.; European Commission Joint Research Centre 2016, 54.
[171] Rule 118.2 *UPCRoP (16th Draft)* reads as follows: "Without prejudice to the general discretion provided for in Articles 63 and 64 of the Agreement, in appropriate cases and at the request of the party liable to the orders and measures provided for in paragraph 1 the Court may order damages or compensation to be paid to the injured party instead of applying the orders and measures if that person acted unintentionally and without negligence, if execution of the orders and measures in question would cause such party disproportionate harm and if damages or compensation to the injured party appear to the Court to be reasonably satisfactory."

replacement, as it was debated on a political level.[172] The deletion was justified by
the consideration that a scenario of damages in lieu of injunctions would have been
difficult to imagine in practice, in particular because of the prerequisite that the
infringement action would have to be not only unintentional but also without any
negligence which – under the very strict negligence standard in a number of
continental European countries, including Germany – is rare.[173] Further, the
deletion was held to be in line with EU law since the Enforcement Directive did
not make implementation of Art. 12 obligatory for the member states.[174] Accordingly,
in the current eighteenth draft of the UPCRoP there is no provision on compensation in lieu of injunctions.

9. *Consideration of Validity Concerns*

Under the UPCA, the court is competent to hear not only infringement proceedings, but also to adjudicate the validity of a patent on the basis of an action for
revocation or a counterclaim for revocation according to Arts. 32(1)(d), (e) and 65 of
the UPCA. While local and regional divisions of the UPC are competent to hear
infringement proceedings,[175] independent revocation actions are brought before the
central division.[176] The specific relationship between pending revocation actions,
counterclaims for revocation and pending infringement proceedings and the
respective competences, possibilities and procedural options and obligations of the
local/regional divisions and the central division in such cases are further regulated in
Art. 33(3)–(5) of the UPCA.

As for the relationship between infringement proceedings and pending revocation
actions or opposition proceedings before the EPO, Rule 118.2 of the UPCRoP
provides that during a pending revocation action before the central division or a
pending opposition before the EPO, the infringement court may (a) render its
decision under the condition of the (partial) validity ruled in a final decision or
(b) may stay the infringement proceedings.[177] In case the court is of the view there is
high likelihood that the patent will be held invalid on any ground by the final
decision, it "shall" stay the infringement proceeding.

Through making the infringement process procedurally independent of the
revocation proceedings (including the possibility of "absorption" by the

---

[172] *See* Rule 118 UPCRoP *(17th Draft)*, cf. also *Responses on the Rules of Procedure of the UPC*
(2014, 95 et seq.).
[173] *Table with Explanatory Notes to the Changes of the Rules of Procedure* (2014, 11); Blok 2016, 57
et seq.
[174] Id.
[175] Art. 33(1) UPCA.
[176] Art. 33(4) UPCA.
[177] *Cf.* also the subsequent paragraphs of Rule 118 UPCRoP on the consequences of a later
decision on the merits of the revocation action.

infringement court)[178] and in particular when allowing the court to set any term or condition for the ruling in the infringement process, in practice validity concerns will of course have significant impact on the grant of permanent or provisional injunctive relief. As there is no case law yet, it is hardly possible, however, to reliably predict how this will be specified in the future practice of the UPC. After the withdrawal of the United Kingdom, it seems reasonably likely, however, that the respective case law of the German courts[179] will deliver influential guidance in that regard.

In the specific case of provisional injunctive relief when weighing the interests of the parties[180] according to Rule 211.2 of the UPCRoP, the court is guided to take into account inter alia whether the applicant can provide reasonable evidence to satisfy the court with a sufficient degree of certainty that the patent in question is valid.

10. *Form of Court Order*

As for the UPCA, one of the main questions is how court orders in regard to injunctive relief will be framed.

According to the German tradition, specific infringing products or elements would have to be described by the claimant as a basis for a specific injunction relating to these products or elements.[181] Such an injunction would then primarily cover further infringing acts with regard to these specifically defined infringing products or elements. Beyond that scope, infringing acts which are "in core" comparable (*Kerntheorie*), i.e. products or elements only subject to insignificant change compared to the scope of the injunction, would also be covered by the injunction. By contrast, specifics of the infringed patent (scope and duration etc.) would not be included in the court's judgment granting injunctive relief.

According to the English tradition, orders granting injunctive relief will be worded more broadly and typically cover any infringement of patent "xyz" without being specifically limited to a concretely defined infringing product.[182] If the infringing product or service is changed during the proceedings, any claimant who has knowledge of this will have to introduce the respective facts into the proceedings in order to justify the grant of a comprehensive injunction. Vice versa, the defendant will have to prove a material difference as a defence if the infringing product or service has been changed after the original proceedings. The defence might be denied, however, if the infringing product or process had already been changed during the original proceedings and if the defendant had already had the chance to introduce this change into the original proceedings. Therefore, the

---

[178] *Cf.* Section B.9 on Art. 33(3)–(5) UPCA.
[179] *See* Chapter 8 (Germany).
[180] Art. 62(2) UPCA.
[181] *See* Chapter 8 (Germany).
[182] *See* Chapter 13 (United Kingdom).

defendant also has an interest in introducing material changes to the product or service into the original proceedings, because otherwise any defence with regard to such changes might be pre-empted if the defendant had the chance to do so but did not act accordingly.

At present, it seems unclear which tradition the UPC will follow in regard to the form of an injunctive relief order. Likewise, it is unclear how a claim for the granting of an injunction would have to be formulated by the claimant. With the withdrawal of the United Kingdom from the system it might seem more likely that the German tradition's influence will increase. However, with the system not even enacted and no serious timeline present at the time of writing, any further attempt to predict the future development in this area would be mere guesswork.

For now, only some procedural guideposts can be outlined. If in the future the UPC were to grant injunctions specifically related to an infringing product or process, and the defendant changed the product insignificantly later on, the claimant, in order to clarify the scope of the injunction, would have to apply to the court to sanction the defendant with a penalty according to Art. 82(4) of the UPCA, Rule 354.4 of the UPCRoP. If this was denied by the Court of First Instance, the plaintiff could then file an appeal against this order to the Court of Appeal under Art. 73(2) (b)(ii) of the UPCA. If leave to appeal were denied by the court or the appeal itself were denied, the plaintiff would have to file a new infringement action. If in turn legal certainty was needed with regard to (significantly) changed products or services, the defendant would have to file an action for declaration of non-infringement to the Court of First Instance, according to Art. 32(1)(b) of the UPCA.

If in the future the UPC were to grant injunctions related to the infringement of patent "xyz" without being limited to specific infringing products or services, such injunctions would presumably cover more or less significantly changed infringing products anyway. In this case, within the procedural framework as described, it would be the defendant who would have to prove that there is a "material difference" compared to the original infringing product that was the object of the infringement proceedings, and that it was not able to introduce relevant facts concerning the materially changed products or processes in the original proceedings.

C. CONCLUSION

Patent enforcement in the EU is governed by the Enforcement Directive which partially harmonizes the national laws of the member states in this area. Given that the Enforcement Directive follows a method of so-called minimum harmonization, it has been a matter for discussion in legal literature whether the Enforcement Directive also sets a certain ceiling in regard to the grant of injunctive relief, namely taking into account proportionality considerations and preventing the abuse of rights. Meanwhile, literature and in particular the CJEU's as well as influential national courts' case law predominantly assume that under the Enforcement Directive, according to the proportionality principle as well as the general prohibition of abuse of rights (both laid down in Art. 3(2) of the Enforcement Directive), the denial or curtailing of injunctive relief is possible due to proportionality considerations and will even be required by the law in certain exceptional cases on the basis of an individual case-by-case analysis.

With regard to private rights and interests of the defendant, this particularly applies to injunctive relief which leads to entire closure of manufacturing and loss of large stocks due to only minor, limited patent infringement and thus to disproportionately substantial losses compared to the economic interest of the patent holder. With regard to public interests, the situation is less clear, as many national laws provide for certain alternative instruments in this field, such as compulsory licences. However, the predominant and appropriate view seems to be that under the guiding principle of proportionality, public interests can also require the denial or curtailing of injunctions in exceptional cases. According to the CJEU's case law in other areas of intellectual property, moreover, a fair balancing of the involved parties' fundamental rights (namely the right to protection of intellectual property (Art. 17(2) CFR) versus the freedom to conduct a business (Art. 16 CFR) as well as fundamental rights of possibly affected third parties will feed into the tailoring process for injunctions, in particular for injunctions against intermediaries but on principle also for injunctions against the infringer (at least in exceptional cases where the denial or curtailing of injunctive relief can be justified).

While the Enforcement Directive thus allows and even requires the denial or flexible curtailing of injunctive relief in certain exceptional cases where an untailored injunction would be grossly disproportionate, it does not contain any bright-line rules for certain entire case groups (such as NPEs or other categories of rightsholders or technologies which might be regarded as particularly prone to abuse of patent rights). Consequently, while the Enforcement Directive gives the necessary leeway to appropriately treat these cases on the basis of a case-by case approach, it does not go further than that and does not contain any general rules or exemptions from injunctive relief in that regard.

Also, the EU competition law's requirements for a compulsory licensing defence of the defendant in proceedings concerning patent injunctions are generally rather strict and therefore such objections have hitherto not played a prominent role in patent infringement proceedings. This situation has significantly changed, however, for standard essential patents in the wake of the court's *Huawei* v. ZTE judgment. In the area of such standard essential patents, for which the rightsholder has declared its willingness to license the patent under FRAND conditions, a specific negotiation regime now applies throughout the EU which in most cases practically requires the patent holder to offer a licence on FRAND conditions to the infringer before proceeding with an action for injunctive relief.

At the time of writing, the beginning of operations of the UPC is expected for mid-2022. The provisions of the UPCA on permanent and provisional injunctive relief on principle are similar to the Enforcement Directive's general rules. As a matter of course, as the UPCA is directly applicable, many of the procedural rules in the UPCA are much more specific than the Enforcement Directive. However, as regards the basic principles, the evolving system will likely develop similar standards as under the Enforcement Directive. A larger material difference would not be permissible anyway, as EU law takes primacy over the UPCA and its contracting states' laws. Therefore, it seems that the implementation of the future UPCA system will likely not materially change the EU law's general principles on the application and tailoring of injunctions as they have been outlined in this chapter. As for their further specification, after the withdrawal of the United Kingdom from the UPC system, it seems reasonably likely that the UPC will be substantively influenced by German case law in the future. Given that the judges will be chosen from all contracting states, it might take a slightly more liberal stance than the German courts, which still tend to more or less "automatically" grant an injunction against the infringer in cases of patent infringement. However, it remains to be seen whether the actual start of the future European patents with unitary effect and the Unified Patent Court system will take place in 2022.

REFERENCES

Cases

Amministrazione delle Finanze v. *Simmenthal*, CJEU of 9 March 1978, C-106/77, ECLI:EU:
    C:1978:49.
Bayer v. *Richter*, CJEU of 12 September 2019, C-688/17, ECLI:EU:C:2019:722.
Bericap Záródástechnikai Bt. v. *Plastinnova*, CJEU of 15 November 2012, C-180/11, ECLI:EU:
    C:2012:717.
Bonnier Audio v. *Perfect Communication Sweden*, CJEU of 19 April 2012, C-461/10, ECLI:EU:
    C:2012:219.
Costa v. *E.N.E.L.*, CJEU of 15 July 1964, C-6/64, ECLI:EU:C:1964:66.
Coty Germany v. *Stadtsparkasse Magdeburg*, CJEU of 16 July 2015, C-580/13, ECLI:EU:
    C:2015:485.
Edwards Lifescience v. *Boston Scientific Scimed*, [2018] EWHC 664 (Pat).
Funke Medien v. *Germany*, CJEU of 29 July 2019, C-469/17, ECLI:EU:C:2019:623.
Glawischnig-Piesczek v. *Facebook*, CJEU of 3 October 2019, C-18/18, ECLI:EU:C:2019:821.
Herzklappen, LG Düsseldorf of 9 March 2017, 4a O 137/15.
Huawei v. *ZTE*, CJEU of 16 July 2015, C-170/13, ECLI:EU:C:2015:477.
IMS Health, CJEU of 29 April 2004, C-418/01, ECLI:EU:C:2004:257.
Karlsson, CJEU of 13 April 2000, C-292/97, ECLI:EU:C:2000:202.
L'Oréal v. *eBay*, CJEU of 12 July 2011, C-324/09, ECLI:EU:C:2011:474.
LSG v. *Tele2*, CJEU of 19 February 2009, C-557/07, ECLI:EU:C:2009:107.
Marleasing v. *La Comercial Internacional*, CJEU of 13 November 1990, C-106/89, ECLI:EU:
    C:1990:395.

Mc Fadden v. *Sony Music Entertainment*, CJEU of 15 September 2016, C-484/14, ECLI:EU: C:2016:686.
Nokia v. *Wärdell*, CJEU of 14 December 2006, C-316/05, ECLI:EU:C:2006:789.
Pelham v. *Hütter*, CJEU of 29 July 2019, C-476/17, ECLI:EU:C:2019:624.
Promusicae v. *Telefónica*, CJEU of 29 January 2008, C-275/06, ECLI:EU:C:2008:54.
RTE v. *Commission/Magill*, CJEU of 6 April 1995, C-241/91 & C-242/91, ECLI:EU:C:1995:98.
Spiegel Online v. *Beck*, CJEU of 29 July 2019, C-516/17, ECLI:EU:C:2019:625.
Stowarzyszenie v. *Stowarzyszenie*, CJEU of 25 January 2017, C-367/15, ECLI:EU:C:2017:36.
Tommy Hilfiger v. *Delta Center*, CJEU of 7 July 2016, C-494/15, ECLI:EU:C:2016:528.
Twentieth Century Fox v. *BT*, EWHC [2011] EWHC 1981 (Ch).
UPC Telekabel Wien v. *Constantin Film*, CJEU of 27 March 2014, C-314/12, ECLI:EU: C:2014:192.
EPGÜ-ZustG I, BVerfG of 13 February 2020, 2 BvR 739/17.
EPGÜ-ZustG II, BVerfG of 9 July 2021, 2 BvR 2216/20, 2 BvR 2217/20.
Zuckerfabrik Suederdithmarschen v. *Hauptzollamt Itzehoe & Hauptzollamt Paderborn*, CJEU of 21 February 1991, C-143/88 & C-92/89, ECLI:EU:C:1991:65.

Regulatory and Legislative Materials

Analysis of Application of Enforcement-Directive, Analysis of the application of Directive 2004/ 48/EC of the European Parliament and the Council of 29 April 2004 on the enforcement of intellectual property rights in the Member States, Commission Staff Working Document, SEC (2010) 1589.
Annexes Consolidated EU Treaties, Consolidated versions of the Treaty on European Union and the Treaty on the Functioning of the European Union, 2008/C 115/01.
Brussels Ia Regulation, Regulation (EU) 1215/2012 of the European Parliament and of the Council of 12 December 2012 on jurisdiction and the recognition and enforcement of judgments in civil and commercial matters, L 351/1.
CFR, Charter of Fundamental Rights of the European Union, 2000/C 364/1.
Draft of German Copyright Act, Bundestagsdrucksache of 23 March 1962, BT-Drs. IV/270.
Draft of German UPC Act of Approval I, Bundestagsdrucksache of 13 February 2017, BT-Drs. 18/11137.
ECHR, European Convention on Human Rights.
E-Commerce Directive, Directive 2000/31/EC of the European Parliament and of the Council of 8 June 2000 on certain legal aspects of information society services, in particular electronic commerce, in the Internal Market ('Directive on electronic commerce'), L 178/1.
Enforcement Directive, Directive 2004/48/EC of the European Parliament and of the Council of 29 April 2004 on the enforcement of intellectual property rights, L 195/16.
Enforcement of Intellectual Property Rights Proposal, Proposal for a Directive of the European Parliament and of the Council on measures and procedures to ensure the enforcement of intellectual property rights, COM (2003) 46 final, 2003/2004 (COD).
EU Approach to SEPs, Communication from the Commission to the European Parliament, the Council and the European Economic and Social Committee, Setting out the EU approach to Standard Essential Patents, COM (2017) 712.
Explanations Relating to the CFR, Explanations relating to the Charter of Fundamental Rights of the European Union, 2007/C 303/02.
Frequently Asked Questions Proposed Directive, Proposed Directive on enforcement of intellectual property rights: frequently asked questions, MEMO/03/20, published on 30 January 2003.

General Data Protection Regulation, Regulation (EU) 2016/679 of the European Parliament and of the Council of 27 April 2016 on the protection of natural persons with regard to the processing of personal data and on the free movement of such data, and repealing Directive 95/46/EC (General Data Protection Regulation), L 119/1.

German UPC Act of Approval II, Gesetz zu dem Übereinkommen vom 19. Februar 2013 über ein Einheitliches Patentgericht of 7 August 2021, BGBl. II S. 850.

Guidance on Enforcement Directive, Communication from the Commission to the European Parliament, the Council and the European Economic and Social Committee, Guidance on certain aspects of Directive 2004/48/EC of the European Parliament and of the Council on the enforcement of intellectual property rights, COM (2017) 708.

InfoSoc Directive, Directive 2001/29/EC of the European Parliament and of the Council of 22 May 2001 on the harmonisation of certain aspects of copyright and related rights in the information society, L167/10.

Letter to Lord Morris, Solloway, Amanda. 2020. https://committees.parliament.uk/download/file/?url=%2Fpublications%2F446%2Fdocuments%2F1739&slug=astolmupc240320pdf.

Parliamentary Written Statement, Solloway, Amanda. 2020. https://questions-statements.parliament.uk/written-statements/detail/2020-07-20/hcws395.

Responses on the Rules of Procedure of the UPC, Responses to the Public Consultation on the Rules of Procedure of the UPC, published on 6 March 2014. www.unified-patent-court.org/sites/default/files/rop-digest.pdf

Rome II Regulation, Regulation (EC) 864/2007 of the European Parliament and of the Council of 11 July 2007 on the law applicable of non-contractual obligations (Rome II), L 199/40.

Summary of Article 288 TFEU, European Union directives, Summary of Article 288 of the Treaty of on the Functioning of the European Union (TFEU) – directives, Publications Office of the European Union, last updated 28 March 2019. https://eur-lex.europa.eu/legal-content/EN/ALL/?uri=uriserv%3Al14527.

Table with Explanatory Notes to the Changes of the Rules of Procedure, Table with explanatory notes to the changes made by the Legal Group of the Preparatory Committee in the Seventeenth draft of the Rules of Procedure, 31 October 2014. www.unified-patent-court.org/sites/default/files/Digest_Legal_Group_17th_Draft_RoP.PDF

TEU, Consolidated Version of the Treaty on European Union, 2012, C-326/13.

TFEU, Consolidated Version of the Treaty of the Functioning of the European Union, 2012, C-326/47.

The Future Relationship with the EU – The UK's Approach to Negotiations, UK Government, 2020. https://assets.publishing.service.gov.uk/government/uploads/system/uploads/attachment_data/file/868874/The_Future_Relationship_with_the_EU.pdf.

Trade Mark Regulation, Regulation (EU) 2017/1001 of the European Parliament and of the Council of 14 June 2017 on the European Union trade mark.

Trade Secrets Directive, Directive (EU) 2016/943 of the European Parliament and of the Council of 8 June 2016 on the protection of undisclosed know-how and business information (trade secrets) against their unlawful acquisition, use and disclosure, L 157/1.

TRIPS, Trade-Related Aspects of Intellectual Property Rights Agreement, 1994.

Unitary Patent Protection Regulation, Regulation (EU) No 1257/2012 of the European Parliament and of the Council of 17 December 2012 implementing enhanced cooperation in the area of the creation of unitary patent protection.

Unitary Patent Protection – Applicable Translation Arrangements Regulation, Council Regulation (EU) No 1260/2012 of 17 December 2012 implementing enhanced cooperation in the area of the creation of unitary patent protection with regard to the applicable translation arrangements, L 361/89.

UPCA, Agreement on a Unified Patent Court (UPCA), February 2013.

UPCRoP, Eighteenth Draft of the Rules of Procedure of the Unified Patent Court, 19 October 2015. www.unified-patent-court.org/sites/default/files/upc_rules_of_proced ure_18th_draft_15_march_2017_final_clear.pdf

UPCRoP (16th Draft), Sixteenth Draft of the Rules of Procedure of the Unified Patent Court, 31 January 2014. www.unified-patent-court.org/sites/default/files/revised-draft-rules-of-procedure.pdf

UPCRoP (17th Draft), Seventeenth Draft of the Rules of Procedure of the Unified Patent Court, 31 October 2014. www.unified-patent-court.org/sites/default/files/UPC_Rules_of_Procedure_17th_Draft.pdf

Books, Articles and Online Materials

Amschewitz, Dennis. 2008. *Die Durchsetzungsrichtlinie und ihre Umsetzung im deutschen Recht*. Tübingen: Mohr Siebeck.

Bennett, Stephen, Stanislas Roux-Vaillard & Christian Mammen. 2015. "Shifting Attitudes to Injunctions in Patent Cases," *Managing Intellectual Property* 246:22–26.

Block, Jonas & Benjamin Rätz. 2019. "Das FRAND-Angebot – Versuch einer internationalen Definition," *Gewerblicher Rechtsschutz und Urheberrecht* 121(8): 797–801.

Blok, Peter. 2016. "A Harmonized Approach to Prohibitory Injunctions: Reconsidering Article 12 of the Enforcement Directive," *Journal of Intellectual Property Law & Practice* 11(1): 56–60.

Broß, Siegfried & Matthias Lamping. 2018. "Eyes Wide Shut," *International Review of Intellectual Property and Competition Law* 49(8): 887–94.

Cabrera Rodríguez, José. 2018. Interim and Final Remedies in Patent Infringement. https://ssrn.com/abstract=3096943

Contreras, Jorge L. & Peter Georg Picht. 2017. "Patent Assertion Entities and Legal Exceptionalism in Europe and the United States, A Comparative View," *Max Planck Institute for Innovation & Competition Research Paper* No. 17-11.

Chalmers, Damian, Davies Gareth & Giorgio Monti et al. 2019. *European Union Law*. Cambridge: Cambridge University Press.

Cross, James & Janet Strath. 2017. "Unwired Planet v Huawei – the FRAND Injunction," *Computer and Telecommunications Law Review* 23(7): 178–80.

Dijkman, Léon & Cato van Paddenburgh. 2018. "The Unified Patent Court as Part of a New European Patent Landscape: Wholesale Harmonization or Experiment in Legal Pluralism?," *European Review of Private Law* 26: 97–117.

Dinwoodie, Graeme B. & Rochelle C. Dreyfuss. 2017. "Brexit and IP: The Great Unraveling?," *NYU School of Law, Public Law & Legal Theory Research Paper Series Working Paper* No. 17-26.

England, Paul. 2016. "Infringement of Second Medial Use Patents: Europe and the Unified Patent Court," *Journal of Intellectual Property Law & Practice* 11(6): 426–34.

European Commission Joint Research Centre. 2016. JRC Science for Policy Report: Patent Assertion Entities in Europe. https://publications.jrc.ec.europa.eu/repository/bitstream/JRC103321/lfna28145enn.pdf

Furlong, John & Susan Doe. 2006. "Researching European Law – a Basic Introduction," *Legal Information Management* 6(2): 136–46.

Gandía Sellens, María Aránzazu. 2018. "The Viability of the Unitary Patent Package after the UK's Ratification of the Agreement on a Unified Patent Court," *International Review of Intellectual Property and Competition Law* 49(2): 136–52.

Heath, Christopher & Thomas F. Cotter. 2015. "Comparative Overview and the TRIPS Enforcement Provisions," in Christopher Heath ed., *Patent Enforcement Worldwide*. Oxford: Hart.

Heinze, Christian. 2012. "Intellectual Property (Enforcement)," in Jürgen Basedow et al. eds., *The Max Planck Encyclopedia of European Private Law*. Oxford: Oxford University Press.

Husovec. Martin. 2013. "Injunctions against Innocent Third Parties: The Case of Website Blocking," *Journal of Intellectual Property, Information Technology and Electronic Commerce Law* 4(2): 116–129.

2017. *Injunctions against Intermediaries in the European Union: Accountable, But Not Liable*. Cambridge: Cambridge University Press.

Hüttermann, Aloys. 2017. *Einheitspatent und Einheitliches Patentgericht*. Köln: Carl Heymanns Verlag.

Jaeger, Thomas. 2017. "Reset and Go: The Unitary Patent System Post-Brexit," *International Review of Intellectual Property and Competition Law* 48(3): 254–85.

Klein, Susanne. 2012. *Die Durchsetzungs-Richtlinie vom 29. April 2004*. Frankfurt a.M.: Lang.

Lamping, Matthias & Hanns Ullrich. 2018. "The Impact of Brexit on Unitary Patent Protection and Its Court," *Max Planck Institute for Innovation and Competition Law Research Paper* No. 18-20.

Lawrance, Sophie & Francion Brooks. 2018. "Unwired Planet v Huawei: The First UK FRAND Determination," *Journal of European Competition Law & Practice* 9(3):170–75.

Leistner, Matthias. 2014. "Structural Aspects of Secondary (Provider) Liability," *Journal of Intellectual Property Law & Practice* 9(1):75–90.

2016. "Vollstreckung von Urteilen des Einheitlichen Patentgerichts in Deutschland," *Gewerblicher Rechtsschutz und Urheberrecht* 118(3): 217–25.

2017. "Die 'Pirate Bay'-Entscheidung des EuGH: ein Gerichtshof als Ersatzgesetzgeber," *Gewerblicher Rechtsschutz und Urheberrecht* 119(8):755–60.

2018. "FRAND Patents in Europe in the Post-Huawei Era: A Recent Report from Germany." https://papers.ssrn.com/sol3/papers.cfm?abstract_id=3278769

2019a. "'Ende gut, alles gut' . . . oder 'Vorhang zu und alle Fragen offen'? Das salomonische Urteil des EuGH in Sachen 'Pelham [Metall auf Metall]'," *Gewerblicher Rechtsschutz und Urheberrecht* 121(10):1008–15.

2019b. "Das Urteil des EuGH in Sachen 'Funke Medien NRW GmbH/Bundesrepublik Deutschland' – gute Nachrichten über ein urheberrechtliches Tagesereignis," *Zeitschrift für Urheber- und Medienrecht* 63(10):720–26.

Leistner, Matthias & Philipp Simon. 2017. "Auswirkungen des Brexit auf das europäische Patentsystem," *Gewerblicher Rechtsschutz und Urheberrecht. Internationaler Teil* 66 (10):825–34.

Lemley, Mark A. & A. Douglas Melamed. 2013. "Missing the Forest for the Trolls," *Columbia Law Review* 113(8):2117–89.

Love, Brian, Christian Helmers, Fabian Gaessler & Max Ernicke. 2017. "Patent Assertion Entities in Europe," in D. Daniel Sokol ed., *Patent Assertion Entities and Competition Policies*. Cambridge: Cambridge University Press.

Marfé, Mark, Alexander Reetz, Camille Pecnard, Riccardo Fruscalzo & Ruud van der Velden. 2015. "The Power of National Courts and the Unified Patent Court to Grant Injunctions," *Journal of Intellectual Property Law & Practice* 10(3):180–90.

Meier-Beck, Peter. 2014. "Quo vadis, iudium unitarium?," *Gewerblicher Rechtsschutz und Urheberrecht* 116(2):144–47.

Morton, Fiona Scott & Carl Shapiro. 2016. "Patent Assertions: Are We Any Closer to Aligning Reward to Contribution?," *Innovation Policy and the Economy* 16:89–133.

Ohly, Ansgar. 2008. "'Patenttrolle' oder: Der patentrechtliche Unterlassungsanspruch unter Verhältnismäßigkeitsvorbehalt? Aktuelle Entwicklungen im US-Patentrecht und ihre Bedeutung für das deutsche und europäische Patentsystem," *Gewerblicher Rechtsschutz und Urheberrecht. Internationaler Teil* 57(10):787–98.

2009. "Three Principles of European IP Enforcement Law: Effectiveness, Proportionality, Dissuasiveness," in Josef Drexl, Reto M. Hilty, Laurence Boy, Christine Godt & Bernard Remiche eds., *Technology and Competition*. Bruxelles: Larcier.

Ohly, Ansgar & Rudolf Streinz. 2017. "Can the UK Stay in the UPC System after Brexit?," *Gewerblicher Rechtsschutz und Urheberrecht. Internationaler Teil* 66(1):1–11.

Osterrieth, Christian. 2009. "Patent-Trolls in Europa – braucht das Patentrecht neue Grenzen?," *Gewerblicher Rechtsschutz und Urheberrecht* 111(6):540–45.

2018. "Technischer Fortschritt – eine Herausforderung für das Patentrecht? Zum Gebot der Verhältnismäßigkeit beim patentrechtlichen Unterlassungsanspruch," *Gewerblicher Rechtsschutz und Urheberrecht* 120(10):985–95.

O'Sullivan, Kevin T. 2019. "Copyright and Internet Service Provider 'Liability': the Emerging Realpolitik of Intermediary Obligations," *International Review of Intellectual Property and Competition Law* 50(5):527–58.

Petillion, Flip & Alexander Heirwegh. 2019. "Genesis, Adoption andApplication of European Directive 2004/48/EC," in Flip Petillion ed., *Enforcement of Intellectual Property Rights in the EU Member States*. Cambridge: Intersentia.

Picht, Peter Georg. 2017a. "'FRAND wars 2.0' – Rechtsprechung im Anschluss an die Huawei/ZTE-Entscheidung des EuGH ('FRAND wars 2.0' – Survey of Court Decisions in the Aftermath of Huawei/ZTE)," *Wirtschaft und Wettbewerb* 68(5):234–41 (Part I), *Wirtschaft und Wettbewerb* 68 (6):300–09 (Part II). https://papers.ssrn.com/sol3/papers.cfm?abstract_id=2916544

2017b. "Unwired Planet v. Huawei: A Seminal SEP/FRAND Decision from the UK," *Gewerblicher Rechtsschutz und Urheberrecht. Internationaler Teil* 12(10):867–80.

Reetz, Alexander, Camille Pecnard, Riccardo Fruscalzo, Ruud van der Velden & Mark Marfé. 2015. "Die Befugnisse der nationalen Gerichte unter dem EPÜ und des Einheitlichen Patentgerichts (EPG) nach Art. 63 (1) EPGÜ zum Erlass von Unterlassungsverfügungen – eine rechtsvergleichende Untersuchung," *Gewerblicher Rechtsschutz und Urheberrecht. Internationaler Teil* 64(3):210–19.

Schröer, Benjamin. 2013. "Einheitspatente – Überlegungen zum Forum-Shopping im Rahmen der alternativen Zuständigkeit nach Art. 83 Abs. 1 EPGÜ," *Gewerblicher Rechtsschutz und Urheberrecht. Internationaler Teil* 62(12):1102–09.

Sonnenberg, Marcus. 2014. *Die Einschränkbarkeit des patentrechtlichen Unterlassungsanspruchs im Einzelfall*. Wiesbaden: Springer Gabler.

Stierle, Martin. 2018. *Das nicht-praktizierte Patent*. Tübingen: Mohr-Siebeck.

2019. "Der quasi-automatische Unterlassungsanspruch im deutschen Patentrecht. Ein Beitrag im Lichte der Reformdiskussion des § 139 I PatG," *Gewerblicher Rechtsschutz und Urheberrecht* 121(9):873–85.

Streinz, Rudolf & Walther Michl. 2018. "Art. 52 CFR," in Rudolf Streinz ed., *EUV/AEUV*. München: C. H. Beck.

Tietz, Jonathan I. 2019. "The Unified Patent Court and Patent Trolls in Europe," *Michigan Technology Law Review* 25(2):303–30.

Tilmann, Winfried. 2016a. "UPCA and EPUE-Reg – Construction and Application," *Gewerblicher Rechtsschutz und Urheberrecht* 65(5): 409–19.

2016b. "The Future of the UPC after Brexit," *Gewerblicher Rechtsschutz und Urheberrecht* 118(8):753–55.

Ullrich, Hanns. 2012a. "Harmonizing Patent Law: The Untamable Union Patent," *Max Planck Institute for Innovation and Competition Law Research Paper* No 12-03.

2012b. "Intellectual Property: Exclusive Rights for a Purpose – The Case of Technology Protection by Patents and Copyright," *Max Planck Institute for Innovation and Competition Law Research Paper* No 13-01.

US Federal Trade Commission. 2016. Patent Assertion Entity Activity. www.ftc.gov/system/files/documents/reports/patent-assertion-entity-activity-ftc-study/p131203_patent_assertion_entity_activity_an_ftc_study_0.pdf

Voet, Milan. 2018. Trolling the U.S. and EU Patent System: Solved by a Loser-Pays-Attorney-Fees Regime? https://papers.ssrn.com/sol3/papers.cfm?abstract_id=3463481

Von Mühlendahl, Alexander. 2007. "Enforcement of Intellectual Property Rights – Is Injunctive Relief Mandatory?," *International Review of Intellectual Property and Competition Law* 38(4):377–80.

Wimmers, Jörg. 2020. "§ 100," in Gerhard Schricker, Ulrich Loewenheim, Matthias Leistner & Ansgar Ohly eds., *Urheberrecht*. München: C. H. Beck.

Yan, Marlen. 2017. *Das materielle Recht im Einheitlichen Europäischen Patentsystem und dessen Anwendung durch das Einheitliche Patentgericht*. Baden-Baden: Nomos.

4

Injunctions in European Law

Judicial Reflections

Sir Richard Arnold

At the time of writing, the United Kingdom remains a member state of the European Union. Accordingly, this chapter is written from that perspective. My thesis is simply stated: European law not merely enables, but requires, the courts of the member states to be flexible when considering whether or not to grant an injunction in a patent case, and to tailor any injunction to the circumstances of the case. An injunction can only be granted when, and to the extent that, it is proportionate and strikes a fair balance between the fundamental rights that are engaged. All that is needed is for the courts of the member states consistently to apply the principles laid down by the legislature and by the Court of Justice of the European Union.

Recitals (17) and (24) of the Enforcement Directive are clear that the measures and remedies provided in the Directive, including injunctions, must be tailored to the circumstances of the case: recital (17) states that they "shall be determined in each case in such a manner as to take due account of the specific characteristics of each case" while recital (24) provides that "prohibitory measures aimed at preventing further infringements of intellectual property rights" should be granted "[d]epending on the particular case, and if justified by the circumstances". It follows that a case-by-case assessment is required, and automatic rules are prohibited. Similarly, Article 3(1) of the Enforcement Directive requires that the measures and remedies "shall be fair and equitable" and Article 3(2) requires that they "shall also be effective, proportionate and dissuasive and shall be applied in such a manner as to avoid the creation of barriers to legitimate trade and to provide for safeguards against their abuse".

In its 2017 Guidance on the Enforcement Directive, the European Commission emphasised the need for national courts to undertake a case-by-case assessment:[1] "[I]n order to ensure the balanced use of the civil IPR enforcement system, the

---

[1] Guidance on the Enforcement Directive, 9–10.

competent judicial authorities should generally conduct a case-by-case assessment when considering the grant of the measures, procedures and remedies provided for by IPRED."

The Commission also emphasised the case law of CJEU concerning the need for national courts "to strike a fair balance between different conflicting fundamental rights *inter alia* when deciding on . . . the awarding of injunctions":[2]

> Although these decisions were issued in the specific context of litigation relating to copyright infringements, the CJEU's analysis addresses in general the balance between the fundamental rights at issue. Therefore, the Commission believes that the requirement of ensuring a fair balance between such rights, in light of the general principle of proportionality, applies not only in copyright infringement cases, but in cases concerning all the IPR falling within IPRED's scope.

The case law of the CJEU fully supports this analysis. The starting point is its seminal decision in *Promusicae*, in which the Court stated (emphases added):[3]

> [T]he Member States must, when transposing the directives mentioned above, take care to rely on an interpretation of the directives which allows a *fair balance* to be struck between the various fundamental rights protected by the Community legal order. Further, when implementing the measures transposing those directives, the authorities and *courts of the Member States* must not only interpret their national law in a manner consistent with those directives but also make sure that they do not rely on an interpretation of them which would be in conflict with those fundamental rights or with the other general principles of Community law, such as the principle of *proportionality*.

The CJEU has reinforced and elaborated on this statement in a series of subsequent judgments. Although some of these judgments have been concerned with injunctions in copyright cases, and in particular injunctions against online intermediaries, this is not true of all such judgments.

In *L'Oréal SA* v. *eBay*, which was a trademark case, the Court Stated (emphases added):

> 138. The rules laid down by the Member States, and likewise *their application by the national courts*, must also observe the limitations arising from Directive 2004/48 and from the sources of law to which that directive refers.
>
> 139. . . . a general monitoring obligation would be incompatible with Article 3 of Directive 2004/48, which states that the measures referred to by the directive must be fair, *proportionate* and must not be excessively costly.
>
> 141. . . . injunctions which are both effective and *proportionate* may be issued . . .
>
> 143. The measures that are described . . . in the preceding paragraphs, as well as any other measure which may be imposed in the form of an injunction under the

2   Guidance on the Enforcement Directive, 10–11.
3   *Promusicae* (CJEU 2008) [68].

third sentence of Article 11 of Directive 2004/48, must strike a *fair balance* between the various rights and interests mentioned above (see, by analogy, *Promusicae*, paragraphs 65 to 68).

144. ... Those injunctions must be effective, *proportionate*, dissuasive and must not create barriers to legitimate trade.

In *Scarlet Extended* the Court Stated (emphases added):

44. As paragraphs 62 to 68 of ... *Promusicae* ... make clear, the protection of the fundamental right to property, which includes the rights linked to intellectual property, must be *balanced* against the protection of other fundamental rights.

45. More specifically, it follows from paragraph 68 of that judgment that, in the context of measures adopted to protect copyright holders, national authorities and *courts* must strike a *fair balance* between the protection of copyright and the protection of the fundamental rights of individuals who are affected by such measures.

46. Accordingly, in circumstances such as those in the main proceedings, national authorities and *courts* must, in particular, strike a *fair balance* between the protection of the intellectual property right enjoyed by copyright holders and that of the freedom to conduct a business enjoyed by operators such as ISPs pursuant to Article 16 of the Charter.

In *UPC Telekabel* the Court Stated (emphases added):

47. In the present case, it must be observed that an injunction such as that at issue in the main proceedings, ... makes it necessary to *strike a balance*, primarily, between (i) copyrights and related rights, which are intellectual property and are therefore protected under Article 17(2) of the Charter, (ii) the freedom to conduct a business, which economic agents such as internet service providers enjoy under Article 16 of the Charter, and (iii) the freedom of information of internet users, whose protection is ensured by Article 11 of the Charter. ...

63. Consequently, even though the measures taken when implementing an injunction such as that at issue in the main proceedings are not capable of leading, in some circumstances, to a complete cessation of the infringements of the intellectual property right, they cannot however be considered to be incompatible with the requirement that a *fair balance* be found, in accordance with Article 52(1), in fine, of the Charter, between all applicable fundamental rights, provided that (i) they do not unnecessarily deprive internet users of the possibility of lawfully accessing the information available and (ii) that they have the effect of preventing unauthorised access to protected subject-matter or, at least, of making it difficult to achieve and of seriously discouraging internet users who are using the services of the addressee of that injunction from accessing the subject-matter that has been made available to them in breach of the intellectual property right.

In *Coty Germany* the Court Stated (emphases added):

34. ... according to the case-law of the Court, EU law requires that, when transposing directives, the Member States take care to rely on an interpretation of

them which allows a fair balance to be struck between the various fundamental rights protected by the EU legal order. Subsequently, when *implementing the measures* transposing those directives, the authorities and *courts* of the Member States must not only interpret their national law in a manner consistent with those directives but also make sure that they do not rely on an interpretation of them which would be in conflict with those fundamental rights or with the other general principles of EU law (see judgment in *Promusicae*, ... paragraph 70). ...

35. ... it is apparent from the case-law of the Court that a measure which results in serious infringement of a right protected by the Charter is to be regarded as not respecting the requirement that such a *fair balance* be struck between the fundamental rights which must be reconciled (see, as regards an *injunction*, judgments in *Scarlet Extended*, ..., paragraphs 48 and 49 ...).

In *Tommy Hilfiger*, which was not only a trademark case, but also a case concerning offline infringement, the Court Stated (emphases added):

34. [In *L'Oréal*] the Court held that injunctions must be equitable and *proportionate*. ...

35. The Court thus took the view that any injunction within the meaning of the third sentence of Article 11 of Directive 2004/48 may be pronounced only if it ensures a *fair balance* between the protection of intellectual property and the absence of obstacles to legitimate trade (see, to that effect, ... *L'Oréal*... paragraph 143)

36. While ... in *L'Oréal* ... the Court had to interpret the third sentence of Article 11 of Directive 2004/48 in the context of injunctions which may be addressed to an intermediary in an online marketplace, it interpreted that article in the light of the general provisions formulated in Article 3 of that directive ... Moreover, it follows from the wording of Article 3 of the directive that it applies to *any measure* referred to by that directive.

In *McFadden* the Court Stated (emphases added):

83. Where several fundamental rights protected under EU law are at stake, it is for the national authorities or *courts* concerned to ensure that a *fair balance* is struck between those rights (see, to that effect ..., *Promusicae*, ... paragraphs 68 and 70). ...

100. ... a measure consisting in [requiring password] securing a [wifi] connection must be considered to be capable of striking a *fair balance* between, first, the fundamental right to protection of intellectual property and, second, the right to freedom to conduct the business of a[n access] provider ... and the right to freedom of information of the recipients of that service.

I would respectfully suggest that the case law of the CJEU is really crystal clear, and admits of no doubts: The national courts must apply these principles when considering whether to grant an injunction to restrain infringements of all intellectual property rights falling within the scope of the Enforcement Directive, which include patents. Applying these principles requires a case-by-case assessment. Automatic rules are prohibited. Injunctions can only be granted when, and to the extent that, they are proportionate and strike a fair balance between the fundamental rights that are engaged, which include the freedom of defendants to conduct a business protected by Article 16 of the Charter of Fundamental Rights. It follows that injunctions should be tailored to the circumstances of the case. Accordingly, all that is needed is for national courts to comply with European law.

REFERENCES

Cases

Case C-580/13 *Coty Germany GmbH* v. *Stadtsparkasse Magdeburg* [EU:C:2015:485]

Case C-484/14 *McFadden* v. *Sony Music Entertainment Germany GmbH* [EU:C:2016:689]

Case C-324/09 *L'Oréal SA* v. *eBay International AG* [2011] ECR I-6011

Case C-275/06 *Productores de Música de España (Promusicae)* v. *Telefónica de España SAU* [2008] ECR I-271

Case C-70/10 *Scarlet Extended SA* v. *Société Belge des Auteurs, Compositeurs et Editeurs SCRL (SABAM)* [2011] ECR I-11959

Case C-494/15 *Tommy Hilfiger Licensing LLC* v. *DELTA CENTER as* [EU:C:2016:528]

Case C-314/12 *UPC Telekabel Wien GmbH* v. *Constantin Film Verleih GmbH* [EU:C:2014:192]

Regulatory and Legislative Materials

EU Charter of Fundamental Rights

European Parliament and Council Directive 2004/48/EC of 29 April 2004 on the enforcement of intellectual property rights

Guidance on certain aspects of European Parliament and Council Directive 2004/48/EC of 29 April 2004 on the enforcement of intellectual property rights COM(2017) 708 final

5

Canada

Norman Siebrasse

A. OVERVIEW

Canada is a federal system with jurisdiction shared between the federal government and the provinces. Patent law is a matter of exclusive federal jurisdiction and is based on the federal *Patent Act*. The federal nature of Canada is reflected in a bifurcated judicial system. The Federal Courts of Canada, a statutory court system with defined jurisdiction,[1] and the provincial superior courts, courts of inherent jurisdiction, corresponding to the traditional English common law courts, both have jurisdiction over patent infringement.[2] However, the Federal Court has exclusive jurisdiction to declare a patent invalid,[3] and the very substantial majority of patent cases are decided by the Federal Court. Consequently, it is largely the case law of the Federal Courts which governs the grant of injunctive relief in patent cases, subject to the guidance of the Supreme Court of Canada.[4]

While the Federal Court jurisdiction extends well beyond patent law,[5] there is a core of about half a dozen judges who are normally assigned to most major patent cases, as well as another half dozen who hear some patent issues, so these judges, particularly the core patent judges, have considerable specialized patent expertise.

---

[1] The Federal Courts of Canada comprises two courts, the Federal Court and the Federal Court of Appeal: *Federal Courts Act*, ss. 3 and 4. As the names imply, the primary jurisdiction of the Federal Court of Appeal is to hear appeals from the Federal Court: *Federal Courts Act*, s. 27(1). Prior to 2 July 2003, the Federal Court of Canada comprised a single court, with two divisions, the Trial Division and the Appeal Division.

[2] See *Patent Act*, s. 54, granting jurisdiction to the provincial superior court in which the infringement is said to have occurred; *Federal Courts Act*, s. 20(2), granting concurrent jurisdiction to the Federal Court in any case relating to patents.

[3] *Federal Courts Act*, s. 20(1).

[4] Similarly, it is the *Federal Courts Rules* that normally govern procedure, including the issuance of orders and findings of contempt.

[5] The jurisdiction also includes matters such as claims against the Crown, judicial review of federal administrative tribunals, and admiralty law: *Federal Courts Act*, ss. 17–26.

The court also uses specialized case management judges to manage complex patent litigation. Even complex cases may take as little as two years from the time an action is commenced until a trial decision is rendered, but it is not uncommon for litigation to take significantly longer.

In the Canadian system, validity and infringement are never bifurcated. A trial is often bifurcated into liability and monetary remedy, but any injunction is normally granted at the end of the liability phase.

Law firms involved in patent litigation in Canada comprise large national firms with a group specializing in intellectual property or patent litigation, as well as a number of smaller specialized firms. The bar that handles patent litigation in Canada is relatively small.

1. *Permanent Injunctions*

The *Patent Act* provides that a court "may ... make such order as the court or judge sees fit" enjoining "further use, manufacture or sale of the subject-matter of the patent".[6] While this provision gives the courts authority and discretion to grant injunctive relief, it provides no substantive guidance. As a former colony of the United Kingdom, Canada has based its legal system on the English common law, and the grant of injunctive relief is based on the English legal tradition of equitable remedies.[7] The discretionary nature of equitable remedies is consistent with the permissive mandate of the statute.

Thus it is perfectly clear, both on the basis of the Act and the traditional equitable nature of injunctive relief, that the grant of injunctive relief to a successful patentee is a matter of discretion, and not a matter of right, and the discretionary nature of injunctive relief is regularly acknowledged by the courts. Nonetheless, the Canadian courts are of the view that an injunction will normally follow a finding that a valid patent has been infringed, and a permanent injunction will be refused "only in very rare circumstances"[8] with the caveat that an injunction will not normally be granted

---

[6] *Patent Act*, s. 57(1).
[7] The statutory provision provides formal authority for the grant of injunctive relief but is never referred to in establishing the relevant principles, which are based on case law and equitable principles.
[8] *Valence* v. *Phostech* (FC 2011, para. 240), stating "The Court should refuse to grant a permanent injunction where there is a finding of infringement, only in very rare circumstances"; and *see, e.g., Merck* v. *Apotex (lisinopril infringement)* (FCA 2006, para. 68), stating "The decision to award an injunction is a discretionary one entitled to considerable deference by this Court", and also stating that an injunction was appropriate because the patent was valid and infringed; *Janssen-Ortho* v. *Novopharm* (FC 2006, para. 133), noting that "As to an injunction that remedy normally follows a finding that a valid patent has been infringed" and recognizing the discretionary nature of the remedy; *Laboratoires Servier* (FC 2008, para. 500), stating: "The grant of a permanent injunction is a discretionary remedy"; *AbbVie* v. *Janssen (injunction)* (FC 2014, para. 34), noting the discretion in s. 57(1)(a) of the Act, and at para. 35, reviewing the case law and stating that "An injunction normally will follow once the Court has found that a patent

if there is no realistic prospect of future infringement.[9] Indeed, there appears to be only one reported Canadian patent case in which a permanent injunction was refused entirely to a successful patentee.[10] However, this historical pattern does not necessarily imply that Canadian courts would be unwilling to refuse a permanent injunction in appropriate circumstances. Cases which present the strongest argument for refusing injunctive relief, such as those involving patent assertion entities (PAEs), as in *eBay* v. *MercExchange* (US 2008), have seldom been litigated to judgment in Canadian courts.

As discussed in the next section, Canadian law implements a patent linkage regime when a generic pharmaceutical company seeks marketing authorization for a pharmaceutical which has patents listed against that pharmaceutical by the innovator company. This patent linkage regime is unique to pharmaceuticals. There are otherwise no apparent differences concerning injunctions across industries.

There is little specifically Canadian scholarship on the issue of injunctive relief in patent cases.

2. *Interlocutory Injunctions*

Like permanent injunctions, interlocutory injunctions (preliminary injunctions pending trial) are similarly authorized by the rules of the relevant court,[11] but again the legislation is merely permissive and the relevant principles are governed by the case law.

The general test for an interlocutory injunction in Canadian law was set out by Lord Diplock in the House of Lords decision in *American Cyanamid* (HL 1975) and subsequently adopted by the Supreme Court of Canada.[12] It is a three-part test, requiring the applicant to establish that: (1) there is a serious question to be tried on the merits; (2) the applicant would suffer irreparable harm if the application were refused; and (3) the balance of convenience favours granting the injunction.[13] Considerable jurisdictional variation has developed in the appellate case law. In Federal Court, the hurdle at the second stage, irreparable harm, is very high. As

---

is valid and has been infringed" and at para. 36, stating that "an injunction should be refused only in rare circumstances"; *Eurocopter* (FC 2012, at para. 397), noting that the grant of an injunction is discretionary, and that an injunction "will be commonly granted for an infringement or threatened infringement, unless there is some equitable reason not to do so, such as acquiescence, long delay, lack of clean hands, unconscionability, or triviality."

[9] See e.g., *Jay-Lor* (FC 2007, para. 263), declining to grant an injunction as the defendants had not manufactured an infringing unit for two years.

[10] *Unilever* (FCTD 1993) aff'd *Unilever* (FCA 1995). The refusal of injunctive relief was not appealed.

[11] *Federal Courts Rules*, r. 373 (1): "On motion, a judge may grant an interlocutory injunction."

[12] Adopted in *RJR-MacDonald* (SCC 1994) and *Manitoba* (AG) v. *Metropolitan Stores* (SCC 1987).

[13] *RJR-MacDonald* (SCC 1994, p. 334).

almost all patent actions are brought in Federal Court, this means that interlocutory injunctions are almost never granted in patent cases.[14]

However, the substantial majority of decided patent cases involve pharmaceuticals and Canada has a patent linkage system, based on the US Hatch–Waxman system. Marketing authorization in Canada is referred to as a Notice of Compliance[15] or "NOC", and the patent linkage system is known as the Patented Medicines (Notice of Compliance) (PM(NOC)) regime. Under the PM(NOC) regime, a drug manufacturer seeking marketing authorization for a generic drug product based on a comparison with a pharmaceutical which has already obtained authorization must first challenge the patents listed against the reference product. If the patentee responds to the challenge, an automatic twenty-four-month statutory stay of authorization is triggered, which is functionally equivalent to an interlocutory injunction. Consequently, while interlocutory injunctions as such are almost never granted, generic pharmaceuticals are routinely subject to the statutory stay.[16]

B. DRAFTING AND ENFORCING INJUNCTIONS

1. *Drafting*

In Canadian practice, reasons for judgment are distinct from the formal judgment. The reasons for judgment will state whether the patentee is entitled to injunctive relief, in terms that may be more or less precise, depending on the case. Injunctive relief is granted by way of an order made in the formal judgment and is effective from the time that it is endorsed by the judge.[17] The formal judgment may be issued at the same time as the reasons for judgment, typically appended to the reasons; or, particularly when there is any uncertainty as to the precise terms of the order, it may be issued subsequently. When the formal judgment is issued subsequently, the

---

[14] A notice of compliance is granted pursuant to the *Food and Drug Regulations* made under the *Food and Drugs Act*. A notice of compliance for new drugs, for example, is governed by the *Food and Drug Regulations* s. C.08.004.01.

[15] See Siebrasse 2009.

[16] Until recently, the proceeding was by way of an application by the patentee seeking an order prohibiting the Minister of Health from granting marketing authorization on the basis that the generic product would infringe a valid patent. If the order of prohibition was granted, the effect would be to prevent the generic product from entering the market. While an injunction against the generic producer would not be granted, the order of prohibition would have the same effect. A generic producer prohibited from entering the market for this reason could seek a stay of the implementation of the order pending appeal, and such a stay would be decided on the same principles as a stay of an injunction. Decisions on a stay of the implementation of the order of prohibition are therefore also relevant to a stay of an injunction pending appeal. The *PM (NOC) Regulations* were amended by SOR/2017-166, s. 7, which came into force on 21 September 2017, to change the proceeding from an application to an action, with the effect of finally deciding the validity of the patent. The nature of the statutory stay was unaffected.

[17] *Federal Courts Rules*, r. 392(2).

parties may be directed by the court to prepare a draft order in accordance with the reasons for judgment, for endorsement by the court.[18] If the parties cannot agree on the terms of the order, a motion may be brought for judgment so that the particulars of the order will be settled by the court.[19] In some cases, the trial judge may draft a proposed judgment and ask for comment by counsel before issuing the final judgment.[20] Thus, regardless of who drafts the order, counsel for both sides will normally have an opportunity for input as to the precise terms of the injunction. If the order remains unclear, a party may move to have it clarified; however, the courts will not allow motions for clarification to be used to as means of reopening decided issues or litigating infringement by new products.[21]

2. Wording

Permanent injunctions are typically granted in broad terms, enjoining the adjudged infringer from infringing the patent or specific claims of the patent.[22] This is sometimes combined with a prohibition on further manufacture or sale of a specific device or process that was adjudged to infringe, or similar variants that infringe, but narrower orders of this type are rarely the sole form of injunctive relief.[23] The claims specified in the order are not generally only the narrowest claims which cover the specific product at issue; the injunction will commonly extend to any claims which

---

[18] Id., r. 394(1).

[19] Id., r. 394.

[20] See, e.g., *Baxter Travenol* (SCC 1983, pp. 390–91); *Merck v. Apotex (enalapril No. 1)* (FCTD 1995); *Merck v. Apotex (lisinopril infringement)* (FC 2006, paras. 242–43).

[21] *Merck v. Apotex (enalapril No. 3)* (FCTD 1998) aff'd *Merck v. Apotex (enalapril No. 4)* (FCA 1999).

[22] See, e.g., *Merck v. Apotex (enalapril No. 5)* (FCTD 2000, paras. 11–12) var'd *Merck v. Apotex (enalapril No. 6)* (FCA 2003) referring to an injunction of this type, including a broad order against infringing specified claims of the patent at issue, combined with a specific prohibition on making, using or selling a specified product, as "the typical injunctive relief awarded when infringement of patent interests is found". And see also *Trojan* (FCA 2003, para. 4) (enjoining infringement of the patent and the sale of specific products and their equivalents); *Human Care* (FC 2018) at Judgment para. 1(e) (enjoining infringement of the patent); *Bayer* (FC 2016) at Judgment para. 2 (enjoining infringement of specified claims); *Weatherford* (FC 2010) (enjoining infringement of the patent and specified claims); *Valence v. Phostech* (FC 2011) at Judgment para. 7 (enjoining infringement of the patent and also enjoining specified process or any similar process that infringes).

[23] If the order includes broad language enjoining infringement generally, an additional reference in the order to specific products "does not in any way cut down" the broad scope of the injunction: *Apotex v. Merck (enalapril No. 2)* (FCA 1996, p .168). In the taxonomy developed Golden 2012, 1404, 1420–24, Canadian courts normally grant "Type-2" injunctions, which "generally prohibits infringement of a patent or patent claim without tying the scope of the prohibition to products or processes already adjudged to infringe" (1404), sometimes combined with a Type-0 injunction, which "explicitly forbid[s] only future infringement that involves the exact products or processes already adjudged to infringe" (1403), or Type-1 injunctions, which provide "an explicit prohibition of infringement that involves only relatively insignificant variations of the products or processes specified by accompanying Type-0 language" (1404).

were at issue in the litigation.[24] If the infringement at issue includes inducement, the infringer will also be enjoined from inducing infringement in similarly broad terms.[25]

In addition, when the adjudged infringer is in possession of infringing goods, the court will normally grant an ancillary order to ensure the injunction will be respected.[26] Typically, the ancillary order will be for delivery up or destruction of those goods.[27] The patentee does not get a property right in the infringing material, and if feasible, as when the patented invention is one removable component of a larger product, the court may order that the goods be rendered non-infringing.[28] The courts will avoid granting an order for delivery up when the goods have a substantial non-infringing use.[29] Occasionally a carve-out may be granted exempting certain infringing goods from delivery up or destruction, especially if this can be done without prejudice to the patentee's rights during the term of the patent.[30]

Preliminary injunctions are so rarely granted in patent cases that it is not possible to generalize regarding their language.

3. *Enforcement*

An injunction is enforced by a contempt action. The sanction for contempt is a fine or imprisonment,[31] though imprisonment is almost never imposed for a single act of civil contempt. The fine should be sufficient to serve as a specific deterrent to future contempt by the contemnor, and as a general deterrent to dissuade others from breaching court orders.[32] It is therefore appropriate to take into account the value of the sales of the offending product in determining the magnitude of the fine.[33] The presence or absence of good faith may be taken into account in determining the

---

[24] See discussion of *Merck v. Apotex (enalapril No. 4)* (FCA 1999) aff'g *Merck v. Apotex (enalapril No. 3)* (FCTD 1998).

[25] See *Uview* (FC 2009), Order 1(b).

[26] *See, e.g., Diversified Products* (FCTD 1988); *Laboratoires Servier* (FC 2008, para. 496).

[27] *See, e.g., Laboratoires Servier* (FC 2008) Judgment, para. 4; *Human Care Canada Inc. v. Evolution Technologies Inc.* (FC 2018); *Janssen-Ortho v. Novopharm* (FC 2006, para. 231).

[28] See *Diversified Products* (FCTD 1988).

[29] See *Teva v. Novartis* (FC 2013, paras. 399–400), accepting an undertaking that goods would only be used for exempt experimental purposes; *Uponor* (FC 2016, para. 300), refusing to grant an order for delivery up.

[30] See *Bombardier* (FC 2020), enjoining dealers in possession of infringing products from selling those products, but exempting them from the order for delivery up, with the effect that the dealers would be permitted to sell the products after the expiry of the patent; and see *Bombardier (motion)* (FC 2020, paras. 33–35), discussing the effect of the order in *Bombardier* (FC 2020).

[31] *Federal Courts Rules*, r. 472.

[32] See *Merck v. Apotex (enalapril No. 6)* (FCA 2003, paras. 80–89), emphasizing the importance of deterrence in imposing a sentence for contempt.

[33] See id., para 84; *Baxter Travenol* (FCA 1987, p. 453).

penalty to be imposed, but is not relevant to whether there was an act of contempt.[34] Exemplary damages may also be awarded as a sanction for breach of an injunction, in particular an interlocutory injunction, but this is unusual.[35]

Because the sanction for contempt is punitive in nature, the alleged contemnor must have had adequate notice as to the acts that would constitute contempt. Accordingly, contempt is inappropriate if the original order was lacking in detail or otherwise insufficiently particularized.[36] Contempt may therefore be inappropriate when the order incorporates overly broad or unclear language.[37]

While there can be no breach of an injunction before the order granting the injunction is formally made, it will nonetheless be a contempt of court to contravene the prohibitions set out in the reasons for judgment, even before the formal order is issued,[38] provided the party had knowledge of the prohibitions in the reasons for judgment[39] and the reasons are clear.[40]

---

[34] *Baxter Travenol* (FCA 1987, p. 454); *Merck* v. *Apotex* (*enalapril No. 6*) (FCA 2003, para. 60).

[35] See *Pro Arts* (Ont SC 1980, p. 441ff), awarding exemplary damages for breach of an interlocutory injunction for copyright infringement; *Lubrizol* (FCA 1992, p. 478), holding that exemplary damages are an available remedy for a callous disregard for an interlocutory injunction in a patent case.

[36] See *College of Optometrists* (Ont CA 2008, para. 41), citing cases; Sharpe 2017, § 6.187.

[37] *Fettes* (Sask CA 2010, para. 21), citing cases.

[38] *Baxter Travenol* (SCC 1983) noting that the relevant rules of court provide several distinct branches, including disobeying an order and, separately, interfering with the orderly administration of justice. Prior to the order being issued, contempt for disobeying a prohibition set out in the reasons is based on the second branch. This distinction is further clarified in the current *Federal Courts Rules*, r. 466 which sets out these branches in separate paragraphs ((b) and (c), respectively). In *Baxter Travenol* (SCC 1983) the reasons referred to the defendant being enjoined from selling products "as exemplified by" certain exhibits, while the formal order referred to products "including the type exemplified" by the same exhibits: p. 391. Because the terms of the formal order were broader than the reasons, there was no difficulty regarding notice. The matter was remanded for a decision on the merits, and the defendant was ultimately held in contempt for breach of the prohibition set out in the Reasons: *Baxter Travenol* (FCTD 1986) var'd *Baxter Travenol* (FCA 1987). See also *Merck* v. *Apotex* (*enalapril No. 6*) (FCA 2003, para. 73) var'g *Merck* v. *Apotex* (*enalapril No. 5*) (FCTD 2000), finding the appellants in contempt on the second branch for disobeying a prohibition contained in the reasons for judgment.

[39] See *Merck* v. *Apotex* (*enalapril No 6*) (FCA 2003, para 55).

[40] See id., para. 73, stating, "The test to apply [for finding contempt] asks the following two questions: (1) Did the alleged contemner have the knowledge of the prohibitions in the reasons for judgment?; and, (2) Was there an act that constituted a contravention of a prohibition therein?"; and see para. 50, stating that the character of the intent required for contempt by interfering with the orderly administration of justice is the same as that for breach of an order, "provided the Reasons are clear", and paras. 64–70, holding that the Reasons at issue "were clear and unambiguous, and did not reasonably lend themselves to the interpretation alleged by the Appellants". See also *Baxter Travenol* (FCTD 1986, p. 454), as quoted in *Merck* v. *Apotex* (*enalapril No. 6*) (FCA 2003, para. 56).

The question therefore arises as to whether a broad "do not infringe" injunction is sufficiently clear to support a finding of contempt.[41] There are few reported decisions relating to contempt of an injunctive relief order in a patent case, and the issue has not often been raised, but it would appear that broad "do not infringe" injunctions will normally be effective according to their terms. The issue arose tangentially in *Weatherford* (FC 2010). After a trial on the merits that focused on one of the defendant's product lines, the defendant was broadly enjoined from infringing the patent at issue.[42] The defendant then brought a motion amending the order to limit the scope of the injunction to the particular product line which had been at issue in the litigation, out of concern that another product line might be subject to the injunction even though those products were not in evidence at trial.[43] The motion was refused, on the basis[44] that it is standard practice to make orders restraining sale and distribution of infringing products generally,[45] and the scope of the order was not unclear: "The Court has provided a claims construction for the relevant claims; the injunction is directed at the Defendants' conduct in infringing the claims as interpreted whether it uses the named products or not", and "The Defendants are in the best position to know their products and whether they infringe".[46] While this was a motion to amend, and not a contempt hearing, this holding strongly suggests that a broad do-not-infringe order would not be held so vague as to preclude enforcement by way of contempt. With that said, there may be some cases in which such an injunction would be too vague on the particular facts.

It is in any event clear that the scope of the injunction will not be limited simply to the products at issue and equivalents. The point arose in *Merck v. Apotex (enalapril No. 4)* (FCA 1999).[47] The specific product at issue was generic enalapril maleate. Claim 1 was a claim to a genus of chemical compounds, including enalapril maleate, while Claims 2–5 were directed at enalapril maleate specifically. The injunction granted after trial enjoined Apotex from infringing any of Claims 1–5, as well as specifically enjoining the sale of enalapril maleate tablets.[48] Subsequent to that judgment, Apotex became aware of other compounds that fell

[41] See Golden 2012, 1422, noting that in the US Federal Court "Type-2, obey-the-law injunctions are technically prohibited", and they are typically "narrowly construed to apply only to products or processes 'previously admitted or adjudged to infringe, and to other devices which are no more than colorably different therefrom and which clearly are infringements'".

[42] *Weatherford* (FC 2010, para. 3).

[43] Id., para. 1.

[44] The trial judge remarked that he had "grave doubts" as to whether the court had jurisdiction to vary an order that was consistent with the reasons, but he did not decide on the basis of lack of jurisdiction, but rather on the basis that even if the court had jurisdiction, he would not grant the amendment: Id., paras. 12–15.

[45] Id., para. 17.

[46] Id., paras. 20–21.

[47] *Merck v. Apotex (enalapril No. 4)* (FCA 1999) aff'g *Merck v. Apotex (enalapril No. 3)* (FCTD 1998).

[48] *Merck v. Apotex (enalapril No. 3)* (FCTD 1998, p. 379).

within the scope of Claim 1 alone.[49] Apotex therefore brought an application to vary the injunction, essentially by removing the references to Claim 1, so that it would be able to make and sell these new compounds, presumably thereby triggering new litigation in which it could challenge the validity of Claim 1. The application was refused on the basis that Apotex had had the opportunity to challenge the validity of Claim 1 at trial and had failed to do so.[50] Note that Claim 1 was not unclear by virtue of its breadth; Apotex acknowledged that the new products would infringe Claim 1.

An injunction granted in *AbbVie v. Janssen (injunction)* (FC 2014) also received a broad interpretation.[51] As discussed in more detail Section C.6, the products at issue were drugs for the treatment of psoriasis, and AbbVie had been granted an injunction with a carve-out permitting the infringer, Janssen, to continue to supply the infringing product, STELARA, to patients who were not responsive to AbbVie's product. However, the injunction prohibited Janssen from promoting or making any representations or claims respecting the use of STELARA for the treatment of psoriasis. Janssen prepared a "script" to be used to inform dermatologists about STELARA, which contained the following language: "It is important to note that this court order does not impact your ability to prescribe STELARA to your patients. The product itself has not changed and there are no changes from a safety and efficacy standpoint."[52]

Both sentences in this statement were held to constitute prima facie contempt, because they sought to influence the physician's treatment decisions.[53] This is a broad interpretation of the injunction; it is not clear what language might be used to convey basic factual information about STELARA, while avoiding contempt. This suggests that Canadian courts will not be inclined to construe the terms of an injunction narrowly.

C. ALTERNATIVES AND MODIFICATIONS

1. *Overview*

As discussed in Section A.1, it is clear that the grant of a permanent injunction is discretionary in principle and so may be refused entirely. By the same token, it is clear that the court has the authority to tailor or modify the grant of an injunction. Such modifications are occasionally implemented, though they are not common.

---

[49] Id., pp. 381, 384; *Merck v. Apotex (enalapril No. 4)* (FCA 1999, para. 4).

[50] *Merck v. Apotex (enalapril No. 4)* (FCA 1999, para. 12); *Merck v. Apotex (enalapril No. 3)* (FCTD 1998, pp. 385–86).

[51] The injunction was granted by *AbbVie v. Janssen (injunction)* (FC 2014); see Section C.6 for a discussion. The show case hearing for contempt is *AbbVie v. Janssen (contempt)* (FC 2014).

[52] *AbbVie v. Janssen* (FC 2014, para. 29).

[53] Id., paras. 66–67 After a complaint by AbbVie, that language was changed (para. 33), but the change did not affect the analysis and the changed language was also held to constitute contempt (para. 73).

Cases departing from the standard practice of granting an injunction against all forms of infringement, effective immediately, can be divided into three broad categories.

The first category is refusal to grant injunctive relief entirely. The second category is decisions involving appeals, either granting a grace period to allow the infringer to bring an appeal or a stay pending the disposition of an appeal. The third category can be divided into two sub-categories, namely cases tailoring the injunction and those granting a stay for reasons unrelated to an appeal.

2. *Refusing Injunctive Relief*

There appears to be only one reported Canadian case refusing injunctive relief as a remedy for infringement of a valid patent, namely *Unilever* (FCTD 1993).[54] The patent at issue related to a method of softening damp clothing in a laundry dryer. The defendant was Procter & Gamble and its product, which was held to infringe, was Bounce dryer sheets. Though Unilever's patent was held to be valid and infringed, the court refused to grant a permanent injunction, instead awarding "a generous, but non-confiscatory, rate of royalty",[55] which was somewhat increased over the reasonable royalty that was payable for the pre-judgment infringement.[56]

The court's discussion of the refusal to award an injunction in favour of the patentee was relatively brief, but two factors were the main basis for the decision:[57]

- the patentees did not practise their patented invention in Canada, nor did they have a competitive product on the Canadian market;[58]
- the patentees "brandish[ed] their patent as a bargaining tool with P & G".[59]

While the patentees did not practise the invention in Canada, they were an operating company, not a patent assertion entity or non-practising entity. The patentee and the defendant were two of the leading global firms in the relevant market, and it appears the Canadian litigation was part of a global litigation strategy. The reference to the patentee "brandishing" their patent as a bargaining tool with

---

[54] *Unilever* (FCTD 1993) aff'd *Unilever* (FCA 1995) The refusal to grant an injunction was not appealed.

[55] *Unilever* (FCTD 1993, p. 572).

[56] Id., p. 571). The decision was the liability phase of a bifurcated trial, with quantum of damages to be determined on a reference. While the liability phase determined entitlement to various remedies, the actual quantum was not determined. There is no reported decision on the reference as to damages, perhaps because the parties settled after the liability determination, as is common.

[57] Id., pp. 570–71.

[58] Id., pp. 568, 570–72.

[59] Id., pp. 570–71, describing these as being "The two factors which mainly predicate the Court's discretion in this regard."

P & G appears to have been a reference to offers to settle the Canadian litigation as part of a global settlement;[60] there is certainly no suggestion that the patentee exploited the patented technology solely by licensing in other jurisdictions, or that it was not concerned with its own global market share. In this context, it is difficult to see why the first two factors should be sufficient grounds for refusing an injunction. The basic argument in favour of injunctive relief is that it allows the parties, rather than the courts, to determine the value of the technology. That is what the parties were attempting to do in the settlement.

A third factor was also mentioned, namely "the hardship which an injunction would inflict on the infringer's employees in difficult economic times, and the absence of a competing workforce engaged by the patentee".[61] There are two difficulties with this factor. First, there is no particular reason to believe that it is likely that the injunction would have been enforced. As noted, the parties were seeking a global settlement, and the main effect of the injunction would probably have been simply to give the patentee greater bargaining power. In principle, one would have expected the patentee to want to license in the Canadian market, given that it did not have a competing product, so that enforcing the injunction rather than licensing would not have generated compensating profits. Second, while the patentee did not have a Canadian workforce, it did have a global workforce, and the decision implicitly prefers the infringer's Canadian workforce over the patentee's foreign workforce. While this may be understandable on the part of a Canadian court, it may be doubted whether it is wise for a court to use injunctive relief as a tool of industrial policy in a global economy.

While *Unilever* has never been disapproved, neither has it been followed. It does clearly establish the proposition, which was not really in doubt, that the court does have the discretion to refuse injunctive relief to a successful patentee, but it has not otherwise been influential. The refusal of a permanent injunction in *Unilever* is best seen as an idiosyncratic decision by the trial judge, which was upheld as not being an abuse of discretion, rather than on the basis that refusal of the injunction was correct in the circumstances. It would be unwarranted to draw any general lessons from *Unilever* as to when a Canadian court is likely to deny injunctive relief in future cases.

3. *Damages in Lieu*

In the only patent case to refuse a permanent injunction, *Unilever* (FCTD 1993), the trial court instead awarded a royalty in lieu on a "generous, but non-confiscatory,

---

[60] Id., pp. 502–05.
[61] Id., p. 572. An additional factor may have been that the patent had less than two years remaining on the term. This was adverted to by the court in the discussion of injunctive relief at p. 570, but was not expressly mentioned as a consideration in refusing injunctive relief.

rate",[62] which was somewhat increased over the reasonable royalty that was payable for the pre-judgment infringement.[63] The enhancement was not based on notions of wilfulness, as is sometimes the rationale for awarding an enhanced royalty in lieu of an injunction in the US context, since wilfulness as such does not play any role in damages in Canadian law.[64] The reasoning behind the enhancement was very brief: "In return for avoidance of an injunction now, it would be equitable for the defendants to enhance the damages payable by means of an increased rate of royalty from and after the date of these reasons."[65] Thus, the enhanced damages were the price the infringer had to pay as compensation for being relieved of the burden of the injunction.

This award was appealed specifically on the basis that the royalty in lieu should have been confined to the same reasonable royalty that would have been payable for pre-judgment infringement. In Canadian practice, an accounting of profits is commonly awarded as a remedy for patent infringement.[66] In this case, the trial judge refused to grant an accounting. The Court of Appeal held that in awarding damages in lieu of an injunction, the trial judge "chose a middle ground" between an accounting and a reasonable royalty and he was entitled to do so.[67] Thus, the enhanced damages were awarded essentially as a middle ground between a reasonable royalty, and the other two remedies, an accounting or an injunction, which a successful patentee might normally expect.

4. *Stay Pending Appeal*

The trial court which grants an injunction has broad discretion to tailor its timing and implementation,[68] including the ability to delay the effect of its grant of injunctive relief until the determination of any appeal.[69] However, this is seldom done. Instead, the trial court will sometimes provide a "grace period" by delaying the

---

[62] Id., p. 572.

[63] Id., p. 571.

[64] Wilfulness may be relevant to punitive or exemplary damages, but it is very clear that wilfulness alone is not sufficient grounds for awarding punitive damages.

[65] *Unilever* (FCTD 1993, p. 571).

[66] In an accounting, the patentee is awarded that portion of the infringer's profit that is attributable to the infringement, on the basis of "but for" causation, taking into account the availability of non-infringing alternatives: *Monsanto* v. *Schmeiser* (SCC 2004, para. 104); *Apotex* v. *ADIR* (FCA 2017, paras. 24–30); and see Seaman et al. 2019, discussing the "differential profit" method that is used to assess an accounting in Canadian law.

[67] *Unilever* (FCA 1995, p. 524).

[68] See *Janssen* v. *AbbVie (stay)* (FCA 2014, para. 18), noting that a court has discretion over its own order as required in the "interests of justice".

[69] Such a delay is sometimes referred to as a "stay", but strictly it is simply the exercise of the trial court's discretion in drafting its own order, while a stay is an order delaying the order of another body: *Janssen* v. *AbbVie (stay)* (FCA 2014, para. 18). And see *Merck* v. *Canada* (FCTD 1999), granting a stay pending disposition of the appeal on the merits in a PM(NOC) proceeding.

effect of the order for a limited period to allow the adjudged infringer to decide
whether to appeal and to seek a stay of the injunction pending appeal.[70] The Court
of Appeal may similarly stay the effect of its own orders pending the disposition of an
application for leave to appeal to the Supreme Court of Canada.[71]

A motion for a stay pending appeal may also be brought in the Court of Appeal
itself. The granting of a stay is a discretionary remedy, with the ultimate basis of
doing justice to all the parties.[72] Stays pending the disposition of an appeal are
granted on the same basis as interlocutory injunctions. In the Federal Court of
Appeal, this means that the party seeking the stay "must establish that there is an
arguable issue to be decided on the appeal, adduce clear evidence that it will suffer
irreparable harm if the stay is not granted, and demonstrate that the balance of
convenience favours the grant of a stay".[73] This test, and particularly the requirement of irreparable harm, puts a significant burden on the party seeking the stay, so
that there is effectively a presumption against granting the stay. Apart from the effect
of the irreparable harm requirement, it has also been said explicitly that there is a
presumption against granting a stay: "[W]here an injunction has been granted by a
final judgment, prima facie, it should remain in force until that judgment has been
found, on appeal, to be wrong."[74] This presumption is not particularly strong, but it
does mean that if all the factors are equally balanced, the stay will be refused.

If the stay is granted by the Court of Appeal, it may be granted subject to
conditions intended to protect the patentee from adverse effects of the stay in the
event that the infringer's appeal is unsuccessful. Such protections are often aimed at
ensuring the adjudged infringer will be able to pay any damages for infringement
arising during the period of the stay.[75] The Court of Appeal may order the hearing of

---

[70] *See, e.g., Merck v. Apotex (lisinopril infringement)* (FC 2006, para. 230) (thirty-day delay);
Procter & Gamble v. Bristol-Myers (FCTD 1978, pp. 168–69) (delay of approximately twenty
days); *Bombardier* (FC 2020) (delay of twenty days).

[71] See *AstraZeneca* (FCA 2005, para. 35), granting a stay pending the disposition of the leave
application by the Supreme Court. Depending on the order, the stay may be extended until
disposition of the Supreme Court appeal where leave is granted. In *AstraZeneca* (FCA 2005,
para. 35) the FCA held: "If leave is granted, Apotex will have a period of 30 days to apply for a
continued stay in which case the stays hereby given will remain effective until the Supreme
Court disposes of the stay applications."

[72] *Apotex v. Wellcome (stay)* (FCA 1998, para. 5).

[73] *Apotex v. Merck (lisinopril stay)* (FCA 2006, para. 4); and see *Trojan* (FCA 2003, para. 5); *Baker
Petrolite* (FCA 2001, para. 10).

[74] *Marketing International* (FCA 1977, p. 230).

[75] *See, e.g., Phostech v. Valence (stay)* (FCA 2011, para. 6), in which a stay was granted with
conditions including an undertaking as to damages, an undertaking that the infringer will make
no distributions to shareholders, and requiring deposit of a bond; *Trojan* (FCA 2003, paras.
8–10), which limited payments to creditors and ordered security to be posted, as well as
ordering that "Terms of existing contracts shall not be altered by the [adjudged infringer] so
as to reduce its expected revenues or profits"; *Baker Petrolite* (FCA 2001), granting a stay subject
to various conditions intended to preserve the assets of the adjudged infringer, when the assets
of the adjudged infringer appeared to be less than the judgment against it. Similarly, when the
trial court grants a grace period to allow the adjudged infringer to seek a stay, the delay may be

the appeal expedited, either instead of granting a stay or in addition to doing so.[76] The Court of Appeal may also tailor the stay to permit only some infringing activity.[77]

Turning to the three-part test, the threshold for a serious question to be tried on appeal is low and is rarely determinative of the decision to refuse a stay.[78]

The need for the adjudged infringer to establish irreparable harm is a significant hurdle to obtaining a stay pending appeal. If a stay is refused and the adjudged infringer is ultimately successful on appeal, the infringer will have suffered harm, such as lost sales, from having been kept off the market while the injunction was "erroneously" in effect.[79] Because the adjudged infringer is kept off the market by the injunction, and not as a result of any wrong done to it by the patentee, it has no legal cause of action to recover those losses. This uncompensated loss, if substantial, will normally constitute irreparable harm satisfying the second branch of the test, and will carry significant weight in the balance of convenience, favouring a stay.[80] Consequently, the patentee seeking to resist a stay may choose to give an undertaking to indemnify the adjudged infringer against such irrecoverable financial loss that it may suffer in the event that its stay is not granted and its appeal is successful.[81]

---

subject to conditions intended to protect the patentee in the event that the application for a stay is unsuccessful: See, e.g., *Merck* v. *Apotex (lisinopril infringement)* (FC 2006, para. 230), requiring that the adjudged infringer account for all the infringing product during that period and hold the proceeds of any dispositions in a separate trust fund.

[76] See, e.g., *Baker Petrolite* (FCA 2001), granting a stay and expedited appeal; *Apotex* v. *Wellcome (expedite)* (FCA 1998), expediting the appeal because a stay was refused; *Apotex* v. *Merck (lisinopril stay)* (FCA 2006), expediting the appeal and refusing a stay; *Trojan* (FCA 2003, paras. 8–9), granting a stay and expediting the appeal.

[77] See *Trojan* (FCA 2003, paras. 8–9), ordering that the adjudged infringer "shall make no new bids pending the appeal, but will be allowed to fulfill its contracts that have been signed, that are being negotiated at the present time, and any contracts which shall be concluded on the basis of bids that have already been made".

[78] *AstraZenceca* (FCA 2005, para. 5), noting that "it is not usually useful to dwell into the seriousness of the question".

[79] *Apotex* v. *Wellcome (stay)* (FCA 1998, para. 4) rev'g *Apotex* v. *Wellcome (stay)* (FCTD 1998). The injunction would have been issued "erroneously" only with the benefit of hindsight; this is not to say that the trial court was wrong to grant the injunction in light of its own conclusions.

[80] Id.; *Evolution Tech* (FCA 2019, para. 31); but see *Arctic Cat* (FCA 2020), refusing a stay pending appeal even though it appears that no undertaking was provided.

[81] *AstraZenceca* (FCA 2005, para. 19); *Apotex* v. *Merck (lisinopril stay)* (FCA 2006, paras. 7–9); *Merck* v. *Canada* (FCTD 1999, paras. 5 and 7). There is no requirement that the patentee give such an undertaking, but if it does not, the potential irreparable harm to the adjudged infringer will weigh in favour of the stay being granted. Undertakings of this type are almost invariably given by a party seeking an interlocutory (preliminary) injunction pending trial and the relevant law has developed primarily in that context (though outside of the patent context, as interlocutory injunctions are almost never granted). The undertaking is given to the court, not to the other party, and is enforced by an application to the court for an order directing an inquiry as to damages. The court has the discretion to refuse to grant the inquiry, but the inquiry will be ordered absent exceptional circumstances. If there is a question as to the patentee's ability to pay, some form of security, such as a bond, may be provided. Again, there

If the patentee is financially able to pay any loss which might arise, such an undertaking will be a complete answer to this concern.[82] The undertaking may extend to "springboard" damages[83] arising after the disposition of the appeal.[84] While an undertaking to pay any loss incurred by the adjudged infringer is perhaps the most common type of undertaking, undertakings may be used flexibly to address any specific concerns arising on the facts of a particular case.[85]

If such an undertaking is granted, the adjudged infringer must therefore establish some other form of irreparable harm in order to obtain a stay.[86] The administrative burdens of complying with the injunction will not suffice.[87] Nor is the fact that a defendant to a patent infringement action would suffer some other financial harm during the time of appeal in itself a sufficient basis for a stay, as this would make the stay effectively automatic.[88] For example, injury to reputation or permanent loss of market share may constitute irreparable harm, but must be established on the facts.[89] The clearest form of irreparable harm arises when the adjudged infringer can establish that it has insufficient funds to pay the award and would be put out of business if the stay were not granted.[90]

An important consideration is the effect of the injunction on the operations of the adjudged infringer. If the infringing product is one of many, so that the injunction will have little effect on the infringer's overall business, the loss of business will not

---

is no requirement to do so, but if there is a real likelihood that the patentee will be unable to pay if necessary, the court will take this into account in assessing irreparable harm.

[82] *AstraZenceca* (FCA 2005, paras. 18–19); *Apotex v. Merck (lisinopril stay)* (FCA 2006, paras. 7–9); *Novopharm v. Janssen-Ortho* (FCA 2006, paras. 12–13).

[83] Springboard damages are damages awarded for losses caused by infringement during the term, but arising after the term, typically associated with the fact that it may take some time for the competitor to ramp up production after the patent has expired while the patentee still has substantial market power. See also Chapter 13 (United Kingdom), Section H.2, discussing springboard damages.

[84] *Novopharm v. Janssen-Ortho* (FCA 2006, paras. 14–15).

[85] See *Bristol-Myers v. Canada* (FCTD 2002) in which the defendant's business would have been put at risk had it been prevented from selling its only product, and the applicant, Bristol-Myers Squibb, had offered to pay up to $50,000.00 per month for six months to cover operating costs, in mitigation. The stay was nonetheless granted, on the basis that the balance of convenience favoured the adjudged infringer; while the court did not say so expressly, it apparently considered the amount of the undertaking inadequate compensation for potentially being forced out of business.

[86] See, e.g., *Novopharm v. Janssen-Ortho* (FCA 2006), refusing a stay on the basis that irreparable harm had not been established in light of the undertaking.

[87] *Janssen v. AbbVie (stay)* (FCA 2014, para. 25).

[88] *Apotex v. Wellcome (stay)* (FCA 1998, para. 5).

[89] *Janssen v. AbbVie (stay)* (FCA 2014, paras. 26–27); *Apotex v. Merck (lisinopril stay)* (FCA 2006, paras. 11–17); *Bristol-Myers v. Canada* (FCTD 2002), finding injury to reputation likely as a result of substantial business disruption; *Apotex v. Wellcome (stay)* (FCTD 1998) rev'd on other grounds *Apotex v. Wellcome (stay)* (FCA 1998) holding no likelihood of injury to reputation on the facts.

[90] *Evolution Tech* (FCA 2019, para. 29).

normally constitute irreparable harm.[91] Conversely, if the effect would be to shut down all or a substantial part of the adjudged infringer's business, as contrasted with causing lost sales in one product line of many, this will normally constitute irreparable harm, and will also weigh heavily in the balance of convenience.[92] This scenario is perhaps the most common reason for a stay being granted.

The impact on the patentee's business will also be considered in the balance of convenience. If sales lost to the infringer will cause substantial harm to the patentee's business, or if the infringer is unlikely to be able to satisfy a damages judgment, this will be given significant weight in the balance of convenience.[93] However, an adjudged infringer's inability to pay must be established on the facts.[94] Conversely, the balance of convenience is more likely to favour a stay if the parties do not compete in the same market, so that the only harm to the patentee is a longer period during which it will be entitled to damages in the form of a reasonable royalty.[95]

It is sometimes suggested that a stay is less likely to be granted when the adjudged infringer knew of the patent and that its product would likely infringe and took a calculated risk that a validity challenge would be successful. This suggestion has had a mixed reception in the Court of Appeal.[96] As a matter of policy, many granted

---

[91] *Apotex* v. *Wellcome (stay)* (FCTD 1998, para. 11) rev'd on other grounds *Apotex* v. *Wellcome (stay)* (FCA 1998).

[92] See *Phostech* v. *Valence (stay)* (FCA 2011, para. 3), granting a stay; *Trojan* (FCA 2003, paras. 8–9), granting a stay on evidence that the adjudged infringer would be unable to continue to operate if the injunction were not stayed; *Bristol-Myers* v. *Canada* (FCTD 2002), granting a stay where there was a serious risk the defendant would have gone out of business if prevented from selling its product; *Baker Petrolite* (FCA 2001, paras. 12 and 14), granting a stay when substantially all of the adjudged infringer's business consisted of dealing in the infringing product, so that it could not cease the infringement without ceasing to carry on its business. Moreover, if the injunction were immediately enforced, the infringer probably would not have been financially able to bring an appeal; *Merck* v. *Canada* (FCTD 1999), granting a stay, noting that infringing product was a very substantial part of the infringer's assets, and refusal of the stay would jeopardize the infringer's continued viability; *Marketing International* (FCA 1977, p. 231), granting stay when the appellant's business would otherwise be terminated, eliminating the appellant as a competitor even if the appeal were successful.

[93] *Bristol-Myers* v. *Canada* (FCTD 2002); *Baker Petrolite* (FCA 2001), noting that the net value of the adjudged infringer's assets was less than the amount of the judgment against it, but nonetheless granting a stay subject to conditions intended to preserve the infringer's assets, as a stay would have required the infringer to cease operations entirely.

[94] *Apotex* v. *Merck (lisinopril stay)* (FCA 2006, para. 30).

[95] *Phostech* v. *Valence (stay)* (FCA 2011, para. 4); *Marketing International* (FCA 1977, p. 231); *Corning Glass* (FCTD 1984, p. 376)

[96] See *Apotex* v. *Wellcome (stay)* (FCTD 1998, para. 10), refusing a stay in part because the adjudged infringers "knew the business risks they were taking when they decided to produce and market [the infringing product] in the midst of the ongoing litigation in Canada and the United States. For whatever reason, they both calculated that the risks of being found to infringe a valid patent were acceptable". However, on appeal, the stay was granted, with the Court of Appeal remarking that "the idea that the loss was merely a foreseeable normal business risk" was "unwarranted". But see *Apotex* v. *Merck (lisinopril stay)* (FCA 2006, para. 31), refusing a stay in part because the adjudged infringer "took a calculated risk that its challenge to the validity of the "350 patent would prove a good defence to an infringement action". See also

patents are ultimately determined to be invalid, and a knowing infringer who successfully attacks the validity of a patent is doing a public service, which should not be discouraged by unduly harsh sanctions.[97] This suggests that known assumption of risk should be irrelevant. On the other hand, it might be said that even so, the infringer should only be excused if it had a good-faith belief in the invalidity of the patent. However, establishing a good-faith belief in invalidity as a condition for various remedies raises significant difficulties in establishing subjective motivation, as illustrated by the US experience with enhanced damages for wilful infringement,[98] and it would seem unwise to import such considerations into a motion for a stay.

If the adjudged infringer has been selling the product at issue for a lengthy period of time, this will weigh in favour of granting a stay. Whatever impact the infringing competition will have on the patentee's market share has already occurred, so the main effect of the stay is only to extend the period for which the patentee will be owed damages.[99] Also the infringer will often have invested substantially in the product lines, so that the implementation of the injunction is likely to cause loss of reputation and other sunk costs, as well as permanent loss of market share due to unreliability of supply to purchasers.[100]

When the public interest lies only in the reduced prices that will result if the adjudged infringer is permitted to continue selling its product, this will not play any role in the balance of convenience, because the premise of the patent system is that this is more than offset by increased innovation; the public interest lies only in allowing competition after the patent has expired.[101] Some more specific impact on the public must be alleged for the public interest to be relevant. In one case, a stay pending disposition of the appeal was granted and upheld, in part because of the potential effect of the injunction on a third-party supplier to the adjudged infringer. The third party was "a charitable organization employing some physically handicapped persons as well as others, many of whose ability to earn a livelihood would be jeopardized by the injunction".[102] However, in upholding the stay, the Court of Appeal remarked that "great care must be exercised in widening the ambit of factors to be taken into account in the determination of the question of irreparable

---

Corning Glass (FCTD 1984, p. 378), refusing a stay in part because the adjudged infringer "went into this undertaking with its eyes open and fully aware of the risks".

[97] See *Lear* v. *Adkins* (US 1969, 670, 673–74), emphasizing the strong public interest in enabling challenges to bad patents.

[98] See *Read* v. *Portec* (Fed. Cir. 1992, pp. 656–57), discussing role of good faith in the context of enhanced damages for willful infringement in US law; and see Chien et al. 2019, 91–94, discussing the US approach to wilfulness.

[99] *Baker Petrolite* (FCA 2001, para. 14); *Apotex* v. *Wellcome* (stay) (FCA 1998).

[100] *Apotex* v. *Wellcome* (stay) (FCA 1998, paras. 3, 5–6).

[101] *AstraZenceca* (FCA 2005, paras. 20–34).

[102] *Procter & Gamble* (stay) (FCA 1978, p. 177).

harm" when determining whether a stay should be granted.[103] In effect, the trial court is permitted to take such considerations into account, but is not encouraged to do so.[104]

In summary, the Canadian courts are of the view that the patentee is entitled to the enforcement of an injunction granted at trial, and there is in effect a presumption against a stay, which is reflected in the doctrinal test requiring the party seeking the stay to establish irreparable harm. However, a stay will be granted in unusual circumstances, especially when the injunction threatens the adjudged infringer's entire business operations.

5. *Stays Other than Pending Appeal*

A stay pending appeal is the most common reason for a stay of a permanent injunction to be granted. Aside from that scenario, there are a few cases in which the grant of a permanent injunction has been made subject to a short runoff period, during which the infringer can dispose of existing stock. The infringer will still be monetarily liable for those sales, either in damages or for an accounting of profits.[105] The practice does not appear to be common.[106] Presumably it does not appeal to the patentee, which would rather make its own sales, and it does not appeal to the infringer, which will be denied part or all of the profit on the sales made in the runoff period.

An adjudged infringer will be ordered to destroy infringing material in its possession at the time the injunction becomes effective, or to deliver such material to the patentee for destruction. These ancillary orders, like the injunction itself, are discretionary, and they may occasionally be modified to allow the adjudged infringer

---

[103] Id., p. 176.

[104] And see *Arctic Cat* (FCA 2020, para. 32), holding that the public interest is not to be taken into consideration unless the party seeking the stay can establish irreparable harm to itself, apart from any effect on the public. This decision appears to be an outlier in entirely excluding consideration of the public interest, but it does illustrate the general reluctance of the courts to take the public interest into account.

[105] See *Janssen-Ortho* v. *Novopharm* (FC 2006, para. 133), granting a permanent injunction, but delaying the effect for thirty days, during which time "the Defendant's [*sic*] may continue to sell or otherwise dispose of its [infringing] products already in its possession, custody or control, but only in the normal course of business and provided that all monies received in respect thereof are accounted for and held in a separate trust fund to be paid to the Plaintiffs or as they may direct by December 31, 2006"; see also *Weatherford* (FC 2010, para. 3), setting out the order granting a broad injunction against infringement, "except for delivery of any Infringing Items presently contracted to be delivered within thirty (30) days of this Order but without prejudice to the Plaintiffs' right to damages".

[106] See *AbbVie* v. *Janssen (injunction)* (FC 2014, para. 89–90), noting that neither party had requested an order with a runoff period of this type.

to retain the infringing material until the expiry of the patent, particularly when the remaining term of the patent is short.[107]

The use of a stay to allow the infringer to design around the patent or otherwise mitigate the effect of injunctive relief is notable by its absence in Canadian law. An illustration, in a negative sense, is provided by *Valence* v. *Phostech* (FC 2011). The invention in question related to a process for making lithium mixed metal (LiFePO$_4$) cathodes for lithium ion batteries. It was known that lithium mixed metal was a good cathode material, but it had not been commercially adopted, apparently because of the cost of production.[108] Both the plaintiff, Valence, and the defendant, Phostech, had independently developed new processes for making lithium mixed metal cathodes at about the same time. The validity of Valence's patents at issue was conceded,[109] but infringement was strongly contested and presented a very difficult issue on the facts.[110] The court ultimately held that Valence had established on the balance of probabilities that the Phostech process infringed.[111] While the court did not say so expressly, the factual issue was closely decided, and it would have been reasonable for Phostech to have believed that its process did not infringe. There was no copying or any other form of bad faith on the part of Phostech.[112] The infringing process was being used by defendant Phostech in its existing facility. After it had become aware of the patent, it began constructing a new facility designed to produce the cathodes using a non-infringing process.[113] The court delivered its judgment in early 2011 and at that time construction of the new plant was underway and it was scheduled to be ready in 2012. Phostech asked the court to give it a two-year grace period before giving effect to the injunction, to allow the new plant to be completed.[114] As well as the business disruption to Phostech, employees at the existing plant would presumably have been affected as well. Given independent invention, good faith, high sunk costs and the substantial business disruption to the adjudged infringer, this would appear to be a situation in which a short stay to allow design around might have been appropriate as a matter of policy. Nonetheless, the court refused to grant a stay, saying simply that a permanent

---

[107] See e.g. *Merck* v. *Apotex (lisinopril infringement)* (FC 2006, para. 231), permitting the adjudged infringer to choose between delivering up the infringing material to the patentee for destruction, or retaining until after expiry of the patent, subject to a requirement to keep an account of all such material and money received in respect thereof.

[108] *Valence* v. *Phostech* (FC 2011, para. 24).

[109] Id., para. 180.

[110] The key to the patented process was the use of carbothermal reduction. It was established that the compounds used in Phostech's allegedly infringing process could support carbothermal reduction under the right conditions, but it was difficult to determine whether the conditions inside the closed industrial kiln used by Phostech would actually result in carbothermal reduction: Id., para. 158.

[111] Id., para. 166.

[112] Id., paras. 44 and 237.

[113] Id., para. 3.

[114] Id., para. 239.

injunction should be refused "only in very rare circumstances", and it was not satisfied that the facts warranted an exception.[115]

6. Tailored Injunction

There is one recent example of a tailored injunction, granted in *AbbVie* v. *Janssen (injunction)* (FC 2014).[116] The litigation concerned treatments for psoriasis, which, in its severe form, can be disabling.[117] At the time, there were four biologics[118] available on the market for the treatment of psoriasis, including AbbVie's HUMIRA and Janssen's STELARA. AbbVie's patent at issue was ultimately held to be infringed by Janssen's STELARA, but none of the other products on the market, including AbbVie's own HUMIRA, were covered by the patent.[119] While AbbVie did not practise the patent, by keeping STELARA off the market AbbVie sought to preserve the largest possible "footprint" for HUMIRA in the market for psoriasis treatments.[120] However, the products are not perfect substitutes. STELARA had a different mechanism from the other products on the market, and while many patients would respond to either HUMIRA or STELARA, there were some patients for whom only STELARA was effective.[121]

Thus, a permanent injunction would in principle have allowed AbbVie to prevent the sale of a drug that AbbVie itself did not supply and that, for some patients, was the only effective treatment for a disabling condition. In the circumstances, AbbVie did not even ask for a broad permanent injunction prohibiting sale of STELARA. One might speculate that this is because AbbVie did not want to be responsible for depriving some patients of the only effective treatment for a serious disorder, either for moral reasons, or because of fear of bad publicity. It is also possible that AbbVie anticipated that it would not have been granted a broad injunction. In any event, AbbVie instead sought an injunction with an exception for existing patients and restrictions on new patients, with all the sales permitted

---

[115] Id, para. 240. A stay pending disposition of the appeal was granted, but allowing Phostech to finish the new plant was not a consideration in the decision to grant a stay: *Phostech* v. *Valence (stay)* (FCA 2011)). The appeal decision (*Phostech* v. *Valence* (FCA 2011)), affirming the trial decision, was rendered in August 2011, and so would not have had the practical effect of giving Phostech time to finish the new plant.

[116] The trial had been divided into several parts, and the decision in *AbbVie* v. *Janssen (injunction)* (FC 2014) concerned only injunctive relief. The underlying liability decision, holding the patent to be valid and infringed, was subsequently set aside: *Janssen* v. *AbbVie (liability)* (FCA 2014) rev'g *AbbVie* v. *Janssen* (FC 2013) and setting aside *AbbVie* v. *Janssen (liability)* (FC 2014). The decision on injunctive relief was set aside in consequence.

[117] *AbbVie* v. *Janssen (injunction)* (FC 2014, para. 17).

[118] A "biologic" is a pharmaceutical derived from living organisms or their cells. They are often contrasted with "small molecule" drugs which are normally chemically synthesized. While small molecule drugs made by different manufacturers are normally pharmacologically identical, biologics from different sources often have different properties.

[119] *AbbVie* v. *Janssen (injunction)* (FC 2014, para. 15).

[120] Id., para. 45.

[121] Id., paras. 21–23.

under the exception subject to a continuing royalty.[122] The issue in the decision on injunctive relief was therefore not whether there should be a carve-out, but rather the precise terms of the carve-out.[123]

On its face, this seems like a compelling case in which a carve-out should be granted and, given the court's concern over the details of the carve-out, it seems likely that a request for a broad injunction without a carve-out would have been refused. However, there is an argument to be made to the contrary. In principle, granting AbbVie a complete injunction, prohibiting any sales of STELARA without AbbVie's permission would not necessarily mean that patients who need STELARA would be forced to go without. If a patient is not responding to AbbVie's HUMIRA, and does respond to STELARA, it would be in AbbVie's own interest to allow Janssen to sell the STELARA, subject to a royalty negotiated with AbbVie. The only difference is that AbbVie would decide the royalty instead of the court. On the facts, it seems possible, or even likely, that something like this would have happened.

On this view, the real problem with granting a broad injunction is that AbbVie would determine the terms of access. AbbVie sought to require physicians to formally certify that new patients had a medical need for STELARA that could not be met by HUMIRA before prescribing STELARA. The court refused to impose this requirement.[124] The case against a broad injunction, therefore, is not necessarily that it would result in STELARA being taken off the market, but rather that the court is in a better position than AbbVie to determine the terms of access.

One disadvantage of the carve-out is the need for detailed judicial supervision of the terms of access. The carve-out order did give rise to a subsequent contempt hearing over the precise words that Janssen was permitted to use in its communications with physicians.[125]

D. PROCEDURAL ISSUES

1. *Types of Parties*

To date, the types of plaintiffs and defendants do not appear to have any influence on the grant and tailoring of injunctions. The bulk of decided patent cases in

---

[122] Id., para. 43.
[123] AbbVie did not seek to restrain dissemination of technical information regarding STELARA (Id., para. 68), but it sought to restrain active marketing by sales representatives. The trial judge agreed to this (para. 71). AbbVie also proposed that Janssen be required to approach the formularies with new criteria for listing (para. 73), be ordered to comply only with lawful requests from Health Canada (para. 77), and be ordered to write a letter to physicians stating that STELARA infringes AbbVie's patent (para. 78). The trial judge refused all these requests. He did order a prohibition on Phase IV clinical trials of STELARA in Canada, although this apparently turned, at least in part, on the fact that none were planned (para. 87).
[124] Id., paras. 63 and 66.
[125] *AbbVie v. Janssen (contempt)* (FC 2014), discussed in Section B.3 Enforcement.

Canada involve pharmaceutical companies and, in particular, litigation between branded pharmaceutical companies and generics, but successful patentees in all fields are routinely granted a permanent injunction, and similarly, patentees in all fields are routinely denied interlocutory injunctions.

However, very few decided cases have involved PAEs and there are even fewer, if any, in which a PAE has been successful in establishing infringement.[126] It is therefore premature to conclude that the Canadian courts would routinely grant injunctions to PAEs. Canadian courts would probably apply traditional principles to cases involving a successful PAE, without drawing a formal distinction based on the nature of the patentee.[127] However, it is entirely possible that the courts would find that the circumstances typically attending the assertion of patent rights by a PAE would justify refusing injunctive relief on the basis of traditional principles.[128]

The Canadian *Patent Act* had long granted the government the unrestricted right to use any patented invention, subject only to an obligation to pay reasonable compensation, as determined by the Commissioner of Patents, a civil servant.[129] This provision was invoked by Crown corporations using patented inventions in the ordinary course of their operations.[130] This was changed in 1993 with the advent of the North American Free Trade Agreement Implementation Act.[131] Under current law, Canadian patents are binding on the government, and there is no immunity from injunctive relief.[132] The modified provisions on "Use of Patents by Government" permit the government to apply for what amounts to a compulsory licence; that is, on application by the Crown, the Commissioner of Patents may authorize the use of a patented invention by the government,[133] though only for specific purposes and a limited time,[134] and subject to a requirement to pay "adequate remuneration" as determined by the Commissioner.[135] Further, use by

---

[126] There had been no comprehensive analysis of the decisions according to the nature of the parties. PAEs are reputed to be active litigants, but to date few cases have come to trial. But see *Safe Gaming* (FC 2018) in which the plaintiff PAE was unsuccessful on the merits.

[127] But see *T-Rex Property* (FC 2019), raising the issue of whether a PAE should be entitled to elect between damages and an accounting of profits.

[128] Note that in *Safe Gaming* (FCA 2018) the Federal Court of Appeal granted a motion for security for costs, both at trial and on appeal, against a PAE that sought to appeal a trial decision holding its patents to be invalid and not infringed. The motion was granted on standard principles set out in the relevant *Federal Courts Rules*, but the fact that the PAE did not carry on any business and had no assets of material value did come into play; see Siebrasse 2018.

[129] See *Formea Chemicals* (SCC 1968, p. 763), holding that the Crown, under the relevant provision, "has an unrestricted right to use a patent".

[130] See id., holding that a Crown corporation dealing in synthetic rubber was entitled to the benefit of s. 19 to use a patented invention relating to polymers.

[131] *NAFTA Implementation Act*, s. 190, providing that the *Patent Act* is binding on the Crown, and s. 191 implementing the new provisions.

[132] *Patent Act*, s. 2.1.

[133] Id., s. 19–19.1.

[134] Id., s. 19(4).

[135] Id., s. 19(2).

the Crown may only be authorized if the Crown establishes that it has made efforts to obtain a licence from the patentee on reasonable commercial terms and those efforts to obtain a licence were unsuccessful within a reasonable period,[136] although those conditions do not apply in the case of a national emergency.[137] To my knowledge this modern provision has not been used, presumably because the conditions are such that it is normally simpler to obtain a commercial licence.

2. *Effect of Validity*

Ex ante uncertainty as to patent validity has no influence on the tailoring of injunctions. If the patent is found to be valid and infringed, injunctive relief is routinely granted. That the infringer might reasonably have believed the patent to be invalid or not infringed has not, to date, factored into a decision to refuse or tailor injunctive relief.[138]

3. *Public Interest*

The public interest may in principle be taken into account, but it is rarely considered in practice.[139]

4. *Follow-on Innovation*

The courts do not explicitly take into account follow-on innovation. As discussed earlier, permanent injunctions are routinely granted. Whether this implicitly takes account of follow-on innovation depends on one's view of the implications of blocking patents for follow-on innovation. On one view, refusing injunctions is good for follow-on innovation because follow-on innovators will then be able to use the invention without paying any licence fee. On the other hand, an injunction that encompasses follow-on innovation is arguably good for that innovation because it encourages pioneer invention and follow-on innovation cannot occur without the original pioneer invention. To optimally encourage invention, the scope of protection should be commensurate with the value of the invention. In many cases, a substantial part of the value of the pioneer invention is embodied in the follow-on innovation which the pioneer invention enables. Presumably there is some balance to be struck between these effects, but it is not clear that the courts are in a good position to make such an assessment.

---

[136] Id, s. 19.1(1).
[137] Id, s .19.1(2).
[138] See *Valence* v. *Phostech* (FC 2011), discussed in Section C.5 Stays Other Than Pending Appeal.
[139] See the discussion of *Unilever* (FCTD 1993) aff'd *Unilever* (FCA 1995) in Section C.2 Refusing Injunctive Relief; *Valence* v. *Phostech* (FC 2011), discussed above Section C.5 Stays Other Than Pending Appeal; and generally Section C.4 Stay Pending Appeal.

E. CONCLUSION

In summary, preliminary injunctions as such are never granted in patent cases in Canadian law, but the statutory stay under the patent linkage system has the same effect in cases involving patented pharmaceuticals. Permanent injunctions are routinely granted to a prevailing patentee as a remedy for patent infringement, but it is clear that grant of an injunction is discretionary. In some circumstances a permanent injunction may be modified, stayed or, rarely, even refused entirely, but on the whole Canadian courts are disinclined to make such adjustments. *Valence* v. *Phostech* in a noteworthy example where a stay to allow design around was summarily refused, even though the facts appeared to provide a good prima facie case for such a stay. The sole case to deny a permanent injunction to a successful patentee has not been influential. With that said, the Canadian courts have seen very little litigation involving patent assertion entities, and it remains an open question as to what course the Canadian courts will take when faced with the prospect of granting injunctive relief to a patent assertion entity in circumstances where the injunction would allow the patent assertion entity to hold up a practicing entity and extract an excessive royalty.

REFERENCES

Cases

Canada

Abbvie Corp v. *Janssen Inc.*, 2014 FC 863 [*AbbVie* v. *Janssen (contempt)* (FC 2014)]

Apotex Inc v. *ADIR*, 2017 FCA 23 [*Apotex* v. *ADIR* (FCA 2017)]

Apotex Inc. v. *Merck & Co.*, (1996), 66 CPR(3d) 167 (FCA) [*Apotex* v. *Merck (enalapril No. 2)* (FCA 1996)]

Apotex Inc v. *Merck & Co.*, 2006 FCA 198 [*Apotex* v. *Merck (lisinopril stay)* (FCA 2006)]

Apotex Inc v. *Wellcome Foundation Ltd* (1998), 81 CPR(3d) 191 (FCTD) [*Apotex* v. *Wellcome (stay)* (FCTD 1998)] expedited *Apotex Inc.* v. *Wellcome Foundation Ltd* (1998), 81 CPR (3d) 443, 228 NR 355 (FCA) [*Apotex* v. *Wellcome (expedite)* (FCA 1998)] rev'd *Apotex Inc.* v. *Wellcome Foundation Ltd* (1998), 82 CPR(3d) 429 (FCA) [*Apotex* v. *Wellcome (stay)* (FCA 1998)]

Arctic Cat Inc. v. *Bombardier Recreational Products Inc.*, 2020 FCA 116 [*Arctic Cat* (FCA 2020)]

AstraZeneca Canada Inc. v. *Canada (Minister of Health)*, 2005 FCA 208 [*AstraZeneca* (FCA 2005)]

Baker Petrolite Corp. v. *Canwell Enviro-Industries Ltd*, 2001 FCA 288 [*Baker Petrolite* (FCA 2001)]

Baxter Travenol Laboratories of Canada Ltd v. *Cutter (Canada) Ltd*, [1987] 2 FC 557, 14 CPR (3d) 449 (FCA) [*Baxter Travenol* (FCA 1987) cited to CPR] var'g *Baxter Travenol Laboratories of Canada Ltd* v. *Cutter (Canada) Ltd*, [1986] 1 FC 497, 1 CPR(3d) 433 (FCTD) [*Baxter Travenol* (FCTD 1986) cited to CPR]

Baxter Travenol Laboratories of Canada Ltd v. *Cutter (Canada) Ltd*, [1983] 2 SCR 388 [*Baxter Travenol* (SCC 1983)]

Bayer Inc. v. *Apotex Inc.*, 2016 FC 1013 [*Bayer* (FC 2016)]

Bombardier Recreational Products Inc. v. *Arctic Cat Inc.* 2020 FC 691 [*Bombardier* (FC 2020)]

Bombardier Recreational Products Inc. v. *Arctic Cat Inc,* 2020 FC 946 [*Bombardier (motion)* (FC 2020)]

Bristol-Myers Squibb Co. v. *Canada (Attorney General),* 2002 FCT 1319 [*Bristol-Myers* v. *Canada* (FCTD 2002)]

College of Optometrists (Ontario) v. *SHS Optical Ltd,* 2008 ONCA 685 [*College of Optometrists* (Ont. CA 2008)]

Corning Glass Works v. *Canada Wire & Cable Ltd* (1984), 1 CPR(3d) 374 (FCTD) [*Corning Glass* (FCTD 1984)]

Diversified Products Corp. v. *Tye-Sil Corp.,* (1988), 25 CPR(3d) 347 (FCTD) [*Diversified Products* (FCTD 1988)]

Eurocopter v. *Bell Helicopter Textron Canada Ltee,* 2012 FC 113 [*Eurocopter* (FC 2012)]

Evolution Technologies Inc. v. *Human Care Canada Inc.,* 2019 FCA 11 [*Evolution Tech* (FCA 2019)]

Fettes v. *Culligan Canada Ltd,* 2010 SKCA 151 [*Fettes* (Sask CA 2010)]

Formea Chemicals Ltd v. *Polymer Corp. Ltd,* [1968] SCR 754 [*Formea Chemicals* (SCC 1968)]

Human Care Canada Inc. v. *Evolution Technologies Inc.,* 2018 FC 1302 [*Human Care* (FC 2018)]

Janssen Inc. v. *Abbvie Corp,* 2014 FCA 176 [*Janssen* v. *AbbVie (stay)* (FCA 2014)]

Janssen Inc. v. *AbbVie Corp,* 2014 FCA 242 [*Janssen* v. *AbbVie (liability)* (FCA 2014)] rev'g *AbbVie Corp.* v. *Janssen Inc.,* 2013 FC 1148 [*AbbVie* v. *Janssen* (FC 2013)] and setting aside *AbbVie Corp* v. *Janssen Inc.,* 2014 FC 55 [*AbbVie* v. *Janssen (liability)* (FC 2014)]

Janssen Inc. v. *Abbvie Corp,* 2014 FCA 241 [*Janssen* v. *AbbVie (injunction)* (FCA 2014)] setting aside *Abbvie Corp.* v. *Janssen Inc.,* 2014 FC 489 [*AbbVie* v. *Janssen (injunction)* (FC 2014)]

Janssen-Ortho Inc. v. *Novopharm Ltd,* 2006 FC 1234 [*Janssen-Ortho* v. *Novopharm* (FC 2006)]

Jay-Lor International Inc. v. *Penta Farm Systems Ltd,* 2007 FC 358 [*Jay-Lor* (FC 2007)]

Laboratoires Servier v. *Apotex Inc.,* 2008 FC 825 [*Laboratoires Servier* (FC 2008)]

Lubrizol Corp. v. *Imperial Oil Ltd* (1992), 45 CPR(3d) 449 (FCA) [*Lubrizol* (FCA 1992)]

Manitoba (AG) v. *Metropolitan Stores Ltd,* [1987] 1 SCR 110 [*Metropolitan Stores* (SCC 1987)]

Marketing International Ltd v. *SC Johnson & Son Ltd,* [1977] 2 FC 618, 35 CPR(2d) 226 (FCA) [*Marketing International* (FCA 1977) cited to CPR]

Merck & Co. v. *Apotex Inc.* (1995), 60 CPR(3d) 31, 90 FTR 1 (FCTD) [*Merck* v. *Apotex (enalapril No. 1)* (FCTD 1995)]

Merck & Co. v. *Apotex Inc.* (1998), 78 CPR(3d) 376 (FCTD) [*Merck* v. *Apotex (enalapril No. 3)* (FCTD 1998)] aff'd *Merck & Co.* v. *Apotex Inc.* (1999), 5 CPR(4th) 363 (FCA) [*Merck* v. *Apotex (enalapril No. 4)* (FCA 1999)]

Merck & Co. v. *Apotex Inc.* (2000), 5 CPR(4th) 1 (FCTD) [*Merck* v. *Apotex (enalapril No. 5)* (FCTD 2000)] var'd *Merck & Co.* v. *Apotex Inc.,* 2003 FCA 234 [*Merck* v. *Apotex (enalapril No. 6)* (FCA 2003)]

Merck & Co. v. *Apotex Inc.,* 2006 FC 524 [*Merck* v. *Apotex (lisinopril infringement)* (FC 2006)] var'd *Merck & Co.* v. *Apotex Inc.,* 2006 FCA 323 [*Merck* v. *Apotex (lisinopril infringement)* (FCA 2006)]

Merck & Co. v. *Canada (Attorney General)* (1999), 4 CPR(4th) 91 (FCTD) [*Merck* v. *Canada* (FCTD 1999)]

Monsanto Canada Inc. v. *Schmeiser,* 2004 SCC 34 [*Monsanto* v. *Schmeiser* (SCC 2004)]

Novopharm Ltd v. *Janssen-Ortho Inc.*, 2006 FCA 406 [*Novopharm* v. *Janssen-Ortho* (FCA 2006)]

Phostech Lithium Inc. v. *Valence Technology Inc.*, 2011 FCA 107 [*Phostech* v. *Valence (stay)* (FCA 2011)]

Pro Arts v. *Campus Crafts* (1980), 28 OR (2d) 422, 50 CPR(2d) 230 (SC (HCJ)) [*Pro Arts* (Ont SC 1980) cited to OR]

Procter & Gamble Co. v. *Bristol-Myers Canada Ltd* (1978), 39 CPR(2d) 145 (FCTD) [*Procter & Gamble* v. *Bristol-Myers* (FCTD 1978)] aff'd 42 CPR(2d) 33 (FCA)

Procter & Gamble Co. v. *Bristol-Meyers Canada Ltd*, (1978), 39 CPR(2d) 171 (FCA) [*Procter & Gamble (stay)* (FCA 1978)]

RJR-MacDonald Inc. v. *Canada (Attorney General)*, [1994] 1 SCR 311 [*RJR-MacDonald* (SCC 1994)]

Safe Gaming System Inc. v. *Atlantic Lottery Corp.*, 2018 FC 542 [*Safe Gaming* (FC 2018)]

Safe Gaming System Inc. v. *Atlantic Lottery Corp.*, 2018 FCA 180 [*Safe Gaming* (FCA 2018)]

Teva Canada Ltd v. *Novartis AG*, 2013 FC 141 [*Teva* v. *Novartis* (FC 2013)]

T-Rex Property AB v. *Pattison Outdoor Advertising Limited Partnership*, 2019 FC 1004 [*T-Rex Property* (FC 2019)]

Trojan Technologies Inc. v. *Suntec Environmental Inc.*, 2003 FCA 309 [*Trojan* (FCA 2003)]

Unilever PLC v. *Procter & Gamble Inc.* (1993), 47 CPR(3d) 479 (FCTD) [*Unilever* (FCTD 1993)] aff'd *Unilever PLC* v. *Procter & Gamble Inc.*, (1995), 61 CPR(3d) 499 (FCA) [*Unilever* (FCA 1995)]

Uponor AB v. *Heatlink Group Inc.*, 2016 FC 320 [*Uponor* (FC 2016)]

Uview Ultraviolet Systems Inc. v. *Brasscorp Ltd*, 2009 FC 58 [*Uview* (FC 2009)]

Valence Technology Inc. v. *Phostech Lithium Inc.*, 2011 FC 174 [*Valence* v. *Phostech* (FC 2011)] aff'd *Phostech Lithium Inc.* v. *Valence Technology Inc.*, 2011 FCA 237 [*Phostech* v. *Valence* (FCA 2011)]

Weatherford Canada Ltd v. *Corlac Inc.*, 2010 FC 667 [*Weatherford* (FC 2010)]

Other Jurisdictions

American Cyanamid Co. v. *Ethicon Ltd*, [1975] AC 396 (HL) [*American Cyanamid* (HL 1975)]

eBay Inc. v. *MercExchange, LLC*, 547 US 388 (2006) [*eBay* v. *MercExchange* (US 2003)]

Lear Inc. v. *Adkins*, 395 US 653 (1969) [*Lear* v. *Adkins* (US 1969)]

Read Corp. v. *Portec Inc.*, 970 F2d 816 (Fed Cir 1992) [*Read* v. *Portec*, (Fed Cir 1992)]

Regulatory and Legislative Materials

Federal Courts Act, RSC 1985, c F-7 [*Federal Courts Act*]

Federal Courts Rules, SOR/98-106 [*Federal Court Rules*]

Food and Drugs Act, RSC 1985, c F-27

Food and Drug Regulations, CRC c 870

Patent Act, RSC 1985, c P-4 [*Patent Act*]

Patented Medicines (Notice of Compliance) Regulations, SOR/93-133 [*PM (NOC) Regulations*]

North American Free Trade Agreement Implementation Act, SC 1993, c 44 [*NAFTA Implementation Act*]

Books, Articles and Online Materials

Chien, Colleen V. et al., 2019, "Ch 3 Enhanced Damages, Litigation Cost Recovery, and Interest," in C. Bradford Biddle, Jorge L. Contreras, Brian J. Love & Norman V. Siebrasse eds., *Patent Remedies and Complex Products: Towards a Global Consensus* (Cambridge University Press)

Golden, John M., 2012, "Injunctions as More (or Less) than 'Off Switches': Patent-Infringement Injunctions' Scope," *Texas Law Review* 90(6): 1399–1472

Seaman, Christopher B. et al., 2019, "Ch 2 Lost Profits and Disgorgement", in C. Bradford Biddle, Jorge L. Contreras, Brian J. Love & Norman V. Siebrasse eds., *Patent Remedies and Complex Products: Towards a Global Consensus* (Cambridge University Press)

Sharpe, Robert, 2017, *Injunctions and Specific Performance* (5th ed) (Thomson Reuters)

Siebrasse, Norman V., 2009, "Interlocutory Injunctions and Irreparable Harm in the Federal Courts," *Canadian Bar Review* 88(3): 515–43

2018, "Security for Costs against Foreign Patent Assertion Entity," *Sufficient Description blog*, 22 October 2018. www.sufficientdescription.com/2018/10/security-for-costs-against-foreign.html

6

Finland

Marcus Norrgård

A. PATENT LITIGATION IN FINLAND: AN OVERVIEW

1. *Court System*

On 1 September 2013 the jurisdiction in intellectual property matters in Finland was reformed. The Market Court, which was created in 2002 for consumer protection and competition law cases, was now also given exclusive jurisdiction in patent, trademark and design registration appeals, and intellectual property disputes (infringement, invalidity etc.).[1] Previously, the District Court of Helsinki had exclusive jurisdiction in patent disputes and the Finnish Patent Office dealt not only with registration matters but also with registration appeals.

The Market Court is a specialized court with legally qualified judges and, in patent cases, technically qualified judges who take part in the proceedings with voting rights equal to those of legally qualified judges.[2] The judgments of the Market Court can only be appealed to the Supreme Court if leave to appeal is granted.[3] Before the reform, judgments could always be appealed from the District Court to the Helsinki Court of Appeals, which in practice prolonged the overall duration of the proceedings by a further 1–2 years. The total duration of proceedings could thus be several (rough estimate: 3–5) years.

---

[1] Ch. 1 of the Market Court Proceedings Act (100/2013).

[2] Ch. 1, section 2 of the Market Court Proceedings Act. The technically qualified judges may either be full-time technical judges called "Market Court Engineers" or part-time "Expert Members". See Ch. 5 of the Courts Act.

[3] Ch. 7, section 4(1) of the Market Court Proceedings Act. In total, the number of applications for leave to appeal per year is about 2,500. A leave to appeal is granted in less than 10% of all civil and criminal cases. See https://korkeinoikeus.fi/fi/index/muutoksenhakijalle/muutoksenha kemuksenlaatiminen/valituslupahakemusjavalitus.html.

A reform was warranted for a number of reasons. It was felt that the quality of the judgments needed to be higher and the proceedings faster.[4] Furthermore, by consolidating all IP-related cases to one court, fragmentation could be avoided. It is quite clear that these goals have been reached. The quality of judgments is high and fragmentation is avoided. The judges are very knowledgeable and thorough. Their decisions seem to be guided only by legal concerns. Non-legal concerns, have not, at least to my knowledge, played any part in the decision-making of the court.

The quality of the judgments is also in part contingent upon how well the cases are argued. Generally, I would say that the patent bar in Finland is quite know-ledgeable. Half a dozen law firms specialize in patent litigation, and they have partners specializing in intellectual property (IP) law. Of these law firms, only one is a large multinational law firm. The others are large Finnish law firms offering services on all aspects of law relating to companies. There are also a couple of small boutique-type law firms doing patent litigation. In addition, patent attorneys' firms take on patent litigation. In some rare cases, even non-specialist lawyers have argued patent cases.

During the three-year period 2016–2018, the Market Court had on average 235 new IP cases.[5] During that same period, the average number of new patent disputes was eleven per year. Patent litigation is thus not especially common, but patent cases are generally "big" and complex cases that require expertise from different fields (technology, law etc.).[6] The average duration of patent litigation was 14.1 months during 2016–2019; the shortest was 9.6 months (2016) and the longest was 23.1 months (2019).[7]

2. *Types of Actions*

There are different types of patent actions available in Finland. In infringement actions the patent holder typically requests the court to grant a final injunction (section 57(1) of the Patents Act), damages for the economic loss due to an infringement (section 58) and/or destruction of infringing goods (section 59).[8]

---

[4] See Government Bill no. 124/2012, p. 21.

[5] For Market Court statistics, see Vuositilastot.

[6] It is quite common that the legal fees for one party in patent litigation is several hundred thousand euros. In *Neste v. UPM* (Market Court decision MAO:866/15 *Neste v. UPM*), the plaintiff's costs were almost 900,000 euros and the defendant's were as high as 1.4 million euros. The Market Court found for the defendant and ordered the claimant to pay almost 1 million euros in legal fees (including expert's fees).

[7] This figure includes all patent cases (infringement and invalidity actions), regardless of whether they ended with a judgment or were settled. The duration is shorter in years when a larger part of the cases ended through settlement. Type of litigation (invalidity, limitation of patent claims, infringement) may also have impacted the duration. The author wishes to thank Chief Judge Jussi Karttunen at the Market Court for the statistics.

[8] Injunctions, damages and destruction are provided for in the Enforcement Directive. Finland opted for a minimum implementation making only the necessary changes to its legislation,

Sometimes the patent holder requests a positive declaratory judgment (section 63 of the Patents Act), in which the patent holder asks the court to find that the defendant's conduct infringes the patent. It is also, in principle, possible to request the court to order the infringer to pay for the costs of publishing the court decision (section 60a of the Patents Act[9]), but to my knowledge this provision has never been used in a patent case.

In addition, it is possible to apply for final and preliminary injunctions against intermediaries in the context of online infringements of IP rights. According to section 57b of the Patents Act, the court may, when hearing an action for a final injunction, at the right holder's request, prohibit "the keeper of a transmitter, server or other similar device or other service provider acting as an intermediary", under penalty of a fine, from continuing the use alleged to infringe the IP right unless it can be considered disproportionate in view of the rights of the alleged infringer or of the rights of the intermediary or right holder. The provision has never, to my knowledge, been used in a patent case.

Patent infringement may also lead to criminal liability (chapter 49, section 2 of the Criminal Code and section 57(2) of the Patents Act). To my knowledge, the criminal law route is not used in patent infringement cases.

Since patent litigation from start to enforceable judgment takes time, preliminary injunctions are available before and during the trial. Typically, the patent holder applies for a preliminary injunction according to chapter 7, section 3 of the Procedural Code already before instituting the infringement action proper (i.e. before making a request for final injunction, damages and/or destruction).

Although, typically, only the patent holder is in a position to institute infringement actions, an alleged infringer may file for a negative declaratory judgment, in which the claimant/alleged infringer asks the court to declare that the activities of the claimant do *not* infringe the patent-in-suit (section 63(2) of the Patents Act). Anecdotally, negative declaratory actions seem to be rather common in pharmaceutical patent litigation.[10]

The main type of action the alleged infringer can resort to in patent litigation is the invalidity action (section 52 of the Patents Act), in which the claimant requests the Market Court to find that the patent-in-suit is invalid, for instance due to lacking novelty, or inventiveness. It is not possible to question the validity of the patent in the infringement action simply by raising the issue in defence. Rather, for the court to take into account the invalidity of the patent, an invalidity action must be filed.

---

which meant that no changes were made to the provisions on injunctions, damages and destruction. See Government Bill 26/2006.

9   This provision implements Article 15 of the Enforcement Directive 2004/48/EC.

10   See, for example, Supreme Court decision KKO:2015:51, which is a case in point. The claimant had instituted a negative declaratory action, in which it asked the court to find that its generic pharmaceutical product (montelukast) did not infringe M's patent. M had, in turn, sued K for infringement of its patent.

According to chapter 4, section 20(1) of the Market Court Proceedings Act, if a defence of invalidity is raised in an infringement action, the court must set a time limit within which the defendant has to institute an invalidity action. Otherwise the invalidity defence is not taken into account. The Market Court has exclusive jurisdiction in both the infringement action and the invalidity action (sections 52 and 65 of the Patents Act) and both actions are as a rule joined in the same trial (chapter 4, section 20(2) of the Market Court Proceedings Act). Joining of the cases means in practice that the issues of validity and infringement are argued in the same trial and that the Market Court gives its judgment on both validity and infringement at the same time.[11] Exceptionally, the court may decide that the infringement action is to be postponed until the invalidity action has been decided.

The alleged infringer may also request a compulsory licence in accordance with sections 45–48 of the Patents Act. Other types of patent litigation include ownership disputes and contract disputes (licences, patent assignments).[12]

B. THE SYSTEM OF INJUNCTIONS IN FINLAND

Injunctions in intellectual property infringement cases in Finland come in two forms: final and preliminary. The difference between the two types of injunctions is that a final injunction may be granted only after a full trial, whereas a preliminary injunction may be ordered in summary proceedings before or during the trial or even in the judgment until the matter is finally settled on appeal.[13] Generally, however, the wording and scope of the injunction is the same: both types of injunctions prohibit the infringer, or alleged infringer in the case of preliminary injunctions, from continuing certain activities that infringe (or are likely to infringe) the rights of the plaintiff/applicant.

---

[11] In invalidity actions, the patent holder may request the Market Court to limit the patent-in-suit. If the patent holder makes such a request and presents amended patent claims, the question of limitation must be decided before the invalidity action can proceed (section 52(2) of the Patents Act). If the Market Court accepts the limitation, the invalidity action continues on the basis of the amended patent claims. It is also possible to separately limit the patent claims, but such a request is made to the Patent Office, not to the Market Court (section 53a of the Patents Act).

[12] In contract cases the District Court (usually at the defendant's domicile) has jurisdiction (Ch. 10, sections 1–2 of the Procedural Code). A contract law claim may, however, be joined with a claim falling within the exclusive jurisdiction of the Market Court, if it is based on "essentially the same grounds" as the claim falling within the exclusive jurisdiction (Ch. 1, section 5(1) of the Market Court Proceedings Act). This might be the case, for example, in a breach of a licensing contract dispute where the licensor/patent holder wishes to pursue the matter as both infringement and breach of contract.

[13] Preliminary injunctions may also be granted *ex parte* "if the purpose of the precautionary measure can otherwise be compromised". See Ch. 7, section 5(2). Ex parte decisions are quite uncommon in patent cases, and will not be dealt with in this chapter.

The legal basis for *final injunctions* can be found in section 57(1) of the Patents Act, which provides that if someone infringes the exclusive right of the patent holder, the court may forbid that person from continuing or repeating the act. The text of the provision leaves many questions open. The fact that the court "may" enjoin the defendant could be construed as meaning that the court has a wide margin of discretion. In reality, however, an ongoing infringement combined with a risk of continued infringement has sufficed for a final injunction.[14]

Since final injunctions require a full trial, which necessarily takes time (usually 1–2 years), preliminary injunctions, which only require summary proceedings (with a duration of some months[15]), are often the more effective remedy of the two. It is quite common that patent litigation starts with an application for a preliminary injunction; if it is granted, main proceedings must be instituted within a month from the decision to grant the preliminary injunction.[16] It is also possible, although not as common, to include a request for a preliminary injunction in the statement of claim in the main proceedings.

Preliminary injunctions in patent law find their legal basis in chapter 7, section 3 of the Procedural Code. This very general provision provides as follows:

> If the applicant can demonstrate that it is probable that he or she has a right other than one referred to in section 1 or 2 that is enforceable against the opposing party by a decision referred to in Chapter 2, section 2 of the Enforcement Code, and that there is a danger that the opposing party by deed, action or negligence or in some other manner hinders or undermines the realization of the right of the applicant or decreases essentially its value or significance, the court may:
> (1) prohibit the deed or action of the opposing party, under threat of a fine;
> (2) order the opposing party to do something, under threat of a fine;
> (3) empower the applicant to do something or to have something done;
> (4) order that property of the opposing party be placed under the administration and care of a trustee; or
> (5) order other measures necessary for securing the right of the applicant to be undertaken.

---

[14] See Supreme Court decision KKO:2003:127, where it was stated that a denial of an injunction, although the court has found that there is an infringement, is mainly possible when there is no risk of continued infringement. This brief statement means, first, that the main reason for a denial of an injunction is a lack of continued infringement and, second, that there might be other, more uncommon, reasons for denying an injunction. Neither the Supreme Court nor the Market Court has elaborated on what those other reasons might be.

[15] See, for example, Market Court decision MAO:111/19 *F. Hoffman-La Roche AG, Roche Oy and Genentech Inc.* v. *MSD Finland Oy*, in which the applicant had applied for a preliminary injunction on the basis of a pharmaceutical patent, the validity of which the defendant disputed. There was conflicting evidence on the question of validity and infringement. Still, the decision was given in three months from the date of the application.

[16] Chapter 7, section 6 of the Procedural Code.

When deciding on the issue of a prohibition or an order referred to in subsection 1, the court shall see to it that the opposing party does not suffer undue inconvenience in comparison with the benefit to be secured.

A prerequisite for the entry into force of the prohibition or order referred to above in subsection 1 is that the applicant applies for enforcement of a precautionary measure as provided in Chapter 8 of the Enforcement Code.

In essence, the applicant must demonstrate (a) that it is "probable"[17] that there is an enforceable legal right against the defendant (that does not fall under section 1 ("debt") or section 2 ("better right" to some property[18]), (b) that there is a danger that the defendant undermines the exploitation of the right and (c) that the opposing party does not suffer undue inconvenience. Translated into an intellectual property law context, this provision requires that (a) there is a likelihood of an ongoing or threatened infringement of the applicant's exclusive right, (b) there is a risk of continued infringement and (c) the opposing party does not suffer "undue inconvenience".

In preliminary injunction matters, a finding of a likelihood of infringement requires (i) that the patent is valid,[19] (ii) that the court finds there is enough evidence that the technical solution used by the defendant falls within the scope of protection of the patent (section 39 of the Patents Act, Article 69 of the European Patent Convention), (iii) that an infringing act (making, offering, placing on the market, using etc. as specified especially in section 3 of the Finnish Patent Act) has taken place, and (iv) that there are no exceptions allowing the otherwise infringing act.

The Supreme Court has stated that the second requirement – the risk of continued infringement – is at hand if the risk "is not quite improbable".[20] This is a very low standard of proof, and the court generally finds that there is a risk of continued infringement if the infringement is ongoing. The ongoing infringement creates a presumption of continued infringement.[21]

The "undue inconvenience" requirement looks at the consequences of the decision. The Market Court has, following suggestions in legal scholarship,[22] taken the view that both granting and denying a preliminary injunction may have

---

[17] I use "probable", "likely" and "likelihood" interchangeably in this chapter.

[18] "Better right" is a property law notion that comes into play, for example, in a situation where a person does not voluntarily give (back) certain property although the applicant has a stronger legal position. This might be the case, say, if a lessee refuses to return leased goods to the lessor after expiration of the lease period, or if a pledgee does not return a security after the legal basis for the pledge no longer exists.

[19] As discussed below in Section D.6, a patent has traditionally enjoyed a strong presumption of validity. In light of Supreme Court decision KKO:2019:34, the presumption seems to have been weakened, at least to some degree.

[20] Supreme Court decisions KKO:1994:132 and KKO:1994:133.

[21] MAO:457/18 *AstraZeneca* v. *Sandoz*, which was a patent case where Sandoz's generic medicine already was on the Finnish market.

[22] Norrgård 2002.

consequences: if the injunction is granted, the defendant may suffer "inconvenience" and if the injunction is denied, the applicant may suffer. It is then for the Market Court to compare these inconveniences and decide whether the inconvenience to the defendant is "undue". A case in point is MAO:457/18 *AstraZeneca* v. *Sandoz*, where the Market Court stated that, if the preliminary injunction were granted, the defendant would suffer inconvenience in the form of economic loss due to not being able to sell the allegedly infringing product. If the preliminary injunction were refused, the allegedly infringing product could be freely sold, which would decrease the sales of the applicant's product. Further, due to generic substitution, the applicant would be forced to lower the price of its product in order not to lose further market share.[23] Further, the relative importance of the product to the applicant was stressed. Taking into account the inconvenience to both the applicant and the defendant, the Market Court found that the inconvenience to the defendant was not "undue" and granted the preliminary injunction.

If these substantive requirements are met, the court may make an order that in intellectual property law usually is an injunction to stop the infringing activities. It is possible for the court to order a seizure of the infringing products, but this is uncommon.

After the preliminary injunction has been granted, the enforcement of the injunction requires that the applicant post a security for possible loss the defendant may incur if it later turns out the preliminary injunction should not have been issued (chapter 8, section 2(1) of the Enforcement Code).

Final injunctions and preliminary injunctions are separate remedies with different requirements with the main difference being the "undue inconvenience" requirement for preliminary injunctions. Both types of injunctions require a showing of an infringement (or threat of infringement) and a risk of continued infringement. The difference is that in preliminary injunction proceedings a "likelihood" of infringement suffices, whereas "full proof" is required for a final injunction.[24] The difference in requirements stems from the fact that preliminary injunctions are meant to be temporary – in force only before and during the trial until the final judgment – whereas final injunction are, as the name indicates, final.

In principle, the system of prohibitory injunctions in patent law is thus rather straightforward. A patent holder who wishes to put a stop to an infringement applies

---

[23] Generic substitution means that a medicinal product prescribed by a doctor is replaced with the cheapest suitable generic medicine (or with a product that is no more than 0.50 euros more expensive than the cheapest). See section 57b of the Medicines Act (395/1987).

[24] In light of Market Court case law, "likelihood" or "probable" stands for "more likely than not", i.e. that infringement is more likely than non-infringement. See, for example, Market Court decision MAO:16/18 *Merck Sharp & Dohme B.V. and MSD Finland Oy* v. *Exeltis Healthcare S.L. and Exeltis Sverige AB*, where the Market Court did not grant a preliminary injunction. The Market Court found that it was (due to the summary nature of the proceedings) impossible to say whether infringement was more likely than non-infringement.

for a preliminary injunction on the basis of chapter 7, section 3 and continues within a month with a request for a final injunction.

In the 1990s it was exceedingly difficult to obtain a preliminary injunction in patent cases.[25] The infringement had to be very clear, which in practice meant that preliminary injunctions were not granted. Since patent holders knew this, they very seldomly even applied for them. This started changing in the early 2000s. Finally, in HelHO 16.2.2006 no. 421 *Pfizer* v. *Ranbaxy*, the Helsinki Court of Appeals created the more balanced formula for preliminary injunctions requiring, among other things, that "likelihood" is to be interpreted as "more likely than not" (instead of "clear showing" or a similar higher standard of proof). Thus, if the patent holder is able to show that the infringement is "more likely than not", the first requirement – likelihood of infringement – is met. This formula is still applied today (now at the Market Court). This does not, however, mean that obtaining a preliminary injunction is easy. Often the technical issues are complex and it is difficult for the court to have a view on the likelihood of infringement.[26] It is particularly difficult in cases of equivalent infringement.

C. THE PRIVATE AND PUBLIC INTEREST

1. *Proportionality*

As noted, proportionality and balancing of interests has not been discussed in the context of *final injunctions*. The role of proportionality in final injunctions has only been discussed in the context of section 57b of the Patents Act. It provides for an injunction against internet intermediaries as required by Article 11, third sentence, of the Enforcement Directive. The provision has not yet been applied. However, section 60c of the Copyright Act provides for a rather frequently used identical injunction in copyright infringement cases. According to both provision, the court may at the patent holder's request, when hearing an injunction action against an infringer, prohibit a service provider that is acting as an intermediary, under penalty of a fine, from continuing the use alleged to infringe the patent (or copyright) unless the cessation of that use can be considered disproportionate in view of the rights of the alleged infringer of the patent or the rights of the intermediary or patent holder.

Further the first sentence of subsection 4 requires that an "injunction issued under this section must not endanger the right of a third party to send and receive messages". Thus, when discussing whether to issue an injunction against an

[25] Norrgård 2002.
[26] See, for example, MAO:111/19 *F. Hoffman-La Roche AG, Roche Oy and Genentech Inc.* v. *MSD Finland Oy*, where the court stated that – due to the summary nature of preliminary injunction proceedings and conflicting expert evidence – it was impossible to say whether it was more likely than not that MSD Finland's pharmaceutical product Ontruzant® infringed the European patent FI/EP 1 308 455.

intermediary, not only the interests of the rights holder, infringer and intermediary are to be taken into account, but also third-party interests, as far as they relate to the right of the third party to send and receive messages. Thus, the injunction against intermediaries explicitly acknowledges private interests of the parties, but also of third parties and fundamental rights (since the right to send and receive messages is a matter of freedom of speech as guaranteed in section 12 of the Constitution of Finland).[27]

Whether there is a spillover effect from the provision on intermediary injunctions to the regular injunction provision can be debated. The provisions on intermediary liability were drafted in a highly politicized environment in copyright law with different interest groupings lobbying for and against the provisions. Personally I am hesitant to draw analogies from the provision to the "normal" injunction provision since the context of intermediary liability is a very particular one. What is noteworthy, however, is that the legislature has, without any controversy, found that third-party interests and fundamental rights may have to be taken into account in injunction matters. Thus, since the "normal" injunction provision gives the court discretion ("may") to grant an injunction, there is nothing stopping the court from taking into account third-party interests and fundamental rights. However, to my knowledge no case law exists.

Proportionality has a prominent role in *preliminary injunctions* as chapter 7, section 3 of the Procedural Code requires that a preliminary injunction may not unduly inconvenience the defendant. A natural starting point for assessing harm is to look at the relative *economic consequences*, on the one hand, to the defendant if an injunction is issued and, on the other hand, to the applicant, if the injunction is denied.[28] Taking into account the "relative" consequences means that it is not the absolute monetary value that is of interest, but the weight of the consequences to the party at hand.

A fairly standard way of balancing the economic interests of the parties can be found in the preliminary injunction decision MAO:457/18 *AstraZeneca* v. *Sandoz* handed down by the Market Court on 19 September 2018. The injunction was granted and the balancing of interests was conducted as follows:[29]

> According to Chapter 7, Section 3(2) of the Procedural Code, the court shall also see to it that the opposing party does not suffer undue inconvenience in comparison with the benefit to be secured.
>
> In light of the evidence presented, the opposing party's generic medicinal product is already on the market in Finland. In light of the evidence presented, four pieces of the product were sold in July 2018.

---

[27] See also the Government Bill HE 26/2006, 26.
[28] Norrgård 2002, 286.
[29] My translation.

The Market Court notes that, as a starting point, the harm the opposing party may suffer from an injunction is the economic damage arising from lost revenue when the opposing party is unable to market and sell its own generic medicinal product.

The applicants have purported that selling the opposing party's generic product decreases the sales of their own Faslodex® original medicinal product. Further, the applicants have purported that admitting the generic product into the generic substitution system and setting a reference price would lead either to a situation where the applicants have to respond to the price competition by lowering the price of their medicinal product, or to a situation where the applicants' medicinal product would lose market share to the opposing party's generic medicinal product due to generic substitution. According to the applicants, the generic substitution and setting of a reference price could take place beginning on 1 October 2018. The applicants have further stated that their original medicinal product is a very important product in their business, but that the opposing party's generic product is but one of many products sold by the opposing party.

Taking all this into account and the fact that Chapter 7, Section 11 of the Procedural Code provides for strict liability for damages and costs the opposing party suffers from an unnecessary provisional measure, the Market Court finds that the opposing party does not suffer undue inconvenience in comparison with the benefit to be secured as required by Chapter 7, Section 3(2) of the Procedural Code.

It has also been found that putting a stop to an infringement that has only just started or has not yet started leads to less harm to the defendant than stopping an infringement that has continued for some time.

2. Public Interest

It has been suggested in legal scholarship that public interest or third-party interests could and should be taken into account as part of the balancing of interests when deciding a preliminary injunction, although the provision in chapter 7, section 3 of the Procedural Code expressly only recognizes the interests of the defendant.[30] There is thus no explicit public interest requirement in Finland for preliminary injunctions. The argument for taking into account third-party interests is that the law does not prohibit it and that it is likely that a court would, in any case, take into account, for example, the effect of massive layoffs when deciding what to do.[31]

In final injunctions neither public nor private interest is a requirement that the courts have to take into account. Although the provision (section 57(1)) states that the court "may" grant a final injunction, the courts have not exercised discretion,

---

[30] See Norrgård 2002, 329.
[31] Norrgård 2002, 329; Westberg 1990, 174; Johansson 1991, 616.

but granted a final injunction if there has been an infringement and a risk of continued infringement.

D. PROCEDURAL ISSUES

1. *Public Bodies as Defendants*

Whether public bodies are subject to injunctions in patent suits is a question that has been dealt with to a lesser degree. In principle, the matter is rather straightforward. As for final injunctions, the court will in general issue an injunction if it has found that there is an infringement (and the plaintiff has requested an injunction). It should however be noted that the court has some discretion since the provision on final injunctions provides that it "may" order an injunction. The situation is thus, at least in principle, not so rigid that an injunction would necessarily follow a finding of infringement.

In Supreme Court decision KKO:2003:127 the question was whether the City of Pori was infringing a patent to an oil spill recovery apparatus although it was only storing it for a possible oil spill situation. The city had acquired the oil spill recovery device and fitted it in its oil spill recovery ship in order to fulfil its duties according to the legislation on oil spill recovery actions. It had not, however, acquired a licence for the use of the device.

The city contested that it had not infringed the patent since it had never used the patent-protected device. Furthermore, the city highlighted the fact that the use of the device was based on an obligation in oil spill legislation. Thus, the city purported to have a right to use the device without the patent holder's permission.

The patent holder claimed damages and requested that the City of Pori be enjoined from continuing the infringement. As to the injunction, the Supreme Court noted that an injunction is a central remedy available to the patent holder and that, as a general rule, the patent holder has a right to an injunction. As to exceptions to this general rule, the court stated that an injunction may be refused mainly when there is no risk of continued or repeated infringement.

As to the lawful duties of the city to use the device in case of an oil spill, the Supreme Court, rather laconically, noted – taking into account section 47 of the Patents Act on compulsory licensing – that the reasons put forward by the city were not sufficient for a refusal of an injunction. The Supreme Court found that there was no reason to refuse an injunction, since the city still had the device in its possession, and intended to continue using it.

Although the decision is rather brief in some of its key findings, what is important to note is that the Supreme Court leaves the door open as to when an injunction may be refused. It does state the general rule (an injunction ensues when there is an infringement) and the main exception (refusal if no risk of continued infringement), but the decision acknowledges there could be other instances where an injunction may be refused. The court does not, however, even *obiter dicta* mention any cases where this might be the case. What we do learn from the case is that a city/ municipality is not immune from injunctions even where there is a regulatory obligation to supply certain services. According to Finnish public law, cities and municipalities are public legal persons and part of the governmental structure. From this I think it can be inferred that other public bodies, such as government agencies, wholly or partly state-owned companies, or public–private partnerships, may also be the subject of injunctions. So at least in 2003 it was quite clear that public bodies were not shielded from injunctions. It should probably be taken into account that the case predates any discussions on the US *eBay* v. *MercExchange*[32] decision (which was decided in 2006). The general view in those days was that an injunction follows as a matter of principle. The decision KKO:2003:127 is however valid law, and there has been no discussion on the status of public bodies as defendants in injunction actions. Thus, I would say that public bodies can be subjected to injunctions.

The view of the Supreme Court can be criticized. The Supreme Court decision would have put the City of Pori in a tricky situation had there been an oil spill. On one hand, the city was under a legal obligation to render oil spill recovery services but, on the other hand, the injunction enjoined it from using the device. In practice, the patent holder gained, as a result of the injunction, a very strong negotiation position.

2. *Public Bodies as Plaintiffs*

There has been no discussion in Finland on whether public bodies can or cannot be plaintiffs in injunction actions or applicants, if the case concerns preliminary injunctions. Generally, the normal rules apply. If a person is the holder of a patent, it has standing to sue and to apply for a preliminary injunction. This applies also in the case of universities, government agencies, municipalities, state-owned companies, etc.

There has been no discussion whether universities or other similar patent-licensing entities (also called non-practising entities, NPEs) have a different status than other entities. Thus, I would say that general rules apply: an NPE may not be refused standing to sue or to apply for a preliminary injunction. In the case of final injunctions, the status of NPEs would need to be dealt with as part of the exceptions to the final injunction. The only, thus far, explicitly recognized exception to a final injunction in cases where the court has already found that there is an infringement is lack of continued infringement (Supreme Court decision KKO:2003:127). Thus, I would say that an NPE would, at least as a starting point, have the same right to a final injunction as other entities.

[32] *eBay Inc.* v. *MercExchange, LLC*, 547 US 388 (2006).

In the case of preliminary injunctions, the situation might be a bit different due to the requirement of "undue inconvenience". As highlighted in Section B, a preliminary injunction requires a showing of likelihood of infringement, a risk of continued infringement and, lastly, that the "opposing party does not suffer undue inconvenience in comparison with the benefit to be secured". Since the "undue inconvenience" criterion requires the court to assess the negative consequences of the decision to the parties, it is possible that the court would take into account the fact that that the NPE is primarily interested in securing monetary compensation for the use of the patent and not in securing exclusive use of the invention (as is often the situation for manufacturing companies). To my knowledge there is no case that has put this question to the test. I do, however, think that the court could accept that an NPE with extensive licensing activities pertaining to the patent-in-suite does not suffer as much "inconvenience" from not getting an injunction as a company with no licensing activities pertaining to the patent-in-suite that uses the patent-in-suite defensively to fend off competitors.

The view, as it stands now, is that public bodies have a right to apply for and be granted final injunctions, just like any patent holder. As to preliminary injunctions, the situation might be a bit different. As was noted in Section B, one requirement for preliminary injunctions is that the injunction does not cause undue inconvenience to the defendant in light of the benefit to be secured. Although the rather convoluted language may give the impression that only the inconvenience to the defendant is to be taken into account, the Market Court has quite clearly asked, on one hand, what would be the harm to the applicant if the injunction is not granted, and on the other hand, what would be the defendant's harm if the injunction is granted. In this balancing of interests, it is possible (although no apparent case law exists) that the harm to the state or municipalities is held to be low due to its very large capacity to absorb harm.

3. *Abuse of Rights*

The abuse-of-rights doctrine is recognized as a general principle of law in Finland.[33] There are different definitions of the doctrine, but common to them is that abuse of rights is understood as an act which formally is legitimate, but which in the particular situation is unlawful due to the way in which the act is done or the purpose of the conduct.[34] As a general principle of law, the doctrine has not been incorporated into the Constitution of Finland, general civil code (because Finland does not have a civil law codification) or in any other statute. However, it has been enacted for particular purposes, such as section 33 of the Contracts Act, which provides for unenforceability of transactions that are "incompatible with honour and

---

[33] See, for example, Kulmala 2018, 894.
[34] Kulmala 2018, 895.

good faith". Also, chapter 4, section 14 of the Enforcement Code is a particular enactment of the general principle of abuse of rights. It provides that attachment of property for the payment of a debt is not hindered by a plea that the property in question belongs to a third party, if the property arrangement is an artificial arrangement.

The abuse-of-rights principle has been applied or referred to in a number of Supreme Court decisions, none of which are concerned with intellectual property. The Market Court has, however, discussed the abuse-of-rights doctrine in one copyright case. Although it is a copyright case, a similar situation might arise in patent law. In case MAO:85/19 *Crystalis Entertainment and Scanbox Entertainment v. A* the defendant argued that it was a violation of privacy and an abuse of rights that the contact details of the defendant, which the internet service provider had been ordered by the court to give to Crystalis, had been used not only by Crystalis but also by Scanbox. The Market Court stated that it was uncontested that the decision to order the internet service provider to give contact details only covered Crystalis and that the information had also been used for Scanbox's benefit. It was further uncontested that the information was to be kept confidential and that privacy legislation covered the use of the information. Still, the court found that since Scanbox based its infringement claims on its own copyright, the purpose of the plaintiff could not be objectionable as the abuse-of-rights doctrine requires. The court also noted that the way the information had come into the plaintiff's possession was not of relevance when discussing damages for the infringement. All in all, the Market Court dismissed the abuse-of-rights doctrine rather quickly. Nevertheless, it is clear that the abuse-of-rights doctrine may be argued in intellectual property infringement cases, although the threshold seems to be quite high.

Although the doctrine of abuse of rights does exist, it is not something that would normally be argued, at least in final injunctions matters. Finnish law is quite straightforward in this sense: if a patent holder manages to fulfil its burden of proof and the court finds that there is an infringement, it is not very likely that an injunction would be refused on the basis of a doctrine of abuse of rights. It should, however, be remembered that since the court "may" order final injunctions, it is possible for case law to develop in a direction where abuse of rights is taken into account in the tailoring of the injunction. At this moment, however, there are no indications that would be the case.

4. *Unclean Hands*

Finnish law does not recognize an unclean hands defence, i.e. a defence that is based on the plaintiff's bad faith or unethical behaviour. Unclean hands would generally fall under the broad category of abuse of rights.[35]

---

[35] See also for Swedish law, Westberg (2004, 294), who proposes that unfair conduct could be taken into account in Sweden.

There is, however, at least one preliminary injunction decision that takes into account something that might be categorized as bad-faith behaviour, namely ambushing tactics by the plaintiff. In *Novartis v. Actavis*[36] the Helsinki District Court refused a preliminary injunction on the grounds that the generic pharmaceutical company Actavis did not act as it had promised. Actavis had stated that it would give Novartis two months' notice before entering the Finnish market. Actavis disregarded this and entered the market without forewarning. The court took this into account and granted the preliminary injunction. The Helsinki Court of Appeals refused the preliminary injunction on the grounds that the infringement was not likely enough.

Although the Court of Appeals did not decide the case on the basis of ambushing, the argument is, I think, valid and it could also be made and accepted in other situations. Thus "breaking a promise" could be taken into account at least in the preliminary injunction phase.[37]

5. *Delay in Applying for a Final or Preliminary Injunction*

Delay in applying for a preliminary injunction may be taken into account. In 2002 it was suggested by Norrgård that delay should be taken into account in the balancing of interests. It was argued that passivity on the part of the applicant indicates that the applicant's interest in having an injunction or the harm it purports to suffer if the injunction is not granted is not as great as it claims.[38] The Supreme Court has not dealt with the question, but the Helsinki Court of Appeals decided in two cases in 2010 that delays of one year and two years, respectively, do not lead to a refusal of a preliminary injunction. In the preliminary injunction case *Janssen-Cilag v. Actavis*,[39] Janssen claimed that the fentanyl patches brought onto the market by Actavis infringed its patents. In the first instance, the District Court of Helsinki rejected the application on the basis of Janssen's passivity because an injunction would have greatly harmed the goodwill value of its products when the application for a preliminary injunction was brought one year after market launch. The Helsinki Court of Appeals, on the other hand, found that Janssen's laboratory analyses and other investigations were acceptable reasons for not applying for the preliminary injunction sooner.

In *Janssen-Cilag v. ratiopharm*,[40] the District Court rejected the application due to delay. Similarly, as in *Janssen-Cilag v. Actavis*, the Appeals Court found that

---

[36] HelHO 10.6.2010 no. 1612 *Novartis v. Actavis*.
[37] It should be noted that it was never argued that breaking a promise amounted to breach of contract. It was thus not a question of contract law (which would have required, among other things, a showing of the existence of a binding contract).
[38] Norrgård 2002, 320 *et seq.*
[39] HelHO 19.3.2010 no. 740 (S09/1812) *Janssen-Cilag v. Actavis*.
[40] HelHO 19.3.2010 no. 741 (S09/1706) *Janssen-Cilag v. ratiopharm*.

laboratory analyses and other investigations could warrant a two-year delay. Generally, it can thus be said that the passivity rules for preliminary injunctions are lax. Though the Market Court has not taken any stance on the matter yet, I would not be surprised if it held a stricter view on delay. Preliminary injunction matters are to be decided swiftly and granted in situations that need to be dealt with quickly (although Finnish law does not explicitly recognize a requirement of urgency). Filing a preliminary injunction application after a delay of one or two years feels like a very long time since it is likely the court could have given a final injunction in that same time.

There are no similar passivity rules for final injunctions. Also, delay as to final injunctions does not seem to be as big a problem since the question has not been argued, to my knowledge, in any final injunction case law. If a patent holder has a need for an injunction, the dispute will likely start with an application for a preliminary injunction, which must be followed up with an application for a final injunction within thirty days from the grant of the preliminary injunction.

If, however, a defendant raised a passivity defence in a final injunction case, it would likely be based on a theory of implied consent. The argument would then be that the patent holder had through its passivity permitted the activities of the defendant and thus implicitly accepted the infringement. Although this argument in itself is valid and recognized in other fields of law, the delay would probably need to be long.[41]

6. Patent Validity

For preliminary injunctions, the classical view was that the patent's validity presumption was very strong.[42] If the patent had been granted and was still in force, the invalidity defence would not succeed. The reason for this view was that preliminary injunction proceedings, which by their nature are summary (i.e. the court is not supposed to look into the evidence presented as thoroughly as it would have to in a full trial) are not the right place for in-depth argumentation as to the validity of a patent. Instead, the preliminary injunction court should rely on the fact that the patent had been examined, granted and was still valid.

This patentee-friendly view steered the discussion in preliminary injunction proceedings quite quickly away from validity into a discussion of whether the defendant's technical solution was within the scope of protection of the patent or not. A case in point is Helsinki Court of Appeal's decision in *Novartis v. Mylan*.[43] Mylan raised invalidity as a defence in a patent infringement matter. Mylan argued

---

[41] In a real property case (Supreme Court decision KKO:1993:35) a twenty-year period in which a party had accepted the conduct of the other party was seen to be sufficient.

[42] See, for example, HelHO 10.6.2010 no. 1659 *Novartis v. Mylan* and HelHO 19.3.2010 no. 740 *Janssen-Cilag v. Actavis*.

[43] HelHO 10.6.2010 no. 1659 *Novartis v. Mylan*.

that the infringement was not sufficiently likely due to the fact that the parallel patents in the Netherlands and United Kingdom had been invalidated and the patent-in-suit had been revoked by the Opposition Division of the European Patent Office. The Court of Appeal found that the patent's validity is to be presumed and that since the decision by the Opposition Division does not finally settle the question of validity, the patent was to be regarded as valid. Further, the Court of Appeals found that the foreign judgments did not make the infringement so uncertain that the likelihood of infringement was not met.

However, Supreme Court decision KKO:2019:34 *Mylan* v. *Gilead* (decided on 11 April 2019) has, at least on the face of it, changed this approach. The pharmaceutical company Gilead applied, and was granted, a preliminary injunction against the generic pharmaceutical company Mylan in December 2017. Gilead was the proprietor of a supplementary protection certificate (SPC), which was based on a European patent for a combination of tenofivir disproxil and emtricitabine, which is used for the treatment of HIV/AIDS. After the grant of the preliminary injunction, in July 2018 the Court of Justice of the European Union (CJEU) gave its preliminary ruling in C-121/17 *Teva* v. *Gilead*,[44] in which it laid down the criteria for when a medicinal product composed of several active ingredients with a combined effect is "protected by a basic patent in force" as required by Article 3(a) of Regulation 469/2009 concerning the supplementary protection certificate for medicinal products. Applying the criteria set forth in this judgment, the referring court, the English High Court, invalidated the SPC on 18 September 2018.

Four days after the CJEU judgment, on 29 August 2018, Mylan applied to the Market Court for cancellation of the preliminary injunction on the ground that circumstances had changed and that the SPC's invalidity was now more likely than its validity, and that there was thus no longer any basis for the preliminary injunction. Mylan argued that the Market Court should follow the English High Court decision and the decisions in Germany, France and Portugal, where the SPC had also been invalidated. Gilead, for its part, argued that the SPC was valid and there were insufficient reasons to cancel the injunction.

The Market Court followed the classical view (very strong presumption of validity) and rejected the application for cancellation. It stated that in light of the evidence and argumentation, and taking into account the summary nature of preliminary injunction proceedings, it was impossible to find that it was more likely than not that the SPC was invalid. Thus, the validity presumption had not been sufficiently challenged, and the requirements for a preliminary injunction were still met.

The Supreme Court, which granted Mylan leave to appeal, stated that a preliminary injunction may be cancelled due to a change in circumstances, if the requirements for a preliminary injunction are no longer fulfilled. According to the

---

[44] CJEU, 25 July 2018, C-121/17 *Teva* v. *Gilead*, ECLI:EU:C:2018:585.

Supreme Court (*Mylan* v. *Gilead*, para. 13) a change in circumstances may concern not only changes in facts but also in the legal situation.

The Supreme Court noted that preliminary injunction proceedings are summary proceedings, where the question is not whether the right in question is valid and whether the defendant has infringed that right. The question is rather whether the requirement of likelihood of validity and infringement is met.

The Supreme Court noted further the validity presumption in preliminary injunction proceedings. According to the court, the registration as such makes the validity of a registered intellectual property right sufficiently likely. The basis for the validity presumption is the granting office's substantive examination. According to the court, the requirements for effective provisional measures as laid down in Article 50(1)(a) of the TRIPS Agreement and Article 9(1)(a) of the Enforcement Directive 2004/48/EC also support the validity presumption.

From the validity presumption it follows that when the defendant contests a preliminary injunction application or applies for cancellation of the injunction, it has the burden of proof, i.e. it is under an obligation to produce evidence to support the grounds for invalidity of the registration. The strength of the validity presumption is dependent upon the kind of registration and when the registration was made. The Supreme Court further stated that the general principles of weighing evidence apply and that when the defendant has made the invalidity sufficiently likely, the burden of proof shifts to the applicant (*Mylan* v. *Gilead*, para. 17).

As to the application of the norms to the factual situation at hand, the Supreme Court followed the criteria laid down in C-121/17 *Teva* v. *Gilead* and found that it was not likely in light of what could be deduced from the patent that the basic patent protected the combination of tenofivir disproxil and emtricitabine. Thus, the presumption of validity had been sufficiently challenged, and the burden of proof shifted to the applicant. Whether a skilled person, despite the wording of the patent, would understand that the patent covered the combination was, according to the Supreme Court, something that required production of evidence (*Mylan* v. *Gilead*, para. 32). The burden of proof as to whether this was the case was on the applicant since the burden had shifted. Gilead was not able to convince the Supreme Court in these summary proceedings that the patent covered the combination. The preliminary injunction was thus cancelled.

The decision of the Supreme Court poses several interpretative challenges. On one hand, the Supreme Court clearly points out that there is a presumption of validity in preliminary injunction proceedings, which according to the court means that the threshold for likelihood of the patent's validity is met by having a right that has been registered. The court does, however, note that the level of examination and the "age" of the registration play a role. In this case, the SPC had been granted in 2009 and, according to the court, the interpretations as to SPCs had since developed quite significantly (*Mylan* v. *Gilead*, para. 28). The view put forth by the Supreme Court also means – as far as I understand – that Finnish utility models, which are only examined as to formalities and not as to substance, do not enjoy the same level of presumption of validity (if at all).

The problem with the presumption of validity is that the Supreme Court does not very clearly address the question of how much is needed to overturn the presumption. The court, rather laconically, states that the general principles of evidence are applied and the burden of proof may shift when a party has presented "sufficient likelihood". In essence, this means that the only thing we know for certain is that the presumption of validity is not as strong as it used to be. As is evident from the Market Court decision, a patent/SPC that has not been revoked or invalidated was, according to the old interpretation, still presumed valid, although there might have been reasons to view it as invalid. The court simply would not take the arguments for invalidation into account. The new interpretation forces the court to look into the evidence for and against validity and decide whether the patent's or SPC's validity is likely. So from a situation where the preliminary injunction court was effectively shielded from invalidity argumentation we have now moved to a situation where invalidity argumentation must be taken into account. What we do not know, however, is how likely the invalidity must be. It should be remembered that Gilead's SPC had been invalidated in other European countries. Also, the question of invalidity in this case was first and foremost a question of legal interpretation. The Supreme Court clearly stated that due to the summary nature of the proceedings, the applicant had not made it likely that the skilled person might have understood the patent to include emtricitabine despite the patent's language (*Mylan* v. *Gilead*, paras. 32–34).

Trying to understand the decision, my interpretation of the current situation is thus the following. (1) A registered patent is presumed valid. (2) The defendant has the burden to show that the patent is likely invalid. (3) If the defendant fulfils its burden, the burden shifts to the applicant. (4) Showing likelihood of invalidity on grounds of legal interpretation is easier than showing invalidity on the basis of factual grounds. (5) Preliminary injunction proceedings are still summary proceedings, which makes taking into account evidence on complicated technical matters more difficult and leads more easily to a non-showing of likelihood. (6) The value of foreign judgments was not discussed at all by the Supreme Court. It seemingly took the CJEU decision and applied its criteria without any recourse to the foreign judgments. Whether this means that they are of no value or that they have hidden persuasive authority is unclear.

In light of these findings, more traditional situations where invalidity is invoked may still face an uphill battle. Let us assume, for example, that a defendant in a preliminary injunction case argues that a patent lacks novelty and inventiveness. These are standard defences in a patent case, and they usually require technical evidence. This in turn might mean that the court is only under an obligation to look into the evidence summarily and that conflicting evidence might mean that the defendant's burden of proof is not met.

As for final injunctions, there is, in principle, a presumption of validity. The role of the presumption is, however, rather limited since questioning the validity of the patent requires an invalidity action, as was noted. In practice this means that if an invalidity action has been instituted alongside an infringement action, the judgment on validity is given at the same time as the infringement judgment. If the court finds that the patent is invalid, then no final injunction or other remedy will be granted. If, on the other hand, the patent is found to be valid, a final injunction may be granted, if the requirements for a final injunction (infringement and risk for continued infringement) are met. The presumption of validity is thus relevant only in cases where no invalidity action has been instituted. In those cases, the court is under an obligation to presume that the patent is valid.

E. ALTERNATIVES AND MODIFICATIONS

1. *Limited Duration of Final and Preliminary Injunctions*

A preliminary injunction has effect from the moment the applicant posts the security required by the enforcement authority (chapter 8, section 2(1) of the Enforcement Code) or from a later point in time, if the court decided so when issuing the preliminary injunction.

A final injunction follows the normal rules for enforcement of judgments. Market Court judgments may be enforced immediately after they have been rendered unless the court has in its decision decided otherwise. The Market Court may decide that the enforcement of the final injunction is to take place at a later date. This is possible at least in two situations. First, if the claimant has asked for a delay, the court would most likely view this as a narrowing of the claim. Since the court cannot give more than has been asked for, it would have to order the final injunction to start at a later date, even in cases of clear infringement. Party autonomy is a very important and clear-cut principle in these kinds of civil cases, and the court cannot go against the plaintiff's wishes. Second, and perhaps more interestingly, it is at least in principle possible for the court to decide that a final injunction is to take effect only at a later date, especially in case it takes some time for the defendant to wind down its infringing activities. Although possible in theory, no case law exists, as far as I know.

For both preliminary and final injunctions, it is possible to apply for a stay of enforcement. The Supreme Court may decide that a decision may not be enforced or that enforcement that has already started is to be halted (chapter 7, section 4(3) of the Market Court Proceedings Act).

It is also possible for the court to decide on an end date for a final injunction. A natural way of explicitly setting an end date is to refer to the term of the patent-in-suit. In literature there have also been discussions on so-called post-expiry injunctions. It has been held possible that they could be granted in order to stop the defendant from enjoying a springboard effect (i.e. the defendant would not be allowed to take advantage of infringing preparations).[45] Although possible in principle, neither legislation nor case law has acknowledged the possibility. Whether in some cases there might be a need to set an end date before the patent expires has not been discussed.

2. *Ongoing Royalties*

Finnish law does not recognize royalties or damages in lieu of injunctions. It should be noted that Article 12 of the Enforcement Directive on "alternative measures", i.e. pecuniary compensation instead of an injunction or destruction, if the infringer has acted unintentionally and without negligence, was not explicitly implemented in Finland. The relation between injunctions and compensation was never discussed during the implementation. The relation between destruction of infringing products (section 59 of the Patents Act) and compensation was, on the other hand, discussed, albeit briefly. The government argued and the parliament accepted that section 59 (3) of the Finnish Patents Act fulfils the requirements of Article 12 of the Enforcement Directive 2004/48/EC.[46] Section 59(3) provides that "the court may order, on request, if there are special reasons for this, that the holders of [infringing] objects . . . shall be able to dispose of the objects for the remainder of the patent term or for a part thereof, against reasonable compensation and on reasonable conditions". Although this provision has never, to my knowledge, been applied, it still shows quite clearly that there could be cases where the infringer is allowed to keep the infringing product and instead pay a monetary compensation.

Since no such provision was put in place for injunctions, it seems that, in order to reach a similar outcome as for destruction, the patent holder would most likely have to withdraw its request for an injunction and instead claim compensation for future losses.

3. *Compulsory Licences*

Compulsory licences are provided for in sections 45–48 of the Patents Act. A compulsory licence requires a public interest and a decision by the Market Court. The compulsory licence is always a non-exclusive licence, which means that the patent holder is always entitled to use the patented invention and grant licences to other parties. The patent holder is always entitled to a licence fee from the licensee for any use based on a compulsory licence.

Compulsory licences are available in five instances: (1) Non-use (section 45 of the Patents Act); (2) Dependent invention (section 46 of the Patents Act); (3)

---

[45] Norrgård 2002, 75.
[46] Government Bill (HE) 26/2006, p. 13.

Compulsory licence to holder of plant breeder's right (section 46a of the Patents Act); (4) Considerable public interest (section 47 of the Patents Act); and (5) Prior use (section 48 of the Patents Act).

According to section 45 of the Patents Act, if three years have elapsed since the grant of the patent and four years from the filing of the application, and if the invention is not worked or brought into use to a reasonable extent in Finland, any person who wishes to work the invention in Finland may obtain a compulsory licence to do so unless there are legitimate grounds for failing to work the invention.

According to section 46, the proprietor of a patent for an invention whose exploitation is dependent on a patent held by another person may obtain a compulsory licence to exploit the invention protected by such patent if it is deemed reasonable in view of the importance of the invention or for other special reasons.

According to section 46a, if a breeder cannot acquire or exploit a plant variety right without infringing a prior patent, they may apply for a compulsory licence for non-exclusive use of the invention protected by the patent if the licence is necessary for the exploitation of the plant variety. The patent holder is entitled to a cross-licence on reasonable terms to use the protected plant variety.

According to section 47, a person who wishes to commercially exploit a patented invention may obtain a compulsory licence to do so, if there is a considerable public interest.

Section 48 provides for a compulsory licence in cases where a person who, at the time the application documents were made available, was commercially exploiting in Finland an invention which is the subject of a patent application (and which leads to a patent), provided there are special reasons for this and also they had no knowledge of the application and could not reasonably have obtained such knowledge. The same applies if a person has made substantial preparations for commercial exploitation of the invention.

To my knowledge there are no decisions on compulsory licences in Finland. In Supreme Court decision KKO:2003:127 the defendant raised the issue of compulsory licences as a defence. It argued that a final injunction should not be issued since it had, among other things, a right to a compulsory licence. However, the Supreme Court takes the view that raising the issue merely in defence in infringement proceedings is not enough. A denial of a final injunction in a situation where the court has found that there is an infringement and a risk of continued infringement requires a judgment granting a compulsory licence.[47]

---

[47] See also Helsinki Court of Appeals preliminary injunction decision HelHO 30.6.2011 no 2120 *Novozymes A/S v. Genencor International Oy and Finnfeeds Oy*, where the defendant argued that it had a right to a section 48 compulsory licence since it had been commercially using its solution before the utility model applications had become public. The Court of Appeals noted that the right to a compulsory licence "had remained unclear" and therefore the compulsory licence issue had no bearing on the decision to refuse the application for a preliminary injunction.

F. DRAFTING AND ENFORCING INJUNCTIONS

1. *The Wording of Injunctions and Their Interpretation*

The scope of an injunction can be said to have an objective and a subjective dimension. The objective dimension of the scope can further be divided into local and temporal. The objective dimension of the scope of the injunction answers the question of which acts may be enjoined (local), and when the injunction starts and ends (temporal). The subjective dimension of the scope deals with who may be enjoined.

The injunction should always be worded so that it is possible to clearly determine the scope of the injunction as to the objective and subjective reach. An unclearly worded injunction may lead to several problems. First of all, it is difficult for the parties and the enforcement authority to know exactly which acts are allowed and which are prohibited. This, in turn, may lead to unnecessary litigation in the enforcement phase. Second, unclear injunctions are problematic from the point of view of the principle of legality. In criminal law, the principle of legality (which includes for example the rule *nullum crimen sine lege* – no crime without law) has a very strong position. Since breaching an injunction may lead to the payment of a conditional fine, it comes close to a criminal sanction. Therefore, I argue that a similar principle of legality should apply for injunction language. Although this is not settled law, courts try to give injunctions a clear and unambiguous wording. Still in the 1990s and early 2000s it was possible to see injunctions worded in a very broad manner, such as "the defendant is enjoined from infringing the patent". This type of language was rightly criticized.[48]

In accordance with the procedural principle of party autonomy, the plaintiff decides the extent of the injunction. In line with general principles of procedural law, the court may order a narrower injunction than the claimant requested, but it may not broaden it: i.e. the injunction may not go further than what was requested. The court's role, if the wording is contested, is to ensure that only a wording that has support in the grounds of the decision and that can be enforced is allowed. The question of what can be enforced can be a very tricky one and it is rarely discussed. The court, however, needs to ensure that the injunction is specific enough for the enforcement authorities to be able to decide which acts are covered by the injunction. One example of an unenforceable injunction might be the abovementioned overly broad injunctions only stating that the "defendant is enjoined from infringing the patent" since it would not specify which acts fall within the injunction. It would create a very difficult situation for the enforcement authority, which is not specialized in intellectual property law, to try to figure out whether certain acts are infringing or not.

---

[48] Norrgård 2002, 74 *et seq.*

For an injunction to have support in the grounds of the decision, one needs to look at the requirements for injunctions. Simply put, an injunction can, first of all, cover infringing acts that are already taking place and for which there is a sufficient risk of continued infringement. Second, the injunction may also cover acts that have not yet taken place, but the threat of which is deemed to be sufficient. Thus, an injunction may cover not only those acts that are taking place, but also sufficiently probable variants that have not yet taken place. The exact scope of the injunction is decided on a case-by-case basis.

For quite a long time, injunctions have been worded in a fairly standard, but sufficiently clear way. One typical example would be an injunction that is worded as follows (freely translated and simplified): "The court prohibits the defendant from offering, putting on the market or using [product X] during the term of the patent [number N]." If the defendant were to, for example, market and sell a product, the injunction would cover such marketing and selling as long as it takes place during the term of the patent and the marketing and/or selling activities are interpreted as "offering" the product and/or "putting [it] on the market". The injunction is thus not limited to exactly the same infringement that was the object of the infringement trial. On the other hand, the injunction is not a broad "do not break the law" type of order. In our example, "product X" may be identified in a number of ways. A common way is using the trademark of the product ("Ezetimib Sandoz 10 mg"[49]), but far from the only one.

2. Flexibilities in the Enforcement Phase

The National Administrative Office for Enforcement (Enforcement Authority) is the government authority in charge of enforcing decisions in civil and administrative matters and collection of fines in criminal matters (chapter 1, section 2 of the Enforcement Code).

Enforcing a preliminary injunction takes place as follows. The enforcement of the preliminary injunction requires, first, that the applicant posts a security for any damage the defendant may suffer if it later turns out that the preliminary injunction should not have been granted (chapter 8, section 2 of the Enforcement Code).[50] Usually, a government official at the Enforcement Authority called the District Bailiff decides the amount of the security (chapter 3, section 43(1) of the Enforcement Code).[51] No security needs to be posted when enforcing a final

---

[49] See Market Court decision MAO:708/17 *Merck v. Sandoz.*

[50] The applicant may be freed from the obligation to post a security if the applicant lacks means to do so and the applicant's right is "evidently founded". This provision is, as far as I know, applied only in very exceptional cases. Both criteria (lack of means and high standard of proof for right) are very strict.

[51] There are certain other government officials that also have the right to make enforcement decisions. See chapter 1, section 7 of the Enforcement Code.

injunction judgment granted by the Market Court (chapter 7, section 7(3) of the Market Court Proceedings Act).

After the security has been posted or if a security need not be posted, the enforcement continues with notifying the defendant of the injunction. If the defendant complies with the wording of the final or preliminary injunction, nothing further will happen. If, however, the defendant breaches the injunction, the District Bailiff has several options after becoming aware of the breach.

The District Bailiff can enforce the breached injunction by making an application to the court requesting that the defendant shall be ordered to pay the conditional fine set in the injunction decision. If the decision does not include a conditional fine, the enforcement authority has to set it first (chapter 3, section 74 of the Enforcement Code). Then only the *second* breach could lead to the defendant being ordered to pay the conditional fine. When the District Bailiff makes the request to the court, they may at the same time decide on a higher conditional fine.

According to chapter 7, section 17 of the Enforcement Code, if the District Bailiff can put a stop to further breaches of the injunction by using appropriate measures, there is an obligation to take such measures. However, this is only possible after a first breach and only after the defendant has been heard (unless a hearing makes the enforcement significantly more difficult).

In most cases, the defendant will follow the injunction order without any further need for specific enforcement orders by the District Bailiff. However, if a defendant were to oppose a granted injunction and continue its infringing activities, the District Bailiff would have rather wide discretion as to when and how vigorously to pursue the case for payment of the conditional fine and whether or not to make an order for a new, higher, conditional fine. The District Bailiff does not, according to my own personal experience, want to get deeply involved in the substance of the case. The Bailiff's competence is not within intellectual property law, but primarily in the enforcement of different types of payment obligations. Thus, difficult questions relating to the interpretation of the injunction is something the enforcement authority would rather see the courts deal with. Such difficult questions can reach the court either after the District Bailiff has applied for payment of the conditional fine at the court, if the District Bailiff makes a decision that the defendant appeals, or if the defendant contests the enforcement by bringing an action in the court in accordance with chapter 10, section 6 of the Enforcement Code.

All in all, there are some flexibilities in how the District Bailiff deals with the conditional fine and with measures putting a stop to the infringement.

REFERENCES

Cases

Court of Justice of the European Union
CJEU, 25 July 2018, C-121/17 *Teva v. Gilead*, ECLI:EU:C:2018:585

Supreme Court
KKO:1993:35
KKO:1994:132
KKO:1994:133
KKO:2003:127
KKO:2015:51
KKO:2019:34, *Mylan v. Gilead*

Market Court
MAO:866/15 *Neste Renewable Fuels Oy and Neste Oyj v. UPM-Kymmene Oyj*
MAO:708/17 *Merck v. Sandoz*
MAO:457/18 *AstraZeneca AB and AstraZeneca Oy v. Sandoz A/S*
MAO:16/18 *Merck Sharp & Dohme B.V. and MSD Finland Oy v. Exeltis Healthcare S.L. and Exeltis Sverige AB*
MAO:85/19 *Crystalis Entertainment UG & Scanbox Entertainment A/S v. A*
MAO:111/19 *F. Hoffman-La Roche AG, Roche Oy and Genentech Inc. v. MSD Finland Oy*

Helsinki Court of Appeals
HelHO 16.2.2006 no. 421 *Pfizer v. Ranbaxy*
HelHO 19.3.2010 no. 740 (S09/1812) *Janssen-Cilag Oy v. Actavis Oy and Actavis Group hf*
HelHO 19.3.2010 no. 741 (S09/1706) *Janssen-Cilag v. ratiopharm GmbH and ratiopharm Oy*
HelHO 10.6.2010 no. 1612 *Novartis v. Actavis*
HelHO 11.6.2010 no. 1659 *Novartis v. Mylan*
HelHO 30.6.2011 no. 2120 *Novozymes A/S v. Genencor International Oy and Finnfeeds Oy*

USA
eBay Inc. v. MercExchange, LLC, 547 US 388 (2006)

Regulatory and Legislative Materials

International Conventions
Agreement on Trade-Related Aspects of Intellectual Property Rights (TRIPS)
European Patent Convention

European Union
Directive 2004/48/EC of the European Parliament and of the Council of 29 April 2004 on the enforcement of intellectual property rights

Finland

Act on Conditional Fines (1113/1990)
Act on Securing Evidence (344/2000)
Constitution of Finland (731/1999)
Contracts Act (228/1929)
Copyright Act (404/1961)
Courts Act (673/2016)
Criminal Code (39/1889)
Enforcement Code (705/2007)
Government Bill HE 26/2006 on amending the legislation on intellectual property law
Government Bill HE 124/2012 on legislation on the Market Court and proceedings in the
    Market Court
Medicines Act (395/1987)
Market Court Proceedings Act (100/2013)
Market Court Act (99/2013)
Patents Act (550/1967)
Procedural Code (4/1734)

Books, Articles and Online Materials

Johansson, Svante. 1991. "Interimistiska åtgärder vid aktiebolagsrättsliga processer," *Svensk juristtidning* 8: 601–17.
Kulmala,   Samuli.   2018.   "Oikeuden   väärinkäytön   kielto   ja
    oikeudenkäyntikulusanktiosäännökset," *Defensor Legis* 6/2018:891–907.
Norrgård, Marcus. 2002. *Interimistiska förbud i immaterialrätten*. Helsingfors: Kauppakaari
    Juristförbundets förlag.
Valituslupahakemus ja valitus [Application for Leave to Appeal]. https://korkeinoikeus.fi/fi/
    index/muutoksenhakijalle/muutoksenhakemuksenlaatiminen/
    valituslupahakemusjavalitus.html.
Vuositilastot [Yearly Statistics]. www.markkinaoikeus.fi/fi/index/ajankohtaista/vuositilastot
    .html.
Westberg, Peter. (1990). "Civilprocessuella säkerhetsåtgärder – ett instrument för
    konfliktlösning?," *Svensk juristtidning* 3/1990: 161–76.
    2004. *Det provisoriska rättsskyddet i tvistemål*. Vol. IV. Lund: Juristförlaget i Lund.

7

France

Thibault Gisclard and Emmanuel Py

In France, the question of injunctive relief for infringement of patents has only given rise to a very limited number of academic studies.[1] Although there are quite a lot of court decisions dealing with this topic, the courts generally do not explain their reasoning on this particular point. In France, patent injunctions can only be handled[2] by the specialized IP chambers[3] of the general jurisdictions of Paris, which are the Tribunal Judiciaire (formerly known as the Tribunal de Grande Instance) de Paris on first instance, where the judgment is generally delivered within eighteen months, and, on appeal, the Cour d'appel de Paris, where the cases are generally adjudicated within twelve months. The highest court, the Cour de cassation only deals with matters of law, and not fact.[4] On average, 170 court decisions on patent litigation were delivered per year in France between 2015 and 2019.

A major distinction must be made in French law between preliminary injunctions and permanent injunctions, since they are not based on the same legal grounds.[5] Therefore, the requirements to grant permanent injunctions are different from the requirements to grant preliminary injunctions. As discussed in greater detail in Section A.1, permanent injunctions are automatically granted every time a valid patent in force has been infringed, since a patent is a property right. However, a preliminary injunction must be based on other legal grounds,[6] which are more

---

[1] *See*, however, Rodà 2012, and Stenger 2019, 10–34.
[2] In practice, injunctive reliefs for patent infringements are only pleaded by a very limited number of attorneys, who might be partners within an intellectual property (IP) department of a large multinational firm, or in small IP boutiques. Since they are all members of the Paris bar, deontological rules are the same as for any member of the Paris bar.
[3] However, these chambers are composed of judges who are not technicians, but specialists of law, and, like any judicial judge, have studied in the Ecole Nationale de la Magistrature.
[4] Usually, the Cour de cassation only deals a handful of patent cases per year.
[5] In practice, permanent injunctions are almost always requested in infringement procedures, whereas preliminary injunctions proceedings are far less frequent.
[6] Article L. 615-3 of the French Intellectual Property Code.

demanding, hence the relative scarcity of these preliminary injunctions. Indeed, at the time of the litigation for preliminary injunctions, the validity of the patent has not been challenged, and the infringement has not been established by the courts.[7]

More generally, since French law belongs to the civil law tradition, judges only have limited powers, which are granted to them by statutory law. Since the statutory bases for a permanent injunction do not give the judge any significant discretion whether or not to grant that relief, the courts cannot consider the fact that the plaintiff is a non-practising entity, and cannot even apply a balance of interests, contrary to preliminary injunctions, or grant compensatory relief instead of injunctive relief when they deem it more appropriate.[8]

A. THE REQUIREMENTS FOR GRANTING A PERMANENT INJUNCTION FOR INFRINGEMENT OF A PATENT IN FRENCH LAW

Since a patent is a property right, every time a valid patent in force has been infringed, a permanent injunction must be issued, except on very rare occasions.

1. *Permanent Injunctions Must Be Granted Automatically When a Valid Patent in Force Has Been Infringed*

When the infringed patent is in force, the legal grounds of patent law explain why such injunctions must be granted every time.

a. The Legal Basis of Permanent Injunctions

The majority of the countries in the world are bound by international conventions relating to intellectual property rights, such as the Paris Convention for the protection of industrial property, and the Trade-Related Aspects of Intellectual Property Rights (TRIPS) agreement. Nonetheless, some differences still remain between the member states of the European Union, which led to the enactment of the Enforcement Directive[9] number 2004/48 of 29 April 2004 (Directive), which has been transposed into the French Intellectual Property Code (the Code) by law number 2007-1544 of 29 October 2007.[10] Therefore, today, the legal bases of injunctive relief are within the French Intellectual Property Code, which must be interpreted according to the European Directive.

---

[7] On the requirements for preliminary injunctions, *see* Section A.2.b.
[8] *See, e.g.*, Paris Court of First Instance, 12 February 2010, Propriété Industrielle Bulletin Documentaire (PIBD) 919, III, 339 (2010) (affirmed by Paris Court of Appeal, 22 May 2013, PIBD 988, III, 1313 (2013)).
[9] Official Gazette of the European Union dated 30 April 2004, issue L. 157.
[10] Official Gazette of the French Republic (JORF) dated 30 October 2007.

The French Intellectual Property Code does not expressly allow the judge to grant a permanent injunction to stop an infringer from infringing a patent. Nonetheless, the majority of legal writers and case law consider that, because of the legal monopoly which derives from the patent title,[11] and the definition of infringing acts,[12] a judge who is requested by the patent holder to grant a permanent injunction for the future must do so every time a valid patent in force has been infringed. Since a patent gives its holder a property right, the patentee has an exclusive right which allows him to request a remedy in case of any encroachment on that property. The injunction which forbids the infringer from continuing the infringing acts is therefore considered a natural consequence of the infringement ruling.[13] This is why Article 11 of the Enforcement Directive, which provides for such a remedy, did not need to be implemented in French law.[14] As a consequence, case law prior to the Enforcement Directive can still be invoked in such situations.

b. The Infringed Patent Must Be in Force

This is a mandatory requirement for granting an injunction: after the patent expires, the infringer cannot be prohibited from performing acts that would have constituted an infringement of the patent when it was in force.[15]

The invalidation of the patent has an impact upon injunctive relief.[16] When the patent has been invalidated during the course of the infringement proceedings, no infringement can be found, and therefore no injunction can be granted.[17] Similarly, when a patent has been invalidated in a first proceeding, this invalidity can be invoked against the patentee during other court proceedings for infringement which

[11] Article L. 611-1, al. 1er of the French Intellectual Property Code provides that "an industrial property title may be granted by the Director of the National Institute of Industrial Property to any invention, conferring on the holder or his successors in title an exclusive right to work the invention".

[12] Article L. 613-3 of the French Intellectual Property Code provides that: "The following shall be prohibited, save consent by the owner of the patent: a) Making, offering, putting on the market, using, importing, exporting, transshipping, or stocking a product which is the subject matter of the patent; b) Using a process which is the subject matter of the patent or, when the third party knows, or it is obvious in the circumstances, that the use of the process is prohibited without the consent of the owner of the patent, offering the process for use on French territory; c) Offering, putting on the market, using, importing, exporting, transshipping the product obtained directly by a process which is the subject matter of the patent or stocking for such purposes."

[13] Foyer & Vivant 1991, 349.

[14] Rodà 2010, 26; Stenger 2019.

[15] Cass. Com., 1 March 1994, no. 92-11.506; Cass. Com., 17 March 2015, no. 13-15.862, PIBD 2015, no. 1027, III, 335; see also, among others, Paris Court of Appeal, 18 February 2005, no. 02/08524, PIBD 811, III, 388 (2005); Paris Court of Appeal, 23 February 2016, no. 13/20365, Paris Court of Appeal, 27 June 2017, no. 14/25023.

[16] As a principle, there is no bifurcation in French patent law.

[17] Cass. Com., 4 March 1986, no. 83-16.848, Bull. IV, no. 36, *Dossiers brevets* 1986, V, p. 1. More generally, on that question, *see* Py 2008, 618, and Py 2011.

are still pending, and this then precludes any action for infringement.[18] When a decision of invalidity rendered in a first litigation has been appealed, and, meanwhile, there is another litigation concerning infringement of the same patent, the defendant may request the postponement of that decision until the final decision concerning the validity of the patent has been rendered. However, the judge is not required to grant the defendant's request, and may take into account the likelihood of invalidity, as he does when an opposition is filed before the European Patent Office.

A major reform of the grant system for French patents has recently introduced[19] an opposition procedure before the French National Industrial Property Institute (INPI), which is based on the European procedure. It allows any person, except the patentee, to challenge the validity of the patent within nine months of the publication of its grant in the *Bulletin officiel de la propriété industrielle*. The decision of the general director of the INPI produces the same effects as a court decision according to Article L. 111-3 al. 6° of the Code of Civil Execution Procedures,[20] which means that it is an executory title. Whereas the preparatory works stated that the decision of the general director of the INPI had the authority of *res judicata*, the articles which were finally enacted do not use that expression. Whether a decision rejecting the opposition has the authority of *res judicata*[21] would depend on its jurisdictional nature, which is discussed among legal writers.[22] In any case, the decision of the general director of the INPI may be amended by the Paris Court of Appeal, which will consider elements of both fact and law.[23] If several provisions deal with the articulation of the opposition procedure with the limitation procedures,[24] and the revocation procedures,[25] nothing is said concerning the articulation between opposition procedures and actions for infringement. The judge may stay his decision in the interest of proper justice, but, as for the European opposition procedure, is not required to do so. The judge might decide on a stay if the opposition seems serious enough, but if the judge doesn't stay, there is a risk of contradictory decisions, since a patent upon which an infringement decision has been based may later be revoked.

---

[18] At least if the decision of invalidation has become *res judicata*: *see* Cass. Com., 6 December 2017, no. 15-19.726, Propr. industr. 2018, comm. 8, note Py 2018; Gisclard 2018.

[19] Ordinance no. 2020-116 of 12 February 2020 creating an opposition procedure to patents, JORF no. 37 of 13 February 2020: this new regime came into force on 1 April 2020 and applies to patents whose delivery has been published in the *Bulletin officiel de la propriété industrielle* since that day. This ordinance has been complemented by decree no. 2020-225 of 6 March 2020 concerning the opposition procedure for patents.

[20] Article L. 613-23-2 of the French Intellectual Property Code.

[21] Article 1355 of the French civil code.

[22] Galloux 2020; see also Pollaud-Dulian 2020, who claims it is a "quasi-jurisdictional" decision; for a more comprehensive analysis, see Py & Raynard 2021.

[23] Article R. 411-19, al. 2, of the French Intellectual Property Code.

[24] Article L. 613-24 of the French Intellectual Property Code.

[25] Article R. 613-44-10, 1 of the French Intellectual Property Code.

The most difficult question, which is somewhat similar to the latter, concerns what happens when a first decision grants a permanent injunction, and, later on, another decision invalidates the same patent. For the moment, French case law has only had to deal with that question in the case of damages that the infringer had to pay, making a distinction between infringers that had already paid such damages to the patentee and cannot ask for a refund of these damages,[26] and those that had not and will not be requested to pay them.[27] Scholars agree that permanent injunctions cannot be enforced after a court has declared the underlying patent invalid,[28] although they do not generally explain upon which statutory basis such an opinion could be based. The injunction should stop having effect, since there cannot be any infringement of an intellectual property right that does not exist. Since injunctions involve the future, whereas damages concern the past, it follows that the patent invalidation decision produces its effects *ex nunc*, and prevails over the infringement decision for the future, but not *ex tunc*, since it doesn't modify the past effects of the infringement decision.[29] On a procedural level, the *res judicata* of the infringement decision ceases its effects for the future, since such a limit is implicitly but necessarily included in the infringement decision. Similarly, an injunction ceases its effects when the patent becomes part of the public domain, as soon as it has expired.[30] Therefore, and contrary to trade secrecy law, there is no need to make any specific request to the judge.

c. An Automatic Remedy

Since permanent injunctions for infringement of a patent are based on the proprietary nature of the patent, it means that the judge must grant such injunctions whenever requested by the patentee to do so. Courts have been granting permanent injunctions for a long time,[31] even though they do not explain clearly the legal basis of the grant of such permanent injunctions. For example, a decision of the Paris Court of Appeal explained in 2017 that the infringement of patent rights constitutes a violation of the exclusive right of the patentee to authorize or prohibit the exploitation of the product which is the subject matter of the patent, and that a remedy should thus be granted in order to reinstate the patentee's rights, which justifies the injunction.[32]

---

[26] Cass. Ass. plén., 17 February 2012, no. 10-24.282, Bull. Ass. Pl. no. 2, PIBD 959, III, 233 (2012); Propr. industr. 2012, comm. 29, note Py 2020, 536 et seq.
[27] Cass. Com., 12 June 2007, no. 05-14.548, Bull. IV, no. 158, PIBD 858, III, 521 (2007).
[28] Raynard et al. 2016; Azéma & Galloux 2017.
[29] Raynard 2012, 444.
[30] Py 2020, 544–45.
[31] *See, e.g.*, Paris Court of Appeal, 16 May 1927, Ann. propr. ind. 1928, 13.
[32] Paris Court of Appeal, 16 May 2017, no. 15/09506.

2. *When Injunctive Relief Is Not Mandatory*

Contrary to preliminary injunctions, which are strongly regulated, permanent injunctions may only be denied on very rare occasions.

a. Situations Where a Permanent Injunction May Be Denied

On very rare occasions, a court may deny the grant of a permanent injunction. We shall examine first the denial of injunctive relief against a certain type of defendant, or with regard to a certain type of plaintiff, then whether this is the case in situations of partial denial of injunctive relief for a sub-group of infringing acts, the cases of compulsory licences, and finally of other exceptions.

Permanent injunctions are still possible[33] for indirect infringers acting in good faith, who can normally not be held liable for an infringement, since they were not acting knowingly.[34] Indeed, the summons makes them aware of the infringement, so that any subsequent act becomes unlawful, which justifies an injunction for the future.[35] The grant of a permanent injunction against intermediaries might be possible under the general rules of civil procedure.[36]

A very old court decision even granted injunctive relief against the French state.[37] However, nowadays, Article L. 615-10 of the French Intellectual Property Code provides for a notable exception:

> [W]here an invention which is the subject of a patent application or of a patent is worked, in order to meet the requirements of national defense, by the State or its suppliers, subcontractors and subsidiary suppliers, without a license having been afforded to them, the ... Court may order neither the discontinuance nor the interruption of the working nor the confiscation provided for in Articles L. 615-3 and L. 615-7-1.

The principle of equality before the law means that the nature or reputation of the plaintiff cannot be considered in the decision whether or not to grant a permanent injunction.[38] More specifically, the fact that the patent holder is a non-practising entity (NPE) does not prevent the court from granting a permanent injunction. Indeed, in property law in general, case law considers that a mere action against an

---

[33] *See* Mathély 1991, 515; Stenger 2019, quoting Paris Court of First Instance, 13 April 1972, PIBD 89, III, 252 (1972).

[34] Indeed, article L. 615-1, al. 3 of the French Intellectual Property Code provides that remedies for some hypotheses of infringement of patent law, such as selling the invention, requires that the defendant acted knowingly.

[35] Passa 2013, 643.

[36] *Id.*, 644.

[37] Cass. Civ., 1 February 1892, Ann. propr. ind. 1892, 103.

[38] In the absence of any specificity concerning a NPE, see Paris Court of First Instance, 10 March 2017, no. 14/16022.

infringement of a property right cannot amount per se to an abuse of law.[39] It is, however, true that some legal writers are pleading that, as in US law, and more precisely since the *eBay* decision,[40] it might be possible to replace the injunction with damages.[41] Indeed, and despite the automatic nature of permanent injunctions, these authors base their opinion upon the function of the patent, which is to promote research in order to be useful to the community.[42] Therefore, when a person does not use the patented invention for its whole purpose, that person might not be able to use the whole set of available remedies.[43] However, for the moment, applicable French patent law does not take into account such ideas, since, contrary to European trademark law, the way the patent holder uses its right is not taken into consideration.[44] This is quite logical, since the notion of function of rights seems rather difficult to apply to, and be defined in, patent law.[45] Indeed, creating a duty to exploit the invention would seem out of step with current uses of patents, especially for a NPE designed to be the sole entity to deal with future licensees, and this explains why such a situation isn't regarded as an abuse.

In addition, there are some compulsory licences in French law, either ordered by courts or by the government. Among them are compulsory licences for lack of exploitation,[46] for dependent inventions,[47] for exportation of pharmaceutical products,[48] in the interest of public health,[49] to satisfy the requirements of the national economy,[50] and for national defence.[51] In practice, such compulsory licences are rarely used (e.g., we are not aware of any case of compulsory licence in the interest of public health[52] in France). We think that pending proceedings regarding a compulsory licence may have an impact on the grant of permanent injunction in a pending infringement case. Indeed, if the request for a compulsory licence is made during the proceedings for infringement of the same patent, the judge who decides there is an infringement but who grants the licence cannot prohibit exploitation of the invention for the future, at least within the scope of the compulsory licence.

---

[39] Cass. Civ. 3rd, 7 June 1990, Bull. civ. III, no. 140; Cass. Civ. 3^e, 10 November 2016 (three cases), no. 15-19.561, no. 15-21.949, no. 15-25.113. On abuse of law, see *infra* in this section.
[40] *eBay Inc.* v. *MercExchange* (2006). See Chapter 14 (United States).
[41] Le Stanc 2014, 59.
[42] *Id.*
[43] *Id.*
[44] On trademark law, *see* Basire 2015.
[45] Py 2018, 5–27.
[46] Art. L. 613-6 *et seq.* of the French Intellectual Property Code.
[47] Art. L. 613-15 of the French Intellectual Property Code.
[48] Art. L. 613-17-1 of the French Intellectual Property Code.
[49] Art. L. 613-16 of the French Intellectual Property Code. For an example outside France, *see* Gisclard 2014.
[50] Art. L. 613-18 of the French Intellectual Property Code.
[51] Art. L. 613-19 of the French Intellectual Property Code.
[52] Gisclard 2020.

Being an infringer does not preclude requesting a compulsory licence,[53] and, indeed, that could even be a way for the infringer to prove that it is able to work the patented invention in an effective and serious manner,[54] which is a requirement of the French Intellectual Property Code for getting a compulsory licence for lack of exploitation.[55] Finally, when a compulsory licence has been granted after a decision of infringement, a permanent injunction which had been granted by the judge who ruled on infringement can no longer be enforced.

Potential infringers have tried to use anti-suit injunctions issued by American courts in order to avoid injunctions prohibiting future patent infringement by French courts. In a 2020 case,[56] Lenovo had an anti-suit injunction issued by a California court against a patent holder. However, the Paris Court of First Instance has deemed such an injunction illicit as fundamentally contrary to the French and international principles of patent law, and to the protection of property, to the rights to a fair trial and to an effective remedy granted by the European Court of Human Rights (ECHR). Since the anti-suit injunction only ended after the term of the patent, it would have deprived the patentee of the right to get an anti-infringement injunction. Therefore, such an anti-suit injunction constitutes an obviously illicit disturbance, and Article 835 of the French Civil Procedure Code allows the court to force its beneficiary to withdraw its use. Anti-suit injunctions are therefore not an efficient shield against injunctive relief for patent infringement before French courts.

Another situation where the courts may refuse an injunction is the lateness failure. Indeed, an injunction can also be denied to a patentee who requests a permanent injunction and, more generally, sues for infringement too late based on civil procedure rules, since Article L. 615-8 of the French Intellectual Property Code states that an infringement action is subject to a limitation period[57] of five years from the day where the owner of a right has known or should have known the last fact allowing its exercise.

On very rare occasions, a permanent injunction may be refused for other reasons, which are probably based more on practical uselessness rather than on legal grounds. Such situations may happen when infringing goods have been withdrawn from the market when the judicial proceedings began.[58] In addition, some decisions have refused to grant a permanent injunction when the defendant was bankrupt and

---

[53] Rennes Court of Appeal, 12 July 1972, PIBD 1973, III, p. 4.
[54] Paris Court of First Instance, 25 May 1983, Ann. propr. ind. 1984, 274.
[55] Art. L. 613-12 of the French Intellectual Property Code.
[56] Paris Court of Appeal, 3 March 2020, no. 19/21426.
[57] By contrast, article L. 615-8-1 of the same code states nowadays that the action for the revocation of a patent is not subject to any limitation.
[58] On trademark law, *see* Paris Court of Appeal, 30 November 2005, PIBD 824, III, 132 (2006), where the court considered that, since the infringer had decided to remove the goods from the market as soon as the proceedings began, there was no need for an injunction.

stopped their business, since such measures were no longer useful.[59] These situations remain exceptional, and even when the practical risk of infringement becomes very low, since infringing goods are not on the market, judges usually still grant the requested permanent injunction.[60] Thus, in very specific circumstances, it may happen that the court only grants damages for past infringements without prohibiting the infringer from continuing the infringing acts. Otherwise, a permanent injunction cannot be refused on the basis of the public interest, or for lack of proportionality,[61] or due to considerations of follow-on innovation.

The general principle of prohibition of abuse of law[62] might, at least theoretically, be applied in the matter of intellectual property rights. In French civil law, several criteria of such abuse have been suggested by scholars,[63] among them negligence in exercising one's rights,[64] malicious intent,[65] and disregard of the social function of rights. However, according to court decisions, actions against encroachments of property rights cannot generally be considered an abuse of law per se.[66] In practice, albeit sometimes pleaded, abuse of law has only rarely been admitted by the courts, which consider that the patentee may make a mistake about the scope of its rights.[67] And even when an abuse of law is admitted by the court during an infringement procedure, it often results from the fact that there was no infringement in that particular case,[68] and is thus not a ground which would justify the refusal of an

[59] On trademark law, *see* Paris Court of First Instance, 6 September 2006, PIBD 841, III, 785 (2006); for copyright and industrial designs, *see* Paris Court of Appeal, 6 February 2009, no. 07/08965.

[60] Paris Court of First Instance, 12 February 2010, PIBD 919, III, 339 (2010) (affirmed by Paris Court of Appeal, 22 May 2013, PIBD 988, III, 1313 (2013)).

[61] For an example of thoroughly explained denial of a preliminary injunction concerning an essential patent in telecommunications, *see* Paris Court of First Instance, 29 November 2013, no. 12/11922 (Ord. JME). However, if the notions of proportionality and balance of interests are clearly emerging in property law in general (*see, e.g.,* Reboul-Maupin 2018, 274 *et seq.*) and in patent law (Vivant 2016, 15), unfortunately, the courts have not applied it yet in the matter of permanent injunctions for infringement of patents.

[62] *See* Josserand 1939, and the famous *Clément-Bayard* case.

[63] Goubeaux 1994.

[64] *See, e.g.,* Paris Court of First Instance, 10 January 2020, no. 16/04839.

[65] Paris Court of First Instance, 20 February 2001, PIBD 729, III, 530 (2001): as a principle, an action in infringement of industrial property rights cannot be an abuse per se; however, if such an action is not aimed at protecting the said rights, but is aimed at eliminating or hampering a competitor, such an action may be deemed abusive.

[66] Paris Court of First Instance, 24 May 2013, no. 11/09609, and Paris Court of First Instance, 7 June 2013, no. 10/08326: the exercise of an action constitutes as a principle a right, and can only degenerate into an abuse which can lead to damages in the case of wrongful intention, bad faith, or gross mistake. *See also* Paris Court of First Instance, 10 March 2017, no. 14/16022: *a contrario*, an abuse might be inferred from the circumstances of the initiation of the procedure, or from the damages requested.

[67] *See, e.g.,* Paris Court of Appeal, 15 November 2019, no. 16/03486.

[68] Cass. Com., 3 June 2003, no. 01-15740, where the patentee perfectly knew that the patent hadn't been infringed; *see also* Paris Court of First Instance, 10 October 2014, no. 12/06748, where the patentee knew that the patent had entered into the public domain.

injunction in the case an infringement has been ascertained. Therefore, the use of the concept of abuse of law for refusing an injunction seems somewhat theoretical. Since a patent gives the patentee a monopoly, whether exploited or not, rules of competition law prohibiting abuse of dominant position or agreements which constitute restraints of trade may be applied when deciding to grant a permanent injunction.[69]

Nonetheless, as regards essential patents and FRAND (Reasonable And Non-Discriminatory) commitments, it should be noted that the Paris Court of First Instance granted a permanent injunction concerning patents on the *mp3* musical files format (ISO/IEC 11172-3 standard) against an infringer who had never applied for a licence,[70] although without any specific motivation or any balance of interests.[71] The ECJ *Huawei* case,[72] which was decided later, would therefore not change the approach in such a situation.

As regards the possibility of alternative measures, the Enforcement Directive provides in Article 12 that member states may provide that, in appropriate cases and at the request of the person liable to be subject to injunctive relief, the competent judicial authorities may order pecuniary compensation to be paid to the injured party instead of applying injunctive relief if that person acted unintentionally and without negligence, if execution of injunctive relief would cause disproportionate harm and if pecuniary compensation to the injured party appears reasonably satisfactory. However, this is only a possibility offered to member states, which has not been used by the French legislature.[73] Contrary to injunctions, destruction and recall orders in case of a patent infringement are discretionary according to Article L. 615-14-2 al. 2 of the French Intellectual Property Code.

b. Differences between Preliminary and Permanent Injunctions

Preliminary injunctions are regulated by Article L. 615-3 of the French Intellectual Property Code. Any person having the right to bring an action for infringement may bring an action in summary proceedings before the competent civil court for an order, if necessary under penalty payment, against the alleged infringer or the intermediaries whose services used, for any measure intended to prevent an imminent infringement of the rights conferred by the title or to prevent the continuation

---

[69] *See* Paris Court of First Instance, 17 April 2015, no. 14/14124, about the determination of royalties for an essential patent.

[70] Paris Court of First Instance, 9 September 2008, no. 06/09277.

[71] On the other hand, preliminary injunctions, which are subject to specific rules (*cf. infra* in this section), are much more motivated: *see, e.g.*, for a refusal, Paris Court of First Instance, ord. Juge de la mise en état (JME), 29 November 2013, no. 12/11922.

[72] *Huawei* v. ZTE (CJEU 2015).

[73] Compare with, for copyright law, the decision of Cass. Civ. 1ère, 15 May 2015, no. 13-27391, Bull. No. 116, which invited the Court of Appeal to balance the interests between the original work and the derivative work, but whose interpretation remains controversial.

of alleged acts of infringement. In summary proceedings or on application, the court may order the measures requested only if the evidence reasonably available makes it likely that the plaintiff's rights are being infringed or that such infringement is imminent. The court may prohibit the continuation of the alleged acts of infringement, make it subject to the provision of guarantees intended to ensure possible compensation to the plaintiff or order the seizure of or delivery into the hands of a third party the goods suspected of infringing the rights conferred by the title, in order to prevent their introduction into or circulation within the circuits of commerce.

Preliminary injunctions are thus very different from permanent injunctions since they are not automatically granted. The Code provides that the court "may" take such measures. Since those measures are temporary, the judges look at the case prima facie. Therefore, as the Code provides, the preliminary injunction can only be granted if elements of proof, which the defendant can reasonably have access to, make it plausible that the patentee's rights have been infringed or are about to be infringed.

Litigation concerning preliminary injunctions is therefore much more developed than for permanent injunctions since the claimant must prove the likelihood of an infringement. In recent years, case law has somewhat evolved concerning the question of the invocation of the invalidity of the patent at that stage of the proceedings. Beforehand, judges considered that they could not deny a preliminary injunction unless the patent was obviously invalid.[74] Nowadays, case law seems to be more rigorous as regards the likelihood of the infringement, by saying that it may be ruled out when there are serious issues of validity[75] or infringement.[76] This means that if the judge ruling on the merits subsequently denies any infringement, the patent holder that had enforced the preliminary injunction will be strictly liable towards the defendant, according to Article L. 111-10 of the French Code of Civil Execution Procedures. In addition, Article L. 615-3 of the French Intellectual Property Code states that the court may subject the grant of a preliminary injunction to a deposit of the patent holder.

B. THE EFFECTS OF PERMANENT INJUNCTIONS FOR INFRINGEMENT OF A PATENT IN FRENCH LAW

A permanent injunction may be formulated in more or less extensive ways, and its duration may vary. When those injunctions are not being complied with by the infringer, remedies are available.

---

[74] *See, e.g.,* Paris Court of Appeal, 21 March 2012, no. 11/12942.

[75] Paris Court of Appeal, 16 January 2009, no. 08/12281; Paris Court of First Instance, summary judgment, 10 August 2012, PIBD 974, III, 823 (2012); Cass. com., 21 October 2014, no. 13-15.435.

[76] On these questions, *see* Galloux 2009, 350; Galloux 2013; Drillon 2015.

1. *The Scope of Permanent Injunctions*

Since there is no statutory basis for permanent injunctions in French patent law, the judge has some latitude to formulate them, provided they comply with the fundamental rules of civil litigation.

For example, some permanent injunctions refer to specific products with a very precise reference to infringing products,[77] notably for illicit imports.[78] In other situations, permanent injunctions refer both to the infringed claims and to the infringing objects, and to the prohibited acts: see, for example, a case where the Paris Court of Appeal "prohibit[ed] company D. to continue the sale of hand pieces and cartridges reproducing the claims 1, 5, 6, 7, 10 and 11 of the French part of European Patent 1 547 538".[79]

Other injunctions remain quite vague in their formulation, but nonetheless refer to the precise acts which have been committed by the defendant: for example, after having said that the defendant, "by importing and selling on the French territory, 'Get Locky' sealing rods that reproduced the claims of patent EP 1 572 548, has infringed the first, third and seventh claims of that patent", the Paris Court of First Instance decided to "prohibit the continuation of such activities".[80] Other injunctions seem more general at first glance, by "prohibit[ing] corporations M. and N. from continuing the patent infringing and unfair competition activities",[81] although one should probably consider that this was an implicit reference to the activities that were previously mentioned in the judgment.

Some injunctions have been granted with a somewhat wider scope by prohibiting, more generally, infringement of specific claims of a specific patent, such as a case of the Paris Court of Appeal, "prohibit[ing] corporation E. to sell products which reproduce the claims 1, 2, 5, 6 and 8 of French patent n°19.01136 owned by

---

[77] Paris Court of First Instance, 20 April 2017, no. 15/05831: "fait interdiction à la société R. de détenir et de commercialiser le déambulateur SPIDO EVOLUTION contrefaisant les revendications du brevet français FR 2 959 663".

[78] *See, e.g.*, Paris Court of First Instance, 7 September 2017, no. 15/07242: "interdit à la SARL W. ... d'importer, d'exporter depuis la France, de fabriquer, d'utiliser, d'offrir en vente, de vendre et de transborder sur tout le territoire français, directement ou indirectement, des tondeuses à gazon référencées TDTAC46T-BS625E ou tout produit comportant un boîtier de transmission identique ou reproduisant les caractéristiques des revendications 1 à 5 du brevet français no. 2 822 916 de la SAS F."; see *also* Paris Court of First Instance, 20 April 2017, no. 14/14832: "fait interdiction à la société B. et à la société S. d'importer et de commercialiser en France les laminateurs à plat 'B. Multi Applicator' contrefaisants, dans un délai de 8 jours à compter de la signification du jugement à intervenir, et ce sous astreinte provisoire de 1000 euros par infraction constatée".

[79] Paris Court of Appeal, 27 October 2017, no. 15/09926.

[80] Paris Court of First Instance, 19 May 2017, no. 15/15406. *See also* Paris Court of First Instance, 5 May 2017, no. 15/16348: "fait interdiction à la société défenderesse de proposer à la vente en France des ensembles bras et balais d'essuie-glace, reproduisant ces revendications".

[81] Paris Court of Appeal, 20 March 2018, no. 16/11444.

Mr. R."[82] The wording was probably suggested by the patent holder, and reproduced as such or with some modifications by the court in its decision.

It should be noted that sometimes injunctions also prohibit unfair competition acts which are linked to patent infringement activities, such as free-riding on the investments of the patent holder by making very similar technical documentations and catalogues.[83]

2. *Duration of Permanent Injunctions*

According to Article L. 613-1 of the French Intellectual Property Code, the exclusive right of exploitation takes effect as of the filing of the application, even though it is only considered as perfect and definitive once granted. That's the reason why Article L. 615-4 of the same code provides that, notwithstanding this former article, acts committed prior to the date on which the patent application has been made public or prior to the date of notification to any third party of a true copy of such application shall not be considered to prejudice the rights deriving from the patent. Moreover, as we have seen previously, the injunction stops as soon as the patent expires.

In addition, the judge may adjust the duration of the scope of an injunction. First, it is possible to postpone the effectiveness, as the Paris Court of First Instance did by "prohibit[ing] corporation R to possess and to sell the Spido Evolution walker which infringes the claims of French patent FR 2 959 663 within 8 days after the notification of the judgment".[84] Other cases have a somewhat more ambiguous formulation, where one can wonder whether it is the injunction itself which begins after a period of time, or whether – which seems much more likely – the injunction begins as soon as the judgment has been issued to the defendant, but the *astreinte* (which is a daily penalty for refusal to comply with that injunction) can only be enforced after such a period of time has passed since the judgment has been issued.[85]

---

[82] Paris Court of Appeal, 22 September 2017, no. 15/09651.

[83] Paris Court of Appeal, 20 March 2018, no. 16/11444.

[84] Paris Court of First Instance, 20 April 2017, no. 15/05831.

[85] Paris Court of First Instance, 11 July 2016, no. 15/0319: "fait interdiction aux sociétés C et CP de fabriquer, d'utiliser, de détenir, d'offrir en vente, de vendre, de livrer ou d'offrir de livrer des coffres et corps de coffres de volets roulants reproduisant les caractéristiques de la revendication 1 du brevet français n° 0958029, ce sous astreinte de 200€ par mètre linéaire de coffre et corps de coffre fabriqué, utilisé, détenu, offert en vente, vendu, livré ou offert à la livraison, passé un délai de 2 mois à compter de la signification du jugement". See also, for an extinctive term, Paris Court of First Instance, 8 June 2017, no. 15/14899: "fait interdiction à la société défenderesse de poursuivre de tels agissements, et ce sous astreinte de 50 euros par infraction constatée un mois à compter de la signification du présent jugement pendant 3 mois". Extinctive (i.e. extinguishing) terms can be combined with suspensive terms: *see, e.g.*, Paris Court of First Instance, 24 February 2017, no. 15/02169: "interdit à Monsieur Ludovic P. d'importer, d'offrir en vente, de vendre, de commercialiser et de détenir à ces fins des baguettes de scellage reprenant les caractéristiques du brevet EP 1 572 548, sous astreinte provisoire de 50 euros par infraction constatée passé le délai de 1 mois après la signification du jugement, et ce pendant 4 mois".

Postponing the effectiveness of the *astreinte* can be justified when it is practically difficult for the infringer to put an immediate end to the infringement (e.g., by replacing an infringing component by a substitute), or when it appears reasonable[86] to allow the infringer to sell its remaining stocks.[87]

Until recently, pursuant to the then applicable general civil procedure rules, an appeal stayed the execution of first-instance judgments,[88] which means that a permanent injunction only became effective once the Court of Appeal has affirmed it. However, at the request of the patent holder, the Court of First Instance could have ordered provisional execution of the decision, which renders the injunction enforceable as soon as the judgment has been issued, despite the appeal.[89] A decree of 11 December 2019 introduced a major change by reverting that principle.[90] Henceforth, provisional execution is the principle, since it automatically applies to first-instance decisions, unless the law or the judge decides otherwise. In that latter situation, the judge will have sole discretion to decide if provisory execution is not compatible with the nature of the case.[91] If a decision which benefits from provisional execution is reversed on appeal, the patent holder that enforced the injunction granted in first instance will be held strictly liable[92] for the damage caused by the enforcement of the injunction.[93] In order to mitigate the amount of such liability, the new legislation states that, in case of appeal, the first president of the appellate court can be asked to stop provisory execution "when there is a serious argument in favor of reversal and that there is a risk that the execution may lead to obviously excessive consequences".[94]

3. *Remedies for Violation of Permanent Injunctions*

Since French civil law has no equivalent for the notion of contempt of court, an injunction may be accompanied by an *astreinte*, which is a recurring penalty for

---

[86] On the discretionary character of the astreinte and its modalities, see *infra*.

[87] Stenger 2019.

[88] Former Art. 539 of the Code of Civil Procedure: "The time-limit for ordinary means of review action will stay the execution of the judgement. The review action brought within the time-limit will likewise suspend execution."

[89] Previous versions of Art. 514 et seq. of the Code of Civil Procedure.

[90] Art. 514 of the Code of Civil Procedure: "As a matter of law, first instance decisions benefit from provisory execution unless otherwise stated by the law or the court decision."

[91] Art. 514-1 of the Code of Civil Procedure.

[92] Art. L. 111-10 of the Code of Civil Execution Procedures: "Subject to the provisions of article L. 311-4, compulsory execution may be extended until its end pursuant to a provisional writ of execution. Such an execution is performed at the peril and risk of the creditor. Shall the title be later modified, the creditor shall reinstate the debtor in his rights in nature or by equivalent."

[93] *See* Paris Court of Appeal, 31 January 2014, no. 2012/05485, where the patent was finally deemed invalid, and Paris Court of Appeal, 2 July 2019, no. 2016/18780. At this time, the impact on French law of the ECJ case of *Bayer* v. *Richter* (CJEU 2019), is not known yet.

[94] New Art. L. 514-3, al. 1 of the *CPCEx*.

refusal to comply with the injunction, in order to encourage the infringer to comply with that order.[95] Article L. 131-1 of the French Code of Civil Execution Procedures (CPCEx) provides that "any judge may, even of its own motion,[96] order an *astreinte* in order to ensure the enforcement of its decision". The determination of the *astreinte* is a discretionary power of the judge, and does not require any motivation.[97] Such an *astreinte*, which may also be ordered by the specialized judge for the enforcement of court decisions,[98] is however not automatically ordered when requested.[99]

Pursuant to the CPCEx, an *astreinte* may be provisional or irrevocable.[100] Whereas a provisional *astreinte* is liquidated later by the judge considering the behaviour of the debtor and their creditworthiness,[101] the amount of an irrevocable *astreinte* is determined definitively by the judge when ordered.[102]

Therefore, when a permanent injunction has been violated, the patent holder may ask the relevant judge to liquidate the *astreinte* which has been ordered, and, in practice, the patentee will generally also request a new *astreinte*.[103] Article L. 131-2 of the CPCEx provides that "the astreinte is independent from the damages", which means that the amount of the *astreinte* has no relationship whatsoever to the amount

---

[95] If somebody refuses to comply with an injunction in a court order, they will only be requested to pay this daily fine, which requires asking the court to liquidate the *astreinte*, and, if refusal to pay continues, to ask for the seizure of that amount, which might not be possible in practice if the debtor is insolvent.

[96] *See* already the abovementioned case of Paris Court of Appeal, 16 May 1927, Ann. propr. ind. 1928, 13.

[97] Cass. Civ. 3, 9 November 1983, no. 82-14.775, Bull. III, no. 219; Cass. Civ. 2, 7 June 2006, no. 05-18.332.

[98] Art. L. 131-1, al. 2 CPCEx: "The specialized judge for the enforcement of court decisions may add an astreinte to a decision pronounced by another judge if the circumstances make it appear necessary."

[99] Paris Court of First Instance, 10 March 2017, no. 15/16137, where the *astreinte* was denied since the patentee did not prove that the infringing products were sold.

[100] Art. L. 131-2 CPCEx: "The *astreinte* is provisional or irrevocable. Any *astreinte* is deemed to be provisional, unless the judge has said that it was irrevocable. A definitive *astreinte* can only be ordered after a provisional *astreinte* has been ordered, and for a duration that the judge determines. If one of these two conditions has not been met, the astreinte shall be liquidated as a provisional *astreinte*."

[101] Art. L. 131-3 CPCE: "The *astreinte*, even when irrevocable, shall be liquidated by the specialized judge for the enforcement of court decisions, unless the judge who ordered it is still dealing with the case, or expressly mentioned that he should enforce it himself." On the liquidation of an *astreinte* in the mater of a trademark infringement, *see* Cass. Com. 14 November 2006, no. 04-11.344, Bull. IV, no. 221.

[102] Art. L. 131-4 CPCF: "The amount of the provisional *astreinte* is liquidated by taking into account the behavior of the person against whom the injunction has been granted, and the difficulties he has run into when complying with it. The rate of the irrevocable *astreinte* can never be modified during its liquidation. The provisional or irrevocable *astreinte* is lifted wholly or in part if it is established that the non-performance or delay in performance of the injunction of the judge derives, wholly or in part, from external events."

[103] Guerchoun 2017.

of losses suffered by the patent holder, and that it cannot be deducted from the damages to be paid, and must therefore be in addition to them.[104] New patent infringement proceedings may also be brought in case these injunctions are not complied with.[105]

REFERENCES

Cases

Cour de cassation

Cass. Civ., 1 February 1892, Ann. propr. ind. 1892, 103
Cass. Civ. 3rd, 9 November 1983, no. 82-14.775, Bull. III, no. 219
Cass. Com., 4 March 1986, no. 83-16.848, Bull. IV, no. 36
Cass. Civ. 3rd, 7 June 1990, Bull. civ. III, no. 140
Cass. Com., 1 March 1994, no. 92-11.506
Cass. Com., 3 June 2003, no. 01-15740
Cass. Civ. 2nd, 7 June 2006, no. 05-18.332
Cass. Com. 14 November 2006, no. 04-11.344, Bull. IV, no. 221
Cass. Com., 12 June 2007, no. 05-14.548, Bull. IV, no. 158
Cass. Ass. plén., 17 February 2012, no. 10-24.282, Bull. Ass. Pl. no. 2
Cass. Com., 21 October 2014, no. 13-15.435
Cass. Com., 17 March 2015, no. 13-15.862
Cass. Civ. 1st, 15 May 2015, no.13-27391, Bull. no. 116
Cass. Civ. 3rd, 10 November 2016, no. 15-19.561 & no. 15-21.949 & no. 15-25.113
Cass. Com., 6 December 2017, no. 15-19.726

Courts of Appeal

Paris Court of Appeal, 16 May 1927, Ann. propr. ind. 1928, 13
Paris Court of Appeal, 18 February 2005, no. 02/08524, PIBD 811, III, 388
Paris Court of Appeal, 30 November 2005, PIBD 824, III, 132
Paris Court of Appeal, 16 January 2009, no. 08/12281
Paris Court of Appeal, 6 February 2009, no. 07/08965
Paris Court of Appeal, 21 March 2012, no. 11/12942
Paris Court of Appeal, 22 May 2013, PIBD 988, III, 1313
Paris Court of Appeal, 31 January 2014, no. 2012/05485
Paris Court of Appeal, 23 February 2016, no. 13/20365
Paris Court of Appeal, 16 May 2017, no. 15/09506
Paris Court of Appeal, 27 June 2017, no. 14/25023
Paris Court of Appeal, 22 September 2017, no. 15/09651
Paris Court of Appeal, 27 October 2017, no. 15/09926
Paris Court of Appeal, 20 March 2018, no. 16/11444
Paris Court of Appeal, 2 July 2019, no. 2016/18780
Paris Court of Appeal, 15 November 2019, no. 16/03486
Paris Court of Appeal, 3 March 2020, no. 19/21426

---

[104] Stenger 2019.
[105] Passa 2013.

Courts of First Instance
Paris Court of First Instance, 13 April 1972, PIBD 89, III, 252
Paris Court of First Instance, 25 May 1983, Ann. propr. ind. 1984, 274
Paris Court of First Instance, 20 February 2001, PIBD 729, III, 530
Paris Court of First Instance, 6 September 2006, PIBD 841, III, 785
Paris Court of First Instance, 9 September 2008, no. 06/09277
Paris Court of First Instance, 12 February 2010, PIBD 919, III, 339
Paris Court of First Instance, 10 August 2012, PIBD 974, III, 823
Paris Court of First Instance, 24 May 2013, no. 11/09609
Paris Court of First Instance, 7 June 2013, no. 10/08326
Paris Court of First Instance, 29 November 2013, no. 12/11922
Paris Court of First Instance, 10 October 2014, no. 12/06748
Paris Court of First Instance, 17 April 2015, no. 14/14124
Paris Court of First Instance, 11 July 2016, no. 15/0319
Paris Court of First Instance, 24 February 2017, no. 15/02169
Paris Court of First Instance, 10 March 2017, no. 14/16022
Paris Court of First Instance, 10 March 2017, no. 15/16137
Paris Court of First Instance, 20 April 2017, no. 15/05831
Paris Court of First Instance, 20 April 2017, no. 14/14832
Paris Court of First Instance, 5 May 2017, no. 15/16348
Paris Court of First Instance, 19 May 2017, no. 15/15406
Paris Court of First Instance, 8 June 2017, no. 15/14899
Paris Court of First Instance, 7 September 2017, no. 15/07242
Paris Court of First Instance, 10 January 2020, no. 16/04839

Regulatory and Legislative Materials

French Civil Code: Art. 1355
French Code of Civil Procedure: Art. 514, 514-1
French Code of Civil Execution Procedures: Art. L. 111-10, L. 131-1, L. 131-2, L. 131-3, L. 131-4, L. 514-3
French Intellectual Property Code: Art. L. 613-12, L. 613-15, L. 613-16, L. 613-17-1, L. 613-18, L. 613-19, L. 613-6 et sq., L. 611-1, L. 613-23-2, L. 613-24, L. 613-3, L. 615-1, L. 615-3, L. 615-8-1, R. 411-19, R. 613-44-10.

Books, Articles and Online Materials

Azéma, Jacques & Galloux, Jean-Christophe. 2017. *Droit de la Propriété Industrielle*. Paris: Dalloz.
Basire, Yann. 2015. *La Fonction de la Marque*. Paris: LexisNexis.
Drillon, Sébastien. 2015. "Actions Complémentaires à l'Action en Contrefaçon," in *Jurisclasseur Brevets*, Fasc. 4650. Paris: LexisNexis.
Foyer, Jean & Vivant, Michel. 1991. *Le Droit des Brevets*. Paris: Presses Universitaires de France.
Galloux, Jean-Christophe. 2009. "Premier Bilan de l'Application de la Loi 2007-1544, dite 'de lutte contre la contrefaçon'," in *Propriété Intellectuelle* no. 33, p. 350. Paris: LexisNexis.
   2013. "Quelques Précisions Relatives aux Mesures Provisoires en Matière de Contrefaçon" in *Propriété Industrielle*, Étude no. 3. Paris: LexisNexis.

2020. "La réforme du droit français des brevets" in *Revue Trimestrielle de Droit Commercial*, Paris: Dalloz.

Gisclard, Thibault. 2014, "La brevetabilité des inventions pharmaceutiques en Inde", in *Propriété Industrielle*, Étude no. 6. Paris: LexisNexis.

2018. "Les Brevets de Nouvelle Application Thérapeutique et la Description de l'Effet Thérapeutique", in *Propriété Industrielle*, Étude no. 11. Paris: LexisNexis.

2020. "Le Droit des Brevets à l'Épreuve du SARS-CoV-2" in *Propriété Industrielle*, Étude no. 10. Paris: LexisNexis.

Goubeaux, Gilles. 1994. *Traité de Droit Civil, Introduction Générale.* Paris: LGDJ.

Guerchoun, Frédéric. 2017. *Astreinte, in Répertoire de Procédure Civile.* Paris: Dalloz.

Josserand, Louis. 1939. *De l'Esprit des Lois et de leur Relativité: Théorie dite de l'Abus des Droits.* Paris: Dalloz.

Le Stanc, Christian. 2014. "Les Patent Trolls" in Gasnier, Jean-Pierre & Bronzo, Nicolas, eds., *Les Nouveaux Usages du Brevet d'Invention: Entre Innovation et Abus*, vol. 1. Aix-en-Provence: Presses Universitaires d'Aix-Marseille.

Mathély, Paul. 1991. *Le Nouveau Droit Français des Brevets d'Invention.* Paris: JNA.

Passa, Jérôme. 2013. *Droit de la Propriété Industrielle vol. 2.* Paris: LGDJ.

Pollaud-Dulian, Frédéric, "La nouvelle procédure d'opposition en droit des brevets français" in *Dalloz IP/IT*, p. 372, Paris: Dalloz.

Py, Emmanuel. 2008. "L'annulation du brevet d'invention, " PhD Thesis, Strasbourg.

2011. "Annulation du brevet" in *Jurisclasseur Brevets*, Fasc. 4495. Paris: LexisNexis.

2018. "Les Limites et Exceptions aux Prérogatives Conférées par le Brevet : Analyse Sous L'angle des Fonctions du Brevet" in Assafim, João Marcelo de Lima, ed., *Inovacão, Propriedade Intelectual e Livre Concorrência.* Rio de Janeiro: Lumen Juris.

2020. "Sanction des Conditions de Brevetabilité : sur la décision d'annulation" in Vivant, Michel, ed., *Les Grands Arrêts de la Propriété Intellectuelle.* Paris: Dalloz.

Py, Emmanuel & Raynard, Jacques. 2021, *Un an de droit des brevets, in Propriété Industrielle.* Paris: LexisNexis.

Raynard, Jacques. 2012. *Note under Cass. Ass. plén., 17 February 2012*, in *La Semaine Juridique, Edition générale.* Paris: LexisNexis.

Raynard, Jacques, Py, Emmanuel & Tréfigny, Pascale. 2016. *Droit de la Propriété Industrielle.* Paris: LexisNexis.

Reboul-Maupin, Nadège. 2018. *Droit des Biens.* Paris: Dalloz.

Rodà, Caroline. 2010, *Les Conséquences Civiles de la Contrefaçon des Droits de Propriété Industrielle.* Paris: LexisNexis.

Stenger, Jean-Pierre. 2019. "Sanctions de la Contrefaçon" in *Jurisclasseur Brevets*, Fasc. 4680. Paris: LexisNexis.

Vivant, Michel. 2016. "L'irruption de la Notion de Balance des Intérêts en Droit des Brevets" in Gasnier, Jean-Pierre & Bronzo, Nicolas, eds., *Les Nouveaux Usages du Brevet d'Invention.* Aix-en-Provence: Presses Universitaires d'Aix-Marseille.

8

Germany

Peter Georg Picht and Anna-Lena Karczewski

For patent litigation, Germany is among the most frequented venues in Europe.[1] Both large, international law firms and highly specialized boutique firms are active before German courts. Not only the Federal Supreme Court (Bundesgerichtshof – BGH) but also a handful of major first- and second-instance venues, such as Düsseldorf, Hamburg, Mannheim and München, play an important role in shaping German patent law. Stakeholders, such as patentees, licensees, inhouse and outside counsel, scholars and non-German courts or lawmakers, therefore have a strong interest not only in the established legal framework for patent litigation in Germany, but also in shifts this framework is, of late, undergoing. At the same time, the language barrier complicates insights on these matters, not least for Anglo-American stakeholders, although a slowly increasing part of scholarship, and even of case law, is available in English. Against that background, this chapter sets out to explain basic structures and recent developments in German patent injunction law. It covers the main types of and requirements for such injunctions under German law (Section A), the injunction's scope as claimed and granted (Section B), bifurcation and stays (Section C), defences and limitations (Section D), as well as alternatives to injunctive relief (Section E), before a conclusion and an outlook (Section G) round off the chapter.

A. PATENT INJUNCTIONS: MAIN TYPES AND REQUIREMENTS

1. Main Types

As a rule of thumb, all acts infringing a patent can trigger injunctive relief under German law. This goes, hence, not only for direct infringements (Sec. 9 German

---

[1] Commission of the European Communities. 2007. "Communication from the Commission to the European Parliament and the Council, Enhancing the patent system in Europe," COM (2007) 165 final, 8; Ann 2009; Klos 2010; Kühnen & Cleassen 2013.

Patent Act – GPA) but also for contributory infringements (Sec. 10 GPA), for acts that enable or promote the infringement, and for uses not falling within the literal scope of a patent claim but which are captured by the doctrine of equivalents.[2] Requirements for an injunction can, however, slightly vary depending on the type of infringing act (see Section A.2). Furthermore, decisions granting injunctive relief can differ in the parallel claims they award to the patentee, such as damages (Sec. 139(2) GPA), recall or destruction (Sec. 140a GPA).

Besides injunctions granted as part of a final court decision ("final injunctions"), interim relief is available in the form of "preliminary injunctions" (see Section A.3). Injunctions can also form part of a court settlement, based either on a court-recorded party agreement (Sec. 794(1) No. 1 Code of Civil Procedure – CCP, Sec. 779 German Civil Code – GCC) or on a court proposal (Sec. 278(6) CCP).

2. *General Requirements and Specific Requirements for Preliminary Injunctions*

Some requirements must be fulfilled for all types of patent injunctions. For instance, the patent, Supplementary Protection Certificate (SPC) or patent application at issue must not be exhausted and the defendant must have used it in the sense of Sec. 9, 10 or 14 GPA. Absent a contractual (Sec. 15(2) GPA) or compulsory (Sec. 24 GPA) licence and absent a (general) declaration of willingness to license (Sec. 23 GPA), there must be a risk of first-time (Sec. 139(1)(2) GPA) or recurrent (Sec. 139(1) (1) GPA) infringement.[3] To give a last example, an injunction is only warranted where the defendant cannot raise a defence, such as the free state-of-the-art defence (also called "Formstein" defence; cf. BGH, 29.04.1986, X ZR 28/85 – Formstein).

Some other requirements depend, however, on whether the injunction sought is of an interim nature. The injunction stipulated in Sec. 139(1) GPA is a final, as

---

[2] On the doctrine of equivalents in German patent law, see Hasselblatt 2012, § 38 para. 199; Osterrieth 2015b, para. 109.

[3] Only infringing acts which have actually taken place, or which are likely to happen, can be enjoined, i.e. injunctions are not granted with regard to theoretical settings; on the requirements for a sufficient first-time infringement risk, see Grabinski & Zülch 2015, paras. 28, 32; Keukenschrijver 2016b, para. 263 (in particular on negative statements regarding the patent); regarding logistics providers: BGH, 19.09.2009, Xa ZR 2/08 – MP3-Player-Import; OLG Hamburg, 16.10.2008, 5 W 53/08 – iPod II. Injunction claims are too broad and will remain unsuccessful if they exclusively try to capture future infringing acts; Kraßer & Ann 2016, § 35 para. 8 et seq.; Grabinski & Zülch, 2015, para. 32. Furthermore, infringing acts do not justify an injunction if there is no risk of a recurrent infringement. This risk is, however, presumed in the event of an infringement, the presumption is rebuttable but the threshold for a rebuttal is high; see Grabinski & Zülch 2015, para. 30. One option is a cease-and-desist declaration, secured by a contractual penalty; Kraßer & Ann 2016, § 35 para. 6 et seq. Note further that the risk of a recurrent infringement can be removed by a court decision granting (preliminary) injunctive relief; OLG Karlsruhe, 10.04.1991, 6 U 164/90 – Erbenermittlung; OLG Karlsruhe, 22.02.1995, 6 U 250–94; OLG Hamburg, 20.06.1984, 3 W 103/84; KG Berlin, 20.08.1992, 25 U 2754/92; KG Berlin, 25.10.1996, 5 U 4912/96; dissent OLG Hamm, 19.02.1991, 4 U 231/90, para. 26.

opposed to a preliminary injunction. "Final" is, however, not the same as "infinite" since it is, by definition, not possible to enjoin a defendant from the use of a patent beyond the patent's protection period.[4] The duration of patent protection constitutes, hence, a built-in time limitation for injunctions.

Much more limited in time are injunctions granted as preliminary injunctive relief under Sec. 935, 940 CCP.[5] This limitation can be caused not only by the fact that the preliminary injunction is replaced by a final decision[6] but also by a time-limited scope of the preliminary injunction itself,[7] or by a legal remedy[8] curtailing the injunction.

For a preliminary injunction, the patentee has to show an obvious claim to an injunction and a reason why the injunction ought to be granted as preliminary relief.[9] To fulfil the first requirement, both patent validity and infringement need to be evident to the court.[10] Unclear validity of the asserted patent may prevent the court from issuing a preliminary injunction.[11] As a general rule, courts do not issue a preliminary injunction where they would stay (Sec. 148 CCP) the main proceedings (on stays see Section C) because of pending validity proceedings and a high

---

[4] Grabinski & Zülch 2015, para. 34, with reference to BGH, 22.11.1957, I ZR 152/56 – Resin, para. 19, BGH, 20.5.2008, X ZR 180/05 – Tintenpatrone, para. 7.

[5] Voß 2019, para. 276. As to TRIPS and EU law background, see in particular: Sec. 50, 41(1) TRIPS; Sec. 9 Enforcement Directive 2004/48/EC; Gesetz zur Verbesserung der Durchsetzung von Rechten des geistigen Eigentums vom 7. Juli 2008, PMZ 2008, 274. The core, general requirements for preliminary relief under Sec. 935, 940 CCP are the existence of a claim (*Verfügungsanspruch*); here mainly: requirements for an injunction, as described in Section A.2 and of sufficient grounds/urgency for issuing a preliminary decision (*Verfügungsgrund*; here e.g. occurrence of an infringement alone not sufficient, further aspects necessary that intensify need for immediate relief; OLG Düsseldorf, 18.05.2009, 2 U 140/08 – Captopril; much depends on expeditious conduct of patentee, OLG München, Mitt. 2001, 85, 89 – Wegfall der Dringlichkeit). The patentee does not have to fully prove that these requirements are fulfilled (*Vollbeweis*), it suffices for it to show prima facie evidence, i.e. preponderance of the evidence (*überwiegende Wahrscheinlichkeit*), Sec. 940, 936, 920(2) CCP. Furthermore, the court has to balance the involved interests (here of infringer and patentee). For legal remedies against a preliminary injunction, *See, e.g.,* Sec. 924, 926, 927 CCP. On the – for the patent context quite important – instrument of a "protective brief" submitted by the (alleged) infringer, see Deutsch 1990.

[6] On the specific constellation that, after the granting of a preliminary injunction, an injunction is denied in the final decision, see BGH, 01.04.1993, I ZR 70/91 – Verfügungskosten.

[7] Grabinski & Zülch 2015, para. 153b, 153h, with case law. One example are preliminary injunctions regarding trade fairs, LG Düsseldorf, 11.05.2004, 4a O 195/04.

[8] E.g., Sec. 927, 929 CCP.

[9] Haft et al. 2011, 927.

[10] Voß 2019, para. 281 et seq.; Osterrieth 2015b, para. 79; cf. OLG Düsseldorf, 29.04.2010, I 2 U 126/09 – Harnkatheterset. In a way, these requirements, together with the ensuing balancing of interests, soften bifurcation and the infringement–injunction nexus as far as preliminary relief is concerned.

[11] Validity concerns are usually considered as removing the grounds/urgency for preliminary relief (*Verfügungsgrund*); OLG Düsseldorf, 29.04.2010, I 2 U 126/09 – Harnkatheterset; OLG Karlsruhe, 08.07.2009, 6 U 61/09 – Vorläufiger Rechtsschutz.

likelihood of invalidation of the patent.[12] The same is usually[13] true where a first-instance ruling has held the patent to be invalid, even though the decision is not yet final.[14] Conversely, a first-instance (although not final) confirmation of validity supports the justification for preliminary relief.[15]

The second requirement is fulfilled where preliminary relief appears suitable and necessary to protect the applicant from substantial disadvantage (*Verfügungsgrund* – grounds for preliminary relief).[16] This usually requires that an element of urgency is present and that the interests of the patentee outweigh – in a balancing exercise – the interests of the infringer.[17] For the determination of urgency, both the pre-litigation conduct of the patentee and its conduct during the litigation are relevant.[18] For instance, the patentee must not, without good reason, allow an extended time-span to pass between learning of the infringement and its circumstances and the filing of the injunction.[19] Nor must it fail to litigate in an active and timely manner, e.g., by defaulting[20] or by delaying an injunction request until publication of the full-fledged reasoning of a decision in parallel nullity proceedings.[21] Factors relevant in the balancing of interests include the impact of an injunction on the infringer's business, the likelihood for the patentee to successfully collect damages later on, and the question whether the patentee engages in patent-based production itself or merely collects royalties.[22]

All in all, the requirements for a preliminary injunction are rather strict since this relief severely impairs the rights of the alleged infringer.[23] Consequently, preliminary injunctions are a well-established, but – at least traditionally[24] – not a very frequent feature of German patent law.[25]

---

[12] OLG Düsseldorf 21.10.1982, 2 U 67/82; OLG Düsseldorf, 05.10.1995, 2 U 43/95; OLG Frankfurt, 27.03.2003, 6 U 215/02 – Mini Flexiprobe.
[13] But not where the decision is evidently flawed; OLG Düsseldorf, 29.05.2008, 2 W 47/07 – Olanzapin.
[14] Grabinski & Zülch 2015, para. 153b.
[15] OLG Düsseldorf, 29.04.2010, I 2 U 126/09 – Harnkatheterset.
[16] Voß 2019, para. 284.
[17] *Id.*
[18] *Id.*
[19] OLG Düsseldorf, 17.01.2013, I-2 U 87/12 – Flupirtin-Maleat.
[20] Voß 2019, para. 290.
[21] OLG Düsseldorf, 29.06.2017, I-15 U 4/17 – Olanzapin II.
[22] Voß 2019, para. 303 with further references.
[23] Osterrieth 2015b, para. 79.
[24] On recent tendencies to grant preliminary injunctions more frequently, see Böhler 2011, 965.
[25] On numbers, see von Falck 2002, 429. On preliminary injunctions in general, see also Böhler 2011, 965; Wuttke 2011, 393. Prominent court decisions have held that it can be difficult to assess the requirements for an injunction in preliminary proceedings and that, therefore, this relief is to be granted with caution, *See, e.g.,* OLG Karlsruhe, 27.04.1988, 6 U 13/88 – Dutralene; OLG Karlsruhe, 08.07.2009, 6 U 61/09 – Vorläufiger Rechtsschutz, para. 13; OLG Düsseldorf, 29.05.2008, 2 W 47/07 – Olanzapin (especially on the relevance of first-instance decisions on patent validity); OLG Hamburg, 03.09.1987, 3 U 83/87; OLG Frankfurt, 03.05.1988, 6 U 207/87.

B. SCOPE AS CLAIMED AND GRANTED: ENFORCEMENT

The usual patent infringement litigation in Germany includes an oral hearing and is decided by a judgment on the merits,[26] including a decision on costs and provisional enforcement.[27] The operative part (*Tenor/Urteilstenor*)[28] of such a judgment is based on the plaintiff's motion, reflects its pleas,[29] and provides the legal basis for the enforcement of the ruling.[30] An infringement decision must state clearly the actions from which a defendant has to refrain.[31] Wording and interpretation of the decision's operative part (*Tenor*) are crucial since they determine the (range of) acts which a defendant is not allowed to repeat/undertake.[32] The operative part must not be so abstract as to cover acts which were not in dispute.[33] By way of interpretation, the scope of an injunction is oftentimes delineated according to the so-called core theory: The infringer cannot evade an injunction by making minor changes to the infringing act/product if the core of the (form of the) infringement remains unchanged.[34]

Whether and in which cases the patent claims can be used to identify the infringing acts is a complex and highly debated issue.[35] Although a plaintiff is not procedurally barred from asserting broad claims for patent infringement, even claims as comprehensive as the patent claims themselves,[36] the action will be dismissed unless the plaintiff specifies the infringement,[37] in particular the infringing product, in the initial complaint or during[38] the proceedings. While the court may not award more than the plaintiff has requested (Sec. 308(1) CCP), it is possible for the court to reframe the claim, to grant less than requested, or to base the decision on different legal grounds than submitted.[39] Inadmissible actions will be thrown out by means of a procedural ruling.[40]

As key means for the enforcement of patent injunction decisions, such decisions regularly impose both a penalty payment (maximum EUR 250,000) for each case of

---

[26] On wording regarding claims and subclaims of the infringed patent, see Voß, 2019, para. 198.

[27] *Id.*, para. 197.

[28] Summarizes the core content of the decision, e.g. the (partial) approval or rejection of the plaintiff's motion as well as the costs. For examples, see the cited decisions, the operative part precedes the reasoning..

[29] Voß 2019, para. 36.

[30] BGH, 30.03.2005, X ZR 126/01 – Blasfolienherstellung.

[31] Grabinski & Zülch 2015, para. 32.

[32] Pitz 2010, para. 134.

[33] Grabinski & Zülch 2015, para. 32.

[34] Pitz 2010, para. 134.

[35] See in detail BGH, 29.04.1986, X ZR 28/85 – Formstein; BGH, 30.03.2005, X ZR 126/01 – Blasfolienherstellung; OLG München, 06.10.1958, 6 W 607/58; Meier-Beck 1998, 277; Grabinski & Zülch 2015, para. 32.

[36] Grabinski & Zülch 2015, para. 32.

[37] BGH, 23.02.1962, I ZR 114/60 – Furniergitter, para. 20; BGH, 29.04.1986, X ZR 28/85 – Formstein.

[38] BGH, 24.11.1999, I ZR 189/97, para. 38.

[39] Voß 2019, para. 36.

[40] Pitz 2010, para. 134.

culpable non-compliance and custody (maximum two years) in case of repeated non-compliance or failure to make a penalty payment.[41]

C. BIFURCATION AND STAYS

In Germany, patent litigation is a civil law dispute subject, in principle, to the same procedural rules as other civil law cases.[42] As a very important exception to this rule, however, German patent litigation is "bifurcated": Court proceedings are split into validity matters[43] on the one hand and all other patent-related disputes, infringement disputes in particular, on the other hand.[44] As one of the reasons for this approach, the relatively thorough patent granting procedure is perceived to justify a presumption of validity of the patent, permitting the infringement court to grant relief without having itself assessed patent validity. Furthermore, the effectiveness of infringement proceedings would be reduced if the infringement court had to deal with validity matters because assessing validity would delay the grant of injunctions, damages or other remedies.[45]

1. *Stay of Infringement Proceedings Pending Validity Proceedings*

Due to bifurcation, it is possible (and frequent) that injunction proceedings and validity proceedings run in parallel and that the infringement court awards an injunction before the validity court ascertains whether the patent in question is valid or not.[46] A key instrument for avoiding contradictory results in the two prongs of the bifurcated system – grant of injunction on the one hand, invalidation of the patent on the other – is a stay of the infringement proceedings according to Sec. 148 CCP.

Courts may grant a stay of infringement proceedings in the first, second[47] or third[48] instance. They have some discretion based on a balancing of the parties'

---

[41] *See further* Grabinski & Zülch 2015, para. 160 et seq.
[42] Osterrieth 2015b, para. 2.
[43] The main relevant types of validity proceedings are opposition proceedings (Sec. 59, 81 GPA) or an action for revocation (Sec. 22, 81 GPA). The German Patent Office, the Federal Patent Court, and the Federal Court of Justice have exclusive jurisdiction over validity, infringement courts are bound by their decision. See Osterrieth 2015b, para. 2 et seq.; Mes 2015, § 139 para. 353.
[44] Osterrieth 2015b, para. 1.
[45] On both reasons, see *id.*, para. 3.
[46] *Id.*, para. 4.
[47] *Id.*, para. 5; Kraßer & Ann 2016, § 36 para. 71. On the particularities of a second-instance assessment, e.g. on the lower threshold for a stay if the patentee *won* the first instance, can as a result enforce the injunction based on the provisionally enforceable first-instance decision, and is, therefore, less severely affected by a stay, see OLG Düsseldorf, 20.06.2002, 2 U 81/99 – Haubenstrechtautomat, para. 128; OLG Düsseldorf, 21.12.2006, 2 U 58/05 – Thermocycler, para. 130.
[48] BGH, 28.09.2011, X ZR 68/10 – Klimaschrank; BGH, 06.04.2004, X ZR 272/02 – Druckmaschinen-Temperierungssystem, e.g. holding that the interests of the patentee ought to prevail the more clearly the later the infringer has attacked the patent's validity.

interests.[49] As a general tendency, German courts use this discretion to take a rather patentee-friendly position; they are restrictive in the grant of stays.[50] According to one of the standard tests, an infringer requesting a stay must show a high likelihood that the patent will be invalidated.[51] A stay is considered appropriate if the patent scope has already been limited as a result of opposition (Sec. 21, 59 GPA) or nullity (Sec. 22, 81 et seq. GPA) proceedings in the first instance, at least where this restriction has the challenged form of execution no longer covered.[52] Some scholars argue that opposition proceedings suggest a stay more strongly than actions for revocation since, in opposition proceedings, it is the patentee who bears the burden of proof.[53] Generally speaking, a stay seems more likely where novelty of the infringed patent is questionable,[54] and less likely where opposition/revocation proceedings focus on inventiveness.[55] If one action for revocation has failed but a second action been filed (on similar grounds), infringement proceedings will usually not be stayed any longer, unless imminent success of the second action for revocation is evident.[56] The suspension will not be granted if the defendant has delayed in initiating the invalidity proceedings (Sec. 296 CCP).[57] Neither the mere possibility of destruction or revocation nor a threat of an action for annulment justify a stay.[58] The same goes for a compulsory licence action,[59] since such action can legitimate use of the patent for the future only.[60]

As to the standards by which the infringement courts determine the likelihood of patent invalidation, there is no formal taking of evidence. However, the defendant should not be significantly worse off than if the infringing court also had the jurisdiction to decide on validity, and the courts do engage in a serious examination of the likelihood of success.[61] For instance, if a stay is requested on the grounds that the patented invention has been in use prior to the granting of the patent and that, therefore, the patent must be nullified, the infringer must produce conclusive and

---

[49] BGH, 28.09.2011, X ZR 68/10 – Klimaschrank; OLG München, 29.12.2008, 6 W 2387/08 – Abstrakte Vorgreiflichkeit.

[50] Mes 2015, § 139 para. 354.

[51] *Id.*, § 139 para. 352, 354; Grabinski & Zülch 2015, para. 107; Osterrieth 2009, 543. On the lower threshold before appeal courts, see BGH, 11.11.1986, X ZR 56/85 – Transportfahrzeug; Grabinski & Zülch 2015, para. 107.

[52] Grabinski & Zülch 2015, para. 107 with reference to OLG Düsseldorf, 22.02.12, I 2 U 26/05.

[53] Mes 2015, § 139 para. 359.

[54] For instance, because the opposing party raises elements of the state of the art which have not been reviewed in the verification procedure; LG München I, 24.08.2007, 21 O 22456/06 – Antibakterielle Versiegelung.

[55] Mes 2015, § 139 para. 355 w.f.r.

[56] BGH, 17.07.2012, X ZR 77/11 – Verdichtungsvorrichtung.

[57] LG München I, 19.05.2011, 7 O 8923/10; BGH, 28.09.2011, X ZR 68/10 – Klimaschrank; Grabinski & Zülch 2015, para. 107.

[58] Grabinski & Zülch 2015, para. 107.

[59] On compulsory licences, see Section D.1.b.

[60] Grabinski & Zülch 2015, para. 109.

[61] *Id.*, para. 107.

detailed evidence of the alleged prior use.[62] Stays may be decided without oral hearing, but this is not the rule.[63] The decision on a stay can be appealed (Sec. 252, 567 et seq. CCP) but review is limited by the principle that the appeal court is not supposed – at this stage – to question the first instance court's preliminary view on whether an infringement has taken place.[64]

Especially in recent times, bifurcation has drawn criticism,[65] not least because a considerable patent invalidation rate and substantial time gaps between the decisions in infringement and validity proceedings can harm alleged infringers who are enjoined from using a technology the patent on which is subsequently declared invalid.[66] The need to wait for the decision of the – usually slower – validity court delays the overall resolution of the case[67] and alleged infringers may be forced into settlement by the costs and other disadvantages they would incur during this period.[68] On the other hand, the swifter decision on and termination of an infringement which bifurcation permits does generate strong patent protection and it certainly makes Germany an attractive venue for patentees.[69]

2. *Other Types of Stays and Procedural Reactions to Patent Invalidation*

Usually, even a permanent injunction issued by a court of first instance is provisionally – i.e. until (and if) overturned by the second instance – enforceable on the condition that the plaintiff lodges sufficient security.[70] Enforcement of the injunction can, as an exception, be stayed until a final decision in the case at the request of the defendant[71] where (i) the defendant provides security (Sec. 719, 707 CCP), (ii) an enforcement threatens to inflict serious, irreparable damage upon the defendant, and (iii) a balancing of interests shows that the defendant's interests outweigh the plaintiff's interests given the facts of the case, including validity concerns.[72]

Other reasons for delaying or staying injunctions in time are, in particular, so-called torpedo actions in other EU member states under Sec. 27, 30 of the Brussels

---

[62] Critical of the high requirements for suspension and with further references, see *id.*, para. 107.

[63] *Id.*, para. 108.

[64] OLG Düsseldorf, 27.05.2003, 2 W 11/03 – Vorgreiflichkeit; OLG Düsseldorf, 08.12.1993, 2 W 79/93 – Prüfungskompetenz des Beschwerdegerichts, para. 8; OLG München, 29.12.2008, 6 W 2387/08 – Abstrakte Vorgreiflichkeit.

[65] See Meier-Beck 2015, 929; Thambisetty 2010, 144; Lemely 2013, 1732; Practical Law Arbitration, 2019.

[66] E.g., BGH, 08.07.2014, X ZR 61/13.

[67] Practical Law Arbitration 2019, 6.

[68] Meier-Beck 2015, 932.

[69] *Id.*, 932.

[70] One way of providing security is to submit a bank guarantee. Roughly speaking, the amount of the security is calculated to cover costs and damages incurred by the defendant in case the first-instance decision is overturned on appeal. For details, see Lackmann 2021, paras. 1 et seq.

[71] See for granting of a use-by period according to considerations of proportionality Section D.6.

[72] Haft et al. 2011.

I Regulation (recast),[73] a pending constitutional complaint against a ruling that grants annulment of the patent,[74] or a referral for a preliminary ruling to the Court of Justice of the European Union pursuant to Sec. 267 TFEU.[75]

If the patent lapses during infringement proceedings, but without retroactive[76] effect, the patentee must limit its claims to the period of patent validity.[77] If the infringement court issues an injunction and the patent is subsequently invalidated, the infringer may file an "action raising an objection to the claim being enforced" (Sec. 767 CCP) based on the grounds that the patent, the use of which has been enjoined, lacks validity. Furthermore, the infringer may file for an interim order staying enforcement (Sec. 769 CCP).[78] If the infringement decision is final and has already been enforced before the invalidation/lapse of the patent,[79] an action for retrial according to Sec. 580 No. 6 CCP (by way of analogy)[80] or claims based on undue enrichment (Sec. 812 et seq. GCC) may be raised. An action for retrial based on a decision (partly) invalidating the patent can, however, only be brought after the invalidating decision has become final.[81]

D. DEFENCES AND LIMITATIONS

1. *Considerations of Public Interest*

a. Relevance and Types of Public Interest Considerations

Sec. 139(1) GPA itself, German patent law's core provision on injunctions, does not foresee the consideration of public interest as far as the latter is not embodied in the requirements the provision establishes for the grant of an injunction. Nor does a strong tradition of wide judicial discretion exist[82] which would enable courts to broadly introduce public interest considerations.

---

[73] "Torpedos" are actions in another EU member state, seeking a declaratory judgment that the patent is not infringed and aiming to block infringement proceedings, using the principle that the infringement court must stay its proceedings until the declaratory judgment court has decided whether it has jurisdiction. See, for details, Osterrieth 2015b, para. 34; Kühnen 2017, § C para. 177.

[74] See LG Düsseldorf, 27.08.2004 – Suspension on constitutional complaint.

[75] Mes 2015, § 139 para. 352. This can apply not only where the referral resulted from proceedings concerning the patent whose (alleged) infringement caused the infringement proceedings to be stayed, but also where the referral concerns another patent but raises the same issue which is relevant to the infringement proceedings to be stayed; BGH, 24.01.2012, VIII ZR 236/10.

[76] There is no retroactive effect, if, for instance, the patent lapses because the protection period is over.

[77] Kühnen 2009, 289 et seq.

[78] Osterrieth 2015b, para. 6.

[79] BGH, 29.07.2010, Xa ZR 118/09 – Bordako.

[80] BGH, 17.04.2012, X ZR 55/09 – Tintenpatrone III; BGH, 29.07.2010, Xa ZR 118/09 – Bordako.

[81] OLG Düsseldorf, 11.11.2010, I 2 U 152/09 – Tintenpatronen.

[82] Ohly 2008, 795.

The balancing of interests required for an interim injunction, however, and in particular the provisions in Sec. 24(1) No. 2 GPA,[83] Sec. 11 GPA, and Sec. 13(1) GPA, are important settings in which public interest considerations can be brought to bear. The general concept of public interest, which is embodied in these provisions, changes over time and cannot be lumped into a single, general formula.[84] It is a broad and multifaceted concept, encompassing, for instance, technical, economic, socio-political and medical aspects,[85] which factor into an assessment of whether an injunction would be proportional[86] under the circumstances of the case.[87] To give an idea, aspects hitherto considered (not only in interim injunction settings) were:

- the patent holder did not satisfy or could not satisfy domestic needs;[88]
- improvement of the trade balance[89] and promotion of exports;[90]
- improvement of the currency situation;[91]
- likely insolvency of the licensee and resulting increase in unemployment;[92]
- increase in workplace safety;[93]
- promotion of public health;[94]
- continuous availability of a particular medicinal product,[95] in particular one that has major advantages (therapeutic properties, efficacy, reduced side effects) over similar products;[96]
- the simultaneous pursuit of financial interests does not prevent presence of a public interest and the granting of a compulsory licence;[97]
- the mere promotion of competition is not sufficient as a public interest.[98]

[83] On the compatibility of this provision with Sec. 30 TRIPS, see Wilhelmi 2019, para. 24.

[84] BGH, 05.12.1995, X ZR 26/92 – Polyferon, para. 45.

[85] Rogge & Kober-Dehm 2015, para. 17; BGH, 05.12.1995, X ZR 26/92 – Polyferon, para. 50; BGH, 13.07.2004, KZR 40/02 – Standard-Spundfass, para. 21.

[86] See also, on proportionality-related modifications to the German legal framework, Section F.

[87] BGH, 05.12.1995, X ZR 26/92 – Polyferon, para. 50.

[88] RG, 27.05.1918, I. 89/17, para. 5; RG, 18.01.1936, I 90/35.

[89] RG, 27.06.1928, I 271/27, para. II.3.

[90] RG, 21.12.1935, I 18/35.

[91] RG, 01.02.1938, I 173 174/36.

[92] RG, 11.03.1926, I 243 244/25 – Stapelfaser, para. 2.a; RG, 24.01.1934, I 37/33 – Tonaufnahmeverfahren.

[93] RG, 11.02.1903, I 291/02.

[94] RG, 16.08.1935, I 44/35.

[95] BGH, 05.12.1995, X ZR 26/92 – Polyferon, para. 56; BPatG, 07.06.1991, 3 Li 1/90 – Zwangslizenz.

[96] Rogge & Kober-Dehm 2015, para. 21.

[97] Id., para. 16.

[98] Id., para. 16.

b. Compulsory Licences on Public Interest Grounds

Based on Art. 5A of the Paris Union Convention for the Protection of Industrial Property and Sec. 31 TRIPs almost all European countries have incorporated legal standards which provide for the right to a compulsory licence.[99] Under German law, if the patentee is unwilling to grant a licence for reasonable remuneration and if there is a public interest in such a licence, a compulsory licence shall be granted to the licence seeker (Sec. 24(1) No. 2 GPA). The presence of a public interest is determined according to the general criteria mentioned in Section D.1.a. So far, Sec. 24(1) GPA has gained traction mainly in the pharmaceutical field[100] and recent case law seems to indicate its relevance is growing there, although the provision is not applied regularly.[101] An abusive exploitation of the patent by the patentee is not a necessary requirement for the grant of a compulsory licence under Sec. 24 GPA.[102] Nor does the licence seeker's unsuccessful offer of licensing conditions (Sec. 24(1) No. 1 GPA) have to meet the requirements for a compulsory licence (defence) under competition law (e.g., dominance, FRAND or Orange Book requirements regarding content and timeframe; see Section D.3).[103] A compulsory licence is not warranted, however, where equivalent ways exist to satisfy the public interest.[104]

The compulsory licence is an exception to the principle that the patent holder remains free to decide whether and how to grant licences enabling use of the patented invention for the benefit of the public interest.[105] Hence, the burden of proving the prerequisites for a compulsory licence lies with the licence seeker.[106] If it can show they are fulfilled, there is no judicial discretion, the licence seeker has a claim to the compulsory licence (Sec. 24 (1), 81 (1), 84 GPA)[107] and the court has to grant it.[108]

The licence seeker can enforce its compulsory licence claim by way of an action before the Federal Patent Court (Sec. 81 GPA). The Patent Act also allows, in case

[99] Pitz 2019, 78.

[100] See Mes 2015, para. 2; BPatG, 31.8.2016, 3 LiQ 1/16; BPatG, 07.06.1991, 3 Li 1/90 – Zwangslizenz: permission to start selling infringing arthritis medication for a limited time period to patients not reactive to other medication, 8% royalty, revoked on the basis of different assessment of facts in BGH, 05.12.1995, X ZR 26/92 – Polyferon.

[101] BPatG, 31.8.2016, 3 LiQ 1/16; BGH, 11.7.2017, X ZB 2/17 – Raltegravir: permission to continue selling patent infringing HIV medication in the territory and to the extent previously covered; Wilhelmi 2019, para. 7 with further references.

[102] Mes 2015, para. 14.

[103] BPatG, 31.8.2016, 3 LiQ 1/16 (EP).

[104] Rogge & Kober-Dehm 2015, para. 16.

[105] E.g., if the possible uses are sufficiently researched or evaluated by the patentee himself, if an equivalent medicinal product or therapy is available for treatment, see BGH, 05.12.1995, X ZR 26/92 – Polyferon, para. 17, 19. Wilhelmi 2019, para. 5 et seq.

[106] See BGH, 05.12.1995, X ZR 26/92 – Polyferon, para. 68.

[107] Mes 2015, para. 30, 33; Wilhelmi 2019, para. 5, 48.

[108] Wilhelmi 2019, para. 25 with reference to RG, 29.06.1943, I 79/42.

of urgency, for the grant of a compulsory licence as an interim measure (Sec. 84 GPA).[109] The result of the court decision granting a compulsory licence is not an outright licence contract between the parties but the legalization of the patent use[110] and a statutory, non-exclusive licence on the conditions[111] – especially the royalties – determined by the court.[112] Hitherto, patent infringers could not use pending proceedings regarding a compulsory licence under Sec. 24 GPA as a defence against the patentee's claim for an injunction.[113] This may change in the future given the case law on competition law-based compulsory licences (see Section D.3). A decision – including preliminary rulings – granting a compulsory licence can, however, be raised in the infringement proceedings and prevent an injunction.[114] Furthermore, the infringer can try to have the infringement court stay the injunction proceedings with regard to the pending compulsory licence proceedings if the compulsory licence is requested with retroactive effect and the court sees a sufficient likelihood – with regard to the requirements mentioned in Section C.1– that it will be awarded.[115]

c. Expropriation Orders on Public Interest Grounds

Another key provision on public interest considerations is Sec. 13(1) GPA which states, in pertinent part:

> (1) The patent shall have no effect in a case where the Federal Government orders that the invention is to be used in the interest of public welfare. Further, it shall not extend to a use of the invention which is ordered in the interest of the security of the Federal Republic of Germany by the competent highest federal authority or by a subordinate authority acting on its instructions. ...
>
> (3) In the cases referred to in subsection (1), the proprietor of the patent shall be entitled to equitable remuneration from the Federal Republic of Germany.

As to its legal nature, Sec. 13 GPA is – today mainly[116] – considered not as a provision foreseeing a contract-based compulsory licence for the benefit of other market participants but as a provision permitting an expropriation of the patentee in the sense of Sec. 14(3) GC, by way of a state order and in exchange for an equitable remuneration. The expropriation order does not, however, invalidate the patent

---

[109] On details, see Mes 2015, para. 33; Wilhelmi 2019, para. 77.

[110] BGH, 11.07.1995, X ZR 99/92 – Klinische Versuche, para. 22 et seq.

[111] See Mes 2015, para. 35 et seq.; Wilhelmi 2019, para. 52 et seq. for typical contents of a compulsory licence. Inter alia, the licence can be limited in scope and subject to case-specific obligations on the licensee.

[112] Mes 2015, paras. 33, 43.

[113] Pitz 2012, para. 198.

[114] Cf. Rogge & Kober-Dehm 2015, para. 36; Wilhelmi 2019, para. 85.

[115] Nieder 2001, 401; Pitz 2012, para. 198.

[116] Compulsory licence: RG, 28.09.1921, I 46/21, RGZ 102, 391; reflecting the public-good limitations to property following from Sec. 14(2) FL.

altogether; it is –and must strictly be[117] – limited to the timespan and forms of use necessary to achieve the public interest goals.[118] Sec. 13 GPA is considered to be coherent with Sec. 31 TRIPS.[119] Its practical relevance is quite low[120] and the most interesting aspects regarding Sec. 13 GPA do (today) probably relate not so much to how the provision plays out in practice but to what it tells us about the possibility of and requirements for a limitation of patent exclusivity and property rights in the public interest, in particular from a constitutional and economic viewpoint.

As to some details of the provision, "public welfare" (Sec. 13(1)(1) GPA) is interpreted in a narrower sense than "public interest" in Sec. 24 GPA, addressing natural disasters, epidemics, attacks using biological weapons, and similar gruesome events.[121] "Interest[s] of the security" (Sec. 13(1)(2) GPA) mainly addresses police or military concerns, as well as the protection of the population during catastrophic events.[122] The expropriating "order" must be cloaked in the form of an administrative act specifying the (extent of the) public use to be made of the invention.[123] Importantly, an order under Sec. 13 GPA may only be issued if use of the patented invention cannot be ensured by other means, such as a (compulsory) licence or less extensive administrative orders.[124]

2. Compulsory Licence According to Sec. 24(2) GPA

Sec. 24(2) GPA provides for the grant of a compulsory licence in situations where "a licence seeker cannot exploit an invention for which he holds protection under a patent with a later filing or priority date without infringing a patent with an earlier filing or priority date". Instead of a specific public interest, the provision requires that the dependent patent embodies an important technical progress of considerable economic potential compared with the invention underlying the earlier patent.[125] In addition, the conditions of Sec. 24 (1) No. 1 GPA must be fulfilled (except public interest), namely the licence seeker must have made unsuccessful efforts within a reasonable period of time to obtain the consent of the patentee to use the protected invention on reasonable commercial terms (see Section D.1.b). By way of compensation for the grant of a compulsory licence, the owner of the earlier patent may request a counter-licence from the licence seeker on reasonable terms (Sec. 24 (2)).

---

[117] Scharen 2015, para. 8.
[118] BGH, 21.02.1989, X ZR 53/87 – Ethofumesat, para. 31.
[119] Scharen 2015, para. 2.
[120] One of the very few cases: OLG Frankfurt PMZ 1949, 330.
[121] Lenz & Kieser 2002, 401, 402 li.Sp. For a pre-World War II case-law example, see RG, 03.03.1928, I 242/27, RGZ 120, 267: protection of miners.
[122] Scharen 2015, para. 6.
[123] *Id.*, para. 3.
[124] *Id.*, para. 4; Keukenschijver 2016a, para. 8.
[125] Mes 2015, para. 20; Wilhelmi 2019, para. 37.

3. *Competition Law*

It is, meanwhile, a well-established principle in German and EU law that competition law rules can impact patent law, especially by limiting the claims and exclusivity rights of patent holders.[126] The focus of this chapter is, however, not on competition law as another part of this book deals with the topic.[127]

4. *General Abuse of Rights Doctrine, Sec. 242 GCC*

In general German civil law, the abuse of a right is usually interpreted as one form of violating the duty to "perform according to the requirements of good faith, taking customary practice into consideration" (Sec. 242 GCC).[128] Courts have considered the exercise of patent rights to constitute such an abuse in a number of settings, including the enforcement of claims based on a patent which had been acquired by way of misrepresentations to the patent office;[129] contradictory positions the patentee defends in the infringement proceedings and in the validity proceedings respectively;[130] or the forfeiture of rights due to lapse of time.[131] On the relevance of Sec. 242 GCC in the context of recent discussions about injunction law reform, see Section D.6.

5. *Personal Characteristics of the Patentee or Infringer*

a. Infringers

In some cases, injunctions are not successful because of who claims them or against whom they are claimed. Indirect/contributory infringers and co-liable persons (*Störer*) cannot be targeted as long as the specific requirements for an injunction against them are not met. The same goes for other groups in the holding to which the infringing company belongs.[132] Furthermore, injunctions are not possible against civil servants who have committed an infringement, as long as the state takes liability (*Amtshaftung* – public liability).[133] The situation is similar for those

---

[126] See BGH, 6.5.2009, KZR 39-06 – Orange Book-Standard; CJEU, 16.07.2015, C-170/13 – Huawei Technologies; CJEU, 05.10.1988, C-238/87 – AB Volvo/Veng; Unwired Planet v. Huawei, [2017] EWHC 711 (Pat); Commission Decision, 29.04.2014, AT.39939 – Samsung; Drexl, 2008, XV; Heinemann 2002, 1, 178 et seq., 321 et seq.; Pregartbauer 2017, 2.

[127] See, with a view specifically to the impact on German injunction case law Picht 2019b, S. 324; Picht 2019a, 1097.

[128] Sutschet 2019, para. 47 et seq.

[129] RG, 25.03.1933, I 226/32, RGZ 140, 187 et seq; Kohler 1888, 162 et seq. This position has been criticized in the academic literature, see e.g., Schulte 2017, § 9 para. 79; Mes 2015, § 9 para. 79.

[130] BGH, 05.06.1997, X ZR 73/95 – Weichvorrichtung II.

[131] BGH, 19.12.2000, X ZR 150/98 – Temperaturwächter, para. 15.

[132] OLG Düsseldorf, 16.02.2006, I-2 U 32/04 – Permanentmagnet; Buxbaum 2009.

[133] BGH, 21.09.1978, X ZR 56/77 – Straßendecke I, para. 24.

protected by a licence contract (Sec. 15(2) GPA), (the right to) a compulsory licence (Sec. 24 GPA), or some other legal position as a result of which they are not considered to have committed an infringement. To the extent the economic effects of an injunction on the defendant are considered in gauging the proportionality of the injunction, characteristics such as the SME status of the defendant can become relevant. We will say more on this aspect in Section D.6.

b. Plaintiffs

On the side of the plaintiff/patent owner, a focus in case law and literature is on the treatment of so-called non-producing entities (NPEs).[134] It follows from the almost "automatic nexus" between infringement and injunction (on limitations see Section D.7) in German statutory patent law, as well as from a relatively patentee-friendly tradition in German case law,[135] that – so far – courts do not systematically deny injunctive relief to a certain type of plaintiff.[136] Some decisions have been restrictive in granting injunctions to NPEs in the context of temporary relief[137] or the provisional enforcement of first-instance decisions.[138] However, with regard to NPEs enforcing patents in the particularly sensitive field of SEPs regarding Information and Communication Technologies (ICT-SEPs), the Düsseldorf Higher Regional Court has underscored, in a high-profile FRAND case, that they should not a priori be treated differently from other patentees.[139]

In a more recent decision,[140] though, the same court has established some boundaries regarding the enforcement of SEPs acquired by an NPE from the original patent holder. It is of vital importance, in such cases, whether a FRAND declaration made by the previous patent owner obliges the acquirer to offer licences on FRAND conditions to standard implementers as well, or whether the acquirer remains free to seek an injunction even though an implementer proves willing to take such a licence. Sometimes, an acquiring NPE will have made its own FRAND declaration, for instance because the relevant standard was set only after the patent acquisition or because the acquirer contractually undertook to do so, but there is no guarantee and implementers may, hence, have to seek refuge from an injunction in the previous patentee's FRAND declaration. Coming to their rescue, the Düsseldorf court held that the acquirer of a SEP is directly and necessarily bound to the FRAND declaration of its predecessor, even absent an express or implied declaration

---

[134] There is no obligation to use a patent in German patent law; Pitz 2012, para. 75.
[135] Contreras & Picht 2017, 6.
[136] See Osterrieth 2009, 542, in particular on NPEs.
[137] LG Düsseldorf, 08.07.1999, 4 O 187/99 – NMR-Kontrastmittel.
[138] OLG Karlsruhe, 11.05.2009, 6 U 38/09 – Patentverwertungsgesellschaft.
[139] OLG Düsseldorf, 13.01.2016, I-15 U 66/15 – Sisvel/Haier, para. 11.
[140] OLG Düsseldorf, 22.03.2019, 4b O 49/14.

to this effect.[141] In the court's view, the FRAND licensing commitment has the effect that the patentee no longer holds an exclusivity right which would allow its holder discretion to permit or prohibit use of the patent. Instead, as a result of the FRAND declaration, the rights from the patent are now limited by the obligation to allow access on FRAND terms. Very importantly, the court seems – the language of the decision is somewhat ambiguous regarding the doctrinal level but it may draw on a similar proposal in the literature[142] – to derive this limitation not from a contractual promise, the lack of which could remove the limitation, but from a modification of the patent *in rem* due to a waiver contained in the patentee's FRAND declaration. Hence, the owner can transfer its patent only together with the FRAND "encumbrance" and the presence or absence of an additional FRAND declaration by the acquirer has no impact on the FRAND licensing obligation. Nor, according to this Düsseldorf decision,[143] can the acquirer usually claim an injunction if an implementer refuses to license the SEP on terms incompatible with those offered by the previous patentee. This is because the court finds, based inter alia on Sec. 15(3) GPA,[144] that the previous FRAND commitment binds the acquirer not only in a general way, but also regarding the licensing practice of the previous patent holder. Existing licence agreements, in particular, do not end or alter their terms and conditions only because of the transfer. As another – and, for once, patentee-friendly – implication of these findings, the Düsseldorf court perceives no competition law violation where the contractual arrangements between patent seller and buyer do not explicitly oblige the buyer to make or honour a FRAND commitment since the FRAND obligation travels with the patent anyway,[145] arguably even if the purchaser is unaware of the FRAND declaration. In consequence, an implementer, especially one who is not willing to take a FRAND licence, cannot raise the absence of such a contractual obligation as a competition law defence against the acquirer's injunction claim.

6. *Proportionality*

a. Traditional Legal Framework

German courts do take proportionality into consideration where they have judicial discretion, such as in the granting of interim injunctions or in the decision on provisional enforceability of injunctions.[146] However, according to German statutory

---

[141] On this and the following, see OLG Düsseldorf, 22.03.2019, 4b O 49/14, para. 203 et seq.

[142] See, in particular, Ullrich 2010a, 14, 90 et seq.

[143] On this and the following, see OLG Düsseldorf, 22.03.2019, 4b O 49/14, para. 240.

[144] Sec. 15(3) GPA: "A transfer of rights or the grant of a licence shall not affect licences previously granted to third parties."

[145] OLG Düsseldorf, 22.03.2019, 4b O 49/14, para. 242.

[146] Haft et al. 2011, 928; Pitz 2012, para. 76.

patent law, the claim to an injunction was, hitherto, not subject to a general proportionality requirement or a balancing of the parties' interests.[147] While proportionality is explicitly mentioned in Sec. 140a GPA (claim for destruction of products) and Sec. 140b GPA (claim for information), Sec. 139 GPA, as the core provision on injunctions, did not explicitly establish a proportionality threshold.[148] Nor is there anything like a broadly available, US-style "eBay" balancing test.[149] Apart from the settings just mentioned, German courts tended – and may well continue to tend – to create an almost automatic link between the establishment of a patent infringement and the granting of an injunction.[150] Many scholars agree that there was no such thing as a general, effective proportionality threshold in traditional German patent injunction law.[151] This has, as noted, made Germany an attractive venue to patentees. Recent developments and a revision of the GPA may, however, increase the relevance of proportionality notions, as we will discuss in the following Section.

b. Revision of Sec. 139 GPA

In August 2021, a revised version of the Patent Act took effect[152] and modified German patent injunction law in mainly three respects. First, the bill adds flexibility to Sec. 139(1) GPA by stating in Sec. 139(1)(3) GPA that the claim to injunctive relief is precluded to the extent it would, due to the special circumstances of the individual case and in view of the principle of good faith (*Gebote von Treu und Glauben*), lead to disproportionate hardship on the infringer or third parties which would not be justified by the patent exclusivity right.

Second, in case and to the extent an injunction is thus precluded, the injured party is entitled to appropriate monetary compensation (*angemessener Ausgleich in Geld*, Sec. 139(1)(4) GPA). Such compensation leaves "unaffected" (*unberührt*) a claim for damages, Sec. 139(1)(5) GPA.[153]

Third, in bifurcated proceedings, the Federal Patent Court is supposed to send a qualified opinion on the validity of a patent to the parties and the infringement court

---

[147] Hessel & Schnellhorn 2017; Haft et al. 2011, 928.
[148] Osterrieth 2009, 543; cf. Pitz 2019a, para. 74.
[149] Contreras & Picht 2017, 4. See also Chapter 14 (United States).
[150] Osterrieth 2018, 987.
[151] Hessel & Schnellhorn 2017, 672; Osterrieth 2015a, para. 119.
[152] Zweites Gesetz zur Vereinfachung und Modernisierung des Patentrechts.
[153] In German, the wording of Sec. 139(1)(3)–(5) GPA is as follows: "Der Anspruch ist ausgeschlossen, soweit die Inanspruchnahme aufgrund der besonderen Umstände des Einzelfalls und der Gebote von Treu und Glauben für den Verletzer oder Dritte zu einer unverhältnismäßigen, durch das Ausschließlichkeitsrecht nicht gerechtfertigten Härte führen würde. In diesem Fall ist dem Verletzten ein angemessener Ausgleich in Geld zu gewähren. Der Schadensersatzanspruch nach Absatz 2 bleibt hiervon unberührt".

within six months from the filing of an action for annulment (Sec. 83(1)(2), (3) GPA), a timeframe that did not hitherto exist.[154]

To a certain extent, the wording of and rationale behind Sec. 139(1)(3) GPA[155] implements a proportionality limitation introduced by the Federal Supreme Court in its *Heat Exchanger (Wärmetauscher)* decision.[156] In this decision, the BGH firmly settled[157] that, in principle, injunctions can be subject to a use-by period during which the infringer has, in particular, the opportunity to sell off infringing products before the injunction takes effect.[158] The court drew this limitation from the general principle of good faith (Sec. 242 GCC) and from similar unfair competition case law[159] and perceives it to be in line with Art. 30 TRIPS, Art. 3 of the Enforcement Directive, and the case law of the UK courts.[160] At the same time, the BGH defined a rather restrictive threshold for the granting of such a use-by period, stating that it can only be considered if the immediate enforcement of the injunction would, due to special circumstances of the individual case, constitute a hardship that is disproportionate and therefore contrary to good faith even in view of the patentee's interests, of the exclusivity of the patent right, and of the regular consequences of its enforcement.[161] Aspects relevant for this test are, inter alia, whether the infringing item constitutes an essential component of a complex product, whether there was an acceptable option for licensing the infringed patent, whether the remaining protection period for the patent is long or short, whether an immediate injunction would have a grave and disproportionate impact on the (entire) business of the infringer, and whether the infringement was a culpable one.[162] Importantly, the fact that the lower instances did not consider the challenged embodiment to infringe the patent does not – according to the BGH – give rise to an assessment more favourable to the infringer as it cannot legitimize the expectation that these decisions will not be overturned.[163]

While the revised Sec. 139(1) GPA is clearly rooted in this case law, it goes a step beyond it. In particular, it arguably introduces a somewhat more general proportionality requirement, allows for the consideration of third-party interests (see also below

---

[154] In German, the wording of Sec. 83(1)(2), (3) is as follows: "Dieser Hinweis soll innerhalb von sechs Monaten nach Zustellung der Klage erfolgen. Ist eine Patentstreitsache anhängig, soll der Hinweis auch dem anderen Gericht von Amts wegen übermittelt werden".

[155] Entwurf eines Zweiten Gesetzes zur Vereinfachung und Modernisierung des Patentrechts, 2020, p. 50 et seq. For key excerpts from this passage in English, see Cotter 2020.

[156] BGH, 10.05.2016, X ZR 114/13 – Wärmetauscher (the decision is sometimes also called "Air Scarf", after the name of the product at issue).

[157] Previous decisions by the Federal Supreme Court had left this open, see BGH, 02.12.1980, X ZR 16/79 – Heuwerbungsmaschine II.

[158] BGH, 10.05.2016, X ZR 114/13 – Wärmetauscher, para. 40 et seq.

[159] *Id.*, para. 42, 45.

[160] *Id.*, para. 46 et seq.

[161] *Id.*, para. 41.

[162] *Id.*, para. 52 et seq.

[163] *Id.*, para. 53.

in this section), and grants a claim to financial compensation without the need for the patentee to show damages or, in fact, any of the requirements for a claim to damages.

The envisaged modification to Sec. 139(1) GPA triggered a broad range of reactions. Some criticized the new provision as a measure cementing the status quo instead of raising the bar for injunctions.[164] Those who suggested, in view of the initial draft, taking third-party interests into consideration and relaxing the link between an injunction stay and the fulfilment of the *Heat Exchanger* criteria[165] were sympathetic towards the reform bill's subsequent modifications.[166] The Max Planck Institute welcomed the introduction of a proportionality test but criticized the precedence it grants the patentee's interests.[167] Other commentators deemed the new provision to strike a good compromise between firmness and flexibility in the granting of injunctive relief, not least by dispelling German judges' hesitations to take into account considerations of proportionality in Sec. 139 GPA.[168] There were, however, also those who denied any need for a modification of Sec. 139 GPA, for instance because they deemed it to inappropriately weaken patent protection and Germany's attractiveness as a patent (litigation) venue, to violate the TRIPS and the EU Enforcement Directive, or to be unnecessary in view of the EU Enforcement Directive's proportionality precept.[169]

Given the intense, controversial debate over whether and how a proportionality defense should be introduced into German patent injunction law, it is worthwhile to look at what the legislature has to say in the legislative materials:[170] It considers the modifications to be, first and foremost, a legislative clarification of a principle rooted in the German constitution, in civil law provisions on good faith and relief from unreasonable obligations, as well as in the EU Enforcement Directive. According to Art. 3(2) of said Directive, measures, procedures and remedies for the enforcement of intellectual property rights must be not only effective and dissuasive, but also proportionate. The legislative materials concur with the view that the principle of proportionality – at least by way of an interpretation in conformity with EU law – already applies to the claim for injunctive relief and that the reluctance of German (lower instance) courts to apply it renders a clarification to this effect worthwhile. At the same time, a proportionality defence must be restricted to exceptional settings as

---

[164] Müller 2020.

[165] Ohly 2020.

[166] *Id.*

[167] Desaunettes-Barbero et al. 2020, 3 et seq., 6 et seq.

[168] Dijkman 2020.

[169] See, for instance, Stellungnahme Deutsche Vereinigung für gewerblichen Rechtsschutz, 29 September 2020; Stellungnahme Bundesverband Deutscher Patentanwälte, 23 September 2020; Stellungnahme Prof. Dr. Winfried Tilmann, 2 September 2020, all available at www.bmjv.de/DE/Startseite/Startseite_node.html.

[170] On the following, see Justification of the government in Entwurf eines Zweiten Gesetzes zur Vereinfachung und Modernisierung des Patentrechts, p. 58 et seq.

it interferes with the core of patent exclusivity rights. In line with such a restrictive application, the patent infringer bears the burden of proof for the disproportionality of the claim and the court must engage in a thorough weighing of all relevant circumstances, taking into account also the paramount, legitimate interest of the patentee in enforcing its right to an injunction. While the recast Sec. 139(1) GPA refrains from listing exemplary settings or criteria for a proportionality defence, the legislative materials identify as relevant (i) the legitimacy of the patentee's interest in an injunction, depending inter alia on whether the patentee manufactures patent-based products itself or merely monetizes the patent, and on whether the patentee's royalty claims seem exaggerated; (ii) the severity of the injunction's economic effects on the infringer, resulting for instance from substantial R&D that went into the infringing product; (iii) the complexity of the infringing product, especially where an injunction based on the infringing nature of one of its many patented components would – possibly in combination with market approval requirements for the product – necessitate the infringer to invest much time and resources in a design-around and to suspend production for a longer period of time; (iv) "subjective" aspects, for instance the nature and extent of the infringer's culpability, including whether it undertook a freedom-to-operate analysis and made sufficient efforts to obtain a licence, as well as the patentee's compliance with good-faith principles, which may for instance be questionable where the patentee deliberately delays the assertion of its injunction until the infringer has made considerable investments in the infringing product; (v) severe harm to fundamental third-party interests,[171] for instance where an injunction would endanger the supply of vital drugs or the maintenance of important infrastructure.

As to the consequences of a successful proportionality defence, the legislature underlines that, instead of denying the injunction entirely, use-by or work-around periods may be the appropriate remedy. To the extent an injunction is denied, the patentee must usually receive monetary compensation, to be determined in the court decision. In addition to this compensation, the patentee remains free to claim damages under Sec. 139(2) GPA.

It remains to be seen whether these changes will profoundly alter the course of German patent injunction law. As to the proportionality requirement, this will very much depend on whether the courts interpret the provision as a prompt to stay, or even refuse, injunctions more frequently and whether they limit its application to a narrow set of cases[172] displaying facts similar to the *Heat Exchanger* case. Initial

---

[171] With this consideration, the legislature rejects, at the same time, German case law which considered compulsory licences under Sec. 24 PatG as the only appropriate option for protecting such third-party interests, see Justification of the government in Entwurf eines Zweiten Gesetzes zur Vereinfachung und Modernisierung des Patentrechts, p. 62.

[172] For a discussion on what the Heat Exchanger criteria mean for FRAND cases, see Picht 2019b, 1097.

reactions by the judiciary do, indeed, indicate such a restrictive approach.[173] As to the claim for financial compensation, some judges and scholars have already argued[174] that, for the sake of deterrence, the level of compensation should be substantially higher than a reasonable royalty rate, while others consider the reasonable royalty as the appropriate starting point, to be complemented by damages claims and augmented in appropriate settings, for instance where third-party interests are the main basis for the proportionality defence and, hence, the infringer seems not entitled to any profits from the continuing use of the patented invention.

7. Further Limitations

There are some further limitations to injunctions worth mentioning. According to Sec. 712(1) CCP, a patent infringer can, in its capacity as addressee (debtor) of the claim to an injunction, file a petition for protection "insofar as the enforcement would entail a disadvantage for the debtor that it is impossible to compensate or remedy ... The court is to allow him, upon a corresponding petition being filed, to avert enforcement by providing security or by lodgement, without taking account of any security that the creditor may have provided". Sec. 712(2) CCP states that "the petition filed by the debtor shall not be complied with if an overriding interest of the creditor contravenes this". In practice, hurdles for success of such a petition are quite high in the patent injunction field.[175]

The infringer can raise a complaint based on a violation of their right to be properly heard in the infringement proceedings (*Anhörungsrüge*, Sec. 321a CCP, Sec. 103(1) FL). If successful, the complaint results in a continuation of the (infringement) proceedings and the infringer can request that the enforcement of the injunction be stayed (Sec. 707 CCP).

Failure to send a warning/cease and desist letter prior to filing for an injunction will, in principle, not limit the patentee's right to an injunction. The main legal consequence (strategic disadvantages aside) of not sending such warning/cease and desist letter can be that the patentee has to bear the litigation costs if the infringer acknowledges the infringement (Sec. 93 CCP).[176]

[173] Views expressed and referred to during the CIPLITEC Conference on "Patentrecht: Der Anspruch auf Unterlassen nach dem 2. PatMoG", 21/22 October 2021, notes on file with the authors and materials partially available at www.ciplitec.de/veranstaltung/der-patentrechtliche-unterlassungsanspruch-nach-dem-2-patmog/.
[174] Views expressed and referred to during the CIPLITEC Conference on "Patentrecht: Der Anspruch auf Unterlassen nach dem 2. PatMoG", 21/22 October 2021, notes on file with the authors and materials partially available at www.ciplitec.de/veranstaltung/der-patentrechtliche-unterlassungsanspruch-nach-dem-2-patmog/.
[175] Osterrieth 2009, 543, reference to BGH, 20.06.2000, X ZR 88/00 – Spannvorrichtung; OLG Düsseldorf, 16.11.1978, 2 U 15/78 – Flachdachabläufe.
[176] Osterrieth 2015a, para. 1060. On the reduced (e.g., oral warning sufficient) requirements for a sufficient warning before the filing for a preliminary injunction, see LG München I,

Enforcement of an injunction under Sec. 890 CCP can become problematic if the infringer subsequently modifies the contested embodiment (*angegriffene Ausführungsform*) against which the injunction has been issued: While it is admissible to work around the patent, to develop and sell a non-infringing product, the infringer must not continue to market products which have been modified only to such a slight extent that the core of the enjoined infringing [177] conduct remains the same (*kerngleiche Handlung*).[178]

General patent protection requirements obviously have an impact on patent injunctions as well. Examples are acts of use permitted under Sec. 11 GPA,[179] priority rights (Sec. 12 GPA), lapse (Sec. 20 GPA) or exhaustion of the patent, usurpation of the invention by the patentee vis-à-vis the "infringer", (Sec. 8 GPA), or the free state-of-the-art defence.[180] At least some German scholars contend that an injunction, being a future-oriented remedy, should not be granted where the patent is about to expire.[181]

Use-by periods, permitting an infringer to sell or use infringing products within a certain time period after the injunction has been granted, were arguably always possible under German patent law, but the option remained a rather theoretical one as courts were reluctant to grant such deferrals.[182] However, use-by periods may become somewhat more frequent due to the modification of Sec. 139 GPA (see Section D.6).

E. ALTERNATIVES TO INJUNCTIVE RELIEF

The injunction is a core remedy in case of patent infringement, but it is by no means the only one. The patentee can combine its injunction claim with other civil and criminal patent infringement claims.[183] These include, in the case of intentional or negligent infringement, claims for compensation according to Sec. 139(2) GPA.

09.06.2011, 7 O 2403/11 – Lawinenschutzrucksack; LG München I, 10.11.2010, 21 O 7656/10 – Messeauftritt, para. 18; OLG Düsseldorf, 12.01.2004 – INTERPACK.

[177] Whether a modified product continues to realize the core of the enjoined, infringing conduct must, to a large extent, be determined by interpreting the injunction decision, Voß 2019, para. 400.

[178] OLG Frankfurt, 14.04.1978, 6 W 12/78 – Küchenreibe; OLG Karlsruhe, 30.11.1983, 6 W 88/83 – Andere Ausführungsform; OLG Düsseldorf, 10.06.2010, 2 U 17/09 – Münzschloss II; LG Düsseldorf, 22.07.2005, 4b O 327/04 – Rotordüse; BGH, 08.11.2007, I ZR 172/05 – Euro und Schwarzgeld; BGH 23.02.1973, I ZR 117/71 – Idee-Kaffee I.

[179] Sec. 11 GPA permits in principle acts privately done, acts for experimental purposes, the extemporaneous preparation for individual cases, the use on-board vessels and the use in the construction or the operation of aircraft or land vehicles of another state party to the Paris Convention for the Protection of Industrial Property, and finally the acts specified in Art. 27 of the Convention on International Civil Aviation of 7 December 1944.

[180] The so-called Formstein defence; see BGH, 29.04.1986, X ZR 28/85 – Formstein.

[181] Kraßer & Ann 2016, § 35 para. 12.

[182] Grabinski & Zülch 2015, para. 136a.

[183] Kraßer & Ann 2016, § 33 para. 25; Grabinski & Zülch 2015, para. 27; Hofmann 2018, 1291.

Additionally, patentees may – subject to a proportionality test (Sec. 140a(4) GPA) – request reparative measures in the form of claims for destruction (Sec. 140a(1), (2) GPA), "for recall of the products which are the subject-matter of the patent[,] or for definitive removal of the products from the channels of commerce" (Sec. 140a(3) GPA).[184] In specific situations, these reparative measures may be granted although the patentee is not entitled to an injunction. In particular, the German Federal Court of Justice has held that destruction of infringing products can be requested even after expiration of the infringed patent.[185] Furthermore, a patentee can – if the respective requirements are fulfilled – claim the provision of information (Sec. 140b GPA), the "production of a document or inspection of an item which lies in [the infringer's] control or of a process which is the subject-matter of the patent" (Sec. 140c(1) GPA), the production of or access to bank, financial or commercial documents (Sec. 140d(1) GPA), as well as the publication of a judgment in its favour (Sec. 140e GPA). In addition to the GPA claims, the patentee may have claims under general civil law.[186] Such GCC claims are declared applicable by Sec. 141a GPA. Last but not least, an infringement can trigger criminal and customs sanctions according to Sec. 142 GPA and Sec. 142a GPA. These additional claims are distinct from and parallel to the injunction, i.e. they are not merely a facet and consequence of the claim for an injunction and the patentee can petition for them independently. For a long time, it had been firmly established in German case law that other infringement remedies do not constitute an alternative to injunctions in the sense that courts would award them in lieu of injunctive relief. Instead, injunctions were, and largely still are, regarded as an almost indispensable consequence of patent infringement.[187] Of late, however, a discourse has evolved on whether German injunction rules ought to be more flexible, including the award of other remedies in lieu of an injunction. As described in Section D.6., this has even induced changes to the German Patent Act, the practice impact of which remain, however, to be seen.

REFERENCES

Cases

BGH, 22.11.1957, I ZR 152/56 – Resin
BGH, 23.02.1962, I ZR 114/60 – Furniergitter
BGH 23.02.1973, I ZR 117/71 – Idee-Kaffee I
BGH, 21.09.1978, X ZR 56/77 – Straßendecke I
BGH, 02.12.1980, X ZR 16/79 – Heuwerbungsmaschine II,

[184] Osterrieth 2015b, para. 26.
[185] BGH, 21.02.1989, X ZR 53/87 – Ethofumesat; Kühnen 2017, para. 1405 et seq.
[186] In particular removal of the consequences of an infringement, Sec. 823(1), 1004 GCC; unjust enrichment, Sec. 812 et seq. GCC; and/or accounting, Sec. 242, 677, 681, 666 GCC (by way of analogy).
[187] Osterrieth 2018, 987.

BGH, 29.04.1986, X ZR 28/85 – Formstein
BGH, 11.11.1986, X ZR 56/85 – Transportfahrzeug
BGH, 21.02.1989, X ZR 53/87 – Ethofumesat
BGH, 01.04.1993, I ZR 70/91– Verfügungskosten
BGH, 11.07.1995, X ZR 99/92 - Klinische Versuche
BGH, 05.12.1995, X ZR 26/92 – Polyferon
BGH, 05.06.1997, X ZR 73/95 – Weichvorrichtung II
BGH, 24.11.1999, I ZR 189/97
BGH, 20.06.2000, X ZR 88/00 – Spannvorrichtung
BGH, 19.12.2000, X ZR 150/98 – Temperaturwächter
BGH, 06.04.2004, X ZR 272/02 – Druckmaschinen-Temperierungssystem
BGH, 13.07.2004, KZR 40/02 – Standard-Spundfass
BGH, 30.03.2005, X ZR 126/01 – Blasfolienherstellung
BGH, 08.11.2007, I ZR 172/05 – Euro und Schwarzgeld
BGH, 20.05.2008, X ZR 180/05 – Tintenpatrone
BGH, 6.5.2009, KZR 39-06 – Orange Book-Standard
BGH, 19.09.2009, Xa ZR 2/08 – MP3-Player-Import
BGH, 29.07.2010, Xa ZR 118/09 – Bordako
BGH, 28.09.2011, X ZR 68/10 – Klimaschrank
BGH, 24.01.2012, VIII ZR 236/10
BGH, 17.04.2012, X ZR 55/09 – Tintenpatrone III
BGH, 17.07.2012, X ZR 77/11 – Verdichtungsvorrichtung
BGH, 08.07.2014, X ZR 61/13
BGH, 10.05.2016, X ZR 114/13 – Wärmetauscher
BGH, 11.7.2017, X ZB 2/17 – Raltegravir
BPatG, 07.06.1991, 3 Li 1/90 – Zwangslizenz
BPatG, 31.8.2016, 3 LiQ 1/16
CJEU, 05.10.1988, C-238/87 – AB Volvo/Veng
CJEU, 27.3.2014, C-314/12 – UPC Telekabel
CJEU, 16.07.2015, C-170/13 – Huawei Technologies
Commission Decision, 29.04.2014, AT.39939 – Samsung
eBay Inc. v. MercExchange, L.L.C., 126 S. Ct. 1837 (2006)
KG Berlin, 20.08.1992, 25 U 2754/92
KG Berlin, 25.10.1996, 5 U 4912/96
LG Düsseldorf, 08.07.1999, 4 O 187/99 – NMR-Kontrastmittel
LG Düsseldorf, 11.05.2004, 4a O 195/04
LG Düsseldorf, 27.08.2004 – Suspension on constitutional complaint
LG Düsseldorf, 22.07.2005, 4b O 327/04 – Rotordüse
LG München I, 24.08.2007, 21 O 22456/06 – Antibakterielle Versiegelung
LG München I, 10.11.2010, 21 O 7656/10 – Messeauftritt
LG München I, 19.05.2011, 7 O 8923/10
LG München I, 09.06.2011, 7 O 2403/11 – Lawinenschutzrucksack
OLG Düsseldorf, 16.11.1978, 2 U 15/78 – Flachdachabläufe
OLG Düsseldorf 21.10.1982, 2 U 67/82
OLG Düsseldorf, 08.12.1993, 2 W 79/93 – Prüfungskompetenz des Beschwerdegerichts
OLG Düsseldorf, 05.10.1995, 2 U 43/95
OLG Düsseldorf, 20.06.2002, 2 U 81/99 – Haubenstrechtautomat
OLG Düsseldorf, 27.05.2003, 2 W 11/03 – Vorgreiflichkeit
OLG Düsseldorf, 12.01.2004 – INTERPACK

OLG Düsseldorf, 16.02.2006, I-2 U 32/04 – Permanentmagnet
OLG Düsseldorf, 21.12.2006, 2 U 58/05 – Thermocycler
OLG Düsseldorf, 29.05.2008, 2 W 47/07 – Olanzapin
OLG Düsseldorf, 18.05.2009, 2 U 140/08 – Captopril
OLG Düsseldorf, 29.04.2010, I 2 U 126/09 – Harnkatheterset
OLG Düsseldorf, 10.06.2010, 2 U 17/09 – Münzschloss II
OLG Düsseldorf, 11.11.2010, I 2 U 152/09 – Tintenpatronen
OLG Düsseldorf, 13.01.2016, I-15 U 66/15 – Sisvel/Haier
OLG Düsseldorf, 29.06.2017, I-15 U 41/17
OLG Düsseldorf, 22.03.2019, 4b O 49/14
OLG Frankfurt PMZ 1949, 330
OLG Frankfurt, 14.04.1978, 6 W 12/78 – Küchenreibe
OLG Frankfurt, 03.05.1988, 6 U 207/87
OLG Frankfurt, 27.03.2003, 6 U 215/02 – Mini Flexiprobe
OLG Hamburg, 20.06.1984, 3 W 103/84
OLG Hamburg, 03.09.1987, 3 U 83/87
OLG Hamburg, 16.10.2008, 5 W 53/08 – iPod II
OLG Hamm, 19.02.1991, 4 U 231/90
OLG Karlsruhe, 30.11.1983, 6 W 88/83 – Andere Ausführungsform
OLG Karlsruhe, 27.04.1988, 6 U 13/88 – Dutralene
OLG Karlsruhe, 10.04.1991, 6 U 164/90 – Erbenermittlung
OLG Karlsruhe, 22.02.1995, 6 U 250-94
OLG Karlsruhe, 11.05.2009, 6 U 38/09 – Patentverwertungsgesellschaft
OLG Karlsruhe, 08.07.2009, 6 U 61/09 – Vorläufiger Rechtsschutz
OLG München, 06.10.1958, 6 W 607/58
OLG München, Mitt. 2001, 85, 89 – Wegfall der Dringlichkeit
OLG München, 29.12.2008, 6 W 2387/08 – Abstrakte Vorgreiflichkeit
RG, 11.02.1903, I 291/02
RG, 27.05.1918, I. 89/17
RG, 28.09.1921, I 46/21, RGZ 102, 391
RG, 11.03.1926, I 243 244/25 – Stapelfaser
RG, 03.03.1928, I 242/27
RG, 27.06.1928, I 271/27
RG, 25.03.1933, I 226/32
RG, 24.01.1934, I 37/33 – Tonaufnahmeverfahren
RG, 16.08.1935, I 44/35
RG, 21.12.1935, I 18/35
RG, 18.01.1936, I 90/35
RG, 01.02.1938, I 173. 174/36
Unwired Planet v. Huawei, [2017] EWHC 711 (Pat)

Regulatory and Legislative Materials

Agreement on Trade Related Aspects of Intellectual Property Rights, "TRIPS".
Code of Civil Procedure – CCP, Zivilprozessordnung, ZPO, "Code of Civil Procedure as promulgated on 5 December 2005 (Federal Law Gazette I p. 3202; 2006 I p. 431; 2007 I p. 1781), last amended by Article 1 of the Act dated 10 October 2013 (Federal Law Gazette I p. 3786)".

Directive 2004/48/EC of the European Parliament and of the Council of 29 April 2004 on the enforcement of intellectual property rights, L-195/16, "Enforcement Directive".

Entwurf eines Zweiten Gesetzes zur Vereinfachung und Modernisierung des Patentrechts, "Draft of a Second Law on the Simplification and Modernization of Patent Law, 14 January 2020," www.bmjv.de/SharedDocs/Gesetzgebungsverfahren/Dokumente/DiskE_2_PatMoG.pdf;jsessionid=E172A46A42A970B69EE1C522CC61937F.1_cid289?__blob=publicationFile&v=1.

German Civil Code – GCC, Bürgerliches Gesetzbuch, BGB, "Civil Code in the version promulgated on 2 January 2002 (Federal Law Gazette I p. 42, 2909; 2003 I p. 738), last amended by Article 4 para. 5 of the Act of 1 October 2013 (Federal Law Gazette I p. 3719)".

German Patent Act – GPA, Deutsches Patentgesetz, PatG, "Patent Act as published on 16 December 1980 (Federal Law Gazette 1981 I p. 1), as last amended by Article 4 of the Act of 8 October 2017 (Federal Law Gazette I p. 3546)".

Gesetz zur Verbesserung der Durchsetzung von Rechten des geistigen Eigentums vom 7. Juli 2008, PMZ 2008, 274.

Paris Convention for the Protection of Industrial Property of March 20, 1883, last amended on September 28, 1979.

Zweites Gesetz zur Vereinfachung und Modernisierung des Patentrechts, "Second Law on the Simplification and Modernization of Patent Law as published on 8 December 2021 (Federal Law Gazette 2021 p. 3490), entered into force on 18 August 2021".

Books, Articles and Online Materials

Ann, Christoph. 2009. "Verletzungsgerichtsbarkeit – zentral für jedes Patentsystem und doch häufig unterschätzt," *Gewerblicher Rechtsschutz und Urheberrecht (GRUR)* 3(4):205–09.

Böhler, Roland. 2011. "Einstweilige Verfügungen in Patentsachen," *Gewerblicher Rechtsschutz und Urheberrecht (GRUR)* 11:965–71.

Buxbaum, Carmen. 2009. "Konzernhaftung bei Patentverletzung durch die Tochtergesellschaft," *Gewerblicher Rechtsschutz und Urheberrecht (GRUR)* 3(4):240–45.

Contreras, Jorge L. & Picht Peter Georg. 2017. Patent Assertion Entities and Legal Exceptionalism in Europe and the United States, A Comparative View. Max Planck Institute for Innovation & Competition Research Paper No. 17-11.

Cotter, Thomas F. 2020. "More on the German Ministry's Proposal Regarding Injunctions", Blog, 15 January. http://comparativepatentremedies.blogspot.com/2020/01/more-on-german-ministrys-proposal.html.

Desaunettes-Barbero, Luc, Reto Hilty, Daria Kim, Matthias Lamping, Peter Slowinski & Hanns Ullrich. 2020. "Stellungnahme zum Diskussionsentwurf eines Zweiten Gesetzes zur Vereinfachung und Modernisierung des Patentrechts," Max-Planck-Institut für Innovation und Wettbewerb.

Deutsch, Volker. 1990. "Die Schutzschrift in Theorie und Praxis," *Gewerblicher Rechtsschutz und Urheberrecht (GRUR)* 5:327–32.

Dijkman, Léon. 2020. "Patent Injunctions Update: German Ministry of Justice Publishes Draft Amendment to Patent Act and Hague Court of Appeal Decides in Further Philips FRAND Cases," http://ipkitten.blogspot.com/2020/01/patent-injunctions-update-german.html.

Drexl, Josef. 2008. *Research Handbook on Intellectual Property and Competition Law.* Cheltenham: Elgar.

Grabinski, Klaus & Carsten Zülch. 2015. "§139 PatG," in Georg Benkard ed., *Patentgesetz, Gebrauchsmustergesetz, Patentkostengesetz.* München: C. H. Beck.

Haft, Klaus, Ralph Nack, Anja Lunze, Clemens-August Heusch, Stefan Schohe & Björn Joachim. 2011. "Unterlassungsgebote in Fällen der Verletzung von Rechten des Geistigen Eigentums (Q219)," *Gewerblicher Rechtsschutz und Urheberrecht International (GRUR Int.)* 11: 927–30.

Hasselblatt, Gordian N. ed. 2012. *Münchener Anwalts Handbuch, Gewerblicher Rechtsschutz.* München: C. H. Beck.

Heinemann, Andreas. 2002. *Immaterialgüterschutz in der Wettbewerbsordnung, Eine grundlagenorientierte Untersuchung zum Kartellrecht des geistigen Eigentums.* Tübingen: Mohr Siebeck.

Hessel Tobias J. & Maximilian Schnellhorn. 2017. "Die Rückabwicklung des vorläufig vollstreckten Unterlassungstitels im Patentrecht," *Gewerblicher Rechtsschutz und Urheberrecht (GRUR)* 7:672–77.

Hofmann, Franz. 2018. "Unterlassungsanspruch und Verhältnismäßigkeit – Beseitigung, Löschung und Rückruf," *Neue Juristische Wochenschrift (NJW)* 18:1290–92.

Klos, Mathieu. 2010. "Unsere Stars für Europa, Deutschlands Patentexperten wählen ihre Favoriten für das europäische Patentgericht," *Juve Rechtsmarkt* 4:72–83.

Kohler, Josef. 1888. *Lehrbuch des Patentrechts.* Mannheim: Bensheimer.

Kraßer, Rudolf & Christoph Ann. 2016. *Patentrecht, Lehrbuch zum deutschen und europäischen Patentrecht und Gebrauchsmusterrecht.* München: C. H. Beck.

Keuekenschijver, Alfred. 2016. "§13 (Staatliche Benutzungsanordnung)," in Rudolf Busse & Alfred Keukenschrijver eds., *Patentgesetz, unter Berücksichtigung des Europäischen Patentübereinkommens, der Regelungen zum Patent mit einheitlicher Wirkung und des Patentzusammenarbeitsvertrags mit Patentkostengesetz, Gebrauchsmustergesetz und Gesetz über den Schutz der Topographien von Halbleitererzeugnissen, Gesetz über Arbeitnehmererfindungen und Gesetz über internationale Patentübereinkommen.* Berlin: Walter de Gruyter GmbH.

——— 2016. "§139 (Unterlassungsanspruch, Schadenersatz)," in Rudolf Busse & Alfred Keukenschrijver eds., *Patentgesetz, unter Berücksichtigung des Europäischen Patentübereinkommens, der Regelungen zum Patent mit einheitlicher Wirkung und des Patentzusammenarbeitsvertrags mit Patentkostengesetz, Gebrauchsmustergesetz und Gesetz über den Schutz der Topographien von Halbleitererzeugnissen, Gesetz über Arbeitnehmererfindungen und Gesetz über internationale Patentübereinkommen.* Berlin: Walter de Gruyter GmbH.

Kühnen, Thomas. 2009. "Das Erlöschen des Patentschutzes während des Verletzungsprozesses, Materiell-rechtliche und verfahrensrechtliche Folgen," *Gewerblicher Rechtsschutz und Urheberrecht (GRUR)* 3(4):288–93.

——— 2017. *Handbuch der Patentverletzung.* Köln: Carl Heymanns Verlag KG.

Kühnen, Thomas & Rolf Cleassen. 2013. "Die Durchsetzung von Patenten in der EU – Standortbestimmung vor Einführung des europäischen Patentgerichts," *Gewerblicher Rechtsschutz und Urheberrecht (GRUR)* 6:592–97.

Lackmann, Rolf. 2021. "§ 709 ZPO," in Hans-Joachim Musielak, & Wolfgang Voit ed., *Zivilprozessordnung mit Gerichtsverfassungsgesetz, Kommentar.* München: Verlag Franz Vahlen.

Lemley, Mark A. 2013. "Why Do Juries Decide If Patents Are Valid?," *Virginia Law Review* 99 (8):1673–736.

Lenz, Christofer & Timo Kieser. 2002. "Schutz vor Milizbrandangriffen durch Angriffe auf den Patschtschutz?," *Neue Juristische Wochenschrift (NJW)* 6:401–03.

Müller, Florian. 2020. "German Ministry of Justice Outlines Patent 'Reform' Bill: Thick but Void Smokescreen, Designed only to Cement the Status Quo on Injunctions," *FOSS PATENTS*, www.fosspatents.com/2020/01/german-ministry-of-justice-outlines.html.

Meier-Beck, Peter. 1998. "Probleme des Sachantrags im Patentverletzungsprozeß," *Gewerblicher Rechtsschutz und Urheberrecht (GRUR)* 3(4):276–80.

2015. "Bifurkation und Trennung, Überlegungen zum Übereinkommen über ein Einheitliches Patentgericht und zur Zukunft des Trennungsprinzips in Deutschland," *Gewerblicher Rechtsschutz und Urheberrecht (GRUR)* 10:929–36.

Mes, Peter. 2015. *Patentgesetz, Gebrauchsmustergesetz*. München: C. H. Beck.

Nieder, Michael. 2001. "Zwangslizenzklage – Neues Verteidigungsmittel im Patentverletzungsprozess?," *Mitteilungen der Deutschen Patentanwälte* 9(10):400–03.

Ohly, Ansgar. 2008. "'Patenttrolle' oder: Der patentrechtliche Unterlassungsanspruch unter Verhältnismäßigkeitsvorbehalt?, Aktuelle Entwicklungen im US-Patentrecht und ihre Bedeutung für das deutsche und europäische Patentsystem," *Gewerblicher Rechtsschutz und Urheberrecht International (GRUR Int.)* 10:787–98.

2020. "Stellungnahme zum Diskussionsentwurf des BMJV eines Zweiten Gesetzes zur Vereinfachung und Modernisierung des Patentrechts: Ergänzung des § 139 Abs. 1 PatG und Einfügung eines neuen § 145a PatG", Ludwig-Maximilians Universität München, 10 March. www.bmjv.de/SharedDocs/Gesetzgebungsverfahren/Stellungnahmen/2020/Downloads/03102020_Stellungnahme_Ansgar-Ohly_DiskE_PatMoG.pdf;jsessionid=55E567FC74716FB16AA359CDDDD7BB0A.2_cid289?__blob=publicationFile&v=2

Osterrieth, Christian. 2009. "Patent-Trolls in Europa – braucht das Patentrecht neue Grenzen?," *Gewerblicher Rechtsschutz und Urheberrecht (GRUR)* 6:540–45.

Osterrieth Christian. 2015. *Patentrecht*. München: C. H. Beck.

2015. "Patent Enforcement in Germany," in Christopher Heath ed., *Patent Enforcement Worldwide, Writings in Honour of Dieter Stauder*. Oxford: Hart.

2018. "Technischer Fortschritt – eine Herausforderung für das Patentrecht? Zum Gebot der Verhältnismäßigkeit beim patentrechtlichen Unterlassungsanspruch," *Gewerblicher Rechtsschutz und Urheberrecht (GRUR)* 10:985–95.

Picht, Peter. 2019a. "Neues SEP/FRAND-Recht vom englischen Court of Appeal: Unwired Planet ./. Huawei und Conversant ./. Huawei & ZTE," *Mitteilungen der deutschen Patentanwälte* 4:146–50.

2019b. "The Future of FRAND Injunctions," *Gewerblicher Rechtsschutz und Urheberrecht (GRUR)* 11:1097.

Pitz, Johann. 2010. *Patentverletzungsverfahren*. München: C. H. Beck.

2012. "§ 139," in Uwe Fitzner, Raimund Lutz & Theo Bodewig eds., *BeckOK Patentrecht*. München: C. H. Beck.

2019. "Compulsory Licensing in the 'Public Interest'," *Acta Scientific Medical Sciences* 3:77–80.

Practical Law Arbitration. 2019. *Damages in International Arbitration, Practical Law UK Practice Note*.

Pregartbauer, Maria. 2017. "Der Anspruch auf Unterlassung aus standardessentiellen Patenten im Telekommunikationssektor," Dissertation Juristische Fakultät der Humboldt-Universität zu Berlin.

Rogge, Rüdiger & Helga Kober-Dehm. 2015. "PatG § 24 [Zwangslizenz; Patentrücknahme]," in Georg Benkard ed., *Beck'sche Kurzkommentare, Band 4, Patentgesetz, Gebrauchsmustergesetz, Patentkostengesetz*. München: C. H. Beck.

Scharen, Uwe. 2015. "PatG § 13 [Beschränkung der Wirkung für öffentliche Wohlfahrt und Staatssicherheit]," in Georg Benkard ed., *Beck'sche Kurzkommentare, Band 4, Patentgesetz, Gebrauchsmustergesetz, Patentkostengesetz*. München: C. H. Beck.

Schulte, Rainer. 2017. *Patentgesetz mit Europäischem Patentübereinkommen, Kommentar.* Köln: Carl Heymanns Verlag.

Sutschet, Holger. 2019. "BGB § 242 Leistung nach Treu und Glauben," in Georg Bamberger, Herber Roth, Wolfgang Hau & Roman Poseck eds., *BeckOK BGB.* München: C. H. Beck.

Thambisetty, Sivaramjani. 2010. "SMEs and Patent Litigation: Policy-Based Evidence Making?," *European Intellectual Property Review* 32(4):143–45.

Ullrich, Hanns. 2010a. "Patente und technische Normen: Konflikt und Komplementarität in patent- und wettbewerbsrechtlicher Sicht," in Matthias Leistner ed., *Europäische Perspektiven des Geistigen Eingentums.* Tübingen: Mohr Siebeck.

von Falck, Andreas. 2002. "Einstweilige Verfügungen in Patent- und Gebrauchsmustersachen," *Mitteilungen der deutscher Patentanwälte* 10:429–38.

Voß, Ulrike. 2019. "Vor §§ PatG § 139–PatG § 142b [Verletzungsprozess]," in Uwe Fitzner, Raimund Lutz & Theo Bodewig eds., *BeckOK Patentrecht.* München: C. H. Beck.

Wilhelmi, Rüdiger. 2019. "PatG § 24 [Zwangslizenz; Patentrücknahme]," in Uwe Fitzner, Raimund Lutz & Theo Bodewig eds., *BeckOK Patentrecht.* München: C. H. Beck.

Wuttke, Tobias. 2011. "Die aktuelle gerichtliche Praxis der einstweiligen Unterlassungsverfügung in Patentsachen – zurück zu den Anfängen?," *Mitteilungen der deutschen Patentanwälte* 9:393–98.

9

Israel

Orit Fischman-Afori

A. INJUNCTIVE RELIEF IN ISRAELI LAW: AN OVERVIEW

1. *Injunction as Equitable Relief*

Israeli law, in general, is based on the principles of English common law, in which an injunction is perceived as a form of equitable, discretionary relief.[1] Historically, injunctive relief was granted based on discretionary criteria, including the irreparable injury rule (in the absence of an injunction, the plaintiff would be caused an irreparable injury, which could not be compensated for by monetary relief); the balance of hardships between the plaintiff and defendant (known also as the "balance of convenience"); and the clean hands rule (equitable relief is only granted if the plaintiff acted in a decent and moral manner, disclosing the relevant facts).[2] Another important criterion was the public interest.[3]

In many common law countries, including Israel, these equitable considerations have survived with respect to temporary injunctions, where they are known as the four-factor test,[4] but they have become only a rhetoric with respect to final injunctions.[5] Nevertheless, according to Israeli law, both temporary and permanent

---

[1] Worthington 2006, 13. For additional discussion of the English common law basis for injunctive relief, see Chapters 13 (United Kingdom), and 14 (United States).

[2] *See* Fischer 2006, 201–02. For the origins of the different considerations see Fiss & Rendleman 1984, 104–08; Bean 2004, 3.

[3] *Id.*

[4] Goren 2015, 862 (in Hebrew) (explaining that under Israeli law the main considerations for granting temporary remedies are the chances for success at the final proceedings, the balance of convenience and other equitable considerations).

[5] Douglas Laycock conducted comprehensive research concerning the irreparable injury rule, which is a major equitable factor. His conclusion was that this factor became "dead" in US case law, in the sense that though it is used rhetorically, in fact it does not play a significant role, see Laycock 1991, 7 (concluding that "I do not argue merely that the irreparable injury rule *should* be abandoned; I argue that it *has been* abandoned in all but rhetoric"). Laycock further

---

injunctions, at least *de jure*, are subject to the courts' discretion. Under section 75 of the Courts Act 1984, any court, ruling in a civil law matter, is authorized to grant an injunction and any other remedy as it deems appropriate under the circumstances. The Civil Law Procedure Regulations (1984) anchors the Israeli version of the four-factors test with respect to temporary remedies: Under section 362 of the Regulations, in granting temporary remedies a court should take into consideration, inter alia, these factors: the injury to the plaintiff if the remedy were not to be granted as opposed to the injury to the defendant if the remedy were to be granted, as well as injury that may be caused to a possessor or third party; whether the application was submitted in good faith, if it is justified and appropriate to grant the remedy, and if the remedy is proportionate.[6] The enforcement of injunction, as all other court orders, is based on the Court Contempt Ordinance, setting the authority to enforce obedience to court orders by fines and imprisonment.[7]

2. *Property Rights and Tort Law Remedies*

Injunctions in the field of intellectual property law raise complex questions regarding the relationship between the nature and scope of property rights and the protection over proprietary interests through tort law and other remedial means. In a nutshell, under Israeli law, property rights are set by laws such as land, chattels or intellectual property laws, but the protection of ownership and possession over assets is determined, inter alia, by tort law. For example, while land law defines ownership of land, the injury to land by trespass is a tort civil wrong. The tension between the proprietary nature of a right and its protection, inter alia, by tort civil wrongs is reflected in the realm of remedies, because the framework for the grant of remedies is set in tort law, which addresses uniformly all remedies, without differentiation

---

explained that since the historical separation between the two parallel courts was abolished and the court was authorized to grant equitable remedies as well as entitled monetary remedies, the discretionary nature of the injunctive relief was in fact diminished and became part of the plaintiff's entitlements. In other words, injunction became a "legal" and not an "equitable" remedy, see, *id.* at 7. This conclusion is relevant to Israeli reality as well, because since the establishment of the state of Israel in 1948 all courts are authorized to grant equitable remedies.

[6] See Civil Law Procedure Regulations (1984), sect. 362. This section is shifted into section 109 to the new Civil-Law Procedure Regulations (2018) which entered into force in 2021. Under the new section, a temporary injunction may be granted on the basis of its necessity to the execution of the final court decision.

[7] Court Contempt Ordinance (1929), art. 6. The enforcement of injunctions in patent cases by court contempt procedures is not rare, yet the claims are examined carefully. For example, already in 1965 the court ruled that the infringement of the injunction was not made by the defendant or his agents, but by a third party that the defendant was only indirectly linked to him, see, CC HMR. 8292/65 *Anshel Cohen* v. *Shlomo Ben-David* [1965]. In another case, concerning an injunction based on unjust enrichment, the Supreme Court ruled that because the validity of the injunction was not clear and it had already expired, the infringement would be considered within the calculation of the monetary remedy, see CA 2287/00 *Shoham Mechonot (Machines) and Mavletim (Dies) LTD* v. *Harar* [2005].

between civil wrongs aimed at protecting ownership and possession, such as trespass, and other civil wrongs, such as negligence. The question, therefore, is whether there are policy considerations supporting differentiation of remedies in cases involving property rights in contrast to other civil wrongs and, in addition, the question of what exactly is the meaning of the notion of "property right" in Israeli law.[8] In a long series of decisions, the Israeli judiciary has consistently categorized various intellectual property rights as "property rights."[9] Therefore, the discourse over remedies in the intellectual property realm is inevitably driven into the comprehensive perceptions of the legal meaning of property rights and its consequences.[10] More specifically, in land law, property rights are perceived under Israeli law as "robust," which confers their owner an almost absolute prerogative to control the protected asset. For

[8] For such discussion by Israeli Supreme Court see: LCA 6339/97 *Roker* v. *Solomon* 55(1) PD 199 [1999] – a case which is further discussed below, see footnotes 11–13 and the accompanying text. See also Lewinsohn-Zamir 2006, 19–25 (analyzing the *Roker* v. *Solomon* decision and supporting its final outcome from an economic perspective); Dagan 2009, 41, 47 (in Hebrew) (stressing the need to understand property rights as non-absolute, which are subject to social needs, and the necessity for the same approach with respect to copyright).

[9] For example, with respect to intellectual property rights in general see: LCA 5768/94 *ASIR Import, Manufacture, and Distribution* v. *Accessories and Products Ltd* [1989] (handed down by a special panel of seven judges); With respect to patent right see: HCJ 5379/00 *Bristol-Myers Squibb Company* v. *The Minister of Health* [2001] (the Supreme Court acknowledged the patent right as a protected property right under the Israeli constitutional provisions); LCA 8127/15 *The Israeli Manufacturers Corporation* v. *Merck Sharp & Dohme Corp. f/k/a* [2016] (the Supreme Court acknowledged the patent extension term as creating a property right); With respect to copyright see: LCA 6141/02 *ACUM (Israeli Collecting Society)* v. *GLZ (IDF Broadcast)* [2003] (Justice Dorner acknowledged copyright as a property right protected under the constitutional provision for the protection of property rights).

[10] This discourse is reflected both in court decisions and in scholarly writings. For example, see *ACUM (Israeli Collecting Society)* v. *GLZ (IDF Broadcast)* [2003], in which Justice Dorner explained that since copyright is a property right, its holders are entitled to prevent future infringements by way of injunction. The most prominent example for such discourse held by a court is in the case LCA 5768/94 *ASIR Import, Manufacture, and Distribution* v. *Accessories and Products Ltd* [1989], which is further discussed in Section C. In this case, the Supreme Court discussed the question of whether intellectual property rights are exclusive in the sense that protection over the subject matter could be enforced only through intellectual property laws. This question further led to a normative debate as to the meaning of the classification of a right as a "property right," and whether the grant of injunction creates a *de facto* property right. Justice Cheshin held the view that injunction generates a property rights, since it would effectively be understood as an *in rem* remedy. In contrast, former Chief Justice Barak stressed that injunction may be granted on a non-property right basis, such as unjust enrichment cause of action, and therefore would have a limited *in personam* impact, that would not create a "new" intellectual property right. Following this ruling, in a subsequent decision, the Supreme Court held that in determining the appropriate remedy the court should consider the field in which the case is "located": is it property, tort, or contract; and the remedy should be adjusted accordingly in order to maintain the legislative harmony, namely legal consistency, see: CA 2287/00 *Shoham Mechonot (Machines) and Mavletim (Dies) LTD* v. *Harar* [2005, para. 16]. For such discourse in the literature see, for example, Dagan 2009, 41, 47 (proposing to understand all property rights, including intellectual property rights, as non-absolute, which are subject to social interests, and therefore as not necessarily including an entitlement to injunction).

instance, in the landmark decision *Roker* v. *Solomon*,[11] the Supreme Court held that although remedies, in general, are always subject to the court's discretion, the injunctive force underlies the basic essence of a property right, and therefore as a matter of principle an owner of a property right should not be deprived of the injunctive prerogative. In this case, the question was whether a landowner in a condominium could insist on preventing a neighbor from using and occupying a section of a shared area on the premises, and whether such action could be characterized as an abusive misuse of a property right. The Supreme Court ruled that a landowner, having a property right, is usually entitled to injunctive relief, and the insistence on enforcing an entitled remedy could not be ruled as a lack of good faith or abusive misuse of a right.[12] Though property rights are not absolute, the Supreme Court concluded, injunctive remedies would rarely be deprived.[13] In the following sections of this chapter, it will be demonstrated that this rigid perception of the scope of property rights has percolated into intellectual property case law.

Moreover, the perception of entitlement to injunctive relief, deriving from the classification of intellectual property rights as property rights, should be settled with another classification – that of intellectual property infringement claims as being part of the broad legal field of tort law.[14] In other words, while intellectual property rights are classified as "property rights," the legal framework for the grant of remedies when such rights are infringed is tort law. The challenge is significant considering section 74 to the Torts Ordinance (New Version),[15] according to which the court should not grant an injunction in cases where the injury or damage to the plaintiff is small and could be evaluated monetarily and offset by compensation, and when granting the injunction would be abusive to the defendant. However, the court may grant monetary relief in lieu of the injunction. The question, therefore, is which of

---

[11] *Roker* v. *Solomon* [1999] (handed down by a special panel of seven judges).

[12] *Id.*

[13] All seven judges deciding the case held that discretion in granting injunction, in principle, exists. They differed, however, as to its appropriate scope, and its application to the case at hand. Six of the seven judges held that the discretion to refuse injunction is narrow and is based on the general principle that every right and remedy, including the right of landowners, must be exercised in good faith, see *Roker* v. *Solomon*, [1999, pp. 238, 240, 241–42, 286, 287]. Justice England, in a dissenting opinion, expressed the view that an injunction should be granted according to a cost–benefit analysis, as is the case with all injunctions granted in tortious civil wrongs, and in the specific case at hand, monetary compensation to the landowners should suffice, see *Roker* v. *Solomon* [1999, pp. 221, 230–31]. See also Lewinsohn-Zamir 2006, 19–21 (explaining the differences between the various majority's opinions).

[14] With respect to Copyright Law, see section 52 of the Copyright Act 2007, according to which infringement of copyright is a civil wrong and the provisions of the Torts Ordinance shall apply. With respect to Patent Law, see: CA 3400/03 *Ruhama Rubinstein and others* v. *Ein-Tal (1983) Ltd* [2005] (holding that patent infringement is akin to a tortious act and the purpose of compensation in case of tort wrongs and patent infringement cause of action is similar).

[15] It should be noted that the Torts Ordinance (New Version) is based on the British torts law that was in force during the British Mandate until 1948, when the state of Israel was established. Namely, torts law in Israel is still based on the British law.

the two perceptions prevails in intellectual property actions – the rigid proprietary perception of an (almost) absolute entitlement to an injunction or rather the tort law perception of a balance of interests and a cost–benefit analysis regarding injunctions? In the following, Israeli courts' approach to patent law actions are examined. It generally appears that the proprietary perception is governing; however, some mild exceptions will be presented.

B. INJUNCTIVE RELIEF IN ISRAELI PATENT LAW

1. *The Patents Act*

Under section 183(a) of the Patents Act – 1967 (the "Patents Act"),[16] a plaintiff is "entitled to relief by way of an injunction and damages." Namely, a permanent injunction is perceived as the major remedy that follows from the patent right, conferring exclusivity over prevention of use of the protected invention.[17] However, as explained in the previous section, the granting of injunctive relief is subject to the court's discretion, being an equitable remedy in essence. Therefore, the use of the term "entitled" may denote a presumption according to which the grant of injunction is the *default* remedy once infringement has been proven, and the court should express a solid reasoning why, upon the specific facts of the case, it is justified to deny the grant of the junctive relief. In that sense, section 183(a) of the Patents Act does not present a *lex specialis* to the general rule, which acknowledges courts' full discretion to grant or to refuse to grant equitable remedies.

The explanatory part of the Patents Act Bill, dated 1965, is rather laconic in the sections concerning remedies.[18] The only explanation given is as follows: "Thus far, the only substantial law governing claims of patent infringement is British common law. It is proposed to set comprehensive rules with respect to jurisdiction, the power to file an infringement lawsuit, exceptions and defense claims, and remedies. All these are new sections."[19] There is not much we can learn from the Patents Act Bill, except that it is proposed to codify British common law rules and not necessarily deviate from them. The term "entitled" in section 183(a) of the Patents Act should not, therefore, be interpreted as overruling the general British common law tradition with respect to courts' discretion in granting injunctive relief.

The common law legacy preceding the Patents Act was acknowledged anew by the early Israeli Supreme Court decision in the case of *American Cyanamid*

---

[16] The patent system in Israel is governed by the Patents Act, 1967 and the Regulations thereunder, as amended from time to time.

[17] The patent right is a "negative right" conferring exclusive preventive prerogative and not a positive right to use the invention, see Patents Act, sect. 49.

[18] Patents Act Bill – 1965, H"H 637, January 20, 1965, p. 98.

[19] *Id.* at p. 123 (unofficial translation).

Company NY USA v. *Lepetit SPT*,[20] which discussed a patent owner's petition to amend the claims of an already registered patent. Justice H. Cohn, handing down the decision, ruled that the Israeli Supreme Court is free to adopt British common law rules as it deems fit. Furthermore, remedies are subject to courts' discretion, and could be denied on the basis of delay or unclean hands. Courts' "discretion" means weighing the conflicting interests at stake and presenting the reasons that justify the refusal to grant remedies that the court is authorized to grant.[21]

The question, therefore, is whether the Israeli judiciary applies its vested, inherent discretion in matters of injunction in patent cases, and if yes, how.

It should be noted that compulsory license schemes are set out in chapter 7 of the Patents Act and include a compulsory license for cases of misuse of a monopoly,[22] and a compulsory license for dependent patent.[23] The terms for the grant of a compulsory license by the Patent Registrar are specified in detail. Chapter 7 was amended in 1999 in order to comply with the TRIPs requirement.[24] Compulsory licenses based on misuse of a monopoly are occasionally granted, but a compulsory license for a dependent patent has not been reported thus far, to the best of our knowledge.[25]

2. Court Decisions

a. Supreme Court

According to Israeli law, patent cases are heard at the District Court (of the relevant jurisdiction) in the first instance, and therefore appeals upon the courts' decisions are directly filed at the Supreme Court, at the second instance. Under a judicial system in which the Supreme Court serves as the appellate instance, there is a relatively high volume of Supreme Court patent cases.[26] Most Supreme Court cases

[20] CA 245/60 *American Cyanamid Company NY USA* v. *Lepetit SPT* PD 16, 788[1962].
[21] *Id.* at p. 803.
[22] Patents Act, sect. 117–19.
[23] Patents Act, sect. 121.
[24] Act for the Amendment of Intellectual Property Rights (in Accordance to the TRIPs Agreement) 1999; Tur-Sinay 2017, 318–19 (in Hebrew).
[25] See Tur-Sinay 2017, 318 (in Hebrew).
[26] The survey was based on the Israeli database Nevo, which includes Israeli court decision of all instances, commencing in 1950, and it included all the decisions that were located as relevant in the database. As explained below in note 30, we have located seventy final decisions at the District Court level. On appeal, approximately forty-five Supreme Court final decision were located, yet it should be clarified that some of these final decisions are without reasoning (i.e. technical decision), and some relate to patent infringement only as a secondary issue to another major claim, such as ownership of a patent. These forty-five decisions do not include interim decisions and permitted appeals concerning Patent Registrar decisions, which occasionally were identified as appeals (twenty-eight located decisions). However, these forty-five decisions include permitted appeals on interim decisions which were turned into a final decision by a determination of the court. Therefore, the amount only reflects an approximation. Out of these

focus on routine patent litigation questions, including the initial qualification of patent registration, validity of the registered patent, interpretation of the patent claims, and inspection of the alleged infringing acts. In cases concluding that the patent was infringed, the Supreme Court approves the injunction order, whether preliminary or permanent, issued by the lower instance. There are no Supreme Court decisions discussing up-front the question whether it is proper, under the circumstances, to deny the grant of permanent injunctive relief, yet as will be presented in the following sections the traces of some hidden flexibilities may nevertheless be found. Moreover, the decisions are focused on the material questions of patent law; the injunctive remedial consequences, in contrast with the monetary remedial consequences, are left with no in-depth reasoning.[27] In other words, final injunctions are generally approved *de facto* by the Supreme Court on an automatic basis, albeit a few mild exceptions could be sketched. The Supreme Court functions as an appellate instance, therefore it can either uphold or reverse the determination of the District Court concerning the patent validity and infringement. However, the operative part of the decision concerning the injunction is viewed as if it is merely a technical matter, which does not merit a normative evaluation. District courts' decisions reflect the same view. In that sense, Supreme Court approach echoes in District Court approach, and vice versa.

Moreover, the characteristics of the parties involved in patent cases seem to be irrelevant: the parties in Israeli patent litigation are both multinational corporations, particularly pharmaceutical companies, and local corporations and individuals; however, we have not found evidence concerning a linkage between that factor and courts' discretion regarding injunctions. Furthermore, there is no special rule exempting the state. In fact, in one of the seminal decisions handed down by the Supreme Court – discussing a patented invention of combat pilot's helmet – a final injunction was issued against the state.[28]

Nevertheless, there are a few slight exceptions, relating to specific situations. The most prominent decision by the Supreme Court, denying the grant of an injunctive relief, relates to the interim period, in which a patent application is still pending (i.e.

forty-five Supreme Court final decisions, in thirty-nine cases the appeal was rejected, and in sixteen cases the appeal was accepted in whole or in part.

[27] Sometimes a court bifurcates the issues of patent infringement liability and remedies, and it is in the court's discretion to determine on the matter. However, while the scope of the monetary relief was extensively discussed in a few Supreme Court decisions, there is no similar discussion regarding injunctions. See for example: CA 2634/09 *Rotenberg* v. *Algo Hashkaya LTD* [2011]; CA 3400/03 *Ruhama Rubinstein* v. *Ein-Tal (1983) Ltd* [2005]; CA 2972/95 *Joseph Wolf and CO. Ltd* v. *Be'eri Print Ltd* [1999]; CA 817/77 *Beecham Group Ltd* v. *Bristol-Myers Co.*, 33 (3) PD 757 [1979].

[28] CA 345/87 *Hughes Aircraft Company* v. *the State of Israel* [1990]. The injunction granted against the state does not differ in any term from injunction against a private entity. The Supreme Court articulated the injunction very briefly (non-official translation): "We order hereby the defendants to refrain from infringing the patent, by themselves or by the aid of others."

the "pendency period"). Under section 179 of the Patents Act, an action for infringement can be brought only *after* the patent has been granted. Once a patent is granted, the court may grant relief for pre-grant infringement. Namely, during the patent pendency period, no remedies may be granted, and only post-grant actions are possible, yet the compensation would be evaluated on a retroactive basis as well. In 2011, the Supreme Court handed down a seminal decision in the case of *Merck & Co. Inc. et al. v. Teva Pharmaceutical Industries Ltd et al.*,[29] ruling that section 179 represents an exhaustive rule, prohibiting the grant of injunctive relief (whether temporary or final) during the patent pendency period. Such a rule applies to other legal mechanisms as well, including the Unjust Enrichment Law, which cannot circumvent the Patents Act provisions. The Supreme Court's reasoning was based on the complex balance of interests reflected by the Patents Act, which takes into consideration both the need to protect inventors' incentives and the public interest in free markets. According to this ruling, the Patents Act equilibrium of interests is clear: The exclusive proprietary power of the patent right begins only after the grant of the patent. The intertwined relation of intellectual property law and unjust enrichment law in Israel will be further discussed in Section C.

Another mild exception, reflecting a not completely automatic approach to permanent injunctions, relates to orders for stay, which seek to temporarily suspend the execution of the lower court injunctive order until the decision in the appeal is made (i.e. "stay order"). In the case of *Neka Chemicals (1952) LTD and others v. Sano Industries Bruno LTD*,[30] the Supreme Court held that while the general rule is that there is no reason to grant a stay order with respect to ordinary injunctions granted by lower courts in patent cases – since otherwise the plaintiff's injury may increase – there is a justification to suspend the delivery up (seizure) order of the infringing products in the case at stake. The reason for such an exception was that delivery up (seizure) orders may injure the defendant's reputation, beyond the direct monetary injury in case the appeal is upheld, and it would be very hard to retroactively evaluate the reputational damages. In contrast, if the appeal is rejected, the plaintiff will be fully compensated for their loss. Therefore, a stay order was issued in part. This decision nevertheless reflects a reasoning that underlies temporary injunctions, weighing harm to the parties as part of the equitable discretion.

A third case, representing somewhat of a deviation from the automatic approach for granting injunctions, is the 1971 decision in the case of *Trisol LTD v. Moses Kobobi*.[31] This decision concerns pre-Patents Act events that occurred in the 1950s and 1960s relating to an allegedly permitted use of a patented invention. Based on severe delay in filing the action, which was decided on the basis of laches, alleged misrepresentation of approval of use and alleged implied license, the Supreme

---

[29] LCA 6025/05 *Merck & Co. Inc. et al. v. Teva Pharmaceutical Industries Ltd et al.* [2011].
[30] CA 4705/05 *Neka Chemicals (1952) LTD v. Sano Industries Bruno LTD* [2005].
[31] CA 689/69 *Trisol LTD v. Moses Kobobi* [1971].

Court ruled that there was no basis for granting an injunction, particularly since at the time the decision was handed down the patent had already expired. Though exceptional, this decision may signal the court's early approach of applying equitable considerations concerning delay with respect to permanent injunctions as well. Yet it could not be ignored that since the patent had already expired at the time of ruling, the court could not grant an injunctive relief. Moreover, the Supreme Court explicitly ruled that delay, in principle, does not deprive a patent owner from their right,[32] but in cases where delay is accompanied by an implied equitable license which is based on the plaintiff's behavior, the patent infringement claim should be entirely rejected. As explained in Section A, with respect to temporary injunctions, Israeli law preserves the British common law legacy, according to which courts apply full discretion on the matter, based on the various traditional factors. Patent law decisions follow these lines.[33] Many Supreme Court decisions foster this legacy,[34] and moreover stress the general rule according to which the appellate instance would not overrule the factual basis underlying the lower court decision to grant or refuse to grant temporary injunction.[35]

[32] Supporting such conclusion with British references: *Van Der Lely (C.) NV v. Bamfords, Ltd RPC* (1964, p. 54).
[33] See, for example: LCA 920/05 *Hasin Ash Industries Ltd v. Konial Antonio (Israel) LTD* [2005].
[34] See, for example: CA 342/64 *American Cyanamid Company USA v. Hirshhorn-Gilerman Partnership* [1965] (holding that the principles for granting a temporary injunction in patent cases are no different from other cases. One of these principles is the "balance of convenience," referring to *Chattender v. Royle* (1887), 36 Ch. D. 425, 436. Moreover, it was explained that the appellate instance usually will not intervene with the lower court determination. Such intervention shall be conducted only if the lower instance was not led by these principles or applied these principles wrongly, referring to Blanco White, Patents For Inventions (3d ed.), 338. Finally, the court overruled the lower court refusal to grant the temporary injunction, since the balance of convenience was not considered properly); LCA 5248/90 *Reuven Antin v. Benjamin Frankel* [1991] (holding that the principles for granting temporary injunction in patent cases are no different from other cases, referring to *id.* CA 342/64 *American Cyanamid Company USA v. Hirshhorn-Gilerman Partnership* [1965], and approving the lower-instance determination with regard to the "balance of convenience" principle at stake); LCA 920/05 *Hasin Ash Industries Ltd v. Konial Antonio (Israel) LTD* [2005] (approving lower instance's decision not to grant temporary injunction on the basis of laches); LCA 11964/04 *Tzefi Profil Chen (1983) LTD v. Azulai* [2005] (holding that the appellate instance usually will not intervene with lower-instance decisions concerning temporary remedies. Patent cases are not an exception referring to CA 342/64 *American Cyanamid Company USA v. Hirshhorn-Gilerman Partnership*, and therefore approving the lower court decision); LCA 4788/08 *Cellopark Technologies LTD v. Mobidum LTD* [2008] (holding that the appellate instance usually will not intervene with lower-instance decisions concerning temporary remedies, considering its vast consideration of the matter and its ability to assess the relevant evidence directly. Patent cases are not an exception and in the case at hand there was no basis for deviation from the general rule of non-intervention).
[35] See, for example, *id.*: LCA 11964/04 *Tzefi Profil Chen (1983) LTD v. Azulai* [2005]; LCA 4788/08 *Cellopark Technologies LTD v. Mobidum LTD* [2008].

b. District Court

In almost all District Courts decisions, once a patent infringement is determined, a final injunction is granted upon request.[36] Namely, the lower courts' approach to final injunctions is predominantly an automatic one as well. The rare cases in which injunction was not granted although the court held that the patent was infringed do not reflect an exception to the automatic approach on the matter, but rather were based on a specific factual situation in which the grant of injunction was irrelevant. For example, in two cases, the court held that the patent was infringed, but nevertheless because at the time the decision was handed down the patent had already expired no injunction could be granted and the only remedy left for the plaintiff was a monetary one.[37] Other examples relate to cases in which injunction was not requested due to various factual circumstances.[38] In contrast, temporary

[36] The survey was based on the Israeli database Nevo, which includes Israeli court decision of all instances, commencing 1950, and it included all the decisions that were located as relevant in the database. We have differentiated between interim decisions (which may include very technical short decisions and reasoned decision with respect to grants of temporary remedies) and final decisions (which include final determination). Within this latter group of final decisions, we have differentiated between final decisions concerning patent infringement and other final decisions, discussing only the validity of an already granted patent; appeals on the Patent Registrar decisions; final decisions concerning various issues except from patent infringement (such as validity of a license, or conflicts relating to the ownership of inventions). The group of final decisions concerning patent infringement is the one that stands at the heart of this survey. We have reviewed seventy District Court final decisions, out of which in thirty-one decisions the court held that the patent at stake was valid and was infringed. In all these thirty-one cases, injunction was granted upon request. In the other thirty-eight decisions, it was held that there was no infringement and therefore no injunction was granted. The following is the result of the survey by year (the year division is set by the Nevo database):

> 1950–1989: seventeen District Court final decisions, out of which seven held patent infringement;
> 1989–2005: twenty-seven District Court final decisions, out of which fifteen held patent infringement;
> 2005–2013: eighteen District Court final decisions, out of which eight held patent infringement;
> 2013–2017: five District Court final decisions, out of which one held patent infringement;
> 2017–2019: three District Court final decisions, out of which none held patent infringement.

[37] See, CC 1512/93 *The Wellcome Foundation Limited* v. *Teva Pharmaceutical Industries* [1995] and CC 881/94 *Eli Lilly Company* v. *Teva Pharmaceutical Industries* [1998]. It should be further noted that at the time these decisions were handed down, time extension orders for expired patents were not yet acknowledged by the Israeli legislation and therefore the court concluded that it could not grant a post-expiration injunction. In a third case, handed down in September 2019, the District Court ruled that the time extension period of a patent had expired, and therefore injunction was no longer a relevant remedy, yet in this case the court also ruled that there was no infringement due to judicial estoppel, see CA 28676-05-13 *Pfizer Inc.* v. *Unifarm LTD* [2019] (under appeal).

[38] See, CC 121/06 *Kapoza* v. *Y. Cochav & Son Construction LTD* [2009] (injunction was not requested, apparently since the case concerned a single act – construction of a system – which was held as a patent infringement); CC 6160/08/07 *Rotenberg* v. *Algo Hashkaya LTD* [2009,

injunctions are subject to close inspection, and courts consider the traditional factors: the balance of convenience, the irreparable harm rule, and equitable considerations of clean hands and laches.[39]

The specific phrasing of injunctive orders is usually included within the court's final decision, and there is no special form for such remedy. The common phrases used are very short, and there is no evidence for flexibilities in the texts. For example, the phrasing of one of the earliest injunctions granted in Israel, in 1952, was (non-official translation): "I order the two defendants and each one of them, to refrain from infringing patent Exhibit 1, directly or indirectly, whether by themselves, by their providers, agents and in general."[40] A later phrasing would typically include more specific prohibited acts, such as the following order granted in 2004 (non-official translation): "The defendants and any one in their behalf will refrain from any commercial act, including acquisition, production, advertising, distribution, marketing, sale, supply and/or offer of the product protected by Israeli patent number 88373, without the plaintiff's in-advance approval in writing."[41] In some cases, the plaintiff is requested to submit separately a phrasing of the injunction for the approval of the court, and in such cases the final injunction is not open to the public.

c. Flexibilities within the Interpretation of Substantive Law

While the Israeli judiciary perceives final injunctions as an automatic outcome to the determination of patent infringement, it nevertheless applies profound discretion as to substantive patent questions involving interpretation of the Patents Act and of the patent claims. The courts have stressed in a long line of decisions that patent cases always entail the application of judicial discretion with respect to substantive issues, such as the qualification of the registered patent and the interpretation of the patent claims, in light of the balance of interests underlying patent law.[42] In other words, in clear contrast to the question of granting injunctions, when determining substantive conclusions, Israeli courts demonstrate great flexibility.

Since there is such a significant difference between the judiciary's rigid approach to final injunctions and its broad, inherent discretion applied with respect to other

---

p. 48] (the court explains that injunction is the usual remedy in cases of patent infringement. In this case injunction was not requested since it concerned termination of a patent license and the plaintiff did not think that the defendant would cause any further harm).

[39] See, for example: CC 7438-11-11 *Kwalata Trading Limited* v. *Regensal Laboratories LTD* [2012]; CC 18514-12-13 *Magnetica Interactive LTD* v. *Ambrozia Superherb LTD* [2014] (temporary injunction was denied due to lack of full disclosure of relevant facts).

[40] CC 1003/51 *Park Davis and Company, Detroit,* v. *Abik Chemical Laboratories LTD* [1952].

[41] CC 2168/00 *SDR Shiryun Yevu and Shivuk LTD* v. *F. B. Sochnuyot Shivuk LTD* [2004].

[42] See, for example: CA 345/87 *Hughes Aircraft Company* v. *the State of Israel* [1990]; CA 407/89 *Tzuk Or Ltd* v. *Car Security Ltd* [1994]; CA 2626/11 *Hasin Ash Industries Ltd* v. *Konial Antonio (Israel) LTD* [2013].

legal questions arising in patent cases, we should ask whether there are *hidden* flexibilities concerning final injunctions as well.

A *possible* phenomenon, proposed here, could be that since the perception of patent cases is binary and a patent was either infringed (and therefore its owner is entitled to an injunction) or there was no patent infringement at all, then in the specific cases in which we could have expected a midway conclusion where despite the finding of patent infringement the granting of an injunction was not justified, the court nevertheless ruled that there was no patent infringement. Namely, the extreme binary way patent law is operated may lead, *de facto*, to the shifting of all the judicial flexibilities to the substantive part of the decision, discussing the infringement. Thus, the proposed hypothesis is that in "gray area" cases, to avoid the ill-consequences of final injunction affecting the public interest at large, the court may rule that there was no infringement at all.[43]

A possible evidentiary basis which may, somewhat, support such a proposition is the finding of this project, which reviewed located final decisions of Israeli district courts (first-instance courts) discussing *inter partes* patent infringement lawsuits in the years 1950–2019.[44] Out of seventy courts' final decisions, in thirty-one cases the lawsuit succeeded, namely the court ruled that the patent was valid and was infringed (in full or in part), and therefore injunction was granted upon request. This finding represents a ratio of 44 percent success in patent lawsuits reaching a court's final decision, which should be understood as a non-accurate ratio, considering many unknown variables, such as the number of patent cases settled outside court (especially after interim proceedings), the number of patent cases resolved in arbitration and other alternative dispute resolutions methods, and other reasons for the cancelation of lawsuits.[45] Nevertheless, this finding is remarkable, considering the general average ratio of success in civil lawsuits reaching a final decision in

---

[43] By way of analogy, former Chief Justice Shamgar expressed a similar fear in a decision discussing the statutory damages scheme that was in force at that time in copyright law. This scheme included a minimum damages threshold, of a significant amount, that courts were compelled to grant. Chief Justice Shamgar expressed his view that this minimum sum did not reflect "light" copyright infringements, therefore courts would inevitably use their discretion and refrain from granting damages at all in such "light" cases. Hence, in his view, the legislature had to amend the statutory damages scheme to give greater flexibility to courts in a way that would allow adjustment of the damages granted to the relevant circumstances, see CA 592/88 *Shimon Sagy v. The late Abraham Ninyo Estate*, p. 271 [1992]. In other words, Chief Justice Shamgar's view was that a rigid approach to remedies may lead to rejection of intellectual property infringement lawsuits in order to avoid the negative consequences of granting overcompensation. It should be further noted that the statutory damages scheme was indeed amended in the new Israeli Copyright Act enacted in 2007, and the minimum threshold for statutory damages was abolished, see Copyright Act 2007, sect. 56.

[44] See *supra* note 36.

[45] According to an Israeli research, an average of 18 percent of civil cases reaches a final reasoned court decision, see, Weinshall & Taraboulos 2017, 763 (in Hebrew).

Israeli courts, which is much higher.[46] How can such a gap be explained? One *possible* explanation is that courts are aware of the gap between the vast legal flexibilities with respect to questions of patent validity and infringement in contrast to the rigid approach with respect to injunctions. And, since the determination in patent cases has a profound impact on the public interest, although the conflict is between private parties, courts may be drawn to entirely reject lawsuits to avoid far-reaching negative consequences of an injunction that may harm the public interest. In other words, the nature of patent litigation, involving the public interest, in contrast to "ordinary" *inter partes* civil lawsuits, may generate a different approach.[47]

A few Israeli cases could fit within such a proposition. A putative example is the case of *Tzhori and Sons Industries LTD and others* v. *"Regba" Communal Agricultural Village LTD*,[48] in which the court had to interpret section 50 of the Patents Act, according to which, if the invention is a process then the scope of the patent covers the "direct product" of the process as well. In this case, the invention concerned the process of cutting a surface (such as marble or stone) that allows for a sink to be installed into the surface in such a manner that the sink and the working surface create a flat platform. The invention related to the cutting process and (implicitly) to the installation of compatible sinks. The question was whether the compatible sink falls within section 50 of the Patents Act, as being a "direct product" of the patented process. The defendant imported and sold compatible sinks without the plaintiff's approval, and therefore competed on the same market. The installation of the imported compatible sinks was done by various freelancers.

It should be noted that these kinds of situations are known in design law as the "must fit/must match" problem, in which the protected design right may give rise to claims of exclusivity over secondary market products (i.e. aftermarket products), such as printers and cartridges, or machines and technological devices and spare

---

[46] The Research Department of the Israeli court system conducted a statistical research concerning civil cases in first-instance courts in Israel and published the full data in 2014. The data includes a sample of 2,000 cases from various Magistrate and District Courts that were "closed files" between December 2008 and December 2011. The sample consists of 2 percent of the entire files at the respective period and, according to the statistical information reported by the Research Department, it reflects an accuracy of over 95 percent and error sampling of less than 6 percent, see Weinshall & Taraboulos 2014. Out of the 2,000 sampled cases, 815 cases have reached a final decision in court (the rest were withdrawn, technically closed, or transferred to arbitration and most were settled with the court's approval). Out of the 815 cases that have reached a final decision in court, in 247 cases the lawsuit was rejected and in 568 cases the lawsuit was accepted in full or in part (401 cases in full and 167 cases in part). This statistical sample represent an average ratio of 70 percent success when a civil case reaches the stage of a court final decision. Clearly this is not an accurate ratio, but it may indicate a scale.

[47] This hypothesis could not be proven or rebutted, but other explanations for the drop of success in patent litigation would lack solid evidence as well.

[48] CA 7614/96 *Tzhori and Sons Industries LTD* v. *"Regba" Communal Agricultural Village LTD* [2000].

parts.[49] The "must fit/must match" problem, however, may be relevant in patents law as well, and has given rise to complex questions concerning the limits of intellectual property monopolist rights vis-à-vis free competition.[50] The District Court in *Tzhori* held that the compatible sink is a direct product of the patented process, since, at least in some periods, it could be installed into surfaces only if they were cut by the patented process. The District Court Judge explicitly explained that considering free competition, not all compatible sinks should fall within the monopoly's scope, but rather only those that would possibly be installed by the patented process. Moreover, the court was aware of the fact that the installation of the compatible sinks was done by third parties – the freelance installers – and the defendant had no control over their acts. During the hearings the defendant had developed its own process for installation of compatible sinks, which was approved by the court as non-infringing. Therefore, a final injunction was ordered, referring only to sinks that were aimed to be installed by the patented process and not by other newly developed methods.[51] On appeal, the Supreme Court reversed the decision, holding that the direct product of the cutting process was only the aperture (i.e. the opening) in the surface, while the compatible sink was a "later" product. The defendant imported and sold the compatible sinks, yet the customer was responsible for the installation of the sink they bought, and the installation was done by third parties for whose acts the defendant was not liable. The Supreme Court rejected the application of the joint tortfeasors doctrine in this case and ruled that the doctrine of contributory infringement was not yet adopted in Israeli patent law. Therefore, the Supreme Court clarified that even if the installation done by third parties was a patent infringement, considering a broad interpretation of the patent, the defendant could not be held liable for such infringing acts since was merely importing the sinks.[52] It should be noted that one year later, in a different case, the Supreme Court

---

[49] In England there is a special exclusion, according to which such objects do not fall within the scope of the design right. Section 213(3)(b)(i) of the Copyright Design Patent Act (1988) is often referred to as the "must fit" exclusion and section 213(3)(b)(ii) as the "must-match" exclusion ("Design right does not subsist in – (a) ..., (b)features of shape or configuration of an article which – (i) enable the article to be connected to, or placed in, around or against, another article so that either article may perform its function, or (ii)are dependent upon the appearance of another article of which the article is intended by the designer to form an integral part").

[50] In the United States there is a significant movement calling for legislating special provisions that would protect consumers' "right to repair," and that would limit the control over spare parts and the aftermarket through patent rights, see Grinvald & Tur-Sinai 2019; Joshua D. Sarnoff, White Paper on Protecting the Consumer Patent Law Right to Repair and the Aftermarket for Exterior Motor Vehicle Repair Parts: The PARTS Act, S. 812, HR 1879, 115th Congress, November 2017.

[51] CC 505/94 *"Regba" Communal Agricultural Village LTD v. Tzhori and Sons Industries LTD* [1986].

[52] CA 7614/96 *Tzhori and Sons Industries LTD v. "Regba" Communal Agricultural Village LTD*, pp. 742–42, 745–47 [2000].

did adopt the doctrine of contributory infringement in patent law.[53] Moreover, the Supreme Court reasoning in the *Tzhori* case was that the Patents Act is subject to interpretation according to the law's initial purpose, and a balance of competing interests should exist: the need to set limits to the monopoly of the patent right which may limit the freedom of occupation and of competition, versus the proprietary interests of patent owners and the public interest in incentivizing the development of inventions.[54] Therefore, the Supreme Court concluded that the defendant did not infringe the patent, and consequently the injunction was revoked. Without discussing the issue of "direct products" and the proper rule for compatible parts, it is clear that the Supreme Court was concerned by the closure of the relevant market to competition, and thus it determined that there was no infringement at all. However, this was, potentially, an appropriate case in which even if the court had concluded that the patent was infringed – since the patent could have been interpreted as including the process of installation and the importation of compatible sinks could have been concluded as contributory – the court could have justified the denial of an injunction as being a far-reaching remedy under the circumstances, which would disproportionally close the market. Such result could have been justified particularly considering the defendant's contributory liability.

C. INJUNCTIVE RELIEF IN PATENT SUBJECT-MATTER CASES BASED ON UNJUST ENRICHMENT LAW

In 1979, the Unjust Enrichment Act was enacted in Israel, based on continental principles.[55] The Act establishes the grounds for monetary restitution; however, it was developed extensively in Israeli case law as a basis for a cause of action as well, particularly in intellectual property subject-matter cases which did not qualify for a fully fledged intellectual property right. Moreover, in a District Court decision of 1989, it was held that unjust enrichment may serve as grounds for granting final injunction, and not only for restitution. The Supreme Court further developed the principle of unjust enrichment as a vehicle for claims in situations in which products were copied, but there was no infringement of any other established intellectual property right.[56]

In 1998, a seminal decision was handed down by the Supreme Court in the case of *ASIR*,[57] which concerned an industrial design that had not been registered and an

[53] CA1636/98 *Rav-Bariach LTD v. Beit Mischar Leavizarey Rechev (Car Accessories Store) Havshush LTD* [2001].
[54] CA 7614/96 *Tzhori and Sons Industries LTD v. "Regba" Communal Agricultural Village LTD* [2000, p. 741].
[55] Unjust Enrichment Act 1979.
[56] LCA 371/89 *Leibovitz v. A & Y. Eliyahu Ltd, et al.* [1990].
[57] LCA 5768/94 *ASIR Import, Manufacture, and Distribution v. Accessories and Products Ltd,* [1989].

invention for which no patent had been registered. The question was whether copying these unregistered products created grounds for a claim of unjust enrichment (which, as mentioned in Section C, entitles the plaintiff to both monetary restitution and injunctive relief). It should be noted that until the new Designs Act was enacted in 2017, there was no established, unregistered design right under Israeli law. The Supreme Court considered the principal question of whether intellectual property is regulated exclusively by the established intellectual property rights, such as patents and designs, or if it may be protected by other legal means. The majority ruled that unjust enrichment may serve as an independent cause of action in cases featuring an "additional element," variously referred to as "unfair competition" or "unfairness."[58]

In the aftermath of the *ASIR* ruling, there have been further cases in which claims based on unjust enrichment were accepted, even though no design had been registered.[59] The injunctions in these cases were occasionally non-perpetual and limited to a certain period. The *ASIR* ruling did not discuss the time period of injunctions, but the Supreme Court referred to this issue in later decisions. For instance, a Supreme Court decision that followed one of the cases discussed in the *ASIR* holding, ruled that the monetary remedies should be limited in a way that would reflect *eight years* of protection over the non-registered design, and that this period already included the injunction that had been granted by the District Court for a limited time.[60] The Supreme Court explained that granting remedies in cases based on unjust enrichment is complex, since, on the one hand, there is no fully fledged (intellectual) property right and, on the other hand, the plaintiff's interest that their design would not be copied justifies protection.[61] Therefore, various factors should be considered in tailoring the adequate remedy, including the behavior, intentions and good faith of the infringer, the investment in the design and the reason the design was not registered. The Supreme Court further emphasized that injunction is an equitable remedy which is subject to the court's discretion.[62] In another case, the Supreme Court stressed that considering the proper balance of interests underlying intellectual property laws, between incentivizing

---

[58] *Id.*

[59] See for example: CC 16218/97 *Single Fashion Design 1994 Ltd* v. *Moses Ben Isaac Kuba* [not published] (injunction was granted against imitation of unregistered design for trousers); CA 3894/03 *Doitch* v. *Israflowers Ltd* [2004] (injunction against imitation of unregistered design for jewelry).

[60] CA 2287/00 *Shoham Mechonot (Machines) and Mavletim (Dies) LTD* v. *Harar* [2005]. The District Court granted an injunction which was effectively in force for three years, due to various interim decisions limiting the injunction during the hearings of the *ASIR* case. This Supreme Court decision, concerning remedies, was handed down ten years later. Therefore, the Supreme Court had to calculate the monetary relief retroactively, taking into consideration that during the term of eight years of protection the injunction was valid for only three years.

[61] See *id.* at paras. 27–28.

[62] See, CA 2287/00 *Shoham Mechonot (Machines) and Mavletim (Dies) LTD* v. *Harar* [2005] at paras. 27–28, 30–31.

creators and allowing free competition, there is no justification to grant perpetual injunction based on unjust enrichment, and the time period should not exceed the term of protection over a registered design. This conclusion was supported by the fact that no explanation was given for the non-registration of the design.[63] However, twenty years after the *ASIR* ruling's legacy was applied extensively in the area of design law, the new Designs Act enacted in 2017 foreclosed the possibility to use unjust enrichment as a cause of action in cases of design infringement, since an explicit provision states the exclusivity of the Designs Act over protection of both registered and non-registered designs.[64]

In the area of patents, nevertheless, the courts are more cautious in their application of the *ASIR* ruling. For example, in a case where no patent had been registered for a medicine, the District Court dismissed a claim of copying based on unjust enrichment.[65] Moreover, as discussed above, the Supreme Court ruled that the Patents Act unequivocally determines that the use of invention cannot be prevented during the pendency period of a patent application, and that this rule cannot be circumvented on the grounds of unjust enrichment. In explaining its decision, the Supreme Court stated that the Patents Act has established a delicate balance of interests that should not be interfered with, and that in the current case the law should be viewed as exhaustive and exclusive.[66]

D. ANALOGIES FROM CLOSE LEGAL AREAS: COPYRIGHT AND PLANT BREEDERS' RIGHT LAW

1. *Analogies from Copyright Law*

The most significant development concerning discretionary final injunctions in the field of intellectual property law concerns an explicit authorization in the new Israeli Copyright Act (enacted in 2007) not to grant injunctive relief. Section 53 of the Copyright Act 2007 provides that: "In an action for copyright infringement the claimant shall be entitled to injunctive relief, unless the court finds that there are reasons which justify not doing so."

---

[63] CA 3894/03 *Deutsch v. Israflowers Ltd* [2012]. In this case, the District Court had granted an injunction in 1996. The Supreme Court decision, rejecting the appeal in part, was handed down in 2012. The one and only claim that was accpted referred to the time period of the injunction. The term of design protection was at that time fifteen years, therefore the Supreme Court ruled that the injunction should not reflect a longer period of time. Considering the passage of time since the injunction was first granted by the District Court in 1996, the Supreme Court did not see reason to keep it valid. The injunction, therefore, was revoked.

[64] Designs Act 2017, sect. 2 provides that: "There shall be no right in a design except under the provisions of this Law." It was explicitly explained in The Designs Act Bill 2015 that this section is aimed at blocking the legal path created by the *ASIR* ruling.

[65] CC 2417/00 *Smithkline Beecham Plc v. Unifarm Ltd* [2006].

[66] See Patents Act Bill – 1965, H"H 637, January 20, 1965, p. 129.

According to legislative history, the original Copyright Act Bill included only a general section according to which "infringement of copyright is a civil wrong and the provisions of the Torts Ordinance shall apply."[67] This section is currently included under section 52 of the Copyright Act. The explanatory part of the bill clarified that without prejudice to the proprietary nature of the copyright, the general appropriate framework for remedies in case of infringement is tort law.[68] During parliamentary committee discussions, there was an outcry over this section and the possibility that it may hinder the nature of copyright as a property right. In particular, the fear was that such a section may give rise to claims based on section 74 of the Torts Ordinance anchoring the rule that injunctions are subject to various equitable considerations headed by the balance of convenience. As a compromise, the current section 53 was added, clarifying that entitlement to an injunction is the general default.[69] During the final vote in parliament, the committee chair explained that injunctive relief may be denied based on prevailing public interest, such as freedom-of-expression and freedom-of-occupation considerations.[70] These considerations, and other appropriate circumstances for denying injunctive relief, were reviewed in Israeli scholarly literature.[71] Yet, after thirteen years, there is still very scant reference to section 53 of the Copyright Act by the judiciary; in fact, courts maintain the automatic approach to final injunctions in the copyright realm as well.[72]

The few court decisions referring to section 53 of the Copyright Act reflect a very cautions and mild change of approach. For instance, the Supreme Court noted only in *obiter dictum* that where a photographic work of historical importance is concerned, the owner of the work may not be entitled to an injunction and may only receive damages for the infringement.[73] In some cases, lower courts were conflicted with the possibility of granting injunction. For example, in one case the District Court considered denying an injunctive relief due to the plaintiff's failure to conduct themselves in good faith and their contributory fault; however, it eventually granted the injunction since the proprietary nature of the copyright should have prevailed in its view.[74] In another case, the District Court held that a *temporary* injunction against the broadcast of a television series should be denied since a *final*

---

[67] The Copyright Act Bill 2005, H"H 196, July 20, 2005, sect. 55 at 1116.

[68] *Id.* at p. 1136.

[69] Minutes no. 353 Economic Committee meeting, Israeli Parliament (seventeenth Parliament, October 9, 2007), p. 23.

[70] Minutes no. M/196 Meeting 170 of the Israeli seventeenth Parliament. (November 19, 2007). According to Article 3 to the Israeli Basic Law – Freedom of Occupation [1994]: "Every Israel national or resident has the right to engage in any occupation, profession or trade", see: www .knesset.gov.il/review/data/eng/law/kns13_basiclaw_occupation_eng.pdf.

[71] See Fischman-Afori 2009, 529 (in Hebrew).

[72] *Id.*

[73] CA 7774/09 *Weinberg v. Weishoff* [2012].

[74] CC 2545/07 *Miriam Bilu and others v. Holon municipality* [2012].

injunction would be rejected as well, as (except from the fact it was not requested) under the circumstances freedom of expression and the public's interest in access to the protected content prevails.[75] Following this later decision, a Magistrate's Court ruling explained the refusal to grant *temporary* injunction against the broadcast of a documentary film due to the high likelihood that the court would deny a final injunction in this case as well, since freedom of expression and the public's interest in access to the film at stake might prevail.[76] In other words, in these two latter cases, lower courts refused to grant temporary injunctions, as occasionally happens, yet the only change of approach lay in the reasons for such denial which referred to a potential justified denial of the final injunction in the future. Finally, recently, the District Court refused to grant an injunctive relief, stressing it was an unapplicable remedy under the specific circumstances, yet with no reference to section 53 and without elaborating on the matter.[77]

2. *Analogies from the Plant Breeders' Right Law*

Another analogy is taken from a very close legal area – the protection of plant breeds. The Plant Breeders' Rights Act (1973) regulates the established, registered plant breeders' right in Israel. This intellectual property right is governed by legal principles akin to those underlying patent law. Moreover, the wording of section 65 of the Plants Breeders' Rights Act is the same as that of section 183 of the Patent Act, according to which in case of infringement the plaintiff is "entitled" to injunctive relief. Thus, when the courts concluded that a plant breeder's right was infringed, its owner was automatically entitled to injunctive relief.

However, in a single and rare Supreme Court decision, in the case of *Florist De Kwakel v. Baruch Hajaj*, handed down in 2013,[78] the scope and nature of the entitlement to injunctive relief in the Plant Breeder's Rights Act was discussed. The Supreme Court eventually granted a limited injunction, therefore most of the discussion is *obiter dictum*. However, since it reflects the first thorough analysis by the Supreme Court of the issue of discretionary permanent injunctions, it has a significant importance. Justice Hanan Meltzer, delivering the opinion of the court, opened by reviewing the adoption of the British common law tradition with respect to equitable remedies, headed by injunctive relief, into Israeli law, and that *de facto* this tradition is applied only with respect to interim injunctions. Nevertheless, Justice Meltzer emphasized that despite the decisive wordings of section 65 of the Plant Breeder's Rights Act and section 183 of the Patent Act, there is an *inherent*

---

[75] CC 57955-12-16 *DBS Satellite Services (1988) Ltd and others v. Noga Communication (1995) Ltd* [2018].
[76] CC 14106-06-19 *Doe v. Jonathan Ofek* [2019].
[77] CC 53689-10-17 *Bardugo v. D. Eithan & R. Lahav-Rig Architectures and Urban Planners Ltd* [2020].
[78] CA 10717/05 *Florist De Kwakel et al. v. Baruch Hajaj et al.* [2013].

vested discretion to the court in matters of injunctions. Such court's general discretionary power could be concluded from both section 75 of the Courts Act, according to which courts are authorized to grant such remedies as are proper under the circumstances, and from section 74 of the Torts Ordinance, according to which injunctive relief is subject to the balance-of-convenience principle. Furthermore, Justice Meltzer stressed that, according to the principle of interpreting various pieces of legislation in a harmonious way, section 53 of the new Copyright Act (clarifying that courts' discretion in granting final injunctions is vested) should be taken into consideration while interpreting the parallel sections on other intellectual property laws, being close legal subject matter. Justice Meltzer specified a few potential reasons for denying injunctive relief that are discussed in the literature,[79] including resolving severe market failures, promoting free competition, and striking a proper balance of interests aimed at promoting access to work. Justice Meltzer added that the court may deny injunctive relief in extreme and rare cases of *misuse of right* where the plaintiff's lack of good faith was apparent and abusive – or, alternatively, in *de minims* cases. Nevertheless, under the specific circumstances, such exceptions did not arise – even though the initial use at stake was under license, a later cancelation of it and the insistence of the right owner on putting an end to the licensed use could not be perceived as abusive or misuse of right, nor as a *de minims* infringement (inter alia, based on the *Roker* v. *Solomon* holding). The Supreme Court also rejected the claim of balance of convenience at stake, since it may hinder the propriety nature of the intellectual property right.

The final ruling of the Supreme Court in the case of *Florist De Kwakel* v. *Baruch Hajaj* was that a final injunction should be granted only to a limited scope of acts that are a clear and direct infringement of the core of the plant breeder's right, in order not to hinder competition and the defendant's right to conduct his business freely (i.e. freedom of occupation).

It should be noted that there was no "follow-up" to the *Florist De Kwakel* v. *Baruch Hajaj* ruling, in the sense that no other court ruling took its legacy a step further.

E. CONCLUSIONS

Litigation concerning patent infringement is held between private parties, but its results have major impact on the public at large. The monopolistic nature of patents affects free competition, freedom of occupation and innovation, and it touches individuals' quality of life, especially when it comes to pharmaceuticals. Therefore, patent law needs to balance various competing interests: on the one hand, the public interest by granting patent rights to incentivize innovation and, on the other hand, the public interest by minimizing the negative consequences

---

[79] Referring to Fischman-Afori 2009 (in Hebrew).

stemming from the patent monopoly. Israeli patent law incorporates vast legal mechanisms that allow discretion in pursuit of the appropriate balance, from the initial stage of the patent registration to the final stage of patent enforcement by court. In all these stages, patent law uses legal measures that are subject to interpretation according to the underlying rationale of patent law. However, when it comes to the very last stage of the judicial process in court, the approach changes sharply – the Israeli judiciary grants final injunctions on an almost automatic basis, as if these were merely a technical matter. Therefore, equitable considerations and the public interest are not a major factor in granting final injunctions, in contrast to temporary injunctions which are still governed by equitable principles. This approach stems from the classification of patents as property rights. Property rights are perceived under Israeli law as "robust" rights that incorporate the injunctive power. While some mild exceptions to this approach have been reported, it nevertheless seems that the governing approach to final injunctions is rigid. A proposed hypothesis is that this rigid approach may lead courts to entirely reject patent infringement claims considering the negative consequences of an injunction. The Israeli patent system has much to gain from expanding the discretion of courts regarding final injunctions as well, since such discretion could serve as an additional, powerful legal means for balancing competing interests in an appropriate and wise manner. The rigid view of patent right as a property right may be relaxed by a complementary perception, according to which patent infringement claims are subject to the flexible equitable and tort law principles regarding injunctions.

REFERENCES

Cases

CA 245/60 *American Cyanamid Company NY USA v. Lepetit SPT and others* [1962] (PD 16, 788)

CA 342/64 *American Cyanamid Company USA v. Hirshhorn-Gilerman Partnership* [1965]

CC 53689-10-17 *Bardugo v. D. Eithan & R. Lahav-Rig Architectures and Urban Planners Ltd* [2020]

CA 817/77 *Beecham Group Ltd v. Bristol-Myers Co.,* 33 (3) PD 757 [1979]

Chattender v. Royle (1887), 36 Ch. D. 425

CA 3894/03 *Deutsch v. Israflowers Ltd* [2012]

CA 3894/03 *Doitch v. Israflowers Ltd* [2004]

CA 10717/05 *Florist De Kwakel et al. v. Baruch Hajaj et al.,* [2013]

CA 2626/11 *Hasin Ash Industries Ltd v. Konial Antonio (Israel) LTD* [2013]

CA 345/87 *Hughes Aircraft Company v. the State of Israel* [1990]

CA 2972/95 *Joseph Wolf and CO. Ltd v. Be'eri Print Ltd* [1999]

CA 4705/05 *Neka Chemicals (1952) LTD and others v. Sano Industries Bruno LTD* [2005]

CA 28676-05-13 *Pfizer Inc. v. Unifarm LTD* [2019] (under appeal)

CA 1636/98 *Rav-Bariach LTD v. Beit Mischar Leavizarey Rechev (Car Accessories Store) Havshush LTD* [2001]

CA 2634/09 *Rotenberg v. Algo Hashkaya LTD* [2011]

CA 3400/03 *Ruhama Rubinstein and others v. Ein-Tal (1983) Ltd* [2005]

CA 592/88 *Shimon Sagy v. The late Abraham Ninyo Estate* [1992] at p. 271

CA 2287/00 *Shoham Mechonot (Machines) and Mavletim (Dies) LTD v. Harar* [2005]

CA 689/69 *Trisol LTD v. Moses Kobobi* [1971]

CA 7614/96 *Tzhori and Sons Industries LTD and others v. "Regba" Communal Agricultural Village LTD* [2000]

CA 407/89 *Tzuk Or Ltd v. Car Security Ltd* [1994]

CA 7774/09 *Weinberg v. Weishoff* [2012]

CC HMR. 8292/65 *Anshel Cohen v. Shlomo Ben-David* [1965]

CC 57955-12-16 *D.B.S. Satellite Services (1988) Ltd and others v. Noga Communication (1995) Ltd and others* [2018]

CC 14106-06-19 *Doe v. Jonathan Ofek* [2019]

CC 881/94 *Eli Lilly Company v. Teva Pharmaceutical Industries* [1998]

CC 121/06 *Kapoza v. Y. Cochav & Son Construction LTD* [2009]

CC 7438-11-11 *Kwalata Trading Limited v. Regensal Laboratories LTD and others* [2012]

CC 18514-12-13 *Magnetica Interactive LTD v. Ambrozia Superherb LTD and others* [2014]

CC 2545/07 *Miriam Bilu and others v. Holon municipality and others* [2012]

CC 1003/51 *Park Davis and Company, Detroit v. Abik Chemical Laboratories LTD* [1952]

CC 505/94 *"Regba" Communal Agricultural Village LTD v. Tzhori and Sons Industries LTD and others* [1986]

CC 6160/08/07 *Rotenberg v. Algo Hashkaya LTD*, at p. 48 [2009]

CC 2168/00 *SDR Shiryun Yevu and Shivuk LTD v. F. B. Sochnuyot Shivuk LTD* [2004]

CC 16218/97 *Single Fashion Design 1994 Ltd v. Moses Ben Isaac Kuba* [not published]

CC 2417/00 *Smithkline Beecham Plc v. Unifarm Ltd* [2006]

CC 1512/93 *The Wellcome Foundation Limited v. Teva Pharmaceutical Industries* [1995]

Chattender v. Royle (1887)

HCJ 5379/00 *Bristol-Myers Squibb Company v. The Minister of Health* [2001]

LCA 6141/02 *ACUM (Israeli Collecting Society) v. GLZ (IDF Broadcast)* [2003]

LCA 5768/94 *ASIR Import, Manufacture, and Distribution v. Accessories and Products Ltd* [1989]

LCA 4788/08 *Cellopark Technologies LTD v. Mobidum LTD* [2008]

LCA 920/05 *Hasin Ash Industries Ltd v. Konial Antonio (Israel) LTD* [2005].

LCA 371/89 *Leibovitz v. A & Y. Eliyahu Ltd, et al.* [1990]

LCA 6025/05 *Merck & Co. Inc. et al. v. Teva Pharmaceutical Industries Ltd et al.* [2011]

LCA 5248/90 *Reuven Antin v. Benjamin Frankel* [1991]

LCA 6339/97 *Roker v. Solomon* 55(1) P.D. 199 [1999]

LCA 8127/15 *The Israeli Manufacturers Corporation v. Merck Sharp & Dohme Corp. f/k/ a* [2016]

LCA 11964/04 *Tzefi Profil Chen (1983) LTD v. Azulai* [2005]

Van Der Lely (C.) NV v. Bamfords, Ltd. RPC (1964)

Regulatory and Legislative Materials

Act for the Amendment of Intellectual Property Rights (In Accordance to the TRIPs Agreement) 1999

Article 6, Court Contempt Ordinance (1929).

Article 3 to the Israeli Basic Law – Freedom of Occupation [1994]

Civil Law Procedure Regulations (2018)

Copyright Act 2007

Joshua D. Sarnoff, White Paper on Protecting the Consumer Patent Law Right to Repair and the Aftermarket for Exterior Motor Vehicle Repair Parts: The PARTS Act, S. 812, HR 1879, 115th Congress, November 2017. https://papers.ssrn.com/sol3/papers.cfm?abstract_id=3082289

Minutes no. 353 Economic Committee meeting, Israeli 17 the Parliament, p. 23, October 9, 2007

Minutes no. M/196 Meeting 170 of the Israeli 17 the Parliament. November 19, 2007

Patents Act Bill – 1965

Section 362 to the Civil Law Procedure Regulations (1984)

Copyright Act 2007

Section 55 to the Copyright Act Bill 2005, H"H 196, July 20, 2005, 1116

Section 213 (3) (b) (i) to the Copyright Design Patent Act (1988)

Section 2 to the Designs Act 2017

Unjust Enrichment Act, 1979

Books, Articles and Online Materials

Bean, David. 2004. *Injunctions*. 8th ed. (Sweet & Maxwell).

Dagan, Hanoch. 2009. "Proprietary Reading: The Renewed Property Institution of Copyright," in Michael Birnhack & Guy Pessach, eds., *Creating Rights – Readings in the Copyright Act* 39 (Nevo).

Fischer, James F. 2006. *Understanding Remedies* (LexisNexis).

Fischman Afori, Orit . 2009. "The Silent Revolution: Judicial Discretion in Granting Permanent Injunctive Relief," in Michael Birnhack and Guy Pessach, eds., *Creating Rights – Essays on the New Copyright Act in Israel* (Nevo).

Fiss, Owen & Doug Rendleman. 1984. *Injunction* (West Academic Pub.).

Goren, Uri. 2015. *Issues in Civil-Law Procedures* (Nevo).

Grinvald, Leah Chan & Ofer Tur-Sinai 2019. "Intellectual Property Law and the Right to Repair," *Fordham Law Review* 88: 63.

Laycock, Douglas. 1991. *The Death of the Irreparable Injury Rule* (Oxford University Press).

Lewinsohm-Zamir, Daphna. 2006. "The Impact of Economic Theory on the Israeli Case Law on Property," *Israel Law Review* 39: 5.

Weinshall, Keren & Ifat Taraboulos. 2014. *Database of Civil Proceedings, The Research Department of the Israeli Court System.*

Weinshall, Keren Margal & Ifat Taraboulos. 2017. "Litigation Costs and Cost-Shifting Practices," *Hebrew University Law Review* 47: 763.

Tur-Sinay. 2017. *Successor Inventions in Patent Law* (Nevo).

White, Blanco. 1962 *Patents for Inventions and the Registration of Industrial Designs*. 3rd ed. (Stevens).

Worthington, Sarah. 2006. *Equity* (Oxford University Press).

10

Italy

Alessandro Cogo and Marco Ricolfi*

A. THE LEGAL CONTEXT

Injunctive relief made its first appearance in Italian legislative texts with the adoption of the 1939 Law on Patents, which empowered a court dealing with an infringement action to issue, on request of the interested party and, at court's discretion, upon payment of a bond, an interim[1] injunction preventing the fabrication and use of the patented invention for the time needed to reach a decision on the merits and for such decision to become final.[2] For a long time, this has been the only provision mentioning injunctive relief in the Law on Patents.

Towards the end of the twentieth century, due to several factors, this started to change. Firstly, the Trade-Related Aspects of Intellectual Property Rights (TRIPS) Agreement, establishing an obligation for the member countries to make available provisional and final injunctive relief (see Chapter III of TRIPS). Secondly, the codification of the Italian laws on industrial property, which brought a unitary set of rules on remedies, including preliminary[3] and final injunctions.[4] Thirdly, harmonization thanks to European Union law, which approached the matter vertically, with the rules on remedies included in the community trademark[5] and design[6] regulations, and horizontally, with the Enforcement Directive. Fourthly, the revival of the project of a unitary European patent, which led to the Unified Patent Court

---

[*] Sections A–D were written by Alessandro Cogo; Section E by Marco Ricolfi.
[1] In the following, We will use the adjective "preliminary" for injunctions issued at the end of a summary proceeding; "interim" for injunctions issued during the proceeding on the merits; "final" for injunctions issued at the end of the proceeding on the merits.
[2] See Art. 83 of the 1939 Law on Patents. Interim injunctions could not be supplemented with penalties for non-compliance: see, e.g., *Eurofarmaco* v. *Glaxo* (App. Roma 1996).
[3] Art. 131 of the Industrial Property Code enacted by the Legislative Decree no. 30 of 2005 (IPC).
[4] Art. 124 IPC.
[5] Art. 130 and Art. 131 of the Regulation on the EU trade mark (EUTMR).
[6] Art. 89 and Art. 90 of the Regulation on Community Designs (CDR).

Agreement (UPCA) containing rules on both provisional[7] and permanent[8] injunctions.[9]

1. *Preliminary and Interim Injunctions*

Until the reform of the 1939 Law on Patents prompted by the TRIPS Agreement, it remained uncertain whether injunctive relief could be obtained, as an urgent and provisional measure, before starting a proceeding on the merits of the case.

According to one view, the answer should have been positive, considering that a general provision of civil procedure law allowed the judiciary to grant any order that, given the circumstances, appeared appropriate to anticipate the effects of the decision on the merits of the case, when the right to be protected was threatened by an imminent and irreparable prejudice.[10]

Others came to the opposite conclusion[11] on the basis of the residual nature of this general provision, which made it inapplicable whenever a specific remedy was available. As the Law on Patents expressly provided for interim injunctions, which were meant to deal urgently with the same risk but according to different rules, allowing preliminary injunctions seemed to run against the intention of the legislator.[12] Interim injunctions had to be issued by a panel of judges,[13] not by a single judge. In their case, the start of the infringement action was a prerequisite for the order to be issued,[14] and not just a condition to prolong its effects; they were issued by a decision of the court provisionally executive and susceptible of being immediately appealed in front of the Court of Appeal, not by an order of the examining judge.[15] Their effects lasted until the decision on the merits of the case became final, unless revoked by the same,[16] and not for the term assigned to the rightsholder to institute a proceeding on the merits of the case.

---

[7] Art. 62 of the Unitary Patent Court Agreement (UPCA).

[8] Art. 63 UPCA.

[9] Art. 1 of the law no. 214/2016 authorized the president of the Italian republic to ratify the UPCA. Art. 2 of the same law gave full execution to the UPCA starting from its entering into force.

[10] *See* Ascarelli 1960, 635; Frigani 1974, 364, 394 ff.; *Alaska* v. *Sammontana* (Trib. Firenze 1993), arguing that preliminary injunctive relief was admissible if, in view of the circumstances of the case, the other preliminary measures provided for by the 1939 Law on Patents, namely description and seizure of infringing goods and of equipment used in their production, would have been inadequate.

[11] Back in the mid-1980s, there were still decisions denying preliminary injunctions, although they were in the minority. *See, e.g., Matessi* v. *Aluminia* (Pret. Milano 1986).

[12] *See Sifa Sitzfabrik* v. *Miotto* (T. Milano 1995) and *W. R. Grace & Co.* v. *Foreco* (Trib. Milano 1994).

[13] *See W. R. Grace & Co.* v. *Foreco* (Trib. Milano 1994).

[14] *See Sifa Sitzfabrik* v. *Miotto* (Trib. Milano 1995).

[15] *See id.*; Greco & Vercellone 1968, 370 f.

[16] *See id.*

For all these reasons, the opinion opposing preliminary injunctions went well beyond the expression of mere formalism. On the contrary, it seemed to articulate a certain degree of resistance against the idea of making available a remedy with potentially disruptive effects for the defendant through a summary proceeding and by way of a provisional order.

The problem of preliminary injunctions was still open in the mid-1990s, although the reform of civil procedure laws regarding precautionary proceedings in general offered new arguments in favour of their availability.[17]

Then, almost sixty years after its enactment, the Law on Patents was amended to include preliminary injunctions, in connection with the implementation of the TRIPS Agreement.[18] Shortly thereafter, their regime was innovated with the enactment of the Industrial Property Code,[19] which established that a preliminary injunction continues to produce effects even if the patentee does not institute a proceeding on the merits of the case.[20] While it remains uncertain whether this rule is compatible with international and European obligations, it has significantly expanded the practical relevance of preliminary measures.

2. *Final Injunctions*

Despite the lack of legislative recognition, which happened only recently, little doubt has ever existed on the capacity of courts to issue final injunctions. On the one hand, the exclusive nature of intellectual property (IP) rights[21] seemed to call for a remedy specifically aimed at preventing the engaging in,[22] continuation or repetition of infringing acts. On the other hand, it would have made little sense to let courts issue preliminary or interlocutory orders that could not be confirmed at the end of the trial.[23] At the end of the day, the law already provided for remedies clearly aimed at indirectly preventing further infringements. In particular, infringing goods, as well as means used to make them, could be assigned to the patentee or seized until the expiration of the patent;[24] an order to pay damages could also include the obligation to pay a fixed amount of money for post-decision infringements or in case of delay in complying with the decision.[25] Against this background, it did not seem

---

[17] *See* Spolidoro 2005, 241. Not all decisions confirm this opinion, however: cf. *W. R. Grace & Co. v .Foreco* (Trib. Milano 1994) for the opposite view.

[18] *See* Art. 26 of the Legislative Decree no. 198 of 19 March 1996.

[19] *See* Art. 132(4) IPC.

[20] *See* Section D.1.

[21] *See* Frignani 1974, 310 ff., 437, ff. 443, who mentions a decision of the Supreme Court of Cassation dated 3 October 1968, n. 3073, that connects the availability of injunctive relief to the exclusive nature of IP rights (in this case a trademark); Vanzetti 2010, 28.

[22] *See* Frignani 1974, 317–18 and 430–31.

[23] *See id.*, 457; Vanzetti 2010, 28.

[24] *See* Art. 85 of the 1939 Law on Patents.

[25] *See* Art. 86 of *id.*

particularly hard to imply a power of the court to issue final injunctions[26] and to safeguard their effectiveness through the provision of astreintes.[27]

This traditional view assumes that injunctive relief – i.e. an order of the court enjoining the defendant from accomplishing, continuing or repeating an act that infringes a claimant's IP right – can be distinguished in some material way from a mere declaratory relief – i.e. a declaration of the court that an act prepared or already committed by the defendant infringes a claimant's IP right. This assumption was challenged under the pre-2005 laws but also thereafter.[28] On the one hand, it has been observed that a finding of infringement necessarily implies an obligation not to accomplish, continue or repeat the act that has been judged unlawful.[29] On the other hand, it has been pointed out that a judicial order to stop and never again repeat an unlawful act does not produce effects that go beyond those of a mere finding of infringement, apart from the fact that it concerns future acts instead of past ones.[30] The command issued by the court does not differ from the one already contained in the law, apart from the fact that it is addressed to a specific entity.[31] Compliance with the court's injunctive order depends on the infringer's voluntary cooperation, no different from compliance with the legislative command on which the finding of infringement and the injunctive order are based. If the infringer does not comply voluntarily, the legal system does not provide for any legal means to enforce the injunction and impose compliance on the wrongdoer. Penalties are a separate, and discretionary, remedy; moreover, they can induce compliance by making it more convenient than infringement[32] but cannot avoid disobedience as such.[33] Criminal sanctions should be considered as inappropriate in case of mere disobedience to the court's order and, at any rate, the wording of current laws allows their application – at the most – only in case of fraudulent behaviour.[34]

This opinion has never been challenged openly. However, there seems to be a general understanding reflected in the current legislative provisions[35] that injunctive relief is a remedy that goes beyond a mere declaration of infringement and has to be

---

[26] See, e.g., *Anzolin* v. *Officina Meccanica MM* (Trib. Vicenza 1990), and the comment published with the decision for further references.

[27] See Ascarelli 1960, 256, 635. *See also*, e.g., *Ing. Bono* v. *Ialchi* (Trib. Milano 1994). Penalties could be issued only to reinforce a final injunction, not an interlocutory or preliminary one: *see* Spolidoro 1982, 242.

[28] See Spolidoro 1982, 41 ff.; Spolidoro 2008a, 174 ff; *see also*, e.g., *Sassi Arredamenti* v. *Gemelli Gualtieri* (Trib. Reggio Emilia 1994).

[29] See Spolidoro 1982, 31–33.

[30] See *La Bruciata* v. *Podere della Bruciata* (App.. Firenze 2017), which qualifies as "declaratory" the judgment issuing an injunction.

[31] Spolidoro 1982, 34.

[32] The amount to be paid is determined at the discretion of the court (Scuffi 2009, 544); however, it should be consistent with the aim of deterring further infringements (Ricolfi 2005, 101–02).

[33] Spolidoro 2008a, 179.

[34] *Id.*, 182–88.

[35] Final injunctions have entered the legislative texts with the enactment of the IPC (*see* Art. 124).

expressly sought by the claimant.[36] Admittedly, injunctive orders cannot be enforced against the will of their addressees. At the same time, the role of penalties is emphasized, as well as the availability of criminal sanctions. Indeed, there have been cases in which criminal courts punished non-compliance with injunctions aimed at protecting intellectual property rights, based on the assumption that these are orders protecting some kind of "property" as required by Article 388 of the Criminal Code.[37] Recently, Article 9 of the legislative decree on 11 May 2018 no. 63 inserted a new specific provision in Article 388 of the Criminal Code to expressly punish as a criminal offence the violation of injunctive orders issued by civil courts in disputes regarding intellectual property rights. As the only requirement for the criminal offence to arise is that disobedience be intentional, it seems that this rule offers a new argument in favour of the traditional view already reported.

As mentioned, injunctive relief is perceived as extending the effects of the finding of infringement, which by nature concerns acts that occurred before the judgment, to future acts of the same kind performed by the same defendant. Disobedience to the court's order leads to the application of penalties and/or grant of damages without considering anew the question about infringement.[38] As the Supreme Court of Cassation affirmed,[39] the authority of *res judicata* also covers the final injunction, with the consequence that the court addressed with a request for penalties or damages should only consider whether the defendant engaged in activities that are substantially the same as those already prohibited.[40]

B. REQUIREMENTS FOR THE GRANT OF INJUNCTIVE RELIEF

1. *Preliminary and Interim Injunctions*

In general, preliminary and interlocutory injunctions can be granted if two requirements are fulfilled: *fumus boni iuris*, i.e. if success on the merit of the case appears

---

[36] An injunction granted without having been solicited by the claimant should be considered *ultra petitum* according to Frignani 1974, 311; *see also* Rovati 2019, 777.

[37] O. A. *and* V. M. (Cass. pen. 1997); K. R. (Cass. pen. 2015); *Kauber Rodolfo* (Trib. Milano sez. pen. 2012). Such cases have been extremely rare (Spolidoro 2005, 242; Scuffi 2009, 545; Di Cataldo 2012, 69). For an attempt to reduce the impact of this case law in the field of intellectual property, *see* Spolidoro 2008b, 171 ff.

[38] *See* Scuffi 2009, 542–43.

[39] And previously *Alessandro Zegna* v. *Ermenegildo Zegna* (App. Torino 1989), which held that a final injunction issued in an earlier proceeding covers later infringements of the same trademark, and of the same kind, performed by the same defendant.

[40] *See Metra* v. *Indinvest* (Cass. 1995) and *Scifoni Renata* v. *Scifoni Fratelli* (Cass. 2008). The relevance of this principle should not be overestimated. As A. Vanzetti 2007, 170, points out, there remains room for disputes between the parties regarding the interference of new allegedly infringing acts with the content of the injunction. An example is offered by *Lodolo* v. *Netafim* (Trib. Bologna 2017), in which the exception of *res judicata* was disregarded because it remained unclear whether the products were the same as those previously deemed non-infringing. It is interesting to note that, even if they had been the same, a new trial would have been necessary because the parties of the two proceedings were not the same, as they involved two different distributors of goods originating from the same producer, who was party only to the first proceeding.

likely, and *periculum in mora*, i.e. risk that delaying relief until the end of the trial would cause irreparable harm to the claimant.

In patent infringement cases, the patentee profits from the rule established by Article 121(1) of the Industrial Property Code (IPC), which places on the alleged infringer the burden of proving that the patent is invalid, if the wish is to offer such a defence.[41] Over the years, courts have become increasingly inclined to imply from this rule a rebuttable presumption of validity of the patent,[42] particularly after the introduction in 2008 of substantive examination of national applications,[43] which approximated the perceived "strength" of titles granted by the Italian IP office to that traditionally attributed to European patents.[44] Such presumption can be enjoyed also in preliminary and interlocutory proceedings,[45] as long as they pertain to patents already examined and granted.[46]

While it is certainly true that the allocation of the burden of proof operated by Article 121(1) of the IPC makes more sense after the reform of examination procedures,[47] it must be stressed that the impact of this reform on the quality of patents granted by our national IP office should not be overestimated. National applications are examined on the basis of a search report and opinion outsourced to the European Patent Office, which finds itself in the difficult position of having to deal with patent applications written in a language other than its official working languages. This, in turn, seems to lead not infrequently to misunderstandings that put the prior art search and evaluation in question. Moreover, patents tend to be granted despite a negative report of the European Patent Office (EPO) examiner if the applicant provides reasonable counterarguments, without further inquiries from the national office. All this considered, courts might be advised to apply Article 121(1) of the IPC *cum grano salis*, particularly in preliminary and interim proceedings,

---

[41] A court seized with an action for infringement can adjudicate upon the plea as to alleged invalidity of the patent, which can be raised by the defendant either by way of an action or a plea in objection. Although the court does not have the power the declare the invalidity *ex officio*, it can prompt the intervention of the public prosecutor who can promote the action for invalidation. See *Buonvicino* v. *MISE* (Cass. 2020).

[42] On the link between the two see the editorial comment to *Salus Researches* v. *Allen & Hambury's Limited* (Trib. Roma 1991).

[43] See Di Fazzio 2019, 726–29, for a summary of the opinions expressed specially before the introduction of substantive examination.

[44] Opposition might play a role, i.e. reducing the strength of the presumption, only for European patents, considering that national patents cannot be opposed. See, e.g., *Innovapac* v. *Barberan* (Trib. Bologna 2008), which denied a preliminary injunction mentioning *obiter* that the European patent actioned by the claimant had been opposed by the defendant.

[45] See *Signature* v. *Axel Weinbrecht* (Trib. Milano 2019). Obviously, the same reasoning does not apply to patents granted without substantive examination (Di Cataldo 2012, 16–17), in respect of which the court has to make a prima facie assessment of validity in case of objection by the alleged infringer. This seems to be adequately reflected in the relevant case law: see for instance *Unknown* v. *Selex* (Trib. Roma 2017).

[46] See *Hair Products* v. *Diffitalia* (Trib. Napoli 2017).

[47] See Di Cataldo 2012, 16–18; Vanzetti & Di Cataldo 2018, 536, 551–52.

considering the disruptive effects that an injunction might have on the defendant's business. In practice, objective elements offered by the alleged infringer that lead to doubt of the validity of the actioned patent should normally be considered sufficient to overcome the presumption of validity within preliminary and interlocutory proceedings, particularly if the prosecution history shows that such elements have not been considered by the EPO examiner or if the reply of the patentee to the objections raised by the examiner does not appear entirely persuasive.

In this connection, it should be considered that validity and infringement are typically assessed with the support of a technical expert appointed by the court, who is requested to provide an opinion on the case after having examined the documents filed by the experts appointed by the parties and heard their arguments. Until 2010 it was unclear, and therefore disputed, whether this could also happen in preliminary and interim proceedings, considering that the law was silent on this point and that the implicit, inevitable delays appeared at odds with the intrinsic urgency characterizing these proceedings. Since 2010, Article 132(5) of the IPC expressly allows courts to order a summary technical evaluation in all precautionary proceedings. Generally, courts tend to make use of this power, which helps them avoid a dismissal of cases that would otherwise appear too complex from a technical point of view to be decided without a full trial. This is not always the case though. Despite the legislative clarification, some courts have recently dismissed claims for injunctive relief considering the case unfit for a summary evaluation.[48]

In this respect it should be considered that preliminary and interim injunctions, by essence, have to be granted on the basis of a summary evaluation of the case. The risk of false positives or negatives is unavoidable and, arguably, greater than in the case of final injunctions. This leads to a question, which is sometimes reflected in the relevant case law:[49] Does the gravity of the consequences for the defendant of a preliminary or interim injunction authorize the court to adopt a more rigorous approach in the evaluation of the *fumus boni iuris*? It is probably a futile question, as a prudent judge will never grant a provisional or interim injunction with potentially disruptive effects on the defendant's business unless thoroughly convinced as to the prima facie validity and infringement of the relevant patent. Whether we should call this a flexibility or not seems scarcely relevant. As to its substance, it seems better to have it than not.

A dispute exists on the other precondition already mentioned, namely, *periculum in mora*, i.e. risk that delaying injunctive relief until the end of the trial would cause

---

[48] See *Hair Products* v. *Diffitalia* (Trib. Napoli 2017); *SFC Intec* v. *Unifix SWG* (Trib. Genova 2014), both regarding disputes in which the defendant also held a patent, or a patent application, covering the allegedly infringing goods. In its reasoning, the court in *SFC Intex* v. *Unifix SWG* (Trib. Genova 2014) mentions the protection of third parties' interests (such as consumers and free competition) as a reason to avoid a summary decision that would have involved a complex and lengthy technical assessment of the case.

[49] See, for instance, *SFC Intec* v. *Unifix* (Trib. Genova 2014).

the patentee a harm that could not be repaired by a judgment to pay damages and disgorge profits. *Periculum in mora* is required by Article 700 of the Code of Civil Procedure (CPC), which was invoked – with mixed fortunes[50] – to claim preliminary injunctions before the amendment of the Law on Patents.[51] As the specific provisions introduced in the Law on Patents and then confirmed in the Industrial Property Code (IPC) do not mention this requirement, some argue that it is no longer in the law[52] and, at any rate, should be considered as running against the monopolistic nature of intellectual property rights. According to this view, courts cannot tolerate an ongoing infringement for the time needed to reach a decision on the merits of the case, which can take up to three years. Others highlight that preliminary injunctions have the same precautionary nature of orders issued under Article 700 CPC and, on this basis, argue that they should be made conditional on the same requirement of *periculum in mora*, which should be considered as applicable by analogy.[53]

Courts tend to sit in between. A considerable number of decisions consider *periculum in mora* irrelevant or, at any rate, *in re ipsa*, i.e. a natural consequence of infringement that should be taken for granted.[54] However, a more nuanced approach seems to be gaining ground. On the one hand, courts frequently claim that *periculum in mora* needs to exist. On the other hand, they are ready to accept that it can be presumed *juris tantum*, considering that damages caused by a violation of an exclusive right are not easy to calculate and repair.[55] The burden of proof returns to the claimant if there are reasons to believe that during the time needed to reach a decision on the merits the patentee will not suffer any (additional) prejudice that cannot be repaired *ex post*. This is the case, according to some decisions, if the parties are not operative in the same geographic area,[56] or if infringing activity stopped, particularly if desistence is accompanied by a pledge not to use the invention in the wake of the proceedings on the merits[57] or if use of

---

[50] *See* above, Section A.1.

[51] *See* above, Section A.1.

[52] *Periculum in mora* is required by Art. 700 of the Code of Civil Procedure, which was used to issue preliminary injunctions before the introduction of specific provisions in the IPC.

[53] *See Job Joint* v. *Lectra* (Trib. Milano 1996).

[54] *See* Frignani 1974, 357 *See, e.g., Millauro* v. *Betamed* (Trib. Roma 2012); *IMT* v. *TVA* (App. Milano 1989), considering use of the invention to make and sell infringing products incompatible with the exclusive nature of the patentee's right.

[55] *See, e.g., Signature* v. *Axel Weinbrecht* (Trib. Milano 2019); *Fiat* v. *Great Wall* (Trib. Torino 2008), in a case regarding threatened infringement of a registered community design; *4B-Four Bind* v. *KGS* (Trib. Torino 2013).

[56] *See Unknown* v. *Pref.Edi.L. I and II* (Trib. Catania 2005 and 2006) and (probably, as the description of the case appears rather deficient) *SFC Intex* v. *Unifix WG* (Trib. Genova 2014).

[57] A declaration of the defendant, stating that production and/or distribution stopped and will not start again, has been considered insufficient in *Signature* v. *Axel Weinbrecht* (Trib. Milano 2019); *La Marzocco* v. *Nuova* Simonelli (Trib. Ancona 2018); *Sisvel* v. *ZTE* (Trib. Torino 2016), which quotes the decision taken by the ECJ on 14 December 2006 in *Nokia* v. *Joacim Wärdell* (ECJ 2006), without giving weight to the fact that it concerns Community trademarks and

the invention cannot restart easily,[58] for instance due to redesign of the allegedly infringing device.[59] Also, if the patentee delayed action without an objective justification,[60] it could be argued that no serious harm is being suffered[61] or the consequences of the infringement on the market have already become irreversible.[62]

A denial of precautionary injunctive relief based on an evaluation of the seriousness of the harm or the effects of infringement in the market postulates the idea that the interest of the patentee to immediately stop an ongoing infringing activity does not enjoy absolute protection. This is far from obvious, considering the exclusive nature of patent rights, and shows a tendency to embed in the test for *periculum in mora* an assessment of the hardships that the patentee and the alleged infringer would encounter should the injunction be denied or granted. In fact, the relatively few decisions that dismissed patentees' claims on this ground usually refer to the invasiveness of the requested remedy, accepting therefore as relevant, and sometimes pre-eminent, the interest of the alleged infringer to carry on its business.[63]

The same tendency seems to inspire another small group of decisions that denied precautionary injunctive relief on the basis of a (supposed) mere economic nature of

---

might reflect their specificities; *Plein Air* v. *Providus* (Trib. Milano 2015), in respect of an interim injunction. On the contrary, a formal pledge undertaken by the legal representative of the defendant has been accepted as relevant to deny *periculum in mora* in *Alaska* v. *Sammontana* (Trib. Firenze 1993) and in *Job Joint* v. *Lectra* (Trib. Milano 1996). Criticism has been expressed by Scuffi 2009, 364, considering that the pledge can be broken by the defendant if it has not led to a settlement or a court decision.

[58] Desistance from commercialization of the allegedly infringing goods does not prevent the grant of provisional injunctions: see *Cartier* v. *Iannetti* (Trib. Roma 2017); *BMW* v. *Cassini* (Trib. Bologna 2008), which considered insufficient a withdrawal from eBay of offers regarding the allegedly infringing goods. Desistance due to the suspension or revocation of the required ministerial authorization to market a pharmaceutical product was not considered decisive to deny an interim injunction in *Pieffe* v. *Janssen-Cilag* (Trib. Monza 1995), considering that disobedience to an injunction would have led to consequences more serious than the marketing of the product without the required ministerial authorization.

[59] *Biesse* v. *Macotec* (Trib. Milano 2014). In this case, the court considered relevant the fact that redesign required relevant planning and financial efforts. Therefore, the court considered sufficient to deny interim injunctive relief a mere undertaking (without penalty) of the defendant that infringement would not occur again. An interim injunction was granted despite redesign of the infringing machine in *Stefanati* v. *Dominioni* (T. Genova 1993) in view of the ongoing state of belligerency of the parties and the allegation by the patentee that the redesigned machine should be considered as infringing.

[60] Dismissals based on delayed action are not frequent. Usually, the idea prevails that the right-holder should be allowed some time to ponder over the case before taking action. For instance, in *Nestec* v. *Casa del Caffè Vergnano* (Trib. Torino 2012), nine months of delay was deemed acceptable given the complexity of the case.

[61] See *Audi* v. *Pneusgarda* (Trib. Milano 2012). According to Spolidoro 2005, 244–45, delayed action should be considered under the principles concerning tolerance or inaction in intellectual property law and, therefore, as a matter regarding *fumus boni juris* more than *periculum in mora*.

[62] Other decisions went so far as to require evidence that infringement had already caused irreversible consequences: see, e.g., *4B-Four Bind* v. *KGS* (Trib. Torino 2013).

[63] See *Unknown* v. *Pref.Edi.L. I and II* (Trib. Catania 2005 and 2006).

the prejudice suffered by the patentee during the time needed to get a decision on the merits. The idea here is that if the alleged infringer is not a direct competitor of the patentee, the latter cannot suffer a trade diversion due the violation of the patent. The prejudice the patentee suffers consists – according to this opinion – only in the loss of royalties that the alleged infringer would have had to pay. As it is neither impossible nor particularly difficult to calculate *ex post* the amount of royalties due, it is not necessary to grant precautionary injunctive relief to avoid the risk that a decision on the merits in favour of the patentee would come too late to adequately protect his right, particularly if the infringer appears solvent.[64]

This reasoning has been applied to cases in which the patentee was a natural person – usually the inventor – who exploited the patent only through licensing, and in consideration of the fact that the parties failed to settle their dispute because they disagreed on the amount of royalties due.[65] The same approach offered a framework to deal with disputes regarding standard essential patents, in which the reference to concepts such as proportionality and balancing of rights became commonplace.[66] Finally, an attempt was made to extend the reach of the reasoning to cases in which a failure to agree on royalties occurred in a dispute between direct competitors, just as happens in many disputes regarding standard essential patents, but with the relevant difference that the owner of the right had not committed to grant licences on FRAND terms. A decision on first instance denying precautionary injunctive relief was reversed on appeal precisely for this reason.[67] However, on appeal the court did not confine itself to distinguishing these two cases and offered arguments that brings us back to a more orthodox approach, according to which the strategy of exploitation of the patent adopted by the owner of the right – apart from the specific case of standard essential patents – seems to remain irrelevant for the availability of precautionary injunctive relief. In particular, the court observed that even when a patentee exploits the patent through licensing deals, this does not mean that the

---

[64] See *Samsung* v. *Apple* (Trib. Milano 2012).

[65] *See Hakan Lans* v. *Dell* (Trib. Monza 1997), which considered also the rapid obsolescence of the products targeted by the injunction, and *Rolando Nannucci* v. *Renault* (Trib. Firenze 2003).

[66] *See* in particular *Samsung* v. *Apple* (Trib. Milano 2012); *Intec* v. *Unifix* (Trib. Genova 2014). Proportionality is sometimes also mentioned in decisions that do not regard standard essential patents. Often it is used as a synonym for reasonableness. *See, e.g., Aqvadesign* v. *G. M. Rubinetteri* (Trib. Torino 2019); *Ericsson* v. *Onda* (Trib. Trieste 2011). Attempts to balance interests can be found also in *Audi* v. *Pneusgarda* (Trans. Milano 2012). A rather articulated evaluation of the potential effects of granting or denying relief on the interests of the parties (but not of third parties, such as drugs providers and users) can be found in *Teva* v. *Mylan* (Trib. Milano 2017), which confirmed – for the time required to make a preliminary assessment as to the validity and infringement of a patent – an injunction already granted *ex parte* against the marketing of an allegedly infringing compound but at the same time lifted an order to freeze the request for authorization to sell the product on the Italian market presented by the defendants to the Italian Medicine Agency.

[67] *See JP Steel Plantech Corp.* v. *Danieli & C. Officine Meccaniche* (Trib. Venezia 2018).

prejudice in case of infringement would be "merely economic" and easy to calculate, as the trade diversion caused by the infringer would affect the licensee and, indirectly, the patentee, diminishing the amount of royalties that the patentee is able to earn and damaging the attractiveness of the patent for prospective licensees.

Not surprisingly, the same decision also refused to relax the protection granted to the patentee if the expiry date of the patent is relatively close and the alleged infringer commits to pay a bond,[68] which should protect the interest of the patentee to obtain damages at the end of the trial, if due. The message seems to be that exclusivity is exclusivity, so long it lasts.

A denial of injunctive relief, whatever the reason, comes with an obligation to pay the expenses of the proceedings, including the costs borne by the defendant to resist. The court might decide to compensate the expenses afforded by the parties but only if none of them could be considered entirely successful.[69] These principles have been generally observed in the decisions examined but not without exceptions.[70]

2. Final Injunctions

The general assumption[71] seems to be that a court reaching a finding of infringement must also grant injunctive relief,[72] if requested to do so,[73] unless the patent has expired[74] or infringement has definitively stopped.[75] Intent or fault by the infringer and harm caused to the rightsowner are not required,[76] considering the preventive function of this remedy.[77]

It has been held that a final injunction, being a future-oriented remedy, presupposes the risk of continuation, or repetition of an infringing activity.[78] As the legal system is certainly oriented towards the prevention of the accomplishment of

---

[68] As the court in *id.* mentions, our law does not provide for such an option (which is however contemplated in Art. 9.2 of the Enforcement Directive). On the other hand, a bond can be imposed by the court on the claimant in order to protect the interest of the defendant to obtain the payment of damages suffered if the remedy turns out later to be unjustified. *See* Art. 669-*undecies* CPC and Art. 81 of the 1939 Law on Patents.

[69] *See* Rossi 2020.

[70] *See Rolando Nannucci* v. *Renault* (Trib. Firenze 2003).

[71] *See*, for instance, Greco & Vercellone 1968, 375.

[72] It is disputed whether a court requested to declare infringement can also issue an injunctive order without adopting a decision *ultra petitum*. In favour, *see* Spolidoro 1982, 46, 178; against Frignani 1974, 311.

[73] Frignani 1974, 311, stressing that the court does not have a discretionary power to deny the injunction.

[74] Scuffi 2009, 488; Sena 2011, 379. *See also Pfizer* v. *Dott. Bonapace* (Trib. Milano 1987); *Staar* v. *Nuova Autovox* (Trib. Milano 1992).

[75] Scuffi 2009, 488–89.

[76] Frignani 1974, 312.

[77] Spolidoro 1982, 161–63; Nivarra 2000, 325; Scuffi 2009, 488; Sena, 2011, 379–80; Di Cataldo 2012, 69.

[78] Frignani 1974, 428 ff.

wrongful acts, it is also accepted that injunctive relief can be granted to stop preparatory acts that would otherwise lead to an infringement.[79] Although current legal texts mention "imminent" infringements only in connection with provisional injunctions,[80] it does not seem reasonable to imply that such orders cannot be confirmed at the end of the proceeding on the merits.

Some argue that courts must grant final injunctions even if continuation, or repetition, of the infringement appears unlikely.[81] A first argument supporting this view comes from the legal nature of injunctive orders. Being of the same nature as declaratory decisions, they depend on the same precondition, namely, the mere finding of infringement. More prosaically, it has been added that an injunction would do no harm to a defendant that is truly committed to respecting the plaintiff's property.[82]

Courts seem to be of the opposite opinion,[83] although cases in which final injunctive relief has been denied due to lack of risk of continuation or repetition of the infringement are extremely rare.[84] Mere desistence from infringement pending the trial, either spontaneously or in compliance with a preliminary or interim injunction, has not always been considered a valid reason to deny injunctive relief.[85] Also, redesign of the product and modification of moulds are not enough, considering that they express a reversible decision.[86] In the field of designs, injunctive relief has been denied because garments bearing the infringing design were meant to be marketed for one season only.[87] Apparently, there seems to be little room for arguments like this in the field of utility patents.

In view of the evolution of the legal texts that started at the end of the last century, a relatively large consensus emerged in the relevant Italian literature on the idea that

[79] Ascarelli 1960, 256 and 634; Frignani 1974, 430, noting that if the infringement has been already accomplished, this would speak in favour of the existence of a risk of continuation or repetition; otherwise, it would be harder to prove the risk which the injunction is meant to cure; Spolidoro 1982, 176–177.
[80] Compare Art. 124 and Art. 131 IPC, which correspond to Art. 9 and Art. 11 of the Enforcement Directive.
[81] Spolidoro 1982, 178 ff.; *Job Joint* v. *Lectra* (Trib. Milano 1996), as *obiter dictum*. Contra Frignani 1974, 408, 418.
[82] Spolidoro 1982, 180; Spolidoro 2008. See also *Plein Air* v. *Providus* (Trib. Milano 2015), in respect of an interim injunction, confirmed on appeal (Trib. Milano 2016); *Sisvel* v. *ZTE* (Trib. Torino 2016).
[83] *See* Scuffi 2009, 363.
[84] Scuffi 2009, 488.
[85] In *Metallurgica Bugatti* v. *Framplast* (App. Milano 2012) injunctive relief was granted; on the contrary, in *Gruppo* v. *Specialized Bicycle Components* (App. Milano 2019) the court gave weight to the fact that the infringer had not been using the contested trademark for the previous ten years, having desisted when the proceeding on the merits began.
[86] *See Lasar* v. *Betonform* (Trib. Venezia 2009); *Vibram* v. *Gommar* (Trib. Bologna 2009), considering that products and corresponding moulds could be reversed to their original infringing shape.
[87] *See Fuzzi* v. *Commerciale Stib* (Trib. Bologna 2009). Similar arguments have been used to deny a preliminary injunction by *Diesel* v. *Industria de Dieseno Texil* (Trib. Milano 2016).

a court should be considered entitled to adapt injunctive relief in view of the circumstances of the case, in particular if the infringer acted in good faith.[88] Some authors referred explicitly to proportionality as the guiding criterion to deploy courts' discretion in tailoring injunctive relief.[89] It remains unclear whether proportionality could also support a denial of injunctive relief in cases in which there is a risk of accomplishment, continuation or repetition of the infringing activity.[90] Considering the choice of the Italian legislator not to introduce alternative measures as allowed by Article 12 of the Enforcement Directive, some have argued that a denial of injunctive relief cannot be based on the "disproportionate harm" that the remedy would cause to the infringer.[91] Others have gone as far as to deny the applicability of Article 12 of the Enforcement Directive to injunctive relief, arguing that an injunction – i.e. an order to behave in conformity with the law – cannot cause a juridically relevant "disproportionate harm".[92] On the contrary, others maintain that Article 12 of the Enforcement Directive offers an argument to hold that injunctive relief could be denied – in relatively exceptional circumstances and despite the choice of our legislator not to introduce the alternative measures mentioned therein – on the theory of abuse of intellectual property rights.[93]

Although this is certainly a relevant question,[94] it should not be forgotten that – particularly in the field of patents, in which the duration of the exclusive rights is limited, the time needed to bring technologies to the market is not negligible, and litigation tends to be lengthy – the flexibility that courts already enjoy in administering provisional injunctions might considerably alleviate the risk that a final injunction would come too soon and cause disproportionate damage to the infringer. This circumstance, which might be seen as an implicit flexibility of the current system as practised, helps in understanding why a demand to reconsider the traditional equation of exclusivity/injunctive relief in conventional situations has not emerged so far.

Both provisional and final injunctions are typically supplemented by an order to pay penalties in case of non-compliance. Although penalties are discretionary

---

[88] *See* Spolidoro 2005, 246.

[89] *See* Auteri 2007, 40. For a similar opinion *see also* Spaccasassi 2005, 81; Vanzetti 2010, 68. This view finds support in Art. 124(6) IPC, which may be read as extending to all remedies, including final injunctions, the principle affirmed by Art. 10(3) Enf. Dir. in relation to corrective measures.

[90] On the other hand, proportionality has been used to support a denial of injunctive relief in a case in which such risks were absent: *see Gruppo* v. *Specialized Bicycle Components* (App. Milano 2019).

[91] *See* Spolidoro 2005, 246 and 251.

[92] *See* Sarti 2004, 136.

[93] *See* Bertani 2017, 486 ff. and 503–04. Among the cases considered by the author there is the exercise of intellectual property rights in such a manner as to bring undue prejudice to other fundamental rights: see on this point *infra*, Section E).

[94] There has also been extensive use of the principle of proportionality by the Italian Agency for Communications (AGCOM) in administering blocking orders: *see* Cogo & Ricolfi 2020, §5.5.

remedies,[95] it is hard to find cases in which they have not been ordered to protect the exclusivity granted by a patent. Rare examples of injunctions not supplemented by penalties can be found in the field of copyright, both in traditional settings[96] and in the relatively new realm of online intermediaries' liability.[97] Particularly in the second case, the dismissal of the request of the claimant to provide for penalties seems to express an attempt to balance the hardships of the parties,[98] considering that an order to "stay down" infringing contents from a sharing platform already places a serious burden on the enjoined party.

C. CONTENT OF COURTS' ORDERS

Usually, orders refer explicitly or implicitly to the facts of the case and enjoin the infringer from doing the same again. Despite their apparent narrowness, such orders have been considered capable of extending their effects beyond the specific facts of the case.

Occasionally, there have been decisions more carefully defining the content of the injunction granted. In the field of trademarks, orders worded to cover "similar" or "analogous" cases have been issued and confirmed on appeal.[99] The same happened in the field of registered designs, with the important qualification that, in case of multiple designs, the order concerns only designs identical or similar to those which have been actioned. In other cases, serial numbers identifying infringing goods are mentioned; however, where this is the case, the order might be supplemented by a reference to identical goods not bearing the said codes.[100]

The approach usually followed by courts does not seem to be overly problematic in the case of preliminary injunctions, as the court which issued the order retains the power to define its reach more precisely, if need be, in particular in respect of behaviours that present minor differences from the one considered prima facie infringing.[101]

In respect of final injunctions, the usual, generic reference to the facts of the case causes some degree of uncertainty, which may lead to further litigation when the rightsholder tries to enforce the injunction by asking the court to apply penalties. In such a case, any variations attributed to the allegedly infringing product requires the

---

[95] *See ex multis* Rovati 2019.

[96] *Martino v. Menegatti* (Trib. Venezia 2007), which considered relevant the small number of products already marketed and the lack of evidence regarding the manufacturing of new items.

[97] *Dailymotion v. Delta TV* (Trib. Torino 2018).

[98] Such attempts seem to find a theoretical support in the arguments developed in Ricolfi 2005, 107 ff.

[99] *See Simod v. Asics* (Trib. Venezia 2006).

[100] *See Ennepi v. Gaudì* (Trib. Bologna 2011); *Gaudì v. Ennepì* (Trib. Bologna 2015); *Canon v. Alphaink* (Trib. Roma 2019).

[101] Scuffi 2009, 540.

court to decide whether the injunction already issued applies or a new trial is due. In this respect, the Supreme Court of Cassation pointed out that minor variations, which do not fall outside the "genus and species" of the infringement already ascertained, are not enough to escape the effects of an injunction already granted.[102] This does not seem to mean that the court that issued the injunction and has competence on the application of penalties[103] can make a new assessment of the scope of the exclusive right and the interference of the (new) allegedly infringing acts.[104] It should limit itself to comparing the facts of the case leading to the grant of the injunction with the new facts that entail, according to the claimant's view, a repetition of the enjoined behaviour. In this regard, whether a difference could be considered as irrelevant seems to depend on the arguments on which the finding of infringement had been based.[105]

The relevant literature has frequently highlighted the importance of an accurate definition of the prohibited behaviour.[106] In particular, it has been stressed that an order too narrowly framed can be easily circumvented, while a broad command is equally ineffective,[107] considering that it imposes a new trial of the case if the defendant circumvents the injunction. However, the same literature stressed the difficulty of finding a proper balance and suggested a close look at the models emerged in other countries, particularly Germany, to help develop a catalogue of formulations to be selected depending on the facts of the case.[108]

Greater attention is required by contributory infringement cases, in which court orders need to be drafted in such a way as to prevent further contributions to downstream infringements, while leaving the defendant free to perform activities that might be legal. Italian courts do not seem to have a lot of experience in this field, considering that until 2016 our patent law did not deal with indirect infringement.[109] Before then, courts did not care much about the extent of orders issued, probably because in most instances the means supplied by the defendant had no other significant use than that covered by the claimant's patent.[110]

---

[102] *See Metra v. Indinvest* (Cass. 1995).

[103] *See Art. 124(7) IPC.*

[104] *See, e.g., General Vacuum v. Sela Cars* (Trib. Torino 2014).

[105] *See Edizione Property v. S.I.G.A.T.* (Cass. 2017).

[106] *See* Vanzetti & Di Cataldo 2018, 553–54.

[107] *See,* for instance, *Lasar v. Betanform* (Trib. Venezia 2009), which enjoined the defendant from making, selling, offering to sell, and advertising the infringing product or any other product that infringes on the patent.

[108] Spolidoro 2008a, 183.

[109] Now the issue is getting more attention: *see* Cuonzo & Ampollini 2018, §4.

[110] A noteworthy exception is *Eurosider v. Carrozzeria Stefano Carservice* (Trib. Genova 2016), which differentiated the position of the supplier from that of the maker of means capable of non-infringing uses.

D. VALIDITY OF COURT ORDERS

1. *Preliminary and Interim Injunctions*

Once granted, a preliminary injunction continues to produce its effects until the exclusive right expires, unless (a) the decision issuing the preliminary injunction is successfully appealed;[111] (b) the preliminary injunction is lifted, on request of the enjoined party, due to a change in the circumstances or the emergence of facts previously unknown;[112] or (c) either of the parties institutes a proceeding on the merits which ends with a decision denying the existence of the right protected by the injunction.[113] Either party has the right to institute a proceeding leading to a decision on the merits but none of them has an obligation to do so.[114] Therefore, the preliminary injunction can produce its effects indefinitely, i.e. until any of the above-mentioned situations occurs. It remains to be seen whether this rule, which was introduced in 2010, is compatible with Article 50, paragraph 6 of the TRIPS and Article 9, paragraph 5 of the Enforcement Directive. So far, courts have taken for granted that it does.[115] Recently, however, a decision of the court in Florence refused to insist the infringer pay penalties theoretically due on the basis of a preliminary injunction not followed by the institution of a proceedings on the merit by the patentee.[116]

If the injunction is supplemented by penalties, as is usually the case, the court might delay their application for the time needed for the enjoined party to comply.[117]

2. *Final Injunctions*

Article 282 of the CPC establishes that first-instance decisions are immediately executive; however, according to Article 283 of the CPC, they may be stayed pending appeal if grave and well-founded reasons support the motion for suspension. Similarly, Article 373 of the CPC allows suspension of the effects of the decision of second instance pending appeal in front of the Supreme Court of

---

[111] *See* Art. 131 IPC and Art. 669-*terdecies* CPC.
[112] *See* Art. 669-*decies* paras. 1 and 2 CPC.
[113] *See* Art. 669-*novies* para. 3 CPC. If the proceedings end in favour of the patentee, the preliminary or interim injunction ceases to produce effects when the decision becomes final. *See A. O. and V. M.* (Cass. pen. 1997).
[114] *See* Art. 132 para. 4 IPC.
[115] The same view has been expressed by Vanzetti & Di Cataldo 2018, 552. *Contra see* Ricolfi 2005, 97–98; Spolidoro 2008a, 187–88.
[116] *Mangusta* v. *Service de Navigation de Plaisance* (Trib. Firenze 2016).
[117] *See Thun* v. *Casati* (Trib. Milano 2019), in a trademark case regarding sale of genuine goods by a seller not (any longer) part of a selective distribution network.

Cassation if immediate execution of the decision would cause a grave and irreparable harm to the losing party.

These rules are prevalently interpreted as referring only to decisions that can be enforced against the will of their addressees.[118] Injunctions, as already mentioned, do not fall into this category and therefore cannot be suspended in their effects.[119]

Broader interpretations of Article 282 of the CPC are nonetheless attested[120] and offer support for the idea that injunctions are immediately effective, unless suspended pending appeal.[121] In the field of intellectual property rights, this opinion does not seem to be opposed by the courts.[122] Motions for suspension are relatively frequently presented and courts decide them without raising objections as to their admissibility and relevance from the point of view of the applicant's interest.[123] Suspension, if granted, impacts on the obligation of the enjoined party to voluntarily comply with the court's order.[124] If the order was supplemented by the provision of penalties, the latter would not apply either. Criminal sanctions are also out of question, lacking an effective court order that can be disobeyed.[125]

The effects of a first-instance decision can be suspended if the chances of revision on appeal appear high and/or the execution of the decision would cause an irreparable harm to the losing party. In the case of second-instance decisions, the only ground for suspension is grave and irreparable harm.[126] Room for the exercise of discretionary power by the court appears greater in respect of first-instance decisions.[127] Reported decisions seem to ordinarily engage in the balancing of the respective inconveniencies of the parties. At the beginning of the 1990s, the attitude of the courts was openly in favour of the alleged infringer, on the assumption that the prejudice suffered by the infringer to comply with an injunction subsequently lifted could have been irreparable, while the patentee could always be compensated

---

[118] *See* Canella 2020, 1384.

[119] *See* Scuffi 2009, 551, 559, where the author mentions at fn. 50 an unpublished decision of the Court of Appeal of Milan dated 8 May 1996 affirming that an injunction not accompanied by restitutionary remedies cannot be enforced against the will of the injuncted party and, therefore, is not capable of being stayed pending appeal. The same conclusion is reached by *La Bruciata* v. *Podere della Bruciata* (App. Firenze 2017) on the basis of the declaratory nature of decisions issuing an injunction (see Section A.2), which implies that they become effective only when they are final and, in turn, that the enjoined party does not have interest to obtain the suspension pending appeal.

[120] *See* Izzo 2020, §3.

[121] Further references in Rovati 2019, 781.

[122] *See* Vanzetti, 2010, 40 ff.; Rovati 2019, 781.

[123] *See* the comment to *La Bruciata* v. *Podere della Bruciata* (App. Firenze 2017) for further references.

[124] *See* the comment to *Industrie Meccaniche CGZ Almec* v. *Macchine Soncini Alberto* (App. Bologna 1990).

[125] *Cf., a contrario, K. R.* (Cass. pen. 2015).

[126] Scuffi 2009, 555, 557–58.

[127] *Id.*, 557.

with damages.[128] Then, when all first- and second-instance decisions became immediately effective *by default*, the attitude of the courts changed.

In consideration of its precautionary nature, suspension depends on the two prerequisites already discussed with reference to preliminary and interim injunctions, i.e. *fumus boni iuris* and *periculum in mora*. Also in this case it is accepted that the court can take into account the respective inconveniences of the parties.[129]

Little attention has been paid to the issue regarding the duration of a final injunction. In this regard, it has been affirmed that an injunction lasts as long as the effects of the decision in which it is stated.[130] As the effects of the decision cannot endure longer than the substantive right on which it is based, this seems to correspond to the – apparently obvious – idea that an invention in the public domain can be freely used by everybody, including the (once) infringer.

E. CONCLUSIONS

After having discussed thoroughly the theoretical reasons which favour or oppose judges' discretion in granting final injunctions, let us just add a practical one which is patent-specific. It has been convincingly shown that granting patents on components of multi-component products is not really a novelty: this was already current practice in the car and aircraft industries in the United States between the two world wars.[131] However, today, patents on individual components of multi-component products have become the rule in whole areas, such as information and communication technology (ICT). Actually, a smartphone is composed of tens of thousands of patented components. If violation of any of these patents were to lead to an injunction, or maybe to an insufficiently well-crafted injunction, then all innovation in the area would grind to a screeching halt. Royalties in the form of assessment of damages seem the better solution, as Judge Posner has convincingly shown. Surprisingly, this crucial matter never turns up before Italian courts. Now we also have a textual ground to come back to the issue, at least as far as patent law is concerned.[132]

---

[128] For instance, the interest of the enjoined party not to stop production of a machine has been protected against the interest of the rightsholder to prevent a theoretical decline in sales, considering that the latter could be adequately compensated by paying damages. *See Morra Macchine Agricole v. Maschinenfabriecken Bernard Krone* (App. Milano 1989) with reference to past rules, according to which the court had to decide, if required by the winning party, whether the decision should be declared immediately effective. A similar point of view seems to be reflected by *Industrie Meccaniche CGZ Alimec v. Macchine Soncini Alberto* (App. Bologna 1990).

[129] Scuffi 2009, 555–56.

[130] Frignani 1974, 407.

[131] *See* Merges 1996, 1293 ff., 1341 ff.

[132] *See* the very pertinent comments to Art. 63(1) chapter IV UPCA by Leistner and Pless; and their notations on the – long overdue – emergence of the principle of proportionality also in connection with injunctive relief.

Turning to a different issue, if an injunction is issued, be it final, temporary or interim, the question arises as to establishing its scope. Let us try to add two dimensions which may lead in opposite directions. First, we are fascinated by the unerring pragmatism of British courts, which, after issuing an injunction, are also prepared to devise "dynamic" orders and set up an updating machinery which delegates to service providers the task of monitoring whether new violations occur.[133] We wonder whether in Italy we could set up something along these lines: a fact-finding expert witness, reporting to court and, given opportunity for the parties to comment, providing a basis for an automatic extension of the order.[134] Second, from efficiency to respect of fundamental rights. Indeed, we suspect that the perspective of fundamental rights has a lot to tell us here: much more than the mere reference to proportionality can convey. Here we are mainly referring to the online world, on which, it seems to us, we have to think hard about the dangers of blocking and filtering orders. It is high time too, as the implementation of the Copyright Digital Single Market Directive is possibly taking us towards the next step: algorithmic decision making which has the same effect as courts' injunctive orders. So, in a nutshell, we should make progress along two dimensions: more efficiency, yes; but also more respect for fundamental rights. Injunctions need not be a blunt instrument; they should resemble the lancet, not the hammer, as the saying goes.

Finally, we end with a remark about innocent infringers and costs. Let us just say that the matter of costs is fundamental here; and we should not leave it forever to a footnote. The importance of the issue can hardly be overstated.[135] Here European courts seem to diverge to some extent. An Italian administrative court held that it is only natural that innocent infringers such as internet service providers (ISPs) should bear the costs of the "negative externalities" they generate.[136] Similarly Cour de Cassation 6 July 2017, *SFR, Orange, Free, Bouyegues* v. *Union des producteurs de cinéma* and others,[137] comes to the same conclusion under French law by arguing that the basis is not the liability of the ISP, which may well be lacking, but its duty to avoid violation of private legal rights. In contrast, British courts resort to differentiating, under relevant English law, between rules applicable to access and hosting providers, and holding the former entitled to be reimbursed their own costs by claimant rightsholders.[138] On the other hand, the possibility for rightsholders to recover costs incurred in giving notice to ISPs is considered in *Mc Fadden* v. *Sony*.[139]

[133] See *Cartier* v. *BSkyB* (EWHC 2014), para. 122 ff.
[134] We have given some thought to this in connection with "dynamic" orders, on which also Prof. Husovec has written extensively (*see* Husovec 2017, *passim*), in Cogo & Ricolfi 2020.
[135] See again Husovec 2017.
[136] *Altroconsumo* v. *AGCOM* (TAR Lazio 2014), para. 15.
[137] Available at www.courdecassation.fr/jurisprudence_2/premiere_chambre_civile_568/909_6_37275.html
[138] *Cartier* v. *British Telecommunications* (UK Supreme Court 2018), at para. 37.
[139] *Mc Fadden* v. *Sony Music* (EUCJ 2016), paras. 72–79.

We know that legal costs are not so sexy as an issue for legal scholarship and young brilliant scholars; but still they play a paramount role in litigation strategies.

REFERENCES

Cases

EU Court 14 December 2006 (First Chamber), case C-316/05, *Nokia Corp.* v. *Joacim Wärdell.*

EU Court 15 September 2016 (Third Chamber), case C-484/14, *Tobias Mc Fadden* v. *Sony Music Entertainment Germany GmbH.*

UK Supreme Court 13 June 2018, *Cartier Int. AG. and others* v. *British Telecommunications Plc and another*, [2018] UKSC 28, per Lord Sumption).

England and Wales High Court of Justice (Chancery Division) 17 October 2014, *Cartier Int. AG. Montblanc-Simplo GmbH, Richemont Int. SA* v. *BSkyB Ltd., BT PLC, EE Ltd., Talktalk Ltd., Virgin Media Ltd. and Open Rights Group*, per Justice Arnold [2014] EWHC 3354 (Ch), available at www.bailii.org/ew/cases/EWHC/Ch/2003/3354.html

Cour de Cassation 6 July 2017, *SFR, Orange, Free, Bouyegues* v. *Union des producteurs de cinéma* and others.

Cass. 25 July 1995, no. 8080, *Metra Metallurgica Trafilati Alluminio spa* v. *Indinvest spa*, in *Giurisprudenza Annotata di Diritto Industriale*, 3205.

Cass. pen. 1997 no. 4298, *O. A. and V. M.*, in *DeJure.*

Cass. 21 May 2008, no. 13067, *Scifoni Renata di Scifoni Carlo & C. s.a.s., già Scifoni Renata s. r.l.* v. *Scifoni Fratelli Organizzazione Internazionale per le Onoranze Funebri di Scifoni Patrizia s.a.s.*, *Giurisprudenza Annotata di Diritto Industriale*, XXXVII (2008), 5220.

Cass. pen. 17 February 2015 n. 15646, *K. R.*, in *DeJure.*

Cass, 7 February 2017 n. 3189, *Edizione Property s.p.a., Edizione Alberghi s.r.l. e Monaco & Gran Canal* v. *S.I.G.A.T. – Società Italiana Gestione Alberghi e Turismo s.r.l.*, in *Giurisprudenza Annotata di Diritto Industriale*, XLVI (2017), 6468.

Cass. 15 January 2020 n. 735, *Buonvicino et al.* v. *Ministero dello Sviluppo Economico and Fruitgrowing Equipment & Service s.r.l.*

App. Torino, 12 May 1989, *Alessandro Zegna spa* v. *Ermenegildo Zegna & Figli*, in *Giurisprudenza Annotata di Diritto Industriale*, XVIII (1989), 2417.

App. Milano, 19 September 1989, *IMT – Internato s.r.l.* v. *TVA Holding s.p.a.*, in *Giurisprudenza Annotata di Diritto Industriale*, XIX (1990), 2492.

App. Milano, 12 December 1989 (ord.), *Morra Macchine Agricole s.n.c.* v. *Maschinenfabrieken Bernard Krone GmbH and Gebrüder Welger GmbH*, in *Giurisprudenza Annotata di Diritto Industriale*, XIX (1990), 2498.

App. Bologna, 10 May 1990, *Industrie Meccaniche CGZ Alimec s.p.a. & Ditta Cavatorta Aldo di Cavatorta Primo* v. *Macchine Soncini Alberto s.p.a. & Soncini Alberto*, in *Giurisprudenza Annotata di Diritto Industriale*, XIX (1990), 2538.

App. Roma, 5 February 1996, *Eurofarmaco s.r.l.* v. *Glaxo Group Limited*, in *Giurisprudenza Annotata di Diritto Industriale*, XXV (1996), 3462.

App. Milano, 11 September 2012, *Metallurgica Bugatti Filippo srl* v. *Franplast srl*, in *Giurisprudenza Annotata di Diritto Industriale*, XLII (2013), 5993.

App. Firenze, 30 May 2017 (ord.), *Azienda Agricola La Bruciata di Duchini Laura* v. *Podere della Bruciata di Rossi Andrea*, in *Giurisprudenza Annotata di Diritto Industriale*, XLVI (2017), 6541.

App. Milano, 28 May 2019, *Gruppo s.r.l.* v. *Specialized Bicycle Components Italia s.r.l.*, in *Darts IP.*

Trib. Milano, 28 December 1987, *Pfizer Inc. and Pfizer Italiana s.p.a.* v. *Dott. Bonapace & C. s.p.a.*, in *Giurisprudenza Annotata di Diritto Industriale*, XVII (1988), 2279.

Trib. Vicenza, 8 October 1990, *Roberto Anzolin* v. *Officina Meccanica M.M. dei F.lli Maggiolino Sergio e Giovanni s.n.c.*, in *Giurisprudenza Annotata di Diritto Industriale*, XX (1990), 2633.

Trib. Roma, 27 March 1991, *Salus Researches s.p.a.* v. *Allen & Hambury's Limited*, in *Giurisprudenza Annotata di Diritto Industriale*, XX (1991), 2656.

Trib. Milano, 9 April 1992, *Staar s.a.* v. *Nuova Autovox s.p.a. and Ermanno Rogledi*, in *Giurisprudenza Annotata di Diritto Industriale*, XXI (1992), 2819.

Trib. Genova, 3 June 1993, *Paola Stefanati, Roberta Stefanati, Andrea Stefanati, Emilia Leonardi ved. Stefanati, Officina DEA s.r.l.* v. *Pietro Dominioni and Punto e Pasta s.r.l.*, in *Giurisprudenza Annotata di Diritto Industriale*, XXIII (1994), 3060.

Trib. Firenze, 31 July 1993 (ord.), *Alaska Industria Gelati di Guarini e C. s.n.c.* v. *Sammontana s.r.l.*, in *Giurisprudenza Annotata di Diritto Industriale*, XXII (1993), 2989.

Trib. Milano, 3 October 1994 (ord.), *W. R. Grace & Co. and Grace Italiana s.p.a.* v. *Foreco s.r.l.*, in *Giurisprudenza Annotata di Diritto Industriale*, XXIII (1994), 3153.

Trib. Reggio Emilia, 3 October 1994, *Sassi Arredamenti s.r.l.* v. *Gemelli Gualtieri di Gualtieri Pasquino & C. s.n.c.*, in *Giurisprudenza Annotata di Diritto Industriale*, XXIV (1995), 3256.

Trib. Milano, 17 November 1994, *Ing. Bono s.p.a.* v. *Ialchi s.p.a.*, in *Giurisprudenza Annotata di Diritto Industriale*, XXIV (1995), 3271.

Trib. Monza, 10 May 1995, *Pieffe Depositi s.a.s.* v. *Janssen-Cilag s.p.a.*, in *Giurisprudenza Annotata di Diritto Industriale*, XXIV (1995), 3314.

Trib. Milano, 20 July 1995 (ord.), *Sifa Sitzfabrik GmbH* v. *Miotto & Associates International Ltd. s.r.l. and Brevetti Amphor di Carlo Ezio Bonetti & C. s.a.s.*, in *Giurisprudenza Annotata di Diritto Industriale*, XXIV (1995), 3335.

Trib. Milano, 30 October 1996 (ord.), *Job Joint s.r.l.* v. *Lectra Systemes Italia s.p.a.*, in *Giurisprudenza Annotata di Diritto Industriale*, XXV (1996), 3519.

Trib. Monza, 6 December 1997 (ord.), *Hakan Lans* v. *Dell Computer Corporation Ltd., Compaq Computer s.p.a., Hewlett-Packard Italiana s.p.a., Telcom s.r.l., Computer Discount 2, Daniela De Giorgio titolare della ditta Computer Time*, in *Giurisprudenza Annotata di Diritto Industriale*, XXVII (1998), 3786.

Trib. Firenze, 27 March 2003 (ord.), *Rolando Nannucci* v. *Renault filiale di Firenze s.p.a. and Renault s.a.s.*, in *Rivista di Diritto Industriale*, LIII (2004), II, 27.

Trib. Catania, 8 September 2005, *Unknown* v. *Pref.Edi.L. s.p.a.*, in *Darts IP*.

Trib. Catania, 19 January 2006, *Unknown* v. *Pref.Edi.L. s.p.a.*, in *Darts IP*.

Trib. Venezia, 13 June 2006, *Simod spa* v. *Asics Corporation and Asics Italia*, in *Giurisprudenza Annotata di Diritto Industriale*, XXXV (2006), 5026.

Trib. Venezia, 19 October 2007, *Tiziana A. Martino* v. *F.lli Menegatti s.p.a.*, in *Annali Italiani di Diritto d'Autore della Cultura e dello Spettacolo* (AIDA), XVIII (2009), 1271.

Trib. Bologna, 15 July 2008, *Innovapac srl* v. *Barberan sa*, in *Giurisprudenza Annotata di Diritto Industriale*, XXXVII (2008), 5300.

Trib. Torino, 15 July 2008, *Fiat Group Automobiles spa* v. *Great Wall Motors Co. Ltd.*, in *Giurisprudenza Annotata di Diritto Industriale*, XXXVII (2008), 5302.

Trib. Bologna, 21 October 2008, *Bayerische Motoren Werke AC* v. *Cassini Fiorella*, in *Giurisprudenza Annotata di Diritto Industriale*, XXXVII (2008), 5312.

Trib. Bologna, 30 March 2009, *Fuzzi s.p.a.* v. *Commerciale Stib s.r.l.*, in *Giurisprudenza Annotata di Diritto Industriale*, XXXVIII (2009), XXXVII (2008), 5416.

Trib. Bologna, 17 July 2009, *Vibram s.p.a.* v. *Gommar s.p.a.*, in *Giurisprudenza Annotata di Diritto Industriale*, XXXVII (2008), 5447.

Trib. Venezia, 13 October 2009, *Lasar s.r.l.* v. *Betonform s.r.l. and Jemmbuild s.r.l.*, in *Giurisprudenza Annotata di Diritto Industriale*, XXXVII (2008), 5460.

Trib. Bologna, 2 February 2011 (ord.), *Ennepi s.r.l.* v. *Gaudì Trade s.r.l.*, in *Dejure*.

Trib. Trieste, 23 August 2011 (ord.), *Telefonaktiebolaget L. M. Ericsson* v. *Onda Communications spa*, in *Giurisprudenza Annotata di Diritto Industriale*, XLII (2013), 5951.

Trib. Milano, 5 January 2012, *Samsung Electronics Co. Ltd and Samsung Electronics Italia s.p. a.* v. *Apple Inc., Apple Italia s.r.l., Apple Retail Italia s.r.l. and Apple Sales International*, in *Giurisprudenza annotata di diritto industriale*, XLIII (2014), 6069.

Trib. Roma, 20 April 2012, *Roberto Millauro e Service 2001 srl* v. *Betamed srl*, in *Giurisprudenza Annotata di Diritto Industriale*, XLII (2013), 5975.

Trib. Torino, 13 May 2012, *Nestec SA, Sociéte des Produits Nestlé SA and Nespresso Italiana spa* v. *Casa del Caffè Vergnano spa*, in *Giurisprudenza Annotata di Diritto Industriale*, XLI (2012), 5880.

Trib. Milano, criminal division, 20 July 2012, *Kauber Rodolfo*, in *Giurisprudenza Annotata di Diritto Industriale*, XLII (2013), 5988.

Trib. Milano, 2 November 2012 (ord.), *Audi AG* v. *Pneusgarda s.r.l. and Acacia s.r.l.*, in *Giurisprudenza Annotata di Diritto Industriale*, XLII (2013), 6003.

Trib. Torino, 21 February 2013, *4B-Four Bind srl* v. *KGS srl, Graphot di Giachino Roberto & C. and MP Stampa srl*, in *Giurisprudenza Annotata di Diritto Industriale*, XLII (2013), 6020.

Trib. Milano, 4 February 2014, *Biesse s.p.a.* v. *Macotec s.r.l.*, in *Giurisprudenza Annotata di Diritto Industriale*, XLIII (2014), 6131.

TAR Lazio, 26 September 2014, *Altroconsumo, Assoproviders et al.* v. *AGCOM, RAI et al., SIAE, Confindustria cultura et al.*, available at www.giustizia-amministrativa.it

Trib. Torino, 10 October 2014, *General Vacuum s.r.l. and Innova s.n.c.* v. *Sela Cars s.r.l.*, in *Giurisprudenza Annotata di Diritto Industriale*, XLIV (2015), 6252.

Trib. Genova, 29 December 2014 (ord.), *SFC Intec AG* v. *Unifix SWG s.r.l. and Heco Italia EFG s.r.l.*, in *Giurisprudenza Annotata di Diritto Industriale*, XLIII (2014), 6176.

Trib. Bologna, 30 April 2015, *Gaudì Trade s.p.a.* v. *Ennepi s.r.l.*, in *Giurisprudenza Annotata di Diritto Industriale*, XLIV (2015), 6285.

Trib. Milano, 13 November 2015, *Plein Air International s.r.l.* v. *Providus srl and Guilbert Express SA*, in *Giurisprudenza Annotata di Diritto Industriale*, XLV (2016), 6370.

Trib. Torino, 18 January 2016 (ord.), *Sisvel International SA* v. *ZTE Italy and Europhoto s.r.l.*, in *Giurisprudenza Annotata di Diritto Industriale*, XLVI (2017), 6481.

Trib. Milano, 3 February 2016 (ord.), *Plein Air International s.r.l.* v. *Providus s.r.l. and Guilbert Express SA*, in *Giurisprudenza Annotata di Diritto Industriale*, XLV (2016), 6385.

Trib. Milano, 4 March 2016 (ord.), *Diesel spa unip., Marni Group srl, Marni Holding spa and OTB spa* v. *Industria de Diseno Texil sa and Zara Home Espana sa*, in *Giurisprudenza Annotata di Diritto Industriale*, XLVI (2017), 6484.

Trib. Firenze, 8 June 2016, *Mangusta s.r.l., Overmarine s.p.a. and Overmarine Due s.r.l.* v. *Service de Navigation de Plaisance Boat Service S.A.*, in *Rivista di Diritto Industriale*, XLVII (2018), 1, II, 53.

Trib. Genova, 21 July 2016, *Eurosider s.a.s.* v. *Carrozzeria Steano Carservice s.n.c. and Emme. Bi. s.n.c.*, in *Darts IP*.

Trib. Napoli, 31 January 2017, *Hair Products* v. *Diffitalia Group s.p.a.*, in *Darts IP*.

Trib. Roma, 12 April 2017, *Unknown* v. *Selex Es s.p.a.* and *Aeroporti di Roma s.p.a.*, in *Darts IP.*

Trib. Roma, 22 May 2017, *Cartier International AG, Officine Panerai AG and Richement Italia s.p.a.* v. *Iannetti s.r.l., Negri s.r.l.* and *Sara Iannetti s.r.l.*, in *Giurisprudenza Annotata di Diritto Industriale*, XLVI (2017), 6539.

Trib. Milano, 18 June 2017 (ord.), *Teva Pharmaceutical Industries Ltd. and Teva Italia srl* v. *Mylan spa, Synthom bv and Syntom Hispania sl*, in *Darts IP* and in *Giurisprudenza Annotata di Diritto Industriale*, XLVI (2017), 6546.

Trib. Bologna, 28 June 2017, *Lodolo Alberto and Ellix s.r.l.* v. *Netafim Italia s.r.l.*, in *Giurisprudenza Annotata di Diritto Industriale*, XLVI (2017), 6550.

Trib. Torino, 24 January 2018, *Dailymotion SA* v. *Delta TV Programs s.r.l.*, in *Annali Italiani di Diritto d'Autore della Cultura e dello Spettacolo* (AIDA), XXVII (2018), 1866.

Trib. Ancona, 18 September 2018 (ord.), *La Marzocco s.r.l.* v. *Nuova Simonelli s.p.a.*, in *Giurisprudenza Annotata di Diritto Industriale*, XLVII (2018), 6683.

Trib. Venezia, 1 October 2018, *JP Steel Plantech Corporation* v. *Danieli & C. Officine Meccaniche s.p.a. and Ferriere Nord s.p.a.*, in *Darts IP.*

Trib. Torino, 11 January 2019 (ord.), *Aqvadesign s.r.l.* v. *G. M. Rubietterie s.r.l.*, in *Darts IP.*

Trib. Roma, 25 February 2019 (ord.), *Canon Kabushiki Kaisha* v. *Alphaink s.r.l.*, in *Darts IP.*

Trib. Milano, 11 November 2019 (ord.), *Thun s.p.a.* v. *Casati F.lli di Casati Alessandra*, in *Sprint.*

Trib. Milano, 18 December 2019 (ord.), *Signature s.r.l.* v. *Axel Weinbrecht GmbH and C'Art Group s.r.l.*, in *Darts IP.*

Pret. Milano, 23 December 1986, *Matessi* v. *Soc. Aluminia*, in *Giurisprudenza Annotata di Diritto Industriale*, XVI (1986), 2150.

Regulatory and Legislative Materials

Royal Decree no. 1127 of 29 June 1939, Law on Patents.

Legislative Decree no. 198 of 19 March 1996, Adaptation of the Internal Legislation on Industrial Property to the Binding Provision of the TRIPS Agreement – Uruguay Round.

Legislative Decree no. 30 of 10 February 2005, Industrial Property Code.

Council of the European Union, Agreement on a Unified Patent Court of 19 February 2013.

Law no. 214 of 3 November 2016, Ratification and Execution of the Agreement on the Unitary Patent Court.

Books, Articles and Online Materials

Ascarelli, Tullio. 1960. *Teoria della Concorrenza e dei Beni Immateriali*. Milano: Giuffrè.

Auteri, Paolo. 2007. "Novità in Tema di Sanzioni," in Luigi Carlo Ubertazzi, ed., *Il progetto di novella del cpi: Le biotecnologie*. Milano: Giuffrè.

Bertani, Michele. 2017. "Abuso dei Diritti di Proprietà Intellettuale," *Rivista di Diritto Commerciale* 115(3): 443–505.

Canella, Maria Giulia. 2020. "Sub art. 282 c.p.c.," in Federico Carpi and Michele Taruffo, eds., *Commentario breve al codice di procedura civile*. Milano: Wolters Kluwer-CEDAM.

Cogo, Alessandro & Ricolfi, Marco. 2020. "Administrative Enforcement of Copyright Infringement in Europe," in Giancarlo Frosio, ed., *Oxford Handbook of Online Intermediary Liability*. Oxford: Oxford University Press, 586–610.

Cuonzo, Gabriel & Ampollini, Daniela. 2018. "Generic Medicines and Second Medical Use Patents: Regulation Instead of Litigation? An Overview of Recent European Case Law and Practice," *IIC – International Review of Intellectual Property and Competition Law* 49(8): 895–915.

Di Cataldo, Vincenzo. 2012. *I Brevetti per Invenzione e per Modello di Utilità. I Disegni e Modelli.* Milano: Giuffrè.

Di Fazzio, Giulia. 2019. "Sub Art. 121 CPI," in Luigi Carlo Ubertazzi, ed., *Commentario Breve alle Leggi su Proprietà Intellettuale e Concorrenza.* Milano: CEDAM.

Frignani, Aldo. 1974. *L'Injunction nella Common Law e l'Inibitoria nel Diritto Italiano.* Milano: Giuffrè.

Greco, Paolo & Vercellone, Paolo. 1968. *Le Invenzioni e i Modelli di Utilità.* Torino: UTET.

Husovec, Martin. 2017. *Injunctions against Intermediaries in the EU. Accountable but not Liable?* Cambridge: Cambridge University Press.

Merges, Robert P. 1996. "Contracting Into Liability Rules: Intellectual Property Rights and Collective Rights Organisations," *California Law Review* 84: 1293–394.

Nivarra, Luca. 2000. "Dolo, Colpa e Buona Fede nel Sistema delle Sanzioni a Tutela della Proprietà Intellettuale," *Annali Italiani di Diritto d'Autore della Cultura e dello Spettacolo (AIDA)* IX: 325 ff.

Ricolfi, Marco. 2005. "Le Misure Compulsorie," in Luca Nivarra, ed., *L'Enforcement dei Diritti di Proprietà Intellettuale.* Milano: Giuffrè.

Rossi, Raffaele. 2020. "Commento all'Art. 91 CPC," in *Leggi d'Italia – Commentario al Codice di Procedura Civile.* Milano: Kluwer.

Rovati, Angelo Maria. 2019. "Art. 124 CPI," in Luigi Carlo Ubertazzi, ed., *Commentario Breve alle Leggi su Proprietà Intellettuale e Concorrenza.* Milano: CEDAM.

Sarti, Davide. 2004. "Il Terzo e la Contraffazione: Profili Civilistici," in Luca Nivarra, ed., *L'Enforcement dei Diritti di Proprietà Intellettuale.* Milano: Giuffrè.

Scuffi, Massimo. 2009. *Diritto Processuale della Proprietà Industriale ed Intellettuale.* Milano: Giuffrè.

Sena, Giuseppe. 2011. *I Diritti sulle Invenzioni e i Modelli di Utilità.* Milano: Giuffrè.

Spaccasassi, Francesco. 2005. "Inibitoria e Ordine di Ritiro dal Commercio nel Progetto di Novella del C.P.I.," in *Studi in Onore di Gerhard Schricker.* Milano: Giuffrè.

Spolidoro, Marco Saverio. 1982. *Le Misure di Prevenzione nel Diritto Industriale.* Milano: Giuffrè.

2005. "La Tutela della Proprietà Intellettuale: l'Evoluzione del Diritto Italiano e del Diritto Europeo," in *Studi in Onore di Gerhard Schricker.* Milano: Giuffrè.

2008a. "Profili Processuali del Codice della Proprietà Industriale," *Il Diritto Industriale* 2008(2):174–89.

2008b. "Un'Importante Sentenza delle Sezioni Unite Penali della Cassazione sul Delitto di Elusione dei Provvedimenti del Giudice Civile: Conseguenze e Riflessioni nella Prospettiva del Diritto Industriale," *Rivista di diritto industriale* LVII(3), I: 171–88.

Vanzetti, Adriano. 2007. "Brevi considerazioni in tema di inibitoria," *Rivista di diritto industriale* LVI(4–5), I: 167–71.

Vanzetti, Adriano & Di Cataldo, Vincenzo. 2018. *Manuale di diritto industriale.* Milano: Giuffrè.

Vanzetti, Michelle. 2010. "Contributo allo Studio delle Misure Correttive e delle Sanzioni Civili nel Diritto Industriale: i Profili Processuali dell'Art. 124 cpi," *Rivista di diritto industriale* LIX(1): 26–71.

11

Netherlands

Willem A. Hoyng and Léon E. Dijkman

A. PROCEDURAL ISSUES

1. Merits Proceedings

All patent cases are heard by the specialized IP chamber of the District Court of the Hague. Appeals (which are *de novo*) are heard by the specialized chamber of the Court of Appeal of the Hague. Thereafter an appeal (on points of law) is possible without the necessity of leave to the Supreme Court. The specialized chamber in first instance issues between about fifty and seventy decisions each year. The Court of Appeal issues about twenty and the Supreme Court around five. Of course, numbers vary from year to year. The courts have a good reputation in patent matters. The UK, German and Dutch courts take into consideration each other's decisions in cases invoking the same European Patent and normally give reasons if they do not follow each other's decision (which is more the exception than the rule). The Netherlands does not have a bifurcated system for patent cases: validity and infringement are always dealt with in the same proceedings. Thus, if an infringer challenges the validity of the patent, the court will normally first decide on the validity of the patent and only turn to infringement if the validity of the patent is upheld. In other words, a Dutch court will not order an injunction unless it has first established that the patent is valid, and the only way that an injunction can be granted on the basis of a patent that is later invalidated is if the decision on validity is overturned on appeal.[1]

---

[1] This may also happen if the injunction is granted in interim proceedings but the patent is invalidated in merits proceedings; this happened, e.g., in *AstraZeneca/Sandoz* (DC The Hague 2018), which decision was overturned on appeal in *AstraZeneca/Sandoz* (CoA The Hague 2018). A strict liability standard for all damages arising out of enforcement has long been the rule if the injunction is enforced but the patent is later invalidated (or infringement denied), but it is questionable whether this is still tenable after the decision in *Bayer Pharma* (CJEU 2019).

This is true in proceedings on the merits, where the court will always rule on the validity of the patent if it is challenged, but also in interim relief proceedings, where the court will make a preliminary assessment of the patent's validity before imposing interim relief, denying it if there is a reasonable, not-to-be-ignored chance that the patent will be revoked or invalidated.

Once validity and infringement are established, the key provision relating to final patent injunctions under Dutch law is Article 3:296 Dutch Civil Code (DCC), which reads as follows: "'Unless the law, the nature of the obligation or a legal act require otherwise, a person obliged to give, do or refrain from doing something to another person, **shall** be so ordered by the court upon request of the entitled party" (our translation; emphasis ours).

This provision is not specific to patent law but covers all civil law obligations. It was newly introduced in the revised civil code, which entered into force in 1992. Since the old civil code did not contain a similar provision, the question whether courts enjoyed discretion to issue injunctions was subject to extensive academic discussion.[2] The issue had long been resolved for contract law, where the Supreme Court had ruled that courts must order performance of a contract if the existence of the obligation is established.[3] In 1985, the Supreme Court resolved the controversy for torts in its landmark decision *Claas/Van Tongeren*, when it held that "once the unlawfulness of acts which are requested to be enjoined is established, the injunction is, principle, allowable right away and is not subject to a further balance of interests, save for exceptions not relevant here".[4] Thus, these decisions by the Supreme Court make clear that, when it comes to injunctions in proceedings on the merit, Dutch law leaves no room for a balance-of-hardships test. This was codified in Article 3:296 DCC, which now governs all obligations under law, including those arising under foreign law and/or in foreign territory.[5]

However, the reference in Article 3:296 DCC to the law, the nature of the obligation or a legal act, and especially the Supreme Court's reference to "exceptions not relevant here" in its statement in *Claas/Van Tongeren*, make clear that this is not an absolute rule. Indeed, five exceptions to this rule have been identified by

---

[2] The discussion is summarized in Van Nispen 1978, no. 174 *et seq.*, with ample citations.

[3] *Meegdes/Meegdes* (HR 1956).

[4] *Claas/Van Tongeren* (HR 1985, para. 3.3) (our translation).

[5] *Lincoln/Interlas* (HR 1989, para. 4.2.4). Dutch courts will also deal with the infringement of foreign patents if the court has jurisdiction over the defendant. If validity is raised, the court will suspend the proceedings on the merit (until validity has been decided by the courts of the country for which the patent has been granted) but will grant a provisional injunction, which can immediately be executed, if it feels that there is no reasonable possibility that the patent will be invalidated. The court will apply the law of the patent but for procedural questions (such as whether or not an injunction should be granted) the courts apply Dutch law.

Advocate-General[6] Vranken in his conclusion before the Supreme Court's decision in *Kimberly Clark/Procter & Gamble*:[7]

(a) A lack of standing (Article 3:303 DCC);
(b) Forfeiture of rights (*rechtsverwerking*);
(c) Abuse of rights (Article 3:13 DCC);
(d) Substantial public interests (Article 6:168 DCC); and
(e) Reasonableness and fairness (*redelijkheid en billijkheid*, Articles 6:2 and 6:248(2) DCC).

An in-depth treatment of these exceptions is not intended here;[8] only some observations on how these exceptions might apply to patent law will be made. Put briefly, in theory each of these exceptions could lead to refusal of an injunction, even if infringement of a valid patent is established and damages are awarded. However, most of these exceptions appear to leave courts insufficient leeway to perform a proportionality assessment as required by Article 3(2) Enforcement Directive. Crucially, all exceptions under (a)–(d) suffer from self-containment. That is, they justify departure from the main rule of Article 3:296 DCC if – and only if – the conditions relevant for the specific exception are fulfilled, disregarding other circumstances that may weigh in favour of denying an injunction. In other words, these exceptions do not allow courts to take into consideration *all* circumstances of a case when deciding whether an injunction is justified, but only those pertinent to the specific exception. It is submitted that this contravenes a court's duty to ensure patent enforcement measures are proportional as per Article 3(2) Enforcement Directive, which necessarily implies taking stock of all relevant circumstances.

Only the exception under (e) – derogation by way of "reasonableness and fairness", two foundational concepts in Dutch private law – allows courts to take into account all circumstances of the case. It has been argued in the literature that this means taking into account not just the parties' interests, but also third-party and public interests.[9] However, Articles 6:2 DCC and 6:248(2) DCC, on which this exception is based, are traditionally applied more specifically in contractual relations. Even though it has been accepted by the Supreme Court that they also apply in tort law, it is uncertain whether in this context they relate only to the tortfeasor's obligation to pay damages (which is construed as an obligation under Dutch law), or *also* to the injured party's entitlement to an injunction.[10] The issue has never been

---

[6] The Advocate-General is an independent lawyer nominated by the government which advises the Supreme Court. The Supreme Court follows the Advocate-General in the majority of cases.

[7] *Kimberly Clark/Procter & Gamble* (HR 1995, para. 20 of the A-G's opinion).

[8] See in more detail Van Nispen 2018a, 15–17.

[9] Wolters 2013, chs. 6.3 and 6.4.

[10] See, e.g, Schelhaas 2017, 2.10 ("In other words, Article 6:2 DCC renders applicable reasonableness and fairness to all legal relations of a contractual nature, whereby it is irrelevant whether they arise out of a contract or from another source (such as tort)"; translation ours). The

put before the Supreme Court and perhaps this is why reasonableness and fairness are only very rarely invoked in the context of patent proceedings; in any event, an injunction in a patent case was never denied because imposing it would contravene these principles.

2. *Interim Relief Proceedings*

The principles discussed apply to merits proceedings, i.e. court proceedings according to the ordinary procedural regime which end in a final decision that can acquire *res judicata*. Thus, Article 3:296 DCC is not applicable in interim relief proceedings, in which an injunction can be rendered much more quickly than in merits proceedings.[11] In interim relief proceedings, the situation is different and the Supreme Court has explicitly stated that the grant of interim relief, including an interim injunction, is always subject to a balance of interest.[12] Courts have long used this additional leeway sparsely and until recently the only case where the preliminary relief judge considered the patent valid and infringed but nonetheless refused an injunction dated from 1989.[13] However, when hearing claims for preliminary relief, the Dutch patent courts have become decidedly more critical when granting injunctions. The best example is a 2020 decision by the Court of Appeal which held, in the context of a FRAND dispute, that the patentee's interest in immediate relief was outweighed by the substantial damage it would cause to the infringer, particularly because the patentee ultimately sought to recover a license fee.[14] The sophistication of the balance of interests that the Court of Appeal applied, as well as the importance it attached to it (it declined to rule on the substance of the patentee's claim), were unprecedented in Dutch patent practice. This decision and a few others may indicate a less absolutist approach to injunctive relief by Dutch courts, at least in preliminary relief proceedings.

Interim injunction proceedings are separate proceedings and can be filed when proceedings on the merits have not (yet) been filed. Appeals to the Court of Appeal and the Supreme Court are possible. At the request of the plaintiff the court sets a day on which the writ of summons has to be served and the date of the hearing. In

---

doctrinal question, then, is whether the duty to cease infringing a patent is "of a contractual nature".

[11] See, e.g., *Euromedica/Merck* (HR 2005, para. 3.5.1).

[12] *Kimberly Clark/Procter & Gamble* (HR 1995, para. 3.4).

[13] *Schneider/ACS* (Prel. Rel. DC The Hague 1989, paras. 5.5.4–5.5.5) (upheld in appeal). In that case, the defendant had filed an affidavit by a doctor who declared that treating patients without the patented device would place patients at risk of receiving poor treatment, possibly even risking their lives in severe cases. According to the court, this was not sufficiently disputed by the patentee so it held that the interests of the patients outweighed those of the patentee. Note that this decision was rendered before the *Boehringer Mannheim/Kirin Amgen* decision of the Supreme Court, which is discussed below (Section B).

[14] *Sisvel/Xiaomi* (CoA The Hague 2020).

extremely urgent cases hearings can take place in a matter of days. In the meantime, the court can issue an *ex parte* injunction in order to preserve the status quo, for instance. A decision normally follows after one or two weeks, but in very urgent cases a decision may follow immediately after the hearing.

In practice, interim relief proceedings take the form of a "mini-trial", often including written rounds, expert statements and oral argument. However, to qualify for an interim injunction a patentee must demonstrate an urgent interest.[15] Dutch courts are generally quite lenient when it comes to the urgency requirement, though it can bar claims for provisional relief, particularly where the patentee is not diligent in pursuing its claim.[16] It must be noted, though, that in this case normally all claims are dismissed. Thus, the urgency requirement has so far not been used to deny an injunction specifically in a case where infringement is otherwise established.

An important feature of preliminary relief proceedings is that they allow for swift cross-border relief. In the 1990s, the Dutch courts famously pioneered cross-border injunctions in patent cases, but this practice was halted by a pair of decisions by the Court of Justice of the European Union (CJEU).[17] However, a subsequent decision clarified that cross-border *preliminary* relief remains allowable.[18] Since then, the District Court of the Hague has repeatedly granted cross-border (preliminary) injunctions in patent cases, either in summary proceedings or as interim relief within the context of pending proceedings on the merits.[19]

B. THE PRIVATE AND PUBLIC INTEREST

The Supreme Court's formula in its *Claas/Van Tongeren* decision and the principle of Article 3:296 DCC, that unlawful acts *shall* be enjoined by the courts, are fully applicable in patent cases. In fact, some years later the Supreme Court suggested that they are *particularly* applicable to patent cases by finding that the duration of a patent is limited and that "this right normally can only be effectively protected by the expeditious grant of an injunction to prevent further infringements".[20] Since then, a successful patentee's entitlement to an injunction has become so commonly accepted that it is hardly ever challenged in patent cases.

---

[15] See, e.g., *DSM/Novozymes* (Prel. Rel. DC The Hague 2017, para. 4.2.1).
[16] See, e.g., *Becton/Braun* (Prel. Rel. DC The Hague 2016, para. 5.2) (waiting for three years after grant of patent to file infringement claims insufficiently diligent).
[17] *Roche/Primus* (CJEU 2006) and *GAT/LUK* (CJEU 2006).
[18] *Solvay/Honeywell* (CJEU 2012).
[19] *DSM/Novozymes* (Prel. Rel. DC The Hague 2017) offers an example of a cross-border injunction in summary proceedings; *Carl Zeiss/VSY* (DC The Hague 2017) offers an example of a cross-border injunction granted within the context of proceedings on the merits.
[20] *Vredo/Veenhuis* (HR 1993, para. 3.4); note that the decision was about the duty of the specialized preliminary relief judge to hear a case. The judge had refused to do so because he ruled that the case was too complicated for preliminary relief proceedings.

Exceptions are few and far between, particularly in merits proceedings. The only outright refusal of an injunction where a valid patent was found to be infringed was in a Standard Essential Patent (SEP) case against a licensee willing to accept a licence on Fair, Reasonable, And Non-Discriminatory (FRAND) terms, while the patentee had given to the standard-setting body (ETSI) a declaration to grant licences on FRAND conditions to its SEPs.[21] Prior to the decision of the Court of Justice of the European Union (CJEU) in *Huawei/ZTE*,[22] such conduct was considered an abuse of rights under Dutch law (3:13 DCC).[23] After *Huawei*, it is generally assumed that FRAND cases should primarily be assessed under Article 102 Treaty on the Functioning of the European Union (TFEU).[24] Conversely, if a licensee is unwilling to accept a licence on FRAND terms, Dutch courts have no qualms about granting an injunction under a FRAND-encumbered patent.[25] In the first FRAND cases decided by the Court of Appeal of the Hague, this court has struck a fair and pragmatic balance between the interests of SEP holders and implementers in its interpretation of their respective obligations arising under the *Huawei/ZTE* framework.[26]

There is only one other decision where requesting an injunction was (implicitly) considered an abuse of rights, but that was outside the context of patent law and mostly related to the way the case was brought before the court.[27] The requirements for finding an abuse of rights are so stringent that it is indeed unlikely that this ground will ever lead to refusal of an injunction in a case of infringement: a patentee that prevails in an infringement suit will always have a considerable interest in exclusivity which will be difficult for defendant to overcome.[28]

---

[21] *Apple/Samsung II* (DC The Hague 2012, para. 4.31) (finding that requesting an injunction against a willing licensee would put undue pressure on them to agree to non-FRAND terms). Infringement of Samsung's patent was later established but an injunction refused for reasons set forth in the decision of 14 March 2012 (see *Apple/Samsung III* (DC The Hague 2012, para. 3.5.11). The decision was preceded by preliminary relief proceedings where the same outcome was reached; see *Samsung/Apple I* (Prel. Rel. DC The Hague 2011, para. 4.36).

[22] *Huawei/ZTE* (CJEU 2015).

[23] See also, *Philips/SK Kassetten* (DC The Hague 2010), which set out the Dutch approach to FRAND patents (with an explanation why it differed from the German approach).

[24] See e.g., *Archos/Philips* (DC The Hague 2017, para. 3.2).

[25] *Philips/Asus* (CoA The Hague 2019); *Philips/Wiko* (CoA, The Hague 2019).

[26] See generally, Larouche and Zingales 2018.

[27] *Media Monkeys* (DC Amsterdam 2014, para. 4.4). In this case, a web developer sued its client for copyright infringement after they refused to pay part of the agreed price, but the contractual dispute was not brought before the court. It therefore held that it could not hear the claim for an injunction "because of the way Media Monkeys had presented the case", fearing it would be used as undue leverage to obtain a disputed payment.

[28] To be sure, there are various situations in which suing for patent infringement can constitute abuse of rights within the meaning of Art. 3:13 DCC and where all claims will be rejected, including a damages claim; an example is *Medinol/Cordis* (Prel. Rel. DC The Hague 2004), in the context of double patenting. However, this chapter is not concerned with such cases and only relates to cases where requesting an injunction could be abusive where a valid patent is found infringed.

The legitimate interests of third parties have likewise almost never sufficed to persuade courts to refuse a final injunction. In a controversial decision – *Boehringer Mannheim/Kirin Amgen* (HR 1995, para. 3.7) – the Supreme Court refused even to consider the fact that an injunction would threaten the availability of a certain drug, preventing patients from receiving that drug for which there was no satisfactory alternative on the market, holding that "the protection of the interests of third parties such as patients should not take place through allowing patent infringement". It is submitted that this holding is hard to accept. Apart from the fact that it is questionable whether this decision remains valid in light of recent case law from the CJEU (to which we return in Section E.2), the decision seems incorrect insofar as it suggests the interests of third parties are protected by "allowing patent infringement". The infringement is not "allowed" since the patentee would be entitled to payment of damages, which, in light of the possibility for a patentee to claim forfeiture of profits (Article 70(5) Dutch Patent Act), can be quite substantial. In addition, it is not an all-or-nothing matter: the injunction could also be suspended, e.g. subject to an escrow payment or for a limited time period, so as to allow switching patients to a substitute pharmaceutical (if available).[29] Be that as it may, a "tailored" injunction to protect patient interests was granted only once. In that case, the District Court proved willing to withhold an injunction until infringement and validity were definitively established, subject to a royalty payment; however, it appears from the decision that at the hearing the patentee agreed this moratorium on the normally immediately enforceable decision of the District Court until the final decision (on appeal) on validity and infringement.[30] In all other cases, patient interests have either been considered insufficiently proven or not capable of justifying refusal of an injunction.[31]

Nor have other societal interests that could fall within the ambit of Article 6:168 DCC ever been able to convince courts to refuse an injunction.[32] The most interesting case in this respect is *Schneider/Cordis*, which involved a medical device where the (specialized IP chamber of the) District Court of the Hague had granted an injunction, immediately enforceable, to Schneider.[33] Cordis thereupon immediately applied to the Court of Assen, where their manufacturing facility was located,

---

[29] See, in the United Kingdom, *Edwards* v. *Boston* (EWHC 2018) where Mr Justice Arnold granted an injunction but stayed it for twelve months to safeguard patient interests.

[30] *Medinol/Boston Scientific* (DC The Hague 2003, para. 3.29). It probably also helped that a licence agreement had previously entered into by the parties, so that the reasonable royalty payable for the duration of the proceedings could be taken from it.

[31] *Cordis/Medinol* (Prel. Rel. DC The Hague 2003, paras. 11–13); *Roche/Primus* (CoA The Hague 2002, para. 11); *C. R. Bard/TD Medical* (Prel. Rel. DC The Hague 1995, para. 25); and *Cook/Fujinon* (Prel. Rel. DC The Hague 1995, paras. 14–15).

[32] It has been questioned whether Article 6:168 DCC can even be applied in IP cases; see the opinion of Advocate-General Franx under *Stichting CAI/Columbia Pictures* (HR 1984, para. 6) and Gielen 1994. Both believe the application of Article 6:168 DCC is precluded by provisions on compulsory licensing in the various IP laws.

[33] *Schneider/Cordis* (DC The Hague 2005).

for a stay of enforcement, stating that enforcement of the injunction would force it to fire around 300 of its employees and possibly relocate its operations from the Netherlands entirely. The preliminary relief judge granted the stay.[34] However, the decision was reversed on appeal, primarily because Cordis had apparently refused to conclude a licence when Schneider offered one, but also under reference to the Supreme Court's holding on the protection of interests of third parties in *Boehringer Mannheim/Kirin Amgen*.[35] Thus, employees' interests have in principle also been found insufficient to even suspend the immediate enforceability of an injunction, pending appeal. In principle, a party that enforces a preliminary injunction which is later quashed in merits proceedings will be fully liable for the damages suffered as a result of the wrongful enforcement.[36] But a decision on the merits can take a long time to obtain and during this time the injunction will remain in full force, which can substantially harm an undertaking and even lead to bankruptcy. In addition, the difficulty of calculating damages suffered as a result of wrongful enforcement makes obtaining full compensation (very) difficult. This means the prospect of a damages claim will not always suffice to safeguard the infringer's interests.

Another interesting case is *Monsanto/Cefetra*, which concerned patented soybeans that had been planted on a large scale in Argentina.[37] Because of the importance of this case for its agricultural sector, the state of Argentina intervened in the proceedings on the side of Cefetra and argued that an injunction in the Netherlands preventing imports from Argentina because of alleged infringement of a European patent would substantially harm its exports, after Monsanto had allegedly made Argentina dependent on this soybean by encouraging the use of the genetically modified seed for growing these soybeans. However, also here the court would not give in: it held that even if the soybeans were not patented in Argentina, it could reasonably have expected that Monsanto would enforce its patents in Argentina's export markets where possible. The situation is not much different in interim relief proceedings, where an injunction was denied only once, in that case to safeguard patient interests.[38] This decision, however, is rather old (1989) and pre-dates the aforementioned Supreme Court decision in *Boehringer Mannheim/Kirin Amgen*, which held that patient interests cannot outweigh a patentee's interest in an injunction.

To be sure, this is not to say that the injunctions were wrongfully granted in *Schneider/Cordis* and *Monsanto/Cefetra*: it is just to show that various attempts have

---

[34] *Schneider/Cordis* (Prel. Rel. DC Assen 2005).

[35] *Schneider/Cordis* (CoA Leeuwarden 2005, paras. 12–13).

[36] See Jansen 2017, 3.10. The principle was accepted specifically for patent law early on: *X/Y* (HR 1934). See also *Voorbraak-Ciba Geigy* (HR 1986). However, it seems that applying such strict liability is not in accordance with the recent decision in *Bayer Pharma* (CJEU 2019). See also Dijkman 2019a, 918.

[37] *Monsanto/Cefetra* (DC The Hague 2008, paras. 4.32–4.33).

[38] *Schneider/ACS* (Prel. Rel. DC The Hague 1989, paras. 5.5.4–5.5.5). Note that the decision carries the suggestion that the case was poorly argued on this point by the patentee.

been made to persuade Dutch courts that third-party interests should lead to refusal of an injunction, but never with any success. Most recently, this strict approach was confirmed in the *Nikon/ASML* decision.[39] It was one of eleven cases brought by Nikon against its Dutch competitor ASML on the basis of patents that related to various aspects of immersion lithography, a technology used in highly complex machines to make computer chips. ASML argued that the grant of an injunction would be disproportional as it would force it to accept Nikon's (allegedly) unreasonable royalty demands, despite the fact that Nikon's patents related only to minor aspects of its machines so that it would effectively be forced to pay to use its own innovations.[40] The court refused to grant ASML's request for relief: tellingly, it assessed each (strict) ground that ASML had invoked to support refusal of an injunction one by one, rather than taking into account all circumstances of the case in one general proportionality test.[41]

Dutch courts and commentators have traditionally assumed, implicitly or explicitly, that the compulsory licensing provision in the Dutch Patent Act (DPA) (Article 57) and Article 6:168 DCC determine the extent to which third-party interests can be taken into account in patent infringement cases.[42] Article 57 of the DPA gives the possibility to ask for a compulsory licence in three situations: (1) for the general interest; (2) for being able to exploit one's own (dependent) patent which has a great economic benefit; and (3) because of non-use during three years after grant without good reason in any country that is part of the World Trade Organization (WTO and part of the agreement on Trade Related Aspects of Intellectual Property (TRIPS)). The provision is basically a dead letter. Over the last 100 years very few compulsory licences have been granted. Under one view, third-party interests cannot be taken into account separately at the injunction stage and cannot lead to denial of an injunction if the requirements under these provisions are not met. We think this is incorrect: under these provisions, an injunction is straight-out denied and the patentee must make do with a reasonable remuneration. By contrast, proportionality need not always lead to a denial of injunctive relief but may instead result in temporary suspension thereof. And, in any case, the patentee retains its auxiliary claims and in particular its damages claim, which may far exceed the payment that would have been due as a reasonable royalty because Dutch patent law allows for disgorgement of profits.[43]

---

[39] *Nikon/ASML* (DC The Hague 2018, para. 4.40 *et seq.*).
[40] See Siebrasse et al. 2019, which contains a theoretical and economic analysis of this problem as well as a comparative study. *Nikon/ASML* is the only Dutch case to date where the small-component issue was raised as an argument to deny an injunction, but the argument was refused by the court.
[41] *Nikon/ASML* (DC The Hague 2018, para. 4.44). Nikon's patent was invalidated by the court, so it did not actually grant the injunction.
[42] See Van Nispen 2018b for references to cases and literature outside the field of intellectual property law.
[43] See in more detail Dijkman 2019b, para. 33; and Stierle 2019, at 353 *et seq.*

The Netherlands does not know immunity for injunctions for the state. So injunctions could be granted against the state if the state cannot successfully invoke misuse/proportionality under Article 168 DCC or obtain a compulsory licence under Article 57 DPA.[44]

C. ALTERNATIVES AND MODIFICATIONS

As stated in Section B, Dutch courts have so far been reluctant to tailor injunctions to specific cases or to substitute the injunction by another remedy. This is largely due to the mandatory language of Article 3:296 DCC: courts *shall* grant the injunction in case of unlawful behaviour. Traditionally, Dutch law did not recognize exceptions to this principle that would allow courts to substitute or modify the injunction.

In theory, a court could suspend the effect of an injunction pending appeal. Under Dutch law, the effect of a merits decision is suspended once an appeal is filed, unless the court declares its decision provisionally enforceable (Article 350(1) Dutch Code of Civil Procedure (DCCP)). Although the Supreme Court has held that the judgement whether to declare a decision provisionally enforceable is subject to a balance of interests; in practice courts virtually always allow provisional enforceability of a decision.[45] Still, a court wishing to avoid disproportionate consequences of an injunction could suspend its effect pending appeal.[46] Another option is for the infringer to appeal the decision and to request the Court of Appeal to suspend the enforceability of the injunction. Such requests have rarely been granted as the traditional test required evident mistakes in the first-instance decision or extreme hardship on the part of the infringer. However, in a recent decision the Dutch Supreme Court relaxed these requirements to a balance of interest between the parties.[47] Just two weeks prior, the Court of Appeal of the Hague had suspended the enforcement of a first-instance decision in a patent case where some of the infringer's arguments had apparently not been considered, the enforcement would cause significant damage to the infringer and the patentee was unlikely to provide recourse for these damages.[48] The case is unusual as the Court of Appeal does not normally find that important arguments of a party were not considered, and such decisions remain rare. But the Supreme Court's relaxation of the standards for suspension, coupled with the Court of Appeal's taking into account the severity of the

---

[44] Art. 57 DPA contains three grounds for grant of a compulsory licence: general interest, non-use of the invention and dependency licenses. Contrary to other jurisdictions, "Crown" or government-use licences are not provided for in the DPA.

[45] *Gommans/Evers* (HR 1996, para. 3.4).

[46] See, e.g., *Medinol/Boston Scientific* (DC The Hague 2003, rov. 3.29), where the district court suspended the injunction until infringement and validity were definitively established, subject to a licence payment along the terms of an earlier licence agreement between the parties.

[47] *X/Y* (HR 2019, para. 5.8 (a)).

[48] *VG Colours/HE Licenties* (CoA The Hague 2019).

consequences of the decision for the infringer, may herald a more liberal approach to the grant of stays pending appeal in the Netherlands.

Alternatively, a court could safeguard the interests of the infringer by making provisional enforcement subject to a security deposit (Article 233(3) DCCP).[49] This possibility was used by interim relief judges in some older decisions, where the injunction was suspended subject to payment by the defendant of an amount in escrow.[50] These cases would have involved particular hardship to the defendant if an injunction were imposed which, taking into account the preliminary nature of the injunction, led the court to this solution. The mere fact that the injunction would cause substantial damage to the defendant, however, is not enough to refuse or suspend it.[51] The situation is different for *ex parte* procedures, but those are no longer granted by the District Court of the Hague in patent cases,[52] with an exception for clearly exceptional cases (exhibitions).

Judicial discretion was also already accepted before the adoption of the Enforcement Directive when it comes to claims for recall or destruction of infringing goods. This discretion is explicitly provided for in the DPA.[53] Thus, in cases where recall or destruction of infringing goods would be particularly oppressive, for instance where this would incur enormous costs, these claims may be refused. However, such refusals remain relatively rare.[54] In this respect, there is no real difference between proceedings on the merits and preliminary relief proceedings since in both cases courts are granted discretion, although the preliminary nature of the decision may of course influence the use of this discretion.[55]

---

[49] See e.g., *Kirin Amgen/Boehringer Mannheim* (CoA The Hague 1994, para. 36), where the Court of Appeal made enforcement of the injunction subject to payment of a security deposit of EUR 5 million.

[50] *BT/Plumettaz* (Prel. Rel. DC The Hague 1994, para. 30); and *Huss/Van de Wiel* (Prel. Rel. DC The Hague 1996, para. 9).

[51] See *Vredo/Veenhuis* (HR 1993), as well as *Dutch Mobile/Sisvel* (Prel. Rel. DC The Hague 2005, para. 10) (where the court accepted that allowing the marketing of infringing products would constitute an "unacceptable precedent" vis-à-vis competitors who had concluded licences with the patentee).

[52] See *Glaxo/Pharmachemie* (Prel. Rel. DC The Hague 2009), where the patent was unopposed before the European Patent Office and not challenged anywhere in Europe, while infringement became apparent from the Summary of Main Product Characteristics (SMPC). Still, the court refused an *ex parte* injunction because the patentee had not offered the infringer a chance to voluntarily remove its product from the market or challenge the infringement claim by sending a summons letter.

[53] Article 70, section 7 DPA provides that "when considering the prayer for relief [for recall or destruction, authors], the gravity of the infringement and the requested measures, as well as the interests of third parties, must be balanced".

[54] Some examples are *Sharp/Samsung* (DC The Hague 2009, para. 4.45); *Bornemann/Houttuin* (DC The Hague 2003, para. 32); and *Aralco/Prefair* (CoA The Hague 1999, para. 13).

[55] An amusing example of a refusal in preliminary relief proceedings is *Gouda Holland/Janse* (CoA 's-Hertogenbosch 1987, para. 4.13), where a recall of infringing heaters would also have affected the courthouse; the CoA discerned "contra-indications from an economic point of

D. DRAFTING AND ENFORCING INJUNCTIONS

It is up to the patentee's attorneys to state, in the writ of summons, what the court is requested to enjoin. It is customary to ask for a general prohibition on the infringement of the invoked patent, which is justified by the infringing acts discussed and evidenced in the writ of summons (and throughout the rest of the proceedings). If infringement is accepted, a court will normally grant a general injunction, containing a general prohibition not to infringe the relevant patent, subject to a penalty. The following would be a typical formulation of the injunction:

> The court ... prohibits [infringer] from infringing [patent number] in the Netherlands, subject to a penalty of EUR 50,000 per violation of this prohibition, or, at the choice of [patentee], of EUR 5,000 per infringing product or per day that [infringer] does not comply with this order, effective 24 hours after service of this order, with a maximum of EUR 1,000,000.

The wording shows that the injunction is formulated very broadly. There is no difference between injunctions in merits and interim proceedings. Courts generally assume that proven infringement gives rise to a threat of further infringement. Because the way in which the further infringement may occur is uncertain, a generally worded injunction is justified.[56] It is enough that infringement by a single product is proven: there is no need for the patentee to prove other products also infringe the patent, and the fact that the infringer states it has comparable products that do not infringe the patent is insufficient ground to limit the injunction.[57] Products that, depending on the consumer, may be used in an infringing manner are also covered by the scope of the injunction.[58] More generally, the Supreme Court has held that the injunction covers all acts which cannot be reasonably doubted to infringe the patent, in light of the court's reasoning in the decision and the interest that the injunction seeks to protect.[59]

Once the decision granting the injunction is served on the defendant, all infringing acts must be ceased. As becomes clear from the sample formulation shown above, the timeframe to stop infringing acts may be (and usually is) quite short. If the infringement nonetheless continues, the patentee may start collection of forfeited penalty sums by seizing bank accounts or further assets of the patentee by a bailiff. The onus is then on the infringer to challenge the alleged forfeiture of penalty sums in separate enforcement proceedings. The penalty amount varies between proceedings, but must in any case be set at an amount that will effectively deter further

---

view" to removal of installed heaters. Another example is *Westo/Railtechniek van Herwijnen* (Prel. Rel. DC The Hague 2001, paras. 21–22).

[56] *Lexington* (HR 1964).

[57] *Carl Zeiss/VSY* (DC The Hague 2017, para. 6.60).

[58] *DSM/Novozymes* (Prel. Rel. DC The Hague 2017, para. 4.17).

[59] *Klokkenspel* (HR 1966).

infringements; if the infringer continues the infringements despite the injunction, the penalty amount may be increased.[60] If a defendant wants to introduce an altered product and to make sure that penalty sums will not be forfeited, the defendant can file summary proceedings and ask the judge to rule that the product is not covered by the judgment (because the judgment does not make clear that the altered product should be considered infringing). If there is doubt, the patentee can file a conditional cross-complaint asking for a new injunction if the court rules that the altered product is not covered by the original injunction arguing that the altered product is also infringing the patent.

E. A LOOK AHEAD

1. *The Enforcement Directive and the Proportionality Requirement*

Directive 2004/48/EC (the Enforcement Directive), which aims to "approximate legislative systems so as to ensure a high, equivalent and homogeneous level of [IP] protection in the internal market", was transposed into Dutch law on 29 April 2006.[61] Article 11 of the Enforcement Directive stipulates that member states shall ensure that, when an intellectual property right is found to be infringed, "the judicial authorities *may* issue against the infringer an injunction" (emphasis ours). In addition, Article 3(2) states that all IP enforcement measures shall be "effective, proportionate and dissuasive". The Enforcement Directive establishes minimum standards with which all member states must comply: thus, the tripartite requirement for IP remedies must be met in all national legal systems.

The open-ended formulation of Article 11, as well as the proportionality requirement in Article 3(2), are suggestive of judicial discretion. Indeed, it has been argued that together these provisions require refusal of an injunction if granting it would be disproportionate.[62] This appears to have been acknowledged by the Dutch legislator who, in the explanatory memorandum to the implementing legislation of the Enforcement Directive, remarked that "it is at all times up to the judge to assess whether a requested measure is proportional to the established infringement".[63] On the other hand, the legislator did not consider transposition of Article 11 necessary, finding that Article 3:296 DCC empowers the court to grant an injunction in case of

---

[60] See, e.g., *Ajinomoto/GBT* (Prel. Rel. DC The Hague 2014).
[61] See recital (10). It led, inter alia, to the introduction of a new chapter in the Dutch Code of Civil Procedure, comprising Articles 1019a–1019i DCCP.
[62] See, e.g., Ohly 2009 ("Article 3 of the Enforcement Directive Requires a flexible approach rather than an all-or-nothing solution"); García Perez 2016, 101 ("the courts may issue an injunction or not, discretionarily").
[63] Kamerstukken II 2005/06, 30392, 3, 7 ("Het is overigens te allen tijde aan de rechter om te beoordelen of een gevorderde maatregel proportioneel is ten opzichte van de geconstateerde inbreuk").

infringement.[64] As we have seen, this is correct but not the end of the story. After all, Article 3:296 DCC and the interpretation given to it by the Supreme Court do not allow precisely that which the legislator believes a court should "at all times" do, i.e. assess whether an injunction might be disproportional in relation to the infringement. This is reflected in the difference in wording: whereas Article 3 Enforcement Directive states that judicial authorities "may" issue an injunction, Article 3:296 DCC states that the injunction "shall" be issued. In light of the legislator's explicit acknowledgement that courts must assess the proportionality of requested measures, it would appear that the failure to introduce a corresponding exception to Article 3:296 DCC might be an omission.

2. *The CJEU's Case Law on Proportionality as Interpreted by the Dutch Supreme Court*

As is well known to IP scholars and practitioners alike, the CJEU has revolutionized European IP through a series of decisions in which it interprets and weaponizes the proportionality requirement in Article 3(2) Enforcement Directive, primarily through its developing jurisprudence of balancing fundamental rights in the context of IP cases. A comprehensive analysis of this case law and how the proportionality doctrine emerges from it will not be undertaken here.[65] It is merely observed that Article 17(2) Charter of Fundamental Rights makes clear that intellectual property is considered a fundamental right. However, when a conflict arises with other fundamental rights (such as the freedom of information, the freedom of carrying out a business) such protection of IP rights is not (and cannot be) absolute. This means that when IP rights are enforced, they must be weighed against other fundamental rights at stake in the case at hand, as provided for in Article 52 of the Charter.[66] The goal of this exercise is to ensure a fair balance is struck between, on the one hand, IP rights holders and, on the other, the rights of users of protected subject matter.[67] This means that in certain circumstances an injunction will have to be refused because granting it would constitute a disproportional interference with the rights of others.[68]

[64] *Id.* at 15.
[65] See esp. Husovec 2016, 250 ("After Promusicae, the proportionality exercise grew into a firm part of the IP case law"; the author proceeds to analyse this case law and the proportionality requirement that emerges from it).
[66] *Sky Österreich* (CJEU 2013, para. 60) ("Where several rights and fundamental freedoms protected by the European Union legal order are at issue, the assessment of the possible disproportionate nature of a provision of European Union law must be carried out with a view to reconciling the requirements of the protection of those different rights and freedoms and a fair balance between them"); *Promusicae* (CJEU 2008, para. 68) confirmed that enforcement of fundamental rights must also not be in conflict "with the other general principles of Community law, such as the principle of proportionality").
[67] *Telekabel Wien* (CJEU 2014, para. 47).
[68] See, e.g., *Scarlet Extended* (CJEU 2011). The case concerned enforcement measures against an intermediary which was an important consideration for the CJEU, but nothing in the CJEU's

This interpretation of the CJEU's case law (generally in the field of copyright law and more especially in regard to providers of access to the internet) has been explicitly embraced by the Dutch Supreme Court in its landmark *GeenStijl/Sanoma* decision.[69] In those proceedings, the Court of Appeal had ruled that it is inappropriate to weigh copyright protection against the fundamental right to freedom of speech, because the balance between these two rights is already reflected in the Dutch Copyright Act and its exceptions.[70] The Supreme Court reversed and held that, if the defendant invokes fundamental rights, these should always be weighed against the intellectual property right invoked:

> 5.2.5. Part II.4 of the cassation complaint correctly takes as its point of departure that the court, if this defence is raised, must investigate whether in the case at hand the enforcement of an intellectual property right is restrained by another fundamental right. It is true that in the enactment of intellectual property laws a correct balance between the various fundamental rights must already be guaranteed, but that does not alter the fact that also the court in a case brought before it must investigate whether, in the circumstances of the case, granting the requested measure, in light of the principle of proportionality, does not detract too much from the fundamental right invoked by the accused party. [translation ours]

The decision has since been followed by lower courts; recently, the Amsterdam Court of Appeal held that when an injunction is requested, "a specific balancing of interests, taking into account the circumstances of the case" must be performed.[71] None of these cases were patent cases, but the Supreme Court's holding in *GeenStijl* is not limited to copyright, instead expressly referring to "an intellectual property right". Thus, the authors of this chapter assume that it applies fully to patent cases. Recent decisions in preliminary relief proceedings that devote much attention to the entitlement to injunctive relief may be a sign of things to come also in proceedings on the merits; in Section B, the Court of Appeal's important decision in *Sisvel/Xiaomi* was already mentioned. Another notable example is *Douwe Egberts/Belmoca*, a preliminary relief case before the District Court.[72] The decision contains a lengthy paragraph discussing the circumstances of the case and concluding that, in light of them, the threshold for granting injunctive relief should be set "relatively high".[73] Even if in the context of a preliminary injunction, it is nonetheless

---

reasoning suggests its holding is limited to intermediaries. See also *McFadden/Sony* (CJEU 2016, para. 90).

[69] *GS Media/Sanoma* (HR 2015).

[70] *GeenStijl/Sanoma* (CoA Amsterdam 2013, para. 2.5.5).

[71] *Anne Frank Stichting* (CoA Amsterdam 2018, para. 3.11.2); see also *Gemeente Rotterdam/Stichting Pictoright* (CoA Amsterdam 2017, para. 3.4.3). A weighing of fundamental rights with reference to the proportionality principle was also undertaken in *Moulinsart/Hergé Genootschap* (CoA The Hague 2015, para. 37).

[72] *Douwe Egberts/Belmoca* (Prel. Rel. District Court The Hague 2018).

[73] *Id.*, para. 6.3. The circumstances were that the defendant had already been on the market for two years before the grant date of the patent without having been informed of the application

interesting that the court is so explicit about how the circumstances of the case influence the use of its discretion to impose an injunction, particularly because it found the patent to be invalid so that the paragraph on the threshold for injunctive relief is technically *obiter dictum*.

3. *Implications for Dutch Patent Law*

What are the implications of these developments for the Dutch approach to patent injunctions? It seems that the importance of the Supreme Court's landmark decisions in *Claas/Van Tongeren* and *Kirin Amgen/Boehringer* is substantially diminished. *Claas/Van Tongeren*'s rule that the grant of an injunction is not subject to a balance of interests once the illegality of an act is established appears to be strongly nuanced by the Supreme Court's decision in *GeenStijl/Sanoma*. The holding in *Kirin Amgen/Boehringer* states that third-party interests cannot be protected by allowing patent infringement to continue is at odds with the CJEU's case law in which the fundamental rights of all parties that are affected by an enforcement measure are considered.[74] The waning of these two foundational principles of Dutch patent law opens up new avenues to courts not just to assess whether injunctions constitute proportional measures, but also to tailor them to ensure that they do.

Although the argument has been that Dutch courts ought to assume discretion to refuse an injunction in patent cases more freely, it is not suggested here that they should use this discretion without restraint. To the contrary: a successful patentee ought normally to be entitled to injunctive relief in the vast majority of cases. But it stands to reason that as innovation changes from nineteenth-century inventions to twenty-first-century technology, the role patents should play to foster this innovation also changes. We believe that increased discretion for patent courts when considering remedies is a key development, mandated by the CJEU's case law, to ensure patent law stays in tune with modern innovation.

REFERENCES

Cases

Court of Justice of the European Union (CJEU)

CJEU 12 September 2019, C-688/17 (*Bayer Pharma*)
CJEU 15 September 2016, C-484/14 (*McFadden/Sony*)
CJEU 16 July 2015, ECLI:EU:C:2015:477, C-170/13 (*Huawei/ZTE*)

by the patentee; that the case was a "bet-the-company" case for the defendant on which its future was staked because an injunction would mean its end; that the defendant was a much smaller company than the patentee; and that damages as a result of an unjustified denial of an injunction could more easily be calculated than damages as a result of an unjustified grant of an injunction.

[74] See the explicit reference to third-party interests in *Scarlet Extended* (CJEU 2011, para. 50), and *McFadden* (CJEU 2016, para. 90).

CJEU 27 March 2014, C-314/12 (*Telekabel Wien*)
CJEU 22 January 2013, C-283/11 (*Sky Österreich*)
CJEU 24 November 2011, C-70/10 (*Scarlet Extended*)
CJEU 29 January 2008, C-257/06 (*Promusicae*)

Dutch Supreme Court (HR)

HR 20 December 2019, ECLI:NL:HR:2019:2026 (*X/Y*)
HR 3 April 2015, ECLI:NL:HR:2015:841 (*GS Media/Sanoma*)
HR 15 April 2005, ECLI:NL:HR:2005:AS5238 (*Euromedica/Merck*)
HR 29 November 1996, NJ 1997/684 (*Gommans/Evers*)
HR 15 December 1995, NJ 1996/509 (*Kimberly Clark/Procter & Gamble*)
HR 21 April 1995, ECLI:NL:HR:1995:ZC1705, NJ 1996/462 (*Boehringer Mannheim/Kirin Amgen*)
HR 4 June 1993, ECLI:NL:HR:1993:ZC0986, NJ 1993/659 (*Vredo/Veenhuis*)
HR 24 November 1989, NJ 1992/404 (*Lincoln/Interlas*)
HR 28 June 1985, NJ 1986/356 (*Claas/Van Tongeren*)
HR 16 November 1984, NJ 1985/547 (*Ciba Geigy/Voorbraak*)
HR 25 May 1984, NJ 1984/697 (*Stichting CAI/Columbia Pictures*)
HR 18 February 1966, NJ 1966/208 (*Klokkenspel*)
HR 3 January 1964, NJ 1964/446 (*Lexington*)
HR 21 December 1956, NJ 1957/126 (*Meegdes/Meegdes*)
HR 26 January 1934, NJ 1934, p. 1021 (*X/Y*)

Dutch Courts of Appeals (CoA)

CoA The Hague 17 March 2020, ECLI:NL:GHDHA:2020:711 (*Sisvel/Xiaomi*)
CoA The Hague 24 December 2019, ECLI:NL:GHDHA:2019:3537 (*Philips/Wiko*)
CoA The Hague 2 December 2019, ECLI:NL:GHDHA:2019:3709 (*VG Colours/HE Licenties*)
CoA The Hague 7 May 2019, ECLI:NL:GHDHA:2019:1065 (*Philips/Asus*)
CoA The Hague 27 November 2018, case no. 200.237.828/01 (*AstraZeneca/Sandoz*)
CoA Amsterdam 6 February 2018, ECLI:NL:GHAMS:2018:395 (*Anne Frank Stichting*)
CoA Amsterdam 21 February 2017, ECLI:NL:GHAMS:2017:523 (*Gemeente Rotterdam/ Stichting Pictoright*)
CoA The Hague 27 October 2015, ECLI:NL:GHDHA:2015:2910 (*Moulinsart/Hergé Genootschap*)
CoA Amsterdam 19 November 2013, ECLI:NL:GHAMS:2013:4019 (*GeenStijl/Sanoma*)
CoA Leeuwarden 12 October 2005, ECLI:NL:GHLEE:2005:AU4338, NJF 2005/446 (*Schneider/Cordis*)
CoA The Hague 27 June 2002, published under HR 19 December 2003, NJ 2008/75 (*Roche/ Primus*)
CoA The Hague 4 February 1999, ECLI:NL:GHSGR:1999:AM2684, BIE 1999/90 (*Aralco/ Prefair*)
CoA The Hague 3 February 1994, case no. 93/960 (*Kirin Amgen/Boehringer Mannheim*)
CoA 's-Hertogenbosch 24 February 1987, ECLI:NL:GHSHE:1987:AM1406, BIE 1990/59 (*Gouda Holland/Janse*)

Dutch District Courts (DC)

Prel. Rel. District Court The Hague 28 December 2018, ECLI:NL:RBDHA:2018:15453, BIE 2019/2 (*Douwe Egberts/Belmoca*)

DC The Hague 18 July 2018, ECLI:NL:RBDHA:2018:8777 (*Nikon/ASML*)

DC The Hague 11 April 2018, ECLI:NL:RBDHA:2018:4127 (*AstraZeneca/Sandoz*)

DC The Hague 7 June 2017, ECLI:NL:RBDHA:2017:6136 (*Carl Zeiss/VSY*)

DC The Hague 8 February 2017, ECLI:NL:RBDHA:2017:1025 (*Archos/Philips*)

Prel. Rel. DC The Hague 6 January 2017, ECLI:NL:RBDHA:2017:110 (*DSM/Novozymes*)

Prel. Rel. DC The Hague 17 June 2016, ECLI:NL:RBDHA:2016:6803 (*Becton/Braun*)

DC Amsterdam 21 July 2014, ECLI:NL:RBAMS:2014:4617 (*Media Monkeys*)

Prel. Rel. DC The Hague 17 February 2014, KG ZA 13-1178 (*Ajinomoto/GBT*)

DC The Hague 20 June 2012, ECLI:NL:RBSGR:2012:BW8964 (*Apple/Samsung III*)

DC The Hague 14 March 2012, ECLI:NL:RBDHA:2012:BV8871 (*Apple/Samsung II*)

Prel. Rel. DC The Hague 14 October 2011, ECLI:NL:RBSGR:2011:BT7610, *IER* 2012/10 (*Apple/Samsung I*)

DC The Hague 17 March 2010 (unpublished), case no. HA ZA 08-2522 (*Philips/SK Kassetten*)

DC The Hague 16 December 2009, unpublished case HA ZA 08-2775 (*Sharp/Samsung*)

Prel. Rel. DC The Hague 24 July 2009 (unpublished), request no. KG RK 09-1943 (*Glaxo/Pharmachemie*)

DC The Hague 19 March 2008, ECLI:NL:RBSGR:2008:BH1019, *BIE* 2008/39 (*Monsanto/Cefetra*)

Prel. Rel. DC The Hague 9 November 2005, ECLI:NL:RBSGR:2005:AX8641, *BIE* 2006/47 (*Dutch Mobile/Sisvel*)

Prel. Rel. DC Assen 23 June 2005, ECLI:NL:RBASS:2005:AT8164, *NJF* 2005/291 (*Schneider/Cordis*).

DC The Hague 8 June 2005, ECLI:NL:RBSGR:2005:BA0329, *BIE* 2007/13 (*Schneider/Cordis*)

Prel. Rel. DC The Hague 5 August 2004, ECLI:NL:RBSGR:2004:AQ6495, *IER* 2004/95 (*Medinol/Cordis*)

DC The Hague 17 December 2003, ECLI:NL:RBSGR:2003:AO6764, *BIE* 2004/16 (*Medinol/Boston Scientific*)

Prel. Rel. DC The Hague 26 August 2003 (unpublished), case no. KG 03/835 (*Cordis/Medinol*)

DC The Hague 2 July 2003, ECLI:NL:RBSGR:2003:AO3481, *BIE* 2004/3 (*Bornemann/Houttuin*)

Prel. Rel. DC The Hague 26 October 2001 (unpublished), case no. KG 01-1197 (*Westo/Railtechniek van Herwijnen*)

Prel. Rel. DC The Hague 18 December 1996, ECLI:NL:RBSGR:1996:AM2559, *BIE* 1998/16 (*Huss/Van de Wiel*)

Prel. Rel. DC The Hague 3 May 1995, ECLI:NL:RBSGR:1995:AM2628, *BIE* 1996/83 (*C.R. Bard/TD Medical*)

Prel. Rel. DC The Hague 17 March 1995, ECLI:NL:RBSGR:1995:AK3500, *IER* 1995/28 (*Cook/Fujinon*)

Prel. Rel. DC The Hague 31 March 1994 (unpublished), case no. KG 94/269 (*BT/Plumettaz*)

Prel. Rel. DC The Hague 21 November 1989, *published under* CoA The Hague 25 October 1990, *BIE* 1992/89 (*Schneider/ACS*),

Other

Edwards Lifesciences LLC v. Boston Scientific Scimed Inc [2018] EWHC 1256 (Pat)

Books, Articles and Online Materials

Dijkman, Léon. 2019a. "CJEU Rules That Repeal of Provisional Measure Does Not Automatically Create Liability for Wrongful Enforcement," *Journal of Intellectual Property Law & Practice* 2019: 917–18.

2019b. "Het octrooirechtelijk verbod: heilig huisje in de storm?," *BerichtenIE* 2019: 186–92.

García Perez, Rafael. 2016. "Injunctions in Intellectual Property Cases: What Is the Power of the Courts?," *Intellectual Property Quarterly* 87(1): 87–101.

Gielen, Charles. 1994. *Volghende het rechte oordeel van redene*. Zwolle: W. E. J. Tjeenk Willink.

Husovec, Martin. 2016. "Intellectual Property Rights and Integration by Conflict: The Past, Present and Future," *Cambridge Yearbook of European Legal Studies* 18: 239–69.

Jansen, Kasper. 2017. *GS Onrechtmatige Daad: Executie van kort geding-vonnissen*. Deventer: Wolters Kluwer.

Larouche, Pierre & Zingales, Nicolo. 2018. "Injunctive Relief in the EU – Intellectual Property and Competition Law at the Remedies Stage," in Contreras, Jorge, ed., *The Cambridge Handbook of Technical Standardization Law*. Cambridge: Cambridge University Press.

Ohly, Ansgar. 2009. "Three Principles of European IP Enforcement Law: Effectiveness, Proportionality, Dissuasiveness," in Drexl, Josef, ed., *Technology and Competition: Contributions in Honour of Hanns Ullrich*. Brussels: Larcier.

Schelhaas, Harriet. 2017. *Redelijkheid en billijkheid (Mon. BW A5)*. Deventer: Wolters Kluwer.

Siebrasse, Norman, Sikorski, Rafal, Contreras, Jorge, Cotter, Thomas, Golden, John, Jong, Sang Jo, Love, Brian & Taylor, David. 2019. "Injunctive Relief," in Biddle, Bradford, Contreras, Jorge, Love, Brian & Siebrasse, Norman, eds., *Patent Remedies and Complex Products: Towards a Global Consensus*. Cambridge: Cambridge University Press.

Stierle, Martin. 2019. "Patent Injunctions – Identifying Common Elements," *Zeitschrift für Geistiges Eigentum* 11: 334–61.

Van Nispen, Constant. 1978. *Het rechterlijk verbod en bevel*. Deventer: Wolters Kluwer.

2018a. *Sancties in het vermogensrecht*. Deventer: Wolters Kluwer.

2018b. *GS Onrechtmatige Daad: Commentaar op art. 6:168 DCC*. Deventer: Wolters Kluwer.

Wolters, Pieter. 2013. *Alle omstandigheden van het geval: een onderzoek naar de omstandigheden die de werking van de redelijkheid en billijkheid beïnvloeden*. Deventer: Wolters Kluwer.

12

Poland

Rafał Sikorski and Tomasz Targosz

Injunctive relief can be found in all Polish patent statutes in the twentieth and twenty-first centuries.[1] The Industrial Property Law[2] (IPL) that currently regulates industrial property rights including patents also envisages this form of relief. Article 287 section 1 of the IPL provides that a patentee whose patent has been infringed, as well as exclusive licensees, may – apart from other remedies – demand injunctive relief. Generally, injunctions are perceived as a necessary corollary to patents. Patents, as exclusive rights, provide patentees with exclusivity to use an invention within limits provided in the law. The availability of injunctive relief allows patentees to protect that exclusivity.

Injunctive relief is generally regarded as one of the most important remedies available to the patentee.[3] Most importantly, when granted it allows the patentee to stop further infringement which, if continued, could lead to irreversible consequences for the patent holder.[4] Injunctions can be granted when the infringement is still ongoing or when that infringement has stopped but there is likelihood that the infringer will commence infringing activities in the future.[5] Injunctive relief does not require fault on the part of the infringer. Therefore, it does not matter whether infringement was intentional or merely negligent.

It is generally assumed, often tacitly rather than explicitly, that permanent injunctions should be granted automatically upon establishing infringement. Polish Industrial Property Law does not however require the injunctions to be granted automatically. Article 287 section 1 of the IPL only provides that the patentee *may* demand an injunction in case of infringement. It does not state that the court *must* in such cases grant injunctive relief. Unfortunately, the provisions of Polish law on

[1] Sikorski et al. 2019, 135.
[2] Dz.U. 2017, (poz.) 776, Dz.U. 2018, (poz.) 2302, Dz.U. 2019, (poz.) 501
[3] Du Vall et al. 2017, 618.
[4] Id.
[5] Podrecki & Traple 2017, 389.

patent injunctions are not worded in a similar manner to, for instance, the provisions of US law, where some degree of discretion stems directly from the wording of the patent statute.[6] As will be shown in Sections A and B, Polish law also has tools, including proportionality, that allow for injunctive relief to be applied more flexibly.

So far, however, there are no examples from the case law of the Polish courts where injunctions have been denied or have been tailored to allow for product redesign. Factors such as the nature of the party – for example the fact that a party is a non-practicing entity – have not yet been considered as a justification for denying injunctive relief. As will be shown – this does not mean that tailoring, for instance, would not be possible under Polish law. Rather, the reason for this is that Poland has so far not been a popular venue for patent litigation.

Beginning on July 1, 2020 all intellectual property (IP) disputes will be resolved by specialized IP courts. The reform that introduced specialized IP courts generally abolished the bifurcated system in which infringement proceedings and proceedings related to revocation and invalidity were conducted separately. Interestingly, however, the bifurcated system was not abolished with respect to patents. Thus, although patent infringement disputes will be now adjudicated by specialized IP courts, patents will still be presumed valid unless declared otherwise in separate revocation or invalidation proceedings conducted before the Polish Patent Office.[7] This certainly strengthens the position of patent holders and may also lead to a phenomenon well-known from the German bifurcated patent system and referred to as "an injunctions gap."[8]

Speaking of injunctions, one should not omit interim (preliminary, temporary) injunctive relief. In Polish law, interim relief is regulated in the Civil Procedure Code. Without considering the conditions for obtaining interim relief, it is impossible to properly assess the actual leverage of both the infringer and patentee in the context of a patent dispute. Interim relief – when too easily available – may give significant leverage to the patentee and significantly affect the outcome of a dispute, including the propensity of the defendant to reach an unfavorable settlement agreement. As will be shown later, Polish Civil Procedure Code largely tilts the balance in favor of the patentee.

A. TOOLS ALLOWING FOR FLEXIBILITY IN GRANTING PERMANENT INJUNCTIVE RELIEF

Polish courts have generally not considered the need to apply patent injunctions in a flexible manner. Similarly, Polish patent literature has also only very briefly analyzed

---

[6]   35 USC § 283.

[7]   Targosz 2015, 815.

[8]   On the phenomenon of the "injunctions gap," seen from a German perspective, *see* Cremers et al. 2014.

possibilities for a more flexible approach towards permanent injunctions.[9] Neither the adoption of the TRIPS Agreement, nor the adoption of Directive 2004/48 – which both make express references to the possibility of abuse of IP remedies or the requirements of proportionality[10] – has changed much in this respect.

Courts in other jurisdictions have adopted a more flexible approach towards injunctive relief. They have sometimes denied or tailored injunctive relief in disputes initiated by holders of standard essential patents and patent assertion entities as well as disputes between patentees and manufacturers of complex products implementing numerous patent-protected inventions. In these cases, courts have recognized that injunctive relief may be disproportionately harsh on technology implementers and may also negatively affect the protection of fundamental rights and freedoms such as freedom to conduct business.[11] Consequently, monetary relief was found to be a sufficient remedy for the protection of patentees' interests as well as the primary function of the patent system, namely, promotion of innovation. Unfortunately, because disputes like the ones described have not been initiated before Polish courts, these courts have had no or very little chance to consider injunctive relief more profoundly.

It seems that more and more often, striking a balance between protection of inventions and interests of users will require a more flexible approach towards injunctive relief. It seems that such flexibility could be achieved in a number of ways: Firstly, with the help of the alternative measure defined in Article 287 section 3 of the IPL, the origins of which can be traced to Article 12 of Directive 2004/48. Secondly, abuse of right doctrines, originating both in patent law[12] and the Civil Code,[13] may also be of assistance. Thirdly, competition law[14] – as the experience of other countries clearly shows – may be a useful tool in adapting injunctive relief to the requirements posed primarily by technology standardization and access to standard essential patents. At first glance, this seems to be a set of quite powerful tools, capable of addressing the concerns over patent enforcement already faced by the courts in more popular patent jurisdictions.

However, a deeper analysis shows that relying only on those tools may not suffice. Thus, the crucial question is whether the courts may directly refer to the more general principle of proportionality, based both on EU law – primarily Directive 2004/48 – as well as the provisions of the Polish Constitution. It seems that applying proportionality to patent injunctions would allow for the most comprehensive and systematic approach to justifying denial or tailoring of injunctive relief in cases where granting injunctive relief is not required to safeguard the interests of the rights

---

[9] *See, e.g.,* Du Vall 2008, 410.
[10] Art. 3 and 12 Directive 2004/48; art. 41 TRIPS Agreement.
[11] Sikorski 2019a, 242–47.
[12] Art. 68 IPL.
[13] Art. 5 Civil Code.
[14] Art. 102 TFEU and art. 9 Act on Protection of Competition and Consumers.

holders or the public interest in having a patent system capable of stimulating innovation. Proportionality analysis requires considering interests of the patentee and the implementer, the circumstances of each case – such as the nature and value of the patent-protected technology as well as the circumstances of the particular infringing use, the interests of other parties, fundamental rights and the public interest.[15]

1. *Alternative Measure: Compensation in Lieu of an Injunction*

Article 12 of Directive 2004/48 introduced a measure by virtue of which the courts of the member states may order monetary compensation in lieu of an injunction. Though optional, in Poland Article 12 was implemented in both industrial property and copyright laws. By virtue of Article 287 section 3 of the IPL, the courts may, upon the motion of the liable party, order payment of monetary compensation in lieu of an injunction. This is only possible, however, when certain additional conditions have been satisfied; namely, when the infringer acted unintentionally and without negligence, the execution of an injunction would cause disproportionate harm to the infringer and pecuniary compensation would be satisfactory to the patentee.

This alternative measure has never been used by the courts with respect to patents. There is also no reported case law on its application to other IP rights.[16] Its reception has been much more favorable in legal literature. Scholars and commentators have welcomed the flexibility that comes with the measure,[17] and some have claimed that the measure could be used in disputes with non-practicing entities.[18] When ordering monetary compensation in lieu of an injunction, courts have a substantial degree of discretion.

That discretion would allow the court to tailor the injunctive relief to the circumstances of a given case. Thus, for example, the court would have discretion as to whether to apply the measure at all as well as discretion with respect to the payment arrangements and conditions for use of the relevant invention.[19] In particular, the court could allow use of the invention for a limited period so as to allow redesign or to limit the number of infringing products that could be sold on the market, in particular by allowing only the products already manufactured to be sold.[20]

---

[15] On the factors considered under proportionality analysis *see* Directive (EU) 2016/943 of the European Parliament and of the Council of 8 June 2016 on the protection of undisclosed know-how and business information (trade secrets) against their unlawful acquisition, use and disclosure (Text with European Economic Area (EEA) relevance), OJ L 157, 15.6.2016, 1–18.

[16] Based on searches in leading databases in Legalis and Lex.

[17] Du Vall 2008, 410.

[18] Kubiak 2016, para. 11.

[19] Podrecki & Traple 2017, 415.

[20] Sikorski et al. 2019, 144.

Though the scope of discretion in applying the alternative measure is quite significant, there are boundaries within which such discretion can be exercised. The limitations result particularly from the conditions which must be met if the court is to order monetary compensation in lieu of an injunction. These conditions must be satisfied jointly, which might be difficult in many cases. For example, pecuniary compensation might not be satisfactory for the patentee, if the patentee exploits the patent by manufacturing and selling goods that implement a patent-protected invention or if the patentee grants exclusive licenses only.[21]

The requirement that the infringer acts neither intentionally nor negligently is also problematic. It is not clear when the assessment of the lack of fault should be made. It seems rather that absence or presence of fault should be assessed at the moment the infringement is initiated. Otherwise, if it is assessed at the time court proceedings are initiated, the measure will hardly ever be available for application, as the infringer will usually have been notified of the infringement prior to initiation of proceedings.

In addition, the assessment of the requisite degree of care may be difficult, especially since both jurisprudence and scholarly writings in this area are quite scarce. Though generally there is agreement that the degree of care required depends on the level of distribution or production of a given infringer and that more is required from manufacturers than those operating in distribution channels,[22] it is not entirely clear what standard of care could, for example, be required from a manufacturer of a complex product who uses multiple components obtained from third parties.[23] Should such a manufacturer be treated in the same way as a pharmaceutical manufacturer? Probably not, as it seems quite evident that a pharmaceutical manufacturer will usually be capable of conducting a search of all relevant product, use and process patents at reasonable cost whereas requiring the manufacturer of a complex product to conduct a comprehensive search of all possible inventions implemented in multiple components of such a product could turn out to be unreasonably costly and could also delay entry of new products to the detriment of consumers. However, the lack of case law and scholarly works in this area results in a substantial degree of uncertainty.

In an important case for injunctive relief such as implementation of technologies protected by standard-essential patents (SEPs), the application of the alternative measure will usually be excluded. This is because unlicensed users usually know that they are implementing a standard, so as a result they either know or could easily have learned that they are infringing one or more SEPs. Thus, in this case courts must resort to other tools to justify denying injunctive relief.

---

[21] *Id.*, 143.

[22] Podrecki & Traple 2012, 1407.

[23] Sikorski et al. 2019, 142.

2. *Abuse of Rights Doctrines*

Legal systems generally provide a defense against rights holders who formally act within the limits of their rights as defined in the law, but in a way that is considered abusive.[24] This is achieved by references to sets of non-legal norms introduced through such concepts as morality, fairness, good faith, proportionality and by reference to reasonableness or social and economic functions of particular rights.[25]

Polish law introduces an abuse-of-rights defense in Article 5 of the Civil Code which provides that rights may not be exercised contrary to their socioeconomic purpose and rules of good faith. This provision applies to the exercise of all private rights.[26] Additionally, Industrial Property Law introduced in 2001 an additional patent-abuse defense of its own in Article 68 sections 1 and 2.

Article 68 provides that:

(1) A patentee or a licensee should not abuse their right, in particular by preventing the use of a patented invention by a third party, if such use is necessary to satisfy the demand on the national market, especially when this is in the public interest and the product is not available to the public in proper quantity or quality or is available but at excessively high price.

(2) Preventing third parties from using a patented invention within the period of three years following patent grant shall not be deemed an abuse of right.

Patent abuse within the meaning of Article 68 opens the door to compulsory licenses that are granted by the Patent Office.[27] Article 68 of the IPL provides for a very narrow abuse doctrine. Reference to satisfying demand on the national market suggests that it will be applicable in a very limited number of cases and primarily when public interest is involved.[28] However, abusive exercise of patents does not have to result in not satisfying the demand on the national market. In such cases, the question is whether abusive exercise of a patent that lies outside Article 68 of the IPL could be challenged under Article 5 of the Civil Code.

The application of the general-abuse doctrine, as defined in Article 5 of the Civil Code, to the exercise of IP rights has not generally been questioned by the courts[29] or by commentators in the legal literature. Barta and Markiewicz, for example,

---

[24] Ibid., 144.

[25] Ibid.

[26] Radwański & Olejniczak 2013, 107.

[27] Art. 68 sect. 1(2) IPL.

[28] Du Vall 2008, 291.

[29] *See, e.g.,* Judgment of the Court of Appeals in Warsaw of December 1, 2014, case VI ACa 517/13. The court found that in the circumstances of the case demanding an injunction did not constitute abuse of a patent, but in principle the application of the abuse doctrine was not excluded.

identify a set of factors which could justify the application of Article 5 of the Civil Code to the exercise of both moral and economic rights in the area of copyright.[30] These authors suggest considering whether the right is exercised: (1) without there being a fair and rational justification for such exercise; (2) to cause harm to the other party; (3) in a way that causes a greater burden for other party, when the right could be exercised in a less burdensome manner; (4) in such a manner that the benefits for the rights holder are disproportionate to the burden caused to the other party; (5) in a manner contrary to the right's purpose or function.

Thus, though generally it is accepted that Article 5 may apply to the exercise of IP rights, in the case of patents, things seem to be a bit more complicated. Some authors claim that Article 68 of the IPL precludes the application of Article 5 of the Civil Code to patents.[31] These authors claim that the intention of the legislature was to exclusively regulate the abuse-of-rights defense in IPL. This is a rather controversial conclusion. Article 68 of the IPL has a very different purpose: it regulates abuse of rights that can be detrimental from the perspective of the public interest and which therefore justifies compulsory licensing, whereas an Article 5 of the Civil Code defense does not require a threat to the public interest.

Consequently, one should assume that Article 5 allows for a defense to the exercise of rights by patentees when these are exercised contrary to the principles of good faith. This is the case when patentees induce reliance as to their future conduct but subsequently act contrary to the justified expectations of patent infringers. Thus, according to the literature, it would be abusive to demand an injunction when parties negotiate a license in good faith and with a view to concluding a license agreement and the licensee, in reliance on the ongoing negotiations, already practices the patented technology.[32] It might also be abusive to demand an injunction when the patentee has knowingly tolerated infringement for a period of time only to later exercise its right to cease infringing activities.[33] Equally, it would be abusive to demand an injunction when the patentee has promised to negotiate licenses on certain conditions and later refuses to do so (as in the case of FRAND commitments). In all these cases just described, Article 68 of the IPL would usually be of very little help. However, there is no reason why an Article 5 defense should not apply in such cases.

3. *Competition Law Defense*

Competition law provides a framework for conducting all economic activities on the market. It is also a framework for the exercise of all private rights, including

[30] Barta & Markiewicz 2013, 300–02.
[31] Du Vall 2008, 290; Żakowska-Henzler 2012, 712–13, 730.
[32] Żakowska-Henzler 2012, 729.
[33] Id., 728–29.

patents.[34] Competition law, both national and EU, can provide a defense against patentees seeking injunctive relief. When a patentee holds a dominant position in a given technology market, patent enforcement can, in certain circumstances, constitute an abuse of such a position.[35] Polish and EU law can apply in parallel to a given anticompetitive practice.[36] However, when a given exercise of patent rights does not affect trade between member states, it can only be assessed under national law. Interestingly, national competition law can provide more rigid assessment of unilateral practices than EU law.[37] Generally, Polish competition law provides for similar criteria to EU competition law.[38] However, the experience of Polish courts with cases at the intersection of IP and competition is much smaller than that of the Court of Justice of the European Union (CJEU) or the Commission.

4. Assessment

The tools described above allow a substantial degree of flexibility in the application of permanent injunctions in patent infringement cases. Each of the tools described has some limitations however.

First, the application of the alternative measure, modeled on Article 12 of Directive 48/2004, requires observing very strict conditions. The requirement of lack of fault may preclude the application of that provision even in cases where monetary compensation seems to provide satisfactory relief from the patentee's perspective or where the public interest would override the private interest of the patent owner.

Second, competition law has inherent limitations as well. The application of Article 102 of the Treaty on the Functioning of the European Union (TFEU) (or its national counterparts) requires establishing a dominant market position, which is usually not contested in the case of SEPs, but which may be missing in other typical cases where denying or tailoring of injunctions is usually considered.

Third, the application of the abuse-of-rights doctrine based on the general provisions of the Civil Code's Article 5 is problematic. Indeed, it seems that an abuse-of-rights defense can address a wide, though probably not the whole, spectrum of cases where denying or limiting injunctive relief would be justified. Most importantly, however, the abuse doctrine has always been regarded as an extraordinary measure, one that should find application in exceptional cases only. The problems with

---

[34] Ullrich 2014, 357.

[35] There is quite a significant number of EU Commission and CJEU decisions on the exercise of IP rights that may in certain special circumstances constitute abuse of dominant position. *See, e.g., Microsoft v. Commission of European Communities* (CJEU 2007) (with respect to copyrights in software); *Huawei Technologies Co. Ltd v. ZTE Corp. and ZTE Deutschland GmbH* (CJEU 2015) (with respect to patents).

[36] Art. 3(1) Regulation 1/2003.

[37] Art. 3(2) *in fine* Regulation 1/2003.

[38] Miąsik 2012, 422–95.

injunctive relief are of a systemic nature, as they involve considerations of the central purpose of the patent law, namely its ability to stimulate innovation.

Rigidity and automatism in the application of injunctive relief could result in patents being exercised in a way that may not further the goals of patent law, namely providing a reward to the patentee and more generally stimulating innovation and dynamic competition. Achieving these goals calls for a comprehensive approach from within patent law rather than via measures of exceptional nature found outside of the patent law itself. Seeing the inherent limitations of the tools described, the relevant question seems to be to what extent proportionality could play a role in ensuring a more flexible approach to injunctive relief.

B. PROPORTIONALITY AND PERMANENT INJUNCTIONS

Interestingly, proportionality – derived from both the Polish Constitution and EU law – has already been successfully used by Polish courts in copyright cases, allowing the courts to alleviate the rigidity of some of the monetary remedies available to copyright holders.[39] It has also recently been successfully invoked in a case concerning the right to information under Polish Industrial Property Law. So far it has not been applied directly with respect to injunctive relief in patent cases. However, the analysis of Polish and EU law shows that there are no legal obstacles in applying proportionality to patent remedies, including injunctive relief. In fact, both EU law[40] and the Polish Constitution[41] require that proportionality is considered when deciding whether to grant, deny or tailor injunctive relief.

1. *Proportionality and Industrial Property Law Remedies before the Constitutional Court*

Article 286¹ section 1(3) of the IPL provided industrial property rights holders, including the patentees, with the right to obtain information from parties other than the infringer about the origin and channels of distribution of infringing products. The right to demand information was modeled on Article 8 of Directive 48/2004. However, whereas Article 8 allowed the rights holder to demand information in connection with infringement proceedings, the right to obtain information from third parties enabled information to be gathered irrespective of whether it would later be used in the proceedings against the infringer.

[39] These cases concerned primarily monetary remedies, namely right to remedy loss resulting from copyright infringement by demanding lump-sum payment equivalent to two or three times the amount of reasonable compensation for the use of a copyrighted work – art. 79 Copyright Law.
[40] Art. 3 and. 12 Directive 48/2004.
[41] Art. 31 and 64 Polish Constitution.

This very broad scope of the information right was challenged before the Constitutional Court as limiting the freedom to conduct business guaranteed by Article 22 of the Constitution in a manner that was disproportionate.[42] The court observed that Article 286¹ section 1(3) of the IPL provided for a standalone right to information. It then stated that such a standalone right to information granted to the rights holder may be justified in order to safeguard industrial property rights of rights holders, but since it results in limitation of the third parties' freedom to conduct business, such a limitation must meet the proportionality test described in Article 31 section 3 of the Polish Constitution – which means that it must be adequate, necessary and proportionate *sensu stricto* in the sense that the measure must be the least intrusive one to achieve a legitimate goal.

The court found that the measure did not meet all elements of the proportionality test.[43] In particular it found the measure not to be proportional because it might be used not only for the protection of IP rights in the course of infringement proceedings. The court stressed that once information is obtained, infringement proceedings need not be initiated at all. The court added that the information obtained could later be used outside of IP infringement proceedings and that there were no safeguards against such use. Consequently, the court found that provisions on the right to information were disproportionately limiting the freedom to conduct business of those obliged to disclose the information on origin and channels of distribution of infringing products.

2. *Proportionality and Copyright Law Remedies before the Constitutional Court*

In a number of copyright cases, proportionality of monetary remedies was challenged. Polish copyright law provided the copyright holder whose economic rights were infringed with a choice of monetary remedies. According to Article 79 section 1 (3)(b) of the Copyright Law, the rights holder could either remedy the loss on the basis of general rules of tort law (this would mean that the burden of proof as to the amount of damages as well as fault and causal link, would lie with the plaintiff – the rights holder) or, in the event of a culpable infringement, by demanding payment of three times the amount of the appropriate fee that would have been due if the infringer sought permission from the copyright holder. The appropriate fee, in practice, equaled royalties that would be due had the parties concluded a licensing agreement.

---

[42] Judgment of the Polish Constitutional Court, December 6, 2018, case SK 16/19.

[43] It is interesting that the Constitutional Court in its opinion referred to art. 8 of Directive 2004/48 as the source for the Polish implementation but did not mention the proportionality principle in art. 3 of Directive 2004/48. The whole reasoning is based on the disproportionate character of the remedy in light of the provisions of the Polish Constitution.

The constitutionality of the lump-sum payment remedy was challenged before the Constitutional Court.[44] The main thrust of the claim lay in the argument that the remedy resulted in unduly harsh (disproportionate) consequences for the infringer. This in turn led to different standards of protection of property of the rights holder and infringer unjustly favoring the rights holder. Equal protection of property (Article 64), the equal treatment clause (Article 32) and the principle of proportionality (Article 31) were the legal basis for the constitutional challenge. The court agreed that infringement, if it leads to loss for the copyright holder, must also have negative consequences for the infringer. These consequences should not exceed certain limits however. The court found the right to a lump sum in the amount of three times the appropriate remuneration leads to disproportionate harm to the infringer and found that part of Article 79 section 1(3)(b) of the Copyright Law to be unconstitutional.

Later the Constitutional Court was asked to assess the validity of the right to payment of a sum corresponding to double the amount of fee that would have been paid had the rights holder given permission for the work to be used (Article 79 section 1(3)(b) of the Copyright Law).[45] Just as in the previous case, the appropriate fee corresponds to the amount of royalties that would be due had the parties concluded a licensing agreement. This remedy is available also when there is no fault on the part of the infringer. Again, the disproportionate nature of the remedy was the basis for the challenge of its constitutionality. And again, the principle of proportionality was derived from the Constitution rather than EU law. This time the court found that the right to demand double the amount of the appropriate fee would not be disproportionate from the perspective of the constitutional standards.[46]

3. *Proportionality and IP Remedies before the Supreme Court*

Of course, injunctive relief *as such* does not raise questions with respect to its compliance with the constitutional norms. In the case of injunctive relief, its disproportionate character becomes apparent only in certain types of IP infringement cases. Therefore, the issue is not whether injunctive relief is constitutional as

---

[44] Judgment of the Constitutional Court of June 23, 2015, case SK 32/14.

[45] Decision of the Supreme Court of April 9, 2019, case V CSK 108/18.

[46] Judgment of the Constitutional Court of November 5, 2019, case P 14/19. Interestingly, the CJEU in *OTK* v. *SFP* dealt with the right to demand double fees prior to the decision of the Constitutional Court and found the remedy to comply with the provisions of Directive 48/2004. The CJEU was persuaded by the arguments raised by the Polish government during the proceedings that the remedy of a lump sum in the amount of double compensation was not automatic and could be refused, especially if the court finds that the copyright holder abused its rights see *OTK* v. *SFP* (CJEU 2017), para. 31. These two cases raise an interesting issue as to whether and to what extent the assessment under "constitutional proportionality" might be different from the assessment under "EU proportionality." In the case of the remedy to claim double compensation, the assessment under both principles of proportionality led the CJEU and Polish Constitutional Court to the same results.

such, but whether it is constitutionally applied in particular circumstances when it leads to disproportionate hardships for the IP-infringing defendants. Consequently, one has to ask whether the provisions of Polish law which provide for injunctive relief could be applied in such a way that would allow courts some flexibility in the application of that remedy so as to avoid unconstitutional results.

Polish courts are bound by the provisions of the Constitution. It is no different in the case of the constitutional provisions on proportionality, equal protection of property or freedom to conduct business. Courts are obliged to interpret and apply the statutes in a manner that would comply with the provisions of the Constitution[47]. Thus, if in a particular case the application of a remedy would be disproportionate the court should avoid applying a remedy in such a manner. In a patent dispute, for example, if the court establishes patent infringement but at the same time finds that an injunction would be a disproportionate limitation on the constitutionally protected freedom to conduct business – as would be the case with a SEP implementer – then the court should not grant an injunction.

Polish courts, by virtue of also being EU courts, are bound to interpret and apply their laws in a manner that complies with the provisions of EU law. This covers interpretation in a manner that complies with the EU directives, including Directive 2004/48 and its Article 3, which explicitly requires that remedies in IP law be applied in a proportional manner. The CJEU has repeatedly confirmed the obligation of member state courts to observe proportionality,[48] firstly in a copyright case concerning intermediary liability,[49] and later also in trademark cases –*L'Oreal and Others*[50] and more recently *Hilfiger*.[51]

As the analysis conducted so far shows, the duty of the courts to consider proportionality has very strong basis in both the Constitution and EU law. In fact, the courts have already resorted to the principle of proportionality to deny the application of various remedies in a number of IP cases. Interestingly, it is not always clear whether the courts invoke the Polish Constitution or EU law as the source for this requirement of proportionality. As the case law analysis later in this section shows, sometimes the courts refer to proportionality or the potential disproportionate effects of a remedy without making a direct reference to the source for the proportionality analysis, while on other occasions the courts directly refer Article 3 of Directive 2004/48. What is more, the courts invoke proportionality when deciding on the application of various types of remedies, both pecuniary (damages) and

---

[47] Gutowski 2018, 95–97.
[48] *See also* the presentation by Lord Justice Arnold, who discusses the cases in the following footnotes in Ludwig-Maximillians Universitat International Conference on "Injunctions and Flexibility in Patent Law," see www.en.zr11.jura.uni-muenchen.de/conference-april/index .html.
[49] *Promusicae* (CJEU 2008).
[50] *L'Oreal and Others* (CJEU 2011).
[51] *Hilfiger* (CJEU 2016).

nonpecuniary (injunctions, publication of judicial decisions or statements by infringers).

In case I CSK 563/13,[52] the Supreme Court dealt with a dispute between a software producer and software user concerning the unauthorized use of software. The plaintiff claimed damages and publication of the court decision establishing copyright infringement in one of the national journals as well as on the websites of the defendant and the journal. The court of first instance ruled for the plaintiff. The case was appealed, and the appeals court lowered the amount of damages but otherwise upheld the first-instance ruling. The case was further appealed to the Supreme Court. In its decision, the Supreme Court vacated the decision of the appeals court and explained what factors should be considered by the appeals court when deciding upon the remedies.

In its opinion, the Supreme Court observed that the provisions of the copyright law on remedies available to the rights holder in case of copyright infringement were worded in a very general manner. The court emphasized that these remedies find application to all types of copyright infringements, and when applied in a particular case they need to be adapted to the circumstances of that case. The Supreme Court observed that in each case, the nature of infringement, its intentional or negligent character, effectiveness of protection and proportionality of a remedy must be considered.

In case V CSK 203/12,[53] the Supreme Court dealt with a dispute between a cable network operator and a collecting society representing holders of copyrights to audiovisual works. Polish copyright law requires cable network operators to conclude licensing agreements with collecting societies. Such societies have an obligation to conclude licensing contracts with all willing licensees. The cable network operator and the collecting society were initially bound by the licensing agreement. The collecting society terminated the agreement and proposed to conclude a new contract with higher royalty fees. The parties were unable to conclude a new agreement because they differed with respect to royalty rates.

The collecting society sued and obtained an injunction against the defendant cable operator from the first-instance court. The injunction was later upheld by the appeals court. The injunction was a sweeping one. The court ordered the cable network operator to cease retransmissions of all audiovisual works, even though the collecting society had rights to represent copyright holders of only some of the audiovisual works. Thus, the injunction did not distinguish between audiovisual works whose retransmission required entering into a licensing agreement with the plaintiff and works which could be retransmitted without the permission of the plaintiff.

---

[52] Judgment of the Supreme Court of October 9, 2014, case I CSK 563/13.
[53] Judgment of the Supreme Court of March 27, 2013, case V CSK 203/12.

The Supreme Court again pointed to the fact that the provision on injunctive relief in the copyright law is formulated in a very general manner. Thus, when the remedy is applied, the court has to take into account particular circumstances of the case. Otherwise, there is a risk that the remedy will be disproportionate, excessively burdensome for the defendant and not adequate. The court also added that injunctions that are formulated too broadly affect the freedom to conduct business.

Case V CSK 102/11[54] concerned yet another dispute between a collecting society and a cable network operator. The case is very similar to the case already discussed, but it is interesting because the court in its opinion referred directly to Directive 2004/48 as the source of an obligation to consider proportionality when deciding on the remedies.

The court very clearly pointed to the fact that although EU directives were not capable of producing direct effect in disputes between private parties, even in such cases member state courts were obliged to interpret and apply their own national laws in compliance with the provisions of those directives. Consequently, said the Supreme Court, in copyright cases courts should also interpret the provisions on copyright remedies in the copyright law in a way that complied with the general principles set out in Article 3 of Directive 2004/48. The court cited Article 3 of Directive 2004/48 when stating that the remedies should be fair and equitable, effective, proportionate, dissuasive and applied in a manner so as to avoid barriers to legitimate trade and should also provide safeguards against their abuse.

As these cases show, courts in various cases resort to proportionality to justify granting remedies in IP disputes or to define the scope of the remedies granted. So far, proportionality has mostly been used in copyright disputes, but there are absolutely no reasons for not resorting to proportionality in the case of all other remedies including injunctive relief. Courts have also cited both national constitution or EU law as the source of proportionality, but it seems that the source does not influence how proportionality is understood and later applied by the courts. Thus, there are no substantive differences in the understanding of what proportionality means. Certainly, Polish law does not require automatism in granting injunctive relief in patent infringement cases. No provision of the Polish Industrial Property Law requires that an injunction be granted in all cases where patent infringement is established, and the plaintiff files a claim for injunctive relief. Thus, there are no legal obstacles to adopting a more flexible approach towards injunctive relief in patent law that includes denying such relief or tailoring it to the circumstances of a particular case.

C. ENFORCEMENT OF PERMANENT INJUNCTIONS

A decision of the first-instance court is not final. As such it cannot be enforced. It may however become final if not appealed in due time. Otherwise, only the

---

[54] Decision of the Supreme Court of March 8, 2012, case V CSK 102/11.

decisions of the second-instance courts are final and enforceable. When injunctive relief is granted, and the infringer does not comply with an injunction, the patentee may initiate enforcement proceedings. Such proceedings are conducted within the framework provided by the provisions of the Code of Civil Procedure. The primary objective of the enforcement proceedings in case of a permanent injunction would be to make the infringer obey the injunctive order.

There are two ways to enforce an injunction. Firstly, the patentee may ask the court to impose a fine on the noncompliant defendant.[55] Secondly, the patentee may ask the court to order the defendant to pay a specified amount of money to the patentee for each case of infringement.[56]

In the first case, if the court finds that the defendant has not complied with a permanent injunctive order, it will impose a fine in the amount not exceeding 10,000 Polish PLN (ca. €2,300). Separate fines may be imposed for each case of infringement. The total amount of fines may not exceed 1,000,000 Polish PLN[57] (ca. €230,000). Failure to pay the fine may lead to imprisonment.[58] Total period of imprisonment may not exceed six months. In the second case, the patentee may demand that the court orders the noncomplying defendant to compensate the patentee for each case of infringement. The court has a substantial degree of discretion when deciding on the amount of monetary compensation. However, such compensation should on the one hand deter the infringer, and on the other hand should not be unnecessarily burdensome, yet be capable of providing the patentee with adequate satisfaction.[59]

D. PRELIMINARY INJUNCTIONS

1. *General Picture*

Preliminary injunctions are very important in Polish patent litigation practice. While there is no available statistical data, most litigators would struggle to recall a patent dispute where the patent owner has not applied for a preliminary injunction. Most aspects of the preliminary injunction procedure are favorable to the patentee. Some of the reasons may be explained by the law, but the attitude on the part of the courts seems to be even more significant.

There are no special rules on preliminary injunctions in patent law, or even in intellectual property law.[60] Consequently, courts must act within the general

---

[55] Art. 1051 § 1 CCP.
[56] Art. 1051¹ § 1 CCP.
[57] Art. 1052 CCP.
[58] Art. 1053 § 1 CCP.
[59] Adamczuk 2015.
[60] A first reading of the relevant statutes could suggest otherwise, but these appearances are misleading. *See* Targosz 2019, 66 ff. This is mostly because in industrial property law the applicable provisions misleadingly call the right of information a preliminary injunction.

framework of the Code of Civil Procedure (CCP),[61] which has a chapter on interim relief.[62] These provisions are mostly broad and rely on open concepts. There are two main requirements for the applicant to show: (a) credibility of the claim and (b) legal (legitimate) interest. The credibility of the claim is often described in a rather hazy manner, resorting to *idem per idem* definitions (e.g. "Making a claim credible means justifying ... the assumptions about the existence of a claim to be secured, which creates a conviction of its probability")[63] but it is, in essence, the question of probability.[64] In the main proceedings (on the merits) the plaintiff must prove the claim, whereas in preliminary injunction proceedings it suffices that the claim look credible. Of course, even the former is in fact only a probability assessment, though the probability must be fairly high to justify a preliminary injunction.[65] The leading works in the field of civil procedure[66] show a surprising lack of awareness when it comes to the differences between the required standard of evidence known as "proving the case" and a less demanding standard such as making a claim credible. It is often difficult to infer from them more than that the latter is lower than the former. One could probably settle with the assessment that the credibility of the claim is tantamount to stating that the probability of the applicant's claim being justified is higher than the opposite conclusion. Credibility of the claim in patent infringement cases must be referred to the necessary conditions of a successful claim, i.e. that the applicant owns the infringed right, the defendant/respondent has undertaken actions typically falling within the scope of protection (selling, offering, manufacturing, etc.) and such actions would infringe the litigated patent claims. Since making a claim credible is a lower standard than proving infringement in the main proceedings, types of evidence usually insufficient in the proceedings on the merits (especially private expert opinions)[67] are deemed admissible. The terminology used (credibility of the *claim*) is not accidental. In Poland, it is understood that in any civil litigation, the plaintiff/applicant pursues rights resulting

[61] Kodeks postępowania cywilnego, Journal of Laws 1964 No. 43, it. 296, consolidated text Journal of Laws 2019, it. 1460.
[62] Part II, art. 730 ff.
[63] Jagieła in Marciniak & Piasecki 2015. In the same vein, Jakubecki 2002, 267 (defining credibility as a "justified conviction that the claim exists").
[64] Iżykowski 1980, 73.
[65] In Poland, even in civil cases it is assumed that to prove the case goes beyond the standard of preponderance of evidence, although it cannot, for obvious reasons, mean absolute certainty (no matter what courts and commentators have to say on this matter).
[66] These are often commentaries to the code of civil procedure written by practicing judges.
[67] In civil and commercial litigation in Poland, an expert opinion commissioned by a party, even from a very respected expert, is not regarded as a proper "expert opinion," for the latter must be requested by the court. However, since preliminary injunction proceedings do not have to meet all the requirements of the proceedings on the merits, private expert opinions are widely used.

from substantive law. These are then translated into procedural claims. For example, a patentee whose patent has been infringed has a right to demand that the infringement be stopped. The remedy satisfying this purpose is an injunction. In court proceedings, the patentee files a claim for an injunction, and it is this claim that must be (in preliminary injunction proceedings) made credible.[68]

The requirement of legitimate interest is intended to restrict preliminary injunctions to cases in which the applicant could not achieve the legitimate goals of litigation if it were necessary to wait for the final verdict on the merits[69] (sometimes involving a delay of a few years). The concept of legal interest is very broad (which is in no way specific to IP cases) and may accommodate various considerations related to the need for a court intervention before the final verdict is delivered. In patent infringement cases this addresses situations in which the applicant may lose a large part of the market to an infringing entrant if the infringement is not immediately halted.

As a third layer of legal assessment, preliminary injunctions should strike a balance between offering effective protection to the applicant and avoiding excessive burdens on the respondent.[70] This provision may be read, at first glance, as explicitly introducing the principle of proportionality into the law on interim relief. Its literal interpretation, however, would suggest that proportionality and balancing are only applicable to the scope of the injunction, not the decision whether to grant it in the first place.

Any decision granting or refusing a preliminary injunction may be appealed[71] and there is also a separate measure to have a final injunction revoked due to a change of circumstances.[72]

The general picture of the Polish law on preliminary injunctions, including preliminary injunctions in patent matters, would, therefore, seem to be reassuring in that it makes it possible to have a reasonable and just policy of preliminary injunctions.[73] There seem to be enough built-in flexibilities and corrective measures to arrive at fair and balanced decisions. To reveal the reasons why this has not been the case one must go deeper into the details and the, at first glance innocuous, wording of some crucial CCP provisions. As with permanent injunctions (or even more so) it is not the law itself that is (in our view) primarily responsible for a manifest failure to use preliminary injunctions in patent law fairly and efficiently.

---

[68] And "proven" in the main proceedings.
[69] Art. 730[1] para. 2 CCP.
[70] Art. 730 [1] § 3 CCP; Jakubecki 2002, 318–19.
[71] Art. 741 CCP.
[72] Art. 742 CCP.
[73] This might have been one of the reasons why the legislature did not consider it necessary to amend the CCP when implementing the Enforcement Directive. It was argued that the law already in place was in full compliance with art. 9 of the Directive. *See* Targosz & Tischner 2007, 129.

2. *What Tilts the System in Favor of the Patentee*

The first advantage for the patent owner is the fact that preliminary injunction (PI) decisions are made *ex parte*. Although the law allows for a court hearing, this option is rarely used (i.e. the defendant is not notified of the application and cannot present any arguments, either in writing or orally).The court knows only the plaintiff's point of view unless the defendant has diligently monitored the courts where a PI application can be filed[74] and managed to file a reply.[75] While most courts take such replies into account, some reject the very idea, arguing that the applicable procedure makes no mention of them.[76] Protective briefs are not known as a legal institution.[77] For a non-specialized judge, a well-prepared PI request is hard to resist. To this, a factor rarely featuring in the theoretical analysis should be added: the standards of lawyers' professional integrity. It is unfortunately not unheard of that in preliminary injunction applications applicants present a distorted picture of their case, which exacerbates the usual consequences of the *ex parte* system.

One of the reasons that courts are reluctant to hear the defendant's side of the story is the expectation of speed. Since Polish courts are, for various reasons, not particularly fast,[78] a simple step of, e.g., holding a short hearing during which the respondent could present its case is usually barred by insurmountable organizational obstacles.[79] Consequently, to issue a decision promptly (as is expected in preliminary injunction cases) often *requires* the court to look only at the application.

---

[74] There are often more than one, e.g., the court of the defendant's seat or the court of the place where the damage occurred or where the action causing damage was taken.

[75] This monitoring has become harder since the Supreme Court held in its resolution of December 15, 2017, III CZP 82/17 that courts of the place where the damage occurred also have jurisdiction to hear tort claims. In patent cases, this may sometimes mean any court in Poland.

[76] Decision of the Regional Court in Łódź, August 12, 2019 r., X GCo 176/19 (unpublished).

[77] The difference between a response to a PI application and a protective brief is that to submit the former, one must know the case file number. A "blind" response will not reach the case files and the judge will not even know it has been filed. The European Commission explains that: "With a protective brief, a defendant fearing to be sued for an IPR infringement (for instance, because it has received a warning letter from the rightholder) informs the competent judicial authorities in advance (i.e. even before an application has been made), why the potential infringement claim is, according to the defendant, not founded. The main purpose of the protective brief is to provide the judicial authorities with as much relevant information as possible, without hearing the defendants once the application for a preliminary injunction has been made, before taking a decision on that application." Communication from the Commission to the European Parliament, the Council and the European Economic and Social Committee. Guidance on certain aspects of Directive 2004/48/EC of the European Parliament and of the Council on the enforcement of intellectual property rights, point 6. https://eur-lex.europa.eu/legal-content/EN/TXT/?uri=celex:52017DC0708

[78] A typical IP case will take approximately 3 years before the first instance and 1.5 years on appeal. A permanent injunction granted in the first-instance decision is not enforceable.

[79] Organizing a hearing where the defendant could reply to the plaintiff's claims would usually take at least weeks, if not months, because courts do not have free time slots into which preliminary injunctions cases could be fitted.

A first-instance decision is not final but is, in principle,[80] immediately enforce-able. Appeals take approximately three months, sometimes longer. In some cases (depending on the characteristics of the market), a preliminary injunction, even wrongly granted, may cause the defendant significant financial harm not only before the final judgment is handed down, but before the respondent's appeal against the preliminary injunction is decided.

The second advantage is that – mainly due to bifurcation – courts rarely take the probability of invalidity into account, not only during infringement proceedings, but also when deciding upon preliminary injunctions. There are exceptions[81] and it is possible to find legal grounds for considering the issues of validity, but it is often simpler for the court to hold that it must treat the patent as valid as long as it formally exists. This issue is, of course, more complex in practice. There are two likely reasons that courts are reluctant to consider validity. The first is often spelled out and may be described as formal. Since courts are not allowed to invalidate patents and are bound by decisions granting patents, it is fairly easy to provide a legitimate legal argument that the question of validity cannot be entertained by a court deciding a preliminary injunction case. Courts usually argue that they must treat the patent as valid as there is a presumption of validity of an administrative decision. They also reason that the only relevant date for assessing the credibility of the claim is the date of the preliminary injunction decision.

There would be a simple way around this impediment, though. Since preliminary injunctions of the type issued in patent infringement proceedings are meant to preserve the current state of affairs until the case on the merits is decided (the Polish legal term for a preliminary injunction is the "securing decision" – the securing part referring to the *secured* claim), it would be straightforward to reason that what the court should really consider is the probability that the applicant will prevail on the merits in the main proceeding. Under this approach, if the patent is likely invalid, the probability of success would be insufficient to warrant a preliminary injunction.

Why, then, has this way out of the bifurcation conundrum not been used? While it is impossible to provide a definitive answer, one can speculate that for a non-specialized court, considering the issue of validity has been even more daunting than understanding the infringement itself. There may of course be exceptional situations in which a judge may start doubting the patent's validity, for example because national patents derived from the same European patent have been declared invalid in a

---

[80] When appealing a preliminary injunction, the respondent may request a stay of enforceability until the appeal is decided. This may be granted (though rather exceptionally) if the court finds the arguments raised in the appeal convincing.
[81] Decision of the Appeal Court in Poznań issued in preliminary injunction proceedings in which the plaintiff sought to enforce a patent of dubious validity, September 1, 2016 r., I ACz 1632/16 (unpublished).

number of jurisdictions, but they are not the norm.[82] Consequently, it is much easier to maintain that the question of validity *cannot* be taken into account.

The full implications of this position are even worse than one might initially guess. Invalidation proceedings before the Polish Patent Office may drag on for years. A scenario in which the plaintiff wins before the patent is invalidated is not that rare. Furthermore, decisions of the Patent Office may be appealed to the Regional Administrative Court in Warsaw, and the judgments of this court can be further appealed to the Supreme Administrative Court. In both cases, the nature of judicial control is formal – administrative courts are not supposed to replace administrative decisions with their own but may quash them if they find violations of procedural or substantive law.[83] Consequently, if the appeal is successful, the matter returns to the Patent Office and the Office must issue a "new" decision. During this time a preliminary injunction will stay in force, even in cases where the same patent has been declared invalid in nearly all other jurisdictions.

The third advantage is more general in nature. As explained, there are two conditions that must be met in order to obtain a PI: the credibility of the claim and legal interest. What is manifestly lacking as a condition of *granting* a PI is what the UK courts refer to as "balance of convenience."[84] In other words, in Poland, the prevailing view is that once the plaintiff/applicant has persuaded the court the infringement is more likely than not and there are reasons why waiting for the final decision will cause harm to the applicant, a preliminary injunction should be granted. The proper balancing is practiced only in the context of deciding the *details* of the provisional measures.[85] Thus, according to this interpretation, a preliminary injunction should be granted even if the overall assessment of all implications of such a grant would speak against it. The balancing is therefore limited to the *how* not the *if* or *whether*. In patent cases, the *how* may of course be relevant, but the room for maneuver is limited. In most instances, preliminary injunctions will simply bar the defendant from continuing the alleged infringement. It should also be stressed that the process of balancing applied to the scope of preliminary injunctions should not be overestimated. In the majority of patent cases there is no sophisticated tailoring of the contours of preliminary injunctions. Courts may, e.g., refuse to order seizure of infringing products or make the enforceability of

---

[82] E.g., Decision of Regional Court in Gdańsk, January 12, 2017, IX GC 1008/14, upheld on appeal. In this case, the patent in question had been revoked by European Patent Office, but due to the suspensive effect of appeal, the decision had not yet become final. The court nevertheless held that invalidity seemed likely and stayed the proceedings.

[83] Hauser et al. 2003, 21.

[84] *Merck Sharp Dohme Corp & Anor* v. *Teva Pharma BV & Anor* (COURT 2012). The EU law term would be "balance of interests" – see Castillo de la Torre 2007, 283.

[85] According to art. 730 § 3 CCP: "When deciding on the type of security or injunction, the court shall take into consideration the interests of the parties to or participants in proceedings insofar as is necessary to provide legal protection to the obligee without excessively burdening the obligor."

the injunction subject to the lodging by the applicant of adequate security. While there are valid reasons why one may have some reservations about the constant "balancing"[86] in the context of permanent injunctions,[87] preliminary injunctions are a different matter. A preliminary injunction in patent litigation constitutes a serious interference with the defendant's business and economic freedom before a final decision on the merits has been reached. Thus, the fact that Polish courts have persisted with a literal interpretation of the law, though a different approach is certainly feasible even without statutory intervention, may signal a worrying trend.

Two other issues revolving around the condition of legal interest complete the patentee-friendly picture. The first is the understanding of the legitimate interest as a situation when the claim cannot wait for the regular decision on the merits. A typical justification, as previously mentioned, is a scenario in which the patentee can lose a substantial market share and future actions for damages may be inadequate to reverse all the consequences of the infringement. Unfortunately, another interpretation of legitimate interest remains popular. It posits that since patents are exclusive rights, the interest of the patentee may lie in the exclusivity being enforced regardless of the economic ramifications of the infringement. Future damages will not restore exclusivity, only repair some consequences of its violation. This argument, when applied in its extreme form, renders the condition of legitimate interest almost meaningless in patent cases. If legitimate interest can be derived from the very essence of the exclusive right, the applicant will always be able to demonstrate it. Again, nothing in our view forces courts to follow such a theory, and it must be stressed that some do not. Alas, many decisions and a large part of legal literature seem oblivious to the unfairness of equating legitimate interest with the exclusivity of IP rights.

The other issue that is usually associated with the requirement of legitimate interest is the urgency of issuing a preliminary injunction.[88] It would appear tacitly settled that the applicant should not wait too long[89] as such delay could raise doubts regarding its legitimate interest. Even this, however, seems to be far from obvious. The dispersion of patent cases and the lack of specialized courts (before July 2021) meant that one can find decisions in which a court would consider the condition of urgency reasonable, but at the same time conclude it has not been expressly mandated by the law and consequently refuse to apply it.[90]

---

[86] According to Lev-Aretz 2014, 640 (stating that "Dr. Annette Kur pointed out, the word 'balance' has become so hackneyed in this context that scholars began referring to it as 'the B word' in her Address at the Columbia Law School Kemochan Center Symposium: Who's Left Holding the [Brand Name] Bag? Secondary Liability for Trademark Infringement on the Internet").
[87] Though we generally endorse it – see Section B.
[88] Targosz 2012, 29; Cieśliński 2011, 856.
[89] No specific timelines have been developed.
[90] Decision of the Regional Court in Łódź, August 12, 2019 r., X GCo 176/19 (unpublished).

It should not come as a surprise that what ultimately fails in Poland as far as preliminary injunctions in patent cases are concerned is the human factor. Polish lawyers often like to complain about the law they have to apply, though in many instances it is more than adequate to the task. There is nothing in the law that would preclude courts from hearing the arguments of the defendant, taking the probability of invalidity into account or looking more closely at the real economic interest the plaintiff has demonstrated in obtaining immediate protection. Yet they rarely do. Even a cursory review of the leading jurisdictions reveals that the attitude Polish courts display in patent cases is, judged against the international background, exceptionally patentee-friendly. It remains to be hoped that the introduction of specialized IP courts[91] will rectify most of the highlighted deficiencies.

E. CONCLUSIONS

The fact that Poland is not one of the major patent jurisdictions in the European Union results in a small number of patent disputes and court decisions. It is therefore still largely a theoretical and abstract intellectual exercise to establish how Polish courts would react when faced with aggressive litigation strategies initiated by patentees.

It seems that at least with respect to permanent injunctions, the Polish legal system would be ready to address challenges posed by litigation initiated with respect to standard essential patents, patent assertion entities or in the case of complex products. Similarly, the Polish legal system would be able to address cases when granting an injunction would raise valid public interest concerns. Proportionality, though not practically tested within the context of patent disputes, is by no means a stranger to Polish courts. First, it is expressly recognized in the Polish Constitution. And because courts should interpret statutes in conformity with the Constitution, proportionality already has affected the manner in which courts apply remedies in IP cases. Secondly, courts do recognize an obligation to interpret national laws in line with EU law. Proportionality, derived from Article 3 of Directive 48/2004, has also already been a factor in IP litigation.

Finally, in the Polish courts interim injunctive relief seems to be immune to proportionality concerns. Though Polish courts could theoretically apply preliminary injunctions in a manner that would take into account the interests of alleged infringers, legislative changes are likely to be necessary to change the long-standing practice of granting interim injunctions in what seems to be the most extreme version of *ex parte* proceedings.

---

[91] These courts started operating in July 2020. Only one court (in Warsaw) has been designated to hear patent cases.

REFERENCES

Cases

Judgment of CJEU of January 29, 2008, case C-275/06 *Promusicae*, ECLI:EU:C:2008:54
Judgment of CJEU of July 12, 2011, case C-324/09 *L'Oreal and Others*, ECLI:EU:C:2011:474
Judgment of CJEU of July 7, 2016, case C-494/15 *Hilfiger*, ECLI:EU:C:2016:528
Judgment of CJEU of January 25, 2017, case C-367/15 OTK v. SFP, ECLI:EU:C:2017:36
Judgment of the Constitutional Court of June 23, 2015, case SK 32/14, OTK-A 2015/6/84
Judgment of the Constitutional Court of November 5, 2019
Judgment of the Polish Constitutional Court, December 6, 2018, case SK 16/19, OTK-A 2019/71
Judgment of the Supreme Court of March 8, 2012, case V CSK 102/11, LEX nr 1213427
Judgment of the Supreme Court of March 27, 2013, case V CSK 203/12, LEX nr 1341708
Judgment of the Supreme Court of October 9, 2014, case I CSK 563/13, LEX nr 1573966
Judgment of the Court of Appeals in Warsaw of December 1, 2014, case VI ACa 517/13, LEX nr 1729679
Decision of the Appeal Court in Poznań, September 1, 2016 r., I ACz 1632/16 (unpublished)
Decision of the Regional Court in Gdańsk, January 12, 2017, IX GC 1008/14 (unpublished)
Resolution of the Supreme Court of December 15, 2017, III CZP 82/17, OSNC 2018/10/93
Decision of the Supreme Court of March 8, 2012
Decision of the Supreme Court of April 9, 2019, case V CSK 108/18, LEX nr 2642768
Decision of the Regional Court in Łódź, of August 12, 2019, X GCo 176/19 (unpublished)
Judgment of the England and Wales High Court (Patents Court) of March 15, 2012, *Merck Sharp Dohme Corp & Anor v. Teva Pharma BV & Anor.*
Microsoft v. Commission of European Communities (CJEU 2007)
Huawei Technologies Co. Ltd v. ZTE Corp. and ZTE Deutschland GmbH (CJEU 2015)
Merck Sharp Dohme Corp & Anor v. Teva Pharma BV & Anor (COURT 2012)

Books, Articles and Online Materials

Adamczuk, Andrzej. 2015. "Commentary to Art. 1051," in Małgorzata Manowska ed., *Kodeks postępowania cywilnego. Komentarz. Tom II* (3rd ed.). Warszawa: Wolters Kluwer.
Barta, Janusz & Markiewicz, Ryszard. 2013. *Prawo autorskie*. Warszawa: Wolters Kluwer.
Castillo de la Torre, Fernando. 2007. "Interim Measures in Community Courts: Recent Trends," *Common Market Law Review* 44(2): 273–353.
Cieśliński, Marcin M. 2011. "Kilka uwag na temat interesu prawnego w udzieleniu zabezpieczenia," in Jacek Gudowski & Karol Weitz eds., *Aurea praxis aurea theoria. Księga pamiątkowa ku czci Profesora Tadeusza Erecińskiego. Tom 1*. Warszawa: Wolters Kluwer.
Cremers, Katrin, Gaessler, Fabian, Harhoff, Dietmar & Helmers, Christian 2014. "Invalid but Infringed? An Analysis of Germany's Bifurcated Patent Litigation System." http://ftp.zew.de/pub/zew-docs/dp/dp14072.pdf
Du Vall, Michał 2008. *Prawo patentowe*. Warszawa: Wolters Kluwer.
Du Vall, Michał, Traple, Elżbieta, Kostański, Piotr, Ożegalska-Trybalska, Justyna & Podrecki, Paweł. 2017. *Prawo patentowe*. Warszawa: Wolters Kluwer.
Gutowski, Maciej. 2018. "Bezpośrednie stosowanie konstytucji w orzecznictwie sądowym," *Ruch Prawniczy Ekonomiczny i Socjologiczny* (1): 93–109.
Hauser, Roman, Drachal, Janusz & Mzyk, Eugeniusz. 2003. *Dwuinstancyjne sądownictwo, administracyjne. Omówienie podstawowych zasad i instytucji procesowych. Teksty aktów prawnych*. Warszawa-Zielona Góra: Zachodnie Centrum Organizacji.

Iżykowski, Michał 1980. "Charakterystyka prawna uprawdopodobnienia w postępowaniu cywilnym," *Nowe Prawo* (3): 71–81.

Jakubecki, Andrzej 2002. *Postępowanie zabezpieczające w sprawach z zakresu prawa własności intelektualnej*, Kraków: Zakamycze.

Kubiak, Maciej. 2016. "Commentary to Art. 287," in Arkadiusz Michalak ed., *Prawo własności intelektualnej. Komentarz* (1st ed.). Warszawa: C. H. Beck.

Lev-Aretz, Yafit. 2014. "Combating Trademark Infringement Online: Secondary Liability v. Partnering Facility," *Columbia Journal of Law & the Arts* 37(4): 639–47.

Marciniak, Andrzej & Piasecki, Kazimierz eds. 2015. *Kodeks postępowania cywilnego. Tom III. Komentarz do art. 730–1088*. Warszawa: C. H. Beck.

Miąsik, Dawid. 2012. *Stosunek prawa ochrony konkurencji do prawa własności intelektualnej*. Warszawa: Wolters Kluwer.

Michalak, Arkadiusz, ed. 2016. *Prawo własności przemysłowej: Komentarz*. Warszawa: C. H. Beck.

Podrecki, Paweł & Traple, Elżbieta. 2012. "Roszczenia z tytułu naruszenia praw własności przemysłowej," in Ryszard Skubisz ed., *System Prawa Prywatnego. Tom 14B. Prawo własności przemysłowej* (1st ed.). Warszawa:C. H. Beck.

2017. "Roszczenia z tytułu naruszenia praw własności przemysłowej," in Ryszard Skubisz ed., *System Prawa Prywatnego: Tom 14C. Prawo własności przemysłowej*. Warszawa: C. H. Beck.

Radwański, Zbigniew & Olejniczak, Adam. 2013. *Prawo cywilne – część ogólna*. Warszawa: C. H. Beck.

Sikorski, Rafał. 2019. "Between Automatism and Flexibility: Injunctions in Twenty-First Century Patent Law," in Rafał Sikorski ed., *Patent Law Injunctions*. Aalphen aan den Rijn: Wolters Kluwer.

Sikorski, Rafał, Andrzejewski, Piotr & Ruchała, Piotr. 2019 "Injunctive Relief in Polish Patent Law," in Rafał Sikorski ed., *Patent Law Injunctions*. Aalphen aan den Rijn: Wolters Kluwer.

Targosz, Tomasz. 2012. "Interlocutory injunctions in IP Disputes under Polish Law," in Horst-Peter Götting, Michał du Vall & Heike Röder-Hitschke eds., *Enforcing Intellectual Property Rights*. Baden-Baden: Nomos.

2015. "Ustanie wyłączności," in Ewa Nowińska & Krystyna Szczepanowska-Kozłowska eds., *System Prawa Handlowego. Tom 3. Prawo Własności Przemysłowej*. Warszawa: C. H. Beck.

2019. "Zabezpieczenie roszczeń w prawie własności intelektualnej – przesłanki udzielenia i specyfika postępowania," *Transformacje Prawa Prywatnego* (1): 99–142.

Targosz, Tomasz & Tischner, Anna. 2007. "Dostosowanie polskiego prawa własności intelektualnej do wymogów prawa wspólnotowego. Uwagi na tle projektu z dnia 24 maja 2006 r. ustawy o zmianie ustawy o prawie autorskim i prawach pokrewnych oraz o zmianie innych ustaw," *Zeszyty Naukowe UJ* (1): 79–144.

Ullrich, Hanns. 2014. "Mandatory Licensing under Patent Law and Competition Law: Different Concerns, Complementary Roles," in Reto M. Hilty & Kung-Chung Liu eds., *Compulsory Licensing – Practical Experiences and Ways Forward (MPI Studies on Intellectual Property and Competition Law, 22)*. Berlin: Springer.

Żakowska-Henzler, Helena. 2012. "Nadużycie patent," in Ryszard Skubisz ed., *System Prawa Prywatnego. Tom 14A. Prawo własności przemysłowej*. Warszawa: C. H. Beck.

13

United Kingdom

Lionel Bently and Sir Richard Arnold

A. THE JURISDICTION OF THE COURTS TO GRANT INJUNCTIONS IN PATENT CASES

Most UK patent litigation takes place in England and Wales, where it is heard by either the Patents Court (larger, more complex and/or more valuable cases) or the Intellectual Property Enterprise Court (smaller, less complex and/or less valuable cases). These are both specialised courts. It is normal in both courts for issues of infringement and validity of the patent to be heard together. The intellectual property bar in England and Wales consists of a considerable number of highly specialised and skilful advocates, most of whom have a Science, Technology, Engineering and Mathematics (STEM) degree as well as a legal qualification. They are instructed by both large multinational firms and small boutique firms of lawyers, and they are well known for being innovative, particularly with regard to procedural questions. Although there is a reasonable volume of UK patent litigation, disputes concerning injunctions are relatively infrequent.

Section 61(1) of the Patents Act 1977 provides:

> Subject to the following provisions of this Part of this Act, civil proceedings may be brought in the court by the proprietor of a patent in respect of any act alleged to infringe the patent and (without prejudice to any other jurisdiction of the court) in those proceedings a claim may be made –
>
> > (a) for an injunction or interdict restraining the defendant or defender from any apprehended act of infringement.

This jurisdiction is not new. Injunctions have been granted in cases of infringement of patents since (at the very least) the eighteenth century.[1] Until the second half of the nineteenth century, such relief was only granted by the Court of Chancery, whereas patent cases were tried in Courts of Law. After the Judicature

---

[1] For an early treatment, see Hindmarch 1846, 361.

Acts, all branches of the High Court could grant injunctive relief. This jurisdiction is now recognised by section 37 of the Senior Courts Act 1981,[2] which states that the High Court "may by order (whether interlocutory or final) grant an injunction … in all cases in which it appears to the court to be just and convenient to do so". Provided the court has *in personam* jurisdiction over the person against whom an injunction, whether interlocutory or final, is sought, the court has power to grant it.[3] Nevertheless, the grant of injunctive relief is frequently described as being an "equitable remedy", and therefore as being discretionary. This does not mean that injunctions are granted arbitrarily; they are granted in accordance with established principles. It does mean that those principles have evolved over time and can be adapted to deal with new situations.[4]

1. *Final Injunctions*

In *Coflexip SA v. Stolt Comex Seaway MS Ltd*, Aldous LJ explained the basic principle that a patentee who succeeds in establishing infringement will normally be entitled to a final injunction (also known as a permanent injunction, although such an injunction will expire when the patent expires, as discussed in Section H.1):[5]

> Where a patentee has conclusively established the validity of his patent and that it had been infringed, as a general rule an injunction will be granted. However that will not happen as a matter of course as an injunction is a discretionary remedy. It is for that reason there have been cases where injunctions have been refused, for example, where the defendant satisfied the court that further infringement was not likely.

A final injunction may also be granted, even if the defendant has not yet infringed, if there is a sufficiently strong probability that the defendant will infringe unless restrained.[6]

2. *Interim Injunctions*

Interim injunctions (also known as interlocutory injunctions, preliminary injunctions or temporary restraining orders) are also available even though infringement

---

[2] See *Fourie* v. *Le Roux*, [2007] UKHL 1, [2007] 1 WLR 320, [25] (Lord Scott of Foscote).

[3] *Id.* [30].

[4] See in particular *Cartier International AG* v. *British Telecommunications plc* [2018] UKSC 28, [2018] Bus LR 1417 (holding that the High Court had power to grant injunctions requiring internet service providers to block access by their subscribers to infringing websites regardless of European law).

[5] [2001] RPC 182, 186. For the suggestion that the Court of Chancery had a duty to award an injunction where validity and infringement of a patent had been established at Law, see *Bridson* v. *McAlpine* (1845) 8 Beav 229, 230, 50 ER 90, 90 (Lord Langdale MR) and *Davenport* v. *Jepson* (1862) 4 De G F & J 440, 446, 45 ER 1252, 1257 (Turner LJ).

[6] See *Merck Sharp & Dohme Corp.* v. *Teva Pharma BV* [2013] EWHC 1958 (Pat), [2014] FSR 3.

has yet to be established. Historically, such relief was granted quite readily.[7] Today interim injunctive relief may be granted on the basis of the principles elaborated in *American Cyanamid Co. v. Ethicon Ltd.*[8] In *American Cyanamid* the claimant sought interim relief to restrain the defendant from infringing the claimant's patent for surgical sutures. The defendant company planned to argue at trial either that it had not infringed or that the claimant's patent was invalid. When considering whether to grant interim relief, the High Court and the Court of Appeal said that the key question was whether the claimant had established a strong prima facie case. In the High Court, Graham J found that the claimant had established a strong prima facie case and that the balance of convenience favoured the grant of interim relief. In the Court of Appeal, where argument had lasted for two weeks, Russell LJ held that no prima facie case of infringement had been proved, and so did not go on to consider the balance of convenience.[9] Overturning this approach, the House of Lords rejected previous suggestions to the effect that a prima facie case must be established before a court could grant interim relief. Instead, the Lords laid down a reduced threshold requirement: for a court to be vested with the discretion to grant an interim injunction, it was only necessary for a claimant to establish that there was "a serious question to be tried". Once a claimant has established this, the House of Lords said that the court should then go on to consider a series of other matters. First, it should compare the possible effects of granting and not granting the injunction on the defendant and the claimant. Lord Diplock explained that this involved deciding whether the claimant's or defendant's interests were capable of being satisfied solely by financial means. If these considerations do not produce a clear indication of the best course of action, the court should consider the "balance of convenience". Finally, if there is no clear result from considering the balance of convenience, the court should look at the merits of the case.

The goal of *American Cyanamid* was to reduce the number of mini-trials that occurred at the interim stage and thereby speed up the process of granting interim

---

[7] See Bottomley 2014. For an early example, see *Boulton v. Bull* (1796) 3 Ves 140, 30 ER 937 (Lord Loughborough LC) (maintaining injunction granted to Boulton even after inconclusive trial of action at law). Eldon LC made it a prerequisite that the patent had been in existence for some time: *Harmer v. Plane* (1807) 14 Ves Jr 130, 33 ER 470 (stating that an injunction would usually be granted if the plaintiff could demonstrate "reasonably long and undisputed possession under color of the patent", but that any such relief would be dissolved where there was "such strong doubt" as to the validity of the patent). In *Hill v. Thompson and Foreman* (1817) 3 Mer 622, 624–25, 36 ER 239, 240 Eldon LC again indicated that preliminary injunctive relief might be appropriate in the case of "an exclusive possession of some duration" but not if the patent were "of yesterday", in which case the Chancery court would send the patentee to a court of law while requiring a defendant to keep an account of sales. From the 1840s, courts became even more cautious, focusing on "balance of inconvenience". Soon after, it became normal for a court to require the plaintiff seeking interim relief to give undertakings to compensate the defendant for losses. See, e.g., *Bridson v. McAlpine* (1845) 8 Beav 229, 230, 50 ER 90, 90 (Lord Langdale MR).

[8] [1975] AC 396.

[9] [1974] FSR 312.

relief. In turn, it was thought that this would avoid duplication and produce a more efficient judicial process.

While the general applicability of *American Cyanamid* to intellectual property cases has been accepted, a number of exceptions have been introduced to the *American Cyanamid* approach. The most important of these was the recognition of the principle that, where the interim decision would be determinative of the action, the approach in *American Cyanamid* is not appropriate.[10] This is because the problem which *American Cyanamid* seeks to redress, namely to minimise the harm when a preliminary decision turns out to have been incorrectly made, does not arise where the preliminary decision is going to be the only decision. In such cases the court should simply do its best to resolve the legal and factual issues on the material available.

In general, however, when considering the grant of interim relief the court should operate in two stages. First, the court should decide whether there is a serious question to be tried. In other words, if the evidence reveals that the claimant does not have any real prospect of succeeding in its claim for a permanent injunction at trial, the court will not even consider the balance of convenience. According to Lord Diplock, when determining whether there is a serious question to be tried, the court should only investigate whether a known cause for action is revealed. In so doing it should take account of points of law that necessarily arise on the facts that are revealed at the interlocutory stage. However, the courts should not embark upon mini-trials of disputed questions of fact or difficult questions of law.

Second, if the court decides that this threshold has been passed, it should then go on to consider whether to exercise its discretion to grant an injunction. That is, it will consider whether it would be fair to grant interim relief. The aim is to reduce the chances of the provisional decision providing an unjust result. In so doing, the court will focus on three factors: whether damages would be an adequate remedy for each party, the balance of convenience, and the relative strength of the parties' cases.

Although strictly persuasive rather than binding on English courts, the Privy Council[11] decision in *National Commercial Bank Jamaica Ltd* v. *Olint Corp* usefully explains the rationale for the approach taken to interim injunctions (albeit in a case concerned with bank accounts). It has been treated as authoritative in patent cases, at least by the High Court.[12] Lord Hoffmann giving judgment for the Privy Council stated:[13]

> The purpose of such an injunction is to improve the chances of the court being able to do justice after a determination of the merits at the trial. At the interlocutory

---

[10] *NWL Ltd* v. *Woods* [1979] 1 WLR 1294.
[11] The Judicial Committee of the Privy Council is the final court of appeal for Commonwealth countries that choose to retain it. It is composed of the same judges who formerly sat in the House of Lords and now sit in the UK Supreme Court.
[12] *Warner-Lambert Company LLC* v. *Actavis Group PTC EHF* [2015] EWHC 72 (Pat), [90]; *Warner-Lambert Company LLC* v. *Sandoz GmbH* [2015] EWHC 3153 (Pat), [82]; *Warner-Lambert Company LLC* v. *Sandoz GmbH* [2016] EWHC 3317 (Pat), [71] (Arnold J).
[13] [2009] UKPC 16, [2009] 1 WLR 1405, [16].

stage, the court must therefore assess whether granting or withholding an injunction is more likely to produce a just result. As the House of Lords pointed out in *American Cyanamid Co v Ethicon* [1975] AC 396, that means that if damages will be an adequate remedy for the plaintiff, there are no grounds for interference with the defendant's freedom of action by the grant of an injunction. Likewise, if there is a serious issue to be tried and the plaintiff could be prejudiced by the acts or omissions of the defendant pending trial and the cross-undertaking in damages would provide the defendant with an adequate remedy if it turns out that his freedom of action should not have been restrained, then an injunction should ordinarily be granted.

He went on:[14]

In practice, however, it is often hard to tell whether either damages or the cross-undertaking will be an adequate remedy and *the court has to engage in trying to predict whether granting or withholding an injunction is more or less likely to cause irremediable prejudice* (and to what extent) if it turns out that the injunction should not have been granted or withheld, as the case may be. The basic principle is that the court should take whichever course seems likely to cause the least irremediable prejudice to one party or the other.

Lord Hoffmann listed a number of matters which the court may take into account:[15]

[T]he prejudice which the plaintiff may suffer if no injunction is granted or the defendant may suffer if it is;
the likelihood of such prejudice actually occurring;
the extent to which it may be compensated by an award of damages or enforcement of the cross-undertaking;[16]
the likelihood of either party being able to satisfy such an award; and
the likelihood that the injunction will turn out to have been wrongly granted or withheld, that is to say, the court's opinion of the relative strength of the parties' cases.

In practice, interim injunctions are relatively rare in patent cases these days, because the courts' preference is to order a speedy trial instead. The principal situation in which interim injunctions are granted is where a generic version of a pharmaceutical product is launched for the first time, since it is generally accepted that this will quickly cause the patentee irreparable harm.[17] In such cases the grant of an interim injunction is frequently combined with an order for a speedy trial.

[14] *Id.*, [17] (emphasis added).
[15] *Id.*, [18].
[16] If there is doubt about whether the claimant will have funds available to compensate the defendant pursuant to its cross-undertaking, a possible solution is to require the claimant to fortify the cross-undertaking in some way, e.g., by obtaining a bank guarantee or insurance bond.
[17] See in particular *SmithKline Beecham plc v. Apotex Europe Ltd* [2003] EWCA Civ 137, [2003] FSR 31. For an exception to this general rule, see *Neurim Pharmaceuticals (1991) Ltd v. Generics UK Ltd* [2020] EWCA Civ 793.

In *Novartis AG* v. *Hospira UK Ltd* the Court of Appeal granted an interim injunction pending an appeal in a case where the patent had been held invalid at first instance (no interim injunction had been granted or was necessary prior to the judgment because the party attacking the patent had given a voluntary undertaking). Floyd LJ explained that, provided the appeal stood a real prospect of success, the principles to be applied in such circumstances were similar to the *American Cyanamid* principles.[18]

3. *Enforcement of Injunctions: Contempt of Court*

If an injunction is granted, breach of the injunction is a contempt of court, which renders the defendant (or in the case of a corporate defendant, its directors) liable to be committed (i.e. imprisoned) for up to two years or have its assets sequestered or fined. Whether the injunction has been breached is an objective question. The defendant's intention (or lack of it) is generally relevant only to the sanction, but the court can dismiss a committal application where it is a disproportionate reaction to a trivial or blameless breach of an order.[19] Because breach of the injunction can be punished in this way, it is not the practice of courts in the United Kingdom to specify in advance payments which must be made in the event of non-compliance, as in some member states of the EU such as France and Germany.

The courts have sometimes expressed discomfort where a motion for committal ends up as, in essence, a question of patent interpretation.[20] Instead of bringing an application that the defendant be committed, a party may apply for a declaration of non-compliance. In *Hotel Cipriani Srl* v. *Fred 250 Ltd*,[21] Arnold J described this as "a low key method of enforcing [an] Injunction", where penal sanctions were clearly inappropriate. Such an application is particularly likely to be appropriate in a case where there is a genuine dispute as to whether the defendant is in breach, e.g., where the defendant has redesigned its product in an attempt to work around the injunction.

B. FORM OF COURT ORDERS IN WHICH INJUNCTIONS ARE GRANTED

1. *Final Injunctions against Primary Infringers*

In *Coflexip SA* v. *Stolt Comex MS Ltd*,[22] Laddie J granted an injunction that specified the zone of prohibited behaviour:

---

[18] *Novartis AG* v. *Hospira UK Ltd* [2013] EWCA Civ 583, [2014] 1 WLR 1264, [41]
[19] *Adam Phones Ltd* v. *Goldschmidt* [2000] FSR 163.
[20] See *Multiform Displays Ltd* v. *Whitmarley Displays Ltd* [1956] RPC 143, 154 (Birkett LJ), 157–58 (Romer LJ), [1957] RPC 260, 262 (Viscount Simmonds).
[21] [2013] EWHC 70 (Ch), [2013] FSR 34, [7]. See also *Illumina Inc.* v. *TDL Genetics Ltd* [2019] EWHC 2405 (Pat).
[22] [1999] FSR 473.

The Defendants and each of them be restrained ... from using or offering for use in the United Kingdom (or in an area designated by Order under section 1(7) of the Continental Shelf Act 1964) a process for laying flexible conduit employing a Flexible Lay System of the design installed in the Seaway Falcon and described in the Defendant's Product and Process Description dated 27th March 1997 which process includes at least one occasion on which the flexible conduit being laid incorporates a rigid accessory (whether made from joined end fittings or not) within its length.

In *Nutrinova Nutrition Specialities & Food Ingredients GmbH v. Scanchem UK Ltd (No. 2)*,[23] Pumfrey J granted an injunction in a narrow form against a good-faith infringer:

It seems to me that if an order in the wide form is made there is a substantial possibility that a difficult question of infringement would have to be decided on a motion to commit. I agree with paragraphs 27 and 28 of Laddie J's judgment in the *Coflexip* case in thinking that it is no answer to this objection to say that it is always open to the defendant to approach the court for a decision that his new course of action does not fall within the scope of the wider form of injunction. To advocate such a course is to assume tacitly that it is more likely that the infringer who has been guilty once will be guilty again. If the facts do not otherwise justify this assumption, it should not be made. I do not think that Scanchem is a willing infringer, and I do not consider that it is guilty of taking a Nelsonian approach to the process operated by its supplier. Since I do not consider that Scanchem has conducted itself in bad faith, I have come to the conclusion that a narrower form of injunction is appropriate. The injunction will be against importing acesulphame K from Beijing Vitasweet. There will be an express liberty to apply to both parties.

On appeal in *Coflexip*, Aldous LJ reasserted the traditional English approach and explained why the normal form of the injunction – that the defendant "be restrained from infringing patent number" – was to be preferred:[24]

It is important that an order, such as an injunction, is drafted so as to set out, with such clarity as the context admits, what may not be done. It is for that reason that the standard form of injunction is in the terms restraining the defendant from infringing the patent. Such an injunction is limited in term and confined to the right given by section 60(1) and (2) of the Patents Act. It also excludes acts, carried out by the defendant and which fall within the ambit of the monopoly, but are excluded from infringement by the Act; for example private use coming within section 60(5)(a) of the Act. Such an injunction is confined to the monopoly as claimed. The claim has been construed by the court with the aid of the parties and in the context of the acts alleged by the plaintiff to infringe and any other potentially

---

[23] [2000] EWHC 124 (Pat), [2001] FSR 43, [20].
[24] *Coflexip SA v. Stott Comex Seaway MS Ltd* [2001] RPC 9, [14].

infringing acts which the defendant wishes to bring before the court. Of course a dispute can arise as to whether acts, not brought before the court, amount to a breach of the injunction. But such a dispute arises against the background where the ambit of the claim and therefore the injunction has been the subject of consideration by the court and has been construed by it.

Later he added:[25] "The usual form of injunction which protects the right established by the patentee, with its ambit construed by the court, does in general provide a fair solution. However each case must be determined on its own facts and the discretion exercised accordingly." Although this is the orthodox form of the injunction, different forms may be appropriate where infringement is, for example, by importation.

In *Sun Microsystems Inc.* v. *M-Tech Data Ltd*, a trademark case concerning parallel imports, Kitchin J awarded an injunction qualified so that the defendants could be informed whether the parts had previously been placed on the market in the EU. In the Supreme Court, Lord Sumption described it as follows:[26]

> In the form that Kitchin J granted it, the injunction restrained only the marketing by M-Tech within the EEA of Sun's trade-marked goods which had not previously been marketed there by Sun or with its consent. There is a proviso designed to ensure that Sun does supply information about the provenance of goods potentially affected by the injunction. Its effect is that the injunction is not to apply to goods marketed by M-Tech unless Sun have confirmed within ten days of being told the serial and part numbers of the goods in question that their records show that they have not been put on the EEA market by them or with their consent.

There is no reason to think the same form of injunction would not have been appropriate had importation of the computer parts been patent-infringing.

Although the Court of Appeal suggested in *Warner-Lambert Company LLC* v. *Actavis Group PTC EHF* that an injunction might be qualified (or even refused) in cases involving infringement of a Swiss form claim by the marketing of a generic pharmaceutical under a so-called skinny label (a marketing authorisation for the old, off-patent use of the drug, but not for the patented second medical use),[27] this suggestion has been rejected by the Supreme Court as a solution to the difficulties posed by such cases, since there would remain problems with the financial remedies which flow from a finding of infringement.[28]

---

[25] *Id.*, [20].

[26] *Sun Microsystems Inc.* v. *M-Tech Data Ltd* [2012] UKSC 27, [2012] 1 WLR 2026, [10].

[27] *Warner-Lambert Company LLC* v. *Actavis Group PTC EHF* [2015] EWCA Civ 556, [2015] RPC 25, [130] (Floyd LJ). See also *Generics (UK) Ltd* v. *Warner-Lambert Company LLC* [2016] EWCA Civ 1006, [2017] RPC 1, [187] (Floyd LJ).

[28] *Generics (UK) Ltd* v. *Warner-Lambert Company LLC* [2018] UKSC 56, [2019] Bus LR 360, [80] (Lord Sumption and Lord Reed), [159] (Lord Briggs), [188] (Lord Hodge), [203] (Lord Mance).

2. *Final Injunction against Indirect Infringer*

In *Grimme Landmaschinenfabrik GmbH & Co. KG v. Scott*, Jacob LJ considered whether a different form of injunction was appropriate in a case of indirect infringement, but concluded that normally it would not be appropriate:[29]

> It might be suggested ... that [the court's] practice should be different in the case of contributory infringement where what is sold by the defendant does not itself infringe and has a non-infringing use. The suggestion might be that the court should modify the injunction so as to try to spell out what it is that the defendant can do. We would not have thought that normally appropriate: it will be up to the defendant to work out how to ensure that there is no ultimate infringement. Of course, if he does take reasonable steps but they turn out unexpectedly to be ineffective, enforcement of the injunction by launching proceedings for contempt of court instead of a fresh action for infringement may be inappropriate: see *Multiform Displays* v. *Whitmarly Displays*.

3. *Interim Injunctions*

In contrast with the form of order granted in final injunction cases, in interim injunctive relief cases it is normal for the court to draw up something more specific. *Terrell on Patents* explains:[30]

> With any injunction or undertaking pending trial, it is desirable that the defendant should know, with as much certainty as possible, what they may, or may not do. This is also in the claimant's interest as any breach is easier to identify and enforce. Accordingly the injunction should be directed towards restraining a specific act in relation to a particular product or process rather than infringing the claimant's patent generally.

Terrell relies on the authority of *Staver Co. Inc. v. Digitext Display Ltd*, a decision of Scott J in a copyright case. There, Scott J had granted an interim injunction against the defendant ordering it not to infringe copyright. Having redesigned its product, the defendant sought to vary the injunction, claiming that the redesign did not infringe. In effect, to determine whether the variant avoided infringement, the court was being asked to rule on the substantive issue. As a result, it was clear to the judge that the original form of the injunction was inappropriate. He explained:[31]

> These difficulties arise out of the form of the injunction. ... Mr. Thorley tells me that the form is one commonly used for interlocutory injunctions in breach of

---

[29] *Grimme Landmaschinenfabrik GmbH & Co. KG v. Scott* [2010] EWCA Civ 1110, [2011] FSR 7, [134].

[30] [2020], 19–261.

[31] *Staver Co. Inc. v. Digitext Display Ltd* [1985] FSR 512, 519.

copyright cases. In my judgment, however, the form is not satisfactory. It is essential that a party who is subject to an interlocutory injunction should know what he can and cannot do pending trial. An order which makes the identification of what is permissible and what is prohibited depend on what happens at trial does not satisfy this requirement ...

The discussion in this case has satisfied me that there are grave objections in principle to the granting of interlocutory injunctions in a form that appears to anticipate the plaintiff's success at trial. In my view, interlocutory injunctions ought, in cases like the present, and perhaps in many other types of case, to identify the prohibited acts in a manner which is not dependent on the resolution of factual triable issues.

The order was varied so that it prevented the manufacture and sale by the defendant of the particular items (which had been made by the defendant) which the plaintiff claimed to be infringing copies or of any colourable adaptation thereof. Since *Staver* v. *Digitext* this practice has generally been followed when granting interim injunctions in intellectual property cases.[32] Thus the order will specify precisely the particular acts which are prohibited (such as selling particular identified goods) rather than merely prohibiting infringement in general terms.

C. DENIAL OF A FINAL INJUNCTION, BUT GRANT OF REMEDIAL MEASURES

Where the defendant has committed an infringement but there is no evidence of an intention to infringe again, no injunction will be granted. Thus in *Proctor* v. *Bayley*, the Court of Appeal reversed the grant of an injunction on the basis that it was unlikely that the defendant would infringe again, since it had already stopped the infringing acts for other reasons. Cotton LJ said:[33]

Where a patent is infringed the patentee has a *prima facie* case for an injunction, for it is to be presumed that an infringer intends to go on infringing, and that the patentee has a right to an injunction to prevent his doing so. Again if there has not been any infringement, but an intention to infringe is shewn, an injunction will be granted. In the present case the Defendants have infringed the patent, but we must look at all the circumstances to see whether there is any ground for inferring that they intend to continue to infringe it. ... Now the circumstances are that the Defendants used four of these [infringing] stokers for a short period, and the use of them was finally discontinued in 1883 on the ground that the Defendants found the machines to be useless. Under these circumstances is there any probability that the Defendants will again infringe the patent? I should say certainly not.

---

[32] See *Celgard, LLC* v. *Shenzhen Senior Technology Material Co. Ltd* [2020] EWCA Civ 1293, [2021] FSR 1 [47] (Arnold LJ) (a trade secrets case).
[33] *Proctor* v. *Bayley* (1889) 42 Ch 390, 398.

Fry LJ said,[34] "an injunction is granted for prevention, and where there is no ground for apprehending the repetition of a wrongful act there is no ground for an injunction".

D. GRANT OF ONGOING ROYALTY/DAMAGES IN LIEU OF FINAL INJUNCTIONS

Section 50 of the Senior Courts Act 1981 now provides: "Where the Court of Appeal or the High Court has jurisdiction to entertain an application for an injunction or specific performance, it may award damages in addition to, or in substitution for, an injunction or specific performance." This jurisdiction is normally traced back to Lord Cairns' Act.[35] It enables the courts to refuse an injunction and award damages instead.

Until recently, the applicable principles were established by the late nineteenth-century nuisance case, *Shelfer* v. *City of London Lighting Co. Ltd*, where the Court of Appeal reversed a decision in which Kekewich J had awarded the lessee of a public house damages rather than an injunction against an electric company in relation to noise and structural damage caused by the latter's engines. There, A. L. Smith LJ said that it was "a good working rule" that:[36]

(1) If the injury to the plaintiff's legal rights is small,
(2) And is one which is capable of being estimated in money,
(3) And is one which can be adequately compensated by a small money payment,
(4) And the case is one in which it would be oppressive to the defendant to grant an injunction: – then damages in substitution for an injunction may be given.

On the facts, the court thought it was clearly not a case of exceptional circumstances justifying an award of damages in lieu. Although some of the criteria established by the Court of Appeal are open-textured, and thus imply some judicial flexibility, the fact that they are cumulative produces the opposite effect.

Although originally formulated in a nuisance case, the *Shelfer* principles have been applied in other cases concerning real property, and also (by analogy with real property) to intellectual property cases.[37] In *Navitaire Inc.* v. *easyJet Airline Co. Ltd* (No. 2)[38] (a copyright case) Pumfrey J refused to grant an injunction on this basis, saying: "My understanding of the word 'oppressive' in this context is that the effect of

---

[34] *Id.*, 401.
[35] The Chancery Amendment Act 1858 (21 & 22 Vict c. 27).
[36] *Shelfer* v. *City of London Lighting Co. Ltd* [1895] 1 Ch 287, 322–23.
[37] For example, *Banks* v. *EMI Songs Ltd (No. 2)* [1996] EMLR 452 (a copyright case).
[38] [2005] EWHC 282 (Ch), [2006] RPC 4, [104]. This statement was cited with approval in *Virgin Atlantic Airways Ltd* v. *Premier Aircraft Interiors Ltd* [2009] EWCA Civ 1513, [2010] FSR 15, [25] (Jacob LJ).

the grant of the injunction would be grossly disproportionate to the right protected. The word 'grossly' avoids any suggestion that all that has to be done is to strike a balance of convenience."

In *HTC Corp. v. Nokia Corp. (No. 2)*,[39] Arnold J recognised that, in principle, the case law of Court of Justice of the European Union,[40] interpreting the intellectual property rights (IPR) Enforcement Directive,[41] required the English courts to deviate from the relatively inflexible *Shelfer* principles:[42]

> In my view, the time has come to recognise that, in cases concerning infringements of intellectual property rights, the criteria to be applied when deciding whether or

[39] [2013] EWHC 3778 (Pat), [2014] RPC 30, [27]. This is unaffected by the Court of Appeal's reversal of another part of this judgment: [2013] EWCA Civ, [2014] RPC 31. See also *Sky Ltd v. Skykick UK Ltd* [2020] EWHC 1735 (Ch), [2020] ETMR 50, [27]-[32] (Arnold LJ) (a trademark case).

[40] See Case C-275/06 *Productores de Musica de Espana (Promusicae) v. Telefonica de Espana SAU* [2008] ECR 1-271, [68]–[70]; Case C-235/09 *DHL Express France SAS v. Chronopost SA* [2011] ECR 1-2801, [58]; Case C-324/09 *L'Oreal SA v. eBay International AG* [2011] ECR 1-6011, [140]-[144]; Case C-70/10 *Scarlet Extended SA v. Societe Beige des Auteurs, Composituers et Editeurs (SABAM)* [2011] ECR 1-11959, [36] and Case C-360/10 *Belgische Vereniging van Auteurs, Componisten en Uitgevers CVBA (SABAM) v. Netlog NV* [EU:C:2012:85], [34]. See also four more recent cases: Case C-314/12, *UPC Telekabel Wien GmbH v. Constantin Film Verleih GmbH* [EU:C:2014:192], [46]; Case C-580/13 *Coty Germany GmbH v. Stadtsparkasse Magdeburg* [EU:C:2015:485], [34]-[35]; Case C-494/15 *Tommy Hilfiger Licensing LLC v. Delta Center as* [EU:C:2016:528], [32]-[36]; and Case C-484/14 *McFadden v. Sony Music Entertainment Germany GmbH* [EU:C:2016:689], [83].

[41] Directive 2004/48/EC of the European Parliament and of the Council of 29 April 2004 on the enforcement of intellectual property rights [2004] OJ L195/16 (IPRED). Case-law decided by the CJEU under that Directive prior to 1 January 2020 remains "retained case-law" binding on the lower courts of the United Kingdom as regards the interpretation of "retained EU law" (e.g. EU-derived legislation), though capable of being deviated from by the Court of Appeal or Supreme Court: European Union (Withdrawal) Act 2018 (as amended) (EU(W)A), ss. 2–4 (on "retained EU law"), s. 6(3) ("retained EU case-law") s 6(4) and European Union (Withdrawal) Act 2018 (Relevant Court) (Retained EU Case Law) Regulations 2020 (SI 2020/1525) (on power to deviate). While Article 3(2) of the EU Enforcement Directive had not been expressly implemented (so is not "retained EU law" by virtue of EU(W)A, s. 2), because that Article was directed at the courts, it had so-called "vertical direct effect" to bring it within EU(W)A, s. 4. Moreover, although based on the Directive, that direct effect had been recognised by the courts which had treated it as binding and applied in domestic case-law. As a result, there can be no doubt that Article 3(2) of IPRED, in general, and the proportionality requirement more specifically, constitute "retained EU law". If there were any doubt, it is notable too that Article 3(2) of the IPRED is replicated in the UK–EU Trade and Cooperation Agreement, Article 256, and, this is automatically implemented in UK law through the European Union (Future Relationship) Act 2020, s. 29.
In contrast, the United Kingdom had not implemented the optional provision in Article 12 of the Directive, but being optional, there was no direct effect and it is not retained EU law.

[42] Another factor which supported the same conclusion was Article 16 of the Charter of Fundamental Rights of the European Union (freedom to conduct a business) and the case law of the CJEU holding that a fair balance must struck between this and intellectual property rights protected by Article 17(2): see in particular Case C-484/14 *McFadden v. Sony Music Entertainment Germany GmbH* [EU:C:2016:689], [80]–[101].

not to grant an injunction are those laid down by Article 3(2): efficacy, proportionality, dissuasiveness, the avoidance of creating barriers to legitimate trade and the provision of safeguards against abuse.

However, looking more closely at the effect of a decision to decline injunctive relief, and the rules on compulsory licensing in the Agreement on Trade Related Aspects of Intellectual Property (TRIPS), Arnold J concluded that the difference between *Shelfer* and the approach under the Enforcement Directive in patent cases is probably not that significant:[43]

> Drawing these threads together, I consider that Article 3(2) of the Enforcement Directive permits and requires the court to refuse to grant an injunction where it would be disproportionate to grant one even having regard to the requirements of efficacy and dissuasiveness. Where the right sought to be enforced by the injunction is a patent, however, the court must be very cautious before making an order which is tantamount to a compulsory licence in circumstances where no compulsory licence would be available. It follows that, where no other countervailing right is in play, the burden on the party seeking to show that the injunction would be disproportionate is a heavy one. I suspect that the practical effect of this approach is little different to Pumfrey J's test [in *Navitaire* v. *easyJet*] of "grossly disproportionate".

On the specific facts of the case, he concluded that an injunction should be granted. He summarised his reasons as follows:[44]

> Taking all of the factors relied on by the parties into account, ... I am not persuaded that this is a case in which I should exercise my discretion to award damages in lieu of an injunction. Nokia has a legitimate interest in seeking a final injunction to prevent further exploitation of the patented invention by HTC without its consent. This is not a case in which the injury to the patent is small, capable of being estimated in money and adequately compensated by a relatively small money payment. If an injunction were refused, it would have to be on the basis of an order for a running royalty. In those circumstances, refusal of an injunction would be tantamount to imposing a compulsory licence on Nokia in circumstances where HTC could not obtain a compulsory licence by the proper route.[45] Most importantly, the grant of a final injunction would not be disproportionate. The grant of an injunction will not deliver HTC over to Nokia "bound hand and foot, in order to be made subject to any extortionate demand" Nokia may make, because HTC already has some non-infringing alternatives available to it, could have had more non-infringing alternatives available to it by now if it had acted promptly when first sued by Nokia and will in any event have more non-

---

[43] *HTC Corp.* v. *Nokia Corp.* [2013] EWHC 3778 (Pat), [2014] RPC 30, [32]. This statement was followed in *Evalve Inc.* v. *Edwards Lifesciences Ltd* [2020] EWHC 513 (Pat), [57] (Birss J).
[44] *Id.*, [74].
[45] Under the Patents Act 1977, s. 48A which gives effect to Article 31 of TRIPs.

infringing alternatives available to it in a period which is significantly shorter than the remaining term of the patent.

It can be seen from this reasoning that an important consideration is the availability to the defendant of ways to work around the injunction.

In *Napp Pharmaceutical Holdings Ltd* v. *Dr Reddy Laboratories (UK) Ltd* Arnold J considered the application of *HTC* v. *Nokia* to a hypothetical situation in which the court concluded on the balance of probabilities that production variables meant that the defendant would sell 2,000 infringing products randomly distributed among 1,998,000 non-infringing products, and also concluded that that quantity could not be discounted as *de minimis*:[46]

> I consider that an injunction would be both disproportionate and a barrier to legitimate trade. It would be disproportionate because the harm to the patentee from infringement on such a small scale would be indistinguishable from the harm caused by wholly non-infringing acts. It would be a barrier to legitimate trade because the practical effect of such an injunction would be to require the defendant to operate even further outside the boundaries of the claim, and thus would effectively extend the scope of the patentee's monopoly. In such a case, the appropriate remedy would be a financial one.

Shortly after the decision in *HTC* v. *Nokia*, the Supreme Court held in *Lawrence* v. *Fen Tigers Ltd*[47] that the approach to be adopted by a judge when being asked to award damages in lieu of an injunction in a nuisance case should be much more flexible than that suggested by earlier Court of Appeal authorities such as *Shelfer*. The leading judgment was given by Lord Neuberger, who said that the court's power to award damages instead of an injunction involved a classic exercise of discretion which should not, as a matter of principle, be fettered.[48] He went on:

> [123] Where does that leave A. L. Smith LJ's four tests? While the application of any such series of tests cannot be mechanical, I would adopt a modified version of the view expressed by Romer LJ in *Fishenden* ... First, the application of the four tests must not be such as "to be a fetter on the exercise of the court's discretion". Secondly, it would, in the absence of additional relevant circumstances pointing the other way, normally be right to refuse an injunction if those four tests were satisfied. Thirdly, the fact that those tests are not all satisfied does not mean that an injunction should be granted.
>
> [124] As for the ... public interest, I find it hard to see how there could be any circumstances in which it arose and could not, as a matter of law, be a relevant factor. Of course, it is very easy to think of circumstances in which it might arise but did not begin to justify the court refusing, or, as the case may be, deciding, to award

---

[46] *Napp Pharmaceutical Holdings Ltd* v. *Dr Reddy Laboratories (UK) Ltd* [2016] EWHC 1517 (Pat), [170].

[47] [2014] UKSC 13, [2014] AC 822.

[48] *Id.*, [119]–[120].

an injunction if it was otherwise minded to do so. But that is not the point. The fact that a defendant's business may have to shut down if an injunction is granted should, it seems to me, obviously be a relevant fact, and it is hard to see why relevance should not extend to the fact that a number of the defendant's employees would lose their livelihood, although in many cases that may well not be sufficient to justify the refusal of an injunction.

In *Evalve Inc.* v. *Edwards Lifesciences Ltd*,[49] Birss J held that *Lawrence* required a more flexible approach than that adopted in *Shelfer*, but that, when considering whether an injunction should be denied on public interest grounds, it was still necessary for the court to take into account the considerations identified by Aldous J in the earlier case of *Chiron Corp.* v. *Organon Teknika Ltd (No. 10)*,[50] namely the nature of patent monopolies and the fact that the Patents Act already places limits on patents in order to safeguard the public interest by virtue of the provisions for compulsory licensing, Crown use and exceptions to infringement.

Where damages are awarded in lieu of an injunction, they are to be assessed "once and for all" in respect of all future infringements.[51] The quantum of such damages will be the amount of money which could reasonably have been demanded by the claimant for consent to such acts (sometimes referred to as "negotiating damages"[52]). It appears that this enables the court to order damages assessed as an ongoing royalty,[53] but possibly not to order an account of (the defendant's) profits (which is an alternative remedy to damages in English law).[54] There is no English patent case yet in which such damages have been assessed, but in principle it appears that they would fall to be assessed in the same way as ordinary damages for patent infringement: if the patentee exploits the patent through marketing products, then it can recover lost profits caused by the infringement; if the patentee exploits the patent through licensing, then it can recover the licensee fees the defendant should have paid; otherwise the patentee can recover a reasonable royalty which represents what a willing licensor and a willing licensee would have agreed (based, for example, on comparable licences).[55] Assessing such damages is hard enough (because it tends to involve difficult questions of causation and complex financial evidence) for past infringements, but it would appear likely to be even more challenging in the case of future infringements.[56]

---

[49] [2020] EWHC 513 (Pat), [47]–[58].
[50] [1995] FSR 325. See also *Biogen Inc.* v. *Medeva plc* [1993] RPC 475 and *Kirin-Amgen Inc.* v. *Transkaryotic Therapies Ltd (No. 3)* [2005] FSR 41, [27] (Neuberger J).
[51] See *Jaggard* v. *Sawyer* [1995] 1 WLR 269, 280–81 (Sir Thomas Bingham MR), 285–86 (Millett LJ).
[52] See *Morris-Garner* v. *One Step (Support) Ltd* [2018] UKSC 20, [2018] 2 WLR 1353.
[53] *HTC Corp.* v. *Nokia Corp.* [2013] EWHC 3778 (Pat), [2014] RPC 30, [14].
[54] See *GlaxoSmithKline UK Ltd* v. *Wyeth Holding LLC* [2017] EWHC 91 (Pat).
[55] See in particular *General Tire & Rubber Co. Ltd* v. *Firestone Tyre & Rubber Co. Ltd (No. 2)* [1975] 1 WLR 819.
[56] See *Evalve Inc.* v. *Edwards Lifesciences Ltd* [2020] EWHC 513 (Pat), [59]–[66] (Birss J).

E. PARTIAL DENIAL OF INJUNCTIVE RELIEF FOR A SUB-GROUP OF INFRINGING ACTS

In *Edwards Life Sciences LLC* v. *Boston Scientific Scimed Inc. (No. 3)*,[57] the High Court recognised that there may be circumstances where carve-outs to an injunction are required in the public interest. There, the High Court found that the ELS's transcatheter heart valve (THV) called the Sapien 3 infringed BS's patent.[58] Although HHJ Hacon granted an injunction, he expressed the view that, if the matter were going no further, he would "certainly be limiting that injunction by reference to the cohort of patients whose lives or health would potentially be put at risk by the grant of an injunction". His conclusion on infringement was upheld by the Court of Appeal, which remitted the issue of whether the injunction should be limited to the High Court.[59] At the hearing before the High Court, it was common ground that the injunction should be stayed for a period, and then qualified for a further period, with respect to supplies of the Sapien 3 in the public interest having regard to the impact that the injunction would have upon the health of patients with aortic stenosis. The disputes were as to (i) the length of the stay and (ii) the scope and duration of the qualification.

So far as issue (ii) was concerned, Arnold J held that the court must strike a balance between the patentee's interest in maintaining the monopoly conferred by the patent and the public interest in ensuring that patients with aortic stenosis receive appropriate treatment. Having found that there was a small but growing number of patients for whom the Sapien 3 was the only suitable device, he held that an exception to the injunction was justified by the need to protect the health of those patients. These would be identified by requiring an appropriate declaration from the responsible clinician to the effect that the patient fell into one of the groups for whom there was no alternative to the Sapien 3. Recognising that non-infringing alternatives might come onto the market, the judge gave the patentee permission to apply to terminate the exception should it no longer be essential to the treatment of the relevant groups of patients.

F. DENYING INJUNCTIVE RELIEF AGAINST A CERTAIN TYPE OF DEFENDANT AS SUCH

1. The Crown[60]

Patent law applies to the Crown, which has no immunity from claims for infringement. Thus section 129 of the Patents Act 1977 states that "This Act … binds the Crown". Moreover, section 3 of the Crown Proceedings Act 1947 provides:

[57] [2018] EWHC 1256 (Pat), [2018] FSR 31.
[58] *Edwards Life Sciences LLC* v. *Boston Scientific Scimed Inc. (No. 3)* [2017] EWHC 755 (Pat).
[59] *Edwards Life Sciences LLC* v. *Boston Scientific Scimed Inc. (No. 3)* [2018] EWCA Civ 673, [2018] FSR 29.
[60] In this context "the Crown" means the government.

Civil proceedings lie against the Crown for an infringement committed by a servant or agent of the Crown, with the authority of the Crown, of:–

(a) a patent, ... but save as provided by this subsection no proceedings lie against the Crown by virtue of this Act in respect of an infringement of any of those rights.

However, while an action for damages for patent infringement may be brought against the Crown, it seems no injunctive relief is available. Section 21 of the Crown Proceedings Act states (emphasis added):

(1) In any civil proceedings by or against the Crown the court shall, subject to the provisions of this Act, have power to make all such orders as it has power to make in proceedings between subjects, and otherwise to give such appropriate relief as the case may require:

Provided that:–

(a) where in any proceedings against the Crown any such relief is sought as might in proceedings between subjects be granted by way of injunction or specific performance, *the court shall not grant an injunction or make an order for specific performance, but may in lieu thereof make an order declaratory of the rights of the parties*; and ...

(2) The court shall not in any civil proceedings grant any injunction or make any order against an officer of the Crown if the effect of granting the injunction or making the order would be to give any relief against the Crown which could not have been obtained in proceedings against the Crown.

It appears that the rationale underlying this provision is that the Crown has a duty to obey the law as declared by the courts, and no injunction is necessary.[61] In practice, the use of an invention by the Crown is normally dealt with under the provisions of sections 55–59 of the Patents Act 1977, which enable the terms for such use to be settled by the courts in the event of dispute. These provisions could be regarded as a form of compulsory licensing, and their compatibility with TRIPs remains to be tested.

2. *Compulsory Licensing and Licences of Right*

A patentee may voluntarily choose to make licences available "as of right" and the patent fees offer a (mild) incentive to do so.[62] As a result of such a declaration, any person that wishes to become a licensee under the patent is so entitled on "such terms as may be settled by agreement or, in default of agreement, by the

---

[61] See *R* v. *Secretary of State for Transport ex p. Factortame Ltd* [1990] 2 AC 85, 150 (Lord Bridge of Harwich); but see also *Re M* [1994] 1 AC 377 (holding that an injunction may be granted against a minister acting in his official capacity).

[62] Patents Act 1977, s. 46(1). The renewal fees are halved: s. 46(3)(d).

comptroller". If, after a patent has been endorsed in this way, a patentee brings infringement proceedings and the defendant undertakes to take a licence on such terms, no injunction shall be granted against the defendant.[63] In addition, the amount (if any) recoverable against the defendant by way of damages shall not exceed double the amount which would have been payable as licensee if such a licence on those terms had been granted before the earliest infringement.[64]

Compulsory licences are available under sections 48–53 of the Patents Act 1977 (as amended).[65] Although it is difficult to epitomise these provisions,[66] in essence, section 48A provides for the possibility of such licences being granted when a patented invention is not being exploited so as to meet "demand in the United Kingdom ... on reasonable terms",[67] where as a result of refusal to grant a licence on reasonable terms, exploitation of other inventions are being hindered, or are insufficient,[68] or where the refusal to license or the conditions imposed on licensees prejudice local production or commercial activities.[69] No such application may be made until three years after the date of grant of a patent. Sections 50A and 50B also permit compulsory licensing as a remedy to certain anti-competitive practices.

In response to an application under these provisions, the comptroller may order a licence in favour of the individual applicant or even order the patent to be licensed as of right (with the same effect as if the patentee had voluntarily done so).[70] If the patentee is a World Trade Organization (WTO) proprietor, section 48A(6) sets a number of conditions on the terms of the order or entry (that the patent is licensed of right) (implementing Article 31 of the TRIPs Agreement). These include "conditions entitling the proprietor of the patent concerned to remuneration adequate in

---

[63] Patents Act 1977, s. 46(3)(c).

[64] Cf. Copyright, Designs and Patents Act 1988, s. 239 (remedies for infringement of UK unregistered design right in cases where licences are available as of right and a defendant undertakes to take a licence), which also prohibit orders for delivery up.

[65] Note also compulsory licences available under the Patents and Plant Variety Rights (Compulsory Licensing) Regulations 2002, SI 2002/247, implementing Directive 98/44/EC.

[66] A distinction is drawn between the grounds on which such licences can be granted against a WTO (section 48A) and non-WTO patent proprietor (section 48B). Here we mention only the former.

[67] Patents Act 1977, ss. 48A(1)(a), 48B(1)(b)).

[68] Patents Act 1977, s. 48A(1)(b)(i) ("the exploitation in the United Kingdom of any other patented invention which involves an important technical advance of considerable economic significance in relation to the invention for which the patent concerned was granted is prevented or hindered"). Under s. 48A(4), such an order is conditional on the comptroller being satisfied that the proprietor of the patent for the other invention is able and willing to "cross-license" on reasonable terms.

[69] Patents Act 1977, s. 48A(1)(b) (ii), s. 48A(1)(c) ("that by reason of conditions imposed by the proprietor of the patent concerned on the grant of licences under the patent, or on the disposal or use of the patented product or on the use of the patented process, the manufacture, use or disposal of materials not protected by the patent, or the establishment or development of commercial or industrial activities in the United Kingdom, is unfairly prejudice").

[70] Patents Act 1977, ss. 48(1)(b), 53(4).

the circumstances of the case, taking into account the economic value of the licence": section 48A(6)(d).

Although the provisions on remuneration differ as between WTO proprietors and non-WTO proprietors,[71] the appropriate methodology seems to be much the same. As a result, both likely require a determination of "the royalty that would be agreed between a willing patentee and a willing licensee having regard to the other terms of the proposed licence".[72]

While the relationship between licences of right and remedies is expressly mentioned in the Act,[73] nothing is said about the interaction between compulsory licensing and infringement actions.[74] Theoretically speaking, this presents an inconsistency because infringement is defined in relation to actions "without the consent of the proprietor" (section 60(1)), and in most compulsory licensing situations the patentee has not consented to the acts in question. From the point of view of common sense, it must be the case that a compulsory licensee does not infringe. This result would most likely be achieved by treating "consent" to include the licence/permission the patentee has been ordered to grant (the reasons why the licence was granted being irrelevant.)

In contrast with the provisions on licences of right there is also no guidance on what the relationship is between the court's jurisdiction to grant remedies and pending applications for compulsory licences. If a defendant faced with an infringement action makes an application to the comptroller seeking a compulsory licence then, in principle, that might be considered in deciding whether to award interim or final injunctive relief.[75] That scenario does not seem to have arisen as yet. Indeed, the number of applications for compulsory licences is miniscule, and no such application has been made for many years.

3. *Other Cases*

It does not appear that there are any other cases in which English courts will refuse an injunction purely based on the identity of the defendant.

---

[71] Under section 48A(6), in relation to WTO proprietors, the royalty must confer *adequate remuneration*, whereas the criterion under section 50(1)(b) of the Patents Act 1977, which relates to the determination of the terms of licences required to be granted by non-WTO proprietors), is to ensure that "the inventor or other person beneficially entitled to a patent shall receive *reasonable remuneration* having regard to the nature of the invention".

[72] *Smith, Kline, French Laboratories Ltd's (Cimetidine) Patent* [1990] RPC 203, 236 (Lloyd LJ); *American Cyanamid's (Fenbufen) Patent* [1991] RPC 409, 411 (Dillon LJ) (both under a provision equivalent to that applicable now to non-WTO proprietors).

[73] Patents Act 1977, s. 46(3)(c).

[74] Patents Act, s. 60(6) (making a person entitled to use an invention under section 55 a person entitled to work the invention for section 60(2) on indirect infringement) (presumably a compulsory licensee is a "licensee" within that provision).

[75] Of course, to succeed in obtaining a licence, it would be necessary for the applicant to have made efforts to obtain a licence from the proprietor: Patents Act 1977, s. 48A(2)(a) (where the proprietor is a WTO proprietor).

G. DENYING INJUNCTIVE RELIEF TO A CERTAIN TYPE OF PLAINTIFF

So far, the English courts have not considered whether injunctive relief may be denied to so-called non-practising entities (NPEs). It seems unlikely that an injunction would be refused purely because the patentee is an NPE, but its non-practising status may be relevant to the some of the considerations affecting the grant of injunctions (e.g. because it does not manufacture products protected by the patent and therefore is not suffering lost profits). In interim injunction cases, it seems that relief might well be refused if it is established that damages would be an adequate remedy to the patentee. In final injunction cases where an NPE establishes infringement, it might be that damages would be awarded in lieu of an injunction under *Shelfer/Lawrence* principles, or on proportionality grounds under Article 3 of the Enforcement Directive.

H. ISSUING INJUNCTIONS FOR LIMITED TIME PERIODS ONLY

1. *The Standard Rule: For the Life of the Patent*

In *Coflexip*, Aldous LJ explained that one of the advantages with injunctions formulated in general terms (e.g. "do not infringe the patent") was that they were limited to the term of the patent. Similarly, in *Smith & Nephew plc v. ConvaTec Technologies Inc. (No. 2)*,[76] Birss J recognised that "In a patent case a normal final injunction is time limited in that it will only last until the patent expires".

2. *Post-Expiry or "Springboard" Injunctions*

However, the courts have been willing occasionally to grant injunctions applicable after the patent expires, but formulated as a remedy for activities of the defendant that infringed during the patent term. These are sometimes called "springboard" injunctions and can be traced back to the early case of *Crossley v. Beverley*, in which Lord Lyndhurst LC granted an injunction to restrain sale of meters (for measuring the supply of flammable gas) which had been manufactured by the defendant during the patent term.[77] In 1834, in a case brought by the same patentee though against a different defendant,[78] Lord Brougham LC confirmed the jurisdiction:

[76] [2013] EWHC 3955 (Pat), [2014] RPC 22, [115].
[77] *Crossley v. Beverley* (1829) 1 Russ & M 166 n, 39 ER 65, 1 Websters Patent Cases 119 (Lord Lyndhurst LC).
[78] The bill in the case was filed on 28 November 1829, and the patent expired on 9 December of the same year.

It was objected, that the Court would not interfere, just on the eve of the expiration of a patent, and grant an injunction which would only last a week. The point has never yet been decided; but I am of the opinion that the Court would interfere, even after a patent has expired, to restrain the sale of articles manufactured previous to its expiration in infringement of a patent right; and that a party would not be allowed to prepare for the expiration of a patent by illegally manufacturing articles, and immediately after its expiration to deluge the market with the produce of his piracy; and thus reaping the reward of his improbous [sic] labour in making it. The Court would, I say, in such case restrain him from selling them even after the expiration of the patent.[79]

These injunctions sit uneasily with the oft-repeated claim that injunctions are only granted to prevent infringement, since the aim is really to prevent a defendant from benefiting from past infringements.

In *Smith & Nephew plc* v. *ConvaTec Technologies Inc. (No. 2)*,[80] Birss J reviewed the authorities, and considered the EU Enforcement Directive, and found there was jurisdiction to award injunctions after expiry. He set out five factors that a court should consider before doing so:

i) Caution is required before a final injunction is granted restraining an otherwise lawful activity. Nevertheless in a proper case it will be.

ii) The nature of any unwarranted advantage relied on should be identified. The precise relationship between the unlawful activity in the past and the later acts which are said to exploit that unwarranted advantage needs to be considered.

iii) If an injunction is to be granted it must be in an appropriate form and for a duration which is commensurate with the unwarranted advantage relied on.[81]

iv) The court must be particularly careful not to put the claimant in a better position than it would be if there had been no infringement at all, especially if otherwise lawful competitive activity will be restrained.

v) In considering what relief to grant, the availability of other remedies apart from an injunction needs to be taken into account, not only damages but . . . the availability of an account of profits should be considered too.

On the facts of the case, he declined to grant a springboard injunction, finding that any advantage which Smith & Nephew had obtained from its infringement had already come to an end.

---

[79] *Crossley* v. *The Derby Gas Light Co.* (1834) 4 Law Journal (Ch) 25, 26.

[80] [2013] EWHC 3955 (Pat), [2014] RPC 22, [133].

[81] This factor now finds an echo in Article 13(1) of the EU Trade Secrets Directive (Directive 2016/943/EU of the European Parliament and of the Council of 8 June 2016 on the protection of undisclosed know-how and business information (trade secrets) against their unlawful acquisition, use and disclosure [2016] OJ L157/1).

3. *Conditional Injunctions: The New FRAND Injunction*

In *Unwired Planet Int'l Ltd* v. *Huawei Technologies (UK) Co. Ltd*, Birss J created a
new form of injunction, called a "FRAND Injunction". These are awarded in cases
where a defendant is found to infringe a patent, but the patentee has offered a
licence on FRAND terms. In such cases, an injunction should be awarded unless
the defendant agrees to enter into the FRAND licence. As the judge explained:[82]

> A FRAND injunction should be in the normal form to restrain infringement of the
> relevant patent(s) but ought to include a proviso that it will cease to have effect if
> the defendant enters into that FRAND licence. If, as in this case, the FRAND
> licence is for a limited time, shorter than the lifetime of the relevant patents, then
> the injunction should also be subject to an express liberty to either party to return to
> court in future to address the position at the end of the term of the FRAND licence.
> In any case the FRAND injunction should also be subject to an express liberty to
> apply in the event the FRAND licence ceases to have effect for any other reason.

The effect of "liberty to apply" mentioned here is that the parties do not have initiate
new proceedings: they can simply make an application in existing proceedings.

The order made in the *Edwards* v. *Boston* case discussed previously was to some
extent a conditional injunction in that it provided that the exception to the injunction would cease to apply in the event that a suitable non-infringing alternative THV
became available.

I. DELAYING/STAYING INJUNCTIONS IN TIME

1. *Pending Appeal*

In general, if a court has found infringement and granted an injunction, the
injunction should be maintained even pending appeal.[83] Recognising that such
an injunction may be seriously damaging to a defendant who succeeds on appeal,
the court may well require an undertaking that the patentee compensate the
defendant for loss caused by the injunction (referred to as a "cross-undertaking in
damages" and comparable to the undertaking which must be given by a patentee
seeking an interim injunction). However, the courts recognise that this will not
always do justice, and a court will look closely at the circumstances of the case to
ascertain the "balance of convenience".

---

[82] *Unwired Planet Int'l Ltd* v. *Huawei Technologies (UK) Co. Ltd* [2017] EWHC 1304 (Pat), [2017]
RPC 20, [20].
[83] Cf., in the pre-judicature era, *Hill* v. *Thompson and Foreman* (1817) 3 Mer 622, 631, 36 ER 239,
242 (Eldon LC refused an injunction following the verdict at law at Nisi Prius, where evidently
there was a legal ground for a new trial).

The basic position was stated by Jacob LJ in *Virgin Atlantic Airways Ltd* v. *Premier Aircraft Interiors Ltd*:[84]

> It should be noted the question is not the same when one is considering what to do on an application for an interim injunction pending trial. In that case the patentee has yet to establish his right, whereas after successful trial he has *prima facie* done just that. So in general, when an appeal is pending, the patentee will get his injunction provided he gives a cross-undertaking in damages against the possibility that the defendant's appeal would be successful. The question, however, remains one of a balance of convenience.

In *Novartis AG* v. *Hospira UK Ltd*,[85] Floyd LJ emphasised that whether a stay should be granted, and if so upon what conditions, was dependent on the balance of hardships or convenience and that the court should endeavour to arrange matters so that the Court of Appeal is best able to do justice between the parties once the appeal is heard.

The balance of convenience can (it seems) include the public interest. In *Leeds Forge Co. Ltd* v. *Deighton's Patent Flue and Tube Co. Ltd*,[86] following a finding of infringement of the claimant's patent for a boiler flue or furnace, counsel for the defendant asked for an injunction to be suspended pending appeal, in part because the patentee had stood by while the defendant developed its factories, but also because granting the injunction with immediate effect would lead to the laying off of seventy workers. The High Court granted the stay pending an application to appeal to the Court of Appeal, and following that application the Court of Appeal ordered a further stay until the appeal had been heard.

2. *Selling Off/Fulfilling Existing Orders*

Sometimes injunctions have been stayed for a period allowing the defendant to sell off existing stocks or fulfil existing orders. These are usually cases where an appeal is pending, and so are part of the assessment of the balance of convenience in that context.[87] A recent example is in *Virgin Atlantic Airways Ltd* v. *Premier Aircraft Interiors Ltd*, where the Court of Appeal created a carve-out enabling the defendant to complete existing contracts. As Jacob LJ explained:[88] "All the above seem to me perfectly in accordance with the exercise with the balance of convenience approach.

---

[84] [2009] EWCA Civ 1513, [2010] FSR 15, [22].

[85] [2013] EWCA Civ 583, [2014] 1 WLR 1264, [39].

[86] (1901) 18 RPC 233, 240.

[87] See *Lyon* v. *Goddard* (1893) 10 RPC 121, 136 (suspending operation of injunction pending appeal in relation to orders taken by the defendant but not executed, but with duty to keep account of profits); *Ducketss* v. *Whitehead* (1895) 12 RPC 187, 191 (stay of injunction pending appeal on same terms).

[88] *Virgin Atlantic Airways Ltd* v. *Premier Aircraft Interiors Ltd* [2009] EWCA Civ 1513, [2010] FSR 15, [36].

They are a carve-out to the injunction which is the least likely to cause injustice if the Supreme Court grants permission to appeal and our decision is subsequently reversed."

3. Redesign

In the mid-1970s, in *Illinois Tool Works Inc.* v. *Autobars Co. (Services) Ltd,*[89] having found infringement of the claimant's patent, Graham J withheld the injunction for a period of three months to give the defendant time to launch a non-infringing product. This was explained on the basis of the public interest concerning the possibility of the loss of employment in times of great economic stress, a consideration that had been treated as relevant in some older authorities. Thirty-five years later, in *Virgin Atlantic Airways Ltd* v. *Premier Aircraft Interiors Ltd,*[90] Jacob LJ stated that he was "not entirely convinced that one would go quite that far these days".

A similar order staying an injunction to allowing for redesign for a period of two and a half weeks was, however, made in *Adaptive Spectrum and Signal Alignment Inc.* v. *British Telecommunications plc.* Here, BT's Rate Adaptive Monitoring Box (RAMBo) in its Dynamic Line Management System which controlled its broadband access network was found to have infringed ASSIA's two patents relating to methods for controlling the operation of a digital subscriber line (DSL) for sending digital information over telephone. Floyd LJ stated:[91]

> In these circumstances an injunction would normally be granted. However, we are narrowly persuaded that it would be right to stay the injunction on terms. ASSIA has made it clear that it is primarily interested in a financial remedy, as its business lies in licensing its inventions. That does not mean that it is not entitled to seek an injunction when BT has never sought a licence: otherwise it would never be able to bring a prospective licensee to the table. But it does mean that it will suffer no lasting harm if, for a short period, BT is granted a stay in order to cease use of the invention. On the other hand, given BT's large market share, the public would suffer if an injunction were granted disrupting or reducing the quality of the BT service.

4. Other Cases

We have already noted that, in *Edwards Lifesciences LLC* v. *Boston Scientific Scimed Inc. (No. 3),*[92] the High Court limited the injunction so that it would not

[89] [1974] RPC 337.
[90] [2009] EWCA Civ 1513, [2010] FSR, [27].
[91] *Adaptive Spectrum and Signal Alignment Inc.* v. *British Telecommunications plc* [2014] EWCA Civ 1513, [4].
[92] [2018] EWHC 1256 (Pat), [2018] FSR 31.

affect the cohort of patients for which the patented invention was essential. The court also considered, in respect of other patients, the grant of a stay for a period in which clinicians who had been trained to use the defendant's infringing heart valve (Sapien 3) could be retrained to use alternative heart valves. Because of uncertainty as to the period required for retraining, Arnold J stayed the injunction to permit continued implantation of the Sapien 3 for a period of twelve months and granted the defendant permission to apply to extend the stay if it turned out that the period required for retraining was longer than that.

J. DENYING OR MODIFYING INJUNCTIVE RELIEF DUE TO CONSIDERATIONS OF PUBLIC INTEREST

Occasionally the courts have recognised that an injunction may be inappropriate because of public interest considerations, though in most such cases the patentee has not demanded immediate injunctive relief (presumably either recognising that the court was unlikely to grant an injunction or fearing the public relations consequences if it did). For example, in *Bonnard v. London General Omnibus Ltd*,[93] where the patent related to a device used on omnibuses, the patentee agreed to the injunction being suspended for a reasonable time, and the Court of Appeal suspended it for two months. In *Hopkinson v. The St James and Pall Mall Electric Lighting Co.*,[94] after the court found infringement of the patentee's patent for a method of supplying electricity to consumers, the report states that "considering the inconvenience caused to the public by suddenly stopping the use of the three wire system, it was agreed that the injunction be suspended for six months, an account of profits to be kept". In *GlaxoSmithKline UK Ltd v. Wyeth Holdings LLC*,[95] the patent related to vaccines against bacterial meningitis and was infringed by the defendant's product. The patentee decided not to seek an injunction, recognising the public health requirements for vaccines against meningitis B. We have already noted that in *Edwards Lifesciences LLC v. Boston Scientific Scimed Inc.*[96] the parties agreed that an injunction was inappropriate in relation to patients for whom the infringing heart valves were essential, the court being left to determine the precise modalities and duration of the exception.

In contrast, in *Roussel-Uclaf v. GD Searle & Co. Ltd*,[97] Graham J considered an interim application in relation to a life-saving drug, a drug for treating cardiac disease. The judge refused the injunction on the normal balance of the risk of injustice basis, but suggested that an application would be refused if the drug was

[93] (1919) 36 RPC 307, 325–26.
[94] (1893) 10 RPC 46, 62.
[95] [2017] EWHC 91 (Pat).
[96] [2018] EWHC 1256 (Pat), [2018] FSR 31.
[97] [1977] FSR 125, 131.

not merely life-saving but unique. This suggestion was subsequently doubted by Aldous J, however.[98]

The law was recently reviewed in *Evalve v. Edwards Life Sciences Ltd* by Birss J,[99] who concluded that the power to refuse an injunction on public interest grounds "should be used sparingly and in limited circumstances".

K. DENYING OR MODIFYING INJUNCTIVE RELIEF DUE TO PROCEDURAL CONSIDERATIONS

Interim injunctions are likely to be denied on the basis of delay, but final injunctions may be awarded despite delay in bringing proceedings as "there must be more than mere delay to disentitle a man to his legal rights".[100] In contrast, such delay might be a factor favouring an award of damages in lieu of an injunction (perhaps demonstrating that the claimant is primarily interested in money or that the award of an injunction would be oppressive[101]).

The position is different if there is more than mere delay. Positive acquiescence will bar the right of the patentee to an injunction if it amounts to a representation to the defendant that they are free to do what would otherwise be an infringement. *Terrell on Patents* gives the following example:[102] "Thus, if a defendant constructed machinery, for instance, in ignorance of the existence of the claimant's patent, and the claimant, aware of such ignorance, lay by in silence and later attempted to obtain an injunction, such relief would probably be refused."

L. THE IMPACT OF VALIDITY CONCERNS ON THE GRANT OF AN INJUNCTION

An interim injunction pending trial may be granted even if the validity of the patent is challenged and the attack appears to be a strong one. As we have already noted, the Court of Appeal granted an interim injunction pending appeal in *Novartis AG v. Hospira UK Ltd*[103] even though the patent had been found invalid at first instance.[104]

A court may consider a stay of injunctive relief awarded in the United Kingdom if there are opposition proceedings pending before the European Patent Office (EPO). However, the jurisprudence recognises that the position is different from

---

[98] *Biogen Inc. v. Medeva plc* [1993] RPC 475, 483; *Chiron Corp. v. Organon Teknika Ltd (No. 10)* [1995] FSR 325, 334–35.

[99] [2020] EWHC 513 (Pat), [78].

[100] *C. Van der Lely NV v. Bamfords Ltd* [1964] RPC 54, 81.

[101] See *Banks v. EMI Songs Ltd (No. 2)* [1996] EMLR 452, 459 (a copyright case).

[102] [2020], 21–27.

[103] [2013] EWCA Civ 583, [2014] 1 WLR 1264.

[104] Note that the first-instance decision to revoke the patent was subsequently upheld by the Court of Appeal: *Novartis AG v. Hospira UK Ltd* [2013] EWCA Civ 1663, [2015] RPC 1.

stays pending appeals. In *Adaptive Spectrum and Signal Alignment Inc. v. British Telecommunications plc*, the Court of Appeal refused British Telecom's application for a cross-undertaking in damages to cater for the possibility that the EPO might subsequently revoke or materially amend one of the patents in issue. Floyd LJ stated:[105]

> A cross-undertaking is appropriate to take account of the possibility that an earlier judgment is wrong (e.g., an interim injunction or an injunction pending appeal). In the present case, revocation by the EPO would not show our judgment to be wrong, or the injunction to have been wrongly granted. A subsequent EPO revocation or amendment would mean that the injunction would become ineffective or have to be discharged from the date of revocation/amendment, but not *ab initio*. There is no reason for ASSIA to pay for the harm during the period when the injunction was rightly granted.

Nevertheless, in *Smith & Nephew plc v. ConvaTec Technologies Inc.*,[106] the Court of Appeal did grant such a stay. Kitchin LJ explained:

> We must also consider the position pending the decision of the TBA [Technical Board of Appeal of the EPO]. We are fully conscious that this raises rather different considerations and in that regard have well in mind the decision and reasoning of this court in *Adaptive Spectrum*. However, in our view this is an unusual case in that the Patent has now been revoked by the Opposition Division and we are satisfied that the decision of the TBA is likely to be at most only a few months after the decision of the Supreme Court in relation to the application for permission to appeal. We have also come to the firm conclusion that it would be wholly disproportionate not to grant to Smith & Nephew the further suspension they seek and that such suspension should be granted in the interests of fairness and equity in light of all of the matters to which we have referred in considering the grant of a stay pending the decision of the Supreme Court in relation to the permission application. In our judgment these matters are equally apposite to the further period between the decision of the Supreme Court and the decision of the TBA.

M. MODIFYING INJUNCTIONS

An interim injunction may be set aside or varied due to a change of circumstances. The requirement is for "a material change in circumstances"; if this is established "then the Court must re-exercise its discretion in the light of the changed circumstances".[107] In that case, Arnold J concluded that a decision of the Court of Appeal upholding a first-instance decision that the patent was partially invalid was a change

---

[105] *Adaptive Spectrum and Signal Alignment Inc. v. British Telecommunications plc* [2014] EWCA Civ 1513, [9].
[106] [2015] EWCA Civ 803, [13].
[107] *Warner-Lambert Company LLC v. Sandoz GmbH* [2016] EWHC 3317 (Pat), [56].

of circumstances, but not a material one, while a change of position by the patentee as to the enforcement of the patent should it be successful on a further appeal to the Supreme Court was a material change of circumstances. Reconsidering the matter in the light of the changed circumstances, however, he remained of the view that the balance of the risk of injustice favoured the maintenance of the injunction.

REFERENCES

Cases

Adam Phones Ltd v. Goldschmidt [2000] FSR 163
Adaptive Spectrum and Signal Alignment Inc. v. British Telecommunications plc [2014] EWCA Civ. 1513
American Cyanamid's (Fenbufen) Patent [1991] RPC 409
American Cyanamid Co. v. Ethicon Ltd [1975] AC 396
Banks v. EMI Songs Ltd (No. 2) [1996] EMLR 452
Biogen Inc. v. Medeva plc [1993] RPC 475
Bonnard v. London General Omnibus Ltd (1919) 36 RPC 307
Boulton v. Bull (1796) 3 Ves 140, 30 ER 937
Bridson v. McAlpine (1845) 8 Beav. 229, 50 ER 90
Cartier International AG v. British Telecommunications plc [2018] UKSC 28, [2018] Bus. LR 1417
Case C-360/10 Belgische Vereniging van Auteurs, Componisten en Uitgevers CVBA (SABAM) v. Netlog NV [EU:C:2012:85]
Case C-580/13 Coty Germany GmbH v. Stadtsparkasse Magdeburg [EU:C:2015:485]
Case C-235/09 DHL Express France SAS v. Chronopost SA [2011] ECR 1-2801
Case C-324/09 L'Oreal SA v. eBay International AG [2011] ECR 1-6011
Case C-484/14 McFadden v. Sony Music Entertainment Germany GmbH [EU:C:2016:689]
Case C-275/06 Productores de Musica de Espana (Promusicae) v. Telefonica de Espana SAU [2008] ECR 1-271
Case C-70/10 Scarlet Extended SA v. Societe Beige des Auteurs, Composituers et Editeurs (SABAM) [2011] ECR 1-11959
Case C-494/15 Tommy Hilfiger Licensing LLC v. Delta Center as [EU:C:2016:528]
Case C-314/12, UPC Telekabel Wien GmbH v. Constantin Film Verleih GmbH [EU:C:2014:192]
Celgard, LLC v. Shenzhen Senior Technology Material Co. Ltd [2020] EWCA Civ 1293, [2021] FSR 1
Chiron Corp. v. Organon Teknika Ltd (No. 10) [1995] FSR 325
Coflexip SA v. Stolt Comex MS Ltd [1999] FSR 473
Coflexip SA v. Stolt Comex MS Ltd [2001] RPC 9
Coflexip SA v. Stolt Comex Seaway MS Ltd [2001] RPC 182
Crossley v. Beverley (1829) 1 Russ & M 166 n, 39 ER 65, 1 Websters Patent Cases 119
Crossley v. The Derby Gas Light Co. (1834) 4 Law Journal (Ch) 25
C. Van der Lely NV v. Bamfords Ltd [1964] RPC 54
Davenport v. Jepson (1862) 4 De G F & J 440, 45 ER 1252
Ducketss v. Whitehead (1895) 12 RPC 187
Edwards Life Sciences LLC v. Boston Scientific Scimed Inc. (No. 3) [2017] EWHC 755 (Pat)
Edwards Life Sciences LLC v. Boston Scientific Scimed Inc. (No. 3) [2018] EWCA Civ 673, [2018] FSR 29

Edwards Lifesciences LLC v. *Boston Scientific Scimed Inc. (No. 3)* [2018] EWHC 1256 (Pat), [2018] FSR 31

Evalve Inc. v. *Edwards Lifesciences Ltd* [2020] EWHC 513 (Pat)

Fourie v. *Le Roux* [2007] UKHL 1, [2007] 1 WLR 320

General Tire & Rubber Co. Ltd v. *Firestone Tyre & Rubber Co. Ltd (No. 2)* [1975] 1 WLR 819

Generics (UK) Ltd v. *Warner-Lambert Company LLC* [2016] EWCA Civ 1006, [2017] RPC 1

Generics (UK) Ltd v. *Warner-Lambert Company LLC* [2018] UKSC 56, [2019] Bus LR 360

GlaxoSmithKline UK Ltd v. *Wyeth Holding LLC* [2017] EWHC 91 (Pat)

Grimme Landmaschinenfabrik GmbH & Co. KG v. *Scott* [2010] EWCA Civ 1110, [2011] FSR 7

Harmer v. *Plane* (1807) 14 Ves Jr 130, 33 ER 470

Hill v. *Thompson and Foreman* (1817) 3 Mer 622, 36 ER 239

Hopkinson v. *The St James and Pall Mall Electric Lighting Co.* (1893) 10 RPC 46

Hotel Cipriani Srl v. *Fred 250 Ltd* [2013] EWHC 70 (Ch), [2013] FSR 34

HTC Corp. v. *Nokia Corp. (No. 2)* [2013] EWCA Civ, [2014] RPC 31

HTC Corp. v. *Nokia Corp. (No. 2)* [2013] EWHC 3778 (Pat), [2014] RPC 30

HTC Corp. v. *Nokia Corp.* [2013] EWHC 37778 (Pat), [2014] RPC 30

Illinois Tool Works Inc. v. *Autobars Co. (Services) Limited* [1974] RPC 337

Illumina Inc. v. *TDL Genetics Ltd* [2019] EWHC 2405 (Pat)

Jaggard v. *Sawyer* [1995] 1 WLR 269

Kirin-Amgen Inc. v. *Transkaryotic Therapies Ltd (No. 3)* [2005] FSR 41

Lawrence v. *Fen Tigers Ltd* [2014] UKSC 13, [2014] AC 822

Leeds Forge Co. Ltd v. *Deighton's Patent Flue and Tube Co. Ltd* (1901) 18 RPC 233

Lyon v. *Goddard* (1893) 10 RPC 121

Merck Sharp & Dohme Corp. v. *Teva Pharma BV* [2013] EWHC 1958 (Pat), [2014] FSR 3

Napp Pharmaceutical Holdings Ltd v. *Dr Reddy Laboratories (UK) Ltd* [2016] EWHC 1517 (Pat)

National Commercial Bank Jamaica Ltd v. *Olint Corp.* [2009] UKPC 16, [2009] 1 WLR 1405,

Navitaire Inc. v. *easyJet Airline Co. Ltd (No. 2)* [2005] EWHC 282 (Ch), [2006] RPC 4

Neurim Pharmaceuticals (1991) Ltd v. *Generics UK Ltd* [2020] EWCA Civ 793

Novartis AG v. *Hospira UK Ltd* [2013] EWCA Civ 583, [2014] 1 WLR 1264

Novartis AG v. *Hospira UK Ltd* [2013] EWCA Civ 1663, [2015] RPC 1

Nutrinova Nutrition Specialities & Food Ingredients GmbH v. *Scanchem UK Ltd (No. 2)* [2000] EWHC 124 (Pat), [2001] FSR 43

NWL Ltd v. *Woods* [1979] 1 WLR 1294

Morris-Garner v. *One Step (Support) Ltd* [2018] UKSC 20, [2018] 2 WLR 1353

Multiform Displays Ltd v. *Whitmarley Displays Ltd* [1956] RPC 143 [1957] RPC 260

Proctor v. *Bayley* (1889) 42 Ch 390

R v. *Secretary of State for Transport ex p. Factortame Ltd* [1990] 2 AC 85

Re M [1994] 1 AC 377

Roussel-Uclaf v. *GD Searle & Co. Ltd* [1977] FSR 125

Shelfer v. *City of London Lighting Co. Ltd* [1895] 1 Ch 287

Sky Ltd v. *Skykick UK Ltd* [2020] EWHC 1735 (Ch), [2020] ETMR 50

SmithKline Beecham plc v. *Apotex Europe Ltd* [2003] EWCA Civ 137, [2003] FSR 31

Smith, Kline, French Laboratories Ltd's (Cimetidine) Patent [1990] RPC 203

Smith & Nephew plc v. *ConvaTec Technologies Inc. (No. 2)* [2013] EWHC 3955 (Pat), [2014] RPC 22

Smith & Nephew plc v. *ConvaTec Technologies Inc.* [2015] EWCA Civ 803

Staver Co. Inc. v. *Digitext Display Ltd* [1985] FSR 512

Sun Microsystems Inc. v. *M-Tech Data Ltd* [2012] UKSC 27, [2012] 1 WLR 2026

Unwired Planet Int'l Ltd v. *Huawei Technologies (UK) Co. Ltd* [2017] EWHC 1304 (Pat), [2017] RPC 20

Virgin Atlantic Airways Ltd v. *Premier Aircraft Interiors Ltd* [2009] EWCA Civ 1513, [2010] FSR 15

Warner-Lambert Company LLC v. *Actavis Group PTC EHF* [2015] EWCA Civ 556, [2015] RPC 25

Warner-Lambert Company LLC v. *Actavis Group PTC EHF* [2015] EWHC 72 (Pat)

Warner-Lambert Company LLC v. *Sandoz GmbH* [2015] EWHC 3153 (Pat)

Warner-Lambert Company LLC v. *Sandoz GmbH* [2016] EWHC 3317 (Pat)

Regulatory and Legislative Materials

Agreement on Trade Related Aspects of Intellectual Property, Annex 1C of the Marrakesh Agreement establishing the World Trade Organization, signed in Marrakesh, Morocco on 15 April 1994 ("TRIPS Agreement")

The Chancery Amendment Act 1858 (21 & 22 Vict c. 27)

Charter of Fundamental Rights of the European Union, [2012] OJ C 326/391

Copyright, Designs and Patents Act 1988 (as amended)

Crown Proceedings Act 1947

Directive 98/44/EC of the European Parliament and of the Council of 6 July 1998 on the legal protection of biotechnological inventions [1998] OJ L 213/13

Directive 2004/48/EC of the European Parliament and of the Council of 29 April 2004 on the enforcement of intellectual property rights [2004] OJ L195/16

Directive 2016/943/EU of the European Parliament and of the Council of 8 June 2016 on the protection of undisclosed know-how and business information (trade secrets) against their unlawful acquisition, use and disclosure [2016] OJ L157/1 ("EU Trade Secrets Directive")

European Union (Future Relationship) Act 2020

European Union (Withdrawal) Act 2018 (as amended)

European Union (Withdrawal) Act 2018 (Relevant Court) (Retained EU Case Law) Regulations 2020 (SI 2020/1525)

Patents Act 1977

Patents and Plant Variety Rights (Compulsory Licensing) Regulations 2002, SI 2002/247

The Trade and Cooperation Agreement between the European Union and the European Atomic Energy Community, of the One Part, and the United Kingdom of Great Britain and Northern Ireland, of the Other Part [2020] OJ L444/14

Books, Articles and Online Materials

Bottomley, Sean. 2014. *The British Patent System during the Industrial Revolution 1700–1852* (Cambridge University Press).

14

United States

John M. Golden

United States courts take a context-sensitive approach to the grant of injunctive relief for US patent infringement. Such context-sensitivity is consistent with the *US Patent Act*, which indicates that courts "may grant injunctions in accordance with the principles of equity to prevent the violation of any right secured by patent, on such terms as the court deems reasonable."[1] In common law jurisdictions, "equity" is generally viewed as resistant to strict rules and willing to make exceptions in light of particular circumstances.[2] In accordance with this vision of equity, the generalist trial judges of US district courts[3] consider various factors in determining whether injunctive relief is justified and have great discretion to tailor injunctions in a particular case.[4] On the other hand, US courts have continued to grant injunctive relief in most infringement cases in which a patent owner prevails, particularly when the patent owner is in direct competition with the adjudged infringer.[5] In contrast, US courts commonly deny injunctive relief for patent owners who are

---

[1] 35 USC § 283.

[2] *See eBay* (US 2006, 393–94) (criticizing "expansive principles" tending to require or preclude injunctive relief in "broad swath[s] of cases").

[3] Henderson & Hubbard 2015, S93) ("Federal district court judges are generalists, and it is probable that the minutiae of a specialty area, like securities law, are beyond the ken of the average judge"). In recent years, parties have filed a few thousand patent suits in US district courts annually. *See* Clark 2020, 4 fig. 1 (reporting just under 3,600 patent suit filings in each of 2018 and 2019); United States Courts 2020. "Even before any appeal, district court proceedings that run through trial commonly span about two years." Cohen et al. 2017, 1793; *see also* Clark 2020, 7 fig. 6 (reporting median times to summary judgment of 639 days and to trial of 843 days for the decade from 2010 through 2019).

[4] *See Weinberger* (US 1982, 312) ("Where plaintiff and defendant present competing claims of injury, the traditional function of equity has been to arrive at a 'nice adjustment and reconciliation' between competing claims ... 'The essence of equity jurisdiction has been the power of the Chancellor to do equity and to mould each decree to the necessities of the particular case,'" quoting *Hecht* (US 1944, 329)).

[5] *See* Cotter & Golden 2019.

"nonpracticing entities" or "patent trolls" – forms of patent-owning entities that do not engage in substantial commercialization or use of the patented invention or variants of it.[6] Further, the US Court of Appeals for the Federal Circuit has held that the US Patent Act does not authorize injunctions to correct past patent infringement.[7] Instead, injunctions are to be granted only as a means to prevent future infringement.[8]

A. BASIC STANDARDS WITH RESPECT TO PRELIMINARY AND PERMANENT INJUNCTIONS

In Anglo-American law, injunctions are equitable remedies, traditionally "to be granted only where law damages [and other remedies available at law] were inadequate and, even then, only in the discretion of the court."[9] The requirement of inadequate legal remedies helped justify common statements that an "injunction is an exceptional remedy."[10] But the traditional limitations on injunctive relief left substantial questions of what constitutes inadequacy of legal remedies and how much discretion trial judges retain. In 2006, the Supreme Court of the United States reshuffled understandings on these matters through its decision in eBay Inc. v. MercExchange, LLC,[11] effectively giving trial judges greater discretion to deny injunctive relief after a judgment of patent infringement.[12] This section discusses the courts' basic tests for whether to grant injunctive relief in the wake of the Supreme Court's eBay decision.

A key distinction in US remedies law is that between permanent and preliminary injunctions. A permanent injunction is a court order pursuant to a final judgment.[13] In a patent infringement suit, a court that renders a final judgment in favor of the patent holder may issue a permanent injunction forbidding the adjudged infringer from engaging in specified infringing activities, typically activities involving the particular products or processes that are the basis for the court's infringement judgment.[14] A preliminary injunction comes before a final judgment: its purpose is to prevent irreparable injury to the plaintiff before the court can issue a final judgment and, relatedly, "to preserve the court's power to render a meaningful decision" on the fully presented merits.[15] There is substantial overlap between how

---

[6] See id.
[7] Golden 2012, 1424–25.
[8] Id., 1424–25.
[9] Claus & Kay 2010, 495.
[10] Bray 2015, 1026.
[11] eBay (US 2006).
[12] See infra Section A.1.
[13] Frost 2018, 1070.
[14] Golden 2012, 1420–24; Stroup et al. 2017, 533.
[15] Wright et al. 2019, 11A: § 2947. Another form of "provisional," pre-final injunction is the temporary restraining order (TRO), a form of emergency order that a court may issue without

US courts assess whether to issue a permanent injunction and how they assess whether to issue a preliminary injunction. But because a court must generally decide whether to issue a preliminary injunction at a time when the outcome of the case is uncertain, there is necessary difference as well. Thus, these two main types of injunctions are discussed separately in the subsections that follow.

1. *Permanent Injunctions*

For over a century prior to the US Supreme Court's 2006 decision in *eBay*, US courts were described as issuing permanent injunctions "as a matter of course" upon making a final judgment of patent infringement.[16] This practice tracked a more general presumption in favor of granting injunctions in cases involving "continual infringement" of a right,[17] circumstances in which an injunction might be thought particularly helpful in preventing later relitigation of substantially the same dispute.[18] But the practice and presumption were not absolute: consistent with general equitable principles, there was a general sense that a court would decline to grant an injunction that would inflict "grossly disproportionate hardship on the defendant"[19] or would conflict with a substantial public interest.[20]

The US Court of Appeals for the Federal Circuit reformulated this practice and presumption as amounting to a "general rule that courts will issue permanent injunctions against patent infringement absent exceptional circumstances."[21] In stating this rule, the Federal Circuit repeatedly acknowledged that a court might nonetheless deny an injunction to protect the public interest.[22] The Federal Circuit has also clarified that, where an award of damages compensates a patent holder for use of the invention during the full patent term, a trial court would not abuse its discretion by denying an injunction.[23] But the Federal Circuit was not so active in acknowledging discretion to deny an injunction that would inflict disproportionate hardship on an adjudged infringer.[24] Indeed, within a few years of the Federal Circuit's creation in 1982,[25] the court signaled a lack of sympathy with such a potential basis for denying an injunction by declaring that the fact that an injunction might put a particular infringer out of business "cannot justify denial of [a

---

a hearing at which its target may be heard. Dobbs 1993, 1: 8. TROs are so rare in US patent law that they are not discussed in the body of this chapter.

[16] Golden 2007, 2119–20 & n. 38 (internal quotation marks omitted), 2122 & n. 49.

[17] Gergen et al. 2012, 212–13.

[18] *Id.*, 235.

[19] Smith 2009, 2131; Note 1958, 342–43.

[20] Schwartz 1964, 1042–43.

[21] *MercExchange* (Fed. Cir. 2005, 1339).

[22] *Id.*, 1338.

[23] *Trans-World* (Fed. Cir. 1984, p.1565).

[24] *MercExchange* (Fed. Cir. 2005, 1338).

[25] *South Corp.* (Fed. Cir. 1982, 1369).

permanent] injunction": "One who elects to build a business on a product found to infringe cannot be heard to complain if an injunction against continuing infringement destroys the business so elected."[26]

The Federal Circuit's "general rule" language and practice stood out against a historical background in which the US Supreme Court had said many times "that equitable remedies are exceptional and available only where there is no adequate remedy at law."[27] Hence, in *eBay* the Supreme Court granted *certiorari* to review the Federal Circuit's "general rule."[28]

This review did not favor the general rule. The Supreme Court emphasized the discretion of trial courts in deciding whether to grant injunctive relief.[29] At the same time, however, the court held that, in determining whether to issue a permanent injunction against an adjudged infringer, courts must apply a four-pronged test. Under this test, the party moving for an injunction "must demonstrate":

"(1) that it has suffered an irreparable injury;
(2) that remedies available at law, such as monetary damages, are inadequate to compensate for the injury;
(3) that, considering the balance of hardships between the plaintiff and defendant, a remedy in equity is warranted; and
(4) that the public interest would not be disserved by a permanent injunction."[30]

The first two prongs of this test are somewhat awkward at best. Regarding the first prong, the court presumably meant to indicate that the movant for an injunction must show that it *will* suffer irreparable injury if an injunction does not issue, rather than that it "has suffered irreparable injury" in the past.[31] Moreover, the first and second prongs are fundamentally redundant.[32] These prongs essentially just state and restate the general, threshold requirement that a court find legal remedies such as compensatory damages[33] inadequate before turning to equitable relief such as an injunction.[34]

The Supreme Court did not explicitly say that no presumptions in favor of the movant for an injunction can apply to analysis of any of these factors.[35] But lower courts, including the Federal Circuit, have commonly taken this to be the case, holding that *eBay* required them to drop, for example, presumptions regarding irreparable injury that their preexisting precedent had prescribed.[36]

[26] *Windsurfing* (Fed. Cir. 1986, 1003 n. 12).
[27] Bray 2015, 1002–03.
[28] *eBay* (US 2006, 391).
[29] *Id.*, 391, 394.
[30] *Id.*, 391.
[31] Gergen et al. 2012, 209–10 & n. 30.
[32] Laycock & Hasen 2019, 387.
[33] Rendleman 2013, 570.
[34] Gergen et al. 2012, 233–34.
[35] *Id.*, 204–05.
[36] *Id.*, 205.

Further, the Federal Circuit has added a significant, albeit largely commonsense, gloss to the understanding of the irreparable injury factor. It has held that the patentee must also show a "causal nexus" between the irreparable injury and the infringement – i.e., "that the infringement causes the harm."[37] In short, to obtain an injunction against patent infringement, a patentee needs to show not just that the patentee will suffer irreparable injury in the absence of an injunction, but that the patentee will suffer irreparable injury caused by the infringement in the absence of an injunction.[38] The Federal Circuit has explained that "[t]he causal nexus requirement ensures that an injunction is only entered against a defendant on account of harm resulting from the defendant's wrongful conduct, not some other reason" – such as the defendant's competitive success relative to the patentee based on noninfringing features of the defendant's products or processes.[39]

On the other hand, the Federal Circuit has emphasized that the causal nexus requirement is not to be overly demanding. Determination of whether there is an adequate causal nexus entails "a flexible analysis" of whether there is "'some connection' between the patented features and demand for the infringing products."[40] If irreparable injury in the form of lost sales is alleged, infringing features need not be "the only cause of the lost sales"[41] or even the "predominant" cause.[42] Instead, the key question is whether an infringing feature "impacts customers' purchasing decisions."[43] The Federal Circuit has indicated that evidence of deliberate copying, criticism of non-infringing alternatives to a patented feature, and expert testimony about the value of such a feature can serve as evidence of the requisite causal nexus.[44]

In any event, the first two prongs of the *eBay* test might not be of great interest in jurisdictions that are not rooted in the Anglo-American legal tradition and its historical demand for special justification of equitable as opposed to legal remedies. Thus, for general international purposes, the aspects of the *eBay* test of most significant interest might very well be the third, "balance of hardships," prong and the fourth, "public interest," prong. These prongs embody a court's discretion to deny injunctive relief even when traditional threshold requirements for obtaining a permanent injunction – success on the merits and inadequacy of legal remedies – are met.

---

[37] *Apple* (Fed. Cir. 2015, 639).

[38] *See id.*, 640.

[39] *See id.*, 640 ("The causal nexus requirement ensures that an injunction is only entered against a defendant on account of harm resulting from the defendant's wrongful conduct, not some other reason").

[40] *Id.*, 641 (quoting *Apple Inc. v. Samsung Elecs. Co.*, 735 F.3d 1352, 1364 (Fed. Cir. 2013)).

[41] *Apple* (Fed. Cir. 2015, 641–42).

[42] *Id.*, 642.

[43] *Id.*, 641.

[44] *See id.*, 642–43 (discussing evidence of causal nexus).

The "balance of hardships" prong effectively requires courts to consider the proportionality of an injunction's impact on the defendant to the rightsholder interests that the injunction is meant to vindicate. If the patented invention only constitutes a minor part of an infringing product or process but an injunction against infringement will cause major disruption to an adjudged infringer's business, a court is substantially likely to find that the "balance of hardships" weighs against an injunction as a result of such disproportionate effect and therefore to deny such relief.[45] On the other hand, the Federal Circuit has instructed that "expenses … incurred in creating the infringing products" and "the cost of redesigning the infringing products" are "irrelevant" to the balance-of-hardships analysis: the focus here is apparently on whether the injunction enables a patent holder substantially to tax value that is not causally related to the infringement itself, rather than to be on relieving an adjudged infringer of more direct "consequences … of its infringement."[46] Although in principle a patent owner might seek to mitigate the disproportionate effect by making a payment to the adjudged infringer as a condition of injunctive relief,[47] the author is not aware of a patent case in which such a payment has been offered by a party or demanded by a court.

The "public interest" prong of the *eBay* test can also provide a basis for denying injunctive relief. Traditionally, US courts had tended to focus on public health or safety concerns in relation to this prong.[48] But a district court held in the wake of *eBay* that a permanent injunction against "Microsoft's Windows and Office software products" would likely disserve the public interest because of a risk of a substantial negative "effect on the public due to the public's undisputed and enormous reliance on these products."[49]

Under some selection or combination of the first three prongs of the *eBay* test, courts have also considered the extent to which a patent owner's interests will be satisfactorily protected through monetary remedies, such as a backward-looking reward of damages or a forward-looking award of a royalty for any ongoing infringement. US courts have frequently found that such monetary remedies are sufficient for patent owners who are "non-practicing entities" (NPEs) in the sense that they do not engage in substantial activities to commercialize the patented invention and, instead of looking to exclude others from such activities, primarily look to license their patent rights to others for monetary compensation.[50] The category of NPEs encompasses a wide variety of entities, from universities and other research-oriented

[45] *See eBay* (US 2006, 396) (Kennedy, J., concurring); Seaman 2016, 1996–98 & tab. 3.
[46] *i4i* (Fed. Cir. 2010, 863).
[47] *Cf.* Calabresi & Melamed 1972, 1116–17.
[48] *See* Riley & Allen 2015, 756.
[49] *z4 Techs* (ED Tex. 2006, 443–44); *see also* Riley & Allen 2015, 770–72.
[50] Hovenkamp & Cotter 2016, 875; *see also, e.g., ActiveVideo* (Fed. Cir. 2012, 1337–38) ("Straightforward monetary harm [in the form of a lost licensing fee] is not irreparable harm"); *MercExchange* (ED Va. 2007, 569–70).

institutions to patent assertion entities (PAEs), often called "patent trolls," a deroga-tory moniker for entities that specialize in acquiring and asserting patent rights.[51] Empirical studies indicate that, even though the US Supreme Court prohibited adoption of a general rule disabling a general category of patent owners such as nonpracticing entities from obtaining injunctive relief,[52] NPEs are especially unlikely to satisfy the *eBay* criteria for obtaining injunctive relief for patent infringe-ment.[53] In contrast, direct competition between an infringer and patent owner appears to be positively associated with grants of injunctive relief.[54]

The Federal Circuit has held[55] that the International Trade Commission (ITC), an administrative body, is not subject to the *eBay* test in determining when to issue "(1) an exclusion order prohibiting entry of certain articles [associated with patent infringement] into the United States [or] (2) a 'cease and desist' order that might, for example, prohibit the sale of infringing matter that has been imported."[56] But statutory law instructs the ITC that it may decline to issue an exclusion order and is barred from issuing a cease-and-desist order if, "after considering the effect of such [an order] upon the public health and welfare, competitive conditions in the United States economy, the production of like or directly competitive articles in the United States, and United States consumers, it finds that such order should not be issued."[57] Moreover, Congress has empowered the President of the United States to negate such ITC orders "for policy reasons."[58] In 2013, the US Trade Representative (USTR), to whom the president has assigned the exercise of this authority, abrogated the ITC's exclusion and cease-and-desist orders directed at Apple Inc. in light of a determination that certain Apple tablets and smartphones infringed a patent owned by Samsung Electronics Co.[59] Apparently key concerns for the USTR were that Samsung itself had characterized the relevant patent as standard-essential and had committed to licensing the patent on FRAND terms.[60] More generally, over the past

---

[51] *See* Gabison 2016, 114.

[52] *eBay* (US 2006, 393).

[53] *See* Cotter & Golden 2019; Seaman 2016, 1988–89.

[54] Cotter & Golden 2019; *see also, e.g., Apple* (Fed. Cir. 2015, 640–47); *Canon* (ND Ga. 2018, 1344–52).

[55] *Spansion* (Fed. Cir. 2010, 1359).

[56] Cotter & Golden 2019.

[57] 19 USC § 1337(f)(1); *see also id.* § 1337(d)(1).

[58] *Id.* § 1337(j)(2).

[59] Letter of Michael Froman, US Trade Representative, to Irving A. Williamson, Chairman, US International Trade Commission (August 3, 2013), https://ustr.gov/sites/default/files/08032013% 20Letter_1.PDF; *see also* Certain Electronic Devices, Including Wireless Communication Devices, Portable Music and Data Processing Devices, and Tablet Computers, Inv. No. 337-TA-794, slip op. at 1–2 (July 5, 2013).

[60] *Compare* Letter of Michael Froman, *supra* note 60, at 1–3, *with Certain Electronic Devices, supra* note 60, at 1–2. "Standard-setting in patent-rich environments often requires participants to disclose relevant patents that they own and license patents essential to the standard to all participants on fair, reasonable, and nondiscriminatory (FRAND) terms." Hovenkamp 2020, 1683.

decade, the ITC itself has appeared more willing to take public interest concerns into active account.[61]

Typically, US courts do not invoke general interests in follow-on innovation as a basis for denying an injunction. On the other hand, if an adjudged infringer has engaged in follow-on innovation and thereby generated an infringing product or process whose value is substantially attributable to such follow-on innovation, injunctive relief could be deemed unwarranted due to the balance of hardships, which will potentially entail a disproportionate burden on the infringer given its separate contributions to overall value. Further, the Federal Circuit has indicated that it believes there is commonly a public interest in granting injunctions against infringement to support the research and development that the patent system is generally thought to promote.[62]

2. *Preliminary Injunctions*

US courts similarly consider four factors in deciding whether to issue a preliminary injunction against allegedly infringing activity – i.e., an injunction to prohibit engagement in certain activities that have not yet been adjudged to be infringing.[63] To obtain a preliminary injunction, a patentee must generally show:

(1) a likelihood of success on the merits – i.e., that there is no substantial question about either the validity of a relevant patent claim and that there is no substantial question that this claim is infringed by an accused product or process;

(2) a likelihood of "suffer[ing] irreparable injury in the absence of preliminary relief" (e.g., because of competitive harm that will be difficult to unwind after litigation has run its course);

(3) "that the balance of equities tips in his favor"; and

(4) "that an injunction is in the public interest."[64]

The likelihood-of-success factor calls for courts to consider the possibility that the accused infringer will prevail in challenging the validity of one or more patent claims. There also might be a failure of likelihood of success on grounds of obstacles to the patent owner's proving infringement or the possibility that a court will find a patent unenforceable on grounds such as patent misuse or inequitable conduct in proceedings before the Patent and Trademark Office.[65] The Federal Circuit has held that a patent owner has failed to show a likelihood of success if "an

---

[61] Chien & Lemley 2012, 28.

[62] *Sanofi-Synthelabo* (Fed. Cir. 2006, 1383); *cf. Abbott* (Fed. Cir. 2008, 1362–63) (affirming a district court's grant of a preliminary injunction).

[63] *See* Friedenthal et al. 1993, 703–06.

[64] *Winter* (US 2008, 20), *quoted in Trebro* (Fed. Cir. 2014, 1165).

[65] Mueller 2013, 550–51.

accused infringer … demonstrate[es] a substantial question of validity or infringe-ment" – i.e., about whether the patent owner will prevail with respect to such issues.[66] Thus, despite the presumption of validity of issued patent claims,[67] any substantial question about "validity, enforceability, or infringement" can bar the granting of a preliminary injunction.[68] Unsurprisingly, therefore, preliminary injunctions are generally difficult to obtain under US patent law.[69]

Even if a patent owner succeeds in establishing a likelihood of success on the merits of its infringement case, the owner will still need to address any concerns with respect to the balance of hardships and the public interest. Here, US courts will generally consider the same sorts of circumstances that inform decisions about these factors in the context of a permanent injunction. On the other hand, the Federal Circuit has indicated that the patent holder's likelihood of success on the merits should inform the weight given to the patent holder's interest in relief under the balance-of-hardships analysis,[70] with the result that uncertainty about infringement, patent validity, or patent enforceability can contribute secondarily through the balance-of-hardships analysis to the difficulty in obtaining a preliminary injunction. The Supreme Court has not explicitly said that courts may not take such a "sliding scale" approach to satisfaction of one or more of the four preliminary-injunction factors.[71] Under a "sliding scale" approach, a very strong showing on one factor can lead to a court awarding a preliminary injunction based on "a lesser showing" on another factor than the court would otherwise demand.[72]

Preliminary injunctions bring with them an additional wrinkle regarding require-ments for bonds that the four-part test does not explicitly reflect. In case the movant for a preliminary injunction later loses on the merits, the Federal Rules of Civil Procedure require that a successful applicant for a preliminary injunction "give … security[, commonly in the form of an injunction 'bond,'] in an amount that the court considers proper to pay the costs and damages sustained by any party found to have been wrongfully enjoined or restrained."[73] Likewise, if a court grants a stay of injunctive relief at a preliminary or later stage – for example, because of an anticipated appeal – the court may demand a bond of the accused or adjudged infringer to help ensure compensation of the patent holder for any infringement

---

[66] *Trebro* (Fed. Cir. 2014, 1165).

[67] *Sanofi-Synthelabo* (Fed. Cir. 2006, 1375).

[68] *Genentech* (Fed. Cir. 1997, 1364).

[69] Golden 2010, 514; *see also* Menell et al. 2016, 3–4 fig. 3.1.

[70] *Abbott* (Fed. Cir. 2008, 1367). At least prior to *eBay*, such "sliding scale" analysis had led courts sometimes to permit a lower showing of likelihood of success when the threat of harm from the lack of an injunction is especially great, *see* Gergen et al. 2012, 211 n. 35, but the Federal Circuit's "substantial question" analysis for likelihood of success in patent-infringement cases does not seem generally to weigh the intensity of the threat of harm. *See supra* text accom-panying notes 65–70.

[71] Laycock & Hasen 2019, 453–54.

[72] *Id.*, 453.

[73] Fed. R. Civ. P. 65(c); *see also Hupp* (Fed. Cir. 1997, 1467).

during the period of the stay.[74] The possibility of such bonds and the sense of their likely effectiveness in securing the interests of one party or another could affect a court's assessment of the balance of hardships associated with granting or denying early injunctive relief.

B. OTHER FACTORS IN THE AVAILABILITY OF INJUNCTIVE RELIEF

1. *Sovereign Immunity*

Under US law, both federal and state governments of the United States generally enjoy sovereign immunity from suit in US courts.[75] The US federal government has waived such immunity for suits for patent infringement, but only for purposes of permitting reasonable royalties, not injunctions against the government.[76] State governments also enjoy sovereign immunity with respect to allegations of patent infringement, but a suit against individual state government actors may be brought to seek an injunction against their continued violation of the federal patent laws.[77]

2. *Additional Grounds for Patent Unenforceability or Denial of Injunctive Relief*

US patents are sometimes held to be unenforceable, with the result that no relief, injunctive or otherwise, is available for infringement.[78] For example, a US patent may be held unenforceable due to patent misuse, which can result from behavior in the nature of an antitrust violation or from behavior otherwise seeking to leverage patent rights beyond what courts have held to be the proper reach[79] – for example, certain activities involving "(1) requiring the purchase of unpatented goods for use with patented apparatus or processes, (2) prohibiting production or sale of competing goods, and (3) conditioning the granting of a license under one patent upon the acceptance of another and different license."[80] But as a practical matter, patent misuse is rarely found in the application of US patent law,[81] the Federal Circuit

---

[74] *See Robert Bosch* (Fed. Cir. 2011, 1147 n. 2).

[75] *See Sisk 2005, 443.

[76] 28 USC § 1498(a); *see also* Golden et al. 2018, 1009.

[77] *See* Golden et al. 2018, 1010–11. Multiple district courts have held that Native American Indian tribes similarly enjoy sovereign immunity from patent-infringement suits, *see, e.g., MicroLog* (ED Tex. 2011) (citing additional cases), but the correctness of such rulings is controversial, *see* Robinson 2007, 244; *see also Navajo Nation* (DNM 2014) (noting, in a trademark case, courts' disagreement over the applicability of tribal immunity in the face of general federal statutes).

[78] *See* Mueller 2013, 550–51.

[79] *See id.*, 568–69.

[80] Chisum 2021, 19.04[3] The courts have also "held that a patent holder cannot charge royalties for the use of his invention after its patent term has expired." *Kimble* (US 2015, 2405).

[81] *See* Strandburg 2011, 289 (observing that patent misuse is one of a set of doctrines that "are never or increasingly rarely applied").

having emphasized that the conduct has "narrow scope" and "is not available to a presumptive infringer simply because a patentee engages in some kind of wrongful commercial conduct, even conduct that may have anticompetitive effects" or in fact is proven to involve "an antitrust violation."[82]

Another basis for declaring a patent unenforceable is a finding of inequitable conduct in proceedings before the US Patent and Trademark Office.[83] Inequitable conduct can come in the form of affirmative misrepresentations but can also come from silence in the form of failures to disclose material prior art.[84] Relatedly, but distinctly, a patent may also be found unenforceable for "prosecution laches" – i.e., for "an unreasonable and unexplained delay in prosecution [of a patent application before the US Patent and Trademark Office (PTO)] even though the applicant complied with pertinent statutes and rules."[85]

Beyond bases for declaring a patent unenforceable, there are a variety of additional equitable grounds for denying injunctive relief or blocking suit by a patentee altogether. These include laches in the form of undue delay in bringing an assertion of patent infringement to the courts;[86] equitable estoppel from effectively inviting another party's reliance on nonassertion of patent rights;[87] and unclean hands,[88] which blocks access to equitable relief in situations "where some unconscionable act of one coming for relief has immediate and necessary relation to the equity that he seeks in respect of the matter in litigation."[89] On the other hand, parties are not generally restricted to relief specified in their pleadings.[90]

3. *Parallel Proceedings and Appeals*

Courts may also choose to stay injunctive relief in light of relevant parallel proceedings, such as reexamination, other post-grant proceedings at the PTO, or an appeal, when such proceedings may result in a pertinent holding that, for example, relevant

---

[82] *Princo* (Fed. Cir. 2010, 1329).

[83] *See* Mueller 2013, 551.

[84] *See* Golden et al. 2018, 868.

[85] *Symbol* (Fed. Cir. 2002, 1363–68).

[86] *Ecolab* (Fed. Cir. 2001, 1371) ("Laches requires proof that the patentee unreasonably and inexcusably delayed filing suit and that the delay resulted in material prejudice to the defendant").

[87] *Id.*, 1371 ("Three elements must be established to bar a patentee's suit by means of equitable estoppel: 1) the patentee, through misleading conduct, leads the alleged infringer to reasonably infer that the patentee does not intend to enforce its patent against the alleged infringer, 2) the alleged infringer relies on that conduct, and 3) due to its reliance, the alleged infringer will be materially prejudiced if the patentee is allowed to proceed with its claim").

[88] *Cf. Sanofi-Synthelabo* (Fed. Cir. 2006, 1384) (upholding district court's rejection of assertion of unclean hands defense on the facts).

[89] *Keystone* (US 1933, 245).

[90] Fed. R. Civ. P. 45(c) ("Every other final judgment [distinct from a default judgment] should grant the relief to which each party is entitled, even if the party has not demanded that relief in its pleadings").

patent claims are invalid, unenforceable, or of insufficient scope to encompass an accused product or process.[91] In deciding whether to grant a stay pending appeal, courts apply a four-factor balancing test under which courts consider:

" '(1) whether the stay applicant has made a strong showing that [it] is likely
      to succeed on the merits;
(2) whether the applicant will be irreparably injured absent a stay;
(3) whether issuance of the stay will substantially injure the other parties
      interested in the proceeding; and
(4) where the public interest lies.' "[92]

Sliding-scale analysis applies to consideration of these factors: "When harm to applicant is great enough, a court will not require 'a strong showing' that applicant is 'likely to succeed on the merits.'"[93] More specifically, the Federal Circuit has indicated: "To obtain a stay, pending appeal, a movant must establish a strong likelihood of success on the merits or, failing that, nonetheless demonstrate a substantial case on the merits provided that the harm factors militate in its favor."[94] Instead of staying an injunction for the entire pendency of an appeal, a district court may delay the effective date of the injunction for a set time period – for example, "two weeks . . . to give the Court of Appeals an opportunity to consider any expedited appeal relating to the denial of the stay"[95] or ninety days so that an infringer's merchant-clients have time to adapt their conduct in conformity with the injunction.[96]

Under longstanding precedent, if the PTO cancels a patent claim, a court should refuse any injunctive relief based on that patent claim or dissolve an injunction previously based on that patent claim.[97] As the Federal Circuit has observed, "[i]t is well established that an injunction must be set aside when the legal basis for it has ceased to exist."[98] The Federal Circuit has also held that, once a nonfinal injunction, whose validity was still pending, is set aside, civil contempt sanctions for violating that injunction must also be vacated.[99] In contrast, criminal contempt sanctions would remain enforceable despite the later setting aside of an injunction.[100]

---

[91] *See Amado* (Fed. Cir. 2008, 1358–59); Menell et al. 2016, 9–19.
[92] *Standard Havens* (Fed. Cir. 1990, 512) (quoting *Hilton* (US 1987, 776)).
[93] *Id.*, 513.
[94] *Gen. Protecht* (Fed. Cir. 2011, 451).
[95] *Bio-Rad* (D. Del. 2019, *6).
[96] *Solutran* (D. Minn. 2018, *2–3).
[97] *See ePlus* (Fed. Cir. 2015, 1354).
[98] *Id.*, 1354.
[99] *Id.*, 1361.
[100] *Id.*, 1356.

C. GENERAL JUDICIAL DISCRETION TO TAILOR
INJUNCTIVE RELIEF

United States patent law does not provide for automated compliance fines for patent infringement, and the Federal Circuit has held that courts are not authorized to provide backward-looking, reparative injunctions to remedy or mitigate past harms from patent infringement,[101] such as an injunction to destroy material originally manufactured in the United States in contravention of US patent rights but now only existing abroad with no prospect of future involvement in activity contrary to those same US patent rights.[102] Instead, patent-infringement injunctions are limited to serving the purpose of preventing future infringement.[103] But subject to these limitations and a procedural requirement that the scope of an order of injunctive relief be clear,[104] US trial courts generally have substantial discretion in crafting the details of injunctive relief, including the specific time at which an injunction will become effective.[105] The clarity requirement means, however, that courts are generally forbidden from issuing simple "do not infringe" orders.[106] Instead, injunctions must generally target specific products or processes plus variations no more than "colorably different" from them.[107]

1. *Timing*

Consistent with restriction to the purpose of preventing infringement,[108] US injunctions based on patent infringement generally are available, and extend, only until a patent expires.[109] On the other hand, as noted above, US courts have discretion to stay injunctions when parallel or appellate proceedings might undercut the basis for the injunction.[110] A court might also stay an injunction or otherwise delay relief when such a delay will help prevent an injunction from imposing an undue burden

---

[101] *See supra* text accompanying notes 7–8.

[102] *See* Golden 2012, 1404.

[103] *See id.*

[104] *See id.*, 1422–23.

[105] *Cf. Amado* (Fed. Cir. 2008, 1358) (noting the district courts' "broad equitable authority" with respect to injunctions); *Russell* (US 1881, 441–42) ("Since the discretion of imposing terms upon a party, as a condition of granting or withholding an injunction, is an inherent power of the court, exercised for the purpose of effecting justice between the parties, it would seem to follow that, in the absence of an imperative statute to the contrary, the court should have the power to mitigate the terms imposed, or to relieve from them altogether, whenever in the course of the proceedings it appears that it would be inequitable or oppressive to continue them").

[106] *See* Golden 2012, 1422–23.

[107] *See id.*, 1422–23.

[108] *See supra* text accompanying notes 7–8.

[109] *See Douglas* (Fed. Cir. 2013, 1339) ("Because the [relevant] patent has expired, any permanent injunction as to this patent is now moot, and the ongoing royalty ceases to apply after the date of expiration").

[110] *See supra* text accompanying note 92.

on its target or from substantially harming the public interest.[111] Thus, for example, a US court might stay an injunction to permit an adjudged infringer or its customers time to implement a redesign for an infringing product or otherwise to alter course to avoid further infringement.[112] As when a permanent injunction is denied or an injunction is stayed pending appeal, the district court may order payment of a royalty for infringing activities for the remainder of the patent term or during the intervening time period, respectively.[113]

2. *Tailoring of Scope*

The classic form for a patent-infringement injunction issued by a US district court is that of an order specifically enjoining an adjudged or accused infringer from continuing to engage in statutorily specified activities (e.g., making, using, or selling) with one or more particular products or processes that the court has determined to be infringing or with respect to which, in the preliminary injunction context, the court has found there to be no substantial question as to infringement.[114] According to Federal Circuit precedent, a patent-infringement injunction is generally not supposed to be an "obey the law" injunction, in this case a bare order that its target not violate the patent laws, not infringe one or more specified patents, or not infringe specified patent claims.[115] On the other hand, even an order that specifically forbids only activities involving a particular product or process is generally read to encompass activities involving products or processes no more than colorably different from that specified, and many injunctions explicitly extend their reach to this extent.[116] Moreover, where the trial record supports finding an injunction to be directed at particular products or processes, the courts may read a technically deficient "obey the law" injunction to have the classic scope, tying the injunction to particular products or processes reflected in the record.[117]

Trial courts have discretion to tailor injunctive relief in ways that differ from the classic form. One catalog classifies various injunction variants as "(i) correlated-activity injunctions (type-C); (ii) destruction, disablement, or delivery injunctions

---

[111] See *Apple* (Fed. Cir. 2015, 638 & 646) (observing that a proposed thirty-day delay for the effective date of an injunction helped justify a trial judge's determination that the infringer "would 'not face any hardship'" from the requested injunction); Golden 2007, 2148 n. 136.

[112] See, e.g., *Broadcom* (Fed. Cir. 2008, 687 & 704) (noting that "carefully constructed sunset provisions" "allowing [several months of] continued sales pursuant to a mandatory royalty" helped neuter arguments that the balance of hardships favored denial of a permanent injunction).

[113] Cf. *Broadcom* (CD Cal. 2008, 1188).

[114] See Golden 2012, 1420.

[115] See *id.*, 1421–23.

[116] See *id.*, 1421.

[117] See *id.*, 1423.

(type-D); (iii) 'reformulated-bounds' injunctions (type-B); and (iv) moderated injunctions (type-M)."[118] A study of patent-infringement injunctions issued by US district courts in 2010 found that, among the over 140 injunctions identified, about 20 percent had a type-C aspect, about 5 percent had a type-D aspect, about 5 percent featured type-B tailoring, and about 3 percent had a type-M aspect.[119]

A correlated-activity (type-C) injunction forbids "activities that overlap significantly, but not entirely, with activities that by themselves can constitute infringement."[120] For example, some patent-infringement injunctions in the United States have prohibited the transport of infringing items or the display of images of infringing items even though these activities do not by themselves infringe patent rights.[121] Although technically reaching beyond the scope of patent rights to correlated activities, such "prophylactic" injunctions might advance interests in clarity and enforceability by encompassing activities that are commonly correlated with infringement.[122]

A "destruction, disablement, or delivery" (type-D) injunction also technically reaches beyond patent scope by "requiring the destruction, disablement, or delivery [to another entity] of specified material." Compliance with such an order necessarily eliminates a capacity to engage in further activities with such material that are noninfringing in themselves but that are often correlated with infringement. Thus, like an injunction forbidding correlated activities, an injunction ordering destruction, disablement, or delivery acts as a form of prophylactic order, promoting clarity and enforceability by technically demanding more than general background patent law requires. A court can, however, narrowly tailor a type-D injunction to focus its prophylactic effect: the court might issue an injunction that requires only the disablement or removal of a specified part or aspect of a particular product or process that the court has found to fall within a patent's scope.[123]

For a reformulated-bounds injunction, a district court may specify an injunction's scope by defining the scope of products or processes implicated by an injunction in much the same way that a patent claim seeks to delineate a patent's scope – i.e., by delineating technological specifications or features of the products or processes falling within the injunction's scope.[124] For purposes of clarity, enforceability, protective effect, or equitable balance, these reformulated bounds might be broader

[118] *Id.*, 1449–50.
[119] *See id.*, 1450–55.
[120] *Id.*, 1450.
[121] *Id.*, 1450.
[122] *See id.*, 1450–51.
[123] *Cf. Apple* (Fed. Cir. 2015, 646) (observing that "Apple's proposed injunction was narrowly tailored to cause no harm to Samsung other than to deprive it of the ability to continue to use Apple's patented features"); *TiVo* (Fed. Cir. 2011, 877) (noting that an injunction required EchoStar "to disable the DVR functionality in existing receivers that had already been placed with EchoStar's customers").
[124] *See* Golden 2012, 1452–55.

or narrower than associated patent claims, and they might be broader on one dimension but narrower on another.[125] For example, an injunction issued by a US district court in 2010 prohibited standard forms of infringing activity (e.g., making or using in the United States) involving "a precast concrete block" that had "a recess or notch" satisfying a dimensional requirement – an explicit restriction on width – that did not appear in associated patent claim language and that presumably helped clarify the resulting injunction's scope.[126]

Finally, there are a variety of ways in which a court might design a moderated (type-M) injunction, one "that includes an explicit carve out for [a subset of] infringing (or likely infringing) behavior."[127] A district court might "grandfather" certain already manufactured or already sold products, at least temporarily enabling their distribution, use, or support in order to protect the public interest or to prevent an injunction from imposing a disproportionate impact on an adjudged or accused infringer.[128] Likewise, a district court could limit an injunction so that it permits an infringer, upon paying a court-determined royalty, to continue to provide support, including replacement parts or other "consumables," for systems already sold to customers.[129] Such a limitation could help protect a public interest in avoiding excessive disruption to the customers' work or other activities.[130]

3. Ongoing Royalties

Except in certain situations involving federally funded inventions, the United States Patent Act does not make general provision for compulsory licensing of patent rights.[131] Nonetheless, in lieu of an injunction forbidding specified activities or in association with the stay of such an injunction, a district court may provide a remedy that can operate as a sort of case-specific compulsory license: specifically, the court may order the payment of "ongoing royalties" for continuing activity that would

---

[125] *See id.,* 1453–55.

[126] *Id.,* 1453–54 (quoting order) (internal quotation marks omitted).

[127] *Id.,* 1455.

[128] *Cf. Apple* (Fed. Cir. 2015, 638) ("Apple's proposed injunction included a 30-day 'sunset period' that would stay enforcement of the injunction until 30 days after it was entered by the district court, during which Samsung could design around the infringing features"); *Broadcom* (CD Cal. 2008, 1188) (describing a "sunset provision" for an injunction which stayed the injunction for over one year with respect to "existing or prior customers" for certain infringing products that "were on sale in or imported into the United States" more than seven months before the injunction order).

[129] *See Bio-Rad* (D. Del. 2019, *4–5).

[130] *Id.,* *4 (noting a contention that the infringer's "customers, many of whom are in the middle of long-term studies, would lose valuable data and funding if forced to stop using their 10X systems and switch to new systems mid-study").

[131] *See* Golden 2010, 516 & n. 57. Some other statutory regimes authorize US administrative agencies to order compulsory licensing, but such orders "have been rare." Contreras 2015, 45. A further statutory regime, antitrust law, has sometimes provided occasion for US courts to order compulsory licensing for purposes of promoting competition. Contreras 2015, 45.

otherwise constitute infringement involving products or processes adjudged to infringe or to be no more than colorably different from those adjudged to infringe.[132] Indeed, the availability of such relief may support a court's holding that an injunction forbidding continued infringement is unwarranted because the patent owner's interests may be adequately protected through a combination of backward-looking damages and forward-looking ongoing royalties.[133] The Federal Circuit has indicated that, before ordering a court-set ongoing royalty, a trial judge should first "instruct the parties to try to negotiate" one.[134] Further, an ongoing royalty should not be awarded if already-provided monetary relief covers all found or expected "damages for past, present, and future infringement," as when a jury calculates a lump-sum royalty for all activities involving infringing subject matter for the duration of the patent term.[135]

There has been some question in the United States of whether a court should specify a rate for an ongoing royalty that is higher than necessary to compensate the patent owner, presumably on grounds that continuing infringement by an adjudged infringer is necessarily willful and therefore properly subject to enhanced damages.[136] This reasoning and the associated practice have been criticized on grounds that the adjudged infringer might, through sunk investments, have become effectively "locked into" a course of infringing conduct and thus have become unable to avoid continuing infringement without undertaking undue costs that might have been part of the very reason for denying an injunction against infringement itself.[137]

On more solid ground, the Federal Circuit has indicated that "changed economic circumstances" might mean that the rate for an ongoing royalty should differ from the royalty rate that was the basis for a jury award of past damages.[138] For example, the post-verdict development of a "non-infringing alternative [that] takes market share from the patented products" might "justify the imposition of rates that were lower than the jury's."[139] Alternatively, analysis of standard factors for determining a reasonable royalty could justify "an ongoing royalty amount higher than the jury rate."[140]

D. ENFORCEMENT OF INJUNCTIONS THROUGH CONTEMPT PROCEEDINGS

In the United States, a party may be found in contempt of court for an "act which is calculated to embarrass, hinder, or obstruct [a] court in administration of justice, or

---

[132] *See SRI* (Fed. Cir. 2019, 1311–12); Cotter & Golden 2019; Menell et al. 2016, 9–20.

[133] *See ActiveVideo* (Fed. Cir. 2012, 1340) ("ActiveVideo's loss of revenue due to Verizon's infringement can be adequately remedied by an ongoing royalty").

[134] *Prism* (Fed. Cir. 2017, 1377).

[135] *Id.*, 1378–79.

[136] *See* Lemley 2011, 702–03.

[137] *See* Siebrasse et al. 2019.

[138] *See XY* (Fed. Cir. 2018, 1297).

[139] *Id.*, 1298.

[140] *Artic Cat* (Fed. Cir. 2017, 1370).

which is calculated to lessen its authority or its dignity."[141] Contempt may be civil or criminal, with civil contempts including "failure to do something which a party is ordered by the court to do for the benefit or advantage of another party to the proceeding before the court," whereas a criminal contempt is "an offense against the dignity of the court" itself, "such as willful disobedience of a lawful writ, process, order, rule, or command of court."[142] Hence, if violation of a court's injunction is willful, it could be a basis for both civil and criminal contempt proceedings. In patent-infringement cases, US district courts have authority to enforce injunctions through contempt proceedings in which they may impose monetary sanctions, more burdensome injunctions, coercive imprisonment to bring about compliance, and even punitive criminal penalties.[143] Criminal penalties are rarely imposed, however, perhaps in large part because of the added costs of criminal procedure.[144] Moreover, even civil contempt proceedings appear to be relatively rare.[145]

E. CONCLUSION

The United States' context-sensitive approach to injunctive relief leaves trial judges with substantial discretion but also demands certain findings relating to inadequacy of legal remedies, the balance of hardships between the plaintiff and defendant, and the public interest before such relief is awarded. The courts enforce a demanding requirement of likelihood of success before a preliminary injunction may issue. Trial judges appear to have especially wide discretion in tailoring the timing and scope of injunctive relief, and such tailoring can mitigate potentially disproportionate effects or other negative social impacts from a court's injunction against further infringement. Although the *eBay* decision's disruption of courts' prior approaches to injunctive relief has invited criticism, the resulting rearticulation of the law on injunctive relief has highlighted how many doctrinal tools can be used to guide the deployment of this remedial option – from the substantive showings demanded of proponents or opponents of such relief, to presumptions and burdens of proof associated with those required showings, to the room for structuring a specific injunction so that it better serves the ends that patent law is meant to advance. Even if a jurisdiction rejects use of one of these tools – for example, by choosing to issue injunctions essentially automatically after a final judgment of patent infringement – that jurisdiction might still improve its performance through wise deployment of another – such as the judicious use of stays to prevent disproportionate hardship to the infringer or even widespread social harm from a more immediately effective order.

[141] Nolan & Nolan-Haley 1990, 319.
[142] *Id.*
[143] *See* Golden 2012, 1409–12.
[144] *See id.*, 1409–10.
[145] *See id.*, 2095.

REFERENCES

Cases

Abbott Labs. v. Sandoz, Inc., 544 F.3d 1341 (Fed. Cir. 2008).
ActiveVideo Networks, Inc. v. Verizon Commc'ns, 694 F.3d 1312 (Fed. Cir. 2012).
Amado v. Microsoft Corp., 517 F.3d 1353 (Fed. Cir. 2008).
Apple Inc. v. Samsung Elecs. Co., 809 F.3d 633 (Fed. Cir. 2015).
Arctic Cat Inc. v. Bombardier Recreational Prods. Inc., 876 F.3d 1350 (Fed. Cir. 2017).
Bio-Rad Labs. Inc. v. 10X Genomics, Inc., No. 15-cv-152-RGA, 2019 WL 3322322 (D. Del. July 24, 2019).
Broadcom Corp. v. Qualcomm Inc., 543 F.3d 683 (Fed. Cir. 2008).
Broadcom Corp. v. Qualcomm Inc., 585 F. Supp. 2d 1187 (CD Cal. 2008).
Canon, Inc. v. Color Imaging, Inc., 292 F. Supp. 3d 1339 (ND Ga. 2018).
Douglas Dynamics, LLC v. Buyers Prods. Co., 717 F.3d 1336 (Fed. Cir. 2013).
eBay Inc. v. MercExchange, LLC, 547 US 388 (2006).
Ecolab, Inc. v. Envirochem, Inc., 264 F.3d 1358 (Fed. Cir. 2001).
ePlus, Inc. v. Lawson Software, Inc., 789 F.3d 1349 (Fed. Cir. 2015).
Genentech, Inc. v. Novo Nordisk A/S, 108 F.3d 1361 (Fed. Cir. 1997).
Gen. Protecht Group, Inc. v. Leviton Mfg. Co., 407 Fed. Appx. 450 (Fed. Cir. 2011) (nonprecedential).
Hecht Co. v. Bowles, 321 US 321 (1944).
Hilton v. Braunskill, 481 US 770 (1987).
Hupp v. Siroflex of Am., Inc., 122 F.3d 1456 (Fed. Cir. 1997).
i4i Ltd. P'ship v. Microsoft Corp., 598 F.3d 831 (Fed. Cir. 2010), *aff'd*, 564 U.S. 91 (2011).
Keystone Driller Co. v. Gen. Excavator Co., 290 U.S. 240 (1933).
Kimble v. Marvel Entertainment, LLC, 135 S. Ct. 2401 (2015).
MercExchange, LLC v. eBay, Inc., 401 F.3d 1323 (Fed. Cir. 2005), *vacated in relevant part by* eBay Inc. v. MercExchange, LLC, 547 US 388 (2006).
MercExchange, LLC v. eBay, Inc., 500 F. Supp. 2d 556 (ED Va. 2007).
MicroLog Corp. v. Cont'l Airlines, Inc., No. 6:10-CV-260, 2011 WL 13141413 (ED Tex. July 21, 2011).
Navajo Nation v. Urban Outfitters, Inc., CIV No. 12-195 LH/LAM, 2014 WL 11511718 (DNM Sept. 19, 2014)
Princo Corp. v. Int'l Trade Comm'n, 616 F.3d 1318 (Fed. Cir. 2010) (en banc).
Prism Techs. LLC v. Sprint Spectrum L.P., 849 F.3d 1360 (Fed. Cir. 2017).
Robert Bosch LLC v. Pylon Mfg. Corp., 659 F.3d 1142 (Fed. Cir. 2011).
Russell v. Farley, 105 US 433 (1881).
Sanofi-Synthelabo v. Apotex, Inc., 470 F.3d 1368 (Fed. Cir. 2006).
Solutran, Inc. v. U.S. Bancorp & Elavon, Inc., No. 13-cv-02637, 2018 WL 6681748 (D. Minn. Dec. 19, 2018).
South Corp. v. United States, 690 F.2d 1368, 1369 (Fed. Cir. 1982) (en banc).
Spansion, Inc. v. Int'l Trade Comm'n, 629 F.3d 1331 (Fed. Cir. 2010).
SRI Int'l, Inc. v. Cisco Sys., Inc., – F.3d – (Fed. Cir. 2019), *available at* 2019 WL 3162421.
Standard Havens Prods., Inc. v. Gencor Indus., Inc., 897 F.2d 511 (Fed. Cir. 1990).
Symbol Techs., Inc. v. Lemelson Med., 277 F.3d 1361 (Fed. Cir. 2002).
TiVo Inc. v. EchoStar Corp., 646 F.3d 869 (Fed. Cir. 2011).
Trans-World Manufacturing Corp. v. Al Nyman & Sons, Inc., 750 F.2d 1552 (Fed. Cir. 1984).
Trebro Mfg., Inc. v. Firefly Equipment, LLC, 748 F.3d 1159 (Fed. Cir. 2014).

XY, LLC v. *Trans Ova Genetics, LC*, 890 F.3d 1282 (Fed. Cir. 2018).
Weinberger v. *Romero-Barcelo*, 456 US 305 (1982).
Windsurfing International, Inc. v. *AMF, Inc.*, 782 F.2d 995 (Fed. Cir. 1986).
Winter v. *Natural Res. Def. Council, Inc.*, 555 US 7 (2008).
z4 Techs., Inc. v. *Microsoft Corp.*, 434 F. Supp. 2d 437 (E.D. Tex. 2006).

Regulatory and Legislative Materials

19 USC § 1337.
28 USC § 1498.
35 USC § 283.
Fed. R. Civ. P. 45.
Fed. R. Civ. P. 65.

Books, Articles and Online Materials

Bray, Samuel. 2015. "The Supreme Court and the New Equity," *Vanderbilt Law Review* 68 (4): 997–1054.
Calabresi, Guido & A. Douglas Melamed. 1972. "Property Rules, Liability Rules, and Inalienability: One View of the Cathedral," *Harvard Law Review* 85(6): 1089–128.
Chien, Colleen V. & Mark A. Lemley. 2012. "Patent Holdup, the ITC, and the Public Interest," *Cornell Law Review* 98(1): 1–46.
Chisum, Donald S. 2021. *Chisum on Patents*. Matthew Bender & Co.
Clark, Geneva. 2020. *Lex Machina: Patent Litigation Report*. Available by request at https://pages.lexmachina.com/Patent-Report-2020_LP — Patent-Report-2020.html.
Claus, Laurence P. & Richard S. Kay. 2010. "Constitutional Courts as 'Positive Legislators' in the United States," *American Journal of Comparative Law* 58 Supp.: 479–504.
Cohen, Lauren, John M. Golden, Umit G. Gurun & Scott Duke Kominers. 2017. "Troll Check: A Proposal for Administrative Review of Patent Litigation," *Boston University Law Review* 97(5): 1775–841.
Contreras, Jorge L. 2015. "A Brief History of FRAND: Analyzing Current Debates in Standard Setting and Antitrust through a Historical Lens," *Antitrust Law Journal* 80(1): 39–120.
Cotter, Thomas F. & John M. Golden. 2019. "Remedies," in Peter S. Menell & David Schwartz, eds., *Research Handbook on the Economics of Intellectual Property Law, Vol. 2: Analytical Methods*. Cheltenham: Edward Elgar.
Dobbs, Dan B. 1993. *Dobbs Law of Remedies*. 2nd ed. St. Paul, MN: West Publishing.
Friedenthal, Jack H., Mary Kay Kane & Arthur R. Miller. 1993. *Civil Procedure*. 2nd ed. St. Paul, MN: West Publishing Co.
Frost, Amanda. 2018. "In Defense of Nationwide Injunctions," *New York University Law Review* 93(5): 1065–119.
Gabison, Garry A. 2016. "Spotting Software Innovation in a Patent Assertion Entity World," *Hastings Science and Technology Law Journal* 8(1): 99–136.
Gergen, Mark P., John M. Golden & Henry E. Smith. 2012. "The Supreme Court's Accidental Revolution? The Test for Permanent Injunctions," *Columbia Law Review* 112(2): 203–49.
Golden, John M. 2007. "'Patent Trolls' and Patent Remedies," *Texas Law Review* 85(7): 2111–61.

2010. "Principles for Patent Remedies," *Texas Law Review* 88(3): 505–92.

2012. "Injunctions as More (or Less) than 'Off Switches': Patent-Infringement Injunctions' Scope," *Texas Law Review* 90(6): 1399–472.

Golden, John M., F. Scott Kieff, Pauline Newman & Henry E. Smith. 2018. *Principles of Patent Law: Cases and Materials.* 7th ed. St. Paul, MN: Foundation Press.

Henderson, M. Todd & William H. J. Hubbard. 2015. "Judicial Noncompliance with Mandatory Procedural Rules under the Private Securities Litigation Reform Act," *Journal of Legal Studies* 44(S1): S87–105.

Hovenkamp, Erik & Thomas F. Cotter. 2016. "Anticompetitive Patent Injunctions," *Minnesota Law Review* 100(3): 871–920.

Hovenkamp, Herbert. 2020. "FRAND and Antitrust," *Cornell Law Review* 105(6): 1683–744.

Laycock, Douglas, & Richard L. Hasen. 2019. *Modern American Remedies: Cases and Materials.* 5th ed. New York: Wolters Kluwer.

Lemley, Mark A. 2011. "The Ongoing Confusion Over Ongoing Royalties," *Missouri Law Review* 76(3): 695–707.

Menell, Peter S., Lynn H. Pasahow, James Pooley, Matthew D. Powers, Steven C. Carlson, Jeffrey G. Homrig, George F. Pappas, Carolyn Chang, Colette Reiner Mayer & Marc David Peters. 2016. *Patent Case Management Judicial Guide.* 3rd ed. Federal Judicial Center. www.fjc.gov/sites/default/files/2017/PCMJG3d_2016_final.pdf

Mueller, Janice. 2013. *Patent Law.* 4th ed. New York: Wolters Kluwer Law & Business.

Nolan, Joseph R. & Jacqueline M. Nolan-Haley. 1990. *Black's Law Dictionary.* 6th ed. St. Paul: West Publishing.

Note. 1958. "The Enforcement of Rights against Patent Infringers," *Harvard Law Review* 72 (2): 328–54.

Rendleman, Doug. 2013. "Remedies: A Guide for the Perplexed," *St. Louis University Law Journal* 57(3): 567–84.

Riley, P. Andrew & Scott A. Allen. 2015. "The Public Interest Inquiry for Permanent Injunctions or Exclusion Orders: Shedding the Myopic Lens," *Vanderbilt Journal of Entertainment and Technology Law* 17(3): 751–79.

Robinson, Eagle H. 2007. Comment, "Infringing Sovereignty: Should Federal Courts Protect Patents and Copyrights from Tribal Infringement?", *American Indian Law Review* 32(1): 233–56.

Schwartz, Herbert F. 1964. Note, "Injunctive Relief in Patent Infringement Suits," *University of Pennsylvania Law Review* 112(7): 1025–48.

Seaman, Christopher B. 2016. "Permanent Injunctions in Patent Litigation after *eBay*: An Empirical Study," *Iowa Law Review* 101(5): 1949–2019.

Siebrasse, Norman V., Rafal Sikorski, Jorge L. Contreras, Thomas F. Cotter, John M. Golden, Sang Jo Jong, Brian J. Love & David O. Taylor. 2019. "Injunctive Relief," in Brad Biddle, Jorge L. Contreras, Brian J. Love & Norman V. Siebrasse eds., *Patent Remedies and Complex Products: Toward a Global Consensus.* Cambridge: Cambridge University Press.

Sisk, Gregory C. 2005. "A Primer on the Doctrine of Federal Sovereign Immunity," *Oklahoma Law Review* 58(3): 439–68.

Smith, Henry E. 2009. "Institutions and Indirectness in Intellectual Property," *University of Pennsylvania Law Review* 157(6): 2083–133.

Strandburg, Katherine J. 2011. "Patent Fair Use 2.0," *UC Irvine Law Review* 1(2): 265–305.

Stroup, Richard L., Susan Tull & Mindy Ehrenfried. 2017. "Patent Holder's Equitable Remedies in Patent Infringement Actions Before Federal Courts and the International Trade Commission," *Journal of the Patent and Trademark Office Society* 99(4): 530–608.

United States Courts. 2020. "Just the Facts: Intellectual Property Cases – Patent, Copyright, and Trademark." www.uscourts.gov/news/2020/02/13/just-facts-intellectual-property-cases-patent-copyright-and-trademark

Wright, Charles A., Arthur R. Miller, Mary Kay Kane, Richard L. Marcus, A. Benjamin Spencer & Adam N. Steinman. 2019. *Federal Practice and Procedure.* St. Paul, MN: Thomson/West.

15

Issuing and Tailoring Patent Injunctions

A Cross-Jurisdictional Comparison and Synthesis

Jorge L. Contreras and Martin Husovec

In the preceding chapters of this book, we have seen a variety of national approaches to the issuance and tailoring of injunctive relief, characterized by a range of similarities and differences among jurisdictions. In this chapter, we synthesize the principal features of these different legal systems, provide an analytical framework for comparing them, and offer our observations about trends and the outlook for the future.

I. INJUNCTIVE RELIEF IN PATENT CASES: COMPARING MODALITIES OF FLEXIBILITY

One can compare national approaches to the issuance and tailoring of injunctive relief at several levels: that of the formal doctrine governing injunctive relief, the norms and customs that guide its judiciary, and the overall structural features of the legal system. The use of particular approaches within a jurisdiction varies based on whether the relief sought is preliminary or permanent. We will thus discuss these separately below, and then offer some observations regarding the rationale for the divergence of approaches as between permanent and preliminary relief.

TABLE 15.1. *Factors affecting issuance of injunctions across jurisdictions*

	Adequacy	Party interests	Public interests
Preliminary injunctions	*Minority*	*All countries*	*Majority*
Stays pending appeal	*Minority*	*Majority*	*Minority*
Final injunctions	*Minority*	*Minority*	*Minority*

When the courts consider injunctive relief, they typically assess a wide range of issues. In order to allow for cross-country comparison, we divide these issues into the following three categories:

(1) *Adequacy* – Is an injunction an appropriate remedy for the type of harm suffered by the plaintiff?
(2) *Party interests* – What is the balance of hardships as between the parties from having an injunction issue or not issue?
(3) *Public interests* – Will any important interests of third parties or the public be affected by the issuance of an injunction?[1]

These three categories are considered differently (if at all) across jurisdictions, but also at various procedural stages within the same jurisdiction (preliminary injunctions, stays pending appeal and final or permanent injunctions). Table 15.1 provides a brief overview of how the countries that we studied take these different factors into account at different stages of litigation.

Below, we consider in greater detail the ways in which different jurisdictions approach the issuance and tailoring of injunctive relief at different stages of litigation.

A. ISSUANCE OF INJUNCTIONS

1. *Permanent Injunctions*

a. The Discretion Spectrum and Conceptual Models

With respect to the *issuance* of injunctive relief (i.e., the binary question of whether or not an injunction should be issued), there are two fundamental legal conceptual models on which the countries studied base their practices: one in which injunctive relief is presumed to be available if a patent is infringed as a logical outgrowth of the nature of the exclusive patent right ("Injunction as a Right"), and another in which injunctive relief is evaluated for its appropriateness as one of several available remedies for patent infringement (including monetary damages) ("Injunction as a Remedy"). These two conceptual models generally exist within the boundaries of the two legal traditions studied here – civil law and common law.

While courts in both groups might consider public and party interests, only common law countries appear to view the remedial adequacy or appropriateness of an injunction as a fundamental factor in deciding whether or not an injunction should be issued. Among the countries studied, the United States and the United Kingdom are the only two clearly following this model. Two other countries in the sample that follow at least some common law principles, Canada and Israel, find

---

[1] From a European perspective, the notion of "proportionality" (see Section II.B) usually covers both balancing of party's interests, as well as balancing the public interest against that of the patent holder.

themselves somewhere between the two legal traditions, less because of underlying doctrine than the attitudes of their judiciaries.

To further explore the richness of national approaches represented in this study, we have developed a spectrum that roughly charts the discretion available to judges and how they exercise it. It should be noted, however, that our classification is a snapshot from a particular period. As will be discussed in Section II.D, the emerging legal literature in many countries, along with cases and legislative changes, might cause countries to shift along our spectrum over time. In that sense, the spectrum is not static.

We describe five points along the spectrum as follows:

A *No to little discretion*: automatic issuance upon a finding of infringement (Germany (pre-2021),[2] France, Italy, Netherlands)
B *Discretion, but not used*: automatic issuance upon a finding of infringement owing to attitudes of judges, despite the fact that that the law gives them some discretion (Finland, Poland)
C *Discretion, rarely used*: automatic issuance upon a finding of infringement owing to attitudes of judges, despite the fact that that the law gives them discretion, except for rare circumstances (Canada, Israel)
D *Discretion, sometimes used*: injunctions generally issue, but there is an individualized assessment in some cases (United Kingdom)
E *Discretion, always used*: individualized assessment in all cases (United States)

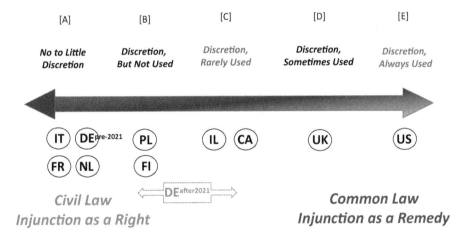

---

[2]   The German legislature amended its patent statute in 2021 in a manner that could affect its future place in our taxonomy. It is possible that Germany will thus move either into category B or C. See Section D and Chapter 8 (Germany).

The foregoing taxonomy is organized according to the remedial theory, and available domestic case law concerning the issuance of permanent injunctions in patent cases. Yet, for practical purposes, one could also view groups A and B, and partly C, as resembling one another. In these countries, injunctions are usually issued when patent infringement is found. Despite the discretion that is afforded to judges in countries in groups B and C, this discretion is never or seldom exercised through a denial of an injunction. However, unlike countries in group A, this is a choice for judges in countries in groups B and C, not black-letter law.

In countries in groups A to C, the default tendency toward the issuance of injunctions is strong, and is overridden rarely (if ever). In countries in group D (comprising only the United Kingdom), the default is weaker and can be overridden more easily. And in group E countries (comprising only the United States), a case-by-case assessment is the default, though individual judges may develop decisional shortcuts and heuristics to simplify the decision-making process.

b. Discretionary Levers When Injunctions Are Issued as of Right

Even in countries that we classify as being in groups A, B, and C, having a strong presumption favoring the issuance of injunctions in patent cases, courts exhibit varying degrees of discretion.

Not surprisingly, the least discretion is observed in group A. There, courts generally take a strong view that permanent injunctions automatically follow a finding of infringement, and extremely limited discretion is afforded to override this presumption: Germany (pre-2021), France, Italy, and the Netherlands represent this approach to varying degrees. The courts in these countries generally see no valid mechanism to balance the interests of the parties in making the injunction decision. As for the public interest, they often view it as sufficiently served by the existence of compulsory licensing schemes or other features of the patent system, as discussed in Section I.C below. If the public interest is at stake, but the defendant did not make use of the procedure for compulsory licensing, the view is that the judge should not try to correct this outcome through remedies. The Dutch courts go as far as to suggest that "the protection of the interests of third parties such as patients should not take place through allowing patent infringement."[3]

Although concepts like general civil law doctrines of abuse of rights and good faith are uniformly available in these countries, they are seldom used to limit the issuance of injunctions. Typically, the only abuse the judges are willing to rely on is one defined by competition law or at least strongly overlapping with competition law. For instance, Dutch courts treated problematic scenarios involving commitments to license patents on fair, reasonable and nondiscriminatory (FRAND) terms

---

[3] *Boehringer Mannheim/Kirin Amgen* (HR 1995, para. 3.7) – see discussion in Chapter 11 (Netherlands).

prior to the Court of Justice of the European Union (CJEU) decision in *Huawei v. ZTE* under the Dutch civil law doctrine of abuse of rights.

Courts in B countries perceive injunctions to be discretionary by nature, but judges predominantly grant them without any significant case-by-case analysis. Finnish law invites judges to consider the issuance of injunctions on a case-by-case basis. Polish law implicitly grants discretion. But despite this, the judges generally issue injunctions in patent cases on a more or less automatic basis.

In the Finnish and Polish literature, it is widely understood that there might be exceptions to this general rule, usually based on the concept of abuse of rights or the principle of proportionality. In both countries, there is other IP case law (e.g., copyright and trademark) that applies such criteria more often. However, no such cases exist to date in patent law.

In 2021 Germany also amended its Patent Act in this direction.[4] Under the new law, a claim to injunctive relief is now precluded to the extent it would, due to the special circumstances of the individual case and in view of the principle of good faith, lead to disproportionate hardship on the infringer or third parties that are not justified by the patent exclusivity right. In cases where an injunction is precluded on these grounds, the patentee will be entitled to monetary compensation in addition to any potential damages in an amount determined by the court. This change is meant to broaden the previously available scope of proportionality considerations in Germany. However, it remains to be seen whether the provision will be construed narrowly or broadly and be relied upon rarely (group C), or never (group B).

An important difference between group B and C countries is the extent of tailoring their judges are willing to undertake. Group C countries, despite being close to civil law countries on the automatic issuance of injunctions, proactively intervene in the tailoring of injunctions, as courts do in common law countries. However, on the issue of denial of injunctions, they remain largely hesitant.

In Israel, there is a significant gap between the judiciary's rigid approach to final injunctions and its broad inherent discretion.

Canada is a special case. Its courts appear to be of the view that, while injunctions are discretionary, as they "normally follow" a finding of infringement, and a permanent injunction will be refused only in "rare circumstances." However, to date, Canadian courts only have had a single patent infringement case in which an injunction was denied. In that case, the court cited local employment concerns, the fact that the patent was not practiced in Canada, and the patent was only used as a negotiation tool. To compensate, the judge awarded damages on "a generous, but non-confiscatory" rate, which was somewhat enhanced compared to reasonable royalties. Unlike US or UK courts, however, Canadian courts have not allowed

---

[4] See Chapter 8, Section D.6.b.

infringers to design around the patent by including stays in their final injunctions. For these reasons, we have included Canada among group C countries, while acknowledging that Canada might at some point shift toward group D. Today, however, Canadian case law does not allow us to make such categorization, which might be caused by the relative scarcity of litigation in Canada by patent assertion entities (PAEs) and the fact that Canadian cases involving tailoring of injunctions have typically involved direct competitors.

Unlike group A countries, therefore, the law in group B and C countries is less an obstacle to the loosening of the automatic issuance of injunctions. The obstacles in these countries are the traditional attitudes of judges, and perhaps a lack of appropriate cases. Although the same can be partly said about the group A countries, the theoretical availability of discretion is an important distinguishing factor.

Philosophically, judges in group A countries often emphasize that the presumption favoring injunctions in patent cases follows from the idea that patent rights are property rights. It is an inherent right of a property owner to exclude others from the enjoyment of that property. This reasoning is explicitly found in a majority of civil law countries in our study (France, Italy, the Netherlands, and Germany).

In France, injunctions do not have an explicit statutory basis, but the proprietary nature of patents is understood to provide an entitlement to such relief. And in Italy, an injunction issued by a court is often seen as equivalent to the prohibition on infringement already contained in the law, apart from the fact that it is addressed to a specific person.

In the future, it will be worth investigating whether the recent patent reform in Germany was sufficient to move the practice of courts in the direction of group C countries. Despite the legislative changes, the attitude of judges and their strong property outlook might limit or eliminate the impact of these changes in daily practice. Such a failure to deliver more flexibility and tailoring in practice would support our thesis that it is often not law but other factors that keep law in action from changing. However, the newly created German claim for compensation in addition to damages could present judges with an attractive new option. It remains to be seen which of these paths German courts eventually take.

c. Judicial Discretion When Injunctions Are Viewed and Practiced as Types of Remedies

Courts in group D and E countries view permanent injunctions as one type of legal remedy that exists alongside other remedies such as compensatory damages, punitive damages, specific performance, and so forth. Given their roots in English common law, these countries generally view equitable remedies as appropriate if they are necessary to address harms that are otherwise inadequately redressed by "legal" remedies such as monetary compensation (i.e., deriving from the historical division between the courts of law and the ecclesiastical courts of equity). Unlike courts in group A countries, the adequacy of injunctive relief is an integral part of the court's analysis of a party's request for an injunction. The difference between groups D and E, then, is the degree to which courts view patent infringement as an irreparable harm as to which a permanent injunction is an appropriate remedy, though in many cases, especially in group D (the United Kingdom), this analysis may be brief or absent in any given case.

While injunctions may also be viewed as remedies in Canada or Israel, this view is seldom adopted by courts in actual practice. Although the two countries differ from group D and E countries on the actual use of discretion, they typically engage in more tailoring than group A and B countries. In most of the common law countries that we studied (United States, United Kingdom, Canada, Israel), judges are more proactive in drafting their injunction orders, and enjoy considerable discretion in doing so.

Courts in the United Kingdom generally view patent infringement as causing irreparable harm to the patent holder, giving rise to a strong presumption of injunctive relief. This view was also held in the United States prior to the US Supreme Court's decision in *eBay* v. *MercExchange* (2006).[5] In *eBay*, however, the Supreme Court rejected the lower courts' presumption of irreparable harm in patent cases, requiring instead that courts apply the "traditional equitable" four-factor analysis when assessing the appropriateness of injunctive relief as a remedy in any given case. As a result, injunctions are refused in a material number of patent infringement cases in the US, particularly those involving nonpracticing entities. In many of these cases, the court will award the patent holder ongoing monetary damages (a royalty) in lieu of the injunction.

The four *eBay* factors, which are discussed at length in Chapter 14 (United States), include irreparable harm, inadequacy of monetary remedies, a balance of hardships between the parties, and the public interest. Though not expressly codified to this degree in the United Kingdom or Canada, some of these principles do enter into judicial consideration of injunctive relief in these countries.

In the United Kingdom, when a patentee has established infringement, an injunction will generally be granted. However, the case law demonstrates that judges can deny injunctions entirely (including an award of damages in lieu of the injunction) or with respect to a part of the infringement; or they can stay enforcement of a permanent injunction for a limited period.

In the United Kingdom, two notable cases concern partial grant of injunctions for a subset of infringements in order to protect the health interests of impacted patients, and a two-and-a-half-week stay of an injunction to allow for redesign of widely used service by the infringer. It is worth noting that in the United Kingdom, many cases which otherwise would have to be argued on grounds of the public interest or balance of hardship, were often resolved by prior agreement of the parties to the dispute, with the judges following the agreement of the parties.

---

[5] *eBay* (2006).

2. *Stays Pending Appeal*

It is a typical feature of many systems that first-instance decisions ordering injunctions can be subject to a stay pending appeal. The courts commonly recognize that such stays provide stronger evidence of infringement than the preliminary injunctions stage. As a consequence, the counter-interests speaking against enforceability have to be stronger. The countries use different defaults: (a) no provisional enforcement, unless the right holder requests it (Italy and France in the past, the Netherlands), or (b) default immediate enforceability, unless the alleged infringer requests a stay (Italy and France today, Canada, United States, Finland, Germany, Israel, and United Kingdom). In Poland, the first-instance decision is never immediately enforceable.

As illustrated by the Italian experience, the default rule may significantly influence outcomes. In the 1990s, the default rule in Italy was that nonfinal injunctions should not be provisionally enforced. Italian courts openly exercised their discretion not to enforce such injunctions in favor of infringers. Their assumption was that the harm suffered by the infringer from an injunction subsequently lifted could be irreparable, while the patentee could always be compensated with damages. Once the default rule changed, the attitude of judges tilted in favor of provisional enforceability. The legislature's choice of default thus influenced the attitude of judges. A similar change of default rules was adopted in France in 2019.

The Netherlands, however, offers a contrary example. Although, by default, appeals suspend enforceability, and the Dutch Supreme Court has held that provisional enforceability is always subject to a balance of interests, in practice the Dutch courts virtually always allow provisional enforceability. In Canada, there is generally a presumption, albeit not too strong, against granting a stay pending appeal.

Regardless of the default rule, injunctions pending appeal are subject to a separate balancing test even in leading civil law jurisdictions. Usually, the infringer has to post a financial guarantee to compensate the patent holder for potential damages caused by the stay. As illustrated by Dutch practice, judges can be reluctant to exercise this discretion.

The balancing usually takes the form of a typical balance of convenience. That is, how much does the potential harm to the defendant outweigh the plaintiff's interests (Germany, United Kingdom)? In the United States, judges can also consider the public interest as a factor in determining whether to grant a stay.[6] Conditions of the financial guarantee, in particular its size, can also act as effective delays on the enforcement of injunctions. For instance, in a recent dispute between Nokia and Daimler,[7] a German court set a bond at the unprecedented rate of €7 billion.

---

[6] See Dobbs 1993, 111–12.
[7] See *LG Manheim*, Case 2 O 34/19.

This brief summary shows that injunctive orders might produce binding effects at different points in time. In countries that frequently grant preliminary injunctions, such orders come very early, but might be more limited in scope. In countries where preliminary injunctions are harder to obtain, patent holders need to await at least a first-instance decision on the merits to obtain an injunction. Such injunctions could be more widely construed than preliminary injunctions and enforced provisionally; but there are also countries in which such injunctions are effectively enforceable only once they become final. Lastly, some countries might offer de facto stays of enforceability during the enforcement stage.

The models employed by different countries might therefore be hard to compare when it comes to temporal effects. A country whose judges often exercise discretion and decide cases very quickly but are less willing to grant stays of final injunctions pending appeal might, at the end of the day, be less generous to infringers than a country whose standards are more rigid but the procedures take much longer and offer numerous delays at the interim stages.

In general, failing to obtain a preliminary injunction means that only a final injunction on the merits will produce any binding effect. Since the merits determination in some countries, such as Poland, might take years to obtain, an infringer effectively enjoys a "stay" during the pendency of the matter. It is therefore understandable that in Poland significant emphasis is put on preliminary injunctions, as these are the only effective injunctive orders that are available for a considerable duration of the patent term.[8]

On the other hand, in countries where preliminary injunctions are rare, such as the United States or Canada, the emphasis is on final injunctions, but these are sometimes provisionally enforceable, subject to different tests of the balance of party interests. In Canada, judges can tailor their stays and temporarily permit part of the infringing activity.

Finally, most of the European jurisdictions, with the exception of Poland, combine available preliminary injunctions with provisional enforceability of first-instance merits decisions. In some countries, such as the Netherlands and Israel, stays might be hard to obtain for the infringers. One Israeli court was of the view that there is ordinarily no reason to grant a stay with respect to injunctions because a failure to enforce the injunction will only increase the plaintiff's injury. However, they are willing to suspend seizure orders as these affect a defendant's reputation, which cannot be *ex post* compensated by damages, while plaintiff's harm of a suspended seizure can be more easily compensated.

3. *Issuance of Preliminary Injunctions*

Unlike permanent injunctions, which are issued only after a finding of infringement, temporary or preliminary injunctive relief is issued during the course of a

---

[8] As discussed in Chapter 14 (Poland), preliminary injunctions are issued in Poland with some frequency, requiring only ex parte proceedings.

proceeding, when an infringement is alleged but not proven. No country in our study has adopted a strong presumption in favor of preliminary relief. Instead, as far as preliminary injunctions are concerned, courts in all countries adopt some form of discretionary procedure.

Generally, the test for preliminary injunctions starts with a determination of the patent holder's probability of success on merits. These standards differ considerably among countries. Some countries, such as the United States, Germany and Finland, require that the patentee demonstrate a substantial likelihood of success on the merits before issuing a preliminary injunction (which we refer to as a "strong" proof requirement), while others, such as the United Kingdom, Canada, Israel and Poland, simply require the existence of a credible claim of infringement (which we refer to as a "weak" proof requirement).

All of the countries that we studied empower judges to exercise discretion when considering the issuance of preliminary injunctions. The central hallmark of such an assessment is the balance of party interests: how the issuance or its refusal will affect the parties. Typical considerations include the impact of an injunctive order on the infringer's business (e.g., closure, customers or insolvency), on the business of the patentee (e.g., on its production, customers or ability to compete), or the likelihood that the patentee will successfully collect damages later in the process. While most countries use such balancing to decide upon issuance, in Poland, for instance, it only shapes the form and scope in which a preliminary injunction is granted.

Unlike parties' hardship, the public interest is not always explicitly mentioned in the legal provisions dealing with preliminary injunctions. For instance, it is not included in the statutory language in Finland. That being said, legal doctrines in the countries studied generally required assessment of the public interest. In the common law countries (United Kingdom, United States, Israel, Canada), public interest is one of the traditional equitable factors. Similarly, major civil law jurisdictions (Germany, France, Italy and the Netherlands) explicitly consider public interest in their decision making about issuance of preliminary injunctions. In Poland, also a civil law country, the public interest is not explicitly considered by the courts, but this seems to be an exception.

Public interest factors considered by judges include issues of employment (e.g., massive and sudden worker layoffs), workplace safety and public health (e.g., availability of products with particular therapeutic properties, increased efficacy or reduced side effects). Pure considerations of follow-on innovation and promotion of competition are usually not sufficient to demonstrate a public interest in favor of injunctions. Nevertheless, courts in some US cases[9] have considered the

---

[9] *See, e.g., Apple* (Fed. Cir. 2015, 647) ("the public interest nearly always weighs in favor of protecting property rights in the absence of countervailing factors, especially when the patentee practices his inventions"). See discussion in Contreras 2019, 3, 11–12.

public interest in the reliable enforcement of patent rights, bringing public interest factors into play in favor of the issuance of injunctions. While employment considerations alone would typically be insufficient to overcome a request for a final injunction, these considerations may be given stronger consideration in the earlier stages (preliminary injunctions and stays pending appeal). In Germany, the courts previously considered issues such as the patent holder's ability to satisfy domestic market needs, improvement of trade balance, or improvement of the currency situation as being covered by the public interest. The net effect of these considerations is that public interest factors usually weigh against the entry of a preliminary injunction.

Similarly, as with stays pending appeal, another hidden flexibility with preliminary relief is its potential to counterbalance the risk of over-enforcement by requiring the party requesting a preliminary injunction to post a bond to compensate the enjoined party should the imposition of the injunction cause injury. A side effect of this requirement is that it potentially makes the enforcement of a preliminary injunction more expensive, thereby incentivizing settlement.

In the EU, this approach is supported by Article 9(6) of the Enforcement Directive, which allows the courts to require adequate security or equivalent assurances to ensure compensation for harms caused by such enforcement. Such security is limited to compensating for harms caused when the preliminary injunction should not have been issued because the patent was later found invalid or not infringed, or when the asserted patent is not renewed or maintained by the patent holder. In some cases, national law might go beyond these scenarios.

The availability of such bonds potentially lessens the severity of a preliminary injunction, reducing the risk to the enjoined party should the injunction be issued in error, and potentially deterring some patent holders from seeking to enforce injunctions when significant harm could arise. If factors such as protecting public health result in the imposition of very high bond requirements, then flexibility may be achieved even when there is little judicial flexibility in the decision whether or not to issue the injunction as an initial matter.

In theory, other forms of security or assurance could be required in addition to monetary bonds. In Europe, such security could be based upon general requirements of proportionality. For instance, a court could require a patent holder to make assurances, subject to pre-agreed compensation, that it will not enforce a preliminary injunction if its supply of products covered by a patent is inadequate to meet public needs, particularly in the case of medical products that are necessary to support public health. Alternatively, a court could assess a high bond requirement in such cases, also with the effect of protecting some public interest.[10]

---

[10] See, for instance, LG Düsseldorf, 9.3.2017, 4a O 137/15 – Herzklappen (security of 90 million euros to allow preliminary enforceability).

Interestingly, the degree of discretion that courts enjoy with respect to preliminary injunctions may, as a practical matter, lessen the need for discretion in permanent injunction cases. That is, the delay and scope of inquiry around preliminary injunctions sometimes act as hidden "flexibilities" of the system. For instance, if the discretion is exercised appropriately on the preliminary and/or stay pending appeal stage, the need for further delays in granting a final injunction might be low, especially if the procedure took years to complete. By the time the final injunction is entered, the patents may have expired, or, at a minimum, the prudent infringer would have had ample time to invent around the infringed patents or prepare for the effects of such an injunction.[11]

B. CONTENT OF INJUNCTION ORDERS

In addition to the processes for determining whether or not an injunction will issue in a particular case, variations exist among courts and jurisdictions with respect to the specific language and terms of injunctions that are issued. The language of injunctions appears to be influenced both by doctrinal rules in a jurisdiction and by its legal norms and customs.

1. *Tailoring the Scope of Injunctions*

In most of the studied common law countries (United States, United Kingdom, Canada, Israel), judges are more proactive in drafting their injunction orders, and enjoy considerable discretion in doing so. These judges are more likely to invite parties to participate in drafting the wording of injunction orders or to draft their orders from scratch. In Canada, for instance, judges may either require the parties to jointly draft the proposed order, or write it themselves and ask the parties to make notes and comments, before issuing it.

In the civil law countries (Germany, France, Finland, Italy, the Netherlands, Poland), the plaintiffs largely predetermine the scope of court orders, and judges can only narrow them, including by reformulating. Hence, they act more as moderators of the proposals of plaintiffs. The process of drafting injunctions is generally less iterative in civil law countries than common law countries.

Varying the discretion of judges, however, does not seem to translate into a shared practice regarding the breadth of resulting orders. We generally observe a spectrum where, on one hand, the judges in some countries issue mere "do not infringe" orders, specifying only the patents infringed (Canada, United Kingdom, Israel, the Netherlands), while judges in other countries tend to specify products or processes along with infringing acts (Italy, Germany, Finland, France, United States).

---

[11] Lemley & Shapiro 2007, 2005 ("The downstream firm cannot adopt a strategy of 'redesign only if the patent is valid' without exposing itself to holdup if the patent is valid").

Some of the countries in which more narrowly worded injunctions are issued sometimes allow enforcement of injunctions beyond their literal wording. For instance, in Germany, the infringer cannot evade an injunction by making minor changes to the infringing act/product if the core of the infringement remains unchanged. In Italy, minor variations falling outside the "genus and species" of the infringement that was already ascertained by the court would also be insufficient to escape the effects of an injunction. On the other hand, in the United States, orders might explicitly envision such equivalent infringements as variations of "no more than colorably different" infringements in addition to those specified in orders.

At the same time, even countries that primarily rely on broader wording of orders sometimes adopt strategies to narrow them or clarify their goals. For instance, judges might accompany broad orders with narrower language specifying products and conduct that are enjoined (Canada), or specifying only the conduct that is enjoined (Israel). In some countries, broad wording of injunctions may eventually be construed more narrowly in light of the court's reasoning (the Netherlands). In the United Kingdom, judges may substitute a default broad form for orders for a form that is more specific if justified by the circumstances of the case. In some countries, prohibitions on indirect infringement and importation are accompanied by more specific orders, as noninfringing activities may be involved in such activities.

Thus, whatever the standard for issuing injunctions in a particular jurisdiction, the scope of injunctive orders seems to reflect some balance between effective protection of patent holders on the one hand, and infringers' right to conduct business, on the other. The overarching goal of all such orders is that infringers should not be able to avoid the effect of such orders. It is commonly feared that overly narrow orders could make enforcement onerous for plaintiffs, as they would need to initiate new litigation for each infringing act not covered by the scope of such narrow orders. On the other hand, as emphasized by the Polish courts, overly broad injunctions can disproportionately limit the rights of infringers by preventing them from taking actions that are not actually infringing. In the United Kingdom, courts will consider the intent of infringers when calibrating the scope of injunctive orders. Similar considerations are present in the Italian literature.

The balance struck by different courts across jurisdictions seems to depend on the broader institutional setup, in particular the availability of an effective procedure to clarify injunctions over time. In some countries, if questions about the scope of an injunction arise, infringers can seek declarations of noninfringement from a court (e.g., Netherlands and United Kingdom). In these models, by default, the costs of clarification and the burden of proof are borne by the infringer. However, different institutional concerns exist in other countries. In Finland, for instance, judges strive for narrow orders because nonspecialist institutions such as the District Bailiff are responsible for subsequent enforcement. The judiciary therefore aims to streamline enforcement as much as possible.

The timeline of injunctive orders is determined not only by a country's attitude toward flexibility in orders for final injunctive relief, but also by the availability of preliminary injunctions, its treatment of stays pending appeal, and eventual enforcement. At each of these stages, additional delays may be introduced. Judges therefore consider the temporal effects of their decisions beyond the actual wording of orders, and in some cases the infringer might have ample time to adapt its operations prior to a final decision on the merits.

2. *The Range of Tailoring Approaches to Injunctive Orders*

At its core, every effort to calibrate the wording of injunction orders is a type of judicial tailoring. For example, mentioning a specific patent or infringing product in an order distinguishes it on a factual basis from other orders. However, there are some tailoring practices that highlight how tailoring can specifically accommodate private and public interests. The country chapters describe several such more advanced types of tailoring: (1) sell-off periods, (2) delays, and (3) additional carve-outs. Notably, each of these types of tailoring derogates from an injunction's otherwise absolute prohibition on the manufacturing and sale of infringing goods – it allows limited infringing activity for the purpose of accommodating reasonable party and public needs.

Sell-off periods are used to allow the infringer to finish distribution of products that were already produced at the time an injunction is entered, or for which orders were placed by the third parties. Such sell-off periods seek to prevent disruption in the distribution of products to the market, particularly when there is a public need for such products (e.g., medical products or drugs).

Delays in the effectiveness of an injunction can, in addition to permitting selling off inventory, allow an infringer to invent around the infringed patent.[12] In some cases, delays in effectiveness are imposed for the benefit of third parties, such as patients, where immediate enforcement could disrupt the functioning of some important public resources (e.g., use of new heart valves requires retraining of the surgeons or adjustment of hospital procedures).[13] It could also mitigate the effects of an injunction on critical infrastructure, such as sewage systems or telecommunication networks, which affect the population at large.

Finally, *carve-outs* often complement these other types of tailoring. They might temporarily exempt the infringer from supplying the infringing product to a group of patients for whom there is currently no noninfringing alternative,[14] exclude the use

---

[12] In the United States, the Federal Circuit in *Broadcom Corp.* (Fed. Cir. 2008) affirmed the District Court decision to delay the effectiveness of permanent injunctive relief by a period of up to twenty months due to the party hardship and public interest.

[13] See *Edwards Lifesciences LLC* ([2018] EWHC 1256 (Pat)) – discussed in Chapter 13 (United Kingdom).

[14] See *id.*; *AbbVie* (FC 2014) – discussed in Chapter 5 (Canada).

of a product by existing consumer users, or simply include conditions on new sales, such as obligations to provide additional information to customers.[15] Apart from individual-oriented carve-outs, one can also imagine geographical carve-outs, e.g., during epidemics, natural catastrophes, or extreme weather.

3. *Compensation by Infringers*

As noted in Section I.B.2, some means of tailoring injunctive relief permit the infringer to continue to infringe for limited periods of time or with respect to limited quantities of products. When an injunction is denied entirely, the infringement may continue indefinitely. Different jurisdictions have considered whether, and to what degree, the infringer must compensate the patent holder for the right to engage in these infringing activities.

When an injunction is denied in the United States after a finding of infringement, the infringer may be required to pay the patent holder ongoing royalties, as though operating under a license from the patent holder. The amount of such ongoing royalties may be determined by the court (often by a jury) or may be negotiated by the parties. An ongoing royalty may not be ordered if the patent holder was awarded lump sum damages to compensate it for all past and future harm associated with the infringement during the patent term.

In Canada, the court in *Unilever* denied an injunction (on the basis that the patent holder had no operations in Canada) and in lieu thereof awarded "a generous, but non-confiscatory, rate of royalty," which was somewhat higher than a reasonable royalty. The court reasoned that the enhancement was given in exchange for the avoidance of an injunction.[16]

Though there is no English patent case to date in which damages have been assessed in lieu of an injunction, it appears that calculation of such damages would follow the criteria for ordinary damages for patent infringement. That is, they would be calculated as lost profits, lost licensing fees, or a reasonable royalty that the parties would have agreed in comparable cases. Disgorgement of the infringer's profits does not seem to be available in such cases.

Article 12 of EU Directive 2004/48 permits the courts of member states to order monetary compensation in lieu of an injunction. Though optional, Poland implemented this provision in Article 287 section 3 of the Polish Industrial Property Law. It provides that a court may, upon the motion of the infringer, order the payment of monetary compensation in lieu of an injunction. This is, however, possible only when the infringer acted unintentionally and without negligence, the issuance of an injunction would disproportionately harm the infringer, and monetary compensation would be satisfactory to the patentee. Despite the existence of this statutory

---

[15] See *id.*
[16] *Unilever* (FCTD 1993, 571).

provision, it has never been exercised with respect to any patent or other intellectual property (IP) case.

Sell-off exceptions permit ongoing infringement with respect to the sale of existing units of an infringing product. In some cases, damages may have been assessed with respect to the manufacture of such infringing products, in which case additional royalties should not be due with respect to their subsequent sale. Thus, sell-off exceptions are usually granted without an obligation by the infringer to compensate the patent holder further. Nevertheless, examples exist in which courts have required compensation by the infringer selling off infringing inventory (Canada). Similarly, in Finland, owners of infringing products can be allowed by a court to continue to use such products if they pay compensation.[17] European law also foresees the opposite scenario, namely that patent holders are asked to shoulder the cost of ancillary orders, such as those requiring the infringer to destroy or recall infringing products.[18]

4. *Enforcement of Injunctions*

The countries studied generally employ a mix of approaches to the enforcement of injunctions. Usually, enforcement mechanisms combine monetary liability (fines, damages and penalties) and criminal penalties. This is the case in Germany, Canada, Israel, Italy, Poland, the United Kingdom and the United States. In the United States, an infringer's failure to comply with the terms of an injunctive order can result in a finding of "contempt of court," which can be a criminal offense, and might result in criminal penalties such as imprisonment as well as a new injunction that is more burdensome. Other countries (Finland, France and the Netherlands), however, only rely on monetary tools to enforce injunctions. Automatic noncompliance fines are more typical for civil law jurisdictions (the Netherlands, Poland, Italy, France and Finland). For instance, in France, the courts use penalties, which they can impose even *ex officio*. Such penalties are often independent of damages and cannot be credited against damages otherwise owed by the infringer.

In the enforcement stage, the effect of an infringer's knowledge and intent to violate an order is not assessed uniformly. While some countries only sanction culpable (Germany), willful (United States) or intentional (Italy) noncompliance, other countries do not take a party's intent into account (United Kingdom). In the United Kingdom, the defendant's intention (or lack of it) is generally relevant only to the sanction, but the court can dismiss disproportionate reactions to trivial or blameless breaches of an order.

[17] Interestingly enough, the compatibility with EU law is supported by Article 12 of the Enforcement Directive – See Chapter 4 (EU).
[18] See Article 10(2) of the Enforcement Directive.

C. INSTITUTIONAL FACTORS

It has already been noted that institutional factors influence the exercise of flexibility both in granting injunctive relief and also in fashioning the terms of injunctions. Most notably, the belief of judges in countries such as Germany (pre-2021) that *compulsory licensing* can resolve public interest issues leads them to adopt a certain kind of "public interest bifurcation." Thus, the public interest is generally set aside when deciding individual cases because the law is construed to create a separate procedure for its evaluation.

Somewhat related to this are rules in some countries that immunize the government and its suppliers from injunctions for patent infringement – United Kingdom (the Crown), France (for national defense), United States (sovereign immunity for federal and state governments). In countries such as the United States, sovereign immunity is a constitutional principle that applies to all claims made against the government. State governments are wholly immune from patent infringement as such claims may be heard only in federal courts, and states may not be sued in federal court without their consent under the 11th Amendment to the Constitution. The federal government is likewise immune from claims brought in its own (federal) courts, though by statute (28 USC § 1498) the federal government has waived its (and its contractors') sovereign immunity for patent infringement claims and permits claims for monetary relief to be brought against it in the specialized Court of Claims. However, no injunction may issue against the federal government or its contractors in such cases.

This *injunction immunity* might provide another type of "public interest bifurcation," as it suggests that the legislature has already considered issues of public interest in immunizing governmental bodies from such injunctions. Although such immunity does not appear common among civil law countries, it may be supplemented *de facto* by compulsory licensing rules, which in some cases are drafted particularly with governmental use in mind. The idea behind such a two-tier system could be explained by the expectation that enjoining actions of public authorities, as opposed to private actors, is more likely to raise public interest concerns. For instance, enjoining fire departments, police corps, military, or public health authorities from using inventions in the course of their public activities appears prima facie more problematic than stopping exploitation by private firms of patents covering typical commercial products or services.

Specifically, Germany, the Netherlands, Finland and Canada, which do not recognize sovereign immunity for patent claims, allow their governments to obtain compulsory licenses under patent rights. Several countries also permit private parties, in addition to governmental entities, to seek compulsory licenses under patent rights under specified conditions. However, several countries, including Germany, report that such compulsory licenses must be applied for specifically and cannot be raised as defenses in an infringement proceeding (Finland, Germany and the Netherlands). Nevertheless, compulsory licenses are reported to be very rarely issued. Therefore, even though some countries that favor an automatic approach to injunctions do have compulsory licensing provisions, they are not often applied in practice, and are not very well integrated with infringement proceedings.

This observation implies that jurisdictions that justify their inflexibility in issuing injunctions by pointing to the availability of compulsory licenses may be relying on a false equivalency. If alleged infringers cannot reasonably rely on the availability of compulsory licenses, they cannot be said to be particularly useful to defend the public interest. Moreover, under such a system, the defense of the public interest is left to the initiative of one of the parties, which may not always be effective or in the best interest of the public. Improving the integration of compulsory licensing procedures into infringement proceedings represents a possible, albeit limited, solution to the general problem of considering the public interest.

Another institutional feature that prominently affects the issuance and tailoring of injunctions is a court's assessment of patent validity and prevailing assumptions about the overall quality of patents in the jurisdiction. If judges believe that the quality of patents is generally high in their jurisdiction, they may presume more strongly that a patentee's argument is likely to prevail. These presumptions impact the availability of preliminary injunctions and possibly stays of enforcement. If the institutional set-up of a country strengthens this presumption further by bifurcating the infringement and validity portions of a proceeding (Germany and Poland), this might also increase the likelihood of final injunctions.

A stronger presumption in favor of granting injunctions might also result from a country's reliance on a nonspecialized judiciary, which may be unwilling to question underlying patents because it is intimidated by their technological aspects. During our workshops, it was suggested that in some countries with a specialized judiciary and patent bar (e.g., the Netherlands and the United Kingdom), one can observe more professional self-restraint in enforcing the rights of their clients. That is, counsel exhibiting self-restraint are more likely to request reasonable remedies, rather than seeking maximal penalties. Such self-restraint would then result in the issuance of more balanced decisions by judges. However, in the United States, professionalization may have the opposite effect, with a specialized patent bar and judiciary leading to a greater number of pro-patent holder decisions as well as rules favoring patent holders.[19]

Naturally, there are a number of additional institutional factors that might influence what we observe in the case law. In particular, legal fees and private costs, the

---

[19] See, e.g., Jaffe & Lerner 2004, 168 ("the failure of federal efforts to reform the patent system is due to several factors: ... (2) the people with the greatest economic stake in retaining a litigious and complex patent system – the patent bar – have proven to be a very powerful lobby"); Holte & Seaman 2017, 145 (finding support for the claim that "the Federal Circuit, as a specialized court with a large number of patent cases, is more pro-patentee than the generalist district courts").

existence of cost-shifting schemes, the likelihood of settlements and the average length of proceedings, all further influence litigation outcomes. For instance, according to one empirical study, German litigants settle 60 percent of patent cases – which is a disproportionately high rate when compared to other jurisdictions (e.g., the settlement rate in the United Kingdom is 35 percent).[20] In the United States, commentators routinely report that the "the vast majority of patent cases settle before trial."[21] Settlement agreements often include cease-and-desist obligations that otherwise would have been adjudicated by the courts. Therefore the fact that we do not observe nuanced tailoring in the case law does not necessarily mean that it is not taking place in the market. In fact, one could argue that such agreements are exactly where such tailoring takes place. Furthermore, some empirical research suggests that German patent courts engage in forum selling by attracting cases through the pro-plaintiff stance of refusals to stay patent infringement proceedings when a patent's validity is being challenged.[22]

Another institutional factor that can affect the frequency and scope of injunctions is the cost of litigation. In the United Kingdom, for example, comparatively high costs of litigation, coupled with fee-shifting rules and high patent invalidation rates, may limit the number of nonpracticing entities (NPEs) invoking their rights in the jurisdiction.[23] As a result, courts in the United Kingdom may have less occasion to consider cases involving NPEs than, say, courts in the United States, in which fee shifting is rare.

To conclude, patent litigation is influenced by a range of systemic factors, and the degree of flexibility and tailoring of injunctive relief in a particular jurisdiction cannot be assessed simply by looking at absolute numbers of decided cases. Sometimes, tailoring may occur before judges make final decisions, because of either built-in delays in the litigation process or settlements. Sometimes other features of the system, such as compulsory licensing, immunities and legal costs, appear to address public and party interests. However, none of these institutional features is perfect or applied uniformly, meaning that there will always be a group of cases that require some form of fine-tuning at the remedial stage.

II. ASSESSING SIMILARITIES, DIFFERENCES AND OUTCOMES

A. TAILORING AND REFUSAL

Judges have two main strategies for giving effect to party interests and public interests when assessing injunctions, while at the same time minimizing encroachments on patent rights: (1) to use discretion in deciding which injunctions to grant and deny, and (2) to tailor final injunctions by allowing delays in effectiveness, sell-off periods

---

[20] Cremers et al. 2016.
[21] *See, e.g.,* Lemley et al. 2013, 171.
[22] See Bechtold et al. 2019.
[23] McDonagh 2016, 30 (studying cases through 2015).

TABLE 15.2. *Notable Cases Involving Injunctions Denial, by Country*

	FR	FI	DE	IT	IL	NL	UK	US	PL	CA
Refusal	n/a	n/a	n/a	n/a	n/a	*Apple v. Samsung II* (2012; willing SEP licensee)	*Edwards v. Boston* (2018; public interest)	Numerous cases since 2006	Yes (in theory, but no case law)	*Unilever* (1993)

or carve-outs.[24] The denial of injunctions, which is often emphasized in policy discussions, seems to be relevant only if tailoring does not offer satisfactory solutions for party or public interests.

Looking at the case law across jurisdictions, we observe that the majority of countries we studied engage in some type of tailoring of injunctive relief – often by introducing delays or sell-off periods in at least some cases.[25] While in other countries tailoring is theoretically possible, there is limited or no case law directly on point. The denial of injunctions after a finding of patent infringement is, except in the United States, very rare.[26] Table 15.2 summarizes notable cases in which injunctions have been denied in patent cases in the countries that we studied.

The most established practice exists in the United States, where courts assess the appropriateness of injunctions on a case-by-case basis and have denied injunctive relief when the factors established in *eBay* v. *MercExchange* are not satisfied. Apart from the United States, United Kingdom courts, despite limited case law, most strongly signal the possibility that injunctive relief may be denied. *Edwards* v. *Boston*[27] shows that such refusal can be also limited to only a subset of infringing actions or be limited in time. In a case involving standards-essential patents, *Unwired Planet* v. *Huawei*,[28] an English court issued a conditional injunction, which would enter into force only if the infringer did not enter into a license with the patent holder on terms prescribed by the court. Lastly, there is a single Canadian case that rejects injunctive relief, in part on the ground that the patentees did not practice their patented invention in Canada.

---

[24] This latter group has been referred to as tailoring of "scope or timing". Siebrasse et al. 2019, 155.

[25] *See also id.* (eliminating existing products from the scope of an injunction has been "occasionally applied or at least considered by courts in the United States, the United Kingdom, and Canada").

[26] Following the framework set forth by the CEJU in *Huawei* v. *ZTE* [C-170/13], courts in Europe may refuse to grant patent injunctions on the basis of competition law when asserted patents are subject to licensing commitments on "fair, reasonable and non-discriminatory" (FRAND) terms. See Larouche & Zingales 2017, 406.

[27] *Edwards Life Sciences LLC* (No. 3) [2018] EWHC 1256 (Pat).

[28] *Unwired Planet Int'l Ltd* [2017] EWHC 1304 (Pat).

B. DISCRETION AND PROPORTIONALITY

Judicial discretion, in the common law countries, and proportionality, in the EU countries, are both types of case-by-case assessment. They might differ in details and the factors that they involve, but ultimately they attempt to deliver individualized justice. This is seen in the English case law, where both of these types of assessment overlap, but often point in the same direction. The combined test developed by Lord Justice Arnold in *HTC* v. *Nokia* blends the two approaches as follows:[29]

> Article 3(2) does not merely require that remedies for infringement should be proportionate and avoid creating barriers to legitimate trade, it also requires that they should be effective and dissuasive. As the jurisprudence of the English courts summarised above recognises, the effect of refusing an injunction to restrain future infringement is, to that extent, to deprive the claimant of its legal right. That is particularly true in the case of patents, which are monopolies and thus the essence of the right is the patentee's right to give or withhold his consent to another person's exploitation of the patented invention. Thus the grant of damages in lieu of an injunction is inevitably less effective and dissuasive than the grant of an injunction. ... Where the right sought to be enforced by the injunction is a patent, however, the court must be very cautious before making an order which is tantamount to a compulsory licence in circumstances where no compulsory licence would be available. It follows that, where no other countervailing right is in play, the burden on the party seeking to show that the injunction would be disproportionate is a heavy one.

From the contributions to this book, it is clear that some judges in common law countries, in particular Israel, share this starting point when exercising their discretion.

The greatest degree of judicial discretion in terms of issuing injunctions is observed in the United States. This result is usually explained by reference to the US Supreme Court's *eBay* decision in 2006. But *eBay* did not emerge in a vacuum. It could be argued that the instrumentalist purpose of patent law established by the US Constitution itself allows US courts to question the normative goals of the patent system, and the remedies that should be available to patent holders, more deeply than is permitted to courts in other countries, including other common law countries.[30] That is, unlike countries in which patents fall under the umbrella of constitutional principles that protect private interests in property, the US Supreme Court, responding to the US Constitution's instrumentalist view of patents, has conceptual-

---

[29] *HTC Corporation* [2013] EWHC 3778 (Pat), paras. 28, 32.

[30] Canada also takes an instrumentalist view of patent law, and the Canadian Patent Act states that "the object of the Patent Act is to promote the development of inventions in a manner that benefits both the inventor and the public." Nevertheless, with respect to injunctions, Canada falls into Group A, giving its judges little discretion not to issue injunctions.

ized patents as "government franchises" rather than traditional property rights.[31] Accordingly, in deciding *eBay*, the US Supreme Court was not constrained by strong constitutional property principles that may limit the authority of courts in other countries to exercise significant discretion in deciding whether or not to grant injunctions in patent cases. In the European Union, judges might be warier of the fact that the legislature's decision to protect an invention through an exclusive right implies that any denial of an injunction would be taking away the "essence" of the patent right.[32]

Significantly, the European proportionality test, which addresses both party interests and public interests, does include a test relating to the adequacy of monetary relief to the patent holder. As illustrated by the passage from *HTC v. Nokia* quoted above, reference to effectiveness and dissuasiveness is, on the contrary, generally understood to highlight the property rationale of patents. From this perspective, it is understandable that European judges do not make the same normative choices, and give much more deference to the legislative authority vested in patents. The proportionality test, as outlined by the case law of the CJEU (see Chapter 4 (EU)), therefore acts as a marginal corrective on the real-world effects of patent enforcement rather than a last-resort corrective on the entire patent system.

As discussed in Chapter 4 (EU), Recital 17 of the EU Enforcement Directive frames proportionality considerations as "tak[ing] into account the specific characteristics of the case, including the specific features of each intellectual property right and, where appropriate, the intentional or unintentional character of the infringement." Article 3(2) provides that "measures, procedure and remedies" used to address the infringement of intellectual property rights must be "effective, proportionate and dissuasive" to ensure their enforcement.

Though the Enforcement Directive includes a specific optional provision on damages in lieu of injunctions, its impact on national law appears to be insignificant at this point. Article 12 of the Enforcement Directive, which is limited to party interest grounds and does not include the public interest element, has not been explicitly implemented in Germany (for patent cases), Finland, France, Italy, the Netherlands, or the United Kingdom. In fact, even Poland, which has implemented it, has not applied it in an IP case. While authors from many of these countries do not dismiss the possibility of refusal of an injunction based on the Enforcement Directive's concept of proportionality, there is no case law showing that this is a

---

[31] *Oil States Energy Services* (2018).

[32] On the notion of essence of intellectual property rights under the EU Charter, see Husovec 2019, 843. For instance, Advocate General Wathelet hints at this in his Opinion in *Huawei v. ZTE* [C-170/13] at fn. 34 ("[t]he essential objective of a patent is to ensure, in order to reward the creative effort of the inventor, that the owner of the patent has the exclusive right to use an invention with a view to manufacturing industrial products and selling them, either directly, or by granting licences to third parties, as well as the right to oppose infringements").

practical possibility. Usually, the only such case law deals with FRAND disputes, drawing on the limits outlined by competition law.

It is notable that the approach of group A countries, which are mostly EU civil law countries, has generally been different with respect to more ancillary orders, such as those relating to destruction and recall of infringing products. These orders are more particularly regulated by the EU law, which explicitly requires that judges always assess "the need for proportionality between the seriousness of the infringement and the remedies ordered as well as the interests of third parties shall be taken into account" (Article 10, EU Enforcement Directive). Thus for these specific ancillary orders it is not uncommon to see refusals, or qualifications, by judges.

The general situation described above contrasts starkly with current interpretations of the Enforcement Directive by the CJEU. As summarized in Chapter 4, "[the Enforcement Directive] allows and even requires the denial or flexible curtailing of injunctive relief in certain exceptional cases where an untailored injunction would be grossly disproportionate, it does not contain any bright-line rules for certain entire case groups."[33] As noted there, even the test outlined in cases concerning injunctions against intermediaries "clearly has an impact on the general question of how to consider and balance the fundamental rights of the parties when applying and specifying injunctions."[34] Even if the member states implemented Article 12 of the Enforcement Directive more broadly (damages in lieu of injunctions), the provision remains conceptually plagued by uncertainties around its scope. In particular, as pointed out in Chapter 4,[35] without an authoritative clarification by the CJEU that for the purposes of assessment of the "innocence" of an infringement only the initial act is relevant, the provision is unlikely to have any practical use.[36]

For these reasons, even if the European courts more fully embrace proportionality in patent law,[37] which they have not done yet, the set of cases that is likely to be considered under the test is much narrower than in the United States. Although European judges have some experience using proportionality for purposes of preliminary injunctions, the interests that they are likely to consider for purposes of final injunctions are more limited. For instance, as suggested in some of the contributions to this book, considerations of employment and follow-on innovation have a smaller role to play under a European proportionality analysis. The reason is not ignorance of these issues, but stronger judicial deference to the legislative design of

---

[33] See Chapter 4 (EU).

[34] See *id.*

[35] See *id.*

[36] It is worth noting that the very idea of an "innocent" patent infringement does not exist in many jurisdictions.

[37] Some commentators have recommended that courts in Europe more fully adopt principles of proportionality in assessing injunctive relief. Siebrasse et al. 2019, at 155 ("we recommend that a proportionality-based test ... be deployed in a system that gives courts latitude to construct injunctions that are tailored to avoid or mitigate disproportionate effects").

the patent law. While at the preliminary stage European judges may try to find a good interim solution in the midst of significant legal uncertainty, in the final stage, when the legal situation is clarified, they feel the need to give full force to the legislator's design. The proportionality test asks them to correct it only at the margin and only as far as a "countervailing right is in play."[38]

C. INTERNATIONAL CONTEXT

International law does not seem to play a major role in tailoring and granting injunctive relief in any of the studied countries. This is in line with the findings of the authors of Chapter 2, who argue that the injunction provisions of the TRIPS Agreement only provide authority to grant injunctions, without significantly constraining the exercise of that authority. They point to the analogous setting of the WTO *China – Enforcement* panel decision, which held that another similarly worded provision of TRIPS provides "the obligation is to 'have' authority, [it is] not an obligation to 'exercise' authority."[39] At the same time, they highlight that the interaction of TRIPS provisions on injunctive relief and compulsory licensing can be become quite complex, depending on the reading that is adopted by the WTO. Nevertheless, the chapter authors, along with other scholars, argue that even the flexible US approach to injunctive relief would very likely be compatible with the TRIPS Agreement.[40]

That being said, two other types of limitations might arise under international law, which are less often appreciated in policy debates. First, they explain that domestic practices around the exercise of authority to grant injunctive relief also need to be consistent with the requirements of national or most-favored-nation (MFN) treatment. They highlight that *de facto* discrimination may thus constitute a violation of TRIPS under some circumstances, for instance when it constitutes a clear feature of the system's design. This could be particularly relevant in cases in which some neutral proxy considerations, such as nonexploitation or local employment, lead to worse enforcement conditions for foreign patent owners. A similar problem could arise in the context of the TRIPS prohibition on discrimination by a field of technology. For instance, when a particular societal issue is being addressed by injunction flexibilities in the area of ICT but remains ignored in other areas of technology (e.g., pharmaceuticals), a compliance issue under the TRIPS Agreement could arise.

Finally, a *lack* of flexibility at the national level could equally constitute a problem because the TRIPS Agreement imposes a ceiling on national enforcement measures. Specifically,

---

[38] *HTC Corp.* v. *Nokia Corp. (No. 2)* [2013] EWHC 3778 (Pat), para. 28.

[39] *China – Enforcement*, at para. 7.236. Article 59 requires that "competent authorities shall have the authority to order the destruction or disposal of infringing goods". See TRIPS, art. 59.

[40] See Chapter 2 (TRIPS).

- Article 7 states that the Objectives of the TRIPS Agreement are to: "contribute to the promotion of technological innovation and to the transfer and dissemination of technology, to the mutual advantage of producers and users of technological knowledge and in a manner conducive to social and economic welfare, and to a balance of rights and obligations."
- Article 41 requires that injunctions must be "be applied in such a manner as to avoid the creation of barriers to legitimate trade and to provide for safeguards against their abuse" and that procedures must be "fair and equitable" and "not ... unnecessarily complicated or costly, or entail unreasonable time-limits or unwarranted delays."

As a result, the TRIPS chapter authors conclude that "excessive enforcement could also raise compliance issues."[41] However, in all of these cases, they observe that there may be a need to prove a pattern or practice, which emerges from domestic decisions, before one can consider underlying compliance with TRIPS obligations.

D. TRENDS AND FUTURE DIRECTIONS

Many of the contributors to this book noted clear or subtle trends in their jurisdictions, indicating that there might be changes on the horizon. The first and most obvious catalyst of change is US judicial practice, which contrasts considerably with that of countries having a strong presumption favoring the issuance of permanent injunctions. A second catalyst may be technological change, which has resulted in increasingly complex technological products, creating more situations in which simple binary decisions regarding injunctions are difficult to justify in light of other interests.[42] A third catalyst, at least in the European Union, is EU law itself, which increasingly emphasizes proportionality, something that can incorporate considerations of both party interest and the public interest.

Equally powerful in reimagining existing approaches to injunctive relief is EU competition law, which has prominently been invoked in FRAND disputes and has directly impacted the remedial toolkit of patent law. Surprisingly, EU competition law has been more successful than the EU Enforcement Directive in influencing

---

[41] *Id.*

[42] See Siebrasse et al. 2019, 156 (recommending "that courts generally be willing to consider such tailoring whenever injunctive relief is sought in relation to a complex product"); Sikorski 2019, 246 ("Comparison of the harm and the elusive benefits of an injunction [for infringing a component of a complex product] would strongly favor monetary compensation in lieu of an injunction or at least tailoring of injunctive relief that would allow for designing around while allowing the manufacturer to stay on the market for the time necessary to switch to a new technology").

European judges regarding the issuance of injunctions. This may be because competition law solutions are more circumscribed than those based on patent law.[43] That is, patent law solutions are often applicable to all patent owners, but competition law solutions are applicable only to a subset of patent owners in a position of dominance. Therefore, there is less worry that any particular decision will have substantial spillover effects. More broadly, it should be emphasized that the EU legislature has limited power to influence other policy layers of the patent system, such as patent quality and scope of rights, which remain outside of EU law.[44]

A number of our European contributors have advocated for greater judicial reliance on the proportionality test in the assessment of injunctions, noting that the literature is sometimes not fully reflected in the case law.[45] Interestingly, European contributors emphasize that other IP domains, in particular copyright law, are more advanced in this respect. There, apparently, internalization of the CJEU's doctrines seems to be in full swing at the domestic level. For example, in the Netherlands, the Amsterdam Court of Appeal has held in a copyright infringement case that when an injunction is requested, "a specific balancing of interests, taking into account the circumstances of the case" must be performed.[46]

The theory that the enforcement of intellectual property rights must be balanced against other fundamental rights (perhaps relating to health, labor or education) could have an impact on injunctions in patent cases too.[47] However, patent judges seem reluctant to extend fundamental rights-inspired balancing to patent law. Usually, they remain convinced that most of the time there is nothing to balance in patent law. In Germany, this attitude has prompted a reaction by the legislature, which recently amended the patent law in a manner that requires courts to consider party interests and the public interest in the analysis of injunctive relief.

This is not to say, however, that the increased use of proportionality by European judges will lead to results that come anywhere close to US practice. As we have shown, there are many shades of flexibility and tailoring that judges can use to consider party and public interests. Based on our survey of the literature, it seems that the existing case law in European countries does not always match the opinions of scholars, who seem less reluctant to internalize EU case law in patent law.

Another important development to watch in this area concerns the creation of the European Unitary Patent Court (UPC) system (see Chapter 4 on the EU). This system will exist independently of and alongside the national legal and judicial

[43] See Husovec 2020 (discussing the use of proportionality in EU patent law).
[44] The principal body that assesses questions of patentability in the EU is the European Patent Office (EPO), an arm of the European Patent Organisation, an international treaty organisation with thirty-eight member states.
[45] CoA Amsterdam 6 February 2018, ECLI:NL:GHAMS:2018:395 (*Anne Frank Stichting*). See also Siebrasse et al. 2019, 155–56 (recommending greater reliance on proportionality principle).
[46] *Anne Frank Stichting* (CoA Amsterdam 2018, para. 3.11.2) – for the discussion, see Chapter 11 (Netherlands).
[47] See Sikorski 2019, 247 (public interest concerns justify tailoring of injunctive relief).

systems studied in this volume, and will be comprised of judges and courts from countries across Europe, with tribunals situated in a few large jurisdictions. It is unclear what institutional and structural preferences will emerge within the UPC system, and the degree to which these features will be influenced, or dominated, by the legal systems of one or more of the remaining UPC member states.

The UPC system, which has not yet been created, is anticipated to grant a degree of discretion to its judges,[48] while leaving the principles underlying the actual practice open. Although the Preparatory Committee expressed the view that the denial of an injunction might be possible only under "very exceptional circumstances,"[49] the final rules of procedure and practice might differ. It is no wonder, therefore, that literature expresses contradictory views on what to expect from the future UPC.[50] In terms of our spectrum, the UPC could easily shift between groups B to E, although only B to D appear likely.

Interestingly, given the recent exit of the United Kingdom from the EU and the UPC system, UK judges, arguably Europe's most ardent champions of proportionality in patent law and influential voices in the original drafting of the UPC's rules, will no longer have a direct say in the new institution's operations or the subsequent evolution of its rules. Their influence might only remain indirect through the interpretation of some common rules under international law, and by setting an example of good practices.[51] After all, the principles of judicial decision making from the UK, and even from non-European countries, may influence the shape of this important new transnational judicial institution.

The predominant concern of patent judges in EU countries seems to be opening the floodgates to a new avenue of pleading at the remedial stage. This would explain why the reference to compulsory licensing, which is dealt with in a separate procedure, still holds sway. However, as demonstrated by countries such as the United Kingdom, the recognition of judicial discretion in injunction cases need not cause major changes in the outcome of cases. As noted in Chapter 13 (United Kingdom), "[a]lthough there is a reasonable volume of UK patent litigation, disputes concerning injunctions are relatively infrequent." Arguably, therefore, in a majority

---

[48] See 63(1) Agreement on a Unified Patent Court (2013) Official Journal C 175, pp. 1–40 ("Where a decision is taken finding an infringement of a patent, the Court *may* grant an injunction against the infringer aimed at prohibiting the continuation of the infringement" – emphasis ours).

[49] "Table with Explanatory Notes to the Changes Made by the Legal Group of the Preparatory Committee in the 17th Draft of the Rules of Procedure" (2014), 11.

[50] See Marfé et al. 2015, 187; Tilmann 2016, 545, 554; and Chapter 8, Section B.

[51] If the UK–EU trade deal is eventually adopted, the United Kingdom and the EU member states participating in the UPC system will remain bound by the general principles for remedies in the IP Enforcement Directive (see Article IP.38(2) of the Trade and Cooperation Agreement Between the European Union and the European Atomic Energy Community, of the one part, and The United Kingdom of Great Britain and Northern Ireland, of the other part (2020) Official Journal L 444, pp. 14–1462).

of cases, the exercise of greater judicial discretion will probably not lead to any large, aggregate difference in outcomes.

At the same time, the view of judges in some countries as mere automatons is not entirely accurate or fair. Courts in countries with strong presumptions favoring the issuance of permanent injunctions sometimes apply proportionality considerations at the preliminary injunction stage, when deciding stays, and when tailoring injunctive relief to the specific cases before them. This tradeoff between the decision to *issue* a permanent injunction (which may be relatively automatic) and the parameters around its *tailoring* (which may be flexible) suggest that any binary view of judicial approaches to injunctive relief is not warranted, and that a jurisdiction's treatment of injunctive relief should be viewed on a holistic basis, taking into account not only doctrinal, but also normative and structural considerations.

REFERENCES

Cases

AbbVie v. *Janssen* (FC 2014).
CoA Amsterdam 6 February 2018, ECLI:NL:GHAMS:2018:395 (*Anne Frank Stichting*)
Apple v. *Samsung*, 809 F.3d 633 (Fed. Cir. 2015).
Apple v. *Samsung*, 678 F. App'x 1012 (Fed. Cir. 2017).
Boehringer Mannheim/Kirin Amgen (HR 1995, para. 3.7).
Broadcom Corp. v. *Qualcomm Inc.*, 543 F.3d 683 (Fed. Cir. 2008).
eBay Inc. v. *MercExchange, LLC*, 547 US 388 (2006).
Edwards Lifesciences LLC v. *Boston Scientific Scimed Inc.* [2018] EWHC 1256 (Pat).
HTC Corporation v. *Nokia Corporation* [2013] EWHC 3778 (Pat).
Huawei v. *ZTE* [C-170/13].
LG Manheim, Case 2 O 34/19.
Oil States Energy Services, LLC v. *Greene's Energy Group, LLC*, 584 U.S. ____ (2018).
Unilever (FCTD 1993).
Unwired Planet Int'l Ltd. v. *Huawei Technologies (UK) Co. Ltd.* [2017] EWHC 1304 (Pat).

Regulatory and Legislative Materials

63(1) Agreement on a Unified Patent Court (2013) Official Journal C 175.
Article 12 of the Enforcement Directive.
Article IP.38(2) of the Trade and Cooperation Agreement

Books, Articles and Online Materials

Bechtold, Stefan, Jens Frankenreiter & Daniel Klerman. 2019. "Forum Selling Abroad," *Southern California Law Review* 92(3):487–556.
Contreras, Jorge L. 2019. "Injunctive Relief in U.S. Patent Cases," in Rafał Sikorski ed., *Patent Law Injunctions*. Wolters Kluwer.
Cremers, Katrin, Max Ernicke, Dietmar Harhoff, Christian Helmers, G. Licht, Luke McDonagh, I. Rudyk, Paula Schliessler, C. Schneider & Nicolas van Zeebroeck. 2016. "Patent Litigation in Europe," *European Journal of Law and Economics* 44: 1–44.

Dobbs, Dan B. 1993. *Dobbs Law of Remedies Vol. 1* (2nd ed.). West Publishing.

Holte, Ryan T. & Christopher B. Seaman. 2017. "Patent Injunctions on Appeal: An Empirical Study of the Federal Circuit's Application of eBay," *Washington Law Review* 92 (1):145–212.

Husovec, Martin. 2019. "The Essence of Intellectual Property Rights under Article 17(2) of the EU Charter," *German Law Journal* 20(6):840–63.

2020. "How Will the European Patent Judges Understand Proportionality?," *Jurimetrics* 60 (4):383–88.

Jaffe, Adam B. & Josh Lerner. 2004. *Innovation and Its Discontents: How Our Broken System Is Endangering Innovation and Progress, and What to Do About It.* Princeton University Press.

Larouche, Pierre & Nicolo Zingales. 2017. "Injunctive Relief in the EU – Intellectual Property and Competition Law at the Remedies State," in Jorge L. Contreras ed., *The Cambridge Handbook of Technical Standardization Law: Competition, Antitrust, and Patents.* Cambridge University Press.

Lemley, Mark A. & Carl Shapiro. 2007. Patent Holdup and Royalty Stacking," *Texas Law Review* 85(7):1991–2050.

Lemley, Mark A., Jamie Kendall & Clint Martin. 2013. "Rush to Judgment: Trian Length and Outcomes in Patent Cases," *AIPLA Quarterly Journal* 41(2):169–204.

Marfé, Mark, Alexander Reetz, Camille Pecnard & Riccardo Fruscalzo. 2015. "The Power of National Courts and the Unified Patent Court to Grant Injunctions: A Comparative Study," *Journal of Intellectual Property Law and Practice* 10(3):180–90.

McDonagh, Luke. 2016. *European Patent Litigation in the Shadow of the Unified Patent Court.* Edward Elgar.

Siebrasse, Norman V., Rafał Sikorski, Jorge L. Contreras, Thomas F. Cotter, John Golden, Sang Jo Jong, Brian J. Love & David O. Taylor. 2019. "Injunctive Relief," in *Patent Remedies and Complex Products.* Cambridge University Press.

Sikorski, Rafał. 2019. "Between Automatism and Flexibility: Injunctions in Twenty-First Century Patent Law," in Rafał Sikorski ed., *Patent Law Injunctions.* Wolters Kluwer.

Tilmann, Winfried. 2016. "The UPC Agreement and the Unitary Patent Regulation – Construction and Application," *Journal of Intellectual Property Law and Practice* 11(7):545.

CPSIA information can be obtained
at www.ICGtesting.com
Printed in the USA
LVHW081529040622
720518LV00003B/42